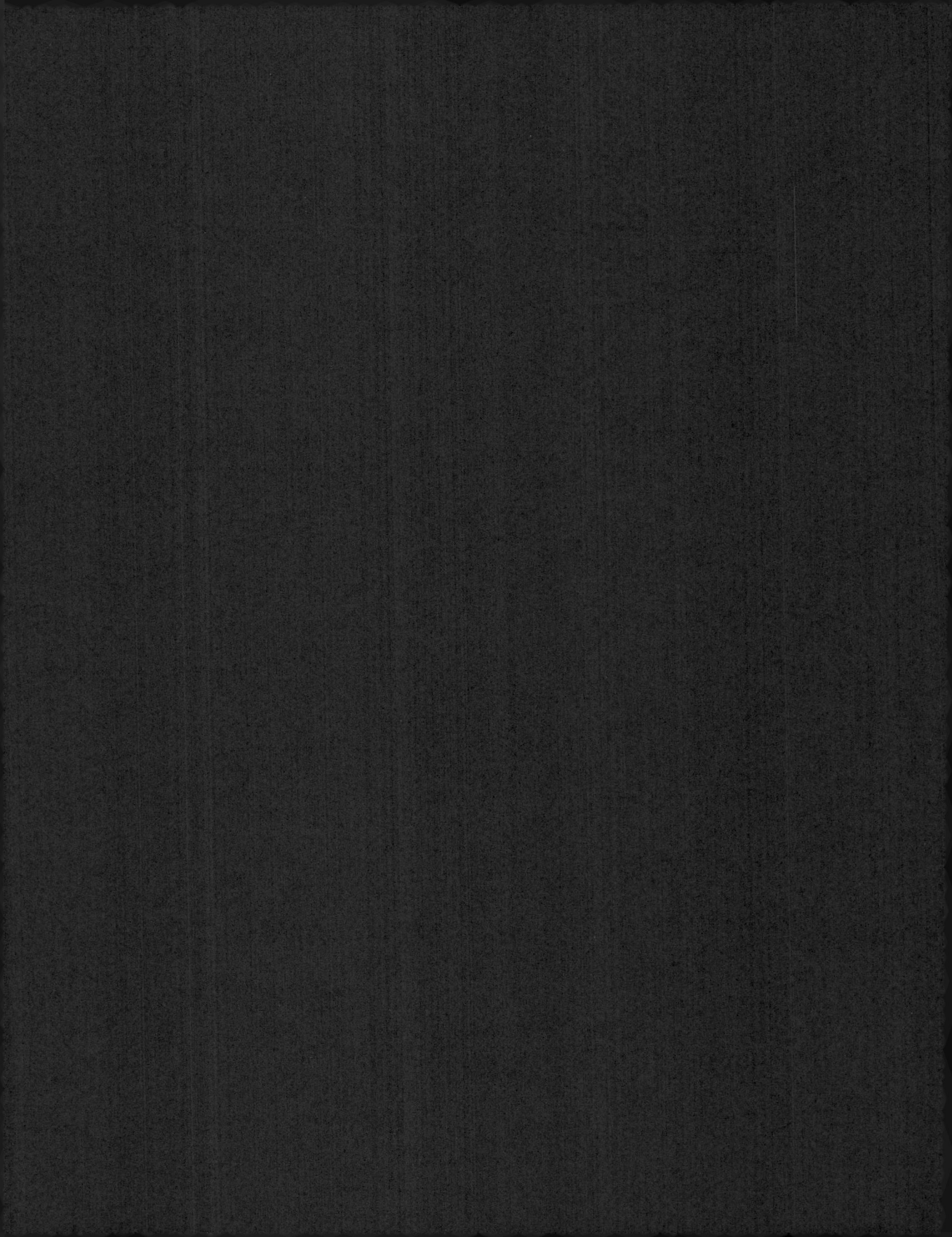

Oracle DB 종사자 및 Oracle DB 업무를 배우고 싶어하는 모든 IT 종사자를 위한 필독서

DBA의 정석

장애 예방 | ASM | RMAN 편

박용석 저

Absolute Performance
axiom™

DBA의 정석 (장애 예방 / ASM / RMAN 편)

- 초 판 2018년 06월 15일 1쇄 발행
- 저 자 박용석
- 총 판 신한전문서적
- 발 행 ㈜ 엑시엄정보시스템
- 주 소 서울시 강남구 역삼로 112, 6층(역삼동, 밀리브지빌딩)
- 전 화 070-8264-9889
- 팩 스 02-6499-9889
- 이메일 oksy@axiominfo.co.kr
- ISBN 979-11-959425-2-7 13000
- 가 격 25,000원

파본은 구입하신 곳에서 교환하여 드립니다.

추천사

RECOMMENDATION

Oracle DB를 관리하는 업무에 종사하는 사람이라면 누구나 탄탄한 기본기에 대한 생각을 많이 해봤을 것이다. 기본적인 업무에는 업무 프로세스를 익히기 위한 다양한 문서가 존재한다. 우리는 직장에서 업무를 수행할 때 수 없이 많은 문서를 참고해서 보게 된다.

특히 DB 엔지니어 및 DBA들은 다양한 매뉴얼을 참고해 가면서 복잡한 직무를 수행하게 된다. 이들 중 현명한 사람들은 직장생활에서 참고가 될 수 있는 자신만의 바이블 몇 권을 책상한 편에 두고 그 바이블을 참고해서 문서작업과 작업계획을 수립하게 된다.

여러분은 고교시절 수학의 정석이라는 책을 가지고 수학의 기본기를 튼튼히 다졌을 것이다.

이 책은 Oracle DB 종사자는 물론 Oracle DB 업무를 배우고 싶어하는 모든 IT 종사자를 위한 Oracle DB 작업의 정석이라고 생각해도 될 것 같다. 이 책이 취업 준비생, 신입사원의 DB 기본기능력을 키우는데 큰 힘을 보탤 것이라 자부하며, 베테랑 DB 엔지니어 및 DBA들에게는 탄탄한 기본기를 보다 강화시키는 데도 도움이 될 것이라 생각한다.

하루에 한 시간, 한 강좌씩만 읽고 실습해 본다면 한 달이 되지 않아 Oracle DB 전문가로서 기본기를 완전히 익힐 수 있을 것이다. 아무쪼록 이 책이 즐겁고 성공적인 직장생활에 도움이 되기를 진심으로 바란다.

2018년 6월

나래인포시스템즈 대표 컨설턴트 정성일

머리말

PREFACE

2005년 Perfect 오라클 실전 튜닝을 출판하고 10년이 넘는 시간이 흘렀다. 처음 Perfect 오라먼저 책을 쓴다는 것은 매우 어렵고 힘든 일이었습니다. 이 책의 주제에 대한 영감은 Oracle 12c에서 ASM을 사용을 해야 하는 이슈들부터 시작되었습니다.

이 책을 완성하기까지 도와준 많은 사람들에게 감사의 인사를 전하고 싶습니다.

이 책이 나오도록 가장 많은 도움을 주신 엑시엄정보시스템 권순용 대표님과 유니원아이앤씨 김도형 대표님, 정훈기 부사장님, 지금은 같은 소속은 아니지만 이 책이 세상에 나오도록 가장 많은 도움을 주신 나래인포시스템 정성일 이사님께 감사의 인사를 드립니다.

그리고 "독자 여러분께 정말 많은 감사드립니다."

본 책은 Oracle 12c의 ASM 지원에 따라서 걱정할 많은 DBA 분들과 이제 막 시작하는 DBA 분들을 위해 그리고 DBA도 아니면서 Oracle DB 운영 일을 겸해야 하는 분들을 위해 작성하였습니다.

Oracle 12c에서는 ASM 사용을 권고하고 있습니다. RMAN과 ASM은 출시가 10년이 넘었지만, 아직도 많은 DBA, 개발자, 관리자들에게 낯설고, 신뢰가 안가는 솔루션이지만, RMAN과 ASM은 여러 분들의 오라클 DB를 한 차원 발전시키는 좋은 솔루션입니다. 필자는 이 솔루션의 좋은 기능과 기능이 사용될 때 이전에 사용 중인 환경과의 장단점을 비교하였습니다.

필자는 ASM과 RMAN으로 된 환경을 경험 하면서 좋은 기능을 알리고 많은 DBA 분들이 ASM과 RMAN의 장점을 알리고 예제를 통한 실습을 하면서 ASM과 RMAN을 경험하도록 내용을 구성하였습니다.

직접 많은 운영 경험과 기술 지원 경험을 통해 자주 발생하는 안타까운 오라클 DB 장애에 대해서 작성하였습니다.

필자는 처음 책을 쓰면서 최대한 명령어 위주로 쉽게 쓰려고 노력하였으며, 많은 정보보다는 정말 필요한 정보만을 담도록 노력하였습니다. 되도록 많은 분들이 이 책을 읽고 이 책의 내용이 좋은 솔루션이 되어 DB 구성 및 운영에 사용되길 바랍니다.

많은 직장에서 필자는 가장 명석한 동료들과 함께 일하고 그들 모두 나름대로 필자에게 도움을 주었지만, 특별히 굿어스 재직 시절의 신종근 이사님 지원에 감사를 전합니다. 아쉽게도 필자와 신종근 이사님은 현재 굿어스에서 일하고 있지 않지만 신종근 이사님의 영향은 오래도록 지속될 것입니다.

마지막으로 끊임없이 도와 준 가족에게 많은 감사를 전합니다. 지속적으로 자원을 아끼지 않은 나의 아내 김선정, 그리고 딸 박소민, 아들 박철우, 박정우가 있었기에 이 책을 마칠 수 있었음을 전하고 싶습니다.

서문

FOREWORD

이 책의 대상 독자

- 오라클 DB를 운영해야하는 DBA
- Oracle 12c 업그레이드를 준비하는 DBA
- 오라클 DB 백업 솔루션 엔지니어
- 오라클 DB 스토리지 기술 지원 엔지니어

이 책의 구성

이 책에의 단원별 내용을 간략히 설명드립니다.

Chapter 1. 장애의 정석 편

이 단원에서는 오라클 DBA로서 DB 운영을 하면서 구성 운영, 변경 작업, 개발 반영 등 오라클 DB가 제공하는 서비스 장애가 자주 발생할 수 있는 오라클 DB 장애 이슈를 정리하였습니다.

Chapter 2. RMAN의 정석 편

이 단원에서는 전통적인 백업과 비교하는 RMAN 백업 내용과 RMAN 백업의 기본적인 명령어 기능, RMAN의 고급 기능을 알아보며, 실제 데이터 유실 시 RMAN 유틸리티로 대처하는 방법에 대해서 실습을 통해 확인하도록 정리하였습니다.

Chapter 3. ASM의 정석 편

기존의 Rawdevice 환경과 ASM 환경의 비교, ASM의 장점에 대해 알아보고 여러 가지 ASM 관리 유틸리티를 관리해보며 단계적으로 실습하며, ASM 구성 방법에 대해서 실습을 통해 확인하도록 정리하였습니다.

차 례

CONTENTS

Chapter 03 ASM의 정석 편

DB 장애의 정석 편

테이블스페이스 장애

오라클의 테이블스페이스(Tablespace)란 테이블이 저장되는 공간입니다. 오라클에서는 테이블스페이스라고 해서 테이블이 저장될 공간을 먼저 만들고 나서 테이블을 생성합니다. 각각의 테이블을 테이블스페이스별로 나누어서 관리합니다.

테이블스페이스를 생성하면 정의된 용량만큼 미리 확보한 테이블스페이스가 생성되며 테이블스페이스에 테이블의 데이터가 저장됩니다.

그럼 오라클 DB의 물리적 저장 단위 구조인 테이블스페이스 관리 중 자주 발생하는 테이블스페이스 장애에 대해서 알아보겠습니다.

1 테이블스페이스 공간 부족

DB 서버를 관리하는 오라클 DBA는 수시로 테이블스페이스를 체크해야 합니다.

```
SQL>SELECT T.NAME , T.BYTES,T.USED,T.FREE,T.PCT_FREE_USED, C.BLOCK_SIZE/1024||'k' BLOCK_SIZE,
      C.CONTENTS, C.LOGGING,
      C.EXTENT_MANAGEMENT,
      C.ALLOCATION_TYPE,
      C.SEGMENT_SPACE_MANAGEMENT,
      C.DEF_TAB_COMPRESSION
FROM
( SELECT
        A.TABLESPACE_NAME                                                    NAME,
        SUM(B.BYTES/1048576)/COUNT( DISTINCT A.FILE_ID||'.'||A.BLOCK_ID )    BYTES,
        SUM(B.BYTES/1048576)/COUNT( DISTINCT A.FILE_ID||'.'||A.BLOCK_ID ) -
        SUM(A.BYTES/1048576)/COUNT( DISTINCT B.FILE_ID )                     USED,
        SUM(A.BYTES/1048576)/COUNT( DISTINCT B.FILE_ID )                     FREE,
        100-(100 * ( (SUM(B.BYTES)/COUNT( DISTINCT A.FILE_ID||'.'||A.BLOCK_ID )) -
                   (SUM(A.BYTES)/COUNT( DISTINCT B.FILE_ID ) )) /
        (SUM(B.BYTES)/COUNT( DISTINCT A.FILE_ID||'.'||A.BLOCK_ID ))) PCT_FREE_USED
FROM    DBA_FREE_SPACE A, DBA_DATA_FILES B
```

```
WHERE      A.TABLESPACE_NAME = B.TABLESPACE_NAME
GROUP BY   A.TABLESPACE_NAME ) T , DBA_TABLESPACES C
WHERE T.NAME=C.TABLESPACE_NAME
ORDER BY T.PCT_FREE_USED ;
```

```
09:14:43 SYS@oracle12> SELECT T.NAME , T.BYTES,T.USED,T.FREE,T.PCT_FREE_USED,
09:15:20   2          C.BLOCK_SIZE/1024||'k' BLOCK_SIZE,
09:15:20   3          C.CONTENTS,
09:15:20   4          C.LOGGING,
09:15:20   5          C.EXTENT_MANAGEMENT,
09:15:20   6          C.ALLOCATION_TYPE,
09:15:20   7          C.SEGMENT_SPACE_MANAGEMENT,
09:15:20   8          C.DEF_TAB_COMPRESSION
09:15:20   9  FROM
09:15:20  10  ( SELECT
09:15:20  11              A.TABLESPACE_NAME                                      NAME,
09:15:20  12              SUM(B.BYTES/1048576)/COUNT( DISTINCT A.FILE_ID||'.'||A.BLOCK_ID )      BYTES,
09:15:20  13              SUM(B.BYTES/1048576)/COUNT( DISTINCT A.FILE_ID||'.'||A.BLOCK_ID ) -
09:15:20  14              SUM(A.BYTES/1048576)/COUNT( DISTINCT B.FILE_ID )                     USED,
09:15:20  15              SUM(A.BYTES/1048576)/COUNT( DISTINCT B.FILE_ID )                     FREE,
09:15:20  16              100-(100 * ( (SUM(B.BYTES)/COUNT( DISTINCT A.FILE_ID||'.'||A.BLOCK_ID )) -
09:15:20  17                              (SUM(A.BYTES)/COUNT( DISTINCT B.FILE_ID ) )) /
09:15:20  18              (SUM(B.BYTES)/COUNT( DISTINCT A.FILE_ID||'.'||A.BLOCK_ID ))) PCT_FREE_USED
09:15:20  19  FROM        DBA_FREE_SPACE A, DBA_DATA_FILES B
09:15:20  20  WHERE       A.TABLESPACE_NAME = B.TABLESPACE_NAME
09:15:20  21  GROUP BY    A.TABLESPACE_NAME ) T , DBA_TABLESPACES C
09:15:20  22  WHERE T.NAME=C.TABLESPACE_NAME
09:15:20  23  ORDER BY T.PCT_FREE_USED ;

                                                                                                      SEGMENT    DEF
                                                                  BLOCK                      EXTENT     ALLOC   SPACE      TAB
Tablespace Name  Total Bytes(MB)  Used (MB)  Free (MB)  Free (%) SIZE  CONTENTS  LOGGING   MANAGEMENT TYPE    MANAGEMENT COMPRESS
---------------- ---------------- ---------- ---------- -------- ----- --------- --------- ---------- ------- ---------- --------
SYSTEM                        800        796          4      .47 8k    PERMANENT LOGGING   LOCAL      SYSTEM  MANUAL     DISABLED
SYSAUX                        480        456         24     4.93 8k    PERMANENT LOGGING   LOCAL      SYSTEM  AUTO       DISABLED
UNDOTBS1                       65         17         48    73.75 8k    UNDO      LOGGING   LOCAL      SYSTEM  MANUAL     DISABLED
USERS                           5          1          4    80.00 8k    PERMANENT LOGGING   LOCAL      SYSTEM  AUTO       DISABLED
09:15:21 SYS@oracle12> █
```

▲ 수시로 테이블스페이스의 남은 공간 체크

서비스 중이던 어플리케이션에서는 "ORA-01653: unable to extend table 〈DML 작업 중인 테이블명〉 by 128 in tablespace 〈테이블스페이스명〉"라는 오류가 발생하게 됩니다. 개발/운영 /현업 팀으로부터 서비스가 이상하다는 메시지를 전달받게 됩니다. DBA 분들이 자주 확인하는 Alert log에도 같은 에러 메시지가 적혀있습니다.

```
Commit complete.

SQL> insert into EMPLOYEES select * from EMPLOYEES ;

54784 rows created.

SQL> commit ;

Commit complete.

SQL> insert into EMPLOYEES select * from EMPLOYEES ;
insert into EMPLOYEES select * from EMPLOYEES
*
ERROR at line 1:
ORA-01653: unable to extend table UNIONE.EMPLOYEES by 128 in tablespace UNIONE


SQL> █
```

▲ 어플리케이션에서 Error 발생

```
[oracle12@yspark-linux trace]$ tail -4 alert_oracle12.log
2017-09-04T15:25:25.861262+09:00
Resize operation completed for file# 3, old size 563200K, new size 573440K
2017-09-04T15:27:43.114026+09:00
ORA-1653: unable to extend table UNIONE.EMPLOYEES by 128 in tablespace UNIONE
[oracle12@yspark-linux trace]$ █
```

▲ Alert log에 Error 발생

사전에 늘려주지 못한 에러로 이 에러는 한국의 인프라 조직에서 DBA의 관리 소홀로 인하여 발생한 장애로 보고 있습니다. 따라서 DBA는 평소 에러를 발생하지 않게 하기 위해 모니터링을 충실히 해야 합니다.

2 Autoextend의 함정

데이터 파일 추가 생성 시 Autoextend on을 켜서 MAX를 unlimited 사이즈로 추가합니다. 테이블스페이스 사이즈 부족으로 인해 장애현상을 받은 DBA는 이제 자동으로 늘어날 테니 테이블스페이스 관리를 안 해도 된다고 생각합니다.

```
SQL>CREATE TABLESPACE MY_TABLESPACE DATAFILE '+DB_DATA' SIZE 10M  AUTOEXTEND ON MAXSIZE
UNLIMITED ;
```

```
09:21:13 SYS@oracle12> CREATE TABLESPACE MY_TABLESPACE DATAFILE '+DB_DATA' SIZE 10M  AUTOEXTEND ON MAXSIZE UNLIMITED ;
Tablespace created.
09:21:26 SYS@oracle12> ▮
```

▲ 자동으로 늘어나길 바라며 데이터 파일 추가

하지만 이런 생각을 하면 안 됩니다. 결국 또 장애가 발생하게 됩니다. 오라클 Database의 Datafile의 개당 최대 크기가 정해져 있기 때문입니다.

```
일반 Tablespace의 최대 DB 사이즈
Block Sz   Max Datafile Sz (Gb)   Max DB Sz (Tb)
--------    ----------------------------
   2,048                   8             512
   4,096                  16           1,024
   8,192                  32           2,048
  16,384                  64           4,096
  32,768                 128           8,192

Bigfile Tablespace의 최대 DB 사이즈
Block Sz   Max Datafile Sz (Gb)  Max DB Sz (Tb)
--------   ------------------   -------------
   2,048               8,192         524,264
   4,096              16,384       1,048,528
   8,192              32,768       2,097,056
  16,384              65,536       4,194,112
  32,768             131,072       8,388,224
```

▲ 오라클 DB 블록 사이즈에 대비한 최대값

Bigfile Tablespace로 만들어진 테이블스페이스는 데이터파일 1개의 크기가 커지는 구조로 장애 시 복구에 더 많은 시간이 걸립니다. 주로 많이 사용하는 8K 블록 DB의 사이즈는 데이터파일

1개당 맥스 값은 30기가로 한정적입니다. 다시 말해 **자동으로 늘어나는 데이터 파일 사이즈 최대값은 30기가 밖에 안 됩니다.** 이렇기 때문에 많은 오라클 DBA가 테이블스페이스 사용 공간 사이즈를 90%에 맞추어 관리하고 수작업으로 추가하고 모니터링 해주어야 합니다.

데이터 2파일 추가 시 오라클의 **Wait Event : Disk file operations I/O**가 발생합니다. 추가하려는 데이터 파일 사이즈가 작을 때나 DB 서버의 Resource가 충분할 때는 문제없지만 한창 배치나 과도한 온라인 트래픽이 들어올 때 이런 이벤트가 발생하면 해당되는 DB가 제공하고 있는 어플리케이션 서비스 지연 현상이 발생됩니다.

```
BHOU EVENT_NAME                          AVG_MS          CT
---- ------------------------------ --------- -----------
1054 Disk file operations I/O             2.00      13,547
1130 Disk file operations I/O             1.52      10,658
1200 Disk file operations I/O             1.57       9,846
1230 Disk file operations I/O             2.45       8,704
1300 Disk file operations I/O             3.84       9,526
1330 Disk file operations I/O             2.39      11,989
1400 Disk file operations I/O             1.68      14,698
1430 Disk file operations I/O             2.89      14,863
1500 Disk file operations I/O           860.85      10,577
1530 Disk file operations I/O            12.97      11,783
1600 Disk file operations I/O           623.88      10,902
1630 Disk file operations I/O           357.75      12,428
1700 Disk file operations I/O           294.84      10,543
1730 Disk file operations I/O            12.97      10,623
1800 Disk file operations I/O           461.91      14,443
1830 Disk file operations I/O            12.83      18,504
1900 Disk file operations I/O           443.37       9,563
1930 Disk file operations I/O           237.39      11,737
2000 Disk file operations I/O           542.44      13,027
2033 Disk file operations I/O             6.11       8,389
2100 Disk file operations I/O            16.85      10,561
2130 Disk file operations I/O           306.17       9,873
2200 Disk file operations I/O            20.83      11,335
2230 Disk file operations I/O            12.92      10,158
2300 Disk file operations I/O            13.42      11,025
2330 Disk file operations I/O            15.01      10,883
0000 Disk file operations I/O             5.33       8,533
1054 db file scattered read               1.50      92,394
1130 db file scattered read               1.33      73,243
1200 db file scattered read               1.82     122,988
1230 db file scattered read               2.53     255,474
1300 db file scattered read               4.26     288,144
1330 db file scattered read               2.47     308,045
1400 db file scattered read               2.60      91,684
1430 db file scattered read               3.56     176,324
1500 db file scattered read               4.95     621,658
1530 db file scattered read               5.11     227,565
1600 db file scattered read               5.86     472,804
1630 db file scattered read               9.44     224,984
1700 db file scattered read               9.40     165,238
1730 db file scattered read               7.78     349,003
1800 db file scattered read               6.93     252,761
1830 db file scattered read               7.79     151,760
1900 db file scattered read               5.48     165,369
1930 db file scattered read               3.09     200,868
2000 db file scattered read               3.45     136,647
2033 db file scattered read               5.17     136,330
2100 db file scattered read              11.16     103,799
2130 db file scattered read              10.44     118,025
2200 db file scattered read              20.02     127,638
2230 db file scattered read              13.66     157,210
2300 db file scattered read              10.95      98,493
2330 db file scattered read               8.39     149,606
0000 db file scattered read               4.16     230,075
```

▲과도한 데이터 추가 트래픽 중 Autoextend 기능으로 인한 extent 확보가 같이 일어나는 경우

항시 DBA는 테이블스페이스의 공간을 체크하고, 해당 DB의 서비스가 안정적일 때 데이터 파일을 추가해 주어야 합니다.

테이블스페이스 공간 추가 시 데이터 파일 resize보다 Autoextend로 데이터 파일 추가를 하면 공간 부족 장애의 골든타임을 확보하게 됩니다.

DB 커넥션 장애

오라클 DB의 연결(커넥션)은 클라이언트 프로세스와 데이터베이스 인스턴스 간의 물리적 경로를 말합니다.
즉 클라이언트와 인스턴스 간의 네트워크 커넥션을 말하는 겁니다. 세션은 인스턴스 안에 있는 논리적인 실체로 현재 유저의 로그인 상태를 나타냅니다.
자주 발생하는 장애인 연결 실패 일명 DB 접속이 안 된다는 장애에 대해서 알아보겠습니다.

1 패스워드 기간 만료로 인한 접속 장애

DBA가 DB에 오라클 유저를 만들어 주고 6개월 정도 지났습니다. 갑자기 개발자로부터 연락이 와서 접속이 안 된다고 합니다. 무슨 문제일까요?

오라클을 설치하고 DB를 생성하고, 유저마다 profile을 만들어 관리정책을 줄 수 있는데, 기본적으로 Default profile에 대해서 수정하지 않았다면 다음의 패스워드 관리 정책이 기본적으로 부여되어 관리됩니다.

```
SQL>SELECT PROFILE, RESOURCE_NAME, RESOURCE_TYPE, LIMIT FROM DBA_PROFILES
WHERE RESOURCE_TYPE='PASSWORD' AND PROFILE='DEFAULT' ;
```

```
09:29:08 SYS@oracle12> SELECT PROFILE, RESOURCE_NAME, RESOURCE_TYPE, LIMIT FROM DBA_PROFILES
09:29:10   2  WHERE RESOURCE_TYPE='PASSWORD' AND PROFILE='DEFAULT' ;

PROFILE                          RESOURCE_NAME                    RESOURCE LIMIT
-------------------------------- -------------------------------- -------- --------------------
DEFAULT                          FAILED_LOGIN_ATTEMPTS            PASSWORD 10
DEFAULT                          PASSWORD_LIFE_TIME               PASSWORD 180
DEFAULT                          PASSWORD_REUSE_TIME              PASSWORD UNLIMITED
DEFAULT                          PASSWORD_REUSE_MAX               PASSWORD UNLIMITED
DEFAULT                          PASSWORD_VERIFY_FUNCTION         PASSWORD NULL
DEFAULT                          PASSWORD_LOCK_TIME               PASSWORD 1
DEFAULT                          PASSWORD_GRACE_TIME              PASSWORD 7
DEFAULT                          INACTIVE_ACCOUNT_TIME            PASSWORD UNLIMITED

8 rows selected.

09:29:12 SYS@oracle12>
```

▲ DB 유저의 프로파일 확인

오라클 DB의 PROFILE을 체크해 보면 패스워드 만료기간이 있는 PASSWORD_LIFE_TIME이란 항목을 확인하게 됩니다. 각 리소스의 의미는 다음과 같습니다.

FAILED_LOGIN_ATTEMPTS	계정을 잠그기 전까지 로그인 시도하다 실패한 횟수
PASSWORD_LOCK_TIME	암호가 기간 만료되어 계정이 잠겨진 채로 남아 있었던 날 수
PASSWORD_LIFE_TIME	날 수로 표시한 암호의 수명으로 이 기간이 지나면 기간 만료됨
PASSWORD_GRACE_TIME	암호 만료된 후 첫 번째 성공 로그인부터 암호 변경을 할 때까지의 유예기간
PASSWORD_REUSE_TIME	암호가 재사용될 때까지의 날 수
PASSWORD_REUSE_MAX	암호가 재사용될 수 있는 최대 회수
INACTIVE_ACCOUNT_TIME	지정된 일 수 내에 인스턴스에 로그인하지 않은 사용자 계정을 잠금 (12C)
PASSWORD_VERIFY_FUNCTION	암호를 할당하기 전 복합성 검사를 수행할 PL/SQL 함수

계정은 지정된 시간(PASSWORD_LOCK_TIME)이 지난 후 자동적으로 잠금이 해제되거나 데이터베이스 관리자가 ALTER USER 명령으로 잠금을 해제해야 합니다. 기본적으로 180일로 세팅되어 있기 때문에 6개월 정도 패스워드가 유효하고 만료되게 됩니다.

2 패스워드 변경으로 인한 접속 장애

기존 DBA가 퇴사를 했고, 새로 입사한 DBA가 패스워드 어느 날 개발자가 특정 유저 패스워드를 알려달라고 했습니다. 하지만 패스워드 기록은 안 되어 있어서 신규 패스워드로 바꾸어도 되냐고 물어보고 허락을 맡아 DB 유저 패스워드 변경해주었습니다. 그러자 서비스 장애가 발생하였습니다. 무슨 문제일까요?

오라클 DB의 profile에는 FAILED_LOGIN_ATTEMPTS라는 항목이 있습니다.

```
SQL>SELECT PROFILE, RESOURCE_NAME, RESOURCE_TYPE, LIMIT FROM DBA_PROFILES
    WHERE RESOURCE_TYPE='PASSWORD' AND PROFILE='DEFAULT'
     AND RESOURCE_NAME='FAILED_LOGIN_ATTEMPTS'
```

```
09:31:35 SYS@oracle12> SELECT PROFILE, RESOURCE_NAME, RESOURCE_TYPE, LIMIT FROM DBA_PROFILES
09:31:45   2  WHERE RESOURCE_TYPE='PASSWORD' AND PROFILE='DEFAULT' AND RESOURCE_NAME='FAILED_LOGIN_ATTEMPTS' ;

PROFILE                        RESOURCE_NAME                    RESOURCE LIMIT
------------------------------ -------------------------------- -------- --------------------
DEFAULT                        FAILED_LOGIN_ATTEMPTS            PASSWORD 10

1 row selected.

09:32:00 SYS@oracle12> 
```

일반적으로 WAS에는 연결 실패 시 자동 재접속(retry connection) 기능이 있습니다. 과거 패스워드로 접속을 성공할 때까지 재시도하게 됩니다. 유저는 Lock 상태로 잠기게 됩니다. 이 경우 개발자가 모든 WAS의 접속 패스워드를 새로 바꾼 신규 패스워드로 변경하여도 unlock 상태로 변경하지 않으면 접속 장애가 계속 발생하게 됩니다.

```
SQL>SELECT PROFILE, RESOURCE_NAME, RESOURCE_TYPE, LIMIT FROM DBA_PROFILES
    WHERE RESOURCE_TYPE='PASSWORD' AND PROFILE='DEFAULT'
     AND RESOURCE_NAME='FAILED_LOGIN_ATTEMPTS'
```

```
09:31:35 SYS@oracle12> SELECT PROFILE, RESOURCE_NAME, RESOURCE_TYPE, LIMIT FROM DBA_PROFILES
09:31:45   2  WHERE RESOURCE_TYPE='PASSWORD' AND PROFILE='DEFAULT' AND RESOURCE_NAME='FAILED_LOGIN_ATTEMPTS' ;
PROFILE                        RESOURCE_NAME                    RESOURCE LIMIT
------------------------------ -------------------------------- -------- --------------------
DEFAULT                        FAILED_LOGIN_ATTEMPTS            PASSWORD 10
1 row selected.
09:32:00 SYS@oracle12>
```

```
SQL>ALTER USER <DB 유저 이름> ACCOUNT UNLOCK;
```

```
09:33:32 SYS@oracle12> ALTER USER HR ACCOUNT UNLOCK ;
User altered.
09:34:52 SYS@oracle12>
```

DB 보안 설정을 강제 하지 않는 환경이라면 FAILED_LOGIN_ATTEMPTS와 PASSWORD_LIFE_TIME의 값을 제한하지 않도록 수정하여 DB 접속 장애 발생 요소를 제거해 놓는 것을 가이드합니다.

```
SQL>ALTER PROFILE DEFAULT LIMIT FAILED_LOGIN_ATTEMPTS UNLIMITED ;
SQL>ALTER PROFILE DEFAULT LIMIT PASSWORD_LIFE_TIME UNLIMITED ;
```

```
09:34:52 SYS@oracle12> ALTER PROFILE DEFAULT LIMIT FAILED_LOGIN_ATTEMPTS UNLIMITED ;
Profile altered.
09:38:31 SYS@oracle12> ALTER PROFILE DEFAULT LIMIT PASSWORD_LIFE_TIME    UNLIMITED ;
Profile altered.
09:38:37 SYS@oracle12>
```

3 DB 세션 허용 parameter 초과로 인한 접속 장애

DBA가 퇴근하려고 하는데 WAS 담당자가 오늘 밤에 WAS 서버를 증설한다고 합니다. 증설 완료 후 다음 날 접속 장애가 났다고 합니다. 무슨 이유일까요?

```
[oracle12@yspark-linux ~]$ sqlplus hr/hr

SQL*Plus: Release 12.2.0.1.0 Production on Wed Sep 6 12:56:20 2017

Copyright (c) 1982, 2016, Oracle.  All rights reserved.

ERROR:
ORA-00603: ORACLE server session terminated by fatal error
ORA-00020: maximum number of processes () exceeded
Process ID: 0
Session ID: 0 Serial number: 0

Enter user-name:
```

▲ DB 접속 에러가 발생

ORA-00603이 발생하면서 DB 접속이 안 되는 이유는 processes란 parameter에 허용된 세션 허용 값 보다 접속 세션이 초과되었기 때문입니다.

```
SQL> show parameter process

NAME                                 TYPE        VALUE
------------------------------------ ----------- ------------------------------
aq_tm_processes                      integer     1
asm_io_processes                     integer     20
cell_offload_processing              boolean     TRUE
db_writer_processes                  integer     1
gcs_server_processes                 integer     0
global_txn_processes                 integer     1
job_queue_processes                  integer     4000
log_archive_max_processes            integer     4
processes                            integer     320
processor_group_name                 string
```

▲ Oracle DB 12c의 processes 기본값은 320

세션이 증가한 원인은 많겠지만 당장 DB 접속이 안 되므로 장애 상황을 벗어나기 위해 특정 세션을 KILL하거나 DB를 재기동해야 합니다. 이런 세션이 다 찬 경우라면 상황 해제를 위해 세션 접속해도 안 됩니다.

```
[oracle12]yspark-linux:/home/oracle12> sqlplus system/oracle

SQL*Plus: Release 12.2.0.1.0 Production on Wed Sep 6 13:19:50 2017

Copyright (c) 1982, 2016, Oracle.  All rights reserved.

ERROR:
ORA-00603: ORACLE server session terminated by fatal error
ORA-00020: maximum number of processes () exceeded
Process ID: 0
Session ID: 0 Serial number: 0

Enter user-name:
```

▲ 세션이 다 찬 경우 관리자 접속 불가

접속이 안 된다는 이상이 있다고 연락을 받고 확인하려 할 때 maximum processes 값을 초과하여 접속을 할 수 없을 경우가 있을 수 있습니다.

아니면 shared pool의 부족 등의 이유도 있을 수 있습니다.
이때 선택하는 방법은 pmon을 kill하고 startup하는 비상조치를 취할 수 있는데 문제는 이 경우 추후 원인을 찾지 못할 수도 있고 이 조치를 취하면 안 되는 즉, DB를 내리면 안 되는 경우도 있을 수 있습니다.
그래서 -prelim 옵션이 존재합니다. preliminary connect의 의미입니다.
일반적으로 정상 상태에서 sysdba 접속 시 새 프로세스를 시작하고, 새 프로세스가 SGA에 접속하고, SGA내에 프로세스와 세션 상태 정보를 넣기 위한 메모리를 할당받아 남깁니다.
하지만 prelim 옵션은 마지막 과정이 없습니다. 그래서 Lock이나 latch나 mutex를 사용하는 작업할 수는 없습니다. prelim 접속 시 shutdown 명령도 abort만 가능합니다.

```
[oracle12]yspark-linux:/home/oracle12>  sqlplus -prelim / as sysdba

SQL*Plus: Release 12.2.0.1.0 Production on Wed Sep 6 13:22:27 2017

Copyright (c) 1982, 2016, Oracle.  All rights reserved.

SQL> oradebug setmypid
Statement processed.
SQL> oradebug hanganalyze 12
Statement processed.
SQL> shutdown abort ;
ORACLE instance shut down.
SQL> startup
ORACLE instance started.
```

▲ preliminary connect 모드로 접속 후 문제 원인을 분석하기 위해 Dump 후 DB 재기동

시퀀스 장애

오라클의 SEQUENCE란 유일(UNIQUE)한 값을 생성해주는 오라클의 Object로 시퀀스를 생성하면 기본키와 같이 순차적으로 증가하는 컬럼을 자동적으로 생성할 수 있습니다. 보통 PRIMARY KEY 값을 생성하기 위해 사용합니다. 메모리에 Cache되었을 때 시퀀스 값의 액세스 효율이 증가합니다. 시퀀스는 테이블과는 독립적으로 저장되고 생성됩니다.

오라클 DB를 운영 중에 자주 발생하는 SEQUENCE 장애에 대해서 알아보겠습니다.

1 NoCycle 시퀀스가 MAX 값 도달로 인한 접속장애

어느 날 갑자기 개발팀에서 연락이 와서 시퀀스가 안 된다고 연락이 옵니다. DBA는 시퀀스에 대해 어떻게 해줘야 할까요?

시퀀스는 자동 증가되는 값으로 순차적으로 값을 증가하여 내부적으로 유일한 값을 만들게 됩니다. 생성할 때 시작 값, 최대값 증가치를 지정하여 자동 증가하도록 생성 가능하며 시작 값과 최대값을 지정하여 자동 증가 컬럼 생성할 수 있고 시작 값과 최대값을 지정하지 않으면 1부터 1씩 증가하게 됩니다.

```
SQL>SELECT
   SEQUENCE_OWNER  "OWNER",
   SEQUENCE_NAME   "SEQUENCE",
   MIN_VALUE       "MIN VALUE",
   MAX_VALUE       "MAX VALUE",
```

```
    INCREMENT_BY     "INCREASE",
    CYCLE_FLAG       "CYCLE",
    ORDER_FLAG       "ORDER",
    CACHE_SIZE       "CACHE",
    LAST_NUMBER      "LAST NUMBER",
    ROUND((LAST_NUMBER/MAX_VALUE)*100) "USED"
FROM      DBA_SEQUENCES
WHERE SEQUENCE_OWNER IN ('HR')
ORDER BY 10 DESC ;
```

```
09:52:43 SYS@oracle12> SELECT
09:53:32   2       SEQUENCE_OWNER   "OWNER",
09:53:32   3       SEQUENCE_NAME    "SEQUENCE",
09:53:32   4       MIN_VALUE        "MIN VALUE",
09:53:32   5       MAX_VALUE        "MAX VALUE",
09:53:32   6       INCREMENT_BY     "INCREASE",
09:53:32   7       CYCLE_FLAG       "CYCLE",
09:53:32   8       ORDER_FLAG       "ORDER",
09:53:32   9       CACHE_SIZE       "CACHE",
09:53:32  10       LAST_NUMBER      "LAST NUMBER",
09:53:32  11       ROUND((LAST_NUMBER/MAX_VALUE)*100) "USED"
09:53:32  12   FROM        DBA_SEQUENCES
09:53:32  13   WHERE SEQUENCE_OWNER IN ('HR')
09:53:32  14   ORDER BY 10 DESC ;

OWNER           SEQUENCE         MIN VALUE  MAX VALUE   INCREASE C O      CACHE LAST NUMBER Used (MB)
--------------- --------------- ---------- ---------- ---------- - - ---------- ----------- ----------
HR              LOCATIONS_SEQ            1       9900        100 N N          0        3300         33
HR              DEPARTMENTS_SEQ          1       9990         10 N N          0         280          3
HR              EMPLOYEES_SEQ            1 1.0000E+28          1 N N          0         207          0

3 rows selected.

09:53:33 SYS@oracle12>
```

▲ 어플리케이션에서 사용 중인 시퀀스 남은 여유 체크

Cycle되지 않는 시퀀스는 MAX 값까지 도달하게 되면 오라클 에러 ORA-08004가 발생합니다.

```
SQL> select DEPARTMENTS_SEQ.NEXTVAL from dual;

   NEXTVAL
----------
      1100

SQL> select DEPARTMENTS_SEQ.NEXTVAL from dual;
select DEPARTMENTS_SEQ.NEXTVAL from dual
*
ERROR at line 1:
ORA-08004: sequence DEPARTMENTS_SEQ.NEXTVAL exceeds MAXVALUE and cannot be instantiated


SQL> 
```

▲ 시퀀스 오라클 에러 발생

시퀀스 범위 도달 에러가 발생하면 조치 방법은 2개입니다.

첫 번째 방법은 시퀀스 MAX 값을 늘려서 해제합니다.

```
SQL> alter sequence DEPARTMENTS_SEQ MAXVALUE 2000 ;
Sequence altered.
SQL>
```

▲ 시퀀스 Max 값을 변경

하지만 시퀀스 MAX값을 늘려 자리수가 변경된 경우 **서비스 어플리케이션에서 시퀀스를 활용한 컬럼 변수값 최대 범위를 초과하는 에러가 발생할 수 있습니다. 이 경우 어플리케이션 코드 수정을 병행해야 합니다.**

두 번째 방법은 현재 시퀀스 값을 초기화하면 됩니다.

```
SQL> alter sequence DEPARTMENTS_SEQ increment by -90 ;
Sequence altered.
SQL> select DEPARTMENTS_SEQ.NEXTVAL from dual;
   NEXTVAL
----------
         1
SQL> alter sequence DEPARTMENTS_SEQ increment by 1 ;
Sequence altered.
```

▲ INCREMENTBY절을 이용하여 시퀀스를 초기화하는 방법

이 방법은 오라클 DB 버전에 따라 차이가 있습니다. 도서의 작성 기준은 Oracle 12c Release 2에 기반 하였습니다.

하지만 이 조치 방법을 해도 장애 상황에서 벗어 날 수 없는 CASE가 있습니다. 두 번째 방법인 현재 시퀀스 값의 초기화의 경우 해당 시퀀스를 이용한 숫자 컬럼에 PK, UK 제약조건이 걸린 경우 unique 한 조건으로 인하여 사전에 들어간 시퀀스의 초기 값으로 인하여 서비스 장애가 발생할 수 있습니다. 최초 개발자는 그래서 No Cycle로 된 시퀀스를 만들었을 겁니다.

결국 시퀀스 에러가 발생하면 개발자와 협의하여 2가지 방법 중 한 방법을 결정해서 처리해야 합니다.
따라서 DBA는 수시로 시퀀스 남은 여유 숫자를 체크하여 장애 발생 사전에 알려주어야 합니다.

2 시퀀스에 과도한 트래픽이 몰려 DB HANG 장애

쇼핑몰 DBA는 혜택 많은 이벤트가 있으면 긴장하게 됩니다. 특히 선착순 이벤트나 한정판매 이벤트의 경우 더 긴장하게 됩니다. 그 이유는 시퀀스 때문입니다. 시퀀스는 자동으로 순서를 정해주니 순서를 정하는 어플리케이션 개발에 많은 도움이 되고, 소스 코드의 간편화가 될 수 있습니다.

하지만 숫자를 생성하고 관리하는 기능은 DBMS 내부에서 동작을 하게 됩니다. 즉 숫자가 중복되거나 순차를 꼭 지켜야 하기 때문에 데이터 정합이라는 RDBMS의 기본 목표로 인하여 오라클은 과도한 트래픽이 몰릴 경우 지연을 통해서라도 이를 지키게 됩니다.

```
SQL>ALTER SEQUENCE <시퀀스 이름> CACHE 1000 ;
```

```
09:53:33 SYS@oracle12> ALTER SEQUENCE HR.LOCATIONS_SEQ CACHE 1000 ;
Sequence altered.
10:03:45 SYS@oracle12>
```

특히 RAC인 경우 DBMS 간 통신에서 Current Block과 CR Block의 높은 전송량을 유발하며 성능 저하 현상이 발생할 수 있습니다. Wait 이벤트 모니터링을 해보면 enq: SQ contention과 DFS lock handle이라는 이벤트가 많이 보이게 됩니다.

CACHE 옵션을 많이 주더라도 단시간 과도한 트래픽이 몰리는 선착순 이벤트인 경우에 채 번 숫자 획득 Logic을 DB의 시퀀스로 하면 엄청난 부하가 DBMS에 존재하기 때문에 이 경우에 어플리케이션 설계 튜닝을 하여 WEB/WAS Layer에서 채 번 숫자 획득 Logic되도록 개선해야 합니다.

아카이브 로그 장애

오라클 DB에 접속을 해서 DML, DDL 등의 데이터 변경 명령어로 작업을 수행하면, 모든 작업의 기록이 온라인 리두 로그 파일에 저장이 됩니다. 오라클 온라인 리두 로그 파일은 계속 증가하는 것이 아니라 몇 개의 리두 로그 파일을 만들어 놓고 번갈아 가면서 기록하는 구조로 되어있습니다.

이렇게 번갈아가면서 기록을 하게 되면 새로운 작업의 내용이 예전의 작업내용을 덮어지므로 예전의 작업한 내용을 잃게 된다는 단점이 있습니다. 그래서 예전의 작업한 내용에 데이터 손실이 발생하면 복구하기 어렵다는 단점이 있습니다. 이런 단점을 해결하기 위한 방법이 온라인 리두 로그 파일의 내용을 다른 디렉토리에 자동으로 복사해서 저장하도록 운영하는 방법이다. 이렇게 운영하는 방법을 아카이브 로그 모드(Archive Log Mode)라고 한다.

아카이브 로드 모드로 운영 하면 온라인 리두 로그 파일 내용을 복사하여 아카이브 로그 파일을 생성합니다.

오라클 DB 아카이브 로그 모드 환경에서 자주 발생하는 장애에 대해서 알아보겠습니다.

1 아카이브 로그 공간이 부족하여 장애 발생

아카이브 로그 모드에서는 가장 주의해야 할 장애입니다. 이 장애현상은 아카이브 로그 모드에서 리두 로그 그룹이 스위치를 할 때, 아카이브 로그를 쓰게 되는데, 아카이브 로그를 저장할 공간이 부족할 경우에 리두 로그 버퍼에 있는 리두 로그를 LGWR 프로세스가 디스크에 쓸 수 없게 됩니다.

이렇게 되면 다음 변경된 DML 내용에 대하여 작업을 하려는 리두 로그 그룹에 대해서는 로그 스위치가 일어나도 작업이 불가능하기 때문에 데이터베이스를 사용할 수가 없습니다. 아카이브가 끝날 때까지 시스템이 기다리게 됩니다.

```
Unable to create archive log file '/oracle/oracle12/arch/1_16_952016687.dbf'
Errors in file /oracle/oracle12/app/oracle/diag/rdbms/oracle12/oracle12/trace/oracle12_arc1_30769.trc:
ORA-19504: failed to create file "/oracle/oracle12/arch/1_16_952016687.dbf"
ORA-27040: file create error, unable to create file
Linux-x86_64 Error: 13: Permission denied
Additional information: 1
ARC1: Error 19504 Creating archive log file to '/oracle/oracle12/arch/1_16_952016687.dbf'
Unable to create archive log file '/oracle/oracle12/arch/1_15_952016687.dbf'
Errors in file /oracle/oracle12/app/oracle/diag/rdbms/oracle12/oracle12/trace/oracle12_arc3_30773.trc:
ORA-19504: failed to create file "/oracle/oracle12/arch/1_15_952016687.dbf"
ORA-27040: file create error, unable to create file
Linux-x86_64 Error: 13: Permission denied
Additional information: 1
ARC3: Error 19504 Creating archive log file to '/oracle/oracle12/arch/1_15_952016687.dbf'
Unable to create archive log file '/oracle/oracle12/arch/1_16_952016687.dbf'
Errors in file /oracle/oracle12/app/oracle/diag/rdbms/oracle12/oracle12/trace/oracle12_arc2_30771.trc:
ORA-19504: failed to create file "/oracle/oracle12/arch/1_16_952016687.dbf"
ORA-27040: file create error, unable to create file
Linux-x86_64 Error: 13: Permission denied
Additional information: 1
ARC2: Error 19504 Creating archive log file to '/oracle/oracle12/arch/1_16_952016687.dbf'
2017-09-05 14:06:51.108000 +09:00
Unable to create archive log file '/oracle/oracle12/arch/1_15_952016687.dbf'
Errors in file /oracle/oracle12/app/oracle/diag/rdbms/oracle12/oracle12/trace/oracle12_arc0_30765.trc:
ORA-19504: failed to create file "/oracle/oracle12/arch/1_15_952016687.dbf"
ORA-27040: file create error, unable to create file
Linux-x86_64 Error: 13: Permission denied
Additional information: 1
ARC0: Error 19504 Creating archive log file to '/oracle/oracle12/arch/1_15_952016687.dbf'
Suppressing further error logging of LOG_ARCHIVE_DEST_1
Suppressing further error logging of LOG_ARCHIVE_DEST_1
```

▲ 아카이빙 실패 시 Alert log에 에러 발생

Alert Log를 확인하여 Archive Log 관련 에러를 확인할 수 있습니다. DBA는 지속적으로 아카이브 로그 공간을 모니터링해서 부족 현상이 없도록 해야 합니다. 가장 좋은 관리 방법은 아카이브 공간에서 아카이브 로그를 백업장치로 백업받고 삭제하는 것입니다.

2 쓰고 있는 마지막 아카이브 로그를 삭제한 경우

DBA가 아카이브 로그 공간 부족 장애 현상에서 빨리 벗어나고 싶어서 다급하게 OS 명령어로 모든 아카이브 로그 삭제하면 어떻게 될까요? 정답은 장애가 발생하게 됩니다.

```
ORA-16038: log 3 sequence# 3716 cannot be archived
ORA-19502: write error on file "", blockno (blocksize=)
ORA-00312: online log 3 thread 1: '+REDO/oracle12/onlinelog/redo03.log'
ORA-00312: online log 3 thread 1: '+FRA/oracle12/onlinelog/redo03.log'
```

```
10:03:45 SYS@oracle12> ALTER DATABASE CLEAR UNARCHIVED LOGFILE GROUP 3;
Database altered.
10:14:01 SYS@oracle12>
```

▲ Alert log에 해당 리두 로그 그룹이 아카이브 되지 않았다고 에러 발생

아카이빙 Write 중인 아카이브 로그 파일을 지우면 결국 오라클은 해당 REDO 로그 그룹 파일은 아카이브 되지 않았다고 판단하게 됩니다. 오라클 DB의 기준은 어떠한 상황 발생에도 복구가 무결함 해야 함이 원칙이기 때문입니다.

따라서 이런 경우 이는 해당 리두 로그 그룹에 마크를 해주는 명령어를 실행하면 됩니다.

```
SQL>ALTER DATABASE CLEAR UNARCHIVED LOGFILE GROUP 3;
```

```
10:03:45 SYS@oracle12> ALTER DATABASE CLEAR UNARCHIVED LOGFILE GROUP 3;
Database altered.
10:14:01 SYS@oracle12> ▮
```

가장 안전한 아카이브 로그 삭제 방법은 바로 RMAN을 통해서 아카이브를 지우는 방법입니다.

```
[oracle12]yspark-linux:/home/oracle12> rman target /
Recovery Manager: Release 12.2.0.1.0 - Production on Tue Sep 5 14:54:24 2017
Copyright (c) 1982, 2017, Oracle and/or its affiliates.  All rights reserved.
connected to target database: ORACLE12 (DBID=2053465567)
RMAN> crosscheck archivelog all ;
using target database control file instead of recovery catalog
allocated channel: ORA_DISK_1
channel ORA_DISK_1: SID=393 device type=DISK
validation succeeded for archived log
archived log file name=/oracle/oracle12/arch/1_6_952016687.dbf RECID=2 STAMP=953906665
validation succeeded for archived log
archived log file name=/oracle/oracle12/arch/1_7_952016687.dbf RECID=1 STAMP=953906664
validation succeeded for archived log
archived log file name=/oracle/oracle12/arch/1_8_952016687.dbf RECID=3 STAMP=953906667
validation succeeded for archived log
archived log file name=/oracle/oracle12/arch/1_9_952016687.dbf RECID=4 STAMP=953906667
validation succeeded for archived log
archived log file name=/oracle/oracle12/arch/1_10_952016687.dbf RECID=5 STAMP=953906673
validation succeeded for archived log
archived log file name=/oracle/oracle12/arch/1_11_952016687.dbf RECID=6 STAMP=953906674
validation succeeded for archived log
archived log file name=/oracle/oracle12/arch/1_12_952016687.dbf RECID=7 STAMP=953906679
validation succeeded for archived log
archived log file name=/oracle/oracle12/arch/1_13_952016687.dbf RECID=8 STAMP=953906679
validation succeeded for archived log
archived log file name=/oracle/oracle12/arch/1_14_952016687.dbf RECID=9 STAMP=953906682
validation succeeded for archived log
archived log file name=/oracle/oracle12/arch/1_15_952016687.dbf RECID=11 STAMP=953906942
validation succeeded for archived log
archived log file name=/oracle/oracle12/arch/1_16_952016687.dbf RECID=10 STAMP=953906942
validation succeeded for archived log
archived log file name=/oracle/oracle12/arch/1_17_952016687.dbf RECID=12 STAMP=953906943
validation succeeded for archived log
archived log file name=/oracle/oracle12/arch/1_18_952016687.dbf RECID=13 STAMP=953909637
Crosschecked 13 objects
```

```
RMAN> delete noprompt archivelog until time 'SYSDATE-1/24' ;

released channel: ORA_DISK_1
allocated channel: ORA_DISK_1
channel ORA_DISK_1: SID=393 device type=DISK
List of Archived Log Copies for database with db_unique_name ORACLE12
=====================================================================

Key     Thrd Seq     S Low Time
------- ---- ------- - ---------
2       1    6       A 04-SEP-17
        Name: /oracle/oracle12/arch/1_6_952016687.dbf

deleted archived log
archived log file name=/oracle/oracle12/arch/1_6_952016687.dbf RECID=2 STAMP=953906665
Deleted 1 objects

RMAN> ▮
```

▲ RMAN을 통해 1 시간 이전에 생성된 아카이브 로그 파일을 삭제

아카이브 로그 백업은 RMAN을 통해서 백업을 받고 3일 보관 및 3일 지난 것은 삭제하는 것으로 구성하는 것이 보통의 백업 구성 방법입니다. 아카이브로그 일일 발생량에 따라 백업 주기와 공간 확보해야 합니다. 일일 아카이브 발생량도 체크해 주세요.

```
SQL> l
select to_char(first_time,'MM-DD') day,
to_char(sum(decode(to_char(first_time,'hh24'),'00',1,0)),'999') "00",
to_char(sum(decode(to_char(first_time,'hh24'),'01',1,0)),'999') "01",
to_char(sum(decode(to_char(first_time,'hh24'),'02',1,0)),'999') "02",
to_char(sum(decode(to_char(first_time,'hh24'),'03',1,0)),'999') "03",
to_char(sum(decode(to_char(first_time,'hh24'),'04',1,0)),'999') "04",
to_char(sum(decode(to_char(first_time,'hh24'),'05',1,0)),'999') "05",
to_char(sum(decode(to_char(first_time,'hh24'),'06',1,0)),'999') "06",
to_char(sum(decode(to_char(first_time,'hh24'),'07',1,0)),'999') "07",
to_char(sum(decode(to_char(first_time,'hh24'),'08',1,0)),'999') "08",
to_char(sum(decode(to_char(first_time,'hh24'),'09',1,0)),'999') "09",
to_char(sum(decode(to_char(first_time,'hh24'),'10',1,0)),'999') "10",
to_char(sum(decode(to_char(first_time,'hh24'),'11',1,0)),'999') "11",
to_char(sum(decode(to_char(first_time,'hh24'),'12',1,0)),'999') "12",
to_char(sum(decode(to_char(first_time,'hh24'),'13',1,0)),'999') "13",
to_char(sum(decode(to_char(first_time,'hh24'),'14',1,0)),'999') "14",
to_char(sum(decode(to_char(first_time,'hh24'),'15',1,0)),'999') "15",
to_char(sum(decode(to_char(first_time,'hh24'),'16',1,0)),'999') "16",
to_char(sum(decode(to_char(first_time,'hh24'),'17',1,0)),'999') "17",
to_char(sum(decode(to_char(first_time,'hh24'),'18',1,0)),'999') "18",
to_char(sum(decode(to_char(first_time,'hh24'),'19',1,0)),'999') "19",
to_char(sum(decode(to_char(first_time,'hh24'),'20',1,0)),'999') "20",
to_char(sum(decode(to_char(first_time,'hh24'),'21',1,0)),'999') "21",
to_char(sum(decode(to_char(first_time,'hh24'),'22',1,0)),'999') "22",
to_char(sum(decode(to_char(first_time,'hh24'),'23',1,0)),'999') "23",
count(*) TOTAL
from v$log_history
group by to_char(first_time,'MM-DD')
order by 1
SQL> /

DAY   00   01   02   03   04   05   06   07   08   09   10   11   12   13   14   15   16   17   18   19   20   21   22   23        TOTAL
----- ---- ---- ---- ---- ---- ---- ---- ---- ---- ---- ---- ---- ---- ---- ---- ---- ---- ---- ---- ---- ---- ---- ---- ---- ----------
08-14    0    0    0    0    0    0    0    0    0    0    0    0    0    0    0    0    0    1    0    0    0    0    1    0          2
08-15    1    0    0    0    0    0    0    0    0    0    0    0    0    0    0    0    0    0    0    0    0    0    0    1          2
08-16    0    0    0    0    0    0    0    0    0    1    0    0    0    0    0    0    0    0    0    0    0    0    0    0          1
09-04    0    0    0    0    0    0    0    0    0    0    0    0    0    0    0    0    0    0    0    0    0    0    0    1          1
09-05    0    0    0    0    0    0    0    0    0    0    0    0    0    0   12    0    0    0    0    0    0    0    0    0         12

SQL> ▮
```

▲ 시각 단위 아카이브 발생 수 체크

```
SQL> select THREAD# , to_date(to_char(first_time,'yyyy/mm/dd'),'yyyy/mm/dd') "per Day"
          ,nvl(sum(1),0) "Log Count"
          ,round(nvl(sum(blocks*block_size),0)/1048576, 2) "Size(Mb)"
from v$archived_log
where      first_time >= trunc(sysdate-7)
group by THREAD# , to_char(first_time,'yyyy/mm/dd')
order by 1,2 desc
/

   THREAD# per Day            Log Count   Size(Mb)
---------- ------------------ ---------- ----------
         1 05-SEP-17                  12        .44
         1 04-SEP-17                   1      134.8

SQL> ▮
```

▲ 일자 단위 아카이브 발생량 체크

3 고속 복구 영역을 사용할 경우 parameter에 의한 장애

RAC인 경우 아카이브 로그 파일을 ASM의 공통 영역에 저장하기 위해 고속 복구 영역을 활성화로 세팅해서 특정 ASM Disk Group에(일반적으로 +FRA Disk Group 사용) 위치하여 사용합니다. 이 경우 디스크 공간은 충분하지만 에러가 발생할 수 있습니다.

```
SYS@unidb11 SQL> select NAME,TOTAL_MB,FREE_MB from v$asm_diskgroup where NAME='ORA_FRA' ;

NAME                                                             TOTAL_MB    FREE_MB
---------------------------------------------------------------- ----------- ----------
ORA_FRA                                                              512000     490574

Elapsed: 00:00:00.04
SYS@unidb11 SQL> archive log list
Database log mode              Archive Mode
Automatic archival             Enabled
Archive destination            USE_DB_RECOVERY_FILE_DEST
Oldest online log sequence     492
Next log sequence to archive   493
Current log sequence           493
SYS@unidb11 SQL> col value for a30
SYS@unidb11 SQL> col name for a30
SYS@unidb11 SQL> select NAME,VALUE from v$spparameter where NAME='db_recovery_file_dest' ;

NAME                           VALUE
------------------------------ ------------------------------
db_recovery_file_dest          +ORA_FRA

Elapsed: 00:00:00.01
SYS@unidb11 SQL>
```

▲ 고속 복구 영역을 사용한 경우

고속 복구 영역을 활성화하여 아카이브 로그 파일 생성 공간으로 사용한 경우 디스크 공간은 충분하지만 공간 부족 에러가 발생할 수 있습니다

```
[unidb11]unione1:/oracle/app/oracle/diag/rdbms/unidb1/unidb11/trace> tail -18 alert_unidb11.log
   DELETE EXPIRED commands.
************************************************************************
ARC0: Error 19809 Creating archive log file to '+ORA_FRA'
Errors in file /oracle/app/oracle/diag/rdbms/unidb1/unidb11/trace/unidb11_arc1_9285.trc:
ORA-19815: 경고: db_recovery_file_dest_size/103809024바이트는 100.00%가 사용 중이므로, 나머지 0바이트를 사용할 수 있습니다.
************************************************************************
You have following choices to free up space from recovery area:
1. Consider changing RMAN RETENTION POLICY. If you are using Data Guard,
   then consider changing RMAN ARCHIVELOG DELETION POLICY.
2. Back up files to tertiary device such as tape using RMAN
   BACKUP RECOVERY AREA command.
3. Add disk space and increase db_recovery_file_dest_size parameter to
   reflect the new space.
4. Delete unnecessary files using RMAN DELETE command. If an operating
   system command was used to delete files, then use RMAN CROSSCHECK and
   DELETE EXPIRED commands.
************************************************************************
ARC1: Error 19809 Creating archive log file to '+ORA_FRA'
[unidb11]unione1:/oracle/app/oracle/diag/rdbms/unidb1/unidb11/trace>
```

▲ 아카이빙 공간은 충분하지만 오라클 에러 발생

그 이유는 db_recovery_file_dest_sizeparameter가 작게 잡혀져 있기 때문입니다. 따라서 이 parameter 수치를 고속 복구 영역의 물리적인 사이즈만큼 증가 시켜주면 장애 상황이 해결됩니다.

```
SYS@unidb11 SQL> show parameter db_recovery_file_dest_size

NAME                                 TYPE                   VALUE
------------------------------------ ---------------------- ------------------------------
db_recovery_file_dest_size           big integer            99M
SYS@unidb11 SQL> alter system set db_recovery_file_dest_size=512000M;

System altered.

Elapsed: 00:00:00.07
SYS@unidb11 SQL>
```

▲ parameter 변경으로 장애 상황 해결

파티션 테이블 장애

오늘날 기업에서 관리하는 데이터는 수 백 테라바이트에 이르는 데이터베이스를 관리합니다. 하지만 이런 데이터들 중 몇몇의 Big Transaction Table이 거의 모든 데이터를 가지고 있고 나머지 테이블들은 이 Big Transaction Table을 경유하여 액세스하는 용도로 사용됩니다.

이렇게 데이터 크기도 크고 중요한 Big Transaction Table을 관리하는 부분에서 문제가 발생될 경우 데이터베이스의 성능 및 관리 작업에 심각한 영향을 받을 수 있습니다.

오라클 파티션 테이블은 이러한 리스크가 있는 Big Transaction Table을 보다 효율적으로 관리하기 위해 Table을 작은 단위로 나눔으로써 데이터 액세스 작업의 성능 향상을 유도하고 데이터 관리를 보다 수월하게 하고자 하는 개념입니다.
대용량 오라클 DB 환경에서 많이 사용하고 있는 파티션 테이블에서 자주 발생하는 장애에 대해서 알아보겠습니다.

1 Range 파티션 테이블의 범위 오류 장애 발생

차세대 DB 서비스를 OPEN하고 1년 후 1일에 파티션 테이블 장애가 날 수 있습니다. 어떤 이유일까요?
Oracle 8i부터 나온 Range 파티션의 경우 다수의 대용량 DB에서 날짜 컬럼 파티션으로 사용하고 있습니다. 개발자가 최초 파티션 키가 날짜로 된 Range 파티션 테이블을 만들면 보통 몇 달/몇 년 후 파티션을 함께 만듭니다. 만들어진 Range 파티션을 넘어선 날짜의 데이터가 들어온다면 장애가 발생합니다.

```
SQL>
SQL> CREATE TABLE sales
          (sales_no NUMBER,
           sale_year INT NOT NULL,
           sale_month INT NOT NULL,
           sale_day INT NOT NULL,
           customer_name  VARCHAR2(30),
           price NUMBER)
         PARTITION BY RANGE (sale_year, sale_month, sale_day)
         (PARTITION sales_q1 VALUES LESS THAN (2016, 01, 01) TABLESPACE USERS,
          PARTITION sales_q2 VALUES LESS THAN (2016, 07, 01) TABLESPACE USERS,
          PARTITION sales_q3 VALUES LESS THAN (2017, 01, 01) TABLESPACE USERS,
          PARTITION sales_q4 VALUES LESS THAN (2017, 07, 01) TABLESPACE USERS );

Table created.

SQL> INSERT INTO sales VALUES(6, 2006, 12, 22, 'tiger', 3300);

1 row created.

SQL> commit ;

Commit complete.

SQL> INSERT INTO sales VALUES(7, 2018, 12, 22, 'tiger', 3300);
INSERT INTO sales VALUES(7, 2018, 12, 22, 'tiger', 3300)
            *
ERROR at line 1:
ORA-14400: inserted partition key does not map to any partition


SQL>
```

▲ Range 파티션 테이블에 장애 발생

DBA는 파티션 사전에 일자 Range 파티션 테이블을 체크해서 ORA-14400 에러가 나서 매월 1일 되는 자정에 일괄 장애 나는 것을 막아야 합니다. 파티션 생성을 사전에 체크해야 하고, 없다면 파티션을 추가해 주어야 합니다.

```
SQL>    ALTER TABLE sales
          ADD PARTITION sales_q7 VALUES LESS THAN (2019, 01, 01 )
          TABLESPACE USERS;

Table altered.

SQL>     INSERT INTO sales VALUES(7, 2018, 12, 22, 'tiger', 3300);

1 row created.

SQL>
```

▲ 해당 데이터가 들어오기 전에 사전에 파티션을 추가

Range 파티션 테이블에 파티션을 사전에 추가하는 것도 DBA가 해야 할 일입니다.
하지만 DBA가 파티션 추가하기 전에 데이터가 들어온다면 ORA-14400이 발생하며 장애 상황을 겪게 될 것입니다.

```
SQL>     ALTER TABLE sales
          ADD PARTITION sales_max VALUES LESS THAN (MAXVALUE, MAXVALUE, MAXVALUE )
          TABLESPACE USERS;

Table altered.

SQL>  INSERT INTO sales VALUES(8, 2040, 12, 22, 'tiger', 3300);

1 row created.

SQL>
```

▲ MAX VALUE 파티션을 추가

만약의 경우를 대비하여 파티션 테이블 초과 데이터 insert를 위해 장애 방지용 파티션인 MAXVALUE 파티션을 추가합니다.

MAXVALUE 파티션으로 인하여 당장 서비스 장애는 발생하지 않지만 데이터를 분할해서 관리해야 하는 파티션 관리 목적으로는 위배되기 때문에 MAXVALUE 파티션을 SPLIT하여야 합니다. SPLIT 하지 않으면 초과되는 데이터가 모두 MAXVALUE 파티션으로 들어가 파티션 별 사이즈가 고르게 있지 못하고 MAXVALUE 파티션 크기만 커져서 쿼리 검색 속도에 영향을 미치게 됩니다.

```
SQL>  INSERT INTO sales VALUES(8, 2040, 12, 22, 'tiger', 3300);

1 row created.

SQL> commit ;

Commit complete.

SQL>     ALTER TABLE sales
  2       SPLIT PARTITION sales_max at (2041, 01, 01 )
  3        into (partition sales_q8, partition sales_max);

Table altered.

SQL> █
```

▲ MAXVALUE 파티션을 SPLIT 분할

2 파티션 테이블 작업 후 INDEX 장애 발생

DBA가 밤새 파티션 테이블 작업을 한 후 다음날 아침에 서비스 장애가 발생하였습니다. 어떤 이유일까요?

```
SQL> CREATE INDEX IX_SALES_GLOBAL ON SALES (SALES_NO, PRICE,sale_year, sale_month, sale_day) ;

Index created.

SQL> drop index IX_SALES_LOCAL ;

Index dropped.

SQL> CREATE INDEX IX_SALES_LOCAL ON SALES (sale_year, sale_month, sale_day,PRICE) LOCAL
  2   (Partition sales_q1 ,
  3     Partition sales_q2 ,
  4     Partition sales_q3 ,
  5     Partition sales_q4 ,
  6     Partition sales_q5 ,
  7     Partition sales_q6 ,
  8     Partition sales_q7 ,
  9     Partition sales_q8 ,
 10     Partition sales_max ) ;

Index created.

SQL> █
```

▲ 파티션 테이블에 Global Index와 Local Partition Index를 생성

```
SQL> EXPLAIN plan FOR
  2  select SALES_NO,PRICE from SALES where SALES_NO=7 ;

Explained.

SQL> SELECT * FROM TABLE(dbms_xplan.display);

PLAN_TABLE_OUTPUT
----------------------------------------------------------------------------------------------------
Plan hash value: 1383442667

-------------------------------------------------------------------------------------
| Id  | Operation         | Name             | Rows  | Bytes | Cost (%CPU)| Time     |
-------------------------------------------------------------------------------------
|   0 | SELECT STATEMENT  |                  |     1 |     6 |     1   (0)| 00:00:01 |
|*  1 |  INDEX RANGE SCAN| IX_SALES_GLOBAL  |     1 |     6 |     1   (0)| 00:00:01 |
-------------------------------------------------------------------------------------

Predicate Information (identified by operation id):
---------------------------------------------------

PLAN_TABLE_OUTPUT
----------------------------------------------------------------------------------------------------

   1 - access("SALES_NO"=7)

13 rows selected.

SQL> ▮
```

▲ Global Index를 잘 타는 SQL 문이 존재

파티션 테이블에 Global Index를 잘 타던 쿼리가 존재하고 있습니다.

```
SQL> ALTER TABLE sales DROP  PARTITION  q7 ;

Table altered.

SQL> ▮
```

▲ 과거 파티션 삭제 작업

DBA는 보관주기 지난 파티션을 삭제하는 작업을 하였습니다.

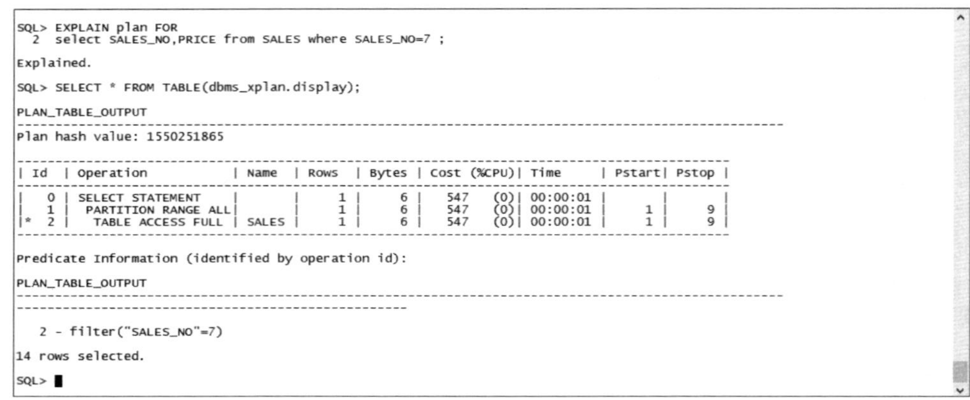

```
SQL> EXPLAIN plan FOR
  2  select SALES_NO,PRICE from SALES where SALES_NO=7 ;

Explained.

SQL> SELECT * FROM TABLE(dbms_xplan.display);

PLAN_TABLE_OUTPUT
----------------------------------------------------------------------------------------------------
Plan hash value: 1550251865

---------------------------------------------------------------------------------------------
| Id  | Operation           | Name  | Rows  | Bytes | Cost (%CPU)| Time     | Pstart| Pstop |
---------------------------------------------------------------------------------------------
|   0 | SELECT STATEMENT    |       |     1 |     6 |   547   (0)| 00:00:01 |       |       |
|   1 |  PARTITION RANGE ALL|       |     1 |     6 |   547   (0)| 00:00:01 |     1 |     9 |
|*  2 |   TABLE ACCESS FULL | SALES |     1 |     6 |   547   (0)| 00:00:01 |     1 |     9 |
---------------------------------------------------------------------------------------------

Predicate Information (identified by operation id):

PLAN_TABLE_OUTPUT
----------------------------------------------------------------------------------------------------
---------------------------------------------------

   2 - filter("SALES_NO"=7)

14 rows selected.

SQL> ▮
```

▲ Index Scan 플랜을 타던 쿼리가 Full Scan 플랜으로 변경

파티션 테이블의 데이터 Rowid가 변경되는 작업을 하면 파티션 테이블의 INDEX가 UNUSABLE 상태로 변경됩니다. 결국 **Index를 타던 쿼리는 Full Table Scan으로 변경되어**

서비스 지연 현상이 발생하고, 야간 파티션 작업 한 다음날 업무 개시부터 장애가 발생하였던 것입니다.

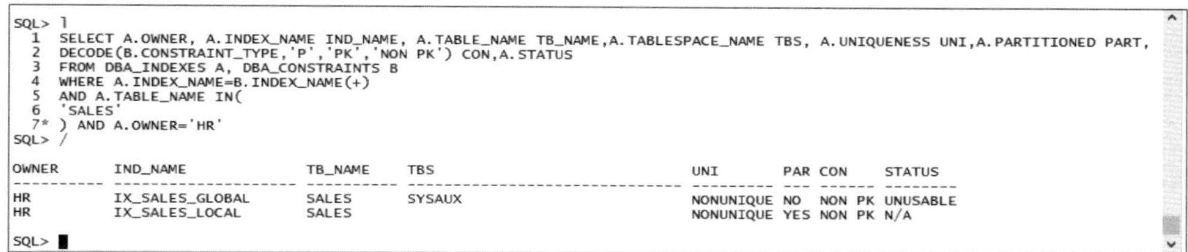

```
SQL> l
  1  SELECT A.OWNER, A.INDEX_NAME IND_NAME, A.TABLE_NAME TB_NAME,A.TABLESPACE_NAME TBS, A.UNIQUENESS UNI,A.PARTITIONED PART,
  2  DECODE(B.CONSTRAINT_TYPE,'P','PK','NON PK') CON,A.STATUS
  3  FROM DBA_INDEXES A, DBA_CONSTRAINTS B
  4  WHERE A.INDEX_NAME=B.INDEX_NAME(+)
  5  AND A.TABLE_NAME IN(
  6  'SALES'
  7* ) AND A.OWNER='HR'
SQL> /

OWNER      IND_NAME             TB_NAME    TBS                            UNI       PAR CON    STATUS
---------- -------------------- ---------- ------------------------------ --------- --- ------ --------
HR         IX_SALES_GLOBAL      SALES      SYSAUX                         NONUNIQUE NO  NON PK UNUSABLE
HR         IX_SALES_LOCAL       SALES                                     NONUNIQUE YES NON PK N/A

SQL>
```

```
SQL> SELECT A.INDEX_OWNER,A.INDEX_NAME,B.UNIQUENESS,A.PARTITION_NAME,A.STATUS,A.TABLESPACE_NAME
  2  FROM DBA_IND_PARTITIONS A, DBA_INDEXES B
  3  WHERE A.INDEX_NAME=B.INDEX_NAME AND A.INDEX_NAME IN
  4  (SELECT INDEX_NAME FROM DBA_INDEXES WHERE TABLE_NAME IN ('SALES'))
  5  ORDER BY A.INDEX_OWNER,A.INDEX_NAME,A.PARTITION_POSITION;

INDEX_OWNE INDEX_NAME                     UNIQUENES PARTITION_NAME                 STATUS   TABLESPACE_NAME
---------- ------------------------------ --------- ------------------------------ -------- ------------------------------
HR         IX_SALES_LOCAL                 NONUNIQUE SALES_Q2                       USABLE   USERS
HR         IX_SALES_LOCAL                 NONUNIQUE SALES_Q3                       USABLE   USERS
HR         IX_SALES_LOCAL                 NONUNIQUE SALES_Q4                       USABLE   USERS
HR         IX_SALES_LOCAL                 NONUNIQUE SALES_Q5                       USABLE   USERS
HR         IX_SALES_LOCAL                 NONUNIQUE SALES_Q6                       USABLE   USERS
HR         IX_SALES_LOCAL                 NONUNIQUE SALES_Q6_5                     USABLE   USERS
HR         IX_SALES_LOCAL                 NONUNIQUE SALES_Q8                       USABLE   USERS
HR         IX_SALES_LOCAL                 NONUNIQUE SALES_Q9                       USABLE   USERS
HR         IX_SALES_LOCAL                 NONUNIQUE SALES_MAX                      USABLE   USERS

9 rows selected.

SQL>
```

▲ 파티션 테이블 index 상태 점검

Global index의 상태는 unusable로 변경되었지만, Local Partition index의 경우에는 변경되지 않았습니다.

파티션 작업 유형	index	Unusable 상태변경
ADD	LOCAL	새로 생성되므로 상관없다.
	GLOBAL	파티션만 추가되므로 상관없다.
DROP	LOCAL	같이 삭제되므로 상관없다.
	GLOBAL	**모든 GLOBAL INDEX가 Unusable**
SPLIT	LOCAL	**SPLIT된 파티션 index Unusable**
	GLOBAL	**모든 GLOBAL INDEX가 Unusable**
MERGE	LOCAL	**머지 되어 남는 파티션 index Unusable**
	GLOBAL	**모든 GLOBAL INDEX가 Unusable**
RENAME	LOCAL	실제 변경이 없으므로 상관없다.
	GLOBAL	실제 변경이 없으므로 상관없다.
MOVE	LOCAL	**MOVE된 파티션 index Unusable**
	GLOBAL	**모든 GLOBAL INDEX가 Unusable**
TRUNCATE	LOCAL	남은 Row가 없으므로 상관없다.
	GLOBAL	**모든 GLOBAL INDEX가 Unusable**
EXCHANGE	LOCAL	**EXCHANGE한 파티션 index Unusable**
	GLOBAL	**모든 GLOBAL INDEX가 Unusable**

▲ 파티션 테이블의 작업별 Index Unusable 상태

Index가 Unusable 상태가 되는 것은 실제 파티션 테이블 데이터의 RowID를 변경시킨 경우, 파티션 단위의 변경이 발생 시에도 해당 파티션에 실제 로우 데이터가 있어서 RowID 변경이 발생된 경우에 발생합니다. 해당 파티션에 실제 로우 데이터가 없으면 발생하지 않습니다.

```
SQL>
SQL> show parameter skip_unusable_indexes

NAME                                 TYPE        VALUE
------------------------------------ ----------- ------------------------------
skip_unusable_indexes                boolean     TRUE
SQL> █
```

skip_unusable_indexes라는 parameter가 있습니다. Oracle DB 12c에서 이 parameter는 TRUE가 기본으로 해당 parameter는 unusable index를 사용하는 DML에 대해서 SKIP (ERROR) 없이 수행하라는 parameter입니다.

보통의 경우 TRUE로 사용하지만 잦은 파티션 테이블 작업이 많은 경우 장애 알림 기능으로 사용할 수 있습니다. 어떤 index가 무슨 이유로 인해 unusable 상태가 되었고, 이것으로 인해 특정 table에 대한 access에 대해 full scan이 반복되고, 그 결과 특정 query의 성능이 매우 나빠지는 경우가 발생할 수 있습니다.

이 parameter를 False로 변경하면 unusable index 존재하여 쿼리 수행 시 error message가 출력되므로 원인을 쉽게 발견할 수 있었지만, 이 parameter를 통해 error message가 출력되지 않게 됨으로써 query 성능이 나빠진 원인을 쉽게 발견하지 못 할 수 있다는 것입니다.

DB 정보 변경 작업 장애

운영 중인 오라클 DB 시스템에 어떤 변경작업을 수행하는 경우에는 가능한 한 충분한 사전 테스트를 거친 후에 작업해야 하며, 롤백 전략을 수립한 다음에 작업하는 것을 원칙으로 합니다. 또한 한 번에 여러 가지 변경 작업을 수행하지 말고, 하나의 변경 작업을 수행하고 그 변경 작업이 미친 영향을 관찰하는 것이 바람직합니다.

모든 변경 작업에 대해서 롤백 전략을 수립하는 것이 원칙이며, 롤백에 필요한 사항들을 문서로 기록하고 롤백에 필요한 스크립트 등을 작성하고 테스트하여 검증합니다. 특히 대용량 데이터베이스의 경우에는 문제 발생 시 복구에 소요되는 시간이 길기 때문에 충분한 사전 테스트와 롤백 전략 수립이 매우 중요합니다.

오라클 DB 안의 테이블 변경/오브젝트 변경/대용량 데이터 변경/통계 정보 변경/파라미터 변경 등 변경 작업을 하면서 발생할 수 있는 장애에 대해 알아보겠습니다.

1 온라인 시간 테이블 변경 작업 이후 장애

점심을 먹고 온 후 DBA는 개발자가 갑자기 요청을 합니다. 너무 급하게 쿼리를 반영했는데 잘못 반영했다고, DB 내에 특정 테이블에 기존 컬럼 삭제 및 신규 컬럼 추가 좀 해달라고 요청을 합니다. DBA는 개발자의 요청대로 개발 DB에서 반영해 보고 운영 DB의 테이블에 변경 작업을 합니다. 서비스의 지연 현상 발생하는 서비스 장애가 발생했습니다. 무슨 이유일까요? 알아보겠습니다.

테스트 프로시저를 만듭니다.

```
SQL> CREATE OR REPLACE PROCEDURE DELEMP(NO in NUMBER) IS
  2  BEGIN
  3  DELETE employees WHERE employee_id = NO;
  4  END;
  5  /

Procedure created.
```

▲ 테스트

첫 번째 세션에서 만든 프로시저에 200을 넣고 수행을 합니다.

```
SQL> exec DELEMP(200);

PL/SQL procedure successfully completed.

SQL> █
```

▲ 첫 번째 세션은 정상 수행

두 번째 세션에서 200을 넣고 수행을 시작하면 완료되지 않고 수행 중인 상태로 대기합니다.

```
[oracle12]yspark-linux:/home/oracle12> sqlplus hr/hr

SQL*Plus: Release 12.2.0.1.0 Production on Fri Sep 22 15:59:12 2017

Copyright (c) 1982, 2016, Oracle.  All rights reserved.

Last Successful login time: Fri Sep 22 2017 15:51:35 +09:00

Connected to:
Oracle Database 12c Enterprise Edition Release 12.2.0.1.0 - 64bit Production

SQL> exec DELEMP(200);
█
```

▲ 두 번째 세션에서 수행

세션 락 상태를 조회해 보면 Row Transaction lock이 걸려있습니다. 200에 해당하는 ROW를 지우려고 하다 보니 첫 번째 세션이 Commit이나 Rollback이 되지 않아 두 번째 세션은 Wait이 되고 있습니다. 어플리케이션이 수행 중 상황을 재현하기 위해서 상황을 만들었습니다.

```
*** LOCK, REQUEST MODE ***
0 : None,     1 : Null,           2 : Row-S (SS),     3 : Row-X (SX)
4 : Share,    5 : S/Row-X (SSX),  6 : Exclusive

                          SID       ORAOSPID                                           SQL
INSTANCE   LOCK_INFO    SERIAL#   CLIENT           PROGRAM          SQL_ID         COMMAN LOCK TYPE
---------- ----------- --------- ---------------- ---------------- ------------- ------ ------------------------------------
DB_1       +Holder:     93,1784   15279,15265      sqlplus@yspark-  96uuxm9njvpys PL/SQL TX(Row Transaction enqueue)
DB_1        ->Waiter:   262,52873 15303,15302      sqlplus@yspark-  auqwphpvnncmj DELETE TX(Row Transaction enqueue)
```

▲ DB LOCK 상태 확인

이제 실제 개발자가 와서 오브젝트 변경 일명 DDL 명령 작업을 DBA에게 요청해서 수행하는 단계입니다.

세 번째 세션에서 해당 프로시저를 DROP 명령어를 수행하면 삭제되지 않고 대기 하게 됩니다.

```
[oracle12]yspark-linux:/home/oracle12> sqlplus hr/hr

SQL*Plus: Release 12.2.0.1.0 Production on Fri Sep 22 16:19:33 2017

Copyright (c) 1982, 2016, Oracle.  All rights reserved.

Last Successful login time: Fri Sep 22 2017 16:19:05 +09:00

Connected to:
Oracle Database 12c Enterprise Edition Release 12.2.0.1.0 - 64bit Production

SQL> drop procedure delemp;
█
```

▲ 세 번째 세션에서 DROP 수행

세션 상황을 확인해 보니 library cache pin 이벤트가 발생하며 대기하게 됩니다.

```
SID          SPID
SERIAL#      CLIENT           DBUSER     OSUSER     MACHINE              PROGRAM                      WAIT_EVENT                                                     SQL_ID          COMMAND
------------ ---------------- ---------- ---------- -------------------- ---------------------------- -------------------------------------------------------------- --------------- -------
17,29285     15955,15954      SYS        oracle12   yspark-linux         sqlplus@yspark-linux         PGA memory operation:131072,1,0                                3jn6rnddkubhm   SELECT
15,15390     15350,15349      HR         oracle12   yspark-linux         SQL*Plus                     library cache pin:1924965648,1922085976,327066054623235        a6bd71gg5tt5x   DrpProc
262,52873    15303,15302      HR         oracle12   yspark-linux         SQL*Plus                     enq: TX - row lock contention:1415053318,393242,1712           auqwphpvnncmj   DELETE
```

▲ Library Cache Pin 이벤트 발생

네 번째 세션에서 해당 프로시저를 ALTER PROCEDURE 명령어로 컴파일을 하게 되면 앞선 상황과 동일하게 대기하게 됩니다.

```
[oracle12]yspark-linux:/home/oracle12/monitor> sqlplus hr/hr

SQL*Plus: Release 12.2.0.1.0 Production on Fri Sep 22 16:20:43 2017

Copyright (c) 1982, 2016, Oracle.  All rights reserved.

Last Successful login time: Fri Sep 22 2017 16:19:33 +09:00

Connected to:
Oracle Database 12c Enterprise Edition Release 12.2.0.1.0 - 64bit Production

SQL> alter procedure DELEMP compile ;
█
```

▲ 네 번째 세션에서 컴파일 수행

세션 상황을 확인해 보니 아까 발생한 library cache pin 이벤트 이외에 library cache lock 이벤트가 발생하며 대기하게 됩니다.

```
SID          SPID
SERIAL#      CLIENT           DBUSER     OSUSER     MACHINE              PROGRAM                      WAIT_EVENT                                                     SQL_ID          COMMAND
------------ ---------------- ---------- ---------- -------------------- ---------------------------- -------------------------------------------------------------- --------------- -------
176,53787    15512,15511      HR         oracle12   yspark-linux         SQL*Plus                     library cache lock:1924965648,1924726856,327066054623235       2qjh83ty59v25   AltProc
96,5431      16683,16682      SYS        oracle12   yspark-linux         sqlplus@yspark-linux         PGA memory operation:131072,1,0                                3jn6rnddkubhm   SELECT
15,15390     15350,15349      HR         oracle12   yspark-linux         SQL*Plus                     library cache pin:1924965648,1922085976,327066054623235        a6bd71gg5tt5x   DrpProc
262,52873    15303,15302      HR         oracle12   yspark-linux         SQL*Plus                     enq: TX - row lock contention:1415053318,393242,1712           auqwphpvnncmj   DELETE
```

▲ Library Cache Lock 이벤트 추가 발생

지금의 부분에서 오라클의 WAIT 이벤트 동작 원리를 상세히 설명하지는 않겠습니다. 본 테스트의 목적은 Object 변경 작업 시 프로시저가 수행 중 일 때 트랜잭션 레벨 락이 수행 중일 때 DB 오브젝트 변경 작업을 하면 장애 상황이 발생할 수 있는 것을 보여드리고자 하였습니다.

결국 이 경우 해결 방법은 선점 하고 있는 원인이 되는 Lock Hold되는 세션을 찾아 alter session kill 명령어로 해당 세션을 제거해 주어 Lock wait된 세션을 release해 주어야 합니다.

하지만 빠른 시간 안에 락 상황을 해결 못하면 Hold되는 세션을 rollback을 하더라도 다음과 같이 변경이 실패하게 됩니다.

```
SQL> drop procedure delemp;
drop procedure delemp
*
ERROR at line 1:
ORA-04021: timeout occurred while waiting to lock object HR.DELEMP

SQL> █
```

▲ ORA-4021 에러 발생

온라인 시간의 DB 오브젝트 변경 작업은 되도록 지양해야 합니다. PM 시간을 잡아 서비스 트래픽을 막은 후 작업을 해야 하고, 만약 긴급의 변경 작업은 수행중인 서비스 트래픽을 파악하면서 온라인 Kill Session이 준비되어 있는 상태에서 진행해야 합니다.

2 테이블 중간에 컬럼 추가 작업 이후 장애

트리거를 이용한 데이터 싱크 대상인 테이블에 컬럼 순서가 변경되어야 할 요청이 들어왔습니다. 야간에 PM 시간을 확보하여 DBA는 기존 테이블을 RENAME으로 백업하고 기존 테이블명으로 CTAS를 이용해 컬럼 순서를 바꾼 테이블을 만들고, 신규 테이블을 만들고 관련된 오브젝트를 COMPILE 해주었습니다. 작업 후 서비스를 OPEN 하였는데 서비스운영자가 연락이 옵니다. 데이터가 틀리다고 합니다. 무슨 이유일까요?

실무 DB 환경에서의 오브젝트 테스트 용 테이블과 PK 인덱스, 어플리케이션 커넥션 유저에 권한과 Synonym, 뷰를 만듭니다.

```
SQL> conn hr/hr
Connected.
SQL> create table def_table (col1 number,col3 number,col4 number);

Table created.

SQL> create unique index def_table_pk on def_table (col1);

Index created.

SQL> alter table def_table add constraint def_table_pk primary key (col1);

Table altered.

SQL> create or replace
  2  TRIGGER def_table_trg
  3  BEFORE update ON def_table
  4  FOR EACH ROW
  5  BEGIN
  6  null;
  7  END;
  8  /

Trigger created.

SQL> grant select on def_table to unione;

Grant succeeded.

SQL> conn unione/unione
Connected.
SQL> create synonym def_table for hr.def_table;

Synonym created.


SQL>  create view def_table_vw as select * from hr.def_table;

View created.

SQL>
```

▲ 테이블과 DEPENDENT 오브젝트

| DEPENDENT 오브젝트란?

특정 object(view, procedure 등)들은 definition에 table과 같은 다른 object를 reference하게 생성됩니다. 이러한 경우 해당 object는 정의문(definition)에서 참조(reference)하는 object에 대하여 디펜던시(dependency)가 걸려있다고 이야기합니다. 이렇게 definition에 다른 object를 reference하는 object를 dependent object라고하며, 참조되는 object를 Referenced Object 라고 합니다.

Dependent and Referenced Objects는 다음과 같습니다.

```
Defendent Object Type : DIMENSION / EVALUATION CONTXT / FUNCTION / INDEX / INDEXTYPE / JAVA CLASS
/ JAVA DATA / MATERIALIZED VIEW / OPERATOR / PACKAGE / PACKAGE BODY / PROCEDURE / RULE / RULE SET
/ SYNONYM / TABLE / TRIGGER / TYPE / TYPE BODY / UNDEFINED / VIEW / XML SCHEMA

Referenced  Object Type : EVALUATION CONTXT / FUNCTION / INDEXTYPE / JAVA CLASS / LIBRARY /
NON-EXISTENT / OPERATOR / PACKAGE / PROCEDURE / SEQUENCE / SYNONYM / TABLE / TYPE / VIEW / XML SCHEMA
```

Referenced object에 대한 alter 작업이 수행되면, dependent object들은 altered type에 따라 그대로 사용되거나 혹은 사용 시 error를 발생시키게 됩니다. 따라서 Alter 작업 후 상태를 확인해서 Compile해야 합니다.

만들어진 Dependent 오브젝트의 상태를 확인해 봅니다.

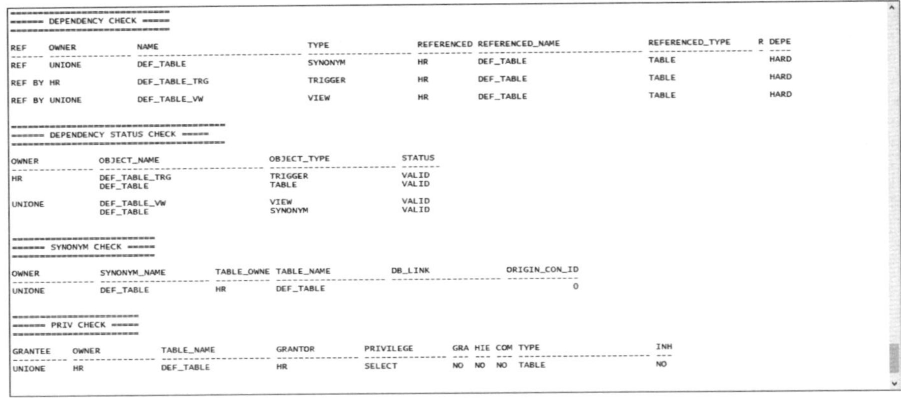

```
============================
====== DEPENDENCY CHECK =====
============================

REF    OWNER           NAME                            TYPE                 REFERENCED REFERENCED_NAME                REFERENCED_TYPE    R DEPE
------ --------------- ------------------------------- -------------------- ---------- ------------------------------ ------------------ - ----
REF    UNIONE          DEF_TABLE                       SYNONYM              HR         DEF_TABLE                      TABLE                HARD
REF BY HR              DEF_TABLE_TRG                   TRIGGER              HR         DEF_TABLE                      TABLE                HARD
REF BY UNIONE          DEF_TABLE_VW                    VIEW                 HR         DEF_TABLE                      TABLE                HARD

=====================================
====== DEPENDENCY STATUS CHECK =====
=====================================

OWNER           OBJECT_NAME                    OBJECT_TYPE          STATUS
--------------- ------------------------------ -------------------- -------
HR              DEF_TABLE_TRG                  TRIGGER              VALID
                DEF_TABLE                      TABLE                VALID

UNIONE          DEF_TABLE_VW                   VIEW                 VALID
                DEF_TABLE                      SYNONYM              VALID

==========================
====== SYNONYM CHECK =====
==========================

OWNER           SYNONYM_NAME         TABLE_OWNE TABLE_NAME           DB_LINK              ORIGIN_CON_ID
--------------- -------------------- ---------- -------------------- -------------------- -------------
UNIONE          DEF_TABLE            HR         DEF_TABLE                                             0

=======================
====== PRIV CHECK =====
=======================

GRANTEE    OWNER           TABLE_NAME           GRANTOR         PRIVILEGE       GRA HIE COM TYPE                     INH
---------- --------------- -------------------- --------------- --------------- --- --- --- ------------------------ ---
UNIONE     HR              DEF_TABLE            HR              SELECT          NO  NO  NO  TABLE                    NO
```

▲ DEPENDENT 오브젝트 상태 확인

테이블을 확인해 보니 Col2 컬럼을 2번째 추가해야 합니다. 이 작업을 할 경우 보통 기존 테이블을 RENAME하고 신규 컬럼을 중간에 위치시켜 Create Table As Select(CTAS)를 이용해 신규 테이블을 생성합니다.

```
SQL> RENAME def_table to def_table_old ;

Table renamed.

SQL> CREATE TABLE DEF_TABLE
  2  AS SELECT COL1,cast(null as number) as COL2,COL3,COL4 from def_table_old ;

Table created.

SQL> select * from DEF_TABLE ;

      COL1       COL2       COL3       COL4
---------- ---------- ---------- ----------
         1                     3          4
         2                     3          4
         3                     3          4

SQL> ▮
```

▲ 테이블 중간에 컬럼을 추가하는 작업

기존 테이블과 환경을 맞추기 위해 이제 신규 테이블에 PK를 만드는 작업부터 시작합니다.

```
SQL> create unique index def_table_pk on def_table (col1);
create unique index def_table_pk on def_table (col1)
                    *
ERROR at line 1:
ORA-00955: name is already used by an existing object


SQL> alter index def_table_pk rename to def_table_old_pk ;

Index altered.

SQL> create unique index def_table_pk on def_table (col1);

Index created.

SQL> alter table def_table add constraint def_table_pk primary key (col1);
alter table def_table add constraint def_table_pk primary key (col1)
                                     *
ERROR at line 1:
ORA-02264: name already used by an existing constraint


SQL> alter table def_table_old rename constraint def_table_pk to def_table_old_pk ;

Table altered.

SQL> alter table def_table add constraint def_table_pk primary key (col1);

Table altered.

SQL> ▮
```

▲ 신규 테이블에 PK와 인덱스를 만드는 작업

하지만 이 작업을 해보면 기존 테이블을 RENAME으로 변경시켜 놓았기 때문에 관련 object name을 변경해야만 신규 테이블에 생성이 가능하다는 것을 확인할 수 있습니다.

PK를 생성하였으니 다른 Dependent 오브젝트의 상태를 확인하기 위하여 STATUS를 조회합니다.

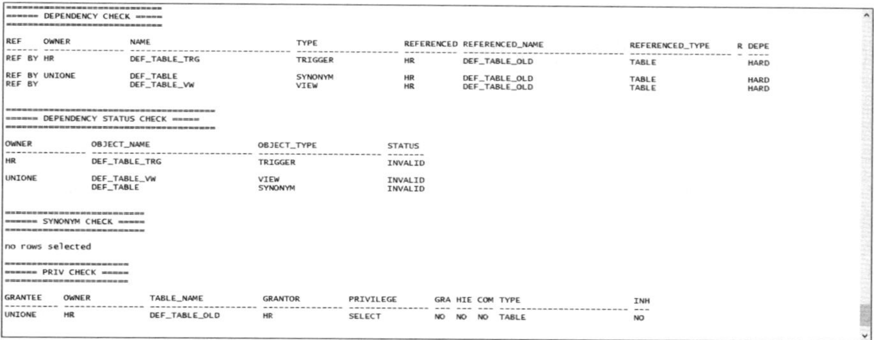

```
============================
====== DEPENDENCY CHECK =====
============================

REF    OWNER           NAME                           TYPE                 REFERENCED REFERENCED_NAME                   REFERENCED_TYPE      R DEPE
------ --------------- ------------------------------ -------------------- ---------- --------------------------------- -------------------- - ----
REF BY HR              DEF_TABLE_TRG                  TRIGGER              HR         DEF_TABLE_OLD                     TABLE                  HARD

REF BY UNIONE          DEF_TABLE                      SYNONYM              HR         DEF_TABLE_OLD                     TABLE                  HARD
REF BY                 DEF_TABLE_VW                   VIEW                 HR         DEF_TABLE_OLD                     TABLE                  HARD

=======================================
====== DEPENDENCY STATUS CHECK =====
=======================================

OWNER           OBJECT_NAME                    OBJECT_TYPE            STATUS
--------------- ------------------------------ ---------------------- -------
HR              DEF_TABLE_TRG                  TRIGGER                INVALID

UNIONE          DEF_TABLE_VW                   VIEW                   INVALID
                DEF_TABLE                      SYNONYM                INVALID

=========================
====== SYNONYM CHECK =====
=========================

no rows selected

======================
====== PRIV CHECK =====
======================

GRANTEE    OWNER           TABLE_NAME           GRANTOR         PRIVILEGE       GRA HIE COM TYPE                     INH
---------- --------------- -------------------- --------------- --------------- --- --- --- ------------------------ ---
UNIONE     HR              DEF_TABLE_OLD        HR              SELECT          NO  NO  NO  TABLE                    NO
```

▲ 기존 OLD 테이블에 걸려 있는 Dependent 오브젝트 상태 확인

컴파일을 통해 기존 테이블에 Defendency가 되어 Invaild되어 있는 Dependent 오브젝트의 상태값을 Vaild로 변경하고 Defendency를 신규 테이블로 변경하기 위해 작업을 합니다.

```
SQL> grant select on def_table to unione;

Grant succeeded.

SQL> conn unione/unione
Connected.
SQL> alter synonym def_table compile ;

Synonym altered.

SQL> alter view def_table_vw compile ;

View altered.

SQL> conn hr/hr
Connected.
SQL> alter trigger def_table_trg compile ;

Trigger altered.

SQL> ▮
```

▲ 기존 OLD 테이블에 걸려 있는 Defendant 오브젝트 컴파일

컴파일 후 신규 테이블의 Dependent 오브젝트 상태 확인을 합니다.

```
============================
====== DEPENDENCY CHECK =====
============================

REF    OWNER           NAME                           TYPE                 REFERENCED REFERENCED_NAME                   REFERENCED_TYPE      R DEPE
------ --------------- ------------------------------ -------------------- ---------- --------------------------------- -------------------- - ----
REF    UNIONE          DEF_TABLE                      SYNONYM              HR         DEF_TABLE                         TABLE                  HARD
REF BY                 DEF_TABLE_VW                   VIEW                 HR         DEF_TABLE                         TABLE                  HARD

=======================================
====== DEPENDENCY STATUS CHECK =====
=======================================

OWNER           OBJECT_NAME                    OBJECT_TYPE            STATUS
--------------- ------------------------------ ---------------------- -------
HR              DEF_TABLE                      TABLE                  VALID

UNIONE          DEF_TABLE_VW                   VIEW                   VALID
                DEF_TABLE                      SYNONYM                VALID

=========================
====== SYNONYM CHECK =====
=========================

OWNER           SYNONYM_NAME         TABLE_OWNE TABLE_NAME           DB_LINK              ORIGIN_CON_ID
--------------- -------------------- ---------- -------------------- -------------------- -------------
UNIONE          DEF_TABLE            HR         DEF_TABLE                                             0

======================
====== PRIV CHECK =====
======================

GRANTEE    OWNER           TABLE_NAME           GRANTOR         PRIVILEGE       GRA HIE COM TYPE                     INH
---------- --------------- -------------------- --------------- --------------- --- --- --- ------------------------ ---
UNIONE     HR              DEF_TABLE            HR              SELECT          NO  NO  NO  TABLE                    NO
```

▲ 컴파일 후 신규 테이블에 걸려있는 Dependent 오브젝트 상태 확인

상태가 모두 VALID가 되었으나 문제가 생겼습니다. 트리거가 보이지 않습니다. 만약 이대로 서비스가 오픈하였다면 장애 상황이 발생됩니다.

트리거의 경우 컴파일을 하면 OLD 테이블로 연결이 됩니다.

```
==============================
====== DEPENDENCY CHECK ======
==============================

REF    OWNER          NAME                           TYPE                REFERENCED REFERENCED_NAME                REFERENCED_TYPE    R DEPE
------ -------------- ------------------------------ ------------------- ---------- ------------------------------ ------------------ - ----
REF BY HR             DEF_TABLE_TRG                  TRIGGER             HR         DEF_TABLE_OLD                  TABLE                HARD

=====================================
====== DEPENDENCY STATUS CHECK ======
=====================================

OWNER          OBJECT_NAME                    OBJECT_TYPE             STATUS
-------------- ------------------------------ ----------------------- -------
HR             DEF_TABLE_TRG                  TRIGGER                 VALID

===========================
====== SYNONYM CHECK ======
===========================

no rows selected

========================
====== PRIV CHECK ======
========================

GRANTEE    OWNER          TABLE_NAME                GRANTOR        PRIVILEGE      GRA HIE COM TYPE                     INH
---------- -------------- ------------------------- -------------- -------------- --- --- --- ------------------------ ---
UNIONE     HR             DEF_TABLE_OLD             HR             SELECT         NO  NO  NO  TABLE                    NO
```

▲ 기존 OLD 테이블에 걸려있는 트리거

Dependent Object 중 트리거의 경우 재컴파일 만하면 안 되며 재생성을 해주어야 합니다.

```
SQL> conn hr/hr
Connected.
SQL> create or replace
  2  TRIGGER def_table_trg
  3  BEFORE update ON def_table
  4  FOR EACH ROW
  5  BEGIN
  6  null;
  7  END;
  8  /
TRIGGER def_table_trg
        *
ERROR at line 2:
ORA-04095: trigger 'DEF_TABLE_TRG' already exists on another table, cannot
replace it


SQL> drop TRIGGER def_table_trg ;

Trigger dropped.

SQL> create or replace
  2  TRIGGER def_table_trg
  3  BEFORE update ON def_table
  4  FOR EACH ROW
  5  BEGIN
  6  null;
  7  END;
  8  /

Trigger created.

SQL> ▮
```

▲ 트리거는 삭제 후 신규 생성

재생성하려고 하면 기존 트리거가 다른 테이블에 걸려있다고 에러가 발생합니다. 따라서 기존 트리거를 완전히 삭제하고 생성해야 합니다.

3 장시간의 대용량 DML 배치 작업 이후 장애

아침에 출근하고 개발팀에서 연락이 왔습니다. "어제 A라는 개발자가 수작업으로 배치를 수행하고 퇴근하였는데, where 절에 기호를 잘못 써서 수행한 내역을 아침 출근해서 확인하였고, 아직도 수행 중으로 나와서 강제 종료시키고 수행 창을 종료 시켰습니다." 개발팀에서는 그 후부터 서비스 장애가 발생하였습니다. DBA는 오늘도 황당합니다. 왜 서비스 장애가 발생한 것일까요? 그리고 Rollback 명령어를 수행하면 장애 상황이 해결 될까요? 지금부터 알아보겠습니다.

건수가 많은 테스트용 테이블을 하나 만듭니다.

```
SQL>  select count(1) from usrinf ;

  COUNT(1)
----------
   6719785

SQL> set timing on
SQL> set time on
16:49:07 SQL>
16:49:09 SQL>
16:49:09 SQL>
16:49:09 SQL> desc usrinf
 Name                                      Null?    Type
 ----------------------------------------- -------- ----------------------------
 ACCOUNTNUM                                NOT NULL NUMBER
 GROUPNUM                                  NOT NULL CHAR(12)
 USERID                                    NOT NULL VARCHAR2(150)
 USERPWD                                            VARCHAR2(96)
 USERNAME                                           VARCHAR2(150)
 USERTYPECODE                                       CHAR(12)
 SEX                                       NOT NULL CHAR(3)
 BIRTH                                              CHAR(24)
 PHONE                                              VARCHAR2(150)
 MOBILE                                             VARCHAR2(150)
 EMAIL                                              VARCHAR2(150)
 ZIPCODE                                            VARCHAR2(30)
 ADDRESS                                            VARCHAR2(600)
 SMS_SEND                                           CHAR(3)
 EMAIL_SEND                                         CHAR(3)
 IPADDR                                             VARCHAR2(45)
 CP_FLAG                                   NOT NULL CHAR(3)
 REGDATE                                            DATE
 LASTCONNECTTIME                                    DATE
 APPLY                                              CHAR(3)
 ADMINLOGNUM                                        NUMBER
 MOTP                                               VARCHAR2(3)
 REGCERT                                            VARCHAR2(3)
 REGCERTDATE                                        DATE
 PIM                                                VARCHAR2(3)
 PIMDATE                                            DATE
```

▲ 다량의 Row 건수 테스트 테이블

원래 개발자가 의도한 DML과 다른 부등호 조건을 바꾼 Update 문을 수행시킵니다. 그리고 긴 시간 동안 수행합니다. 그 후 Rollback 명령어로 수행 결과를 Rollback 하였습니다.

```
14:20:19 SQL>
14:20:20 SQL> -- Currect DML
14:20:50 SQL>
14:20:53 SQL> update usrinf set SMS_SEND='N' where REGDATE > sysdate - 60 ;

0 rows updated.

Elapsed: 00:00:32.49
14:21:29 SQL>
14:21:35 SQL> commit ;

Commit complete.

Elapsed: 00:00:00.01
14:21:38 SQL>
14:21:38 SQL> -- Wrong DML
14:21:45 SQL>
14:21:47 SQL> update usrinf set SMS_SEND='N' where REGDATE <  sysdate - 60 ;
```

▲ 잘못 돌린 긴 시간의 DML 작업

정확한 DML 문을 실행할 경우 32초 만에 0건이 나왔습니다. 60일 이후 등록된 데이터를 수정해야 하는데 부등호 기호가 잘못되어 60일 이전의 모든 데이터를 수정하는 시나리오의 테스트입니다.

이 작업을 하면서 DBMS가 어떤 동작을 했는지 Wait Event, Lock Status, Undo Segment 사용현황을 살펴보겠습니다.

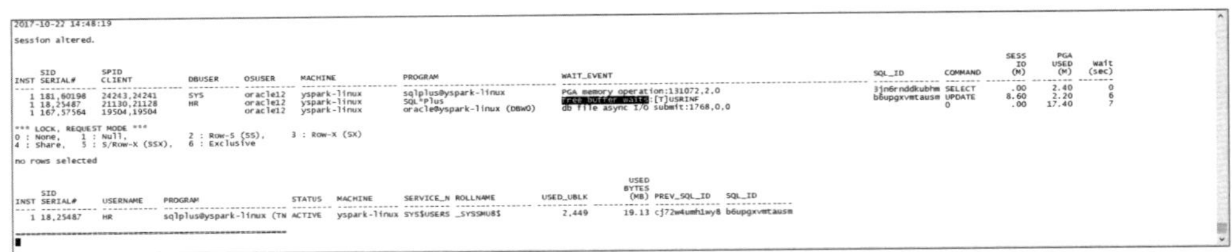

```
2017-10-22 14:48:19

Session altered.

     SID         SPID                                                                                                                                                     SESS      PGA
INST SERIAL#     CLIENT           DBUSER    OSUSER    MACHINE       PROGRAM                        WAIT_EVENT                                  SQL_ID        COMMAND     IO     USED    wait
                                                                                                                                                                           (M)      (M)    (sec)
---- ----------- ---------------- --------- --------- ------------- ------------------------------ ------------------------------------------- ------------- ------- -------- -------- ------
   1 181,60198   24243,24241      SYS       oracle12  yspark-linux  sqlplus@yspark-linux           PGA memory operation:131072,2,0             3jn6rnddkubhm SELECT       .00     2.40      0
   1 18,25487    21130,21128      HR        oracle12  yspark-linux  SQL*Plus                       free buffer waits:[T]USRINF                 b6upgxvmtausm UPDATE      8.60     2.20      6
   1 167,57564   19504,19504                oracle12  yspark-linux  oracle@yspark-linux (DBW0)     db file async I/O submit:1768,0,0                         0            .00    17.40      7

*** LOCK, REQUEST MODE ***
0 : None,    1 : Null,            2 : Row-S (SS),     3 : Row-X (SX)
4 : Share,   5 : S/Row-X (SSX),   6 : Exclusive

no rows selected

                                                                                                              USED
     SID                                                                                                     BYTES
INST SERIAL#     USERNAME   PROGRAM                     STATUS   MACHINE      SERVICE_N ROLLNAME     USED_UBLK  (MB) PREV_SQL_ID   SQL_ID
---- ----------- ---------- --------------------------- -------- ------------ --------- ------------ --------- ----- ------------- -------------
   1 18,25487    HR         sqlplus@yspark-linux (TN    ACTIVE   yspark-linux SYS$USERS _SYSSMU8$        2,449 19.13 cj72w4umh1wy8 b6upgxvmtausm
```

▲ DB 세션 정보, LOCK 정보, Undo 세그먼트 사용 정보 체크

HR 유저로 접속한 Update 세션이 free buffer waits 이벤트와 Undo Segment 사용 현황이 보입니다.

이때 또 다른 세션에서 해당 테이블인 USRINF를 조회합니다.

```
15:10:47 SQL>
15:10:47 SQL>
15:10:47 SQL>
15:10:48 SQL> conn hr/hr
Connected.
15:10:55 SQL>
15:10:55 SQL>
15:10:56 SQL> select REGDATE,BIRTH,SEX from usrinf where REGDATE > to_date('2012/07/24 00:00:00','YYYY/MM/DD HH24:MI:SS') ;

REGDATE            BIRTH                     SEX
------------------ ------------------------- ---
24-JUL-12          19870311                  1
24-JUL-12          19820128                  1
24-JUL-12          19521110                  1
24-JUL-12          19720910                  1
24-JUL-12          19890710                  1
24-JUL-12          19840718                  1
24-JUL-12          19890104                  1
24-JUL-12          19670207                  1
24-JUL-12          19831016                  1
24-JUL-12          19791227                  2
24-JUL-12          19930821                  1

REGDATE            BIRTH                     SEX
------------------ ------------------------- ---
24-JUL-12          19900419                  1
24-JUL-12          19910819                  1
24-JUL-12          19820317                  1
24-JUL-12          19930913                  1
24-JUL-12          19910821                  1
24-JUL-12          19710717                  2
24-JUL-12          19851201                  1
24-JUL-12          19880305                  1
24-JUL-12          19650520                  2
24-JUL-12          19820107                  1
24-JUL-12          19680205                  2

REGDATE            BIRTH                     SEX
------------------ ------------------------- ---
24-JUL-12          19900809                  2
24-JUL-12          19740916                  2
24-JUL-12          19671120                  1
24-JUL-12          19930501                  1
24-JUL-12          19861213                  1
24-JUL-12          19901023                  1
24-JUL-12          19930911                  1
24-JUL-12          19940517                  1
24-JUL-12          19421123                  1
24-JUL-12          19670314                  2
24-JUL-12          19920320                  1

REGDATE            BIRTH                     SEX
------------------ ------------------------- ---
```

▲ UPDATE 중 테이블의 일부 데이터를 조회

SELECT 문을 수행해보니 조회가 바로 잘 실행됩니다.

이번에는 UPDATE 문을 테스트합니다.

```
24-JUL-12          19910627                  2
24-JUL-12          19960321                  1
24-JUL-12          19850112                  1
24-JUL-12          19850219                  2
24-JUL-12          19640525                  1
24-JUL-12          19610103                  2
24-JUL-12          19890420                  1
24-JUL-12          19690226                  2
24-JUL-12          20001108                  2
24-JUL-12          19890913                  1
24-JUL-12          19840512                  1

REGDATE            BIRTH                     SEX
------------------ ------------------------- ---
24-JUL-12          19550830                  2
24-JUL-12          19731102                  2
24-JUL-12          19650125                  1
24-JUL-12          19850307                  1
24-JUL-12          19871102                  1
24-JUL-12          19890720                  1
24-JUL-12          19821212                  2
24-JUL-12          19811204                  1
24-JUL-12          19881102                  1
24-JUL-12          19691102                  1
24-JUL-12          20010914                  1

88 rows selected.

Elapsed: 00:00:00.02
15:11:04 SQL>
15:13:24 SQL> update usrinf set SMS_SEND='N' where REGDATE > to_date('2012/07/24 00:00:00','YYYY/MM/DD HH24:MI:SS') ;
```

▲ 조회한 결과를 토대로 같은 조건으로 UPDATE 문 실행

앞서 나온 결과값을 기준으로 Update 문을 실행하면 그러면 커서는 깜빡이고 기다리게 됩니다. 이때 DB 세션 상태를 확인합니다.

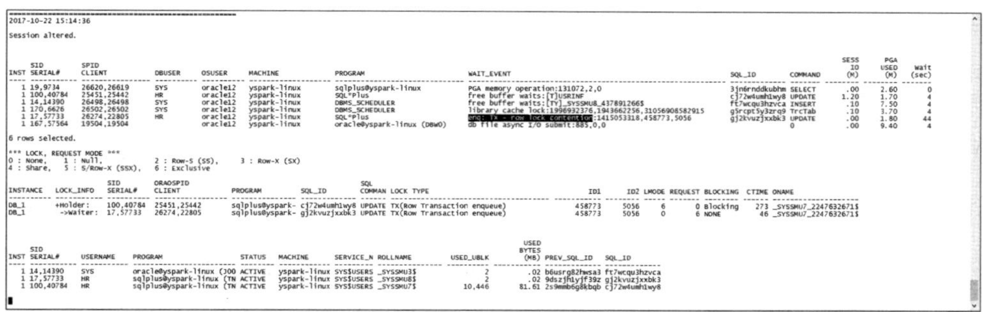

```
2017-10-22 15:14:36

Session altered.

     SID         SPID                                                                                                                                                        SESS     PGA
INST SERIAL#     CLIENT          DBUSER     OSUSER     MACHINE            PROGRAM                      WAIT_EVENT                                              SQL_ID        COMMAND    IO    USED   Wait
                                                                                                                                                                                   (M)     (M)  (sec)
---- ----------- --------------- ---------- ---------- ------------------ ---------------------------- ------------------------------------------------------- ------------- ------- ------- ------- -------
   1 19,9734     26620,26619     SYS        oracle12   yspark-linux       sqlplus@yspark-linux         PGA memory operation:131072,2,0                         3jn6rnddkubhm SELECT      .00    2.60      0
   1 100,40784   25451,25442     HR         oracle12   yspark-linux       SQL*Plus                     free buffer waits:[T]USRINF                             cj72w4umh1wy8 UPDATE     1.20    1.70      4
   1 14,14390    26498,26498     SYS        oracle12   yspark-linux       DBMS_SCHEDULER               free buffer waits:[TY]_SYSSMU8_437891266$               ft7wcqu3hzvca INSERT      .10    7.50      4
   1 170,6626    26502,26502     SYS        oracle12   yspark-linux       DBMS_SCHEDULER               library cache lock:1996932376,1943662256,31056908582915 g5rcpt5y3zrq9 TrcTab      .10    3.70      4
   1 17,57733    26274,22805     HR         oracle12   yspark-linux       SQL*Plus                     enq: TX - row lock contention:1415053318,458773,5056    gj2kvuzjxxbk3 UPDATE      .00    1.80     44
   1 167,57564   19504,19504                oracle12   yspark-linux       oracle@yspark-linux (DBW0)   db file async I/O submit:885,0,0                                      0           .00    9.40      4

6 rows selected.

*** LOCK, REQUEST MODE ***
0 : None,    1 : Null,           2 : Row-S (SS),    3 : Row-X (SX)
4 : Share,   5 : S/Row-X (SSX),  6 : Exclusive

                       SID        ORAOSPID                                           SQL
INSTANCE   LOCK_INFO   SERIAL#    CLIENT           PROGRAM           SQL_ID          COMMAN LOCK TYPE                              ID1      ID2 LMODE REQUEST BLOCKING  CTIME ONAME
---------- ----------- ---------- ---------------- ----------------- --------------- ------ ------------------------------ ---------- -------- ----- ------- --------- ------ ------------------
DB_1       +Holder:    100,40784  25451,25442      sqlplus@yspark-   cj72w4umh1wy8   UPDATE TX(Row Transaction enqueue)      458773     5056     6       0 Blocking     273 _SYSSMU7_2247632671$
DB_1        ->Waiter:  17,57733   26274,22805      sqlplus@yspark-   gj2kvuzjxxbk3   UPDATE TX(Row Transaction enqueue)      458773     5056     0       6 NONE          46 _SYSSMU7_2247632671$


                                                                                                                     USED
     SID                                                                                                            BYTES
INST SERIAL#     USERNAME   PROGRAM                        STATUS   MACHINE      SERVICE_N ROLLNAME       USED_UBLK   (MB) PREV_SQL_ID   SQL_ID
---- ----------- ---------- ------------------------------ -------- ------------ --------- ------------- ---------- ------ ------------- -------------
   1 14,14390    SYS        oracle@yspark-linux (J00       ACTIVE   yspark-linux SYS$USERS _SYSSMU3$              2    .02 b6usrg82hwsa3 ft7wcqu3hzvca
   1 17,57733    HR         sqlplus@yspark-linux (TN       ACTIVE   yspark-linux SYS$USERS _SYSSMU8$              2    .02 9dszjh1yjf39z gj2kvuzjxxbk3
   1 100,40784   HR         sqlplus@yspark-linux (TN       ACTIVE   yspark-linux SYS$USERS _SYSSMU7$         10,446  81.61 2s9mmb6g8kbqb cj72w4umh1wy8
```

▲ row lock 상태의 DB세션

기다리던 다른 세션의 UPDATE 문은 ORA-00060 에러 deadlock를 발생시키면서 실패하였습니다. 테스트 상황이지만 같은 환경의 운영환경이라면 일단 1차 장애가 발생하였습니다.

```
15:18:52 SQL>
15:18:53 SQL>
15:18:53 SQL> update usrinf set SMS_SEND='N' where REGDATE > to_date('2012/07/24 00:00:00','YYYY/MM/DD HH24:MI:SS') ;
update usrinf set SMS_SEND='N' where REGDATE > to_date('2012/07/24 00:00:00','YYYY/MM/DD HH24:MI:SS')
                                      *
ERROR at line 1:
ORA-00060: deadlock detected while waiting for resource


Elapsed: 00:02:03.43
15:21:01 SQL>
```

▲ 문법이 잘못된 문장의 수행 시간이 긴 DML 문으로 인하여 다른 세션에서 발생한 정상 세션 실패

Deadlock 에러 발생으로 인해 LOCK 현상은 해소 되었지만, 문법이 잘못된 DML은 에러 없이 계속 수행 중입니다.

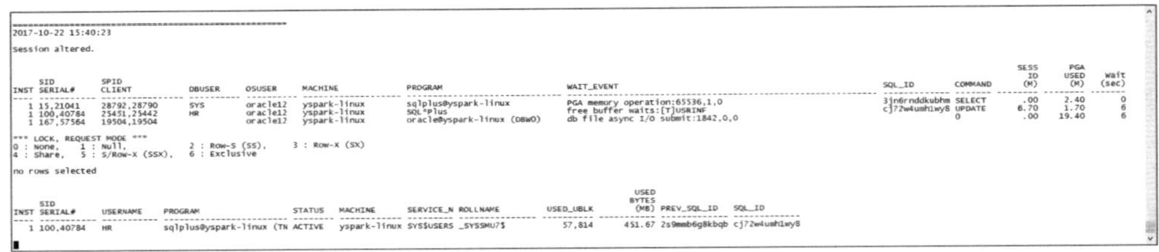

```
----------------------------------------------------------------
2017-10-22 15:40:23

Session altered.

                                                                                                                                                                       SESS      PGA
     SID          SPID                                                                                                                                                  IO     USED    Wait
INST SERIAL#      CLIENT           DBUSER     OSUSER     MACHINE           PROGRAM                       WAIT_EVENT                                SQL_ID        COMMAND     (M)      (M)   (sec)
---- ------------ ---------------- ---------- ---------- ----------------- ----------------------------- ----------------------------------------- ------------- ------- -------- -------- ------
   1 15,21041     28792,28790      SYS        oracle12   yspark-linux      sqlplus@yspark-linux          PGA memory operation:65536,1,0            3jn6rnddkubhm SELECT       .00     2.40      0
   1 100,40784    25451,25442      HR         oracle12   yspark-linux      SQL*Plus                      free buffer waits:[T]USRINF               cj72w4umh1wy8 UPDATE      6.70     1.70      6
   1 167,57564    19504,19504                 oracle12   yspark-linux      oracle@yspark-linux (DBW0)    db file async I/O submit:1842,0,0                       0            .00    19.40      6

*** LOCK, REQUEST MODE ***
0 : None,     1 : Null,          2 : Row-S (SS),     3 : Row-X (SX)
4 : Share,    5 : S/Row-X (SSX), 6 : Exclusive

no rows selected


                                                                                                                USED
     SID                                                                                                       BYTES
INST SERIAL#      USERNAME    PROGRAM                     STATUS   MACHINE      SERVICE_N ROLLNAME      USED_UBLK  (MB) PREV_SQL_ID   SQL_ID
---- ------------ ----------- --------------------------- -------- ------------ --------- ------------- ---------- ----------- ------------- -------------
   1 100,40784    HR          sqlplus@yspark-linux (TN    ACTIVE   yspark-linux SYS$USERS _SYSSMU7$         57,814      451.67 2s9mmb6g8kbqb cj72w4umh1wy8
```

▲ Lock 세션은 없어졌지만 문법이 잘못된 DML 문은 계속 수행

1시간가량 돌린 DML의 문제점을 확인하고 Rollback을 합니다.

```
SQL> set timing on
SQL> set time on
15:02:11 SQL> set echo on
15:02:14 SQL>
15:02:14 SQL>
15:09:49 SQL> -- Wrong DML
15:09:55 SQL>
15:10:04 SQL> update usrinf set SMS_SEND='N' where REGDATE <  sysdate - 60 ;

6719733 rows updated.

Elapsed: 01:03:52.51
16:13:58 SQL>
16:20:32 SQL> rollback ;
```

▲ 잘못된 DML 문의 Rollback 시작

잘못된 DML 문의 Rollback을 시작합니다. 이제 Rollback 단계에서의 DB 상황을 모니터링 합니다.

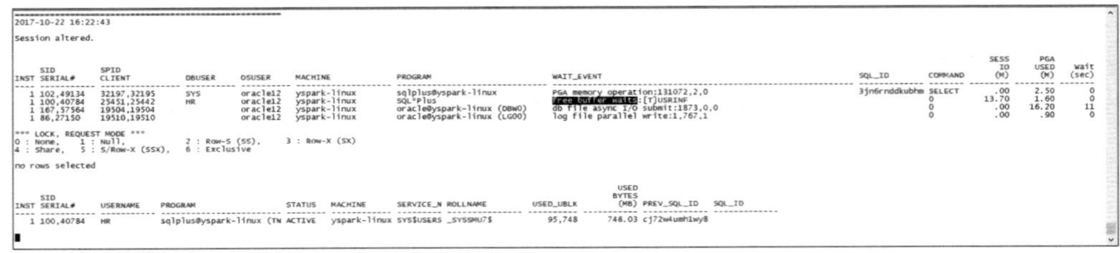

```
----------------------------------------------------------------
2017-10-22 16:22:43

Session altered.

                                                                                                                                                                       SESS      PGA
     SID          SPID                                                                                                                                                  IO     USED    Wait
INST SERIAL#      CLIENT           DBUSER     OSUSER     MACHINE           PROGRAM                       WAIT_EVENT                                SQL_ID        COMMAND     (M)      (M)   (sec)
---- ------------ ---------------- ---------- ---------- ----------------- ----------------------------- ----------------------------------------- ------------- ------- -------- -------- ------
   1 102,49134    32197,32195      SYS        oracle12   yspark-linux      sqlplus@yspark-linux          PGA memory operation:131072,2,0           3jn6rnddkubhm SELECT       .00     2.50      0
   1 100,40784    25451,25442      HR         oracle12   yspark-linux      SQL*Plus                      free buffer waits:[T]USRINF                             0          13.70     1.60      0
   1 167,57564    19504,19504                 oracle12   yspark-linux      oracle@yspark-linux (DBW0)    db file async I/O submit:1873,0,0                       0            .00    16.20     11
   1 86,27150     19510,19510                 oracle12   yspark-linux      oracle@yspark-linux (LG00)    log file parallel write:1,767,1                         0            .00      .90      0

*** LOCK, REQUEST MODE ***
0 : None,     1 : Null,          2 : Row-S (SS),     3 : Row-X (SX)
4 : Share,    5 : S/Row-X (SSX), 6 : Exclusive

no rows selected


                                                                                                                USED
     SID                                                                                                       BYTES
INST SERIAL#      USERNAME    PROGRAM                     STATUS   MACHINE      SERVICE_N ROLLNAME      USED_UBLK  (MB) PREV_SQL_ID   SQL_ID
---- ------------ ----------- --------------------------- -------- ------------ --------- ------------- ---------- ----------- ------------- -------------
   1 100,40784    HR          sqlplus@yspark-linux (TN    ACTIVE   yspark-linux SYS$USERS _SYSSMU7$         95,748      748.03 cj72w4umh1wy8
```

▲ Rollback 단계에서 DBMS 모니터링

다른 세션에서 조회 SQL 문을 수행합니다.

```
16:00:54 SQL>
16:23:41 SQL> select REGDATE,BIRTH,SEX from usrinf where REGDATE > to_date('2012/07/24 00:00:00','YYYY/MM/DD HH24:MI:SS') ;

REGDATE            BIRTH                    SEX
------------------ ------------------------ ---
24-JUL-12          19870311                 1
24-JUL-12          19820128                 1
24-JUL-12          19521110                 1
24-JUL-12          19720910                 1
24-JUL-12          19890710                 1
24-JUL-12          19840718                 1
24-JUL-12          19890104                 1
24-JUL-12          19670207                 1
24-JUL-12          19831016                 1
24-JUL-12          19791227                 2
24-JUL-12          19930821                 1

REGDATE            BIRTH                    SEX
------------------ ------------------------ ---
24-JUL-12          19900419                 1
24-JUL-12          19910819                 1
24-JUL-12          19820317                 1
24-JUL-12          19930913                 1
24-JUL-12          19910821                 1
24-JUL-12          19710717                 2
24-JUL-12          19851201                 1
24-JUL-12          19880305                 1
24-JUL-12          19650520                 2
24-JUL-12          19820107                 1
24-JUL-12          19680205                 2

REGDATE            BIRTH                    SEX
------------------ ------------------------ ---
24-JUL-12          19900809                 2
24-JUL-12          19740916                 2
24-JUL-12          19671120                 1
24-JUL-12          19930501                 1
24-JUL-12          19861213                 1
24-JUL-12          19901023                 1
24-JUL-12          19930911                 1
24-JUL-12          19940517                 1
24-JUL-12          19421123                 1
```

▲ 잘 수행되는 다른 세션의 SELECT 문

조회문인 SELECT 문은 잘 수행이 됩니다.

```
24-JUL-12          19811204                 1
24-JUL-12          19881102                 1
24-JUL-12          19691102                 1
24-JUL-12          20010914                 1

88 rows selected.

Elapsed: 00:00:00.40
16:23:51 SQL>
16:25:23 SQL>
16:25:24 SQL> update usrinf set SMS_SEND='N' where REGDATE > to_date('2012/07/24 00:00:00','YYYY/MM/DD HH24:MI:SS') ;
```

▲ Wait되고 있는 다른 세션의 UPDATE 문

잘못된 세션의 롤백을 시동 중에도 다른 세션의 Update 문으로 인해 Lock 현상이 발생하였습니다. enq: TX-row lock contention 이벤트가 발생합니다.

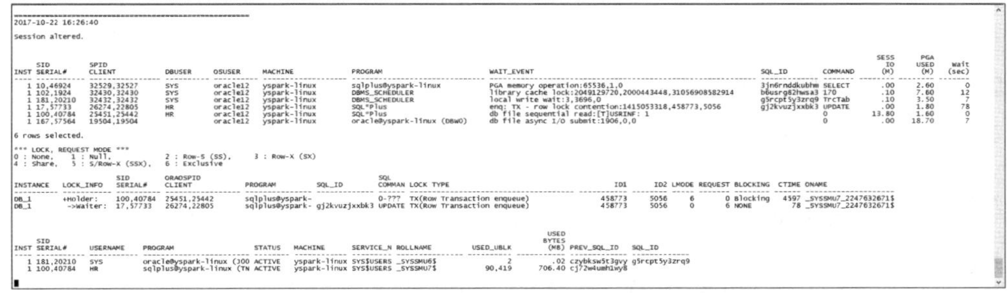

```
--------------------------------------------------------
2017-10-22 16:26:40

Session altered.

                                                                                                                                                                      SESS     PGA
     SID         SPID                                                                                                                                                   IO    USED    wait
INST SERIAL#     CLIENT           DBUSER     OSUSER     MACHINE            PROGRAM                        WAIT_EVENT                                             SQL_ID        COMMAND   (M)     (M)   (sec)
---- ----------- ---------------- ---------- ---------- ------------------ ------------------------------ ------------------------------------------------------ ------------- ------ ------- ------- ------
   1 10,46924    32529,32527      SYS        oracle12   yspark-linux       sqlplus@yspark-linux           PGA memory operation:65536,1,0                         3jn6rnddkubhm SELECT     .00    2.60      0
   1 102,1924    32430,32430      SYS        oracle12   yspark-linux       DBMS_SCHEDULER                 library cache lock:2049129720,2000443448,31056908582914 b6usrg82hwsa3 170        .10    7.60     12
   1 181,20210   32432,32432      SYS        oracle12   yspark-linux       DBMS_SCHEDULER                 local write wait:3,3696,0                              g5rcpt5y3zrq9 TrcTab     .10    3.50      7
   1 17,57733    26274,22805      HR         oracle12   yspark-linux       SQL*Plus                       enq: TX - row lock contention:1415053318,458773,5056   gj2kvuzjxxbk3 UPDATE     .00    1.80     78
   1 100,40784   25451,25442      HR         oracle12   yspark-linux       SQL*Plus                       db file sequential read:[T]USRINF: 1                                 0        13.80    1.60      0
   1 167,57564   19504,19504                 oracle12   yspark-linux       oracle@yspark-linux (DBW0)     db file async I/O submit:1906,0,0                                    0          .00   18.70      7

6 rows selected.

*** LOCK, REQUEST MODE ***
0 : None,    1 : Null,            2 : Row-S (SS),     3 : Row-X (SX)
4 : Share,   5 : S/Row-X (SSX),   6 : Exclusive

                        SID          ORAOSPID                                                 SQL
INSTANCE   LOCK_INFO    SERIAL#      CLIENT           PROGRAM           SQL_ID        COMMAN LOCK TYPE                               ID1      ID2 LMODE REQUEST BLOCKING  CTIME ONAME
---------- ------------ ------------ ---------------- ----------------- ------------- ------ --------------------------------- ---------- -------- ----- ------- -------- ------ -------------------
DB_1       +Holder:     100,40784    25451,25442      sqlplus@yspark-                 0-???  TX(Row Transaction enqueue)           458773     5056     6       0 Blocking   4597 _SYSSMU7_2247632671$
DB_1        ->Waiter:   17,57733     26274,22805      sqlplus@yspark-   gj2kvuzjxxbk3 UPDATE TX(Row Transaction enqueue)           458773     5056     0       6 NONE         78 _SYSSMU7_2247632671$


                                                                                                                       USED
     SID                                                                                                              BYTES
INST SERIAL#     USERNAME   PROGRAM                      STATUS   MACHINE      SERVICE_N ROLLNAME             USED_UBLK   (MB) PREV_SQL_ID   SQL_ID
---- ----------- ---------- ---------------------------- -------- ------------ --------- -------------------- --------- ------- ------------- -------------
   1 181,20210   SYS        oracle@yspark-linux (J00     ACTIVE   yspark-linux SYS$USERS _SYSSMU6$                    2     .02 czybksw5t3gvy g5rcpt5y3zrq9
   1 100,40784   HR         sqlplus@yspark-linux (TN     ACTIVE   yspark-linux SYS$USERS _SYSSMU7$               90,419  706.40 cj72w4umh1wy8
```

▲ Rollback 도중에 발생하는 LOCK 현상

즉 Rollback을 시도하는 중에는 SELECT 문은 잘 수행되지만 DML은 수행이 불가능합니다. 아직 장애 상황인 것을 알 수 있습니다.

```
15:02:14 SQL>
15:02:14 SQL>
15:09:49 SQL> -- Wrong DML
15:09:55 SQL>
15:10:04 SQL> update usrinf set SMS_SEND='N' where REGDATE <  sysdate - 60 ;

6719733 rows updated.

Elapsed: 01:03:52.51
16:13:58 SQL>
16:20:32 SQL> rollback ;


Rollback complete.

Elapsed: 00:40:37.68
17:02:24 SQL> 17:02:24 SQL>
```

▲ 잘못된 쿼리 수행 시간 1시간과 Rollback 시간 40분 후 장애 상황에서 해제

다른 세션의 DML들은 2분 만에 Deadlock 에러로 DML이 취소되는 1차 장애 상황과 달리 이번에는 Lock 세션이 지속됩니다. 테스트 상황에서는 37분 걸렸습니다.

```
Elapsed: 00:00:00.40
16:23:51 SQL>
16:25:23 SQL>
16:25:24 SQL> update usrinf set SMS_SEND='N' where REGDATE > to_date('2012/07/24 00:00:00','YYYY/MM/DD HH24:MI:SS') ;


88 rows updated.

Elapsed: 00:37:00.16
17:02:25 SQL> 17:02:25 SQL> rollback ;

Rollback complete.

Elapsed: 00:00:00.16
17:06:52 SQL>
```

▲ 다른 세션의 DML은 DeadLock 에러가 발생 안 하고 대기하다 수행 완료

결과적으로 잘못된 쿼리로 인한 장애를 인지하고 긴 수행 시간과 긴 Rollback 시간이 완료될 때까지 장애 상황이 지속되는데 Undo 사용 현황을 모니터링하면서 Undo 세그먼트로부터 해당 세그먼트의 Rollback을 확인하며 장애 해제 진행을 확인할 수 있습니다.

즉 Rollback 단계에서도 장애 상황인 것입니다. 사실 이 단계는 모두 출근하고 장애 상황을 인지 한 단계라 오피스의 분위기는 매우 안 좋습니다. 사실 밤사이에도 문제가 발생하였지만 인지가 안 되었습니다.

이런 상황이 빈번히 발생하면 모니터링만 하고 어떤 조치를 취할 수 없을지 고민하게 됩니다. Rollback 단계를 빠르게 하는 방법이 없을까? 생각하게 됩니다.
리소스를 더 투입하여 Rollback과 DML을 빠르게 하는 방법을 지금부터 알려드리겠습니다. 단 CPU, MEMORY 리소스가 남을 경우만 해당됩니다.

저자가 추천하는 방법은 특정 DB 파라미터를 수정하는 방법입니다. 먼저 DB 파라미터를 조회합니다.

_cleanup_rollback_entries, fast_start_parallel_rollback, recovery_parallelism입니다.

```
17:16:19 SQL>
17:20:34 SQL> @hidden_param
Enter parameter_name : _cleanup_rollback_entries

                                  INSTANCE                                                                                ALTER   ALTER
parameter                         VALUE                     DESCRIPTION                                                   SESSION SYSTEM
--------------------------------- ------------------------- ------------------------------------------------------------- ------- ---------
_cleanup_rollback_entries         100                       no. of undo entries to apply per transaction cleanup          FALSE   FALSE

Elapsed: 00:00:01.32
17:20:48 SQL> @hidden_param
Enter parameter_name : fast_start_parallel_rollback

                                  INSTANCE                                                                                ALTER   ALTER
parameter                         VALUE                     DESCRIPTION                                                   SESSION SYSTEM
--------------------------------- ------------------------- ------------------------------------------------------------- ------- ---------
fast_start_parallel_rollback      LOW                       max number of parallel recovery slaves that may be used       FALSE   IMMEDIATE

Elapsed: 00:00:00.02
17:20:54 SQL> @hidden_param
Enter parameter_name : recovery_parallelism

                                  INSTANCE                                                                                ALTER   ALTER
parameter                         VALUE                     DESCRIPTION                                                   SESSION SYSTEM
--------------------------------- ------------------------- ------------------------------------------------------------- ------- ---------
recovery_parallelism              0                         number of server processes to use for parallel recovery       FALSE   FALSE

Elapsed: 00:00:00.02
17:26:51 SQL>
```

▲ DML Recovery와 관련된 파라미터 조회

해당 DB 파라미터를 다음과 같이 변경합니다.

```
SQL*Plus: Release 12.2.0.1.0 Production on Thu Oct 26 18:03:36 2017

Copyright (c) 1982, 2016, Oracle.  All rights reserved.


Connected to:
Oracle Database 12c Enterprise Edition Release 12.2.0.1.0 - 64bit Production

SQL> alter system set "_cleanup_rollback_entries"=50000 scope=spfile ;

System altered.

SQL> alter system set fast_start_parallel_rollback=HIGH scope=spfile ;

System altered.

SQL> alter system set recovery_parallelism=4 scope=spfile ;

System altered.

SQL> shutdown immediate ;
Database closed.
Database dismounted.
ORACLE instance shut down.
SQL> startup
ORACLE instance started.

Total System Global Area  746586112 bytes
Fixed Size                  8625176 bytes
Variable Size             587203560 bytes
Database Buffers           33554432 bytes
Redo Buffers                8151040 bytes
In-Memory Area            109051904 bytes
Database mounted.
Database opened.
SQL>
SQL> @hidden_param
Enter parameter_name : _cleanup_rollback_entries

                                  INSTANCE                                                                                ALTER   ALTER
parameter                         VALUE                     DESCRIPTION                                                   SESSION SYSTEM
--------------------------------- ------------------------- ------------------------------------------------------------- ------- ---------
_cleanup_rollback_entries         50000                     no. of undo entries to apply per transaction cleanup          FALSE   FALSE

SQL> @hidden_param
Enter parameter_name : fast_start_parallel_rollback

                                  INSTANCE                                                                                ALTER   ALTER
parameter                         VALUE                     DESCRIPTION                                                   SESSION SYSTEM
--------------------------------- ------------------------- ------------------------------------------------------------- ------- ---------
fast_start_parallel_rollback      HIGH                      max number of parallel recovery slaves that may be used       FALSE   IMMEDIATE

SQL> @hidden_param
Enter parameter_name : recovery_parallelism

                                  INSTANCE                                                                                ALTER   ALTER
parameter                         VALUE                     DESCRIPTION                                                   SESSION SYSTEM
--------------------------------- ------------------------- ------------------------------------------------------------- ------- ---------
recovery_parallelism              4                         number of server processes to use for parallel recovery       FALSE   FALSE

SQL>
SQL>
```

▲ 파라미터를 변경하고 DB를 재기동하여 적용 후 적용된 파라미터 값 확인

적용 결과를 확인하고 같은 잘못된 DML 쿼리를 수행하고 Rollback 해 봅니다.

```
16:09:08 SQL>
16:09:09 SQL> update usrinf set SMS_SEND='N' where REGDATE < sysdate - 60 ;

6719733 rows updated.

Elapsed: 00:21:11.55
16:30:27 SQL> 16:30:27 SQL> rollback ;

Rollback complete.

Elapsed: 00:13:12.98
16:45:33 SQL>
```

▲ 같은 DML 쿼리의 수행시간이 파라미터 적용 후 단축

파라미터 적용 전 수행 시간 1시간 수행/Rollback 시간 40분 수행되었으나, 해당 파라미터 수치를 변경 후 20분 수행/Rollback 시간 13분 수행되었습니다.

해당 파라미터는 리소스를 병렬처리 프로세스 수를 증가시켜 빠른 DML 성능에 효과를 보여주고 있습니다. 하지만, 리소스가 부족한 상태에서 적용하게 되면 Hang 상태로 변경되므로, 적용 전 테스트를 통해 가용성 확보 후 적용해야 합니다.

개발자의 잦은 실수로 인한 잘못 된 Long DML이 발생할 경우에만 검토 후 적용해야 합니다.

4 통계 정보 데이터 갱신 작업 이후 장애

오라클 DB 내에 테이블의 정보, 데이터의 정보를 가지고 있는 것이 통계 정보라고 합니다. 통계 정보 갱신은 DBA들이 많이 하는 작업입니다. 이 정보가 갱신되었을 때 발생할 수 있는 장애에 대해서 알아보고 대체 방법이 어떻게 되는지 살펴보겠습니다.

테스트용 테이블과 인덱스를 생성합니다.

```
14:37:11 SQL> conn hr/hr
Connected.
14:37:14 SQL> create table STAT_TEST as select BIRTH,REGDATE from USRINF ;

Table created.

Elapsed: 00:00:37.56
14:38:38 SQL> select count(1) from STAT_TEST ;

  COUNT(1)
----------
   6719785

Elapsed: 00:00:06.63
14:38:56 SQL> create index STAT_TEST_N1 ON STAT_TEST (BIRTH) ;

Index created.

Elapsed: 00:03:15.73
14:42:17 SQL> create index STAT_TEST_N2 ON STAT_TEST (REGDATE) ;

Index created.

Elapsed: 00:01:39.70
14:46:16 SQL> BEGIN
14:48:19   2       DBMS_STATS.GATHER_TABLE_STATS('HR','STAT_TEST',
14:48:19   3                                     METHOD_OPT => 'FOR ALL COLUMNS SIZE 1',
14:48:19   4                                     NO_INVALIDATE => FALSE);
14:48:19   5  END;
14:48:19   6  /

PL/SQL procedure successfully completed.

Elapsed: 00:00:23.38
```

▲ 테스트 테이블, 인덱스 생성 후 통계 정보 생성

통계 정보 갱신 시 발생할 수 있는 SQL 성능 저하의 테스트를 위한 테이블과 인덱스를 만들었습니다.

다음은 일반적으로 사용하는 어플리케이션의 SQL을 테스트하겠습니다.

```
14:52:18 SQL>
14:52:55 SQL> VAR B1 VARCHAR2(20);
14:52:55 SQL>
14:52:55 SQL> EXEC :B1 := '20060322220202';

PL/SQL procedure successfully completed.

Elapsed: 00:00:00.00
14:52:55 SQL>
14:52:55 SQL>
14:52:55 SQL> SELECT COUNT(1)
14:52:55   2  FROM   STAT_TEST
14:52:55   3  WHERE  REGDATE IN (SELECT REGDATE
14:52:55   4                     FROM   STAT_TEST
14:52:55   5                     WHERE  REGDATE = TO_DATE(:B1,'YYYYMMDDHH24MISS')
14:52:55   6                     )
14:52:55   7  AND    BIRTH IS NOT NULL ;

  COUNT(1)
----------
         2

Elapsed: 00:00:00.02
14:52:56 SQL> █
```

▲ 어플리케이션이 자주 사용하는 SQL

어플리케이션에서 사용하는 SQL입니다. 0.02초가 걸리고 있습니다. 특정 시간에 생성된 데이터의 NOT NULL 값의 건수를 확인하는 쿼리입니다.

해당 쿼리의 실행 플랜을 살펴보겠습니다.

```
PLAN_TABLE_OUTPUT
--------------------------------------------------------------------------------------------------------------------------------------------
--------------------------------------------------------------
SQL_ID  ccspfmjuzf7vz, child number 0
-------------------------------------
SELECT COUNT(1) FROM   STAT_TEST WHERE  REGDATE IN (SELECT REGDATE
       FROM   STAT_TEST                 WHERE  REGDATE =
TO_DATE(:B1,'YYYYMMDDHH24MISS')               ) AND    BIRTH IS NOT NULL

Plan hash value: 4290807858

--------------------------------------------------------------------------------------------------------------------------------------------
| Id  | Operation                             | Name         | Starts | E-Rows | A-Rows |   A-Time    | Buffers | Reads  |  OMem |  1Mem | Used-Mem |
--------------------------------------------------------------------------------------------------------------------------------------------
|   0 | SELECT STATEMENT                      |              |      1 |        |      1 |00:00:00.02 |       7 |      3 |       |       |          |
|   1 |  SORT AGGREGATE                       |              |      1 |      1 |      1 |00:00:00.02 |       7 |      3 |       |       |          |
|*  2 |   HASH JOIN SEMI                      |              |      1 |      1 |      2 |00:00:00.02 |       7 |      3 |  1995K|  1995K|  459K (0)|
|*  3 |    TABLE ACCESS BY INDEX ROWID BATCHED| STAT_TEST    |      1 |      1 |      2 |00:00:00.02 |       4 |      3 |       |       |          |
|*  4 |     INDEX RANGE SCAN                  | STAT_TEST_N2 |      1 |      1 |      2 |00:00:00.01 |       3 |      2 |       |       |          |
|*  5 |    INDEX RANGE SCAN                   | STAT_TEST_N2 |      1 |      1 |      1 |00:00:00.01 |       3 |      0 |       |       |          |
--------------------------------------------------------------------------------------------------------------------------------------------

Predicate Information (identified by operation id):
---------------------------------------------------

   2 - access("REGDATE"="REGDATE")
   3 - filter("BIRTH" IS NOT NULL)
   4 - access("REGDATE"=TO_DATE(:B1,'YYYYMMDDHH24MISS'))
   5 - access("REGDATE"=TO_DATE(:B1,'YYYYMMDDHH24MISS'))

Note
-----
   - this is an adaptive plan

31 rows selected.

NAME       CHILD_NUMBER   POSITION DATATYPE_STRING      WAS VALUE_STRING         LAST_CAPTURED
---------- ------------ ---------- -------------------- --- -------------------- ---------------
:B1                   0          1 VARCHAR2(32)         YES 20060322220202       20171027 145256

   elapsed       disk      query    current       rows
---------- ---------- ---------- ---------- ----------
   .015697          3          7          0          1

       Row Row_Source_Operation
---------- ---------------------------------------------------------------------------------------------------
         1 SELECT STATEMENT   (cr=7 pr=3 pw=0 time=15697)
         1  SORT AGGREGATE  (cr=7 pr=3 pw=0 time=15697)
         2   HASH JOIN SEMI  (cr=7 pr=3 pw=0 time=15692)
         2    NESTED LOOPS SEMI  (cr=4 pr=3 pw=0 time=15561)
         2     STATISTICS COLLECTOR   (cr=4 pr=3 pw=0 time=15553)
         2      TABLE ACCESS BY INDEX ROWID BATCHED STAT_TEST (cr=4 pr=3 pw=0 time=15504)
         2       INDEX RANGE SCAN STAT_TEST_N2 (cr=3 pr=2 pw=0 time=71)
         0     INDEX RANGE SCAN STAT_TEST_N2 (cr=0 pr=0 pw=0 time=0)
         1    INDEX RANGE SCAN STAT_TEST_N2 (cr=3 pr=0 pw=0 time=10)

9 rows selected.

SQL> █
```

▲ 자주 사용하는 SQL의 실행 PLAN

SQL PLAN의 순서를 보면 REGDATE 컬럼에 생성한 인덱스인 STAT_TEST_N2를 가장 먼저 Range Scan하는 Plan으로 수행되며 1건의 Rows를 만들기 위해 읽는 횟수도 물리적인 디스크 블록 접근 횟수 3번과 변경된 버퍼 블록 수 7번으로 매우 양호하고 좋은 SQL로 풀리고 있습니다.

이 DB에는 Batch 프로그램이 수행되고 있습니다. 이배치의 순서는 다음과 같습니다.

```
SQL>
SQL> -- Daily BATCH
SQL>
SQL>
SQL> CREATE TABLE STAT_TEST_TEMP AS SELECT * FROM STAT_TEST ;
SQL>
SQL> UPDATE STAT_TEST SET BIRTH = NULL ;
SQL>
SQL> commit;
SQL>
SQL> --STAT_TEST TABLE SELECT BATCH APP Start ...
SQL>
SQL> ...
SQL>
SQL> --STAT_TEST TABLE SELECT BATCH APP END ...
SQL>
SQL>
SQL> DELETE FROM STAT_TEST ;
SQL>
SQL> commit ;
SQL>
SQL> insert into STAT_TEST select * from STAT_TEST_TEMP ;
SQL>
SQL> commit ;
```

▲ 테스트 배치 프로그램

배치 프로그램은 매일 STAT_TEST 테이블을 백업받고 BIRTH 컬럼을 NULL로 치환 후 프로그램을 돌리고 종료되면 STAT_TEST 테이블을 원복 시키는 순서의 프로그램입니다.
이제 이배치 프로그램을 실행시킵니다.

```
15:02:27 SQL>
15:02:27 SQL> conn hr/hr
Connected.
15:02:33 SQL> -- Daily BATCH
15:02:38 SQL>
15:02:38 SQL> -- TEMP PART
15:02:39 SQL>
15:02:39 SQL> CREATE TABLE STAT_TEST_TEMP AS SELECT * FROM STAT_TEST ;

Table created.

Elapsed: 00:00:35.04
15:03:20 SQL> UPDATE STAT_TEST SET BIRTH = NULL ;


6719785 rows updated.

Elapsed: 09:22:13.94
00:26:24 SQL>
11:29:24 SQL> commit;

Commit complete.

Elapsed: 00:00:00.32
11:29:27 SQL>
```

▲ 테스트 배치 프로그램 실행 중간 단계

배치 프로그램을 실행시키는 도중에 통계 정보 갱신 작업을 합니다.

```
11:33:12 SQL>
11:33:16 SQL> BEGIN
11:33:33   2       DBMS_STATS.GATHER_TABLE_STATS('HR','STAT_TEST',
11:33:33   3                                     METHOD_OPT => 'FOR ALL COLUMNS SIZE 1',
11:33:34   4                                     NO_INVALIDATE => FALSE);
11:33:34   5  END;
11:33:34   6  /

PL/SQL procedure successfully completed.

Elapsed: 00:01:11.88
11:34:47 SQL>
```

▲ 테스트 배치 프로그램 실행 도중 통계 정보 갱신

BIRTH 컬럼이 Null로 치환이 완료된 다음에 아래의 통계 정보 갱신 작업이 수행되었습니다. 통계 정보 갱신을 On-line 중에 다량의 데이터가 변경되는 도중에 갱신한다고 보면 됩니다.

그 이후 배치 프로그램은 수행이 끝까지 완료되었고, 데이터는 원복 되었습니다.

```
15:02:27 SQL>
15:02:27 SQL>
15:02:27 SQL> conn hr/hr
Connected.
15:02:33 SQL> -- Daily BATCH
15:02:38 SQL>
15:02:38 SQL> -- TEMP PART
15:02:39 SQL>
15:02:39 SQL> CREATE TABLE STAT_TEST_TEMP AS SELECT * FROM STAT_TEST ;

Table created.

Elapsed: 00:00:35.04
15:03:20 SQL> UPDATE STAT_TEST SET BIRTH = NULL ;


6719785 rows updated.

Elapsed: 09:22:13.94
00:26:24 SQL>
11:29:24 SQL> commit;

Commit complete.

Elapsed: 00:00:00.32
11:29:27 SQL>
11:36:17 SQL> DELETE FROM STAT_TEST ;

6719785 rows deleted.

Elapsed: 00:16:54.53
11:54:01 SQL> commit ;

Commit complete.

Elapsed: 00:00:00.02
11:54:25 SQL> insert into STAT_TEST select * from STAT_TEST_TEMP ;


6719785 rows created.

Elapsed: 07:46:37.16
19:41:20 SQL>
21:43:54 SQL> commit ;

Commit complete.

Elapsed: 00:00:00.18
21:44:00 SQL>
```

▲ 테스트 배치 프로그램 실행 완료

BIRTH 컬럼이 Null로 치환이 완료 된 다음에 다음의 통계 정보 갱신 작업이 수행되었습니다. 통계 정보 갱신을 On-line 중에 다량의 데이터가 변경되는 도중에 갱신한다고 보면 됩니다. 그 이후 배치 프로그램은 수행이 끝까지 완료되었고, 데이터는 원복 되었습니다.

이제 배치 프로그램 테스트 이전에 자주 사용하는 쿼리를 수행시켜 봅니다.

```
21:44:32 SQL>
21:44:33 SQL> VAR B1 VARCHAR2(20);
21:44:56 SQL>
21:44:56 SQL> EXEC :B1 := '20060322220202';

PL/SQL procedure successfully completed.

Elapsed: 00:00:00.00
21:44:56 SQL>
21:44:56 SQL>
21:44:56 SQL> SELECT COUNT(1)
21:44:56   2  FROM    STAT_TEST
21:44:56   3  WHERE   REGDATE IN (SELECT REGDATE
21:44:56   4                  FROM    STAT_TEST
21:44:56   5                  WHERE   REGDATE = TO_DATE(:B1,'YYYYMMDDHH24MISS')
21:44:56   6                  )
21:44:56   7  AND     BIRTH IS NOT NULL ;

  COUNT(1)
----------
         2

Elapsed: 00:08:59.23
21:53:56 SQL> █
```

▲ 자주 사용하는 SQL문 재실행

0.02초 수행되었던 SQL이 9분가량 수행되었습니다. 똑같은 SQL의 수행시간이 수백 배 느려졌습니다.

서비스가 느려진 장애가 발생한 상황입니다. 왜 같은 SQL이 느려진 걸까요? PLAN을 살펴보겠습니다.

```
PLAN_TABLE_OUTPUT
-----------------------------------------------------------------------------------------------------------------------------------------------
----------------------------------------------------------------
SQL_ID  ccspfmjuzf7vz, child number 0
-------------------------------------
SELECT COUNT(1) FROM    STAT_TEST WHERE   REGDATE IN (SELECT REGDATE
         FROM    STAT_TEST                  WHERE  REGDATE =
TO_DATE(:B1,'YYYYMMDDHH24MISS')                   ) AND     BIRTH IS NOT NULL

Plan hash value: 108704307

-----------------------------------------------------------------------------------------------------------------------------------------------
| Id  | Operation                              | Name         | Starts | E-Rows | A-Rows |   A-Time    | Buffers | Reads  |  OMem |  1Mem | Used-Mem |
-----------------------------------------------------------------------------------------------------------------------------------------------
|   0 | SELECT STATEMENT                       |              |      1 |        |      1 |00:02:24.48  |   5681K|   4942K|       |       |          |
|   1 |  SORT AGGREGATE                        |              |      1 |      1 |      1 |00:02:24.48  |   5681K|   4942K|       |       |          |
|*  2 |   HASH JOIN SEMI                       |              |      1 |      1 |      2 |00:02:24.48  |   5681K|   4942K|  1995K|  1995K|  720K (0)|
|*  3 |    TABLE ACCESS BY INDEX ROWID BATCHED| STAT_TEST    |      1 |      1 |      2 |00:02:24.46  |   5681K|   4942K|       |       |          |
|*  4 |     INDEX FULL SCAN                    | STAT_TEST_N1 |      1 |      1 |  6718K|00:00:13.20  |   38974 |  38974 |       |       |          |
|*  5 |    INDEX RANGE SCAN                    | STAT_TEST_N2 |      1 |      1 |      1 |00:00:00.02  |       3 |      3 |       |       |          |
-----------------------------------------------------------------------------------------------------------------------------------------------

Predicate Information (identified by operation id):
---------------------------------------------------

   2 - access("REGDATE"="REGDATE")
   3 - filter("REGDATE"=TO_DATE(:B1,'YYYYMMDDHH24MISS'))
   4 - filter("BIRTH" IS NOT NULL)
   5 - access("REGDATE"=TO_DATE(:B1,'YYYYMMDDHH24MISS'))

Note
-----
   - this is an adaptive plan

31 rows selected.

NAME       CHILD_NUMBER   POSITION DATATYPE_STRING      WAS VALUE_STRING         LAST_CAPTURED
---------- ------------ ---------- -------------------- --- -------------------- --------------
:B1                   0          1 VARCHAR2(32)         YES 20060322220202       20171028 220420

   elapsed       disk      query    current       rows
---------- ---------- ---------- ---------- ----------
144.482537    4942879    5681599          0          1

      Row Row_Source_Operation
--------- -------------------------------------------------------------------------------------------------------------
        1 SELECT STATEMENT    (cr=5681599 pr=4942879 pw=0 time=144482537)
        1  SORT AGGREGATE  (cr=5681599 pr=4942879 pw=0 time=144482537)
        2   HASH JOIN SEMI  (cr=5681599 pr=4942879 pw=0 time=144482528)
        2    NESTED LOOPS SEMI  (cr=5681596 pr=4942876 pw=0 time=144458980)
        2     STATISTICS COLLECTOR    (cr=5681596 pr=4942876 pw=0 time=144458970)
        2      TABLE ACCESS BY INDEX ROWID BATCHED STAT_TEST (cr=5681596 pr=4942876 pw=0 time=144458884)
  6718986       INDEX FULL SCAN STAT_TEST_N1 (cr=38974 pr=38974 pw=0 time=13197564)
        0     INDEX RANGE SCAN STAT_TEST_N2 (cr=0 pr=0 pw=0 time=0)
        1    INDEX RANGE SCAN STAT_TEST_N2 (cr=3 pr=3 pw=0 time=23319)

9 rows selected.

SQL> █
```

▲ 갑자기 느려진 동일 SQL문의 수행 PLAN

SQL PLAN의 순서가 REGDATE 컬럼에 생성한 인덱스인 STAT_TEST_N2를 가장 먼저 Range Scan했던 Plan이 바뀌었습니다. BIRTH 컬럼에 생성된 인덱스 STAT_TEST_N1를 가장 먼저 Full Scan하고 있습니다. 그리고 1건의 Rows를 만들기 위해 읽는 횟수도 물리적인 디스크 블록 접근 횟수 3번과 변경된 버퍼 블록 수 7번으로 매우 양호하고 좋았던 SQL이 1건의 Rows를 만들기 위해 읽는 횟수도 물리적인 디스크 블록 접근 횟수 495만 번과 변경된 버퍼 블록 수 568만 건을 읽어야만 하는 악성 SQL로 변경되었습니다.

어마어마한 차이를 보이며 변경되었습니다. 왜 이런 현상이 발생하였는지 통계 정보의 데이터를 보겠습니다.

```
22:09:23 SQL> SELECT S.TABLE_NAME,
22:09:23   2         S.COLUMN_NAME,
22:09:23   3         S.NUM_DISTINCT,
22:09:23   4         S.NUM_NULLS,
22:09:23   5         S.DENSITY,
22:09:23   6         S.LOW_VALUE,
22:09:23   7         S.HIGH_VALUE,
22:09:23   8         S.HISTOGRAM
22:09:23   9  FROM   USER_TAB_COLS S
22:09:23  10  WHERE  S.TABLE_NAME = UPPER('STAT_TEST')
22:09:23  11   AND   s.COLUMN_NAME in ('REGDATE','BIRTH')
22:09:23  12  ;

TABLE_NAME COLUMN_NAME          NUM_DISTINCT  NUM_NULLS    DENSITY LOW_VALUE            HIGH_VALUE           HISTOGRAM
---------- -------------------- ------------ ---------- ---------- -------------------- -------------------- ---------------
STAT_TEST  BIRTH                           0    6719785          0                                           NONE
STAT_TEST  REGDATE                   5474816         52 1.8265E-07 77C70B090B2325       78700718101E35       NONE

Elapsed: 00:00:00.13
22:09:23 SQL> █
```

▲ 테스트 테이블의 통계 정보 값 조회

BIRTH 값의 NULL 통계 정보 값이 높아졌습니다. 즉 배치 프로그램 도중에 NULL 데이터로 치환된 후 통계 정보가 수집되어 현재 데이터 값과 다른 수치를 보이고 있습니다.

왜 옵티마이저는 이런 Plan을 만들었는지 통계 정보 데이터 값과 SQL을 보면 알 수 있습니다.

그건 바로 'BIRTH IS NOT NULL' 조건 때문입니다. 위에 배치 프로그램 수행 중간에 BIRTH 컬럼의 값이 모두 NULL 변경된 후 값을 넣고 통계 정보를 갱신 한 것을 기억하실 겁니다. 옵티마이저 또한 위의 SQL을 가지고 Plan을 만들 때 'BIRTH IS NOT NULL'이 조건을 가지고 통계 정보를 살펴보았고 살펴보니 'BIRTH' 컬럼에 값이 모두 NULL이다는 것으로 확인하였습니다.

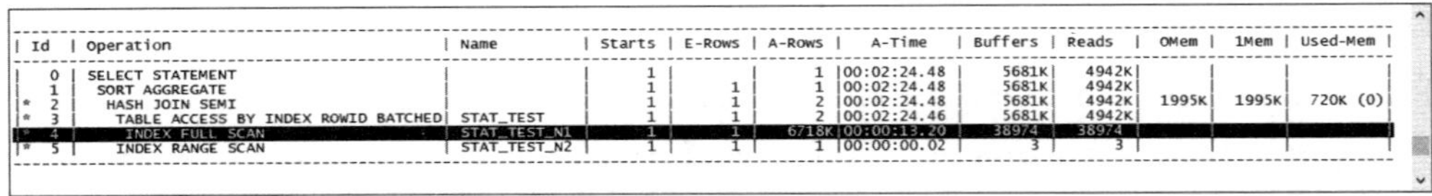

```
--------------------------------------------------------------------------------------------------------------------------------------------------
| Id  | Operation                              | Name          | Starts | E-Rows | A-Rows |   A-Time    | Buffers | Reads  |  OMem |  1Mem | Used-Mem |
--------------------------------------------------------------------------------------------------------------------------------------------------
|   0 | SELECT STATEMENT                       |               |      1 |        |      1 |00:02:24.48  |   5681K|   4942K|       |       |          |
|   1 |  SORT AGGREGATE                        |               |      1 |      1 |      1 |00:02:24.48  |   5681K|   4942K|       |       |          |
|*  2 |   HASH JOIN SEMI                       |               |      1 |      1 |      2 |00:02:24.48  |   5681K|   4942K|  1995K|  1995K|  720K (0)|
|*  3 |    TABLE ACCESS BY INDEX ROWID BATCHED| STAT_TEST     |      1 |      1 |      2 |00:02:24.46  |   5681K|   4942K|       |       |          |
|*  4 |     INDEX FULL SCAN                    | STAT_TEST_N1  |      1 |      1 |  6718K |00:00:13.20  |   38974|   38974|       |       |          |
|*  5 |    INDEX RANGE SCAN                    | STAT_TEST_N2  |      1 |      1 |      1 |00:00:00.02  |       3|       3|       |       |          |
--------------------------------------------------------------------------------------------------------------------------------------------------
```

▲ 옵티마이저의 예상 건수와 실제 건수가 큰 차이

그렇기 때문에 옵티마이저는 INDEX FULL SCAN을 하여 0건을 액세스하는 것이 최적이므로 판단하였고 1건을 액세스 한 뒤 FROM 절의 STAT_TEST에 ACCESS하는 것보다 더 낫다고 판단을 한 것입니다.

이처럼 옵티마이저는 통계 정보를 바탕으로 실행계획을 만든다는 것을 확인할 수 있습니다.

하지만 배치 프로그램 종료 후 BIRTH 컬럼의 데이터는 NULL에서 원복되었기 때문에 정확히 매칭되는 통계 정보 값은 아니어서 예상 건수와 실제 건수는 차이를 보이고 있습니다.

그럼 이렇게 통계 정보를 갱신하고 어플리케이션이 갑자기 느려지는 상황에서 대처 방법은 어떻게 될까요? 지금부터 알아보겠습니다.

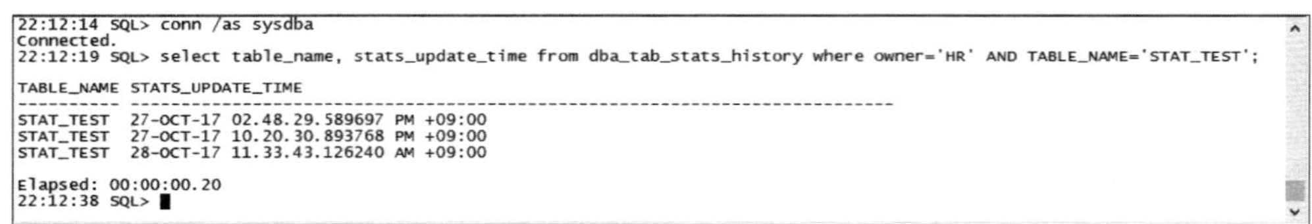

```
22:12:14 SQL> conn /as sysdba
Connected.
22:12:19 SQL> select table_name, stats_update_time from dba_tab_stats_history where owner='HR' AND TABLE_NAME='STAT_TEST';

TABLE_NAME STATS_UPDATE_TIME
---------- ---------------------------------------------------------------------------
STAT_TEST  27-OCT-17 02.48.29.589697 PM +09:00
STAT_TEST  27-OCT-17 10.20.30.893768 PM +09:00
STAT_TEST  28-OCT-17 11.33.43.126240 AM +09:00

Elapsed: 00:00:00.20
22:12:38 SQL>
```

▲ 테이블의 통계 정보 생성 확인

통계 정보의 갱신 이력을 조회합니다. 어느 시간에 통계 정보가 갱신되었는지 확인하고 통계 정보를 원복 시킬 시점을 결정합니다.

```
22:12:38 SQL> exec DBMS_STATS.RESTORE_TABLE_STATS('HR','STAT_TEST','27-OCT-17 10.20.30.893768 PM +09:00',TRUE,TRUE,TRUE) ;

PL/SQL procedure successfully completed.

Elapsed: 00:00:02.31
22:15:24 SQL> SELECT OWNER, TABLE_NAME, TO_CHAR(LAST_ANALYZED,'yyyy-mm-dd hh24:mi:ss') AS LAST_STAT_DATE
22:15:52   2  FROM DBA_TABLES
22:15:52   3  WHERE OWNER='HR'
22:15:52   4  AND  TABLE_NAME='STAT_TEST' ;

OWNER      TABLE_NAME LAST_STAT_DATE
---------- ---------- -------------------
HR         STAT_TEST  2017-10-27 22:20:30

Elapsed: 00:00:00.20
22:15:53 SQL> conn hr/hr
Connected.
22:16:18 SQL> SELECT S.TABLE_NAME,
22:16:19   2         S.COLUMN_NAME,
22:16:19   3         S.NUM_DISTINCT,
22:16:19   4         S.NUM_NULLS,
22:16:19   5         S.DENSITY,
22:16:19   6         S.LOW_VALUE,
22:16:19   7         S.HIGH_VALUE,
22:16:19   8         S.HISTOGRAM
22:16:19   9  FROM   USER_TAB_COLS S
22:16:19  10  WHERE  S.TABLE_NAME = UPPER('STAT_TEST')
22:16:19  11    AND  S.COLUMN_NAME in ('BIRTH','REGDATE');

TABLE_NAME COLUMN_NAME          NUM_DISTINCT  NUM_NULLS    DENSITY LOW_VALUE            HIGH_VALUE           HISTOGRAM
---------- -------------------- ------------ ---------- ---------- -------------------- -------------------- ---------------
STAT_TEST  BIRTH                       36200        799 .000027624 30303030303130312020 32303939303231392020 NONE
                                                                   20202020202020202020 20202020202020202020
                                                                   20202020             20202020

STAT_TEST  REGDATE                   5474816         52 1.8265E-07 77C70B090B2325       78700718101E35       NONE

Elapsed: 00:00:00.19
22:16:20 SQL> █
```

▲ 통계 정보 원복 후 통계 정보 원복 확인

DBMS_STATS 패키지 내에 RESTORE_TABLE_STATS 프로시저를 이용하여 해당 테이블의 통계 정보를 원복 시킵니다. 원복 시킨 이후 해당 테이블의 통계 정보 원복을 확인하고, 문제가 되었던 컬럼의 통계 정보 데이터를 조회합니다.

이제 문제가 되었던 느려졌던 SQL문을 수행해 봅니다.

```
21:53:56 SQL> VAR B1 VARCHAR2(20);
22:18:06 SQL>
22:18:06 SQL> EXEC :B1 := '20060322220202';

PL/SQL procedure successfully completed.

Elapsed: 00:00:00.00
22:18:06 SQL>
22:18:06 SQL>
22:18:06 SQL> SELECT COUNT(1)
22:18:06   2  FROM   STAT_TEST
22:18:06   3  WHERE  REGDATE IN (SELECT REGDATE
22:18:06   4                     FROM   STAT_TEST
22:18:06   5                     WHERE  REGDATE = TO_DATE(:B1,'YYYYMMDDHH24MISS')
22:18:06   6                     )
22:18:06   7  AND    BIRTH IS NOT NULL ;

  COUNT(1)
----------
         2

Elapsed: 00:00:00.05
22:18:08 SQL> █
```

▲ 느려졌던 SQL 수행

9분 정도 걸렸던 SQL문이 0.05초로 수행 시간이 다시 좋아졌습니다.

이제 해당 SQL의 SQL 수행 PLAN도 확인해 봅니다.

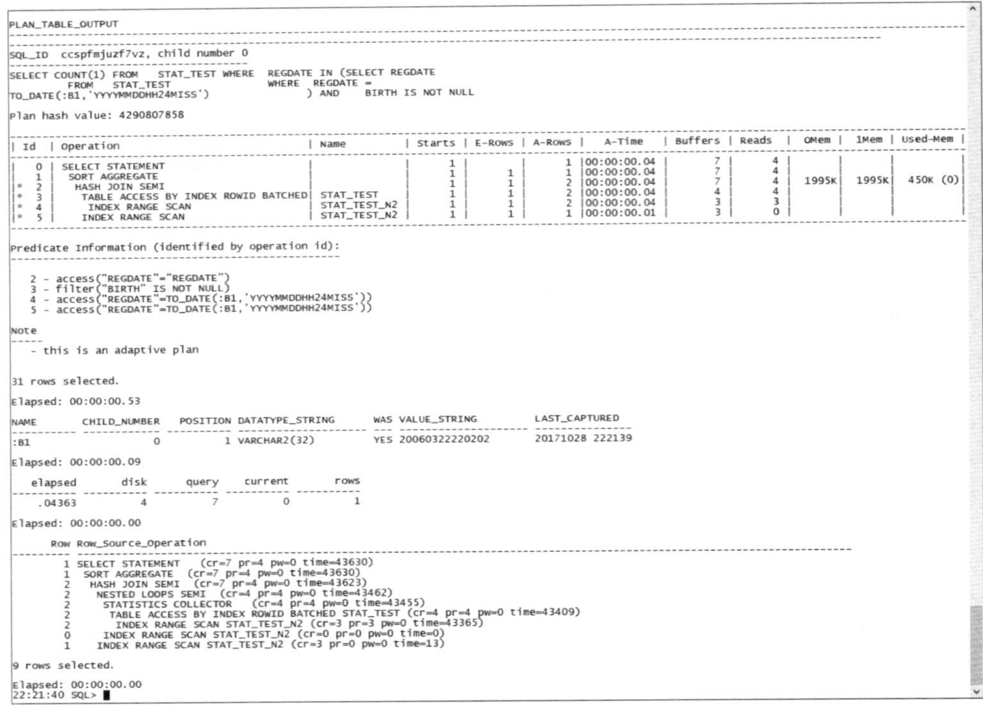

```
PLAN_TABLE_OUTPUT
------------------------------------------------------------------------------------------------------------

SQL_ID  ccspfmjuzf7vz, child number 0
-------------------------------------
SELECT COUNT(1) FROM   STAT_TEST WHERE  REGDATE IN (SELECT REGDATE
        FROM   STAT_TEST                WHERE  REGDATE =
TO_DATE(:B1,'YYYYMMDDHH24MISS')               ) AND    BIRTH IS NOT NULL

Plan hash value: 4290807858

------------------------------------------------------------------------------------------------------------------------------------------------
| Id  | Operation                               | Name         | Starts | E-Rows | A-Rows |   A-Time    | Buffers | Reads  |  OMem |  1Mem | Used-Mem |
------------------------------------------------------------------------------------------------------------------------------------------------
|   0 | SELECT STATEMENT                        |              |      1 |        |      1 |00:00:00.04 |       7 |      4 |       |       |          |
|   1 |  SORT AGGREGATE                         |              |      1 |      1 |      1 |00:00:00.04 |       7 |      4 |       |       |          |
|*  2 |   HASH JOIN SEMI                        |              |      1 |      1 |      2 |00:00:00.04 |       7 |      4 | 1995K | 1995K | 450K (0) |
|*  3 |    TABLE ACCESS BY INDEX ROWID BATCHED| STAT_TEST    |      1 |      1 |      2 |00:00:00.04 |       4 |      4 |       |       |          |
|*  4 |     INDEX RANGE SCAN                    | STAT_TEST_N2 |      1 |      1 |      2 |00:00:00.04 |       3 |      3 |       |       |          |
|*  5 |    INDEX RANGE SCAN                     | STAT_TEST_N2 |      1 |      1 |      1 |00:00:00.01 |       3 |      0 |       |       |          |
------------------------------------------------------------------------------------------------------------------------------------------------

Predicate Information (identified by operation id):
---------------------------------------------------

   2 - access("REGDATE"="REGDATE")
   3 - filter("BIRTH" IS NOT NULL)
   4 - access("REGDATE"=TO_DATE(:B1,'YYYYMMDDHH24MISS'))
   5 - access("REGDATE"=TO_DATE(:B1,'YYYYMMDDHH24MISS'))

Note
-----
   - this is an adaptive plan

31 rows selected.

Elapsed: 00:00:00.53

NAME       CHILD_NUMBER   POSITION DATATYPE_STRING      WAS VALUE_STRING         LAST_CAPTURED
---------- ------------ ---------- -------------------- --- -------------------- ---------------
:B1                   0          1 VARCHAR2(32)         YES 20060322220202       20171028 222139

Elapsed: 00:00:00.09

   elapsed       disk      query    current       rows
---------- ---------- ---------- ---------- ----------
    .04363          4          7          0          1

Elapsed: 00:00:00.00

       Row Row_Source_Operation
---------- -----------------------------------------------------------------------------------------
         1 SELECT STATEMENT   (cr=7 pr=4 pw=0 time=43630)
         1  SORT AGGREGATE  (cr=7 pr=4 pw=0 time=43630)
         2   HASH JOIN SEMI  (cr=7 pr=4 pw=0 time=43623)
         2    NESTED LOOPS SEMI  (cr=4 pr=4 pw=0 time=43462)
         2     STATISTICS COLLECTOR   (cr=4 pr=4 pw=0 time=43455)
         2      TABLE ACCESS BY INDEX ROWID BATCHED STAT_TEST (cr=4 pr=4 pw=0 time=43409)
         2       INDEX RANGE SCAN STAT_TEST_N2 (cr=3 pr=3 pw=0 time=43365)
         0     INDEX RANGE SCAN STAT_TEST_N2 (cr=0 pr=0 pw=0 time=0)
         1    INDEX RANGE SCAN STAT_TEST_N2 (cr=3 pr=0 pw=0 time=13)

9 rows selected.

Elapsed: 00:00:00.00
22:21:40 SQL>
```

▲ SQL PLAN 확인

SQL PLAN의 순서를 보면 REGDATE 컬럼에 생성한 인덱스인 STAT_TEST_N2를 가장 먼저 Range Scan하는 Plan으로 수행되며 1건의 Rows를 만들기 위해 읽는 횟수도 물리적인 디스크 블록 접근 횟수 4번과 변경된 버퍼 블록 수 7번으로 매우 양호하고 좋은 SQL로 다시 수행되고 있습니다.

지금까지 통계 정보 갱신으로 인한 서비스 응답시간 저하 장애에 대해서 알아보았습니다. 본 장의 핵심은 데이터데 통계정보 값이 다를 경우 문제가 될 수 있는 점을 테스트를 통해 알아보았습니다.

통계 정보 갱신은 DB에서 수행 중인 전체 SQL의 95%의 성능 효과 장점과 5%의 성능 저하 Risk를 가지고 있다고 알려져 있습니다.
따라서 저자 또한 통계 정보는 DB내의 데이터와 맞도록 갱신을 추천합니다.

가장 추천하는 안전한 통계 정보 갱신 방법은 데이터 변경이 없을 때 통계 정보 갱신을 하고 통계 정보 갱신 후 DBMS 모니터링 / 서비스 모니터링 / 통계 정보 원복 준비 등 통계 정보 갱신에 따른 SQL PLAN 변경으로 인한 어플리케이션 서비스의 성능 저하 RISK에 대비를 하는 방법을 권합니다.

▶ 참고자료

참고	참고문헌
[1] Oracle OnlineManual (https://docs.oracle.com) [2] My Oracle Support (https://support.oracle.com)	

02
Chapter

RMAN의 정석 편

RMAN의 소개

데이터베이스와 함께 설치되는 복구 관리자(RMAN)는 데이터베이스에서 백업 및 복구 작업을 수행하고 백업 전략관리를 자동화하는 오라클 데이터베이스 클라이언트입니다. 이 툴을 사용하면 훨씬 간단하게 데이터베이스를 백업, 복원 및 복구할 수 있습니다. Oracle에서 백업 및 복구용으로 권장하는 툴인 Oracle 12c RMAN(복구 관리자)의 기본 개념에 대해 설명합니다.

1 Oracle DB 백업

오라클 DB 백업 방식에는 크게 논리적 백업과 물리적 백업이 있으며 서비스 기준으로 오프라인 백업과 온라인 백업이 있습니다. 지금부터 이 백업의 특성과 방법을 알아보겠습니다.

■ 논리적 백업

1. 테이블과 저장 프로시저 등의 정의 정보와 데이터를 추출하고, 장애 시 데이터를 로드하는 방법입니다.
2. 논리적 백업 취득 시에는 Export 유틸리티를 사용하고, 로드 시에는 Import 유틸리티를 사용합니다.
3. 백업 취득 시점의 데이터만 보호할 수 있습니다.
4. 불완전 복구의 백업 방식입니다.
5. 주로 데이터 마이그레이션 시 사용합니다.
6. 논리적 백업의 툴은 2종류입니다.

   ❶ Original Export(exp), Import(imp)
   ❷ Datapump Export(expdp), Import(impdp)

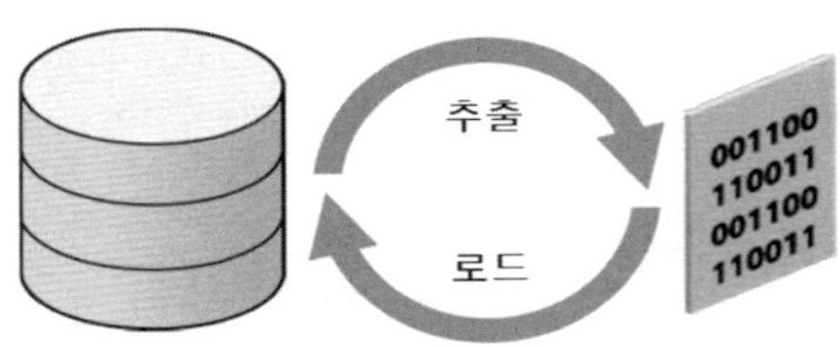

▲ 논리적 백업

■ 물리적 백업

1. Oracle Database를 구성하는 파일 군의 물리적인 복사본을 만들 수 있습니다.
2. Oracle Database 가동 중에 백업을 수행 가능합니다(온라인 백업).
3. 디스크의 물리적 장애(미디어 장애)가 발생하더라도 장애 발생 직전까지 복구할 수 있습니다.
4. 완전 복구가 가능한 백업 방식입니다.
5. 물리적 백업의 툴은 2종류입니다.

❶ Begin/End Backup 사용자 관리 백업 OS 제공 복사 명령+SQL 명령
❷ Oracle RMAN(Recovery Manager) 유틸리티

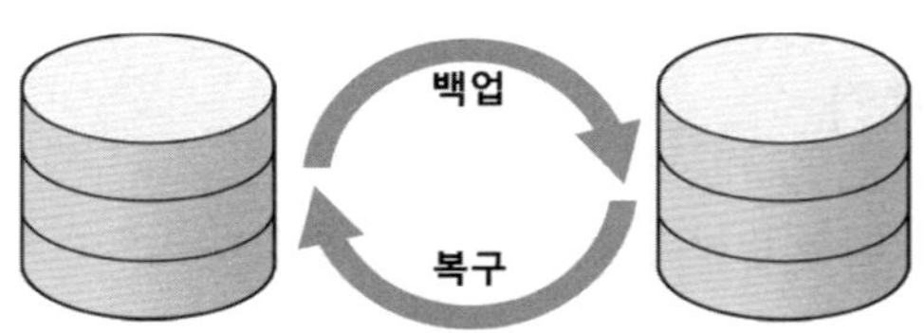

▲ 물리적 백업

그럼 완전 복구가 가능한 물리적 백업의 2가지 방식에 대해서 알아보겠습니다.

■ Begin/End Backup 사용자 관리 백업

1. OS에서 제공하는 복사 명령과 SQL 명령을 함께 사용하는 백업 방법입니다.
2. 백업 관련 파일을 관리자가 관리합니다.

❶ 백업 대상 데이터 파일과 그 위치를 관리해야 합니다.
❷ 백업된 데이터 보관 주기 관리 및 불필요한 파일 삭제를 직접해야 합니다.
❸ 복구 작업 시, 장애에 따른 복원 할 파일을 식별하고 올바른 위치에 복원 작업해야 합니다.

3. 파일 유형에 따라 백업 방법이 다릅니다.

❶ SPFILE/Control File/ 데이터 파일에 따라 백업 방법이 다릅니다.
❷ 온라인 또는 오프라인 상태의 모든 테이블스페이스 또는 개별 데이터파일을 백업합니다.

❸ Control file을 이전 파일로 백업하거나 스크립트를 작성하여 복구 시 Control file을 재생성합니다.
❹ OS에서 제공하는 복사 명령을 이용하기 때문에, 파일 손상이 있어도 감지할 수 없습니다.
❺ 스토리지 기능을 사용하여 백업할 때 사용합니다.

■ Oracle RMAN(Recovery Manager) 백업

1. Oracle Database의 백업, 복원, 복구를 위한 유틸리티입니다.
2. 백업 관련 파일을 Oracle Database 자신이 관리합니다.

❶ 백업 상황을 Oracle Database의 Control File에 저장하고 복원, 복구 시에 활용합니다.
❷ 백업 상황을 외부의 Recovery Catalog에 등록하는 것으로, 여러 백업의 중앙 관리가 가능합니다.

3. 플랫폼에 관계없이 동일한 명령으로 해결 가능합니다.
4. RMAN으로 파일 손상(Block Corruption)의 감지가 가능합니다.
5. "파일" 보다 작은 "Oracle Block" 단위로 백업, 복원, 복구가 가능하여 백업 시간이 단축됩니다.

서비스 기준으로 서비스/DB를 내려서 백업받는 오프라인 백업과 서비스/DB를 내리지 않고 온라인 중에 백업받는 방식입니다.

■ 오프라인 물리적 백업

1. Oracle Database Instance를 정상적으로 정지시킨 상태에서 OS 명령어로 Oracle Database Instance를 구성하는 파일 군의 물리적 사본을 얻는 방법입니다.
2. Oracle Database Instance가 시작되는 동안, Control File만 인식시킨 상태(mount 상태)에서 RMAN으로 이미지 복사본을 수행하는 방법입니다.
3. Database 복구 시, 이전에 취득한 모든 백업을 복원하는 것으로 백업 수행 완료 시점 상태로 복원합니다.
4. 복원 완료 후에 Oracle Database Instance를 사용자에게 Open하게 됩니다.

■ 온라인 물리적 백업

1. Oracle Database Instance를 가동시킨 채 OS 명령어로 물리적 백업을 수행하거나, 또는 RMAN에서 Image Copy, Backup Set 방식으로 백업을 수행하는 방법입니다.
2. 복구 시, 이전에 수행한 백업을 복원한 후 아카이브 로그를 이용한 복구 작업을 할 필요가 있습니다.
3. 장애 발생 직전의 상태까지 복구할 수 있습니다.
4. Oracle Database Instance를 Archive log 모드로 실행시켜야 합니다.

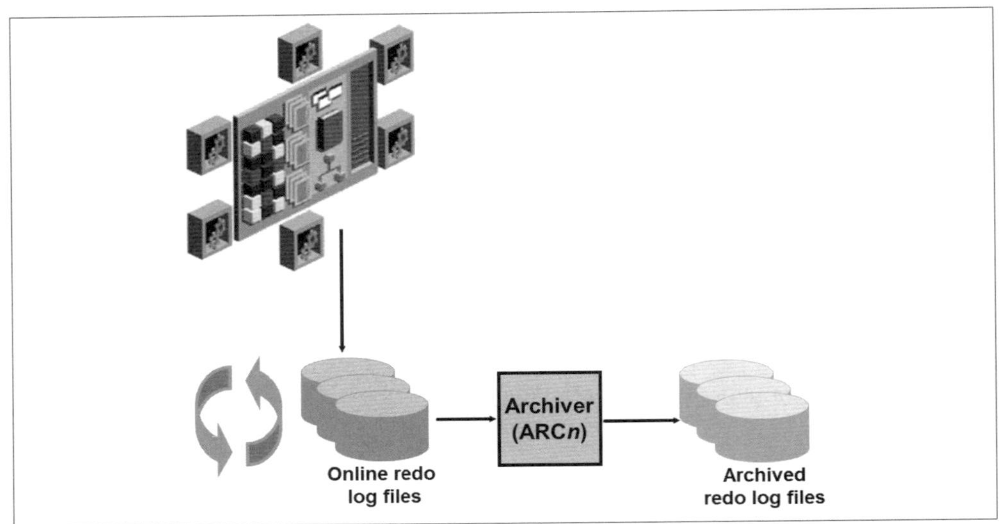

▲ 아카이브 로그 모드

2 RMAN(Recovery Manager)의 개요

Recovery Manager는 DBA가 강력한 운영체제 독립 스크립트 언어로 백업, 복원, 그리고 복구 프로세스를 관리하는데 도움을 주는 오라클 유틸리티입니다. Recovery Manager의 기능은 명령 라인 인터페이스와 Oracle Enterprise Manager Backup Manager(GUI)를 통해서도 사용할 수 있습니다.

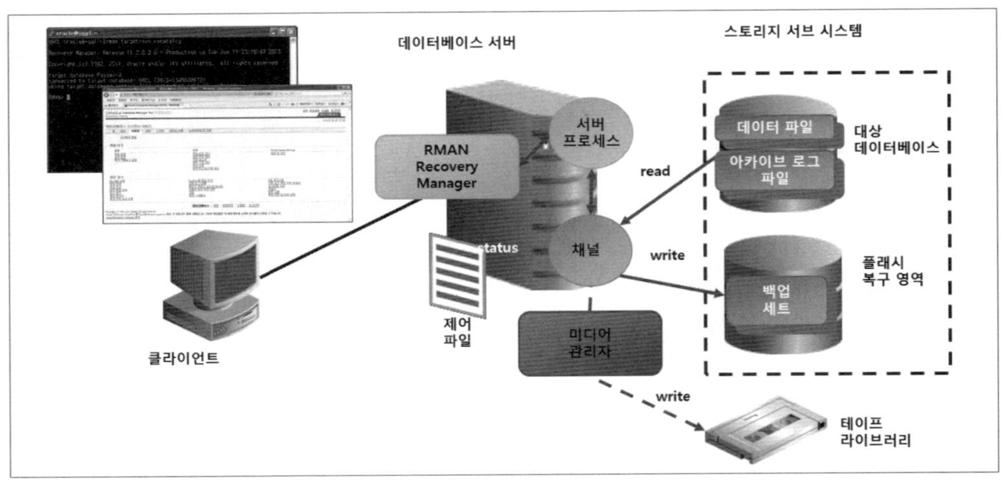

▲ RMAN 기본 구성

■ RMAN 정리

1. RMAN은 데이터베이스의 백업(Backup), 복원(Restore) 및 복구(Recovery)를 수행하기 위한 클라이언트 유틸리티입니다.
2. RMAN은 독립형 애플리케이션으로 오라클 데이터베이스와 클라이언트 연결 방식을 통해 접속됩니다.
3. RMAN은 Interpreter에 불과하여 유저의 명령을 해독한 후, RPC를 통하여 데이터베이스에게 넘겨주어 실제적인 작업의 처리는 대상 데이터베이스에서 수행하게 됩니다.
4. RMAN의 실행 방법은 다음과 같습니다.

❶ OS prompt로부터 RMAN을 기동 커멘드 라인으로 실행합니다(SQL*Plus와 같은 CLI 인터페이스).
❷ Oracle Enterprise Manager(OEM)l를 사용해 GUI 형태로 실행 가능합니다.
❸ 데이터베이스에의 접속은 Net(TCP/IP)를 활용하여 원격지에서도 가능합니다.

5. 백업 대상 파일은 Control File, 데이터 파일, 아카이브 로그 파일이며 온라인 REDO 로그 파일과 Temp 파일은 RMAN 백업 대상에서 제외합니다.
6. RMAN이 접속하려는 대상 데이터베이스는 MOUNT되거나 OPEN되어야만 하며 복구 카탈로그(Recovery Catalog)가 사용되면 카탈로그 데이터베이스가 OPEN되어 있어야 합니다.

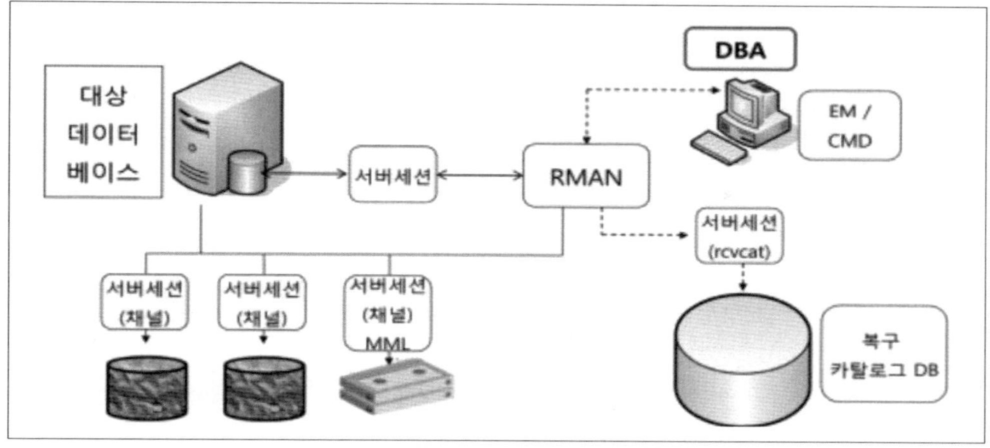

▲ Oracle RMAN

3 RMAN 백업 방식의 장점

Begin/End Backup 사용자 관리 백업에 대비해 여러 가지 측면의 RMAN 백업의 장점을 살펴보겠습니다.

■ RMAN을 이용한 DB 백업 관리

1. Oracle DB 백업에 필요한 설정을 저장하고 관리합니다.
2. Oracle DB가 백업해야 할 데이터/저장 기간을 인식합니다.
3. Oracle DB가 백업 저장 백업 공간을 관리하며 고속 복구 영역(FAST RECOVERY AREA) 이용이 가능합니다.
4. 백업 및 복구 명령을 단순화하며 OS 명령(복잡한 Shell명령)과 함께 사용하지 않아도 됩니다.
5. 명령 스크립트의 가독성 향상 및 DB 백업 운영 가능성이 높아지며 작업 자동화로 인한 실수를 줄일 수 있습니다.

❶ 하나의 Command 명령어로 Oracle Database에서 백업해야 할 모든 데이터를 저장(데이터 파일 /control 파일/SPFILE 파일)
❷ 아카이브로그백업도 RMAN 명령을 통해 Database 백업 시 포함하여 백업이 가능합니다.

▲ DBA가 관리해야 하는 Begin/End Backup 방식

■ RMAN을 이용한 DB 복구

1. 장애 복구의 총 시간은 DBA가 분석하는 시간인 장애 진단, 복구 절차 검토의 시간과 실제 복구 작업으로 이루어집니다.
2. 기존 Begin/End Backup의 경우 Restore를 위해 스토리지/서버/백업 담당자를 모두 필요하게 됩니다.
3. RMAN 백업은 Oracle DB가 복구에 필요한 백업을 자동으로 선택합니다.
4. Data Recovery Advisor 기능으로 복구 방법을 Oracle DB가 추천할 수 있습니다.
5. DBA가 분석하는 장애 분석에 필요한 시간을 줄이게 되어 신속한 복구할 수 있습니다.

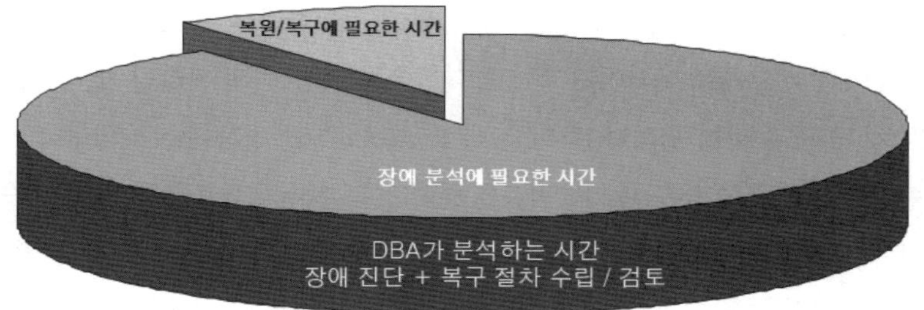

▲ 장애 복구에서 장애 분석 및 복구 전략을 수립하기 위한 시간이 포함

■ Oracle DB 리소스 기준 장점

1. RMAN 백업은 Oracle Database의 구조를 최대한 활용하여 백업받습니다.
2. 운영 DB에서 온라인으로 백업 받을 경우 기존 Begin/End Backup의 Hot Backup 모드의 부하가 없습니다.
3. RMAN은 실제 사용하는 데이터 블록 단위로 읽고 쓰기가 가능합니다(Begin/End BACKUP은 파일 단위).
4. RMAN으로 백업하면 백업 중에 운영 중인 DB의 손상된 블록의 검증이 기본 제공됩니다.
5. 고속 증분 백업 기능을 이용하여 백업 시간을 절감 시킬 수 있습니다.
6. 블록 단위의 블록 미디어 복구가 가능합니다.
7. 백업 압축 기능을 제공하여 백업 양을 줄일 수 있습니다.
8. 미사용 데이터의 압축 및 SKIP 기능을 제공합니다.

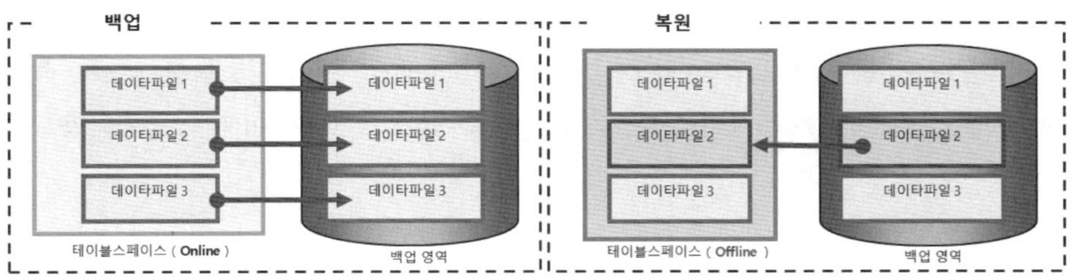

▲ Begin/End Backup 방식의 백업 복구(복원) 단위

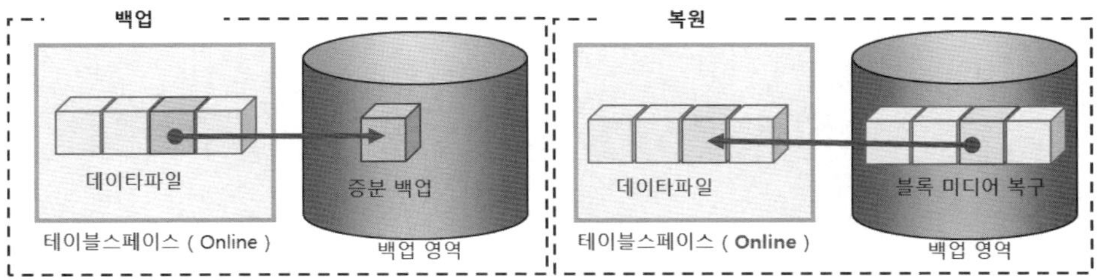

▲ RMAN 방식의 백업 복구(복원) 단위

RMAN에서는 BLOCK-LEVEL BACKUP의 사용이 가능합니다. RMAN의 구조는 INPUT 메모리와 OUTPUT 메모리로 이루어져 각 DB 블록이 백업을 위해 처리될 때, 각 블록에 대해 CORRUPTION 점검을 하게 됩니다(IMAGE COPY로 실행할 경우에는 제외됩니다). 또한 이 처리 절차 단계에서 Null Compression 점검을 하여 블록 헤더가 0으로 잡혀있는, 즉 비어있는 블록에 대해서는 백업에 포함시키지 않아 훨씬 더 효과적인 백업을 수행하게 됩니다.
이때 완벽하게 비어있는 모든 DB 블록들이 백업 대상에서 제외되는 것은 아닙니다. RMAN은 데이터베이스가 다운되어 있을 때에도 수행되어야 하기 때문에, 데이터베이스가 운용되어 있는 중의 Segment Management 정보를 포함하고 있는 뷰에 접근하는 대신(보다 정확한 정보를 얻을 수 있는), OS 레벨에서의 데이터파일 헤더에서 필요한 정보를 얻어 오기 때문에 예를 들어 Truncate 시킨 테이블에 소모되어 있는 DB 블록에 대한 정보들을 얻어올 수 없습니다.
그리고 이러한 방식으로 미사용 된 블록의 백업 불 포함이 시간적인 성능 향상을 불러일으키는 것은 아닙니다. 심각한 병합 현상을 보이는 백업 대상 장치를 제외하고는 시간적으로는 거의 동일한 시간을 소모하게 됩니다. 왜냐하면 RMAN은 여전히 데이터파일 내의 모든 블록을 대상으로 검사를 하여야 하기 때문입니다.
이러한 BLOCK-Level Backup은 Redo의 생성을 적게 합니다. Begin/End Backup 방식의 백업은 많은 양의 Redo Log 생성 및, Archived Redo Log를 위한 Log Switch의 대량 발생 등이 야기되나, RMAN은 DBWR와 연계하여 작업을 수행하기에 Block 레벨의 동기성을 보장할 필요가 없어 이러한 문제가 발생하지 않습니다.
또한 오라클 9i부터는 'ora-1578: block corruption detected' 에러의 발생 시, 파일을 통째로 복구하는 대신, 단순히 Corrupt된 블록만을 교체할 수 있어 그 효용성이 더욱 증가되었습니다.

RMAN의 구성

RMAN은 백업해야 할 Target 데이터베이스, 백업/복구 정보 영역, 고속 복구 영역, 등으로 구성됩니다. RMAN을 구성하고 있는 각 영역을 살펴보겠습니다.

1 RMAN 구조 및 기본 구성 요소

RMAN을 이용한 오라클 DB 백업 구성도와 기본 RMAN 구성은 다음과 같습니다.

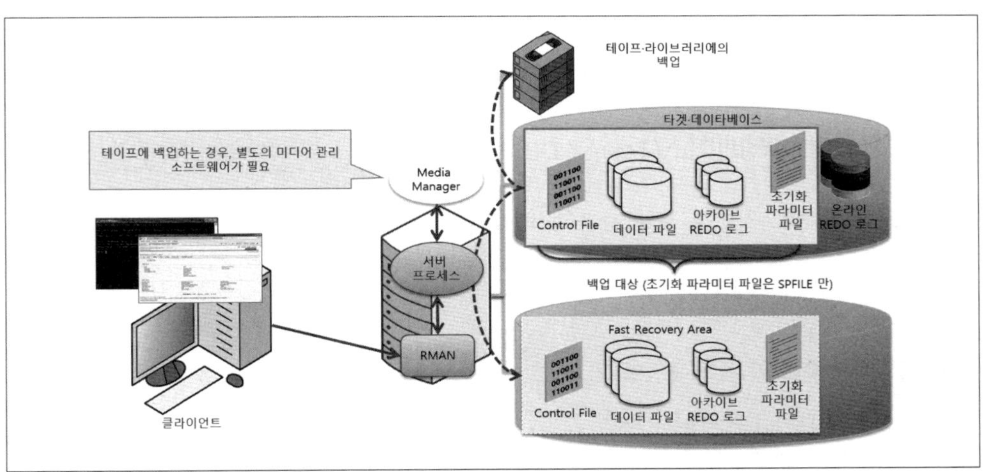

▲ RMAN 백업 구성도

■ RMAN 기본 구성 요소

1. 대상 데이터베이스 : 백업 및 복구 작업을 실행할 데이터베이스입니다.
2. Recovery Manager Client : 유저 명령을 해석하고 명령을 실행 하도록 서버 세션에 지시합니다.

3. 고속 복구 영역(Fast Recovery Area) : 백업/복구에 관련된 파일을 저장하고 있는 디스크 위치입니다.
4. 미디어 관리자(Media Management) : 백업 장치(테이프)와 상호 작용하는데 필요한 응용프로그램입니다.
5. Recovery Catalog(복구 카탈로그) : 컨트롤 파일 또는 Catalog DB에 RMAN 활동을 기록합니다.

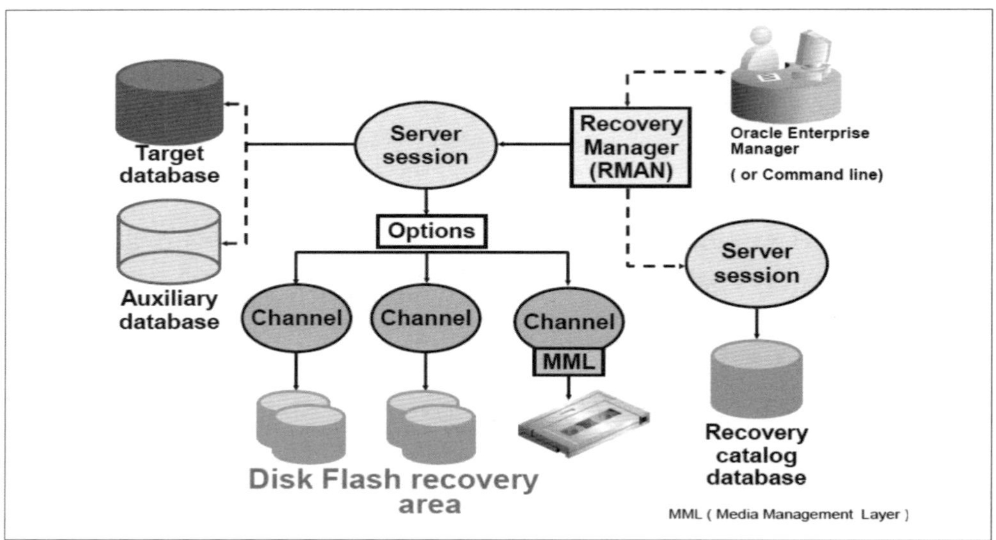

▲ RMAN 기본 구성

2 대상 데이터베이스(Target DB)

RMAN 백업 및 복구 작업을 실행 시 실제 데이터베이스 내부에서 동작하는 내용에 대해 알아보겠습니다.

■ 대상 데이터베이스의 주요 포인트

1. 백업 시에는 데이터 파일에서 사용한 블럭을 읽고 백업 세트를 내보냅니다.
2. 복원 시에는 백업 세트를 읽어서 데이터 파일을 쓰게 됩니다.
3. RMAN은 백업 및 복구를 수행할 때 기본적으로 PGA 메모리를 사용하며, PGA 메모리 공간이 부족할 경우 SGA(Large pool, shared pool)를 사용하여 백업을 수행합니다.
4. RMAN 클라이언트에서 Network를 통해 대상 데이터베이스에 연결되어 있는 경우 백업 대상은 클라이언트 시스템이 아닙니다.
5. RMAN 백업 정보는 카탈로그 DB가 없을 경우 대상 데이터베이스의 Control File에서 관리됩니다.
6. V$ 뷰, RMAN의 CLI 명령어인 LIST 명령에서 백업 상태를 확인 가능합니다.

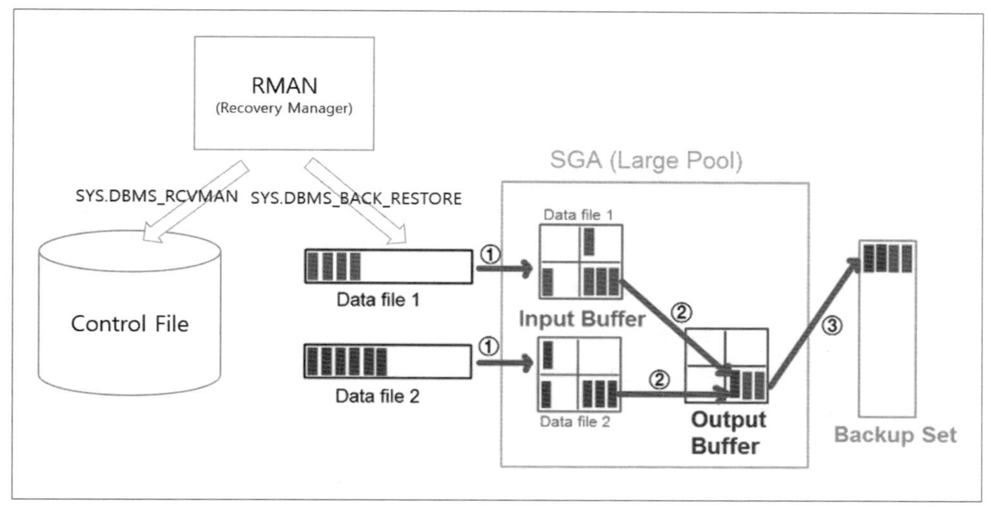

▲ 대상 데이터베이스 내의 RMAN 백업 동작

RMAN 실행 시, 두개의 서버 프로세스와 채널 당 하나의 채널 프로세스가 생성됩니다. 한 개의 서버 프로세스는 대상 데이터베이스에서의 SYS 권한으로 필요한 RMAN 패키지를 호출하며 백업과 복구를 실행하는 채널 프로세스의 작업 양을 coordinate합니다. 두 번째 서버 프로세스는 shadow라고도 불리며, RMAN의 장시간 트랜잭션을 감시하며 필요한 정보들을 로깅합니다. RMAN을 사용할 시 주의해야 하는 것은 shared pool과 large pool입니다. RMAN은 몇 개의 Oracle PL/SQL 패키지들을 기존의 PL/SQL 패키지들과 마찬가지로 Shared Pool에 올려 사용합니다. 이때 Shared Pool의 여유 공간이 부족하거나 단편화 현상이 심할 시에는 RMAN 패키지가 실행되지 않을 수가 있습니다. 항상 Shared Pool 내부에 RMAN의 실행에 충분한 메모리가 존재해야 합니다.

RMAN의 두 가지의 버퍼를 사용합니다. 하나는 INPUT BUFFER로 백업되는 파일들의 데이터 블록이 로딩 되는 곳이며 다른 하나는 OUTPUT BUFFER로써 해당 블록이 백업이 필요한지의 여부를 검사하는 곳입니다.

■ INPUT BUFFER

데이터파일에서 백업해야 하는 블록만 추출해서 메모리로 가져올 때 사용합니다. 백업 셋에 포함될 파일들의 개수가 4, 혹은 이하일 때 RMAN은 파일 당 4개의 버퍼를 1MB 크기로 생성합니다. 전체 크기는 16MB 혹은 그보다 작습니다. 백업 셋에 포함될 파일들의 개수가 4 보다 크고 9 보다 작을 때, RMAN은 파일 당

4개의 버퍼를 512 KB 크기로 생성합니다. 전체 크기는 16MB 혹은 그보다 작습니다. 백업 셋에 포함될 파일들의 개수가 8 보다 클 때 RMAN은 파일 당 4개의 버퍼를 128KB 크기로 생성합니다. 파일 당 할당되는 최대 INPUT 버퍼의 크기는 512KB입니다. 이러한 모든 사항은 채널 당 할당되는 것입니다. 채널 부분에서 정리하겠습니다.

■ OUTPUT BUFFER

Backup Set(백업파일)에 저장하기 위해 사용합니다. 디스크로 쓸 때, 채널 별로 총 4개의 OUTPUT BUFFER가 생성되며 각각의 크기는 1MB가 됩니다. 이리하여 각 채널별 최대 크기는 4MB가 됩니다. 테이프에 쓸 때, 채널 별로 총 4개의 OUTPUT BUFFER가 생성되며 각각의 크기는 256KB가 됩니다. 이리하여 각 채널 별 최대 크기는 총 1MB가 됩니다.

■ RMAN MEMORY 순서

1. Data file 별로 input buffer가 생성됩니다. 이 input buffer에 data file에서 백업받아야 할 블록을 가져옵니다.
2. 여러 개의 input buffer중 하나가 가득 차면 output buffer로 블록을 복사해옵니다.
3. ouput buffer에는 여러 data file의 블록이 혼재하게 되며 output buffer 역시 가득 차면 backup set에 내려쓰게 됩니다. 따라서 RMAN backup set에는 여러 파일들의 블록들이 혼재되어 있습니다.

■ 복구 시 RMAN MEMORY 버퍼

1. 디스크에서의 복구 시, 채널 별로 총 4개의 INPUT BUFFER가 생성되며 각각의 크기는 총 1MB가 됩니다.
2. 테이프에서의 복구 시, 채널 별로 총 4개의 INPUT BUFFER가 생성되며 각각의 크기는 BLKSIZE의 크기에 맞추어 생성됩니다. 기본값은 256KB입니다.
3. 복구 시의 OUTPUT BUFFER의 크기는 채널 별로 총 4개의 OUTPUT BUFFER가 생성되며 항상 128KB 크기로 생성됩니다.

■ RMAN 패키지

1. **SYS.DBMS_RCVMAN** : 이 패키지는 Control File을 읽어 RMAN이 해당 작업을 수행하기 위해 필요한 정보들을 입력하는 역할을 합니다. 백업 및 복구에 필요한 파일들의 위치와 파일 헤더 정보 및 크기 등의 정보 취급을 담당합니다.
2. **SYS.DBMS_BACKUP_RESTORE** : 이 패키지는 백업 및 복구에 필요한 데이터 파일, 컨트롤 파일, ARCHIVE REDO LOG 파일들을 호출하기 위한 SYSTEM CALL을 생성합니다.

■ **채널**

채널은 서버 프로세스로 동작하는 백업과 복구를 하는 경로입니다. 채널을 할당해야 RMAN이 백업, 복구를 수행할 수 있습니다. 복구를 할 때는 채널을 할당하지 않아도 되지만, 백업을 할 경우는 반드시 채널을 할당해 줘야합니다.

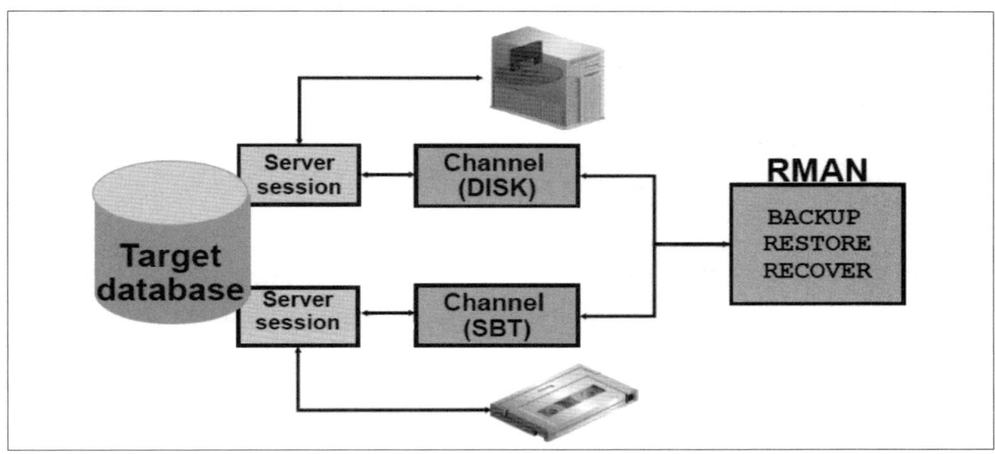

▲ RMAN 백업의 채널

채널은 DATA와 백업 Device 장치까지의 Data 전송 Stream입니다. 채널 프로세스는 실제적으로 백업과 복구를 실행하는 프로세스로서 데이터파일로부터 실지 읽기와 쓰기를 담당합니다. 채널 프로세스의 타입은 DISK CHANNEL과 TAPE CHANNEL 두 가지가 존재합니다.

채널 할당은 보통 Backup해야 할 Data File의 개수에 따라합니다.

1. **4개 이하** : 각 파일에 4개 버퍼 1M 할당 → 4파일 X 4버퍼 X 1M = 16M
2. **5~6개** : 각 파일에 4개 버퍼 512K 할당 → 8파일 X 4버퍼 X 512kb = 16M
3. **9개 이상** : 각 파일에 4개 버퍼 128kb 할당

3 FRA(Fast Recovery Area) 고속 복구 영역

Fast Recovery Area는 Oracle 데이터베이스의 모든 복구 관련 파일 및 활동에 대한 통합 저장 위치입니다. 미디어 장애로부터 데이터베이스를 완전히 복구하는 데 필요한 모든 파일은 빠른 복구 영역의 일부입니다.

백업에 사용할 복구 관련 파일 저장을 위해 사용 가능한 옵션의 디스크 공간을 말합니다.

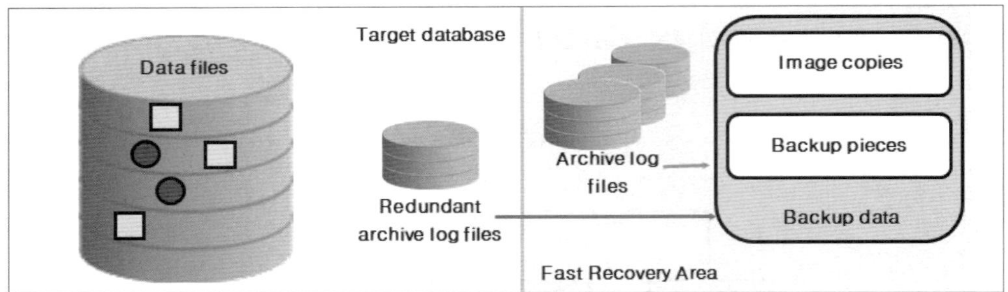

▲ FRA에 놓인 백업 데이터 구성

데이터베이스가 백업 및 복구 관련 파일을 저장하고 관리할 수 있는 디스크 위치입니다 FRA를 활용하여 디스크 백업 및 아카이브 된 리두 로그 등 가능한 한 많은 백업 및 복구 관련 파일을 저장하는 것을 권고 드립니다.

백업 및 복구 관련 파일은 Permanent Item과 Transient Item 두 가지 유형으로 구성됩니다. Permanent Item은 인스턴스에서 활발하게 사용됩니다. Transient Item은 일종의 복구 작업이 발생한 경우에만 필요합니다.

- **Permanent Items** : 다중화 된 Current Control File들, 다중화 된 Online Redo Log File들
- **Transient Items** : Archivelog, Datafile 복사본, Controlfile 복사본, ControlFile Auto 백업, 백업 데이터, Flashback 로그

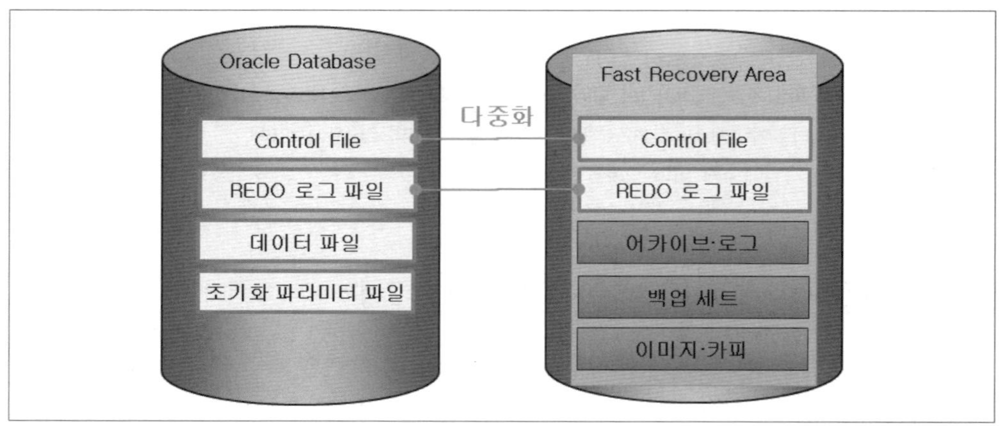

▲ FRA에 놓인 백업 데이터 구성

■ **FRA에 저장되는 파일은 다음과 같으며 Oracle Managed Files(OMF) 기능을 이용하여 Naming되어 관리됩니다.**

1. Control File의 복사본
2. Online Redo Log 복사본
3. Archive log File
4. RMAN 백업 파일
5. Flash Back Log 파일

Oracle Flashback Database 및 Guaranteed Restore Points와 같은 일부 오라클 데이터베이스 백업 기능에서는 반드시 FRA를 사용해야 합니다. 일반 disk나 tape으로도 backup이 가능하나, flashback database 등의 새로운 기능 등을 사용하려면 flash recovery area를 사용하는 것이 바람직합니다.

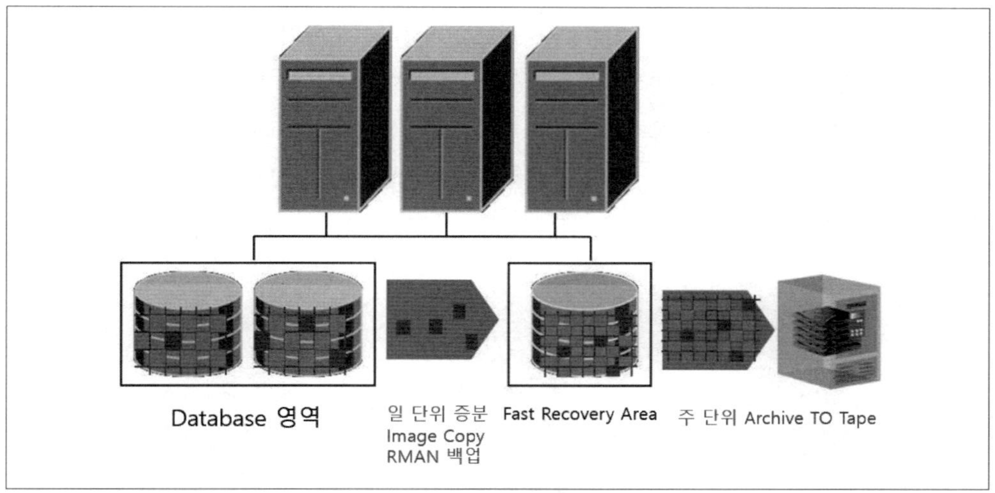

▲ FRA를 활용한 오라클 백업 전략

하지만 이러한 기능을 위해 FRA를 사용하더라도 이를 통해 모든 복구 관련 파일을 저장해야 하는 것은 아닙니다. FRA를 반드시 사용해야 하는 것은 아니지만 이를 사용하면 다른 온 디스크 백업 스토리지 방식보다 많은 이점을 누릴 수 있습니다. RMAN 및 미디어 관리자를 통해 고속 복구 영역에서 테이프로 이동된 백업은 다른 필수 파일을 위해 공간을 비워야 할 때까지 디스크에 보존되므로 테이프에서 백업을 복원할 필요성이 줄어듭니다.

동시에 복구 목표를 기준으로 더 이상 필요하지 않은 폐기된 파일 및 테이프에 백업된 파일은 삭제 대상으로 지정되어 공간이 필요할 때 삭제됩니다. 이러한 삭제 작업은 공간이 필요할 때 자동으로 관리됩니다. DBA는 더 이상 오래된 백업을 수동으로 삭제할 필요가 없으며 DBA가 실수로 중복 집합 파일을 삭제할 가능성도 줄어듭니다.

■ 고속 복구 영역의 초기화 파라미터

1. DB_RECOVERY_FILE_DEST : 고속 복구 영역의 위치를 지정합니다.
2. DB_RECOVERY_FILE_DEST_SIZE : 고속 복구 영역의 사용 용량(단위 : 바이트) 제한합니다. 장애의 정석 편에 기술되어 있지만, 실제 디스크의 남은 공간이 있더라도 이 파라미터 기준으로 공간 사용이 제한됩니다.

4 복구 카탈로그 RMAN Repository와 Recovery Catalog

Recovery Catalog는 RMAN에 의해서 사용되어지고 유지 관리되는 저장소입니다.
RMAN은 recovery catalog에 저장되어 있는 정보를 사용해서 요청되어진 Backup과 Restore의 실행을 어떻게 할지를 결정하게 되는데, 이 catalog의 사용 여부가 우선 결정되어야 합니다. catalog없이 RMAN을 사용할 때의 단점은 recovery catalog의 overhead가 없는 대신, Point-In-Time recovery가 어려우며, control file 손상 시에 recovery 할 수 없고, stored script를 사용할 수 없습니다. 오라클에서는 RECOVERY CATALOG 사용을 권장합니다.

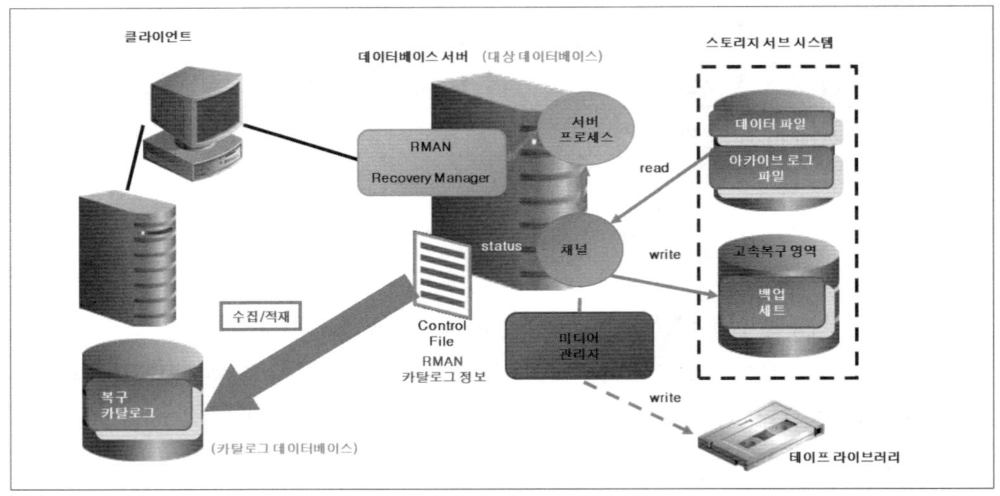

▲ RMAN 카탈로그 저장 흐름

RMAN은 대상 데이터베이스 및 해당 백업/복구 작업에 대한 메타데이터를 RMAN 저장소에 유지 관리합니다.

RMAN은 자체 구성 설정, 대상 데이터베이스 스키마, 아카이브 된 리두 로그 및 모든 백업 파일을 디스크 또는 테이프에 저장합니다. RMAN의 LIST, REPORT 및 SHOW 명령은 RMAN 저장소 정보를 표시합니다.

RMAN 저장소 데이터의 기본 저장소는 항상 대상 데이터베이스의 컨트롤 파일입니다.

CONTROL_FILE_RECORD_KEEP_TIME 초기화 파라미터는 최신 백업에 대한 정보를 저장하기 위해 백업 레코드를 재사용하기 전에 해당 레코드를 컨트롤파일에 유지할 기간을 제어합니다.

RMAN 저장소 데이터의 다른 복사본이 복구 카탈로그에 저장될 수도 있습니다. 복구 카탈로그는 RMAN 저장소 정보를 보존하므로 컨트롤파일이 손실될 경우 복원 및 복구를 더욱 편리하게 수행할 수 있습니다(백업 컨트롤파일에는 사용 가능한 최신 백업에 대한 일부 정보가 포함되어 있지 않을 수 있습니다). 또한 컨트롤 파일 레코드 수에는 제한이 있으므로 복구 카탈로그 DB는 컨트롤파일보다 더 광범위한 백업 내역을 저장할 수 있습니다.

RMAN 저장소 레코드에 추가하여 복구 카탈로그는 일반적인 백업 작업에 대한 RMAN 명령 시퀀스인 RMAN 내장 스크립트를 보유할 수도 있습니다. 복구 카탈로그의 중앙 집중식 스크립트 스토리지를 사용하는 것이 명령 파일로 작업하는 것보다 훨씬 편리할 수 있습니다. 내장 스크립트를 제외하면 모든 RMAN 기능은 복구 카탈로그의 사용 여부에 관계없이 동일하게 동작합니다.

■ RMAN 백업 환경에서 Control file 관리 주의 사항

Control File은 말 그대로 데이터베이스 내의 실제적(Physical) 파일들을 관리하는데 사용됩니다. Control File의 내부적인 정보는 Circular reuse records와 noncircular reuse records로 구분됩니다. Physical Backup을 관장하는 RMAN으로서는 Control File의 사용이 절대적으로 필요합니다. RMAN은 Control File로부터 필요한 파일들의 리스트, checkpoint의 정보 및 복구 가능 여부를 수집합니다. 또한 Control File을 직접 액세스하므로 유저가 수동으로 파일 리스트를 작성할 필요성을 배재 시킵니다.

RMAN은 스스로 행한 백업 작업의 정보들을 일반적으로는 Control File에 기록하여 필요 시 참조하게 됩니다. Control File의 내부적인 정보는 Circular reuse records와 noncircular reuse records로 구분됩니다. RMAN Catalog의 사용 시에는 Control File 대신 Catalog에 이러한 정보들을 기록하게 됩니다.

만약 이러한 백업과 관련된 정보가 Control File에 기록되지 않거나 삭제되었다면 RMAN을 통해 구축해 둔 백업은 사용이 불가능해집니다.

이러한 이유로 인하여 **Control File은 RMAN을 사용하기 위한 절대적 필요 요소**라 말할 수 있습니다.

Control File은 극히 드물지만 디스크 용량의 부족으로 인하여 오래된 내부적인 정보들이 자체적으로 삭제될 수 있습니다. 또한 **CONTROLFILE_RECORD_KEEP_TIME** 파라미터의 적절치 못한 설정으로 인하여 자체 정보들이 삭제될 수도 있습니다. 이 파라미터의 기본값은 7로서 DAY 단위를 나타냅니다. 물론 RMAN의 백업 정보가 삭제되는 것을 방지하기 위해서입니다. **이 파라미터의 값을 RMAN의 BACKUP RETENTION PERIOD의 값보다 길게 잡는 것 또한 문제의 발생 요지가 있어 추천되지 않습니다.**

또한 극히 주의해야 할 사항은 Control File을 백업할 시에 RMAN이 백업한 Control File 대신, '**alter database backup controlfile to trace;**'를 사용하여 생성한 백업용 Control File의 사용입니다. 이와 같이 백업된 Control File은 RMAN이 기록한 백업 정보들을 포함시키지 않습니다.

만약 RMAN Catalog를 사용하지 않는 상태에서 이와 같은 Control File을 사용하여 기존의 Control File을 덮어씌운다면 RMAN을 통한 백업은 전부 사용이 불가능해집니다.

이와 같이 Control File을 재구성해야 할 경우는 흔히 MAXLOGFILES나 MAXLOGHISTORY 파라미터 값 등의 변경과 같은 데이터베이스의 내부적인 구조를 변경시켰을 때 필요한데, 가능하다면 이와 같이 TRACE를 사용하여 Control File을 백업하는 것은 RMAN을 사용할 시에는 최대한 배재해야 합니다. 혹은 Trace 대신 Binary file 자체로서 Control File을 백업하여 RMAN 관련 정보를 보존하면서 Control File을 백업하는 것 또한 가능합니다.

Control File은 Binary File로 데이터베이스 내에서 매우 업데이트 성이 강한 파일입니다. 만약 RMAN을 통한 백업 중에 Control File의 내용이 변경이 된다면 에러가 발생하겠지요. 혹은 Control File의 변경을 잠금 할 수도 있지만 이렇게 된다면 데이터베이스 전체를 잠금하는 것과 다를 바가 없습니다. **이러한 점을 극복하기 위해 RMAN은 Snapshot Controlfile이라는 기법을 사용하여 백업 도중의 Control File과의 동질성을 유지합니다.** 이렇게 생성된 Snapshot Controlfile은 ORACLE_HOME/dbs(UNIX), ORACLE_HOME/database (MS)에 SNCF〈ORACLE_SID〉라는 이름으로 저장되게 됩니다. 이러한 기본적인 위치는 'configure snapshot controlfile name to '〈location/file_name〉'의 사용을 통하여 변경이 가능합니다.

RMAN을 사용한 백업 컨셉

RMAN 유틸리티를 이용하여 백업하는 컨셉에는 백업 세트 방식과 이미지 카피 방식이 있습니다. 그리고 백업 전략으로 전체 백업과 증분 백업이 있습니다. 지금부터는 RMAN 유틸리티를 이용한 백업 컨셉들을 알아보겠습니다.

1 백업 세트(Backup Set)

백업 세트 방식(BACKUP AS BACKUPSET)으로 RMAN 백업을 수행하면 RMAN에서는 해당 백업을 백업 집합에 저장합니다. 하나 이상의 백업 조각으로 구성된 백업 집합은 백업되는 물리적 파일 데이터를 포함합니다. 백업 집합은 RMAN에서만 액세스할 수 있는 형식으로 저장됩니다. 따라서 RMAN에서만 백업 집합을 생성 및 복원할 수 있습니다. 백업 집합은 디스크 또는 테이프에 저장될 수 있으며 백업 집합은 RMAN에서 백업을 테이프에 쓸 때 사용할 수 있는 유일한 백업 유형입니다.

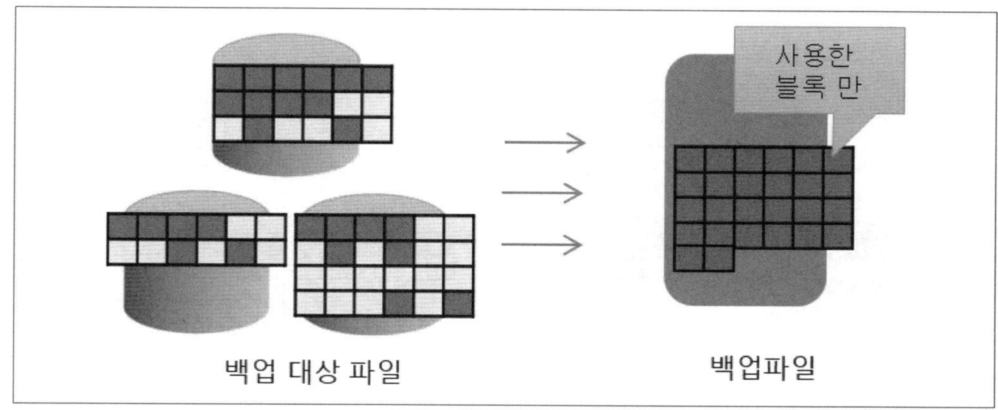

▲ RMAN의 Backup Set 방식 백업

하나 이상의 물리적인 Backup Pieces를 포함하는 논리적 구조로 Data file (including control files), Archive Log 하나의 logical backup set에 포함되어, 하나 이상의 datafile 또는 Archive Log를 포함하는 Single Physical File로 백업 파일이 만들어집니다.

■ **Backup Set 방식의 장점 정리**

1. Tape에 바로 Write가 가능합니다.
2. 사용되지 않은 데이터 블록을 SKIP하여 Empty block없이 압축됩니다(백업 시간 감소/백업 용량 감소).
3. 증분 백업에 사용이 가능합니다.
4. Block Corruption 검사가 포함됩니다.

■ **Backup Set 방식의 단점 정리**

1. RMAN에 의해 생성할 수 있는 독자적인 형식의 파일로 백업되어 RMAN으로만 복원해야 합니다.
2. OS 명령어로 복원하는 백업 솔루션은 사용이 불가합니다.

2 이미지 카피(Image Copy)

이미지 카피 방식(BACKUP AS COPY)으로 RMAN 백업을 수행하면 RMAN에서는 파일을 이미지 복사본(디스크에 생성된 데이터베이스 파일의 비트 단위 복사본)으로 복사합니다. 이 복사본은 Unix의 경우 cp, 윈도의 경우 COPY 등의 운영 체제 명령을 사용하여 생성할 수 있는 파일 복사본과 동일합니다. 하지만 BACKUP AS COPY를 사용하는 경우 RMAN 저장소에 기록되며, RMAN에서는 이 데이터를 사용하여 복원 작업을 수행할 수 있습니다. 이미지 복사본은 테이프에 생성할 수 없습니다.

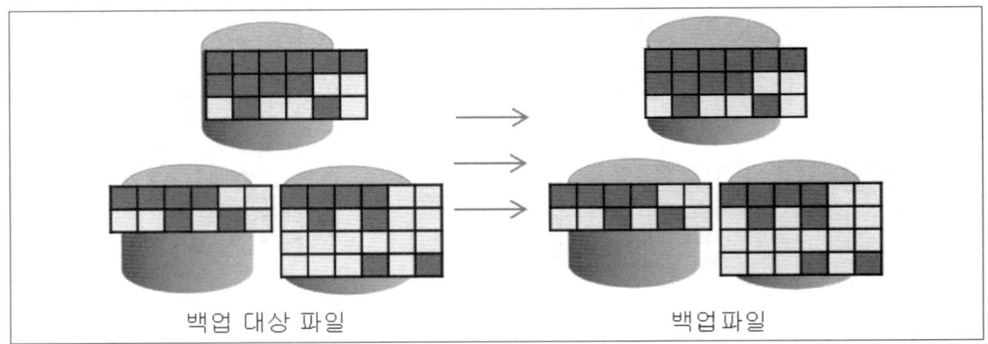

▲ RMAN의 Image Copy 방식 백업

Datafile, Controlfile, ArchiveLog file의 복사가 됩니다. 증분 백업의 기준이 되는 데이터로 사용가능합니다.(Incremental level 0) 백업 대상 파일의 비트 단위 복사로 백업되며 이미지 카피 백업은 "BACKUP AS COPY" 명령어로 수행합니다.

■ Image Copy 방식의 장점 정리

1. Disk에 있을 경우 복구를 위해 바로 Database에 사용가능합니다(복구 시간, 절차 단축).
2. OS 명령어로 복원하는 방법으로 사용가능합니다.

■ Image Copy 방식의 단점 정리

1. TAPE으로 바로 WRITE가 안됩니다.
2. Block corruption 검사는 불가합니다.
3. 사용하지 않는 빈 블록도 포함해서 압축되어 백업됩니다.

3 RMAN의 전체 백업

전체 백업은 모든 할당된 블록을 대상으로 합니다. 백업 방식은 이미지 카피 방식 또는 백업 세트 방식으로 수행 가능합니다. 증분 백업보다 복원 속도가 빠릅니다. 매번 모든 할당된 블록을 복사하기 때문에 많은 공간이 필요합니다.

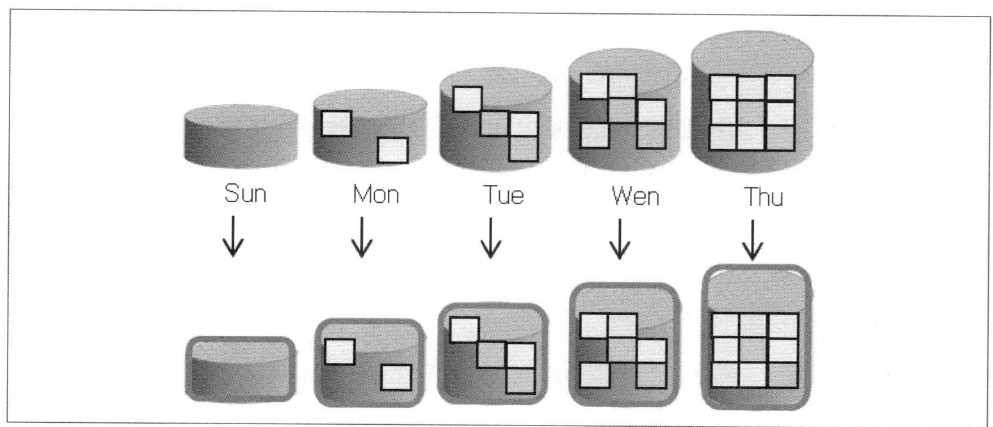

4 RMAN의 증분 백업

증분 백업은 이전의 백업 이후의 변경된 블록만을 대상으로 백업합니다. '차분 증분'과 '누적 증분'의 2종류의 증분 백업이 있습니다. 1회의 백업 양이 적기 때문에 백업 사이즈를 작게 가져가며 백업 시간을 절감할 수 있습니다. 복원 시 전체 백업받은 데이터와 차분 증분 백업 받은 데이터를 적용시켜 복구하게 됩니다.

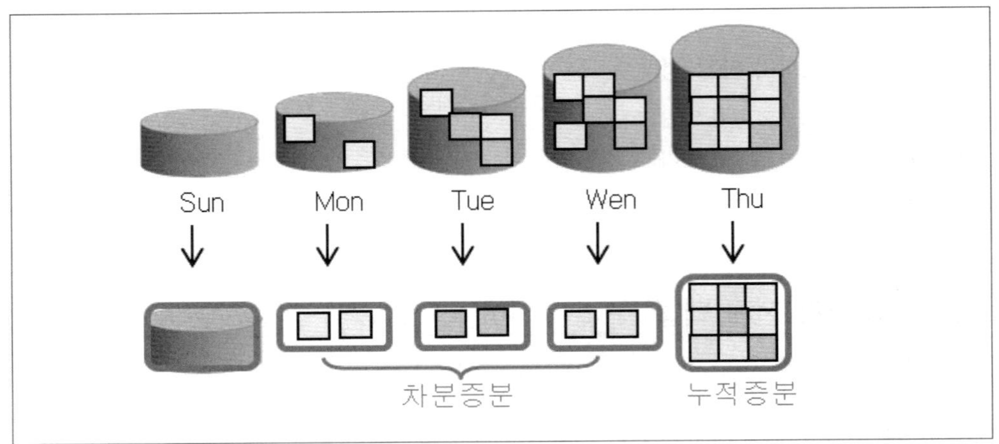

▲ 증분 백업

BACKUP INCREMENTAL을 지정하면 RMAN은 데이터베이스의 증분 백업을 생성합니다. 증분 백업은 이전 증분 백업 이후 블럭 기준으로 데이터베이스에 변경된 내용을 캡처합니다. 증분 백업 전략의 시작점은 레벨 0 증분 백업으로, 이 레벨에서는 데이터베이스의 모든 블럭이 백업됩니다. 정기적으로 수행되는 레벨 1 증분 백업에는 이전 증분백업 이후 변경된 블럭만 포함됩니다. 레벨 1 증분 백업은 누적될 수도 있고(최신 레벨 0 백업 이후 변경된 모든 블럭 포함) 차등을 둘 수도 있습니다(최신 증분 백업이 레벨 0인지 1인지에 관계없이 해당 백업 이후 변경된 블록블 포함).

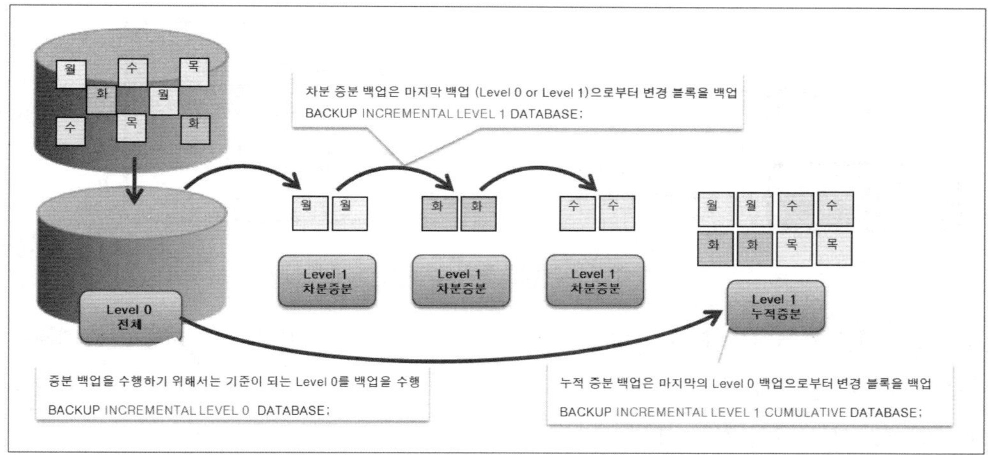

▲ 차분 증분(Incremental)과 누적 증분(Cumulative)

증분 백업은 일반적으로 전체 데이터베이스 백업보다 더 작으며 빠르게 생성됩니다. 증분 백업에서 복구하는 것이 리두 로그만 사용하여 복구하는 것보다 더 빠릅니다. 증분 백업에서 복원하는 중에는 리두의 변경 사항을 하나씩 재 적용하지 않기 위해 레벨 0 백업을 시작점으로 사용한 다음 레벨 1 백업을 기준으로 변경된 블럭을 업데이트합니다.

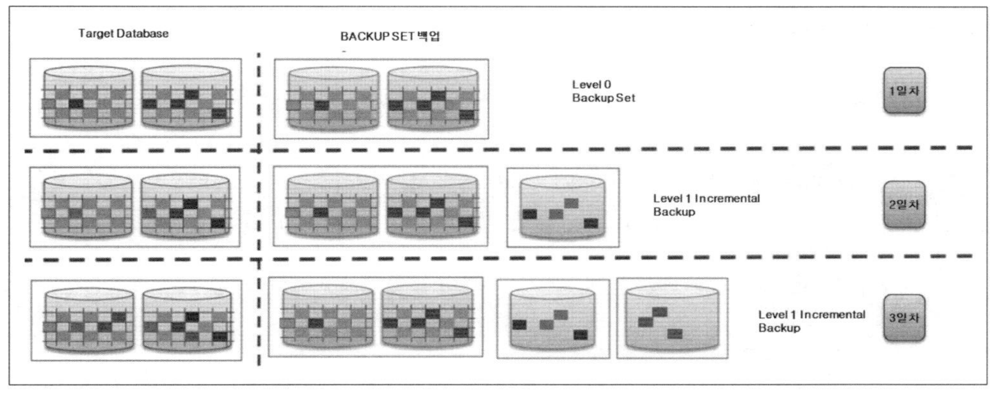

증분 백업으로 복구하는 경우 사용자의 추가 작업이 필요하지 않습니다. 증분 백업을 사용할 수 있는 경우 RMAN은 복구 중 해당 증분 백업을 사용합니다.

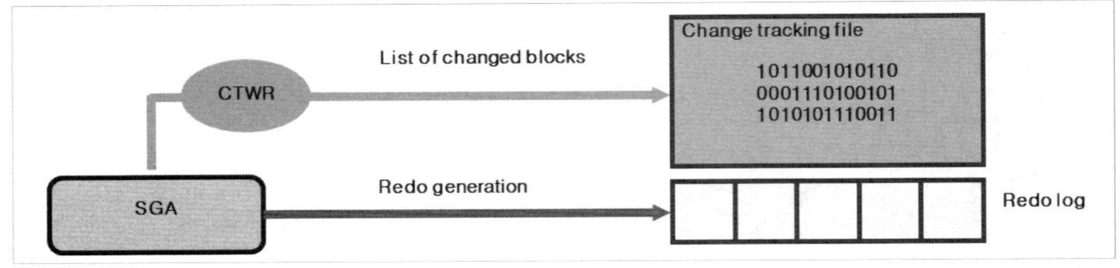

▲ Block Change Tracking

RMAN 백업은 Row단위가 아닌 Block 단위로 받습니다. 증분 백업은 블록을 다 스캔해서 해당 날짜를 우선 찾게 되는데 이럴 경우, 속도가 느리게 됩니다. Oracle 10g부터 Enterprise Edition에는 '블록 체인지 트랙킹' 기능이 추가되었는데, 이는 변경된 블록의 날짜를 List에 저장하여 변경된 블록만 추적하는 기능입니다. Block 들의 변경사항은 Change tracking file에 저장되어 관리됩니다.

Block Change Tracking은 변경 트레이스 기능이 포함되어 있는데 이 기능을 사용하면 각 데이터 파일의 변경된 블럭이 변경 트레이스 파일에 기록되므로 증분 백업의 성능이 향상됩니다.

변경 트레이스가 사용으로 설정된 경우 RMAN은 변경 트레이스 파일을 사용하여 증분 백업의 변경된 블럭을 식별하므로 데이터파일의 모든 블럭을 스캔할 필요가 없어집니다.

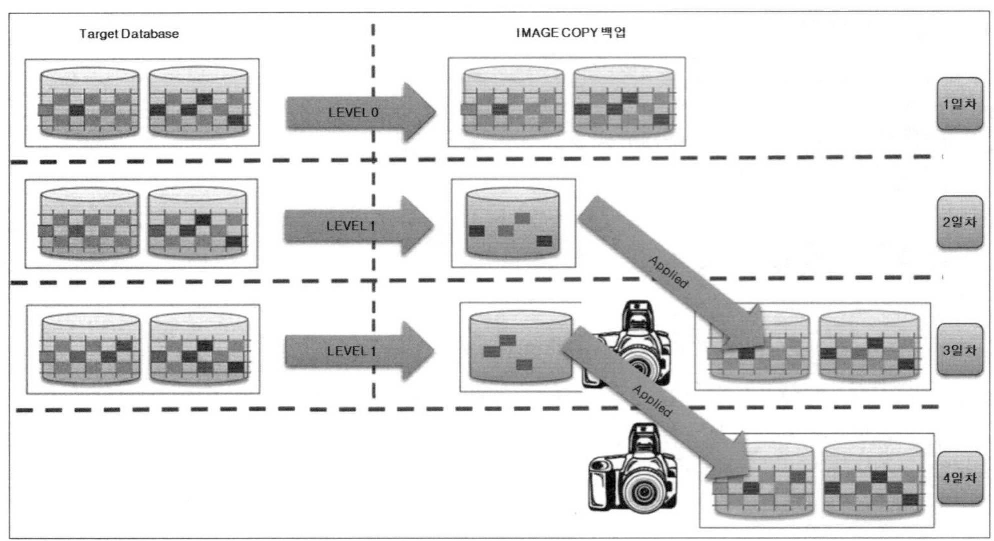

▲ Image Copy 방식의 Incrementally Updated 백업

RMAN의 증분 업데이트 백업 기능을 사용하면 증분 백업 루틴을 더 효율적으로 수행할 수 있습니다. 레벨 1 백업의 변경 내용을 사용하여 레벨 1 증분 백업이 생성된 SCN을 기준으로 모든 변경 사항을 포함하도록 이미지 복사 레벨 0 증분 백업을 롤 포워드 할 수 있습니다. 레벨 1 증분 백업의 모든 변경 내용이 이미 적용되었으므로 업데이트된 레벨 0 증분 백업을 사용하는 복구는 더 빠르게 수행됩니다.

백업 서버와 DB 서버가 분리 되어 있다면, 세 번째부터 이 백업은 DB 서버의 데이터 파일을 직접 읽어내는 것이 아니기 때문에 대용량 데이터베이스 환경에서 가장 효과적인 백업 전략이 될 수 있습니다.

RMAN의 기본 사용 방법

RMAN 유틸리티의 사용을 단계별 실습을 통해 백업 및 복구 기능을 확인하고 주로 사용하는 명령어를 수행하겠습니다.

1 RMAN 주요 명령어

RMAN 유틸리티의 주요 명령어입니다.

RMAN 명령어는 타겟 데이터베이스와 복구 카탈로그, 고속 복구 영역의 리소스를 기준으로 참조하고 변경합니다.

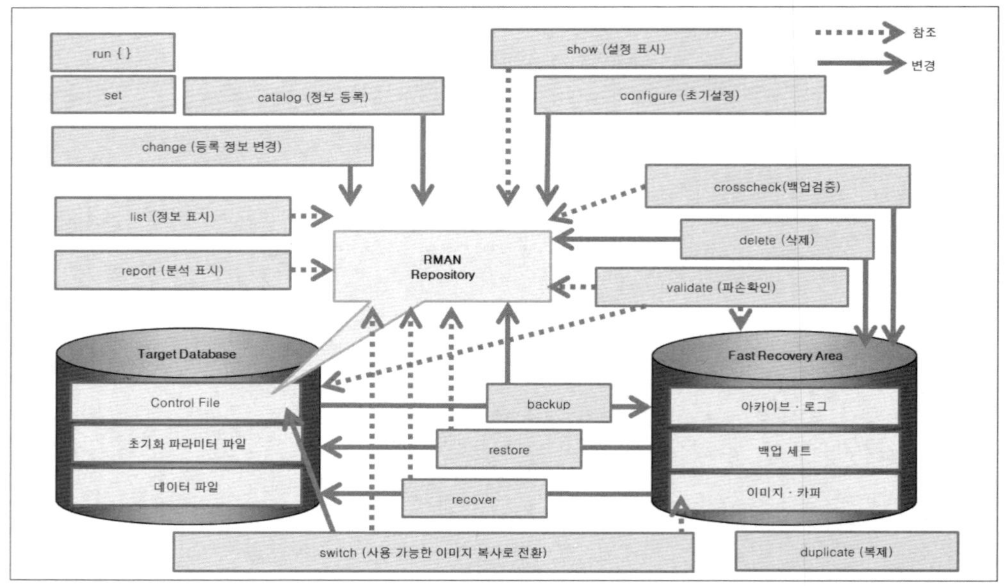

▲ RMAN 유틸리티 주요 명령어 별 결과값을 가져오는 Resource

2 RMAN의 접속 명령어

RMAN CLI 명령어를 통하여 Target Database에 접속하겠습니다.

OS 프롬프트에서 RMAN 명령을 사용해 관리자 권한(SYSDBA 권한)으로 접속합니다.

```
$ rman target sys/<패스워드>
$ rman target /
```

```
[oracle12]yspark-linux:/home/oracle12> rman target sys/oracle
Recovery Manager: Release 12.2.0.1.0 - Production on Tue Nov 14 17:37:42 2017
Copyright (c) 1982, 2017, Oracle and/or its affiliates.  All rights reserved.
connected to target database: ORACLE12 (DBID=2053465567)
RMAN>
RMAN> exit

Recovery Manager complete.
[oracle12]yspark-linux:/home/oracle12> rman target /
Recovery Manager: Release 12.2.0.1.0 - Production on Tue Nov 14 17:37:52 2017
Copyright (c) 1982, 2017, Oracle and/or its affiliates.  All rights reserved.
connected to target database: ORACLE12 (DBID=2053465567)
RMAN>
RMAN> exit

Recovery Manager complete.
[oracle12]yspark-linux:/home/oracle12>
```

RMAN 시작 후 CONNECT 절로 Target DATABASE를 지정하여 접속할 수 있습니다.

```
$ rman
RMAN> CONNECT TARGET SYS/<패스워드>
RMAN> CONNECT TARGET SYS/<패스워드>@<접속기술자>
```

```
[oracle12]yspark-linux:/home/oracle12> rman
Recovery Manager: Release 12.2.0.1.0 - Production on Tue Nov 14 17:44:06 2017
Copyright (c) 1982, 2017, Oracle and/or its affiliates.  All rights reserved.
RMAN> CONNECT TARGET SYS/oracle
connected to target database: ORACLE12 (DBID=2053465567)
RMAN>
RMAN> exit

Recovery Manager complete.
[oracle12]yspark-linux:/home/oracle12> rman
Recovery Manager: Release 12.2.0.1.0 - Production on Tue Nov 14 17:45:03 2017
Copyright (c) 1982, 2017, Oracle and/or its affiliates.  All rights reserved.
RMAN> CONNECT TARGET SYS/oracle@ORACLE12
connected to target database: ORACLE12 (DBID=2053465567)
RMAN>
RMAN>
```

RMAN 명령 파일을 사용하여 접속할 수 있습니다.

```
$ rman target / NOCATALOG @<RMAN 명령파일 이름>
$ rman target / NOCATALOG cmdfile='<RMAN 명령파일 이름>'
```

```
[oracle12]yspark-linux:/home/oracle12> cat show_db_name.rman
SHOW db_unique_name ;
exit ;
[oracle12]yspark-linux:/home/oracle12> rman target / NOCATALOG @show_db_name.rman

Recovery Manager: Release 12.2.0.1.0 - Production on Tue Nov 14 17:53:37 2017

Copyright (c) 1982, 2017, Oracle and/or its affiliates.  All rights reserved.

connected to target database: ORACLE12 (DBID=2053465567)
using target database control file instead of recovery catalog

RMAN> SHOW db_unique_name ;
2> exit
RMAN configuration parameters for database with db_unique_name ORACLE12 are:
RMAN configuration has no stored or default parameters

Recovery Manager complete.
[oracle12]yspark-linux:/home/oracle12> rman target / NOCATALOG cmdfile='show_db_name.rman'

Recovery Manager: Release 12.2.0.1.0 - Production on Tue Nov 14 17:53:46 2017

Copyright (c) 1982, 2017, Oracle and/or its affiliates.  All rights reserved.

connected to target database: ORACLE12 (DBID=2053465567)
using target database control file instead of recovery catalog

RMAN> SHOW db_unique_name ;
2> exit
RMAN configuration parameters for database with db_unique_name ORACLE12 are:
RMAN configuration has no stored or default parameters

Recovery Manager complete.
[oracle12]yspark-linux:/home/oracle12> █
```

실행하기 전에 RMAN 명령 파일의 구문 에러를 확인할 수 있습니다.

```
$ rman CHECKSYNTAX @<RMAN 명령 파일이름>
```

```
[oracle12]yspark-linux:/home/oracle12> rman CHECKSYNTAX @show_db_name.rman

Recovery Manager: Release 12.2.0.1.0 - Production on Tue Nov 14 17:59:23 2017

Copyright (c) 1982, 2017, Oracle and/or its affiliates.  All rights reserved.

RMAN> SHOW db_unique_name ;
2> exit
The cmdfile has no syntax errors

Recovery Manager complete.
[oracle12]yspark-linux:/home/oracle12> █
```

3 RMAN의 환경 설정 명령어

1. RMAN 백업 설정 확인

show 명령어를 통해 RMAN 백업 설정을 확인합니다.

```
[oracle12]yspark-linux:/home/oracle12> rman target / NOCATALOG

Recovery Manager: Release 12.2.0.1.0 - Production on Tue Nov 14 18:07:59 2017

Copyright (c) 1982, 2017, Oracle and/or its affiliates.  All rights reserved.

connected to target database: ORACLE12 (DBID=2053465567)
using target database control file instead of recovery catalog

RMAN> show all ;

RMAN configuration parameters for database with db_unique_name ORACLE12 are:
CONFIGURE RETENTION POLICY TO REDUNDANCY 1; # default
CONFIGURE BACKUP OPTIMIZATION OFF; # default
CONFIGURE DEFAULT DEVICE TYPE TO DISK; # default
CONFIGURE CONTROLFILE AUTOBACKUP ON; # default
CONFIGURE CONTROLFILE AUTOBACKUP FORMAT FOR DEVICE TYPE DISK TO '%F'; # default
CONFIGURE DEVICE TYPE DISK PARALLELISM 1 BACKUP TYPE TO BACKUPSET; # default
CONFIGURE DATAFILE BACKUP COPIES FOR DEVICE TYPE DISK TO 1; # default
CONFIGURE ARCHIVELOG BACKUP COPIES FOR DEVICE TYPE DISK TO 1; # default
CONFIGURE MAXSETSIZE TO UNLIMITED; # default
CONFIGURE ENCRYPTION FOR DATABASE OFF; # default
CONFIGURE ENCRYPTION ALGORITHM 'AES128'; # default
CONFIGURE COMPRESSION ALGORITHM 'BASIC' AS OF RELEASE 'DEFAULT' OPTIMIZE FOR LOAD TRUE ; # default
CONFIGURE RMAN OUTPUT TO KEEP FOR 7 DAYS; # default
CONFIGURE ARCHIVELOG DELETION POLICY TO NONE; # default
CONFIGURE SNAPSHOT CONTROLFILE NAME TO '/oracle/oracle12/app/oracle/product/12.2.0/dbhome_1/dbs/snapcf_oracle12.f'; #
default

RMAN> exit


Recovery Manager complete.
[oracle12]yspark-linux:/home/oracle12> █
```

2. RMAN 설정 변경

CONFIGURE 명령을 통해 RMAN 백업 설정을 변경할 수 있습니다. 변경 후에는 show 명령어를 통해 반영을 확인합니다.

```
RMAN> CONFIGURE 리소스 설정명령어 ;
RMAN> show all ;
```

```
RMAN> configure channel device type disk format '/oracle/oracle12/RMAN_BACKUP/%d_%U_%t_%s' ;

using target database control file instead of recovery catalog
new RMAN configuration parameters:
CONFIGURE CHANNEL DEVICE TYPE DISK FORMAT   '/oracle/oracle12/RMAN_BACKUP/%d_%U_%t_%s';
new RMAN configuration parameters are successfully stored

RMAN> show all ;

RMAN configuration parameters for database with db_unique_name ORACLE12 are:
CONFIGURE RETENTION POLICY TO REDUNDANCY 1;
CONFIGURE BACKUP OPTIMIZATION ON;
CONFIGURE DEFAULT DEVICE TYPE TO DISK; # default
CONFIGURE CONTROLFILE AUTOBACKUP ON;
CONFIGURE CONTROLFILE AUTOBACKUP FORMAT FOR DEVICE TYPE DISK TO '%F'; # default
CONFIGURE DEVICE TYPE DISK PARALLELISM 1 BACKUP TYPE TO BACKUPSET; # default
CONFIGURE DATAFILE BACKUP COPIES FOR DEVICE TYPE DISK TO 1; # default
CONFIGURE ARCHIVELOG BACKUP COPIES FOR DEVICE TYPE DISK TO 1; # default
CONFIGURE CHANNEL DEVICE TYPE DISK FORMAT   '/oracle/oracle12/RMAN_BACKUP/%d_%U_%t_%s';
CONFIGURE MAXSETSIZE TO UNLIMITED; # default
CONFIGURE ENCRYPTION FOR DATABASE OFF; # default
CONFIGURE ENCRYPTION ALGORITHM 'AES128'; # default
CONFIGURE COMPRESSION ALGORITHM 'BASIC' AS OF RELEASE 'DEFAULT' OPTIMIZE FOR LOAD TRUE ; # default
CONFIGURE RMAN OUTPUT TO KEEP FOR 7 DAYS; # default
CONFIGURE ARCHIVELOG DELETION POLICY TO NONE; # default
CONFIGURE SNAPSHOT CONTROLFILE NAME TO '/oracle/oracle12/app/oracle/product/12.2.0/dbhome_1/dbs/snapcf_oracle12.f'; #
default

RMAN> CONFIGURE SNAPSHOT CONTROLFILE NAME TO '/oracle/oracle12/RMAN_BACKUP/snapcf_oracle12.f';

new RMAN configuration parameters:
CONFIGURE SNAPSHOT CONTROLFILE NAME TO '/oracle/oracle12/RMAN_BACKUP/snapcf_oracle12.f';
new RMAN configuration parameters are successfully stored

RMAN> show all ;

RMAN configuration parameters for database with db_unique_name ORACLE12 are:
CONFIGURE RETENTION POLICY TO REDUNDANCY 1;
CONFIGURE BACKUP OPTIMIZATION ON;
CONFIGURE DEFAULT DEVICE TYPE TO DISK; # default
CONFIGURE CONTROLFILE AUTOBACKUP ON;
CONFIGURE CONTROLFILE AUTOBACKUP FORMAT FOR DEVICE TYPE DISK TO '%F'; # default
CONFIGURE DEVICE TYPE DISK PARALLELISM 1 BACKUP TYPE TO BACKUPSET; # default
CONFIGURE DATAFILE BACKUP COPIES FOR DEVICE TYPE DISK TO 1; # default
CONFIGURE ARCHIVELOG BACKUP COPIES FOR DEVICE TYPE DISK TO 1; # default
CONFIGURE CHANNEL DEVICE TYPE DISK FORMAT   '/oracle/oracle12/RMAN_BACKUP/%d_%U_%t_%s';
CONFIGURE MAXSETSIZE TO UNLIMITED; # default
CONFIGURE ENCRYPTION FOR DATABASE OFF; # default
CONFIGURE ENCRYPTION ALGORITHM 'AES128'; # default
CONFIGURE COMPRESSION ALGORITHM 'BASIC' AS OF RELEASE 'DEFAULT' OPTIMIZE FOR LOAD TRUE ; # default
CONFIGURE RMAN OUTPUT TO KEEP FOR 7 DAYS; # default
CONFIGURE ARCHIVELOG DELETION POLICY TO NONE; # default
CONFIGURE SNAPSHOT CONTROLFILE NAME TO '/oracle/oracle12/RMAN_BACKUP/snapcf_oracle12.f';

RMAN> █
```

RMAN 설정 관련 주요 CONFIGURE 명령어는 다음과 같습니다.

❶ CONFIGURE RETENTION POLICY TO REDUNDANCY 1;
- backup본의 개수를 설정합니다. REDUNDANCY는 이중화를 뜻합니다.

❷ CONFIGURE BACKUP OPTIMIZATION ON;
- 이미 backup된 동일한(checkpoint SCN등) datafile, archived redolog, backup set이 있다면 skip합니다.

❸ CONFIGURE CONTROLFILE AUTOBACKUP ON;
- RMAN의 BACKUP이나 COPY 명령 등의 수행 후 자동으로control file backup을 수행

❹ CONFIGURE CONTROLFILE AUTOBACKUP FORMAT FOR DEVICE TYPE DISK TO '/DATA/ORABACKUP/%F';
- CONTROLFILE의 백업 경로를 지정합니다.

❺ CONFIGURE DEVICE TYPE DISK PARALLELISM 1 BACKUP TYPE TO BACKUPSET;
- 특정 device에 automatic channel allocation될 때 channel의 개수를 지정합니다.

❻ CONFIGURE MAXSETSIZE TO 10G;
- backupset의 maximum size를 설정합니다.

❼ CONFIGURE DATAFILE BACKUP COPIES FOR DEVICE TYPE DISK TO 1;
- DATAFILE, CONTROL FILE의 backup set의 copy 본 개수를 지정합니다.

❽ CONFIGURE ARCHIVELOG BACKUP COPIES FOR DEVICE TYPE DISK TO 1;
- ARCHIVELOG FILE의 backup set의 copy 본 개수를 지정합니다.

❾ CONFIGURE ARCHIVELOG DELETION POLICY TO NONE;
- flash recovery area의 archived redo log에 대한 삭제 여부를 설정합니다.

❿ CONFIGURE SNAPSHOT CONTROLFILE NAME TO '〈경로〉/snapcf_RMANTEST1.f';
- resync시 생성되는 임시 snapshot control file의 이름을 지정합니다.

⓫ CONFIGURE CHANNEL DEVICE TYPE DISK FORMAT '/data/orabackup/%U';
- 백업 파일 저장 경로 설정합니다.
- backupset 파일 이름 형식 (FORMAT)은 다음과 같습니다.

  - %c : backup piece의 copy number
  - %p : backup piece number, 1부터 시작하고 1씩 증가
  - %s : backup set number, control file내의 counter, set이 생성될 때 마다 증가
  - %d : database name
  - %n : database name, padded on the right with x char to total length oh 8 char
  - %t : fixed reference time 이후 경과한 시간(초)을 4byte로 나타낸 값으로 %s와 조합하면 backup set에 unique name을 지정
  - %u : backup set 번호와 생성시간에 대한 단축 표기법, 8자 이름 지정
  - %U : %u_%p_%c (default)

4 RMAN의 백업 수행 명령어

1. RMAN 백업 수행(백업 세트 방식)

이제부터 RMAN의 backup 명령어를 통해 DB를 백업해 보겠습니다.
백업 세트 방식으로 아카이브 로그 파일을 포함한 DB 전체를 풀 백업 받는 명령어입니다.

```
RMAN> BACKUP DATABASE PLUS ARCHIVELOG ;
```

```
RMAN> BACKUP DATABASE PLUS ARCHIVELOG ;


Starting backup at 14-NOV-17
current log archived
using channel ORA_DISK_1
channel ORA_DISK_1: starting archived log backup set
channel ORA_DISK_1: specifying archived log(s) in backup set
input archived log thread=1 sequence=321 RECID=316 STAMP=958495309
input archived log thread=1 sequence=322 RECID=317 STAMP=958496957
input archived log thread=1 sequence=323 RECID=318 STAMP=958498539
input archived log thread=1 sequence=324 RECID=319 STAMP=958500118
input archived log thread=1 sequence=325 RECID=320 STAMP=958501619
input archived log thread=1 sequence=326 RECID=321 STAMP=958502420
input archived log thread=1 sequence=327 RECID=322 STAMP=958503718
input archived log thread=1 sequence=328 RECID=323 STAMP=958505225
input archived log thread=1 sequence=329 RECID=324 STAMP=958506263
input archived log thread=1 sequence=330 RECID=325 STAMP=958507858
input archived log thread=1 sequence=331 RECID=326 STAMP=958509376
input archived log thread=1 sequence=332 RECID=327 STAMP=958510946
input archived log thread=1 sequence=333 RECID=328 STAMP=958512429
input archived log thread=1 sequence=334 RECID=329 STAMP=958513622
input archived log thread=1 sequence=335 RECID=330 STAMP=958515669
input archived log thread=1 sequence=336 RECID=331 STAMP=958517661
input archived log thread=1 sequence=337 RECID=332 STAMP=958519905
input archived log thread=1 sequence=338 RECID=333 STAMP=958521700
input archived log thread=1 sequence=339 RECID=334 STAMP=958523297
input archived log thread=1 sequence=340 RECID=335 STAMP=958525910
input archived log thread=1 sequence=341 RECID=336 STAMP=958546972
input archived log thread=1 sequence=342 RECID=337 STAMP=958552333
input archived log thread=1 sequence=343 RECID=338 STAMP=958554849
input archived log thread=1 sequence=344 RECID=339 STAMP=958559559
input archived log thread=1 sequence=345 RECID=340 STAMP=958563447
input archived log thread=1 sequence=346 RECID=341 STAMP=958563493
input archived log thread=1 sequence=347 RECID=342 STAMP=958563542
input archived log thread=1 sequence=348 RECID=343 STAMP=958563594
input archived log thread=1 sequence=349 RECID=344 STAMP=958563653
input archived log thread=1 sequence=350 RECID=345 STAMP=958563699
input archived log thread=1 sequence=351 RECID=346 STAMP=958563761
input archived log thread=1 sequence=352 RECID=347 STAMP=958563808
input archived log thread=1 sequence=353 RECID=348 STAMP=958563861
input archived log thread=1 sequence=354 RECID=349 STAMP=958563919
input archived log thread=1 sequence=355 RECID=350 STAMP=958563977
input archived log thread=1 sequence=356 RECID=351 STAMP=958564039
input archived log thread=1 sequence=357 RECID=352 STAMP=958564111
input archived log thread=1 sequence=358 RECID=353 STAMP=958564163
input archived log thread=1 sequence=359 RECID=354 STAMP=958564221
input archived log thread=1 sequence=360 RECID=355 STAMP=958564277
input archived log thread=1 sequence=361 RECID=356 STAMP=958564333
input archived log thread=1 sequence=362 RECID=357 STAMP=958564394
channel ORA_DISK_1: starting piece 1 at 14-NOV-17
```

```
Starting backup at 14-NOV-17
using channel ORA_DISK_1
channel ORA_DISK_1: starting full datafile backup set
channel ORA_DISK_1: specifying datafile(s) in backup set
input datafile file number=00003 name=/oracle/oracle12/oradata/oracle12/sysaux01.dbf
input datafile file number=00004 name=/oracle/oracle12/oradata/oracle12/undotbs01.dbf
input datafile file number=00001 name=/oracle/oracle12/oradata/oracle12/system01.dbf
input datafile file number=00002 name=/oracle/oracle12/oradata/oracle12/unione02.dbf
input datafile file number=00008 name=/oracle/oracle12/oradata/oracle12/unione03.dbf
input datafile file number=00009 name=/oracle/oracle12/oradata/oracle12/unione04.dbf
input datafile file number=00010 name=/oracle/oracle12/oradata/oracle12/undotbs02.dbf
input datafile file number=00011 name=/oracle/oracle12/oradata/oracle12/undotbs03.dbf
input datafile file number=00007 name=/oracle/oracle12/oradata/oracle12/users01.dbf
input datafile file number=00005 name=/oracle/oracle12/oradata/oracle12/unione01.dbf
channel ORA_DISK_1: starting piece 1 at 14-NOV-17
```

```
Starting backup at 14-NOV-17
current log archived
using channel ORA_DISK_1
channel ORA_DISK_1: starting archived log backup set
channel ORA_DISK_1: specifying archived log(s) in backup set
input archived log thread=1 sequence=413 RECID=408 STAMP=960058381
channel ORA_DISK_1: starting piece 1 at 14-NOV-17
channel ORA_DISK_1: finished piece 1 at 14-NOV-17
piece handle=/oracle/oracle12/RMAN_BACKUP/ORACLE12_07sjil0d_1_1_960058381_7 tag=TAG20171114T185301 comment=NONE
channel ORA_DISK_1: backup set complete, elapsed time: 00:00:01
Finished backup at 14-NOV-17

Starting Control File and SPFILE Autobackup at 14-NOV-17
piece handle=/oracle/oracle12/FRA/ORACLE12/autobackup/2017_11_14/o1_mf_s_960058382_f0oh80np_.bkp comment=NONE
Finished Control File and SPFILE Autobackup at 14-NOV-17

RMAN>
```

특정 테이블스페이스만 백업 세트 형식으로 백업합니다.

```
RMAN> BACKUP TABLESPACE <테이블스페이스명>;
```

```
RMAN> BACKUP TABLESPACE USERS;

Starting backup at 14-NOV-17
using channel ORA_DISK_1
channel ORA_DISK_1: starting full datafile backup set
channel ORA_DISK_1: specifying datafile(s) in backup set
input datafile file number=00007 name=/oracle/oracle12/oradata/oracle12/users01.dbf
channel ORA_DISK_1: starting piece 1 at 14-NOV-17
channel ORA_DISK_1: finished piece 1 at 14-NOV-17
piece handle=/oracle/oracle12/RMAN_BACKUP/ORACLE12_09sjil5t_1_1_960058557_9 tag=TAG20171114T185557 comment=NONE
channel ORA_DISK_1: backup set complete, elapsed time: 00:00:03
Finished backup at 14-NOV-17

Starting Control File and SPFILE Autobackup at 14-NOV-17
piece handle=/oracle/oracle12/FRA/ORACLE12/autobackup/2017_11_14/o1_mf_s_960058561_f0ohflkr_.bkp comment=NONE
Finished Control File and SPFILE Autobackup at 14-NOV-17

RMAN> █
```

데이터 파일만 골라서 백업 세트 방식으로 백업합니다.

```
RMAN> BACKUP DATAFILE 파일번호,파일번호,...
```

```
RMAN> BACKUP DATAFILE 1,2 ;

Starting backup at 14-NOV-17
using channel ORA_DISK_1
channel ORA_DISK_1: starting full datafile backup set
channel ORA_DISK_1: specifying datafile(s) in backup set
input datafile file number=00001 name=/oracle/oracle12/oradata/oracle12/system01.dbf
input datafile file number=00002 name=/oracle/oracle12/oradata/oracle12/unione02.dbf
channel ORA_DISK_1: starting piece 1 at 14-NOV-17
channel ORA_DISK_1: finished piece 1 at 14-NOV-17
piece handle=/oracle/oracle12/RMAN_BACKUP/ORACLE12_0bsjilbg_1_1_960058736_11 tag=TAG20171114T185856 comment=NONE
channel ORA_DISK_1: backup set complete, elapsed time: 00:00:35
Finished backup at 14-NOV-17

Starting Control File and SPFILE Autobackup at 14-NOV-17
piece handle=/oracle/oracle12/FRA/ORACLE12/autobackup/2017_11_14/o1_mf_s_960058772_f0ohn5o1_.bkp comment=NONE
Finished Control File and SPFILE Autobackup at 14-NOV-17

RMAN> █
```

백업 세트 방식으로 이번엔 압축하여 DB 전체 백업을 수행해 보겠습니다.

```
RMAN> BACKUP DATAFILE 파일번호,파일번호,...
```

```
RMAN> BACKUP AS COMPRESSED BACKUPSET DATABASE ;

Starting backup at 16-NOV-17
using channel ORA_DISK_1
channel ORA_DISK_1: starting compressed full datafile backup set
channel ORA_DISK_1: specifying datafile(s) in backup set
input datafile file number=00003 name=/oracle/oracle12/oradata/oracle12/sysaux01.dbf
input datafile file number=00004 name=/oracle/oracle12/oradata/oracle12/undotbs01.dbf
input datafile file number=00001 name=/oracle/oracle12/oradata/oracle12/system01.dbf
input datafile file number=00002 name=/oracle/oracle12/oradata/oracle12/unione02.dbf
input datafile file number=00008 name=/oracle/oracle12/oradata/oracle12/unione03.dbf
input datafile file number=00009 name=/oracle/oracle12/oradata/oracle12/unione04.dbf
input datafile file number=00010 name=/oracle/oracle12/oradata/oracle12/undotbs02.dbf
input datafile file number=00011 name=/oracle/oracle12/oradata/oracle12/undotbs03.dbf
input datafile file number=00007 name=/oracle/oracle12/oradata/oracle12/users01.dbf
input datafile file number=00005 name=/oracle/oracle12/oradata/oracle12/unione01.dbf
channel ORA_DISK_1: starting piece 1 at 16-NOV-17
channel ORA_DISK_1: finished piece 1 at 16-NOV-17
piece handle=/oracle/oracle12/RMAN_BACKUP/ORACLE12_0rsjnkso_1_1_960222104_27 tag=TAG20171116T162144 comment=NONE
channel ORA_DISK_1: backup set complete, elapsed time: 00:02:45
Finished backup at 16-NOV-17

Starting Control File and SPFILE Autobackup at 16-NOV-17
piece handle=/oracle/oracle12/FRA/ORACLE12/autobackup/2017_11_16/o1_mf_s_960222270_f0th9hpx_.bkp comment=NONE
Finished Control File and SPFILE Autobackup at 16-NOV-17

RMAN> █
```

생성된 아카이브 로그 파일만 백업을 수행하겠습니다.

```
RMAN> BACKUP ARCHIVELOG ALL ;
```

```
RMAN> backup archivelog all ;

Starting backup at 16-NOV-17
current log archived
using channel ORA_DISK_1
skipping archived logs of thread 1 from sequence 321 to 413; already backed up
channel ORA_DISK_1: starting archived log backup set
channel ORA_DISK_1: specifying archived log(s) in backup set
input archived log thread=1 sequence=414 RECID=409 STAMP=960112854
input archived log thread=1 sequence=415 RECID=410 STAMP=960123655
input archived log thread=1 sequence=416 RECID=411 STAMP=960158022
input archived log thread=1 sequence=417 RECID=412 STAMP=960222727
input archived log thread=1 sequence=418 RECID=413 STAMP=960222727
input archived log thread=1 sequence=419 RECID=414 STAMP=960222731
input archived log thread=1 sequence=420 RECID=415 STAMP=960222731
input archived log thread=1 sequence=421 RECID=416 STAMP=960222736
input archived log thread=1 sequence=422 RECID=417 STAMP=960222737
input archived log thread=1 sequence=423 RECID=418 STAMP=960222740
input archived log thread=1 sequence=424 RECID=419 STAMP=960222740
input archived log thread=1 sequence=425 RECID=420 STAMP=960222743
input archived log thread=1 sequence=426 RECID=421 STAMP=960222743
input archived log thread=1 sequence=427 RECID=422 STAMP=960222747
input archived log thread=1 sequence=428 RECID=423 STAMP=960222747
input archived log thread=1 sequence=429 RECID=424 STAMP=960222750
input archived log thread=1 sequence=430 RECID=425 STAMP=960222750
input archived log thread=1 sequence=431 RECID=426 STAMP=960222753
input archived log thread=1 sequence=432 RECID=427 STAMP=960222754
input archived log thread=1 sequence=433 RECID=428 STAMP=960222757
input archived log thread=1 sequence=434 RECID=429 STAMP=960222757
input archived log thread=1 sequence=435 RECID=430 STAMP=960222763
input archived log thread=1 sequence=436 RECID=431 STAMP=960222763
input archived log thread=1 sequence=437 RECID=432 STAMP=960222767
input archived log thread=1 sequence=438 RECID=433 STAMP=960222767
input archived log thread=1 sequence=439 RECID=434 STAMP=960222770
input archived log thread=1 sequence=440 RECID=435 STAMP=960222770
input archived log thread=1 sequence=441 RECID=436 STAMP=960222774
input archived log thread=1 sequence=442 RECID=437 STAMP=960222774
input archived log thread=1 sequence=443 RECID=438 STAMP=960222777
input archived log thread=1 sequence=444 RECID=439 STAMP=960223146
channel ORA_DISK_1: starting piece 1 at 16-NOV-17
channel ORA_DISK_1: finished piece 1 at 16-NOV-17
piece handle=/oracle/oracle12/RMAN_BACKUP/ORACLE12_0tsjnltb_1_1_960223147_29 tag=TAG20171116T163907 comment=NONE
channel ORA_DISK_1: backup set complete, elapsed time: 00:00:15
Finished backup at 16-NOV-17

Starting Control File and SPFILE Autobackup at 16-NOV-17
piece handle=/oracle/oracle12/FRA/ORACLE12/autobackup/2017_11_16/o1_mf_s_960223162_f0tj5dht_.bkp comment=NONE
Finished Control File and SPFILE Autobackup at 16-NOV-17

RMAN>
```

2. RMAN 백업 수행(이미지 카피 방식)

데이터파일을 Bit 형식으로 복사하는 이미지 카피(Image Copy) 방식으로 DB 전체를 백업합니다.

```
RMAN> BACKUP AS COPY DATABASE ;
```

```
RMAN> BACKUP AS COPY DATABASE ;

Starting backup at 14-NOV-17
using channel ORA_DISK_1
channel ORA_DISK_1: starting datafile copy
input datafile file number=00003 name=/oracle/oracle12/oradata/oracle12/sysaux01.dbf
output file name=/oracle/oracle12/RMAN_BACKUP/ORACLE12_data_D-ORACLE12_I-2053465567_TS-SYSAUX_FNO-3_0dsjilgh_960058897_13 tag=TAG201
71114T190137 RECID=1 STAMP=960059736
channel ORA_DISK_1: datafile copy complete, elapsed time: 00:14:09
channel ORA_DISK_1: starting datafile copy
input datafile file number=00004 name=/oracle/oracle12/oradata/oracle12/undotbs01.dbf
output file name=/oracle/oracle12/RMAN_BACKUP/ORACLE12_data_D-ORACLE12_I-2053465567_TS-UNDOTBS1_FNO-4_0esjimb3_960059747_14 tag=TAG2
0171114T190137 RECID=2 STAMP=960060426
channel ORA_DISK_1: datafile copy complete, elapsed time: 00:11:22
channel ORA_DISK_1: starting datafile copy
input datafile file number=00001 name=/oracle/oracle12/oradata/oracle12/system01.dbf
output file name=/oracle/oracle12/RMAN_BACKUP/ORACLE12_data_D-ORACLE12_I-2053465567_TS-SYSTEM_FNO-1_0fsjin0d_960060429_15 tag=TAG201
71114T190137 RECID=3 STAMP=960060682
channel ORA_DISK_1: datafile copy complete, elapsed time: 00:04:16
channel ORA_DISK_1: starting datafile copy
input datafile file number=00002 name=/oracle/oracle12/oradata/oracle12/unione02.dbf
output file name=/oracle/oracle12/RMAN_BACKUP/ORACLE12_data_D-ORACLE12_I-2053465567_TS-UNIONE_FNO-2_0gsjin8d_960060685_16 tag=TAG201
71114T190137 RECID=4 STAMP=960060711
channel ORA_DISK_1: datafile copy complete, elapsed time: 00:00:35
channel ORA_DISK_1: starting datafile copy
input datafile file number=00008 name=/oracle/oracle12/oradata/oracle12/unione03.dbf
output file name=/oracle/oracle12/RMAN_BACKUP/ORACLE12_data_D-ORACLE12_I-2053465567_TS-UNIONE_FNO-8_0hsjin9h_960060721_17 tag=TAG201
71114T190137 RECID=5 STAMP=960060743
channel ORA_DISK_1: datafile copy complete, elapsed time: 00:00:25
channel ORA_DISK_1: starting datafile copy
input datafile file number=00009 name=/oracle/oracle12/oradata/oracle12/unione04.dbf
output file name=/oracle/oracle12/RMAN_BACKUP/ORACLE12_data_D-ORACLE12_I-2053465567_TS-UNIONE_FNO-9_0isjinaa_960060746_18 tag=TAG201
71114T190137 RECID=6 STAMP=960060772
channel ORA_DISK_1: datafile copy complete, elapsed time: 00:00:35
channel ORA_DISK_1: starting datafile copy
input datafile file number=00010 name=/oracle/oracle12/oradata/oracle12/undotbs02.dbf
output file name=/oracle/oracle12/RMAN_BACKUP/ORACLE12_data_D-ORACLE12_I-2053465567_TS-UNDOTBS1_FNO-10_0jsjinbe_960060782_19 tag=TAG
20171114T190137 RECID=7 STAMP=960060784
channel ORA_DISK_1: datafile copy complete, elapsed time: 00:00:03
channel ORA_DISK_1: starting datafile copy
input datafile file number=00011 name=/oracle/oracle12/oradata/oracle12/undotbs03.dbf
output file name=/oracle/oracle12/RMAN_BACKUP/ORACLE12_data_D-ORACLE12_I-2053465567_TS-UNDOTBS1_FNO-11_0ksjinbh_960060785_20 tag=TAG
20171114T190137 RECID=8 STAMP=960060788
channel ORA_DISK_1: datafile copy complete, elapsed time: 00:00:03
channel ORA_DISK_1: starting datafile copy
input datafile file number=00007 name=/oracle/oracle12/oradata/oracle12/users01.dbf
output file name=/oracle/oracle12/RMAN_BACKUP/ORACLE12_data_D-ORACLE12_I-2053465567_TS-USERS_FNO-7_0lsjinbk_960060788_21 tag=TAG2017
1114T190137 RECID=9 STAMP=960060790
channel ORA_DISK_1: datafile copy complete, elapsed time: 00:00:03
channel ORA_DISK_1: starting datafile copy
input datafile file number=00005 name=/oracle/oracle12/oradata/oracle12/unione01.dbf
output file name=/oracle/oracle12/RMAN_BACKUP/ORACLE12_data_D-ORACLE12_I-2053465567_TS-UNIONE_FNO-5_0msjinbn_960060791_22 tag=TAG201
71114T190137 RECID=10 STAMP=960060792
channel ORA_DISK_1: datafile copy complete, elapsed time: 00:00:01
Finished backup at 14-NOV-17

Starting Control File and SPFILE Autobackup at 14-NOV-17
piece handle=/oracle/oracle12/FRA/ORACLE12/autobackup/2017_11_14/o1_mf_s_960060794_f0okmd5s_.bkp comment=NONE
Finished Control File and SPFILE Autobackup at 14-NOV-17

RMAN>
```

데이터 파일만 골라서 이미지 카피 방식으로 백업합니다.

```
RMAN> BACKUP AS COPY DATAFILE <파일번호>,<파일번호>,… ;
```

```
[oracle12]yspark-linux:/home/oracle12> rman target /

Recovery Manager: Release 12.2.0.1.0 - Production on Thu Nov 16 16:08:52 2017

Copyright (c) 1982, 2017, Oracle and/or its affiliates.  All rights reserved.

connected to target database: ORACLE12 (DBID=2053465567)

RMAN> backup as copy datafile 1,2 ;

Starting backup at 16-NOV-17
using target database control file instead of recovery catalog
allocated channel: ORA_DISK_1
channel ORA_DISK_1: SID=8 device type=DISK
channel ORA_DISK_1: starting datafile copy
input datafile file number=00001 name=/oracle/oracle12/oradata/oracle12/system01.dbf
output file name=/oracle/oracle12/RMAN_BACKUP/ORACLE12_data_D-ORACLE12_I-2053465567_TS-SYSTEM_FNO-1_0osjnk57_96022135
1_24 tag=TAG20171116T160911 RECID=11 STAMP=960221606
channel ORA_DISK_1: datafile copy complete, elapsed time: 00:04:17
channel ORA_DISK_1: starting datafile copy
input datafile file number=00002 name=/oracle/oracle12/oradata/oracle12/unione02.dbf
output file name=/oracle/oracle12/RMAN_BACKUP/ORACLE12_data_D-ORACLE12_I-2053465567_TS-UNIONE_FNO-2_0psjnkd9_96022160
9_25 tag=TAG20171116T160911 RECID=12 STAMP=960221632
channel ORA_DISK_1: datafile copy complete, elapsed time: 00:00:25
Finished backup at 16-NOV-17

Starting Control File and SPFILE Autobackup at 16-NOV-17
piece handle=/oracle/oracle12/FRA/ORACLE12/autobackup/2017_11_16/o1_mf_s_960221634_f0tgonl8_.bkp comment=NONE
Finished Control File and SPFILE Autobackup at 16-NOV-17

RMAN> █
```

지정된 테이블스페이스만 이미지 카피 방식으로 백업을 수행합니다.

```
RMAN> BACKUP AS COPY TABLESPACE <테이블스페이스명> ;
```

```
RMAN> BACKUP AS COPY TABLESPACE users ;

Starting backup at 16-NOV-17
using channel ORA_DISK_1
channel ORA_DISK_1: starting datafile copy
input datafile file number=00007 name=/oracle/oracle12/oradata/oracle12/users01.dbf
output file name=/oracle/oracle12/RMAN_BACKUP/ORACLE12_data_D-ORACLE12_I-2053465567_TS-USERS_FNO-7_0vsjnnan_9602
24599_31 tag=TAG20171116T170319 RECID=13 STAMP=960224601
channel ORA_DISK_1: datafile copy complete, elapsed time: 00:00:03
Finished backup at 16-NOV-17

Starting Control File and SPFILE Autobackup at 16-NOV-17
piece handle=/oracle/oracle12/FRA/ORACLE12/autobackup/2017_11_16/o1_mf_s_960224603_f0tkldky_.bkp comment=NONE
Finished Control File and SPFILE Autobackup at 16-NOV-17

RMAN> █
```

안전을 위해 백업할 때 "PLUS ARCHIVELOG" 옵션을 사용하십시오. 아카이브 로그 파일이 백업될 때마다 오래된 아카이브 로그 파일을 제거해야 합니다.

5 RMAN을 이용한 증분 백업과 Block Change Tracking

이전에 백업 받았던 백업 데이터와 비교해서 변경된 부분만 골라서 백업을 수행하는 것을 증분 백업(Incremental backup)이라고 합니다. 이제부터 어떻게 증분 백업을 수행하는지 알아보겠습니다.

1. 백업 세트 방식의 증분 백업

아카이브 로그 파일을 포함한 DB의 LEVEL 0 백업으로 차등 증분 백업을 수행합니다.

```
RMAN> BACKUP INCREMENTAL LEVEL 0 DATABASE PLUS ARCHIVELOG ;
```

```
RMAN> BACKUP INCREMENTAL LEVEL 0 DATABASE PLUS ARCHIVELOG;


Starting backup at 16-NOV-17
current log archived
using channel ORA_DISK_1
skipping archived logs of thread 1 from sequence 321 to 444; already backed up
channel ORA_DISK_1: starting archived log backup set
channel ORA_DISK_1: specifying archived log(s) in backup set
input archived log thread=1 sequence=445 RECID=440 STAMP=960224896
channel ORA_DISK_1: starting piece 1 at 16-NOV-17
channel ORA_DISK_1: finished piece 1 at 16-NOV-17
piece handle=/oracle/oracle12/RMAN_BACKUP/ORACLE12_11sjnnk1_1_1_960224897_33 tag=TAG20171116T170816 comment=NONE
channel ORA_DISK_1: backup set complete, elapsed time: 00:00:01
Finished backup at 16-NOV-17

Starting backup at 16-NOV-17
using channel ORA_DISK_1
channel ORA_DISK_1: starting incremental level 0 datafile backup set
channel ORA_DISK_1: specifying datafile(s) in backup set
input datafile file number=00003 name=/oracle/oracle12/oradata/oracle12/sysaux01.dbf
input datafile file number=00004 name=/oracle/oracle12/oradata/oracle12/undotbs01.dbf
input datafile file number=00001 name=/oracle/oracle12/oradata/oracle12/system01.dbf
input datafile file number=00002 name=/oracle/oracle12/oradata/oracle12/unione02.dbf
input datafile file number=00008 name=/oracle/oracle12/oradata/oracle12/unione03.dbf
input datafile file number=00009 name=/oracle/oracle12/oradata/oracle12/unione04.dbf
input datafile file number=00010 name=/oracle/oracle12/oradata/oracle12/undotbs02.dbf
input datafile file number=00011 name=/oracle/oracle12/oradata/oracle12/undotbs03.dbf
input datafile file number=00007 name=/oracle/oracle12/oradata/oracle12/users01.dbf
input datafile file number=00005 name=/oracle/oracle12/oradata/oracle12/unione01.dbf
channel ORA_DISK_1: starting piece 1 at 16-NOV-17
channel ORA_DISK_1: finished piece 1 at 16-NOV-17
piece handle=/oracle/oracle12/RMAN_BACKUP/ORACLE12_12sjnnk2_1_1_960224898_34 tag=TAG20171116T170818 comment=NONE
channel ORA_DISK_1: backup set complete, elapsed time: 00:02:16
Finished backup at 16-NOV-17

Starting backup at 16-NOV-17
current log archived
using channel ORA_DISK_1
channel ORA_DISK_1: starting archived log backup set
channel ORA_DISK_1: specifying archived log(s) in backup set
input archived log thread=1 sequence=446 RECID=441 STAMP=960225034
channel ORA_DISK_1: starting piece 1 at 16-NOV-17
channel ORA_DISK_1: finished piece 1 at 16-NOV-17
piece handle=/oracle/oracle12/RMAN_BACKUP/ORACLE12_13sjnnob_1_1_960225035_35 tag=TAG20171116T171035 comment=NONE
channel ORA_DISK_1: backup set complete, elapsed time: 00:00:01
Finished backup at 16-NOV-17

Starting Control File and SPFILE Autobackup at 16-NOV-17
piece handle=/oracle/oracle12/FRA/ORACLE12/autobackup/2017_11_16/o1_mf_s_960225036_f0tkzy6f_.bkp comment=NONE
Finished Control File and SPFILE Autobackup at 16-NOV-17

RMAN>
```

이번에는 LEVEL 1로 차등 증분 백업을 수행합니다.

```
RMAN> BACKUP INCREMENTAL LEVEL 1 DATABASE PLUS ARCHIVELOG ;
```

```
RMAN> BACKUP INCREMENTAL LEVEL 1 DATABASE PLUS ARCHIVELOG ;

Starting backup at 20-NOV-17
current log archived
using target database control file instead of recovery catalog
allocated channel: ORA_DISK_1
channel ORA_DISK_1: SID=14 device type=DISK
skipping archived logs of thread 1 from sequence 321 to 446; already backed up
channel ORA_DISK_1: starting archived log backup set
channel ORA_DISK_1: specifying archived log(s) in backup set
input archived log thread=1 sequence=447 RECID=442 STAMP=960307262
input archived log thread=1 sequence=448 RECID=443 STAMP=960372751
input archived log thread=1 sequence=449 RECID=444 STAMP=960455218
input archived log thread=1 sequence=450 RECID=445 STAMP=960532360
input archived log thread=1 sequence=451 RECID=446 STAMP=960549673
channel ORA_DISK_1: starting piece 1 at 20-NOV-17
channel ORA_DISK_1: finished piece 1 at 20-NOV-17
piece handle=/oracle/oracle12/RMAN_BACKUP/ORACLE12_15sk1kpd_1_1_960549677_37 tag=TAG20171120T112116 comment=NONE
channel ORA_DISK_1: backup set complete, elapsed time: 00:00:25
Finished backup at 20-NOV-17

Starting backup at 20-NOV-17
using channel ORA_DISK_1
channel ORA_DISK_1: starting incremental level 1 datafile backup set
channel ORA_DISK_1: specifying datafile(s) in backup set
input datafile file number=00003 name=/oracle/oracle12/oradata/oracle12/sysaux01.dbf
input datafile file number=00004 name=/oracle/oracle12/oradata/oracle12/undotbs01.dbf
input datafile file number=00001 name=/oracle/oracle12/oradata/oracle12/system01.dbf
input datafile file number=00002 name=/oracle/oracle12/oradata/oracle12/unione02.dbf
input datafile file number=00008 name=/oracle/oracle12/oradata/oracle12/unione03.dbf
input datafile file number=00009 name=/oracle/oracle12/oradata/oracle12/unione04.dbf
input datafile file number=00010 name=/oracle/oracle12/oradata/oracle12/undotbs02.dbf
input datafile file number=00011 name=/oracle/oracle12/oradata/oracle12/undotbs03.dbf
input datafile file number=00007 name=/oracle/oracle12/oradata/oracle12/users01.dbf
input datafile file number=00005 name=/oracle/oracle12/oradata/oracle12/unione01.dbf
channel ORA_DISK_1: starting piece 1 at 20-NOV-17
channel ORA_DISK_1: finished piece 1 at 20-NOV-17
piece handle=/oracle/oracle12/RMAN_BACKUP/ORACLE12_16sk1kq7_1_1_960549703_38 tag=TAG20171120T112143 comment=NONE
channel ORA_DISK_1: backup set complete, elapsed time: 00:02:06
Finished backup at 20-NOV-17

Starting backup at 20-NOV-17
current log archived
using channel ORA_DISK_1
channel ORA_DISK_1: starting archived log backup set
channel ORA_DISK_1: specifying archived log(s) in backup set
input archived log thread=1 sequence=452 RECID=447 STAMP=960549831
channel ORA_DISK_1: starting piece 1 at 20-NOV-17
channel ORA_DISK_1: finished piece 1 at 20-NOV-17
piece handle=/oracle/oracle12/RMAN_BACKUP/ORACLE12_17sk1ku8_1_1_960549832_39 tag=TAG20171120T112352 comment=NONE
channel ORA_DISK_1: backup set complete, elapsed time: 00:00:01
Finished backup at 20-NOV-17

Starting Control File and SPFILE Autobackup at 20-NOV-17
piece handle=/oracle/oracle12/FRA/ORACLE12/autobackup/2017_11_20/o1_mf_s_960549834_f14h5x9g_.bkp comment=NONE
Finished Control File and SPFILE Autobackup at 20-NOV-17

RMAN>
```

LEVEL 1로 차등 증분 백업이 완료되면 누적 증분 백업을 수행합니다.

```
RMAN> BACKUP INCREMENTAL LEVEL 1 CUMULATIVE DATABASE;
```

```
RMAN> BACKUP INCREMENTAL LEVEL 1 CUMULATIVE DATABASE;

Starting backup at 20-NOV-17
using channel ORA_DISK_1
channel ORA_DISK_1: starting incremental level 1 datafile backup set
channel ORA_DISK_1: specifying datafile(s) in backup set
input datafile file number=00003 name=/oracle/oracle12/oradata/oracle12/sysaux01.dbf
input datafile file number=00004 name=/oracle/oracle12/oradata/oracle12/undotbs01.dbf
input datafile file number=00001 name=/oracle/oracle12/oradata/oracle12/system01.dbf
input datafile file number=00002 name=/oracle/oracle12/oradata/oracle12/unione02.dbf
input datafile file number=00008 name=/oracle/oracle12/oradata/oracle12/unione03.dbf
input datafile file number=00009 name=/oracle/oracle12/oradata/oracle12/unione04.dbf
input datafile file number=00010 name=/oracle/oracle12/oradata/oracle12/undotbs02.dbf
input datafile file number=00011 name=/oracle/oracle12/oradata/oracle12/undotbs03.dbf
input datafile file number=00007 name=/oracle/oracle12/oradata/oracle12/users01.dbf
input datafile file number=00005 name=/oracle/oracle12/oradata/oracle12/unione01.dbf
channel ORA_DISK_1: starting piece 1 at 20-NOV-17
channel ORA_DISK_1: finished piece 1 at 20-NOV-17
piece handle=/oracle/oracle12/RMAN_BACKUP/ORACLE12_19sk1l7j_1_1_960550131_41 tag=TAG20171120T112850 comment=NONE
channel ORA_DISK_1: backup set complete, elapsed time: 00:02:05
Finished backup at 20-NOV-17

Starting Control File and SPFILE Autobackup at 20-NOV-17
piece handle=/oracle/oracle12/FRA/ORACLE12/autobackup/2017_11_20/o1_mf_s_960550256_f14hm24r_.bkp comment=NONE
Finished Control File and SPFILE Autobackup at 20-NOV-17

RMAN>
```

2. 이미지 카피 방식의 증분 백업

이미지 카피(Image Copy) 방식으로 차분 증분 백업을 수행하겠습니다.

LEVEL 0 백업을 시작합니다.

```
RMAN> BACKUP AS COPY INCREMENTAL LEVEL 0 DATABASE;
```

```
RMAN> BACKUP AS COPY INCREMENTAL LEVEL 0 DATABASE;

Starting backup at 20-NOV-17
using channel ORA_DISK_1
channel ORA_DISK_1: starting datafile copy
input datafile file number=00003 name=/oracle/oracle12/oradata/oracle12/sysaux01.dbf
output file name=/oracle/oracle12/RMAN_BACKUP/ORACLE12_data_D-ORACLE12_I-2053465567_TS-SYSAUX_FNO-3_1bsk1nca_960552
330_43 tag=TAG20171120T120530 RECID=14 STAMP=960553151
channel ORA_DISK_1: datafile copy complete, elapsed time: 00:13:45
channel ORA_DISK_1: starting datafile copy
input datafile file number=00004 name=/oracle/oracle12/oradata/oracle12/undotbs01.dbf
output file name=/oracle/oracle12/RMAN_BACKUP/ORACLE12_data_D-ORACLE12_I-2053465567_TS-UNDOTBS1_FNO-4_1csk1o64_9605
53156_44 tag=TAG20171120T120530 RECID=15 STAMP=960553926
channel ORA_DISK_1: datafile copy complete, elapsed time: 00:12:56
channel ORA_DISK_1: starting datafile copy
input datafile file number=00001 name=/oracle/oracle12/oradata/oracle12/system01.dbf
output file name=/oracle/oracle12/RMAN_BACKUP/ORACLE12_data_D-ORACLE12_I-2053465567_TS-SYSTEM_FNO-1_1dsk1ouc_960553
932_45 tag=TAG20171120T120530 RECID=16 STAMP=960554211
channel ORA_DISK_1: datafile copy complete, elapsed time: 00:04:46
channel ORA_DISK_1: starting datafile copy
input datafile file number=00002 name=/oracle/oracle12/oradata/oracle12/unione02.dbf
output file name=/oracle/oracle12/RMAN_BACKUP/ORACLE12_data_D-ORACLE12_I-2053465567_TS-UNIONE_FNO-2_1esk1p7a_960554
218_46 tag=TAG20171120T120530 RECID=17 STAMP=960554242
channel ORA_DISK_1: datafile copy complete, elapsed time: 00:00:25
channel ORA_DISK_1: starting datafile copy
input datafile file number=00008 name=/oracle/oracle12/oradata/oracle12/unione03.dbf
output file name=/oracle/oracle12/RMAN_BACKUP/ORACLE12_data_D-ORACLE12_I-2053465567_TS-UNIONE_FNO-8_1fsk1p83_960554
243_47 tag=TAG20171120T120530 RECID=18 STAMP=960554263
channel ORA_DISK_1: datafile copy complete, elapsed time: 00:00:25
channel ORA_DISK_1: starting datafile copy
input datafile file number=00009 name=/oracle/oracle12/oradata/oracle12/unione04.dbf
output file name=/oracle/oracle12/RMAN_BACKUP/ORACLE12_data_D-ORACLE12_I-2053465567_TS-UNIONE_FNO-9_1gsk1p8s_960554
268_48 tag=TAG20171120T120530 RECID=19 STAMP=960554291
channel ORA_DISK_1: datafile copy complete, elapsed time: 00:00:25
channel ORA_DISK_1: starting datafile copy
input datafile file number=00010 name=/oracle/oracle12/oradata/oracle12/undotbs02.dbf
output file name=/oracle/oracle12/RMAN_BACKUP/ORACLE12_data_D-ORACLE12_I-2053465567_TS-UNDOTBS1_FNO-10_1hsk1p9m_960
554294_49 tag=TAG20171120T120530 RECID=20 STAMP=960554296
channel ORA_DISK_1: datafile copy complete, elapsed time: 00:00:03
channel ORA_DISK_1: starting datafile copy
input datafile file number=00011 name=/oracle/oracle12/oradata/oracle12/undotbs03.dbf
output file name=/oracle/oracle12/RMAN_BACKUP/ORACLE12_data_D-ORACLE12_I-2053465567_TS-UNDOTBS1_FNO-11_1isk1p9p_960
554297_50 tag=TAG20171120T120530 RECID=21 STAMP=960554300
channel ORA_DISK_1: datafile copy complete, elapsed time: 00:00:03
channel ORA_DISK_1: starting datafile copy
input datafile file number=00007 name=/oracle/oracle12/oradata/oracle12/users01.dbf
output file name=/oracle/oracle12/RMAN_BACKUP/ORACLE12_data_D-ORACLE12_I-2053465567_TS-USERS_FNO-7_1jsk1p9s_9605543
00_51 tag=TAG20171120T120530 RECID=22 STAMP=960554303
channel ORA_DISK_1: datafile copy complete, elapsed time: 00:00:03
channel ORA_DISK_1: starting datafile copy
input datafile file number=00005 name=/oracle/oracle12/oradata/oracle12/unione01.dbf
output file name=/oracle/oracle12/RMAN_BACKUP/ORACLE12_data_D-ORACLE12_I-2053465567_TS-UNIONE_FNO-5_1ksk1p9v_960554
303_52 tag=TAG20171120T120530 RECID=23 STAMP=960554304
channel ORA_DISK_1: datafile copy complete, elapsed time: 00:00:01
Finished backup at 20-NOV-17

Starting Control File and SPFILE Autobackup at 20-NOV-17
piece handle=/oracle/oracle12/FRA/ORACLE12/autobackup/2017_11_20/o1_mf_s_960554305_f14mkmcb_.bkp comment=NONE
Finished Control File and SPFILE Autobackup at 20-NOV-17

RMAN>
```

이미지 카피 방식은 차등 증분 백업을 지원하지 않습니다.

RMAN의 고급 사용 방법편에서 증분 업데이트 백업이라는 RMAN 백업을 알아보겠습니다.

3. Block Change Tracking(FAST INCREMENTAL BACKUPS)

Block Change Tracking을 이용한 Fast Incremental backup feature는 Standard Edition 2에서는 지원하지 않고, Enterprise Edition만 가능합니다. Fast Incremental backup은 과거 backup 이후에 변경된 block들만을 backup받습니다. Fast Incremental backup은 RMAN을 통하여 사용가능합니다.

Database block에 대한 변경은 이제 Tracking file을 사용하여 모두 tracking됩니다.

Block Change Tracking 기능이 활성화되면 오라클은 Tracking file 안에 block들에 대한 변화를 기록하게 됩니다. Incremental backup 동안 RMAN은 tracking file을 읽어 변경된 block을 찾게 됩니다. 이것은 datafile 안의 모든 block을 읽지 않아도 되게 해주며 그로 인해 좀 더 빠른 incremental backup이 수행되도록 해줍니다.

이제 사용 방법을 테스트하겠습니다. 먼저 Block Change Tracking을 Enable합니다.

```
SQL> ALTER DATABASE ENABLE BLOCK CHANGE TRACKING USING FILE '<파일이름>' ;
```

```
[oracle12]yspark-linux:/oracle/oracle12/RMAN_BACKUP> sqlplus "/as sysdba"

SQL*Plus: Release 12.2.0.1.0 Production on Mon Nov 20 12:41:32 2017

Copyright (c) 1982, 2016, Oracle.  All rights reserved.

Connected to:
Oracle Database 12c Enterprise Edition Release 12.2.0.1.0 - 64bit Production

SQL> ALTER DATABASE ENABLE BLOCK CHANGE TRACKING USING FILE '/oracle/oracle12/RMAN_BACKUP/change_tracking.f' ;

Database altered.

SQL>
```

Block Change Tracking과 tracking file에 대한 정보는 controlfile 안에 저장되어 있으며 V$BLOCK_CHANGE_TRACKING view에 의해 조회할 수 있습니다.

```
SQL> desc V$BLOCK_CHANGE_TRACKING
 Name
Null?    Type
----------------------------------------------------------------------------------------------------------------
-------- --------------------------------------------------------------------------------
 STATUS
   VARCHAR2(10)
 FILENAME
   VARCHAR2(513)
 BYTES
   NUMBER
 CON_ID
   NUMBER

SQL> select * From V$BLOCK_CHANGE_TRACKING ;

STATUS     FILENAME                                                    BYTES     CON_ID
---------- ------------------------------------------------------- ---------- ----------
ENABLED    /oracle/oracle12/RMAN_BACKUP/change_tracking.f            11599872          0

SQL>
SQL>
```

이 view는 언제나 하나의 record만을 포함합니다. 만약에 STATUS가 ENABLED이면 FILENAME은 tracking file명을 나타내고 BYTES는 tracking file의 크기를 나타내게 됩니다.

만약에 STATUS가 DISABLED 이면 나머지 두 컬럼은 NULL이 됩니다.

V$BACKUP_DATAFILE view는 USED_CHANGE_TRACKING이라는 컬럼을 가지고 있습니다. 이 컬럼의 값이 YES이고 level 0보다 큰 incremental backup이 수행되면 RMAN이 incremental backup을 빠르게 수행하게 위해 tracking file을 사용했다는 의미입니다.

```
SQL> SELECT FILE#, AVG(DATAFILE_BLOCKS), AVG(BLOCKS_READ),
AVG(BLOCKS_READ/DATAFILE_BLOCKS) * 100 AS "READ FOR BACKUP"
FROM V$BACKUP_DATAFILE
WHERE INCREMENTAL_LEVEL >= 0 AND USED_CHANGE_TRACKING = 'YES'
GROUP BY FILE#
ORDER BY FILE# ;
```

```
SQL> SELECT FILE#,
  2  AVG(DATAFILE_BLOCKS),
  3  AVG(BLOCKS_READ),
  4  AVG(BLOCKS_READ/DATAFILE_BLOCKS) * 100 AS "READ FOR BACKUP"
  5  FROM V$BACKUP_DATAFILE
  6  WHERE INCREMENTAL_LEVEL >= 0
  7  AND USED_CHANGE_TRACKING = 'YES'
  8  GROUP BY FILE#
  9  ORDER BY FILE# ;

     FILE# AVG(DATAFILE_BLOCKS) AVG(BLOCKS_READ) READ FOR BACKUP
---------- -------------------- ---------------- ---------------
         1              1310720              373      .028457642
         2               169664            74723      44.0417531
         3              3932160              883      .022455851
         4              3932160              157      .003992716
         5                 1280                1         .078125
         7                 8960                1      .011160714
         8               165408            58523      35.3809973
         9               160568            38131      23.7475711
        10                12800               17        .1328125
        11                12800               25        .1953125

10 rows selected.

SQL> █
```

Block Change Tracking이 활성화 또는 비활성화될 때마다 tracking file이 생성과 삭제에 관한 log가 alert log에 기록됩니다. Tracking file은 'ALTER DATABASE RENAME FILE' 명령을 사용하여 rename할 수 있습니다. Tracking file은 binary file입니다. RMAN은 tracking file의 backup과 recovery를 지원하지 않습니다.

6 RMAN의 복구 수행 명령어

이제 백업 데이터를 이용한 복구(RESTORE, RECOVER) 명령어를 수행해 보겠습니다.

1. 데이터베이스 전체의 RESTORE, RECOVER

```
RMAN> SHUTDOWN;
RMAN> STARTUP MOUNT;
RMAN> RESTORE DATABASE;
RMAN> RECOVER DATABASE;
RMAN> ALTER DATABASE OPEN;
```

```
RMAN> SHUTDOWN IMMEDIATE ;

database closed
database dismounted
Oracle instance shut down

RMAN> STARTUP MOUNT ;

connected to target database (not started)
Oracle instance started
database mounted

Total System Global Area     746586112 bytes

Fixed Size                     8625176 bytes
Variable Size                587203560 bytes
Database Buffers              33554432 bytes
Redo Buffers                   8151040 bytes
In-Memory Area               109051904 bytes

RMAN> RESTORE DATABASE ;

Starting restore at 20-NOV-17
allocated channel: ORA_DISK_1
channel ORA_DISK_1: SID=89 device type=DISK

channel ORA_DISK_1: restoring datafile 00001
input datafile copy RECID=40 STAMP=960558765 file name=/oracle/oracle12/RMAN_BACKUP/ORACLE12_data_D-ORACLE12_I-2053
465567_TS-SYSTEM_FNO-1_1tsk1sf2_960557538_61
destination for restore of datafile 00001: /oracle/oracle12/oradata/oracle12/system01.dbf
```

```
output file name=/oracle/oracle12/oradata/oracle12/undotbs03.dbf RECID=0 STAMP=0
Finished restore at 20-NOV-17

RMAN> RECOVER DATABASE;

Starting recover at 20-NOV-17
using channel ORA_DISK_1
channel ORA_DISK_1: starting incremental datafile backup set restore
channel ORA_DISK_1: specifying datafile(s) to restore from backup set
destination for restore of datafile 00001: /oracle/oracle12/oradata/oracle12/system01.dbf
destination for restore of datafile 00002: /oracle/oracle12/oradata/oracle12/unione02.dbf
destination for restore of datafile 00003: /oracle/oracle12/oradata/oracle12/sysaux01.dbf
destination for restore of datafile 00004: /oracle/oracle12/oradata/oracle12/undotbs01.dbf
destination for restore of datafile 00005: /oracle/oracle12/oradata/oracle12/unione01.dbf
destination for restore of datafile 00007: /oracle/oracle12/oradata/oracle12/users01.dbf
destination for restore of datafile 00008: /oracle/oracle12/oradata/oracle12/unione03.dbf
destination for restore of datafile 00009: /oracle/oracle12/oradata/oracle12/unione04.dbf
destination for restore of datafile 00010: /oracle/oracle12/oradata/oracle12/undotbs02.dbf
destination for restore of datafile 00011: /oracle/oracle12/oradata/oracle12/undotbs03.dbf
channel ORA_DISK_1: reading from backup piece /oracle/oracle12/RMAN_BACKUP/ORACLE12_2ask1tpo_1_1_960558904_74
channel ORA_DISK_1: piece handle=/oracle/oracle12/RMAN_BACKUP/ORACLE12_2ask1tpo_1_1_960558904_74 tag=INCR_UPDATE
channel ORA_DISK_1: restored backup piece 1
channel ORA_DISK_1: restore complete, elapsed time: 00:00:15

starting media recovery
media recovery complete, elapsed time: 00:00:08

Finished recover at 20-NOV-17

RMAN> ALTER DATABASE OPEN ;

Statement processed

RMAN>
```

2. 테이블스페이스 단위의 RESTORE, RECOVER

특정 테이블스페이스만 RMAN으로 복구가 가능합니다.

```
RMAN> ALTER TABLESPACE <테이블스페이스명> OFFLINE ;
RMAN> RESTORE TABLESPACE <테이블스페이스명>  ;
RMAN> RECOVER TABLESPACE USERS, UNIONE ;
RMAN> ALTER TABLESPACE UNIONE ONLINE ;
```

```
RMAN> ALTER TABLESPACE USERS OFFLINE ;

Statement processed

RMAN> ALTER TABLESPACE UNIONE OFFLINE ;

Statement processed

RMAN> RESTORE TABLESPACE USERS, UNIONE;

Starting restore at 20-NOV-17
using channel ORA_DISK_1

channel ORA_DISK_1: restoring datafile 00007
input datafile copy RECID=36 STAMP=960558761 file name=/oracle/oracle12/RMAN_BACKUP/ORACLE12_data_D-ORACLE12_I-2053
465567_TS-USERS_FNO-7_23sk1sub_960558027_67
destination for restore of datafile 00007: /oracle/oracle12/oradata/oracle12/users01.dbf
channel ORA_DISK_1: copied datafile copy of datafile 00007
output file name=/oracle/oracle12/oradata/oracle12/users01.dbf RECID=0 STAMP=0
channel ORA_DISK_1: restoring datafile 00002
input datafile copy RECID=43 STAMP=960558863 file name=/oracle/oracle12/RMAN_BACKUP/ORACLE12_data_D-ORACLE12_I-2053
465567_TS-UNIONE_FNO-2_1usk1soa_960557834_62
destination for restore of datafile 00002: /oracle/oracle12/oradata/oracle12/unione02.dbf
channel ORA_DISK_1: copied datafile copy of datafile 00002
output file name=/oracle/oracle12/oradata/oracle12/unione02.dbf RECID=0 STAMP=0
channel ORA_DISK_1: restoring datafile 00005
input datafile copy RECID=38 STAMP=960558761 file name=/oracle/oracle12/RMAN_BACKUP/ORACLE12_data_D-ORACLE12_I-2053
465567_TS-UNIONE_FNO-5_24sk1suj_960558035_68
destination for restore of datafile 00005: /oracle/oracle12/oradata/oracle12/unione01.dbf
channel ORA_DISK_1: copied datafile copy of datafile 00005
output file name=/oracle/oracle12/oradata/oracle12/unione01.dbf RECID=0 STAMP=0
channel ORA_DISK_1: restoring datafile 00008
input datafile copy RECID=42 STAMP=960558859 file name=/oracle/oracle12/RMAN_BACKUP/ORACLE12_data_D-ORACLE12_I-2053
465567_TS-UNIONE_FNO-8_1vsk1spo_960557880_63
destination for restore of datafile 00008: /oracle/oracle12/oradata/oracle12/unione03.dbf
channel ORA_DISK_1: copied datafile copy of datafile 00008
output file name=/oracle/oracle12/oradata/oracle12/unione03.dbf RECID=0 STAMP=0
channel ORA_DISK_1: restoring datafile 00009
input datafile copy RECID=41 STAMP=960558838 file name=/oracle/oracle12/RMAN_BACKUP/ORACLE12_data_D-ORACLE12_I-2053
465567_TS-UNIONE_FNO-9_20sk1srh_960557937_64
destination for restore of datafile 00009: /oracle/oracle12/oradata/oracle12/unione04.dbf
channel ORA_DISK_1: copied datafile copy of datafile 00009
output file name=/oracle/oracle12/oradata/oracle12/unione04.dbf RECID=0 STAMP=0
Finished restore at 20-NOV-17
```

```
RMAN> RECOVER TABLESPACE USERS, UNIONE ;

Starting recover at 20-NOV-17
using channel ORA_DISK_1
channel ORA_DISK_1: starting incremental datafile backup set restore
channel ORA_DISK_1: specifying datafile(s) to restore from backup set
destination for restore of datafile 00007: /oracle/oracle12/oradata/oracle12/users01.dbf
destination for restore of datafile 00002: /oracle/oracle12/oradata/oracle12/unione02.dbf
destination for restore of datafile 00005: /oracle/oracle12/oradata/oracle12/unione01.dbf
destination for restore of datafile 00008: /oracle/oracle12/oradata/oracle12/unione03.dbf
destination for restore of datafile 00009: /oracle/oracle12/oradata/oracle12/unione04.dbf
channel ORA_DISK_1: reading from backup piece /oracle/oracle12/RMAN_BACKUP/ORACLE12_2ask1tpo_1_1_960558904_74
channel ORA_DISK_1: piece handle=/oracle/oracle12/RMAN_BACKUP/ORACLE12_2ask1tpo_1_1_960558904_74 tag=INCR_UPDATE
channel ORA_DISK_1: restored backup piece 1
channel ORA_DISK_1: restore complete, elapsed time: 00:00:15

starting media recovery
media recovery complete, elapsed time: 00:00:02

Finished recover at 20-NOV-17

RMAN> ALTER TABLESPACE USERS ONLINE ;

Statement processed

RMAN> ALTER TABLESPACE UNIONE ONLINE ;

Statement processed
```

테스트 환경인 Oracle 12c Release 2에서는 SQL*PLUS 명령어가 RMAN CLI 환경에서 수행이 가능합니다.

3. 데이터 파일 단위의 RECOVER

특정 파일이 손상되었을 때 해당 파일만 복구도 가능합니다.

이 테스트를 위해 특정 파일을 임의적으로 손상시킵니다.

```
[oracle12]yspark-linux:/home/oracle12> dd if=/dev/null of=/oracle/oracle12/oradata/oracle12/unione03.dbf bs=8k
0+0 records in
0+0 records out
0 bytes (0 B) copied, 8.0719e-05 s, 0.0 kB/s
[oracle12]yspark-linux:/home/oracle12> sqlplus "/as sysdba"

SQL*Plus: Release 12.2.0.1.0 Production on Mon Nov 20 15:02:01 2017

Copyright (c) 1982, 2016, Oracle.  All rights reserved.


Connected to:
Oracle Database 12c Enterprise Edition Release 12.2.0.1.0 - 64bit Production

SQL> ALTER TABLESPACE UNIONE OFFLINE ;
ALTER TABLESPACE UNIONE OFFLINE
*
ERROR at line 1:
ORA-01115: IO error reading block from file 8 (block # 1)
ORA-01110: data file 8: '/oracle/oracle12/oradata/oracle12/unione03.dbf'
ORA-27072: File I/O error
Additional information: 4
Additional information: 1


SQL> ▮
```

데이터 파일의 블록이 손상되었습니다. 이제 복구를 위해 데이터 파일을 OFFLINE으로 변경합니다.

```
SQL> alter tablespace UNIONE offline ;
alter tablespace UNIONE offline
*
ERROR at line 1:
ORA-01122: database file 8 failed verification check
ORA-01110: data file 8: '/oracle/oracle12/oradata/oracle12/unione03.dbf'
ORA-01210: data file header is media corrupt


SQL> alter tablespace UNIONE offline immediate ;

Tablespace altered.
```

OFFLINE이 안 될 때는 immediate 옵션을 사용하여 강제로 OFFLINE시킵니다.

해당 데이터 파일의 테이블스페이스가 OFFLINE이 되면 RESTORE/RECOVER로 DATAFILE을 복구합니다.

```
RMAN> recover datafile 9 ;

Starting recover at 20-NOV-17
using channel ORA_DISK_1

starting media recovery
media recovery complete, elapsed time: 00:00:00

Finished recover at 20-NOV-17

RMAN> ALTER TABLESPACE UNIONE ONLINE ;

Statement processed

RMAN> ▮
```

7 RMAN의 기본 수행 명령어

지금까지 백업 수행과 복구 수행 명령어에 대해서 테스트 해보았습니다. 이제 백업/복구에 관련된 RMAN의 기본 수행/확인 명령어에 대해서 테스트 해보겠습니다.

1. RUN 명령어

여러 개의 RMAN 명령어를 함께 실행할 때 사용하는 명령어입니다.

초기 설정을 기록(ALLOCATE CHANNEL, RELEASE CHANNEL)하고 SET 명령(SET NEWNAME)과의 연계가 가능합니다.

```
run{
alter tablespace USERS offline;
restore tablespace USERS;
recover tablespace USERS;
alter tablespace USERS online;
}
```

```
RMAN> run{
2> alter tablespace USERS offline;
3> restore tablespace USERS;
4> recover tablespace USERS;
5> alter tablespace USERS online;
6> }

Statement processed

Starting restore at 20-NOV-17
using channel ORA_DISK_1

channel ORA_DISK_1: restoring datafile 00007
input datafile copy RECID=36 STAMP=960558761 file name=/oracle/oracle12/RMAN_BACKUP/ORACLE12_data_D-ORACLE12_I-2053465
567_TS-USERS_FNO-7_23sk1sub_960558027_67
destination for restore of datafile 00007: /oracle/oracle12/oradata/oracle12/users01.dbf
channel ORA_DISK_1: copied datafile copy of datafile 00007
output file name=/oracle/oracle12/oradata/oracle12/users01.dbf RECID=0 STAMP=0
Finished restore at 20-NOV-17

Starting recover at 20-NOV-17
using channel ORA_DISK_1
channel ORA_DISK_1: starting incremental datafile backup set restore
channel ORA_DISK_1: specifying datafile(s) to restore from backup set
destination for restore of datafile 00007: /oracle/oracle12/oradata/oracle12/users01.dbf
channel ORA_DISK_1: reading from backup piece /oracle/oracle12/RMAN_BACKUP/ORACLE12_2ask1tpo_1_1_960558904_74
channel ORA_DISK_1: piece handle=/oracle/oracle12/RMAN_BACKUP/ORACLE12_2ask1tpo_1_1_960558904_74 tag=INCR_UPDATE
channel ORA_DISK_1: restored backup piece 1
channel ORA_DISK_1: restore complete, elapsed time: 00:00:01

starting media recovery

archived log for thread 1 with sequence 467 is already on disk as file /oracle/oracle12/FRA/ORACLE12/archivelog/2017_1
1_20/o1_mf_1_467_f14r1j0d_.arc
archived log for thread 1 with sequence 468 is already on disk as file /oracle/oracle12/FRA/ORACLE12/archivelog/2017_1
1_20/o1_mf_1_468_f14r3oc3_.arc
archived log for thread 1 with sequence 469 is already on disk as file /oracle/oracle12/FRA/ORACLE12/archivelog/2017_1
1_20/o1_mf_1_469_f14x87r0_.arc
archived log file name=/oracle/oracle12/FRA/ORACLE12/archivelog/2017_11_20/o1_mf_1_467_f14r1j0d_.arc thread=1 sequence
=467
media recovery complete, elapsed time: 00:00:01
Finished recover at 20-NOV-17

Statement processed

RMAN>
```

백업/복구 시 디스크 채널을 추가 할당하여 빠른 수행도 가능합니다.

```
run {
allocate channel c1 device type disk;
allocate channel c2 device type disk;
allocate channel c3 device type disk;
alter tablespace UNIONE offline ;
restore tablespace UNIONE ;
recover tablespace UNIONE ;
alter tablespace UNIONE online ;
}
```

```
RMAN> run {
2> allocate channel c1 device type disk;
allocate channel c2 device type disk;
allocate channel c3 device type disk;
3> 4> 5> alter tablespace UNIONE offline ;
6> restore tablespace UNIONE ;
7> recover tablespace UNIONE ;
8> alter tablespace UNIONE online ;
9> }

released channel: ORA_DISK_1
allocated channel: c1
channel c1: SID=89 device type=DISK

allocated channel: c2
channel c2: SID=18 device type=DISK

allocated channel: c3
channel c3: SID=187 device type=DISK

Statement processed

Starting restore at 20-NOV-17

channel c1: restoring datafile 00002
input datafile copy RECID=43 STAMP=960558863 file name=/oracle/oracle12/RMAN_BACKUP/ORACLE12_data_D-ORACLE12_I-2053465
567_TS-UNIONE_FNO-2_1usk1soa_960557834_62
destination for restore of datafile 00002: /oracle/oracle12/oradata/oracle12/unione02.dbf
channel c2: restoring datafile 00005
input datafile copy RECID=38 STAMP=960558761 file name=/oracle/oracle12/RMAN_BACKUP/ORACLE12_data_D-ORACLE12_I-2053465
567_TS-UNIONE_FNO-5_24sk1suj_960558035_68
destination for restore of datafile 00005: /oracle/oracle12/oradata/oracle12/unione01.dbf
channel c3: restoring datafile 00008
input datafile copy RECID=42 STAMP=960558859 file name=/oracle/oracle12/RMAN_BACKUP/ORACLE12_data_D-ORACLE12_I-2053465
567_TS-UNIONE_FNO-8_1vsk1spo_960557880_63
destination for restore of datafile 00008: /oracle/oracle12/oradata/oracle12/unione03.dbf
channel c2: copied datafile copy of datafile 00005
output file name=/oracle/oracle12/oradata/oracle12/unione01.dbf RECID=0 STAMP=0
channel c2: restoring datafile 00009
input datafile copy RECID=41 STAMP=960558838 file name=/oracle/oracle12/RMAN_BACKUP/ORACLE12_data_D-ORACLE12_I-2053465
567_TS-UNIONE_FNO-9_20sk1srh_960557937_64
destination for restore of datafile 00009: /oracle/oracle12/oradata/oracle12/unione04.dbf
```

```
starting media recovery

archived log for thread 1 with sequence 467 is already on disk as file /oracle/oracle12/FRA/ORACLE12/archivelog/2017_1
1_20/o1_mf_1_467_f14r1j0d_.arc
archived log for thread 1 with sequence 468 is already on disk as file /oracle/oracle12/FRA/ORACLE12/archivelog/2017_1
1_20/o1_mf_1_468_f14r3oc3_.arc
archived log for thread 1 with sequence 469 is already on disk as file /oracle/oracle12/FRA/ORACLE12/archivelog/2017_1
1_20/o1_mf_1_469_f14x87r0_.arc
archived log file name=/oracle/oracle12/FRA/ORACLE12/archivelog/2017_11_20/o1_mf_1_467_f14r1j0d_.arc thread=1 sequence
=467
media recovery complete, elapsed time: 00:00:01
Finished recover at 20-NOV-17

Statement processed
released channel: c1
released channel: c2
released channel: c3

RMAN>
```

멀티채널 추가는 Standard Edition은 불가하고 Enterprise Edition만 가능합니다.

2. SWITCH 명령어

사용 가능한 이미지 복사를 수행한 백업 파일로 DATAFILE을 전환해서 복구를 수행하게 해주는 명령어입니다. RESTORE 명령어 수행 시간이 절감되어 빠른 복구가 가능합니다.

먼저 데이터 파일 위치를 확인합니다.

```
SQL> select name from v$datafile ;

NAME
--------------------------------------------------------------------------------
/oracle/oracle12/oradata/oracle12/system01.dbf
/oracle/oracle12/oradata/oracle12/unione02.dbf
/oracle/oracle12/oradata/oracle12/sysaux01.dbf
/oracle/oracle12/oradata/oracle12/undotbs01.dbf
/oracle/oracle12/oradata/oracle12/unione01.dbf
/oracle/oracle12/oradata/oracle12/users01.dbf
/oracle/oracle12/oradata/oracle12/unione03.dbf
/oracle/oracle12/oradata/oracle12/unione04.dbf
/oracle/oracle12/oradata/oracle12/undotbs02.dbf
/oracle/oracle12/oradata/oracle12/undotbs03.dbf

10 rows selected.

SQL> █
```

이제 SWTICH 명령어로 복원 및 RECOVER 명령어로 DATABASE 복구를 수행합니다.

```
STARTUP MOUNT;
SWITCH DATABASE TO COPY;
RECOVER DATABASE;
ALTER DATABASE OPEN;
```

```
RMAN> STARTUP MOUNT;

connected to target database (not started)
Oracle instance started
database mounted

Total System Global Area     746586112 bytes

Fixed Size                     8625176 bytes
Variable Size                587203560 bytes
Database Buffers              33554432 bytes
Redo Buffers                   8151040 bytes
In-Memory Area               109051904 bytes

RMAN> SWITCH DATABASE TO COPY;

datafile 1 switched to datafile copy "/oracle/oracle12/RMAN_BACKUP/ORACLE12_data_D-ORACLE12_I-2053465567_TS-SYSTEM_FNO
-1_1tsk1sf2_960557538_61"
datafile 2 switched to datafile copy "/oracle/oracle12/RMAN_BACKUP/ORACLE12_data_D-ORACLE12_I-2053465567_TS-UNIONE_FNO
-2_1usk1soa_960557834_62"
datafile 3 switched to datafile copy "/oracle/oracle12/RMAN_BACKUP/ORACLE12_data_D-ORACLE12_I-2053465567_TS-SYSAUX_FNO
-3_1rsk1qr0_960555872_59"
datafile 4 switched to datafile copy "/oracle/oracle12/RMAN_BACKUP/ORACLE12_data_D-ORACLE12_I-2053465567_TS-UNDOTBS1_F
NO-4_1ssk1rle_960556718_60"
datafile 5 switched to datafile copy "/oracle/oracle12/RMAN_BACKUP/ORACLE12_data_D-ORACLE12_I-2053465567_TS-UNIONE_FNO
-5_24sk1suj_960558035_68"
datafile 7 switched to datafile copy "/oracle/oracle12/RMAN_BACKUP/ORACLE12_data_D-ORACLE12_I-2053465567_TS-USERS_FNO-
7_23sk1sub_960558027_67"
datafile 8 switched to datafile copy "/oracle/oracle12/RMAN_BACKUP/ORACLE12_data_D-ORACLE12_I-2053465567_TS-UNIONE_FNO
-8_1vsk1spo_960557880_63"
datafile 9 switched to datafile copy "/oracle/oracle12/RMAN_BACKUP/ORACLE12_data_D-ORACLE12_I-2053465567_TS-UNIONE_FNO
-9_20sk1srh_960557937_64"
datafile 10 switched to datafile copy "/oracle/oracle12/RMAN_BACKUP/ORACLE12_data_D-ORACLE12_I-2053465567_TS-UNDOTBS1_
FNO-10_21sk1sta_960557994_65"
datafile 11 switched to datafile copy "/oracle/oracle12/RMAN_BACKUP/ORACLE12_data_D-ORACLE12_I-2053465567_TS-UNDOTBS1_
FNO-11_22sk1str_960558011_66"
```

```
RMAN> RECOVER DATABASE;

Starting recover at 20-NOV-17
allocated channel: ORA_DISK_1
channel ORA_DISK_1: SID=89 device type=DISK
channel ORA_DISK_1: starting incremental datafile backup set restore
channel ORA_DISK_1: specifying datafile(s) to restore from backup set
destination for restore of datafile 00001: /oracle/oracle12/RMAN_BACKUP/ORACLE12_data_D-ORACLE12_I-2053465567_TS-SYSTE
M_FNO-1_1tsk1sf2_960557538_61
destination for restore of datafile 00002: /oracle/oracle12/RMAN_BACKUP/ORACLE12_data_D-ORACLE12_I-2053465567_TS-UNION
E_FNO-2_1usk1soa_960557834_62
destination for restore of datafile 00003: /oracle/oracle12/RMAN_BACKUP/ORACLE12_data_D-ORACLE12_I-2053465567_TS-SYSAU
X_FNO-3_1rsk1qr0_960555872_59
destination for restore of datafile 00004: /oracle/oracle12/RMAN_BACKUP/ORACLE12_data_D-ORACLE12_I-2053465567_TS-UNDOT
BS1_FNO-4_1ssk1rle_960556718_60
destination for restore of datafile 00005: /oracle/oracle12/RMAN_BACKUP/ORACLE12_data_D-ORACLE12_I-2053465567_TS-UNION
E_FNO-5_24sk1suj_960558035_68
destination for restore of datafile 00007: /oracle/oracle12/RMAN_BACKUP/ORACLE12_data_D-ORACLE12_I-2053465567_TS-USERS
_FNO-7_23sk1sub_960558027_67
destination for restore of datafile 00008: /oracle/oracle12/RMAN_BACKUP/ORACLE12_data_D-ORACLE12_I-2053465567_TS-UNION
E_FNO-8_1vsk1spo_960557880_63
destination for restore of datafile 00009: /oracle/oracle12/RMAN_BACKUP/ORACLE12_data_D-ORACLE12_I-2053465567_TS-UNION
E_FNO-9_20sk1srh_960557937_64
destination for restore of datafile 00010: /oracle/oracle12/RMAN_BACKUP/ORACLE12_data_D-ORACLE12_I-2053465567_TS-UNDOT
BS1_FNO-10_21sk1sta_960557994_65
destination for restore of datafile 00011: /oracle/oracle12/RMAN_BACKUP/ORACLE12_data_D-ORACLE12_I-2053465567_TS-UNDOT
BS1_FNO-11_22sk1str_960558011_66
channel ORA_DISK_1: reading from backup piece /oracle/oracle12/RMAN_BACKUP/ORACLE12_2ask1tpo_1_1_960558904_74
channel ORA_DISK_1: piece handle=/oracle/oracle12/RMAN_BACKUP/ORACLE12_2ask1tpo_1_1_960558904_74 tag=INCR_UPDATE
channel ORA_DISK_1: restored backup piece 1
channel ORA_DISK_1: restore complete, elapsed time: 00:00:15

starting media recovery

archived log for thread 1 with sequence 467 is already on disk as file /oracle/oracle12/FRA/ORACLE12/archivelog/2017_11_
_467_f14r1j0d_.arc
archived log for thread 1 with sequence 468 is already on disk as file /oracle/oracle12/FRA/ORACLE12/archivelog/2017_11_
_468_f14r3oc3_.arc
archived log for thread 1 with sequence 469 is already on disk as file /oracle/oracle12/FRA/ORACLE12/archivelog/2017_11_
_469_f14x87r0_.arc
archived log file name=/oracle/oracle12/FRA/ORACLE12/archivelog/2017_11_20/o1_mf_1_467_f14r1j0d_.arc thread=1 sequence=
media recovery complete, elapsed time: 00:00:27
Finished recover at 20-NOV-17

RMAN> ALTER DATABASE OPEN;

Statement processed
```

복구 후에 FILE 위치를 확인해 봅니다.

```
SQL> select name from v$datafile ;

NAME
--------------------------------------------------------------------------------------------------------------
/oracle/oracle12/RMAN_BACKUP/ORACLE12_data_D-ORACLE12_I-2053465567_TS-SYSTEM_FNO-1_1tsk1sf2_960557538_61
/oracle/oracle12/RMAN_BACKUP/ORACLE12_data_D-ORACLE12_I-2053465567_TS-UNIONE_FNO-2_1usk1soa_960557834_62
/oracle/oracle12/RMAN_BACKUP/ORACLE12_data_D-ORACLE12_I-2053465567_TS-SYSAUX_FNO-3_1rsk1qr0_960555872_59
/oracle/oracle12/RMAN_BACKUP/ORACLE12_data_D-ORACLE12_I-2053465567_TS-UNDOTBS1_FNO-4_1ssk1rle_960556718_60
/oracle/oracle12/RMAN_BACKUP/ORACLE12_data_D-ORACLE12_I-2053465567_TS-UNIONE_FNO-5_24sk1suj_960558035_68
/oracle/oracle12/RMAN_BACKUP/ORACLE12_data_D-ORACLE12_I-2053465567_TS-USERS_FNO-7_23sk1sub_960558027_67
/oracle/oracle12/RMAN_BACKUP/ORACLE12_data_D-ORACLE12_I-2053465567_TS-UNIONE_FNO-8_1vsk1spo_960557880_63
/oracle/oracle12/RMAN_BACKUP/ORACLE12_data_D-ORACLE12_I-2053465567_TS-UNIONE_FNO-9_20sk1srh_960557937_64
/oracle/oracle12/RMAN_BACKUP/ORACLE12_data_D-ORACLE12_I-2053465567_TS-UNDOTBS1_FNO-10_21sk1sta_960557994_65
/oracle/oracle12/RMAN_BACKUP/ORACLE12_data_D-ORACLE12_I-2053465567_TS-UNDOTBS1_FNO-11_22sk1str_960558011_66

10 rows selected.

SQL> █
```

데이터 파일의 위치가 RMAN 백업을 이미지 카피(image copy)한 백업 파일로 변경되었습니다.

다시 원복하려면 DB를 내렸다가 MOUNT한 상태에서 SWITCH 명령어를 수행시키면 본래의 데이터 파일로 DB를 복구시킬 수 있습니다.

```
RMAN> SWITCH DATABASE TO COPY;

datafile 1 switched to datafile copy "/oracle/oracle12/oradata/oracle12/system01.dbf"
datafile 2 switched to datafile copy "/oracle/oracle12/oradata/oracle12/unione02.dbf"
datafile 3 switched to datafile copy "/oracle/oracle12/oradata/oracle12/sysaux01.dbf"
datafile 4 switched to datafile copy "/oracle/oracle12/oradata/oracle12/undotbs01.dbf"
datafile 5 switched to datafile copy "/oracle/oracle12/oradata/oracle12/unione01.dbf"
datafile 7 switched to datafile copy "/oracle/oracle12/oradata/oracle12/users01.dbf"
datafile 8 switched to datafile copy "/oracle/oracle12/oradata/oracle12/unione03.dbf"
datafile 9 switched to datafile copy "/oracle/oracle12/oradata/oracle12/unione04.dbf"
datafile 10 switched to datafile copy "/oracle/oracle12/oradata/oracle12/undotbs02.dbf"
datafile 11 switched to datafile copy "/oracle/oracle12/oradata/oracle12/undotbs03.dbf"

RMAN> RECOVER DATABASE;

Starting recover at 20-NOV-17
using channel ORA_DISK_1

starting media recovery
media recovery complete, elapsed time: 00:00:06

Finished recover at 20-NOV-17

RMAN> ALTER DATABASE OPEN;

Statement processed

RMAN> █
```

이번에는 특정 데이터 파일만 이미지 카피(Image Copy)해서 백업 받은 백업 파일로 전환해서 복구해 보겠습니다.

```
RMAN> ALTER DATABASE DATAFILE <파일번호> OFFLINE ;
RMAN> SWITCH DATAFILE <파일번호> TO COPY ;
RMAN> RECOVER DATAFILE <파일번호> ;
RMAN> ALTER DATABASE DATAFILE <파일번호> ONLINE ;
```

```
RMAN> ALTER DATABASE DATAFILE 8 OFFLINE ;

Statement processed

RMAN> SWITCH DATAFILE 8 TO COPY ;

datafile 8 switched to datafile copy "/oracle/oracle12/RMAN_BACKUP/ORACLE12_data_D-ORACLE12_I-2053465567_TS-UNIONE_FNO-
8_1vsk1spo_960557880_63"

RMAN> RECOVER DATAFILE 8 ;

Starting recover at 20-NOV-17
using channel ORA_DISK_1

starting media recovery
media recovery complete, elapsed time: 00:00:00

Finished recover at 20-NOV-17

RMAN> ALTER DATABASE DATAFILE 8 ONLINE ;

Statement processed

RMAN> █
```

데이터베이스가 커서 백업 데이터를 다시 원복하는 시간이 오래 걸리는 경우 빠른 복구를 위해 SWITCH 명령어를 이용하는 경우 이미지 카피 백업으로 수행해야 합니다.

이번에는 RMAN의 RUN 명령어와 SET 명령어를 이용하여 기존 데이터 파일을 새로운 위치에 데이터 파일을 마이그레이션하는 테스트를 해보겠습니다.

```
RMAN> RUN
{
  ALTER TABLESPACE <테이블스페이스명> OFFLINE IMMEDIATE ;
  SET NEWNAME FOR DATAFILE '<원래데이터 파일 경로>' TO '<신규데이터 파일 경로>' ;
  RESTORE TABLESPACE <테이블스페이스명>;
  SWITCH DATAFILE ALL;
  RECOVER TABLESPACE <테이블스페이스명>;
  ALTER TABLESPACE <테이블스페이스명> ONLINE ;
}
```

```
RMAN> RUN
2> {
3>    ALTER TABLESPACE UNIONE OFFLINE IMMEDIATE ;
4>    SET NEWNAME FOR DATAFILE
5>      '/oracle/oracle12/oradata/oracle12/unione01.dbf' TO '/oracle/oracle12/oradata/oracle12/UNIONE/unione01.dbf' ;
  SET NEWNAME FOR DATAFILE
6> 7>      '/oracle/oracle12/oradata/oracle12/unione02.dbf' TO '/oracle/oracle12/oradata/oracle12/UNIONE/unione02.dbf' ;
8>    SET NEWNAME FOR DATAFILE
9>      '/oracle/oracle12/oradata/oracle12/unione03.dbf' TO '/oracle/oracle12/oradata/oracle12/UNIONE/unione03.dbf' ;
10>    SET NEWNAME FOR DATAFILE
11>      '/oracle/oracle12/oradata/oracle12/unione04.dbf' TO '/oracle/oracle12/oradata/oracle12/UNIONE/unione04.dbf' ;
12>    RESTORE TABLESPACE UNIONE;
13>    SWITCH DATAFILE ALL;
14>    RECOVER TABLESPACE UNIONE;
15>    ALTER TABLESPACE UNIONE ONLINE ;
16> }

Statement processed

executing command: SET NEWNAME

executing command: SET NEWNAME

executing command: SET NEWNAME

executing command: SET NEWNAME

Starting restore at 20-NOV-17
using channel ORA_DISK_1

channel ORA_DISK_1: restoring datafile 00002
input datafile copy RECID=89 STAMP=960571414 file name=/oracle/oracle12/RMAN_BACKUP/ORACLE12_data_D-ORACLE12_I-20534655
67_TS-UNIONE_FNO-2_1usk1soa_960557834_62
destination for restore of datafile 00002: /oracle/oracle12/oradata/oracle12/UNIONE/unione02.dbf
channel ORA_DISK_1: copied datafile copy of datafile 00002
```

```
Finished restore at 20-NOV-17

datafile 2 switched to datafile copy
input datafile copy RECID=104 STAMP=960572830 file name=/oracle/oracle12/oradata/oracle12/UNIONE/unione02.dbf
datafile 5 switched to datafile copy
input datafile copy RECID=105 STAMP=960572830 file name=/oracle/oracle12/oradata/oracle12/UNIONE/unione01.dbf
datafile 8 switched to datafile copy
input datafile copy RECID=106 STAMP=960572830 file name=/oracle/oracle12/oradata/oracle12/UNIONE/unione03.dbf
datafile 9 switched to datafile copy
input datafile copy RECID=107 STAMP=960572830 file name=/oracle/oracle12/oradata/oracle12/UNIONE/unione04.dbf

Starting recover at 20-NOV-17
using channel ORA_DISK_1

starting media recovery
media recovery complete, elapsed time: 00:00:01

Finished recover at 20-NOV-17

Statement processed

RMAN>
```

SQL 문장인 ALTER DATABASE RENAME FILE과 OS COPY 명령어를 사용하는 것과 같으며 채널을 추가 할당하면 채널 마다 복구 및 복원 속도를 빠르게 하여 이관이 가능합니다. RMAN의 고급 사용 방법 편에서 자세히 테스트 해보겠습니다.

3. LIST 명령어

LIST 명령어는 수행한 백업 정보를 표시해 주는 명령어입니다.

백업 세트(Backup Sets) 방식으로 백업을 수행한 결과 확인 명령어입니다.

```
RMAN> LIST BACKUP ;
```

```
RMAN> LIST BACKUP ;


List of Backup Sets
===================


BS Key  Type LV Size       Device Type Elapsed Time Completion Time
------- ---- -- ---------- ----------- ------------ ---------------
1       Full    10.19M     DISK        00:00:02     10-OCT-17
        BP Key: 1   Status: AVAILABLE  Compressed: NO  Tag: TAG20171010T163803
        Piece Name: /oracle/oracle12/app/oracle/product/12.2.0/dbhome_1/dbs/c-2053465567-20171010-00
  SPFILE Included: Modification time: 27-SEP-17
  SPFILE db_unique_name: ORACLE12
  Control File Included: Ckp SCN: 1432712265   Ckp time: 10-OCT-17

BS Key  Type LV Size       Device Type Elapsed Time Completion Time
------- ---- -- ---------- ----------- ------------ ---------------
2       Full    10.28M     DISK        00:00:03     22-OCT-17
        BP Key: 2   Status: AVAILABLE  Compressed: NO  Tag: TAG20171022T145202
        Piece Name: /oracle/oracle12/app/oracle/product/12.2.0/dbhome_1/dbs/c-2053465567-20171022-00
  SPFILE Included: Modification time: 10-OCT-17
  SPFILE db_unique_name: ORACLE12
  Control File Included: Ckp SCN: 1433852528   Ckp time: 22-OCT-17

BS Key  Type LV Size       Device Type Elapsed Time Completion Time
------- ---- -- ---------- ----------- ------------ ---------------
3       Full    10.28M     DISK        00:00:03     22-OCT-17
        BP Key: 3   Status: AVAILABLE  Compressed: NO  Tag: TAG20171022T150708
        Piece Name: /oracle/oracle12/app/oracle/product/12.2.0/dbhome_1/dbs/c-2053465567-20171022-01
  SPFILE Included: Modification time: 10-OCT-17
  SPFILE db_unique_name: ORACLE12
  Control File Included: Ckp SCN: 1433862390   Ckp time: 22-OCT-17

BS Key  Size       Device Type Elapsed Time Completion Time
------- ---------- ----------- ------------ ---------------
4       7.18G      DISK        00:03:14     14-NOV-17
        BP Key: 4   Status: AVAILABLE  Compressed: NO  Tag: TAG20171114T184409
        Piece Name: /oracle/oracle12/RMAN_BACKUP/ORACLE12_04sjikfq_1_1_960057850_4
```

이미지 카피(Image Copy) 방식으로 백업을 수행한 결과 확인 명령어입니다.

```
RMAN> LIST COPY ;
```

```
RMAN> LIST COPY ;

specification does not match any control file copy in the repository
List of Datafile Copies
=======================

Key     File S Completion Time Ckp SCN    Ckp Time        Sparse
------- ---- - --------------- ---------- --------------- ------
88      1    A 20-NOV-17       1436695047 20-NOV-17       NO
        Name: /oracle/oracle12/RMAN_BACKUP/ORACLE12_data_D-ORACLE12_I-2053465567_TS-SYSTEM_FNO-1_1tsk1sf2_960557538_61

16      1    A 20-NOV-17       1436476276 20-NOV-17       NO
        Name: /oracle/oracle12/RMAN_BACKUP/ORACLE12_data_D-ORACLE12_I-2053465567_TS-SYSTEM_FNO-1_1dsk1ouc_960553932_45
        Tag: TAG20171120T120530

11      1    A 16-NOV-17       1436141059 16-NOV-17       NO
        Name: /oracle/oracle12/RMAN_BACKUP/ORACLE12_data_D-ORACLE12_I-2053465567_TS-SYSTEM_FNO-1_0osjnk57_960221351_24
        Tag: TAG20171116T160911

3       1    A 14-NOV-17       1435996034 14-NOV-17       NO
        Name: /oracle/oracle12/RMAN_BACKUP/ORACLE12_data_D-ORACLE12_I-2053465567_TS-SYSTEM_FNO-1_0fsjin0d_960060429_15
        Tag: TAG20171114T190137

108     2    A 20-NOV-17       1436696331 20-NOV-17       NO
        Name: /oracle/oracle12/oradata/oracle12/unione02.dbf

89      2    A 20-NOV-17       1436695047 20-NOV-17       NO
        Name: /oracle/oracle12/RMAN_BACKUP/ORACLE12_data_D-ORACLE12_I-2053465567_TS-UNIONE_FNO-2_1usk1soa_960557834_62

17      2    A 20-NOV-17       1436476699 20-NOV-17       NO
```

너무 많은 정보를 보여 주면 SUMMARY 옵션을 주어 요약한 결과를 확인합니다.

```
RMAN> LIST BACKUP SUMMARY ;
```

```
RMAN> LIST BACKUP SUMMARY;


List of Backups
===============
Key     TY LV S Device Type Completion Time #Pieces #Copies Compressed Tag
------- -- -- - ----------- --------------- ------- ------- ---------- ---
1       B  F  A DISK        10-OCT-17       1       1       NO         TAG20171010T163803
2       B  F  A DISK        22-OCT-17       1       1       NO         TAG20171022T145202
3       B  F  A DISK        22-OCT-17       1       1       NO         TAG20171022T150708
4       B  A  A DISK        14-NOV-17       1       1       NO         TAG20171114T184409
5       B  A  A DISK        14-NOV-17       1       1       NO         TAG20171114T184409
6       B  F  A DISK        14-NOV-17       1       1       NO         TAG20171114T185043
7       B  A  A DISK        14-NOV-17       1       1       NO         TAG20171114T185301
8       B  F  A DISK        14-NOV-17       1       1       NO         TAG20171114T185302
9       B  F  A DISK        14-NOV-17       1       1       NO         TAG20171114T185557
10      B  F  A DISK        14-NOV-17       1       1       NO         TAG20171114T185601
11      B  F  A DISK        14-NOV-17       1       1       NO         TAG20171114T185856
12      B  F  A DISK        14-NOV-17       1       1       NO         TAG20171114T185932
13      B  F  A DISK        14-NOV-17       1       1       NO         TAG20171114T193314
14      B  F  A DISK        16-NOV-17       1       1       NO         TAG20171116T161354
15      B  F  A DISK        16-NOV-17       1       1       YES        TAG20171116T162144
16      B  F  A DISK        16-NOV-17       1       1       NO         TAG20171116T162429
17      B  A  A DISK        16-NOV-17       1       1       NO         TAG20171116T163907
18      B  F  A DISK        16-NOV-17       1       1       NO         TAG20171116T163922
19      B  F  A DISK        16-NOV-17       1       1       NO         TAG20171116T170322
20      B  A  A DISK        16-NOV-17       1       1       NO         TAG20171116T170816
21      B  0  A DISK        16-NOV-17       1       1       NO         TAG20171116T170818
22      B  A  A DISK        16-NOV-17       1       1       NO         TAG20171116T171035
23      B  F  A DISK        16-NOV-17       1       1       NO         TAG20171116T171036
24      B  A  A DISK        20-NOV-17       1       1       NO         TAG20171120T112116
25      B  1  A DISK        20-NOV-17       1       1       NO         TAG20171120T112143
26      B  A  A DISK        20-NOV-17       1       1       NO         TAG20171120T112352
27      B  F  A DISK        20-NOV-17       1       1       NO         TAG20171120T112354
28      B  1  A DISK        20-NOV-17       1       1       NO         TAG20171120T112850
29      B  F  A DISK        20-NOV-17       1       1       NO         TAG20171120T113056
30      B  F  A DISK        20-NOV-17       1       1       NO         TAG20171120T123825
31      B  A  A DISK        20-NOV-17       1       1       NO         TAG20171120T130052
32      B  1  A DISK        20-NOV-17       1       1       NO         TAG20171120T130053
33      B  A  A DISK        20-NOV-17       1       1       NO         TAG20171120T130310
34      B  F  A DISK        20-NOV-17       1       1       NO         TAG20171120T130311
35      B  A  A DISK        20-NOV-17       1       1       NO         INCR_UPDATE
36      B  A  A DISK        20-NOV-17       1       1       NO         INCR_UPDATE
37      B  F  A DISK        20-NOV-17       1       1       NO         TAG20171120T134202
38      B  1  A DISK        20-NOV-17       1       1       NO         TAG20171120T134337
39      B  F  A DISK        20-NOV-17       1       1       NO         TAG20171120T134425
40      B  A  A DISK        20-NOV-17       1       1       NO         INCR_UPDATE
41      B  1  A DISK        20-NOV-17       1       1       NO         INCR_UPDATE
42      B  A  A DISK        20-NOV-17       1       1       NO         INCR_UPDATE
43      B  F  A DISK        20-NOV-17       1       1       NO         TAG20171120T135513
44      B  F  A DISK        20-NOV-17       1       1       NO         TAG20171120T145126
45      B  F  A DISK        20-NOV-17       1       1       NO         TAG20171120T154242
46      B  F  A DISK        20-NOV-17       1       1       NO         TAG20171120T164325
47      B  F  A DISK        20-NOV-17       1       1       NO         TAG20171120T173543
48      B  F  A DISK        20-NOV-17       1       1       NO         TAG20171120T175618
49      B  A  A DISK        20-NOV-17       1       1       NO         TAG20171120T182205
50      B  F  A DISK        20-NOV-17       1       1       NO         TAG20171120T185251
```

아카이브 로그 파일의 백업 수행 결과 확인 명령어입니다.

```
RMAN> LIST ARCHIVELOG ALL ;
```

```
RMAN> LIST ARCHIVELOG ALL ;

List of Archived Log Copies for database with db_unique_name ORACLE12
=====================================================================

Key     Thrd Seq     S Low Time
------- ---- ------- - ---------
143     1    148     X 21-OCT-17
        Name: /oracle/oracle12/arch/1_148_952016687.dbf

144     1    149     X 21-OCT-17
        Name: /oracle/oracle12/arch/1_149_952016687.dbf

145     1    150     X 21-OCT-17
        Name: /oracle/oracle12/arch/1_150_952016687.dbf

146     1    151     X 22-OCT-17
        Name: /oracle/oracle12/arch/1_151_952016687.dbf

147     1    152     X 22-OCT-17
        Name: /oracle/oracle12/arch/1_152_952016687.dbf

148     1    153     X 22-OCT-17
        Name: /oracle/oracle12/arch/1_153_952016687.dbf

149     1    154     X 22-OCT-17
        Name: /oracle/oracle12/arch/1_154_952016687.dbf

150     1    155     X 22-OCT-17
        Name: /oracle/oracle12/arch/1_155_952016687.dbf
```

기간을 주어 특정 기간 아카이브 로그 백업 정보를 확인합니다.

```
RMAN> LIST ARCHIVELOG UNTIL TIME 'SYSDATE-7';
```

```
RMAN> LIST ARCHIVELOG UNTIL TIME 'SYSDATE-7';

List of Archived Log Copies for database with db_unique_name ORACLE12
=====================================================================

Key     Thrd Seq     S Low Time
------- ---- ------- - ---------
143     1    148     X 21-OCT-17
        Name: /oracle/oracle12/arch/1_148_952016687.dbf

144     1    149     X 21-OCT-17
        Name: /oracle/oracle12/arch/1_149_952016687.dbf

145     1    150     X 21-OCT-17
        Name: /oracle/oracle12/arch/1_150_952016687.dbf

146     1    151     X 22-OCT-17
        Name: /oracle/oracle12/arch/1_151_952016687.dbf

147     1    152     X 22-OCT-17
        Name: /oracle/oracle12/arch/1_152_952016687.dbf

148     1    153     X 22-OCT-17
        Name: /oracle/oracle12/arch/1_153_952016687.dbf

149     1    154     X 22-OCT-17
        Name: /oracle/oracle12/arch/1_154_952016687.dbf

150     1    155     X 22-OCT-17
        Name: /oracle/oracle12/arch/1_155_952016687.dbf
```

컨트롤 파일의 백업 현황을 확인합니다.

```
RMAN> LIST BACKUP OF CONTROLFILE ;
```

```
RMAN> LIST BACKUP OF CONTROLFILE;


List of Backup Sets
===================


BS Key  Type LV Size       Device Type Elapsed Time Completion Time
------- ---- -- ---------- ----------- ------------ ---------------
1       Full    10.19M     DISK        00:00:02     10-OCT-17
        BP Key: 1   Status: AVAILABLE  Compressed: NO  Tag: TAG20171010T163803
        Piece Name: /oracle/oracle12/app/oracle/product/12.2.0/dbhome_1/dbs/c-2053465567-20171010-00
  Control File Included: Ckp SCN: 1432712265   Ckp time: 10-OCT-17

BS Key  Type LV Size       Device Type Elapsed Time Completion Time
------- ---- -- ---------- ----------- ------------ ---------------
2       Full    10.28M     DISK        00:00:03     22-OCT-17
        BP Key: 2   Status: AVAILABLE  Compressed: NO  Tag: TAG20171022T145202
        Piece Name: /oracle/oracle12/app/oracle/product/12.2.0/dbhome_1/dbs/c-2053465567-20171022-00
  Control File Included: Ckp SCN: 1433852528   Ckp time: 22-OCT-17

BS Key  Type LV Size       Device Type Elapsed Time Completion Time
------- ---- -- ---------- ----------- ------------ ---------------
3       Full    10.28M     DISK        00:00:03     22-OCT-17
        BP Key: 3   Status: AVAILABLE  Compressed: NO  Tag: TAG20171022T150708
        Piece Name: /oracle/oracle12/app/oracle/product/12.2.0/dbhome_1/dbs/c-2053465567-20171022-01
  Control File Included: Ckp SCN: 1433862390   Ckp time: 22-OCT-17

BS Key  Type LV Size       Device Type Elapsed Time Completion Time
------- ---- -- ---------- ----------- ------------ ---------------
8       Full    10.66M     DISK        00:00:02     14-NOV-17
        BP Key: 8   Status: AVAILABLE  Compressed: NO  Tag: TAG20171114T185302
        Piece Name: /oracle/oracle12/FRA/ORACLE12/autobackup/2017_11_14/o1_mf_s_960058382_f0oh80np_.bkp
  Control File Included: Ckp SCN: 1435993800   Ckp time: 14-NOV-17
```

오라클 DB의 파라미터 파일 백업 현황을 확인합니다.

```
RMAN> LIST BACKUP OF SPFILE ;
```

```
RMAN> LIST BACKUP OF SPFILE;


List of Backup Sets
===================


BS Key  Type LV Size       Device Type Elapsed Time Completion Time
------- ---- -- ---------- ----------- ------------ ---------------
1       Full    10.19M     DISK        00:00:02     10-OCT-17
        BP Key: 1   Status: AVAILABLE  Compressed: NO  Tag: TAG20171010T163803
        Piece Name: /oracle/oracle12/app/oracle/product/12.2.0/dbhome_1/dbs/c-2053465567-20171010-00
  SPFILE Included: Modification time: 27-SEP-17
  SPFILE db_unique_name: ORACLE12

BS Key  Type LV Size       Device Type Elapsed Time Completion Time
------- ---- -- ---------- ----------- ------------ ---------------
2       Full    10.28M     DISK        00:00:03     22-OCT-17
        BP Key: 2   Status: AVAILABLE  Compressed: NO  Tag: TAG20171022T145202
        Piece Name: /oracle/oracle12/app/oracle/product/12.2.0/dbhome_1/dbs/c-2053465567-20171022-00
  SPFILE Included: Modification time: 10-OCT-17
  SPFILE db_unique_name: ORACLE12

BS Key  Type LV Size       Device Type Elapsed Time Completion Time
------- ---- -- ---------- ----------- ------------ ---------------
3       Full    10.28M     DISK        00:00:03     22-OCT-17
        BP Key: 3   Status: AVAILABLE  Compressed: NO  Tag: TAG20171022T150708
        Piece Name: /oracle/oracle12/app/oracle/product/12.2.0/dbhome_1/dbs/c-2053465567-20171022-01
  SPFILE Included: Modification time: 10-OCT-17
  SPFILE db_unique_name: ORACLE12

BS Key  Type LV Size       Device Type Elapsed Time Completion Time
------- ---- -- ---------- ----------- ------------ ---------------
8       Full    10.66M     DISK        00:00:02     14-NOV-17
        BP Key: 8   Status: AVAILABLE  Compressed: NO  Tag: TAG20171114T185302
        Piece Name: /oracle/oracle12/FRA/ORACLE12/autobackup/2017_11_14/o1_mf_s_960058382_f0oh80np_.bkp
  SPFILE Included: Modification time: 14-NOV-17
  SPFILE db_unique_name: ORACLE12
```

Data Recovery Advisor 명령어(LIST/ADVISE/REPAIR)

RMAN은 데이터베이스 복구에 관련한 조언, 동일한 파일의 병렬 백업, 보안을 위한 가상 카탈로그와 같은 유용한 신기능을 제공합니다. LIST 명령어를 통해 확인하고 Data Recovery Advisor를 통해 복구 전략을 제시 받고 복구하는 방법을 확인하겠습니다.

먼저 에러 상황을 만듭니다. 특정 DATAFILE의 이름을 변경하고 SELECT 문으로 해당 데이터 파일의 테이블을 조회합니다.

```
[oracle12@yspark-linux UNIONE]$ mv unione03.dbf unione03.dbf.bak
[oracle12@yspark-linux UNIONE]$ ls
unione01.dbf  unione02.dbf  unione03.dbf  unione03.dbf.bak  unione04.dbf
[oracle12@yspark-linux UNIONE]$ █
```

```
ORA-01116: error in opening database file 8
ORA-01110: data file 8: '/oracle/oracle12/oradata/oracle12/UNIONE/unione03.dbf'
ORA-27041: unable to open file
Linux-x86_64 Error: 2: No such file or directory
Additional information: 3


6165 rows selected.

SQL> █
```

LIST 명령어를 통해 데이터 실패 에러를 확인합니다.

```
RMAN> LIST FAILURE ;
```

```
RMAN> LIST FAILURE ;

Database Role: PRIMARY

List of Database Failures
=========================

Failure ID Priority Status    Time Detected Summary
---------- -------- --------- ------------- -------
1662       HIGH     OPEN      20-NOV-17     One or more non-system datafiles are missing

RMAN>
```

자세하게 데이터 실패 에러 내용을 확인합니다.

```
RMAN> LIST FAILURE <실패 확인 ID> DETAIL ;
```

```
RMAN> LIST FAILURE 1662 DETAIL ;

Database Role: PRIMARY

List of Database Failures
=========================

Failure ID Priority Status    Time Detected Summary
---------- -------- --------- ------------- -------
1662       HIGH     OPEN      20-NOV-17     One or more non-system datafiles are missing
  Impact: See impact for individual child failures
  List of child failures for parent failure ID 1662
  Failure ID Priority Status    Time Detected Summary
  ---------- -------- --------- ------------- -------
  3225       HIGH     OPEN      20-NOV-17     Datafile 8: '/oracle/oracle12/oradata/oracle12/UNIONE/unione03.dbf' is missing
    Impact: Some objects in tablespace UNIONE might be unavailable

RMAN>
```

이제 LIST 명령어를 통해 에러 내용을 확인 후 ADVISE 명령을 통해 복구 전략을 도출합니다. Data Recovery Advisor는 에러의 상세한 설명과 그 해결 방법을 제시합니다.

```
RMAN> ADVISE FAILURE ;
```

```
RMAN> ADVISE FAILURE ;

Database Role: PRIMARY

List of Database Failures
=========================

Failure ID Priority Status    Time Detected Summary
---------- -------- --------- ------------- -------
1662       HIGH     OPEN      20-NOV-17     One or more non-system datafiles are missing
  Impact: See impact for individual child failures
  List of child failures for parent failure ID 1662
  Failure ID Priority Status    Time Detected Summary
  ---------- -------- --------- ------------- -------
  3225       HIGH     OPEN      20-NOV-17     Datafile 8: '/oracle/oracle12/oradata/oracle12/UNIONE/unione03.dbf' is missing
    Impact: Some objects in tablespace UNIONE might be unavailable

analyzing automatic repair options; this may take some time
allocated channel: ORA_DISK_1
channel ORA_DISK_1: SID=16 device type=DISK
analyzing automatic repair options complete

Mandatory Manual Actions
========================
no manual actions available

Optional Manual Actions
=======================
1. If file /oracle/oracle12/oradata/oracle12/UNIONE/unione03.dbf was unintentionally renamed or moved, restore it

Automated Repair Options
========================
Option Repair Description
------ ------------------
1      Restore and recover datafile 8
  Strategy: The repair includes complete media recovery with no data loss
  Repair script: /oracle/oracle12/app/oracle/diag/rdbms/oracle12/oracle12/hm/reco_1272191402.hm

RMAN>
```

어드바이저가 에러를 분석합니다. 이번 경우는 그 원인이 명백합니다. 데이터파일이 존재하지 않습니다. 다음으로, 어드바이저가 전략을 제시합니다. 위에서는 전략 또한 매우 간단합니다. 파일을 복구하고 복원하면 됩니다.

마지막 STEP으로 어드바이저가 제시한 복구 전략을 실행합니다. 제시된 복구 스크립트의 검증 후 YES를 입력합니다.

```
RMAN> REPAIR FAILURE ;
```

```
RMAN> REPAIR FAILURE ;

Strategy: The repair includes complete media recovery with no data loss
Repair script: /oracle/oracle12/app/oracle/diag/rdbms/oracle12/oracle12/hm/reco_1272191402.hm

contents of repair script:
   # restore and recover datafile
   sql 'alter database datafile 8 offline';
   restore ( datafile 8 );
   recover datafile 8;
   sql 'alter database datafile 8 online';

Do you really want to execute the above repair (enter YES or NO)? YES
executing repair script

sql statement: alter database datafile 8 offline

Starting restore at 20-NOV-17
using channel ORA_DISK_1

channel ORA_DISK_1: restoring datafile 00008
input datafile copy RECID=110 STAMP=960572831 file name=/oracle/oracle12/oradata/oracle12/unione03.dbf
destination for restore of datafile 00008: /oracle/oracle12/oradata/oracle12/UNIONE/unione03.dbf
channel ORA_DISK_1: copied datafile copy of datafile 00008
output file name=/oracle/oracle12/oradata/oracle12/UNIONE/unione03.dbf RECID=0 STAMP=0
Finished restore at 20-NOV-17

Starting recover at 20-NOV-17
using channel ORA_DISK_1

starting media recovery
media recovery complete, elapsed time: 00:00:02

Finished recover at 20-NOV-17

sql statement: alter database datafile 8 online
repair failure complete

RMAN> ▮
```

4. REPORT 명령어

백업에 필요한 타겟 데이터베이스의 정보를 분석하여 표시해주는 REPORT 명령어입니다.
타겟 데이터베이스의 데이터 파일과 테이블스페이스 이름을 확인합니다.

```
RMAN> REPORT SCHEMA ;
```

```
RMAN> REPORT SCHEMA ;

Report of database schema for database with db_unique_name ORACLE12

List of Permanent Datafiles
===========================
File Size(MB) Tablespace           RB segs Datafile Name
---- -------- -------------------- ------- ------------------------
1    10240    SYSTEM               YES     /oracle/oracle12/oradata/oracle12/system01.dbf
2    1370     UNIONE               NO      /oracle/oracle12/oradata/oracle12/UNIONE/unione02.dbf
3    30720    SYSAUX               NO      /oracle/oracle12/oradata/oracle12/sysaux01.dbf
4    30720    UNDOTBS1             YES     /oracle/oracle12/oradata/oracle12/undotbs01.dbf
5    10       UNIONE               NO      /oracle/oracle12/oradata/oracle12/UNIONE/unione01.dbf
7    70       USERS                NO      /oracle/oracle12/oradata/oracle12/users01.dbf
8    1337     UNIONE               NO      /oracle/oracle12/oradata/oracle12/UNIONE/unione03.dbf
9    1299     UNIONE               NO      /oracle/oracle12/oradata/oracle12/UNIONE/unione04.dbf
10   100      UNDOTBS1             YES     /oracle/oracle12/oradata/oracle12/undotbs02.dbf
11   100      UNDOTBS1             YES     /oracle/oracle12/oradata/oracle12/undotbs03.dbf

List of Temporary Files
=======================
File Size(MB) Tablespace           Maxsize(MB) Tempfile Name
---- -------- -------------------- ----------- --------------------
1    124      TEMP                 32767       /oracle/oracle12/oradata/oracle12/temp01.dbf
2    30720    TEMP                 30720       /oracle/oracle12/oradata/oracle12/temp02.dbf
3    30720    TEMP                 30720       /oracle/oracle12/oradata/oracle12/temp03.dbf
4    30720    TEMP                 30720       /oracle/oracle12/oradata/oracle12/temp04.dbf

RMAN> ▮
```

신규 데이터 파일이 추가되었거나, 백업 정책상 기간이 초과된 파일은 백업이 필요합니다. 백업이 필요한 데이터파일 확인합니다.

```
RMAN> REPORT NEED BACKUP ;
```

```
RMAN> REPORT NEED BACKUP ;

RMAN retention policy will be applied to the command
RMAN retention policy is set to redundancy 1
Report of files with less than 1 redundant backups
File #bkps Name
---- ----- -----------------------------------------------------
12   0     /oracle/oracle12/oradata/oracle12/oracle12_01.dbf

RMAN> █
```

백업 정책 기간/횟수/아카이브로그 등 백업 파일이 보존이 불필요한 내역을 확인합니다.

```
RMAN> REPORT OBSOLETE ;
```

```
RMAN> REPORT OBSOLETE ;

RMAN retention policy will be applied to the command
RMAN retention policy is set to redundancy 1
Report of obsolete backups and copies
Type                 Key    Completion Time    Filename/Handle
-------------------- ------ ------------------ --------------------
Archive Log          143    21-OCT-17          /oracle/oracle12/arch/1_148_952016687.dbf
Archive Log          144    21-OCT-17          /oracle/oracle12/arch/1_149_952016687.dbf
Archive Log          145    22-OCT-17          /oracle/oracle12/arch/1_150_952016687.dbf
Archive Log          146    22-OCT-17          /oracle/oracle12/arch/1_151_952016687.dbf
Archive Log          147    22-OCT-17          /oracle/oracle12/arch/1_152_952016687.dbf
Archive Log          148    22-OCT-17          /oracle/oracle12/arch/1_153_952016687.dbf
Archive Log          149    22-OCT-17          /oracle/oracle12/arch/1_154_952016687.dbf
Archive Log          150    22-OCT-17          /oracle/oracle12/arch/1_155_952016687.dbf
Archive Log          151    22-OCT-17          /oracle/oracle12/arch/1_156_952016687.dbf
Archive Log          152    22-OCT-17          /oracle/oracle12/arch/1_157_952016687.dbf
Archive Log          153    22-OCT-17          /oracle/oracle12/arch/1_158_952016687.dbf
Archive Log          154    22-OCT-17          /oracle/oracle12/arch/1_159_952016687.dbf
Archive Log          155    22-OCT-17          /oracle/oracle12/arch/1_160_952016687.dbf
Archive Log          156    22-OCT-17          /oracle/oracle12/arch/1_161_952016687.dbf
Archive Log          157    22-OCT-17          /oracle/oracle12/arch/1_162_952016687.dbf
Archive Log          158    22-OCT-17          /oracle/oracle12/arch/1_163_952016687.dbf
Archive Log          159    22-OCT-17          /oracle/oracle12/arch/1_164_952016687.dbf
Archive Log          160    22-OCT-17          /oracle/oracle12/arch/1_165_952016687.dbf
Archive Log          161    22-OCT-17          /oracle/oracle12/arch/1_166_952016687.dbf
Archive Log          162    22-OCT-17          /oracle/oracle12/arch/1_167_952016687.dbf
Archive Log          163    22-OCT-17          /oracle/oracle12/arch/1_168_952016687.dbf
Archive Log          164    22-OCT-17          /oracle/oracle12/arch/1_169_952016687.dbf
Archive Log          165    22-OCT-17          /oracle/oracle12/arch/1_170_952016687.dbf
Archive Log          166    22-OCT-17          /oracle/oracle12/arch/1_171_952016687.dbf
Archive Log          167    22-OCT-17          /oracle/oracle12/arch/1_172_952016687.dbf
Archive Log          168    22-OCT-17          /oracle/oracle12/arch/1_173_952016687.dbf
Archive Log          169    22-OCT-17          /oracle/oracle12/arch/1_174_952016687.dbf
Archive Log          170    22-OCT-17          /oracle/oracle12/arch/1_175_952016687.dbf
Archive Log          171    22-OCT-17          /oracle/oracle12/arch/1_176_952016687.dbf
Archive Log          172    22-OCT-17          /oracle/oracle12/arch/1_177_952016687.dbf
Archive Log          173    22-OCT-17          /oracle/oracle12/arch/1_178_952016687.dbf
Archive Log          174    22-OCT-17          /oracle/oracle12/arch/1_179_952016687.dbf
Archive Log          175    22-OCT-17          /oracle/oracle12/arch/1_180_952016687.dbf
Archive Log          176    22-OCT-17          /oracle/oracle12/arch/1_181_952016687.dbf
Archive Log          177    22-OCT-17          /oracle/oracle12/arch/1_182_952016687.dbf
Archive Log          178    22-OCT-17          /oracle/oracle12/arch/1_183_952016687.dbf
Archive Log          179    22-OCT-17          /oracle/oracle12/arch/1_184_952016687.dbf
Archive Log          180    22-OCT-17          /oracle/oracle12/arch/1_185_952016687.dbf
Archive Log          181    22-OCT-17          /oracle/oracle12/arch/1_186_952016687.dbf
```

5. VALIDATE 명령어

RMAN으로 백업 수행이 완료된 후에 백업된 데이터로 복원이 가능한지, 적합하게 정합성은 가지고 있는지 확인을 해야 합니다. 현재 VALIDATE 명령어로 수행이 완료된 백업의 정합성을 확인할 수 있습니다.VALIDATE 명령어를 이용하면 물리적으로 손상된 데이터베이스 블록을 쉽게 확인할 수 있습니다. 손상된 블록이 감지되는 경우, 그 정보는 Automatic Diagnostic Repository에 저장됩니다.

데이터베이스의 데이터 파일들 상태를 확인합니다.

```
RMAN> VALIDATE DATABASE ;
```

```
RMAN> validate database ;

Starting validate at 23-NOV-17
using channel ORA_DISK_1
channel ORA_DISK_1: starting validation of datafile
channel ORA_DISK_1: specifying datafile(s) for validation
input datafile file number=00003 name=/oracle/oracle12/oradata/oracle12/sysaux01.dbf
input datafile file number=00004 name=/oracle/oracle12/oradata/oracle12/undotbs01.dbf
input datafile file number=00001 name=/oracle/oracle12/oradata/oracle12/system01.dbf
input datafile file number=00002 name=/oracle/oracle12/oradata/oracle12/UNIONE/unione02.dbf
input datafile file number=00008 name=/oracle/oracle12/oradata/oracle12/UNIONE/unione03.dbf
input datafile file number=00009 name=/oracle/oracle12/oradata/oracle12/UNIONE/unione04.dbf
input datafile file number=00010 name=/oracle/oracle12/oradata/oracle12/undotbs02.dbf
input datafile file number=00011 name=/oracle/oracle12/oradata/oracle12/undotbs03.dbf
input datafile file number=00007 name=/oracle/oracle12/oradata/oracle12/users01.dbf
input datafile file number=00005 name=/oracle/oracle12/oradata/oracle12/UNIONE/unione01.dbf
input datafile file number=00012 name=/oracle/oracle12/oradata/oracle12/oracle12_01.dbf
channel ORA_DISK_1: validation complete, elapsed time: 00:21:20
List of Datafiles
=================
File Status Marked Corrupt Empty Blocks Blocks Examined High SCN
---- ------ -------------- ------------ --------------- ----------
1    OK     0              1219075      1310721         1437023560
  File Name: /oracle/oracle12/oradata/oracle12/system01.dbf
  Block Type Blocks Failing Blocks Processed
  ---------- -------------- ----------------
  Data       0              72197
  Index      0              14977
  Other      0              4471

File Status Marked Corrupt Empty Blocks Blocks Examined High SCN
---- ------ -------------- ------------ --------------- ----------
2    OK     0              7863         175400          1436483984
  File Name: /oracle/oracle12/oradata/oracle12/UNIONE/unione02.dbf
  Block Type Blocks Failing Blocks Processed
  ---------- -------------- ----------------
  Data       0              151303
  Index      0              15492
  Other      0              742
```

```
File Status Marked Corrupt Empty Blocks Blocks Examined High SCN
---- ------ -------------- ------------ --------------- ----------
12   OK     0              1153         1280            1436805296
  File Name: /oracle/oracle12/oradata/oracle12/oracle12_01.dbf
  Block Type Blocks Failing Blocks Processed
  ---------- -------------- ----------------
  Data       0              0
  Index      0              0
  Other      0              127

channel ORA_DISK_1: starting validation of datafile
channel ORA_DISK_1: specifying datafile(s) for validation
including current control file for validation
including current SPFILE in backup set
channel ORA_DISK_1: validation complete, elapsed time: 00:00:02
List of Control File and SPFILE
===============================
File Type    Status Blocks Failing Blocks Examined
------------ ------ -------------- ---------------
SPFILE       OK     0              2
Control File OK     0              680
Finished validate at 23-NOV-17

RMAN>
```

특정 테이블스페이스를 지정해서 검증 작업을 수행합니다.

```
RMAN> VALIDATE TABLESPACE UNIONE ;

Starting validate at 23-NOV-17
using channel ORA_DISK_1
channel ORA_DISK_1: starting validation of datafile
channel ORA_DISK_1: specifying datafile(s) for validation
input datafile file number=00002 name=/oracle/oracle12/oradata/oracle12/UNIONE/unione02.dbf
input datafile file number=00008 name=/oracle/oracle12/oradata/oracle12/UNIONE/unione03.dbf
input datafile file number=00009 name=/oracle/oracle12/oradata/oracle12/UNIONE/unione04.dbf
input datafile file number=00005 name=/oracle/oracle12/oradata/oracle12/UNIONE/unione01.dbf
channel ORA_DISK_1: validation complete, elapsed time: 00:01:47
List of Datafiles
=================
File Status Marked Corrupt Empty Blocks Blocks Examined High SCN
---- ------ -------------- ------------ --------------- ----------
2    OK     0              7863         175400          1436483984
  File Name: /oracle/oracle12/oradata/oracle12/UNIONE/unione02.dbf
  Block Type Blocks Failing Blocks Processed
  ---------- -------------- ----------------
  Data       0              151303
  Index      0              15492
  Other      0              742

File Status Marked Corrupt Empty Blocks Blocks Examined High SCN
---- ------ -------------- ------------ --------------- ----------
5    OK     0              1            1280            1698602
  File Name: /oracle/oracle12/oradata/oracle12/UNIONE/unione01.dbf
  Block Type Blocks Failing Blocks Processed
  ---------- -------------- ----------------
  Data       0              1126
  Index      0              0
  Other      0              153

File Status Marked Corrupt Empty Blocks Blocks Examined High SCN
---- ------ -------------- ------------ --------------- ----------
8    OK     0              6631         171144          1436483986
  File Name: /oracle/oracle12/oradata/oracle12/UNIONE/unione03.dbf
  Block Type Blocks Failing Blocks Processed
  ---------- -------------- ----------------
  Data       0              149209
  Index      0              14590
  Other      0              714

File Status Marked Corrupt Empty Blocks Blocks Examined High SCN
---- ------ -------------- ------------ --------------- ----------
9    OK     0              10273        166304          1436816379
  File Name: /oracle/oracle12/oradata/oracle12/UNIONE/unione04.dbf
  Block Type Blocks Failing Blocks Processed
  ---------- -------------- ----------------
  Data       0              140188
  Index      0              15130
  Other      0              713

Finished validate at 23-NOV-17
```

특정 데이터 파일을 지정해서 검증 작업을 합니다.

```
RMAN> VALIDATE DATAFILE <파일번호> ;
```

```
RMAN> VALIDATE DATAFILE 10 ;

Starting validate at 23-NOV-17
using channel ORA_DISK_1
channel ORA_DISK_1: starting validation of datafile
channel ORA_DISK_1: specifying datafile(s) for validation
input datafile file number=00010 name=/oracle/oracle12/oradata/oracle12/undotbs02.dbf
channel ORA_DISK_1: validation complete, elapsed time: 00:00:03
List of Datafiles
=================
File Status Marked Corrupt Empty Blocks Blocks Examined High SCN
---- ------ -------------- ------------ --------------- ----------
10   OK     0              1            12800           1437027178
  File Name: /oracle/oracle12/oradata/oracle12/undotbs02.dbf
  Block Type Blocks Failing Blocks Processed
  ---------- -------------- ----------------
  Data       0              0
  Index      0              0
  Other      0              12799

Finished validate at 23-NOV-17

RMAN> █
```

데이터베이스 전체를 기준으로 이미지 카피(Image Copy) 방식으로 백업된 데이터의 정합성을 확인합니다.

```
RMAN> VALIDATE COPY OF DATABASE;

Starting validate at 23-NOV-17
using target database control file instead of recovery catalog
allocated channel: ORA_DISK_1
channel ORA_DISK_1: SID=259 device type=DISK
channel ORA_DISK_1: starting validation of datafile
channel ORA_DISK_1: including datafile copy of datafile 00003 in backup set
input file name=/oracle/oracle12/RMAN_BACKUP/ORACLE12_data_D-ORACLE12_I-2053465567_TS-SYSAUX_FNO-3_2vsk2j9e_9605809
10_95
channel ORA_DISK_1: including datafile copy of datafile 00004 in backup set
input file name=/oracle/oracle12/RMAN_BACKUP/ORACLE12_data_D-ORACLE12_I-2053465567_TS-UNDOTBS1_FNO-4_30sk2k12_96058
1666_96
channel ORA_DISK_1: including datafile copy of datafile 00001 in backup set
input file name=/oracle/oracle12/RMAN_BACKUP/ORACLE12_data_D-ORACLE12_I-2053465567_TS-SYSTEM_FNO-1_31sk2kjm_9605822
62_97
channel ORA_DISK_1: including datafile copy of datafile 00002 in backup set
input file name=/oracle/oracle12/RMAN_BACKUP/ORACLE12_data_D-ORACLE12_I-2053465567_TS-UNIONE_FNO-2_32sk2krm_9605825
18_98
channel ORA_DISK_1: including datafile copy of datafile 00008 in backup set
input file name=/oracle/oracle12/RMAN_BACKUP/ORACLE12_data_D-ORACLE12_I-2053465567_TS-UNIONE_FNO-8_33sk2kt3_9605825
63_99
channel ORA_DISK_1: including datafile copy of datafile 00009 in backup set
input file name=/oracle/oracle12/RMAN_BACKUP/ORACLE12_data_D-ORACLE12_I-2053465567_TS-UNIONE_FNO-9_34sk2kug_9605826
08_100
channel ORA_DISK_1: including datafile copy of datafile 00010 in backup set
input file name=/oracle/oracle12/RMAN_BACKUP/ORACLE12_data_D-ORACLE12_I-2053465567_TS-UNDOTBS1_FNO-10_35sk2kvk_9605
82644_101
channel ORA_DISK_1: including datafile copy of datafile 00011 in backup set
input file name=/oracle/oracle12/RMAN_BACKUP/ORACLE12_data_D-ORACLE12_I-2053465567_TS-UNDOTBS1_FNO-11_36sk2kvn_9605
82647_102
channel ORA_DISK_1: including datafile copy of datafile 00007 in backup set
input file name=/oracle/oracle12/RMAN_BACKUP/ORACLE12_data_D-ORACLE12_I-2053465567_TS-USERS_FNO-7_37sk2kvq_96058265
0_103
channel ORA_DISK_1: including datafile copy of datafile 00005 in backup set
input file name=/oracle/oracle12/RMAN_BACKUP/ORACLE12_data_D-ORACLE12_I-2053465567_TS-UNIONE_FNO-5_38sk2kvt_9605826
53_104
channel ORA_DISK_1: including datafile copy of datafile 00012 in backup set
input file name=/oracle/oracle12/RMAN_BACKUP/ORACLE12_data_D-ORACLE12_I-2053465567_TS-ORACLE12_FNO-12_39sk2kvu_9605
82654_105
```

```
  File Name: /oracle/oracle12/RMAN_BACKUP/ORACLE12_data_D-ORACLE12_I-2053465567_TS-UNDOTBS1_FNO-10_35sk2kvk_96058264
4_101
  Block Type Blocks Failing Blocks Processed
  ---------- -------------- ----------------
  Data       0              0
  Index      0              0
  Other      0              12799

File Status Marked Corrupt Empty Blocks Blocks Examined High SCN
---- ------ -------------- ------------ --------------- ----------
11   OK     0              1            12800           1436809828
  File Name: /oracle/oracle12/RMAN_BACKUP/ORACLE12_data_D-ORACLE12_I-2053465567_TS-UNDOTBS1_FNO-11_36sk2kvn_96058264
7_102
  Block Type Blocks Failing Blocks Processed
  ---------- -------------- ----------------
  Data       0              0
  Index      0              0
  Other      0              12799

File Status Marked Corrupt Empty Blocks Blocks Examined High SCN
---- ------ -------------- ------------ --------------- ----------
12   OK     0              1153         1280            1436805296
  File Name: /oracle/oracle12/RMAN_BACKUP/ORACLE12_data_D-ORACLE12_I-2053465567_TS-ORACLE12_FNO-12_39sk2kvu_96058265
4_105
  Block Type Blocks Failing Blocks Processed
  ---------- -------------- ----------------
  Data       0              0
  Index      0              0
  Other      0              127

Finished validate at 23-NOV-17

RMAN>
```

데이터 파일의 특정 블록을 지정해서 블록 검증 작업을 합니다.

```
RMAN> VALIDATE DATAFILE <파일번호> BLOCK <블록번호> ;
```

```
RMAN> VALIDATE DATAFILE 4 BLOCK 56 ;

Starting validate at 23-NOV-17
using channel ORA_DISK_1
channel ORA_DISK_1: starting validation of datafile
channel ORA_DISK_1: specifying datafile(s) for validation
input datafile file number=00004 name=/oracle/oracle12/oradata/oracle12/undotbs01.dbf
channel ORA_DISK_1: validation complete, elapsed time: 00:00:01
List of Datafiles
=================
File Status Marked Corrupt Empty Blocks Blocks Examined High SCN
---- ------ -------------- ------------ --------------- ----------
4    OK     0              0            1               1406612
  File Name: /oracle/oracle12/oradata/oracle12/undotbs01.dbf
  Block Type Blocks Failing Blocks Processed
  ---------- -------------- ----------------
  Data       0              0
  Index      0              0
  Other      0              1

Finished validate at 23-NOV-17

RMAN>
```

백업 데이터로 복구가 가능한지 조회가 가능합니다. 실제로 복원은 수행되지 않습니다. 2일 전 상태로 복원이 가능한지 확인합니다.

```
RMAN> RESTORE DATABASE UNTIL TIME 'SYSDATE-2' VALIDATE HEADER ;
```

```
RMAN> RESTORE DATABASE UNTIL TIME 'SYSDATE-2' VALIDATE HEADER ;

Starting restore at 23-NOV-17
using channel ORA_DISK_1

List of Datafile Copies
=======================

Key     File S Completion Time Ckp SCN    Ckp Time        Sparse
------- ---- - --------------- ---------- --------------- ------
115     1    A 20-NOV-17       1436809615 20-NOV-17       NO
        Name: /oracle/oracle12/RMAN_BACKUP/ORACLE12_data_D-ORACLE12_I-2053465567_TS-SYSTEM_FNO-1_31sk2kjm_960582262_97
        Tag: INCR_UPDATE

116     2    A 20-NOV-17       1436809870 20-NOV-17       NO
        Name: /oracle/oracle12/RMAN_BACKUP/ORACLE12_data_D-ORACLE12_I-2053465567_TS-UNIONE_FNO-2_32sk2krm_960582518_98
        Tag: INCR_UPDATE

113     3    A 20-NOV-17       1436808536 20-NOV-17       NO
        Name: /oracle/oracle12/RMAN_BACKUP/ORACLE12_data_D-ORACLE12_I-2053465567_TS-SYSAUX_FNO-3_2vsk2j9e_960580910_95
        Tag: INCR_UPDATE

114     4    A 20-NOV-17       1436809341 20-NOV-17       NO
        Name: /oracle/oracle12/RMAN_BACKUP/ORACLE12_data_D-ORACLE12_I-2053465567_TS-UNDOTBS1_FNO-4_30sk2k12_960581666_96
        Tag: INCR_UPDATE

122     5    A 20-NOV-17       1436809936 20-NOV-17       NO
        Name: /oracle/oracle12/RMAN_BACKUP/ORACLE12_data_D-ORACLE12_I-2053465567_TS-UNIONE_FNO-5_38sk2kvt_960582653_104
        Tag: INCR_UPDATE

121     7    A 20-NOV-17       1436809932 20-NOV-17       NO
        Name: /oracle/oracle12/RMAN_BACKUP/ORACLE12_data_D-ORACLE12_I-2053465567_TS-USERS_FNO-7_37sk2kvq_960582650_103
        Tag: INCR_UPDATE

117     8    A 20-NOV-17       1436809887 20-NOV-17       NO
        Name: /oracle/oracle12/RMAN_BACKUP/ORACLE12_data_D-ORACLE12_I-2053465567_TS-UNIONE_FNO-8_33sk2kt3_960582563_99
        Tag: INCR_UPDATE

118     9    A 20-NOV-17       1436809907 20-NOV-17       NO
        Name: /oracle/oracle12/RMAN_BACKUP/ORACLE12_data_D-ORACLE12_I-2053465567_TS-UNIONE_FNO-9_34sk2kug_960582608_100
        Tag: INCR_UPDATE

119     10   A 20-NOV-17       1436809924 20-NOV-17       NO
        Name: /oracle/oracle12/RMAN_BACKUP/ORACLE12_data_D-ORACLE12_I-2053465567_TS-UNDOTBS1_FNO-10_35sk2kvk_960582644_101
        Tag: INCR_UPDATE

120     11   A 20-NOV-17       1436809928 20-NOV-17       NO
        Name: /oracle/oracle12/RMAN_BACKUP/ORACLE12_data_D-ORACLE12_I-2053465567_TS-UNDOTBS1_FNO-11_36sk2kvn_960582647_102
        Tag: INCR_UPDATE

123     12   A 20-NOV-17       1436809940 20-NOV-17       NO
        Name: /oracle/oracle12/RMAN_BACKUP/ORACLE12_data_D-ORACLE12_I-2053465567_TS-ORACLE12_FNO-12_39sk2kvu_960582654_105
        Tag: INCR_UPDATE

validation succeeded for datafile copy and control file copy
Finished restore at 23-NOV-17
```

6. CROSSCHECK 명령어

타겟 데이터베이스와 복구 카탈로그 간의 정보를 동기화 시켜주는 역할을 합니다. OS 명령어로 파일을 지우거나, 물리적인 정보가 수정되었을 때 복구 카탈로그 데이터를 업데이트 해줍니다.
전체 BACKUPSET 백업 파일과 타겟 데이터베이스 서버와 비교하겠습니다.

```
RMAN> CROSSCHECK BACKUPSET ;
```

```
RMAN> CROSSCHECK BACKUPSET ;

using channel ORA_DISK_1
crosschecked backup piece: found to be 'EXPIRED'
backup piece handle=/oracle/oracle12/app/oracle/product/12.2.0/dbhome_1/dbs/c-2053465567-20171010-00 RECID=1 STAMP=957026285
crosschecked backup piece: found to be 'AVAILABLE'
backup piece handle=/oracle/oracle12/app/oracle/product/12.2.0/dbhome_1/dbs/c-2053465567-20171022-00 RECID=2 STAMP=958056725
crosschecked backup piece: found to be 'AVAILABLE'
backup piece handle=/oracle/oracle12/app/oracle/product/12.2.0/dbhome_1/dbs/c-2053465567-20171022-01 RECID=3 STAMP=958057630
crosschecked backup piece: found to be 'AVAILABLE'
backup piece handle=/oracle/oracle12/FRA/ORACLE12/autobackup/2017_11_14/o1_mf_s_960058382_f0oh80np_.bkp RECID=8 STAMP=960058384
crosschecked backup piece: found to be 'AVAILABLE'
backup piece handle=/oracle/oracle12/FRA/ORACLE12/autobackup/2017_11_14/o1_mf_s_960058561_f0ohflkr_.bkp RECID=10 STAMP=960058562
crosschecked backup piece: found to be 'AVAILABLE'
backup piece handle=/oracle/oracle12/FRA/ORACLE12/autobackup/2017_11_14/o1_mf_s_960058772_f0ohn5o1_.bkp RECID=12 STAMP=960058773
crosschecked backup piece: found to be 'AVAILABLE'
backup piece handle=/oracle/oracle12/FRA/ORACLE12/autobackup/2017_11_14/o1_mf_s_960060794_f0okmd5s_.bkp RECID=13 STAMP=960060796
crosschecked backup piece: found to be 'AVAILABLE'
backup piece handle=/oracle/oracle12/FRA/ORACLE12/autobackup/2017_11_16/o1_mf_s_960221634_f0tgonl8_.bkp RECID=14 STAMP=960221636
crosschecked backup piece: found to be 'AVAILABLE'
backup piece handle=/oracle/oracle12/FRA/ORACLE12/autobackup/2017_11_16/o1_mf_s_960222270_f0th9hpx_.bkp RECID=16 STAMP=960222271
crosschecked backup piece: found to be 'AVAILABLE'
backup piece handle=/oracle/oracle12/FRA/ORACLE12/autobackup/2017_11_16/o1_mf_s_960223162_f0tj5dht_.bkp RECID=18 STAMP=960223164
crosschecked backup piece: found to be 'AVAILABLE'
backup piece handle=/oracle/oracle12/FRA/ORACLE12/autobackup/2017_11_16/o1_mf_s_960224603_f0tkldky_.bkp RECID=19 STAMP=960224604
crosschecked backup piece: found to be 'AVAILABLE'
backup piece handle=/oracle/oracle12/FRA/ORACLE12/autobackup/2017_11_16/o1_mf_s_960225036_f0tkzy6f_.bkp RECID=23 STAMP=960225038
crosschecked backup piece: found to be 'AVAILABLE'
backup piece handle=/oracle/oracle12/FRA/ORACLE12/autobackup/2017_11_20/o1_mf_s_960549834_f14h5x9g_.bkp RECID=27 STAMP=960549837
crosschecked backup piece: found to be 'AVAILABLE'
backup piece handle=/oracle/oracle12/FRA/ORACLE12/autobackup/2017_11_20/o1_mf_s_960550256_f14hm24r_.bkp RECID=29 STAMP=960550258
crosschecked backup piece: found to be 'AVAILABLE'
backup piece handle=/oracle/oracle12/FRA/ORACLE12/autobackup/2017_11_20/o1_mf_s_960554305_f14mkmcb_.bkp RECID=30 STAMP=960554307
crosschecked backup piece: found to be 'AVAILABLE'
backup piece handle=/oracle/oracle12/FRA/ORACLE12/autobackup/2017_11_20/o1_mf_s_960555791_f14o017m_.bkp RECID=34 STAMP=960555793
crosschecked backup piece: found to be 'AVAILABLE'
backup piece handle=/oracle/oracle12/FRA/ORACLE12/autobackup/2017_11_20/o1_mf_s_960558125_f14q93ms_.bkp RECID=37 STAMP=960558131
crosschecked backup piece: found to be 'AVAILABLE'
backup piece handle=/oracle/oracle12/FRA/ORACLE12/autobackup/2017_11_20/o1_mf_s_960558265_f14qfc1c_.bkp RECID=39 STAMP=960558266
crosschecked backup piece: found to be 'AVAILABLE'
backup piece handle=/oracle/oracle12/FRA/ORACLE12/autobackup/2017_11_20/o1_mf_s_960558913_f14r1mgg_.bkp RECID=43 STAMP=960558915
crosschecked backup piece: found to be 'AVAILABLE'
backup piece handle=/oracle/oracle12/FRA/ORACLE12/autobackup/2017_11_20/o1_mf_s_960562286_f14vc01j_.bkp RECID=44 STAMP=960562287
crosschecked backup piece: found to be 'AVAILABLE'
backup piece handle=/oracle/oracle12/FRA/ORACLE12/autobackup/2017_11_20/o1_mf_s_960565362_f14yc3t5_.bkp RECID=45 STAMP=960565363
crosschecked backup piece: found to be 'AVAILABLE'
backup piece handle=/oracle/oracle12/FRA/ORACLE12/autobackup/2017_11_20/o1_mf_s_960569005_f151wyyr_.bkp RECID=46 STAMP=960569006
crosschecked backup piece: found to be 'AVAILABLE'
```

수행 결과 AVAILABLE로 표시되어 있다면 사용 가능의 의미입니다. EXPIRED된 것을 보면 이것은 BACKUPSET 목록에 존재하지만 실제 파일은 존재하지 않는다는 의미입니다. 백업 파일을 삭제 할 때도 RMAN 명령어로 삭제해 주어야 합니다.

CROSSCHECK 명령어로 아카이브 로그 파일의 정합성 체크를 합니다.

```
RMAN> CROSSCHECK ARCHIVELOG ALL;
```

```
RMAN> CROSSCHECK ARCHIVELOG ALL;

released channel: ORA_DISK_1
allocated channel: ORA_DISK_1
channel ORA_DISK_1: SID=259 device type=DISK
validation succeeded for archived log
archived log file name=/oracle/oracle12/FRA/ORACLE12/archivelog/2017_11_20/o1_mf_1_470_f157owdw_.arc RECID=465 STAMP=960574925
validation succeeded for archived log
archived log file name=/oracle/oracle12/RMAN_BACKUP/ORACLE12_arch_D-ORACLE12_id-2053465567_S-471_T-1_A-2053448415_2nsk2htf_96057
9503_87 RECID=469 STAMP=960579503
validation succeeded for archived log
archived log file name=/oracle/oracle12/FRA/ORACLE12/archivelog/2017_11_20/o1_mf_1_471_f157q58v_.arc RECID=466 STAMP=960574965
validation succeeded for archived log
archived log file name=/oracle/oracle12/RMAN_BACKUP/ORACLE12_arch_D-ORACLE12_id-2053465567_S-472_T-1_A-2053448415_2msk2htd_96057
9501_86 RECID=468 STAMP=960579502
validation succeeded for archived log
archived log file name=/oracle/oracle12/FRA/ORACLE12/archivelog/2017_11_20/o1_mf_1_472_f15d4x5j_.arc RECID=467 STAMP=960579501
validation succeeded for archived log
archived log file name=/oracle/oracle12/FRA/ORACLE12/archivelog/2017_11_20/o1_mf_1_473_f15f860l_.arc RECID=470 STAMP=960580630
validation succeeded for archived log
archived log file name=/oracle/oracle12/FRA/ORACLE12/archivelog/2017_11_20/o1_mf_1_474_f15fhk3f_.arc RECID=471 STAMP=960580865
validation succeeded for archived log
archived log file name=/oracle/oracle12/FRA/ORACLE12/archivelog/2017_11_20/o1_mf_1_475_f15fjwhf_.arc RECID=472 STAMP=960580908
validation succeeded for archived log
archived log file name=/oracle/oracle12/FRA/ORACLE12/archivelog/2017_11_20/o1_mf_1_476_f15h7k5z_.arc RECID=473 STAMP=960582657
validation succeeded for archived log
archived log file name=/oracle/oracle12/FRA/ORACLE12/archivelog/2017_11_21/o1_mf_1_477_f1770mnf_.arc RECID=474 STAMP=960639784
validation succeeded for archived log
archived log file name=/oracle/oracle12/FRA/ORACLE12/archivelog/2017_11_21/o1_mf_1_478_f17w3ng3_.arc RECID=475 STAMP=960661385
validation succeeded for archived log
archived log file name=/oracle/oracle12/FRA/ORACLE12/archivelog/2017_11_22/o1_mf_1_479_f18k7zp5_.arc RECID=476 STAMP=960683028
validation succeeded for archived log
archived log file name=/oracle/oracle12/FRA/ORACLE12/archivelog/2017_11_22/o1_mf_1_480_f19vf8qo_.arc RECID=477 STAMP=960726205
validation succeeded for archived log
archived log file name=/oracle/oracle12/FRA/ORACLE12/archivelog/2017_11_22/o1_mf_1_481_f19xldh6_.arc RECID=478 STAMP=960728418
validation succeeded for archived log
archived log file name=/oracle/oracle12/FRA/ORACLE12/archivelog/2017_11_22/o1_mf_1_482_f1bjkyh3_.arc RECID=479 STAMP=960747860
validation succeeded for archived log
archived log file name=/oracle/oracle12/FRA/ORACLE12/archivelog/2017_11_23/o1_mf_1_483_f1d5rpoj_.arc RECID=480 STAMP=960802349
Crosschecked 16 objects

RMAN>
```

특정 기간 백업받은 데이터와 카탈로그 정보를 확인할 수 있습니다.

```
RMAN> CROSSCHECK BACKUP COMPLETED BETWEEN '<시작날짜>' AND '<종료날짜>' ;
```

```
RMAN> CROSSCHECK BACKUP COMPLETED BETWEEN '20-NOV-17' AND '20-NOV-17';

using channel ORA_DISK_1
specification does not match any backup in the repository

RMAN> CROSSCHECK BACKUP COMPLETED BETWEEN '20-NOV-17' AND '21-NOV-17';

using channel ORA_DISK_1
crosschecked backup piece: found to be 'AVAILABLE'
backup piece handle=/oracle/oracle12/FRA/ORACLE12/autobackup/2017_11_20/o1_mf_s_960549834_f14h5x9g_.bkp RECID=27 STAMP=960549837
crosschecked backup piece: found to be 'AVAILABLE'
backup piece handle=/oracle/oracle12/FRA/ORACLE12/autobackup/2017_11_20/o1_mf_s_960550256_f14hm24r_.bkp RECID=29 STAMP=960550258
crosschecked backup piece: found to be 'AVAILABLE'
backup piece handle=/oracle/oracle12/FRA/ORACLE12/autobackup/2017_11_20/o1_mf_s_960554305_f14mkmcb_.bkp RECID=30 STAMP=960554307
crosschecked backup piece: found to be 'AVAILABLE'
backup piece handle=/oracle/oracle12/FRA/ORACLE12/autobackup/2017_11_20/o1_mf_s_960555791_f14o017m_.bkp RECID=34 STAMP=960555793
crosschecked backup piece: found to be 'AVAILABLE'
backup piece handle=/oracle/oracle12/FRA/ORACLE12/autobackup/2017_11_20/o1_mf_s_960558125_f14q93ms_.bkp RECID=37 STAMP=960558131
crosschecked backup piece: found to be 'AVAILABLE'
backup piece handle=/oracle/oracle12/FRA/ORACLE12/autobackup/2017_11_20/o1_mf_s_960558265_f14qfc1c_.bkp RECID=39 STAMP=960558266
crosschecked backup piece: found to be 'AVAILABLE'
backup piece handle=/oracle/oracle12/FRA/ORACLE12/autobackup/2017_11_20/o1_mf_s_960558913_f14r1mgg_.bkp RECID=43 STAMP=960558915
crosschecked backup piece: found to be 'AVAILABLE'
backup piece handle=/oracle/oracle12/FRA/ORACLE12/autobackup/2017_11_20/o1_mf_s_960562286_f14vc01j_.bkp RECID=44 STAMP=960562287
crosschecked backup piece: found to be 'AVAILABLE'
backup piece handle=/oracle/oracle12/FRA/ORACLE12/autobackup/2017_11_20/o1_mf_s_960565362_f14yc3t5_.bkp RECID=45 STAMP=960565363
crosschecked backup piece: found to be 'AVAILABLE'
backup piece handle=/oracle/oracle12/FRA/ORACLE12/autobackup/2017_11_20/o1_mf_s_960569005_f151wyyr_.bkp RECID=46 STAMP=960569006
crosschecked backup piece: found to be 'AVAILABLE'
backup piece handle=/oracle/oracle12/FRA/ORACLE12/autobackup/2017_11_20/o1_mf_s_960572143_f154z1dj_.bkp RECID=47 STAMP=960572145
crosschecked backup piece: found to be 'AVAILABLE'
backup piece handle=/oracle/oracle12/FRA/ORACLE12/autobackup/2017_11_20/o1_mf_s_960573378_f1565nds_.bkp RECID=48 STAMP=960573380
crosschecked backup piece: found to be 'AVAILABLE'
backup piece handle=/oracle/oracle12/RMAN_BACKUP/ORACLE12_2isk2ded_1_1_960574925_82 RECID=49 STAMP=960574926
crosschecked backup piece: found to be 'AVAILABLE'
backup piece handle=/oracle/oracle12/FRA/ORACLE12/autobackup/2017_11_20/o1_mf_s_960576771_f159hofo_.bkp RECID=50 STAMP=960576773
crosschecked backup piece: found to be 'AVAILABLE'
backup piece handle=/oracle/oracle12/FRA/ORACLE12/autobackup/2017_11_20/o1_mf_s_960577978_f15bod6x_.bkp RECID=51 STAMP=960577980
crosschecked backup piece: found to be 'AVAILABLE'
backup piece handle=/oracle/oracle12/RMAN_BACKUP/ORACLE12_2qsk2j0m_1_1_960580630_90 RECID=52 STAMP=960580630
crosschecked backup piece: found to be 'AVAILABLE'
backup piece handle=/oracle/oracle12/RMAN_BACKUP/ORACLE12_2rsk2j0o_1_1_960580632_91 RECID=53 STAMP=960580633
crosschecked backup piece: found to be 'AVAILABLE'
backup piece handle=/oracle/oracle12/RMAN_BACKUP/ORACLE12_2ssk2j81_1_1_960580865_92 RECID=54 STAMP=960580866
crosschecked backup piece: found to be 'AVAILABLE'
backup piece handle=/oracle/oracle12/FRA/ORACLE12/autobackup/2017_11_20/o1_mf_s_960580867_f15fhp9o_.bkp RECID=55 STAMP=960580870
crosschecked backup piece: found to be 'AVAILABLE'
backup piece handle=/oracle/oracle12/RMAN_BACKUP/ORACLE12_2usk2j9c_1_1_960580908_94 RECID=56 STAMP=960580908
crosschecked backup piece: found to be 'AVAILABLE'
backup piece handle=/oracle/oracle12/RMAN_BACKUP/ORACLE12_3ask2l01_1_1_960582657_106 RECID=57 STAMP=960582658
crosschecked backup piece: found to be 'AVAILABLE'
backup piece handle=/oracle/oracle12/FRA/ORACLE12/autobackup/2017_11_20/o1_mf_s_960582659_f15h7ocv_.bkp RECID=58 STAMP=960582661
Crosschecked 22 objects
```

7. DELETE 명령어

최근에 백업을 받아서 과거 백업 데이터가 필요 없거나, 백업 보존 기간이 지났거나, 용량이 커져서 과거 아카이브로그를 지워야 한다던가할 때 사용하는 DELETE 명령어입니다.

가장 많이 하는 명령어로는 RMAN을 통한 아카이브 로그 삭제하는 경우입니다.

2일전 이미 백업 받았지만 존재하는 아카이브 로그를 삭제합니다.

```
RMAN> DELETE BACKUP OF ARCHIVELOG UNTIL TIME='SYSDATE-<보관일수>' ;
```

```
RMAN> DELETE BACKUP OF ARCHIVELOG UNTIL TIME='SYSDATE-2' ;

using channel ORA_DISK_1

List of Backup Pieces
BP Key  BS Key  Pc# Cp# Status      Device Type Piece Name
------- ------- --- --- ----------- ----------- ----------
49      49      1   1   AVAILABLE   DISK        /oracle/oracle12/RMAN_BACKUP/ORACLE12_2isk2ded_1_1_960574925_82
52      52      1   1   AVAILABLE   DISK        /oracle/oracle12/RMAN_BACKUP/ORACLE12_2qsk2j0m_1_1_960580630_90
54      54      1   1   AVAILABLE   DISK        /oracle/oracle12/RMAN_BACKUP/ORACLE12_2ssk2j81_1_1_960580865_92
56      56      1   1   AVAILABLE   DISK        /oracle/oracle12/RMAN_BACKUP/ORACLE12_2usk2j9c_1_1_960580908_94
57      57      1   1   AVAILABLE   DISK        /oracle/oracle12/RMAN_BACKUP/ORACLE12_3ask2l01_1_1_960582657_106

Do you really want to delete the above objects (enter YES or NO)? YES
deleted backup piece
backup piece handle=/oracle/oracle12/RMAN_BACKUP/ORACLE12_2isk2ded_1_1_960574925_82 RECID=49 STAMP=960574926
deleted backup piece
backup piece handle=/oracle/oracle12/RMAN_BACKUP/ORACLE12_2qsk2j0m_1_1_960580630_90 RECID=52 STAMP=960580630
deleted backup piece
backup piece handle=/oracle/oracle12/RMAN_BACKUP/ORACLE12_2ssk2j81_1_1_960580865_92 RECID=54 STAMP=960580866
deleted backup piece
backup piece handle=/oracle/oracle12/RMAN_BACKUP/ORACLE12_2usk2j9c_1_1_960580908_94 RECID=56 STAMP=960580908
deleted backup piece
backup piece handle=/oracle/oracle12/RMAN_BACKUP/ORACLE12_3ask2l01_1_1_960582657_106 RECID=57 STAMP=960582658
Deleted 5 objects
```

현재 설정된 백업 정책을 기준으로 불필요하다고 판단하는 파일들을 조회하고 삭제합니다.

```
RMAN> DELETE BACKUP OF ARCHIVELOG UNTIL TIME='SYSDATE-<보관일수>' ;
```

```
RMAN> DELETE OBSOLETE ;

RMAN retention policy will be applied to the command
RMAN retention policy is set to redundancy 1
using channel ORA_DISK_1
Deleting the following obsolete backups and copies:
Type                 Key    Completion Time    Filename/Handle
-------------------- ------ ------------------ --------------------
Datafile Copy        88     20-NOV-17          /oracle/oracle12/RMAN_BACKUP/ORACLE12_data_D-ORACLE12_I-2053465567_TS-SYSTEM_FNO-1_1tsk1sf2_960557538_61
Datafile Copy        91     20-NOV-17          /oracle/oracle12/RMAN_BACKUP/ORACLE12_data_D-ORACLE12_I-2053465567_TS-UNDOTBS1_FNO-4_1ssk1rle_960556718_60
Datafile Copy        93     20-NOV-17          /oracle/oracle12/RMAN_BACKUP/ORACLE12_data_D-ORACLE12_I-2053465567_TS-USERS_FNO-7_23sk1sub_960558027_67
Datafile Copy        96     20-NOV-17          /oracle/oracle12/RMAN_BACKUP/ORACLE12_data_D-ORACLE12_I-2053465567_TS-UNDOTBS1_FNO-10_21sk1sta_960557994_65
Datafile Copy        97     20-NOV-17          /oracle/oracle12/RMAN_BACKUP/ORACLE12_data_D-ORACLE12_I-2053465567_TS-UNDOTBS1_FNO-11_22sk1str_960558011_66
Datafile Copy        108    20-NOV-17          /oracle/oracle12/oradata/oracle12/unione02.dbf
Datafile Copy        110    20-NOV-17          /oracle/oracle12/oradata/oracle12/unione03.dbf
Datafile Copy        111    20-NOV-17          /oracle/oracle12/oradata/oracle12/unione04.dbf
Datafile Copy        109    20-NOV-17          /oracle/oracle12/oradata/oracle12/unione01.dbf
Archive Log          465    20-NOV-17          /oracle/oracle12/FRA/ORACLE12/archivelog/2017_11_20/o1_mf_1_470_f157owdw_.arc
Archive Log          466    20-NOV-17          /oracle/oracle12/FRA/ORACLE12/archivelog/2017_11_20/o1_mf_1_471_f157q58v_.arc
Archive Log          467    20-NOV-17          /oracle/oracle12/FRA/ORACLE12/archivelog/2017_11_20/o1_mf_1_472_f15d4x5j_.arc
Archive Log          468    20-NOV-17          /oracle/oracle12/RMAN_BACKUP/ORACLE12_arch_D-ORACLE12_id-2053465567_S-472_T-1_A-2053448415_2msk2htd_960579501_86
Archive Log          469    20-NOV-17          /oracle/oracle12/RMAN_BACKUP/ORACLE12_arch_D-ORACLE12_id-2053465567_S-471_T-1_A-2053448415_2nsk2htf_960579503_87
Datafile Copy        112    20-NOV-17          /oracle/oracle12/RMAN_BACKUP/ORACLE12_data_D-ORACLE12_I-2053465567_TS-SYSAUX_FNO-3_2osk2htg_960579504_88
Archive Log          470    20-NOV-17          /oracle/oracle12/FRA/ORACLE12/archivelog/2017_11_20/o1_mf_1_473_f15f860l_.arc
Archive Log          471    20-NOV-17          /oracle/oracle12/FRA/ORACLE12/archivelog/2017_11_20/o1_mf_1_474_f15fhk3f_.arc
Backup Set           53     20-NOV-17
  Backup Piece       53     20-NOV-17          /oracle/oracle12/RMAN_BACKUP/ORACLE12_2rsk2j0o_1_1_960580632_91
Archive Log          472    20-NOV-17          /oracle/oracle12/FRA/ORACLE12/archivelog/2017_11_20/o1_mf_1_475_f15fjwhf_.arc

Do you really want to delete the above objects (enter YES or NO)? YES
```

```
Do you really want to delete the above objects (enter YES or NO)? YES
deleted datafile copy
datafile copy file name=/oracle/oracle12/RMAN_BACKUP/ORACLE12_data_D-ORACLE12_I-2053465567_TS-SYSTEM_FNO-1_1tsk1sf2_960557538_61 RECID=88 STAMP=950571414
deleted datafile copy
datafile copy file name=/oracle/oracle12/RMAN_BACKUP/ORACLE12_data_D-ORACLE12_I-2053465567_TS-UNDOTBS1_FNO-4_1ssk1rle_960556718_60 RECID=91 STAMP=960571414
deleted datafile copy
datafile copy file name=/oracle/oracle12/RMAN_BACKUP/ORACLE12_data_D-ORACLE12_I-2053465567_TS-USERS_FNO-7_23sk1sub_960558027_67 RECID=93 STAMP=960571415
deleted datafile copy
datafile copy file name=/oracle/oracle12/RMAN_BACKUP/ORACLE12_data_D-ORACLE12_I-2053465567_TS-UNDOTBS1_FNO-10_21sk1sta_960557994_65 RECID=96 STAMP=960571415
deleted datafile copy
datafile copy file name=/oracle/oracle12/RMAN_BACKUP/ORACLE12_data_D-ORACLE12_I-2053465567_TS-UNDOTBS1_FNO-11_22sk1str_960558011_66 RECID=97 STAMP=960571416
deleted archived log
archived log file name=/oracle/oracle12/FRA/ORACLE12/archivelog/2017_11_20/o1_mf_1_470_f157owdw_.arc RECID=465 STAMP=960574925
deleted archived log
archived log file name=/oracle/oracle12/FRA/ORACLE12/archivelog/2017_11_20/o1_mf_1_471_f157q58v_.arc RECID=466 STAMP=960574965
deleted archived log
archived log file name=/oracle/oracle12/FRA/ORACLE12/archivelog/2017_11_20/o1_mf_1_472_f15d4x5j_.arc RECID=467 STAMP=960579501
deleted archived log
archived log file name=/oracle/oracle12/RMAN_BACKUP/ORACLE12_arch_D-ORACLE12_id-2053465567_S-472_T-1_A-2053448415_2msk2htd_960579501_86 RECID=468 STAMP=96057950
deleted archived log
archived log file name=/oracle/oracle12/RMAN_BACKUP/ORACLE12_arch_D-ORACLE12_id-2053465567_S-471_T-1_A-2053448415_2nsk2htf_960579503_87 RECID=469 STAMP=96057950
deleted datafile copy
datafile copy file name=/oracle/oracle12/RMAN_BACKUP/ORACLE12_data_D-ORACLE12_I-2053465567_TS-SYSAUX_FNO-3_2osk2htg_960579504_88 RECID=112 STAMP=960580408
deleted archived log
archived log file name=/oracle/oracle12/FRA/ORACLE12/archivelog/2017_11_20/o1_mf_1_473_f15f860l_.arc RECID=470 STAMP=960580630
deleted archived log
archived log file name=/oracle/oracle12/FRA/ORACLE12/archivelog/2017_11_20/o1_mf_1_474_f15fhk3f_.arc RECID=471 STAMP=960580865
deleted backup piece
backup piece handle=/oracle/oracle12/RMAN_BACKUP/ORACLE12_2rsk2j0o_1_1_960580632_91 RECID=53 STAMP=960580633
deleted archived log
archived log file name=/oracle/oracle12/FRA/ORACLE12/archivelog/2017_11_20/o1_mf_1_475_f15fjwhf_.arc RECID=472 STAMP=960580908
Deleted 15 objects
```

정기적으로 불필요한 백업한 데이터를 제거해서 백업 영역을 확보할 수 있습니다.

CROSSCHECK 명령어로 확인 후 EXPIRED된 정보를 복구 카탈로그에서 삭제합니다.

```
RMAN> DELETE EXPIRED BACKUP ;
```

```
RMAN> DELETE EXPIRED BACKUP ;

using channel ORA_DISK_1

List of Backup Pieces
BP Key  BS Key  Pc# Cp# Status      Device Type Piece Name
------- ------- --- --- ----------- ----------- ----------
1       1       1   1   EXPIRED     DISK        /oracle/oracle12/app/oracle/product/12.2.0/dbhome_1/dbs/c-2053465567-20171010-00

Do you really want to delete the above objects (enter YES or NO)? YES
deleted backup piece
backup piece handle=/oracle/oracle12/app/oracle/product/12.2.0/dbhome_1/dbs/c-2053465567-20171010-00 RECID=1 STAMP=957026285
Deleted 1 EXPIRED objects

RMAN> ▮
```

백업 세트(Backup Set) 방식으로 백업 파일을 지정해서 지웁니다.

```
RMAN> DELETE BACKUPSET <백업세트KEY> ;
```

```
RMAN> DELETE BACKUPSET 2 ;

using channel ORA_DISK_1

List of Backup Pieces
BP Key  BS Key  Pc# Cp# Status      Device Type Piece Name
------- ------- --- --- ----------- ----------- ----------
2       2       1   1   AVAILABLE   DISK        /oracle/oracle12/app/oracle/product/12.2.0/dbhome_1/dbs/c-2053465567-20171022-00

Do you really want to delete the above objects (enter YES or NO)? YES
deleted backup piece
backup piece handle=/oracle/oracle12/app/oracle/product/12.2.0/dbhome_1/dbs/c-2053465567-20171022-00 RECID=2 STAMP=958056725
Deleted 1 objects

RMAN> ▮
```

8 FAST RECOVERY AREA 관리 명령어

RMAN에서 사용하는 고속 복구 영역 관리를 실습해 보겠습니다.

FRA의 위치를 확인합니다.

```
SQL> SELECT * FROM V$RECOVERY_FILE_DEST ;
```

```
SQL> SELECT * FROM V$RECOVERY_FILE_DEST ;
NAME                                                SPACE_LIMIT SPACE_USED SPACE_RECLAIMABLE NUMBER_OF_FILES     CON_ID
--------------------------------------------------- ----------- ---------- ----------------- --------------- ----------
/oracle/oracle12/FRA/                                1.0727E+12 1587673088                 0              39          0
```

FRA의 사용 현황을 확인합니다.

```
SQL> SELECT * FROM V$RECOVERY_AREA_USAGE ;
```

```
SQL> SELECT * FROM V$RECOVERY_AREA_USAGE ;
FILE_TYPE               PERCENT_SPACE_USED PERCENT_SPACE_RECLAIMABLE NUMBER_OF_FILES     CON_ID
----------------------- ------------------ ------------------------- --------------- ----------
CONTROL FILE                             0                         0               0          0
REDO LOG                                 0                         0               0          0
ARCHIVED LOG                           .12                         0              14          0
BACKUP PIECE                           .03                         0              25          0
IMAGE COPY                               0                         0               0          0
FLASHBACK LOG                            0                         0               0          0
FOREIGN ARCHIVED LOG                     0                         0               0          0
AUXILIARY DATAFILE COPY                  0                         0               0          0

8 rows selected.
```

영역은 충분히 사용 가능한지 확인이 가능합니다. 삭제 가능한 파일은 어느 정도 존재하는지 쿼리문을 통해 확인이 가능합니다.

장애의 정석 부분에서 살펴보았지만, DB_RECOVERY_FILE_DEST_SIZE를 적절한 값으로 설정해야 하고 주기적으로 불필요한 백업을 RMAN의 DELETE 명령어로 삭제해야 합니다.

```
SQL> alter system set db_recovery_file_dest_size=100G;
```

```
SQL> alter system set db_recovery_file_dest_size=100G;

System altered.

SQL> SHOW PARAMETER DB_RECOVERY_FILE_DEST_SIZE

NAME                                 TYPE        VALUE
------------------------------------ ----------- ------------------------------
db_recovery_file_dest_size           big integer 100G
SQL>
```

9 RMAN Block Corruption 체크

DB 운영 중에 BLOCK Corruption 장애가 나면 현재 RMAN 백업을 사용하지 않아도 체크가 가능합니다.

RMAN으로 백업없이 Block Corruption을 체크합니다.

```
RMAN> BACKUP CHECK LOGICAL VALIDATE DATABASE ;
```

```
RMAN> BACKUP CHECK LOGICAL VALIDATE DATABASE ;

Starting backup at 23-NOV-17
using channel ORA_DISK_1
channel ORA_DISK_1: starting full datafile backup set
channel ORA_DISK_1: specifying datafile(s) in backup set
input datafile file number=00003 name=/oracle/oracle12/oradata/oracle12/sysaux01.dbf
input datafile file number=00004 name=/oracle/oracle12/oradata/oracle12/undotbs01.dbf
input datafile file number=00001 name=/oracle/oracle12/oradata/oracle12/system01.dbf
input datafile file number=00002 name=/oracle/oracle12/oradata/oracle12/UNIONE/unione02.dbf
input datafile file number=00008 name=/oracle/oracle12/oradata/oracle12/UNIONE/unione03.dbf
input datafile file number=00009 name=/oracle/oracle12/oradata/oracle12/UNIONE/unione04.dbf
input datafile file number=00010 name=/oracle/oracle12/oradata/oracle12/undotbs02.dbf
input datafile file number=00011 name=/oracle/oracle12/oradata/oracle12/undotbs03.dbf
input datafile file number=00007 name=/oracle/oracle12/oradata/oracle12/users01.dbf
input datafile file number=00005 name=/oracle/oracle12/oradata/oracle12/UNIONE/unione01.dbf
input datafile file number=00012 name=/oracle/oracle12/oradata/oracle12/oracle12_01.dbf
channel ORA_DISK_1: backup set complete, elapsed time: 00:24:24
List of Datafiles
=================
File Status Marked Corrupt Empty Blocks Blocks Examined High SCN
---- ------ -------------- ------------ --------------- ----------
1    OK     0              1219065      1310721         1437036981
  File Name: /oracle/oracle12/oradata/oracle12/system01.dbf
  Block Type Blocks Failing Blocks Processed
  ---------- -------------- ----------------
  Data       0              72202
  Index      0              14982
  Other      0              4471
```

```
File Status Marked Corrupt Empty Blocks Blocks Examined High SCN
---- ------ -------------- ------------ --------------- ----------
10   OK     0              1            12800           1437037033
  File Name: /oracle/oracle12/oradata/oracle12/undotbs02.dbf
  Block Type Blocks Failing Blocks Processed
  ---------- -------------- ----------------
  Data       0              0
  Index      0              0
  Other      0              12799

File Status Marked Corrupt Empty Blocks Blocks Examined High SCN
---- ------ -------------- ------------ --------------- ----------
11   OK     0              1            12800           1437036974
  File Name: /oracle/oracle12/oradata/oracle12/undotbs03.dbf
  Block Type Blocks Failing Blocks Processed
  ---------- -------------- ----------------
  Data       0              0
  Index      0              0
  Other      0              12799

File Status Marked Corrupt Empty Blocks Blocks Examined High SCN
---- ------ -------------- ------------ --------------- ----------
12   OK     0              1153         1280            1436805296
  File Name: /oracle/oracle12/oradata/oracle12/oracle12_01.dbf
  Block Type Blocks Failing Blocks Processed
  ---------- -------------- ----------------
  Data       0              0
  Index      0              0
  Other      0              127

channel ORA_DISK_1: starting full datafile backup set
channel ORA_DISK_1: specifying datafile(s) in backup set
including current control file in backup set
including current SPFILE in backup set
channel ORA_DISK_1: backup set complete, elapsed time: 00:00:01
List of Control File and SPFILE
===============================
File Type    Status Blocks Failing Blocks Examined
------------ ------ -------------- ---------------
SPFILE       OK     0              2
Control File OK     0              680
Finished backup at 23-NOV-17
```

RMAN 백업의 백업 세트(Backup Set) 방식을 수행하면서 Block Corruption을 체크합니다.

```
RMAN> BACKUP CHECK LOGICAL DATABASE ;
```

```
RMAN> BACKUP CHECK LOGICAL DATABASE;

Starting backup at 23-NOV-17
using channel ORA_DISK_1
channel ORA_DISK_1: starting full datafile backup set
channel ORA_DISK_1: specifying datafile(s) in backup set
input datafile file number=00003 name=/oracle/oracle12/oradata/oracle12/sysaux01.dbf
input datafile file number=00004 name=/oracle/oracle12/oradata/oracle12/undotbs01.dbf
input datafile file number=00001 name=/oracle/oracle12/oradata/oracle12/system01.dbf
input datafile file number=00002 name=/oracle/oracle12/oradata/oracle12/UNIONE/unione02.dbf
input datafile file number=00008 name=/oracle/oracle12/oradata/oracle12/UNIONE/unione03.dbf
input datafile file number=00009 name=/oracle/oracle12/oradata/oracle12/UNIONE/unione04.dbf
input datafile file number=00010 name=/oracle/oracle12/oradata/oracle12/undotbs02.dbf
input datafile file number=00011 name=/oracle/oracle12/oradata/oracle12/undotbs03.dbf
input datafile file number=00007 name=/oracle/oracle12/oradata/oracle12/users01.dbf
input datafile file number=00005 name=/oracle/oracle12/oradata/oracle12/UNIONE/unione01.dbf
input datafile file number=00012 name=/oracle/oracle12/oradata/oracle12/oracle12_01.dbf
channel ORA_DISK_1: starting piece 1 at 23-NOV-17
channel ORA_DISK_1: finished piece 1 at 23-NOV-17
piece handle=/oracle/oracle12/RMAN_BACKUP/ORACLE12_3mska007_1_1_960823303_118 tag=TAG20171123T152143 comment=NONE
channel ORA_DISK_1: backup set complete, elapsed time: 00:03:56
Finished backup at 23-NOV-17

Starting Control File and SPFILE Autobackup at 23-NOV-17
piece handle=/oracle/oracle12/FRA/ORACLE12/autobackup/2017_11_23/o1_mf_s_960823539_f1dth6c7_.bkp comment=NONE
Finished Control File and SPFILE Autobackup at 23-NOV-17
```

10 RMAN을 이용한 ASM FILE ↔ FILE 마이그레이션

RMAN의 명령어를 통하여 일반 File System 형식의 File을 ASM 파일로 변경이 가능합니다.

COPY 명령어로 일반 File System 형식의 데이터 파일을 ASM으로 파일 복사합니다.

```
RMAN> COPY datafile '<파일경로>/<파일이름>' to '+<ASM디스크그룹명>/<파일이름>' ;
```

```
Recovery Manager: Release 12.2.0.1.0 - Production on Fri Nov 24 11:11:10 2017

Copyright (c) 1982, 2017, Oracle and/or its affiliates.  All rights reserved.

connected to target database: ORACLE12 (DBID=2053465567)

RMAN> COPY datafile '/oracle/oracle12/oradata/oracle12/UNIONE/unione02.dbf' to '+DATA/ORACLE12/DATAFILE/unione02.dbf' ;

Starting backup at 24-NOV-17
using target database control file instead of recovery catalog
allocated channel: ORA_DISK_1
channel ORA_DISK_1: SID=182 device type=DISK
channel ORA_DISK_1: starting datafile copy
input datafile file number=00002 name=/oracle/oracle12/oradata/oracle12/UNIONE/unione02.dbf
output file name=+DATA/ORACLE12/DATAFILE/unione02.dbf tag=TAG20171124T112257 RECID=124 STAMP=960895584
channel ORA_DISK_1: datafile copy complete, elapsed time: 00:03:50
Finished backup at 24-NOV-17

Starting Control File and SPFILE Autobackup at 24-NOV-17
piece handle=/oracle/oracle12/FRA/ORACLE12/autobackup/2017_11_24/o1_mf_s_960895620_f1h0vsxb_.bkp comment=NONE
Finished Control File and SPFILE Autobackup at 24-NOV-17

RMAN> █
```

이번에는 run 명령어를 통해 테이블스페이스에 포함된 데이터 파일을 모두 옮겨보겠습니다.

먼저 옮길 테이블스페이스의 데이터 파일을 조회합니다.

```
SQL> SELECT FILE_NAME , BYTES/1024/1024 MB FROM DBA_DATA_FILES WHERE TABLESPACE_NAME = 'UNIONE' ;

FILE_NAME
                                                                                        MB
--------------------------------------------------------------------------------------- ----------
/oracle/oracle12/oradata/oracle12/UNIONE/unione01.dbf                                   10
/oracle/oracle12/oradata/oracle12/UNIONE/unione02.dbf                                   1370.3125
/oracle/oracle12/oradata/oracle12/UNIONE/unione03.dbf                                   1337.0625
/oracle/oracle12/oradata/oracle12/UNIONE/unione04.dbf                                   1299.25

SQL>
```

RUN 명령어를 이용하여 데이터 파일을 복사하고 RENAME 해보겠습니다.

```
RMAN> RUN {
ALTER TABLESPACE UNIONE OFFLINE IMMEDIATE ;
  SET NEWNAME FOR DATAFILE '/oracle/oracle12/oradata/oracle12/UNIONE/unione01.dbf' TO
'+DATA/ORACLE12/DATAFILE/unione01.dbf' ;
  SET NEWNAME FOR DATAFILE '/oracle/oracle12/oradata/oracle12/UNIONE/unione02.dbf' TO
'+DATA/ORACLE12/DATAFILE/unione02.dbf' ;
  SET NEWNAME FOR DATAFILE '/oracle/oracle12/oradata/oracle12/UNIONE/unione03.dbf' TO
'+DATA/ORACLE12/DATAFILE/unione03.dbf' ;
  SET NEWNAME FOR DATAFILE '/oracle/oracle12/oradata/oracle12/UNIONE/unione04.dbf' TO
'+DATA/ORACLE12/DATAFILE/unione04.dbf' ;
RESTORE TABLESPACE UNIONE ;
SWITCH DATAFILE ALL;
RECOVER TABLESPACE UNIONE ;
ALTER TABLESPACE UNIONE ONLINE ;
```

```
RMAN> RUN {
2> ALTER TABLESPACE UNIONE OFFLINE IMMEDIATE ;
3>    SET NEWNAME FOR DATAFILE '/oracle/oracle12/oradata/oracle12/UNIONE/unione01.dbf' TO '+DATA/ORACLE12/DATAFILE/
unione01.dbf' ;
4>    SET NEWNAME FOR DATAFILE '/oracle/oracle12/oradata/oracle12/UNIONE/unione02.dbf' TO '+DATA/ORACLE12/DATAFILE/
unione02.dbf' ;
5>    SET NEWNAME FOR DATAFILE '/oracle/oracle12/oradata/oracle12/UNIONE/unione03.dbf' TO '+DATA/ORACLE12/DATAFILE/
unione03.dbf' ;
6>    SET NEWNAME FOR DATAFILE '/oracle/oracle12/oradata/oracle12/UNIONE/unione04.dbf' TO '+DATA/ORACLE12/DATAFILE/
unione04.dbf' ;
7> RESTORE TABLESPACE UNIONE ;
8> SWITCH DATAFILE ALL;
9> RECOVER TABLESPACE UNIONE ;
10> ALTER TABLESPACE UNIONE ONLINE ;
11> }

Statement processed

executing command: SET NEWNAME

executing command: SET NEWNAME

executing command: SET NEWNAME

executing command: SET NEWNAME

Starting restore at 24-NOV-17
using channel ORA_DISK_1

datafile 2 is already restored to file +DATA/ORACLE12/DATAFILE/unione02.dbf
channel ORA_DISK_1: starting datafile backup set restore
channel ORA_DISK_1: specifying datafile(s) to restore from backup set
channel ORA_DISK_1: restoring datafile 00005 to +DATA/ORACLE12/DATAFILE/unione01.dbf
channel ORA_DISK_1: restoring datafile 00008 to +DATA/ORACLE12/DATAFILE/unione03.dbf
channel ORA_DISK_1: restoring datafile 00009 to +DATA/ORACLE12/DATAFILE/unione04.dbf
channel ORA_DISK_1: reading from backup piece /oracle/oracle12/RMAN_BACKUP/ORACLE12_3mska007_1_1_960823303_118
channel ORA_DISK_1: piece handle=/oracle/oracle12/RMAN_BACKUP/ORACLE12_3mska007_1_1_960823303_118 tag=TAG20171123T152143
channel ORA_DISK_1: restored backup piece 1
channel ORA_DISK_1: restore complete, elapsed time: 00:01:37
Finished restore at 24-NOV-17

datafile 2 switched to datafile copy
input datafile copy RECID=128 STAMP=960898851 file name=+DATA/ORACLE12/DATAFILE/unione02.dbf
datafile 5 switched to datafile copy
input datafile copy RECID=129 STAMP=960898851 file name=+DATA/ORACLE12/DATAFILE/unione01.dbf
datafile 8 switched to datafile copy
input datafile copy RECID=130 STAMP=960898852 file name=+DATA/ORACLE12/DATAFILE/unione03.dbf
datafile 9 switched to datafile copy
input datafile copy RECID=131 STAMP=960898852 file name=+DATA/ORACLE12/DATAFILE/unione04.dbf

Starting recover at 24-NOV-17
using channel ORA_DISK_1

starting media recovery
media recovery complete, elapsed time: 00:00:11

Finished recover at 24-NOV-17
```

완료 후에 ASM 형태로 파일이 변경되었는지 DB에서 조회합니다.

```
SQL> SELECT FILE_NAME , BYTES/1024/1024 MB FROM DBA_DATA_FILES WHERE TABLESPACE_NAME = 'UNIONE' ;

                                                                                          MB
FILE_NAME
------------------------------------------------------------------------------- ----------
+DATA/ORACLE12/DATAFILE/unione01.dbf                                                      10
+DATA/ORACLE12/DATAFILE/unione02.dbf                                               1370.3125
+DATA/ORACLE12/DATAFILE/unione03.dbf                                               1337.0625
+DATA/ORACLE12/DATAFILE/unione04.dbf                                                 1299.25
```

일반 File System의 데이터 파일이 ASM을 이용하는 데이터 파일로 변경되었습니다.

11 RMAN 백업 환경에서의 Daily 백업 체크

RMAN 스크립트를 만들어서 오라클 DB의 스케줄러에 등록하면 자동으로 DB 백업을 수행시킬 수 있습니다.
백업 스크립트의 오라클 스케줄러 등록을 실습해 보겠습니다.
먼저 RMAM 환경에서 수행이 되는 RMAN 수행 파일을 만듭니다.
백업 세트 방식으로 압축해서 전체 데이터베이스를 대상으로 RMAN 백업을 받는 파일을 만듭니다.

```
run {
backup as compressed backupset database;
backup as compressed backupset archivelog all delete input;
backup as compressed backupset current controlfile;
delete noprompt obsolete;
}
```

```
[oracle12]yspark-linux:/home/oracle12> vi full_cmd.rman
run {
backup as compressed backupset database;
backup as compressed backupset archivelog all delete input;
backup as compressed backupset current controlfile;
delete noprompt obsolete;
}
```

이번에는 백업용 OS Shell 스크립트를 만듭니다.

```
#!/bin/bash
. /home/oracle12/.bash_profile
rman target / @/home/oracle12/full_cmd.rman
```

```
[oracle12]yspark-linux:/home/oracle12> vi rman.sh
#!/bin/bash
. /home/oracle12/.bash_profile
rman target / @/home/oracle12/full_cmd.rman
~
```

이제 만든 스크립트를 Oracle 스케줄러에 등록합니다. 먼저 JOB을 만듭니다.

```
BEGIN
   DBMS_SCHEDULER.CREATE_JOB (
     job_name=>'RMAN_BACKUP_ZERO',
     job_type=>'EXECUTABLE',
     job_action=>'/home/oracle12/rman.sh',
     repeat_interval=> 'FREQ=DAILY;BYHOUR=1;BYMINUTE=10',
     enabled=>TRUE,
     comments=>'LEVEL 0 ');
END;
/
```

```
SQL> BEGIN
       DBMS_SCHEDULER.CREATE_JOB (
         job_name=>'RMAN_BACKUP_ZERO',
         job_type=>'EXECUTABLE',
         job_action=>'/home/oracle12/rman.sh',
         repeat_interval=> 'FREQ=DAILY;BYHOUR=1;BYMINUTE=10',
         enabled=>TRUE,
         comments=>'LEVEL 0 ');
     END;
     /

PL/SQL procedure successfully completed.

SQL>
```

해당 JOB의 속성을 설정합니다.

```
BEGIN
   DBMS_SCHEDULER.SET_ATTRIBUTE (
     name =>'RMAN_BACKUP_ZERO',
     attribute=>'raise_events',
     VALUE=>DBMS_SCHEDULER.job_started
     +DBMS_SCHEDULER.job_succeeded
     +DBMS_SCHEDULER.job_failed
     +DBMS_SCHEDULER.job_broken
     +DBMS_SCHEDULER.job_stopped);
END;
/
```

```
SQL> BEGIN
  2      DBMS_SCHEDULER.SET_ATTRIBUTE (
  3         name =>'RMAN_BACKUP_ZERO',
  4         attribute=>'raise_events',
  5         VALUE=>DBMS_SCHEDULER.job_started
  6         +DBMS_SCHEDULER.job_succeeded
  7         +DBMS_SCHEDULER.job_failed
  8         +DBMS_SCHEDULER.job_broken
  9         +DBMS_SCHEDULER.job_stopped);
 10  END;
 11  /

PL/SQL procedure successfully completed.
```

3일 정도 지난 후 백업이 정상적으로 되고 있는지 확인하는 단계입니다.

오라클 스케줄러에 등록된 JOB이 잘 수행되었는지 DBA_SCHEDULER_JOB_LOG 뷰를 조회하여 확인합니다.

```
SELECT TO_CHAR(LOG_DATE, 'YYYY/MM/DD HH24:MI:SS') AS JOB_DATE, OWNER,JOB_NAME,STATUS
FROM DBA_SCHEDULER_JOB_LOG
WHERE JOB_NAME='RMAN_BACKUP_ZERO'
AND log_date >= TRUNC(SYSDATE-7) ;
```

```
SQL> SELECT TO_CHAR(LOG_DATE, 'YYYY/MM/DD HH24:MI:SS') AS JOB_DATE, OWNER,JOB_NAME,STATUS FROM DBA_SCHEDULER_JOB_LOG
  2  where JOB_NAME='RMAN_BACKUP_ZERO'
  3  AND LOG_DATE >= trunc(sysdate-7) ;

JOB_DATE            OWNER      JOB_NAME         STATUS
------------------- ---------- ---------------- ------------------------------
2017/11/25 01:16:27 SYS        RMAN_BACKUP_ZERO SUCCEEDED
2017/11/27 01:15:38 SYS        RMAN_BACKUP_ZERO SUCCEEDED
2017/11/26 01:15:39 SYS        RMAN_BACKUP_ZERO SUCCEEDED

SQL>
```

RMAN 백업이 잘 수행되었는지 V$RMAN_BACKUP_JOB_DETAILS 뷰를 조회하여 확인합니다.

```
SELECT SESSION_KEY , INPUT_TYPE , STATUS ,
       TO_CHAR(START_TIME,'YYYY/MM/DD HH24:MI')  START_TIME ,
       TO_CHAR(END_TIME,'YYYY/MM/DD HH24:MI')    END_TIME ,
       TIME_TAKEN_DISPLAY                        JOB_TIME ,
       ROUND(COMPRESSION_RATIO, 0) COMP_RATIO ,
       INPUT_BYTES_PER_SEC_DISPLAY INPUT_SEC ,
       OUTPUT_BYTES_PER_SEC_DISPLAY OUTPUT_SEC
from V$RMAN_BACKUP_JOB_DETAILS
WHERE START_TIME >= TRUNC(SYSDATE-2)
ORDER BY 1 ;
```

```
SQL> SELECT SESSION_KEY,INPUT_TYPE,STATUS,
            TO_CHAR(START_TIME,'YYYY/MM/DD HH24:MI')  START_TIME,
            TO_CHAR(END_TIME,'YYYY/MM/DD HH24:MI')    END_TIME,
            TIME_TAKEN_DISPLAY                       JOB_TIME,
            ROUND(COMPRESSION_RATIO, 0) COMP_RATIO,
            INPUT_BYTES_PER_SEC_DISPLAY INPUT_SEC,
            OUTPUT_BYTES_PER_SEC_DISPLAY OUTPUT_SEC
     from V$RMAN_BACKUP_JOB_DETAILS
     WHERE START_TIME >= TRUNC(SYSDATE-2)
     ORDER BY 1 ;

SESSION_KEY INPUT_TYPE    STATUS    START_TIME       END_TIME         JOB_TIME   COMP_RATIO INPUT_SEC  OUTPUT_SEC
----------- ------------- --------- ---------------- ---------------- ---------- ---------- ---------- ----------
        284 DB FULL       COMPLETED 2017/11/25 01:11 2017/11/25 01:16 00:05:08            4    29.37M      7.47M
        290 DB FULL       COMPLETED 2017/11/26 01:11 2017/11/26 01:15 00:04:29            4    29.11M      7.26M
        296 DB FULL       COMPLETED 2017/11/27 01:11 2017/11/27 01:15 00:04:27            4    29.30M      7.31M
```

오라클 스케줄러를 이용하여 RMAN 백업이 잘 수행되고 있음을 확인할 수 있습니다.

RMAN의 고급 사용 방법

기본 명령어 실습이 완료되면 RMAN을 이용한 증분 업데이트 백업, 카탈로그 DB 생성 DB 복제, 등 RMAN 고급 기능을 실습을 시작합니다.

1 Incrementally Updated 백업(대용량 데이터베이스 RMAN 백업)

대용량 DB의 백업 방식인 Image Copy 방식의 Incrementally Updated 백업을 실습해 보겠습니다. 앞에서 설명하였지만 이 백업은 레벨 1 백업의 변경 내용을 사용하여 레벨 1 증분 백업이 생성된 SCN을 기준으로 모든 변경 사항을 포함하도록 이미지 복사 레벨 0 증분 백업을 롤 포워드할 수 있습니다.
첫 번째 RMAN 백업 RUN 스크립트 실행합니다.

```
RUN {
RECOVER COPY OF DATABASE WITH TAG 'incr_update';
BACKUP INCREMENTAL LEVEL 1 FOR RECOVER OF COPY WITH TAG 'incr_update'
DATABASE;
}
```

```
RMAN> RUN {
2> RECOVER COPY OF DATABASE WITH TAG 'incr_update';
3> BACKUP INCREMENTAL LEVEL 1 FOR RECOVER OF COPY WITH TAG 'incr_update'
4> DATABASE;
5> }

Starting recover at 27-NOV-17
using channel ORA_DISK_1
no copy of datafile 1 found to recover
no copy of datafile 2 found to recover
no copy of datafile 3 found to recover
no copy of datafile 4 found to recover
no copy of datafile 5 found to recover
no copy of datafile 7 found to recover
no copy of datafile 8 found to recover
no copy of datafile 9 found to recover
no copy of datafile 10 found to recover
no copy of datafile 11 found to recover
no copy of datafile 12 found to recover
no copy of datafile 13 found to recover
no copy of datafile 14 found to recover
no copy of datafile 15 found to recover
no copy of datafile 16 found to recover
no copy of datafile 17 found to recover
Finished recover at 27-NOV-17

Starting backup at 27-NOV-17
using channel ORA_DISK_1
no parent backup or copy of datafile 3 found
no parent backup or copy of datafile 4 found
no parent backup or copy of datafile 1 found
no parent backup or copy of datafile 2 found
no parent backup or copy of datafile 8 found
no parent backup or copy of datafile 9 found
no parent backup or copy of datafile 13 found
no parent backup or copy of datafile 14 found
no parent backup or copy of datafile 15 found
no parent backup or copy of datafile 16 found
no parent backup or copy of datafile 17 found
no parent backup or copy of datafile 10 found
no parent backup or copy of datafile 11 found
no parent backup or copy of datafile 7 found
no parent backup or copy of datafile 5 found
no parent backup or copy of datafile 12 found
channel ORA_DISK_1: starting datafile copy
input datafile file number=00003 name=/oracle/oracle12/oradata/oracle12/sysaux01.dbf
```

```
channel ORA_DISK_1: datafile copy complete, elapsed time: 00:00:03
channel ORA_DISK_1: starting datafile copy
input datafile file number=00007 name=/oracle/oracle12/oradata/oracle12/users01.dbf
output file name=/oracle/oracle12/RMAN_BACKUP/ORACLE12_data_D-ORACLE12_I-2053465567_TS-USERS_FNO-7_58skk816_961159846_168 tag=INC
R_UPDATE RECID=160 STAMP=961159849
channel ORA_DISK_1: datafile copy complete, elapsed time: 00:00:03
channel ORA_DISK_1: starting datafile copy
input datafile file number=00005 name=+DATA/ORACLE12/DATAFILE/unione01.dbf
output file name=/oracle/oracle12/RMAN_BACKUP/ORACLE12_data_D-ORACLE12_I-2053465567_TS-UNIONE_FNO-5_59skk819_961159849_169 tag=IN
CR_UPDATE RECID=161 STAMP=961159850
channel ORA_DISK_1: datafile copy complete, elapsed time: 00:00:01
channel ORA_DISK_1: starting datafile copy
input datafile file number=00012 name=/oracle/oracle12/oradata/oracle12/oracle12_01.dbf
output file name=/oracle/oracle12/RMAN_BACKUP/ORACLE12_data_D-ORACLE12_I-2053465567_TS-ORACLE12_FNO-12_5askk81b_961159851_170 tag
=INCR_UPDATE RECID=162 STAMP=961159851
channel ORA_DISK_1: datafile copy complete, elapsed time: 00:00:01
Finished backup at 27-NOV-17

Starting Control File and SPFILE Autobackup at 27-NOV-17
piece handle=/oracle/oracle12/FRA/ORACLE12/autobackup/2017_11_27/o1_mf_s_961159853_f1q2x01h_.bkp comment=NONE
Finished Control File and SPFILE Autobackup at 27-NOV-17
```

최초의 백업이기 때문에 "no parent backup or copy of datafile"이라는 메시지와 함께 LEVEL 0의 풀 백업과 동일하게 백업이 실행됩니다.

두 번째로 같은 스크립트를 재수행합니다.

```
RUN {
RECOVER COPY OF DATABASE WITH TAG 'incr_update';
BACKUP INCREMENTAL LEVEL 1 FOR RECOVER OF COPY WITH TAG 'incr_update'
DATABASE;
}
```

```
RMAN> RUN {
2> RECOVER COPY OF DATABASE WITH TAG 'incr_update';
BACKUP INCREMENTAL LEVEL 1 FOR RECOVER OF COPY WITH TAG 'incr_update'
3> 4> DATABASE;
5> }

Starting recover at 27-NOV-17
using channel ORA_DISK_1
no copy of datafile 1 found to recover
no copy of datafile 2 found to recover
no copy of datafile 3 found to recover
no copy of datafile 4 found to recover
no copy of datafile 5 found to recover
no copy of datafile 7 found to recover
no copy of datafile 8 found to recover
no copy of datafile 9 found to recover
no copy of datafile 10 found to recover
no copy of datafile 11 found to recover
no copy of datafile 12 found to recover
no copy of datafile 13 found to recover
no copy of datafile 14 found to recover
no copy of datafile 15 found to recover
no copy of datafile 16 found to recover
no copy of datafile 17 found to recover
Finished recover at 27-NOV-17

Starting backup at 27-NOV-17
using channel ORA_DISK_1
channel ORA_DISK_1: starting incremental level 1 datafile backup set
channel ORA_DISK_1: specifying datafile(s) in backup set
input datafile file number=00003 name=/oracle/oracle12/oradata/oracle12/sysaux01.dbf
input datafile file number=00002 name=+DATA/ORACLE12/DATAFILE/unione02.dbf
input datafile file number=00005 name=+DATA/ORACLE12/DATAFILE/unione01.dbf
input datafile file number=00008 name=+DATA/ORACLE12/DATAFILE/unione03.dbf
input datafile file number=00009 name=+DATA/ORACLE12/DATAFILE/unione04.dbf
input datafile file number=00004 name=/oracle/oracle12/oradata/oracle12/undotbs01.dbf
```

```
channel ORA_DISK_1: backup set complete, elapsed time: 00:00:03
channel ORA_DISK_1: starting incremental level 1 datafile backup set
channel ORA_DISK_1: specifying datafile(s) in backup set
input datafile file number=00001 name=/oracle/oracle12/oradata/oracle12/system01.dbf
channel ORA_DISK_1: starting piece 1 at 27-NOV-17
channel ORA_DISK_1: finished piece 1 at 27-NOV-17
piece handle=/oracle/oracle12/RMAN_BACKUP/ORACLE12_5dskkakr_1_1_961161883_173 tag=INCR_UPDATE comment=NONE
channel ORA_DISK_1: backup set complete, elapsed time: 00:00:01
channel ORA_DISK_1: starting incremental level 1 datafile backup set
channel ORA_DISK_1: specifying datafile(s) in backup set
input datafile file number=00013 name=/oracle/oracle12/oradata/oracle12/aso_test01.dbf
input datafile file number=00014 name=/oracle/oracle12/oradata/oracle12/UNIONE_ENC_ARIA.dbf
input datafile file number=00015 name=/oracle/oracle12/oradata/oracle12/UNIONE_ENC_SEED.dbf
input datafile file number=00016 name=/oracle/oracle12/oradata/oracle12/UNIONE_ENC_AES.dbf
input datafile file number=00017 name=/oracle/oracle12/oradata/oracle12/UNIONE_ENC_3DES.dbf
input datafile file number=00010 name=/oracle/oracle12/oradata/oracle12/undotbs02.dbf
input datafile file number=00011 name=/oracle/oracle12/oradata/oracle12/undotbs03.dbf
input datafile file number=00007 name=/oracle/oracle12/oradata/oracle12/users01.dbf
input datafile file number=00012 name=/oracle/oracle12/oradata/oracle12/oracle12_01.dbf
channel ORA_DISK_1: starting piece 1 at 27-NOV-17
channel ORA_DISK_1: finished piece 1 at 27-NOV-17
piece handle=/oracle/oracle12/RMAN_BACKUP/ORACLE12_5eskkaks_1_1_961161884_174 tag=INCR_UPDATE comment=NONE
channel ORA_DISK_1: backup set complete, elapsed time: 00:00:01
Finished backup at 27-NOV-17
```

백업 스크립트를 수행시키면 아까와 달리 부모 백업은 있지만 복구할 파일이 없다는 "no copy of datafile .. found to recover" 나오면서 수분 안에 백업이 완료됩니다. 이번 백업을 통해 LEVEL 변경기준이 되는 백업이 완료되었습니다.

이제 기준이 되는 LEVEL 0 백업과 롤 포워드 복구시킬 LEVEL 1 백업이 만들어졌습니다.

세 번째로 같은 스크립트를 재수행합니다.

```
RUN {
RECOVER COPY OF DATABASE WITH TAG 'incr_update';
BACKUP INCREMENTAL LEVEL 1 FOR RECOVER OF COPY WITH TAG 'incr_update'
DATABASE;
}
```

```
RMAN> RUN {
2> RECOVER COPY OF DATABASE WITH TAG 'incr_update';
3> BACKUP INCREMENTAL LEVEL 1 FOR RECOVER OF COPY WITH TAG 'incr_update'
4> DATABASE;
5> }

Starting recover at 27-NOV-17
using channel ORA_DISK_1
channel ORA_DISK_1: starting incremental datafile backup set restore
channel ORA_DISK_1: specifying datafile copies to recover
recovering datafile copy file number=00002 name=/oracle/oracle12/RMAN_BACKUP/ORACLE12_data_D-ORACLE12_I-2053465567_TS-UNIONE_FNO-
2_4uskk8h1_961159713_158
recovering datafile copy file number=00003 name=/oracle/oracle12/RMAN_BACKUP/ORACLE12_data_D-ORACLE12_I-2053465567_TS-SYSAUX_FNO-
3_4rskk6me_961157838_155
recovering datafile copy file number=00004 name=/oracle/oracle12/RMAN_BACKUP/ORACLE12_data_D-ORACLE12_I-2053465567_TS-UNDOTBS1_FN
O-4_4sskk7gn_961158679_156
recovering datafile copy file number=00005 name=/oracle/oracle12/RMAN_BACKUP/ORACLE12_data_D-ORACLE12_I-2053465567_TS-UNIONE_FNO-
5_59skk819_961159849_169
recovering datafile copy file number=00008 name=/oracle/oracle12/RMAN_BACKUP/ORACLE12_data_D-ORACLE12_I-2053465567_TS-UNIONE_FNO-
8_4vskk8hh_961159729_159
recovering datafile copy file number=00009 name=/oracle/oracle12/RMAN_BACKUP/ORACLE12_data_D-ORACLE12_I-2053465567_TS-UNIONE_FNO-
9_50skk8i0_961159744_160
channel ORA_DISK_1: reading from backup piece /oracle/oracle12/RMAN_BACKUP/ORACLE12_5cskkako_1_1_961161880_172
channel ORA_DISK_1: piece handle=/oracle/oracle12/RMAN_BACKUP/ORACLE12_5cskkako_1_1_961161880_172 tag=INCR_UPDATE
channel ORA_DISK_1: restored backup piece 1
channel ORA_DISK_1: restore complete, elapsed time: 00:00:07
```

```
channel ORA_DISK_1: starting incremental datafile backup set restore
channel ORA_DISK_1: specifying datafile copies to recover
recovering datafile copy file number=00001 name=/oracle/oracle12/RMAN_BACKUP/ORACLE12_data_D-ORACLE12_I-2053465567_TS-SYSTEM_FNO-
1_4tskk883_961159427_157
channel ORA_DISK_1: reading from backup piece /oracle/oracle12/RMAN_BACKUP/ORACLE12_5dskkakr_1_1_961161883_173
channel ORA_DISK_1: piece handle=/oracle/oracle12/RMAN_BACKUP/ORACLE12_5dskkakr_1_1_961161883_173 tag=INCR_UPDATE
channel ORA_DISK_1: restored backup piece 1
channel ORA_DISK_1: restore complete, elapsed time: 00:00:01
channel ORA_DISK_1: starting incremental datafile backup set restore
channel ORA_DISK_1: specifying datafile copies to recover
recovering datafile copy file number=00007 name=/oracle/oracle12/RMAN_BACKUP/ORACLE12_data_D-ORACLE12_I-2053465567_TS-USERS_FNO-7
_58skk816_961159846_168
recovering datafile copy file number=00010 name=/oracle/oracle12/RMAN_BACKUP/ORACLE12_data_D-ORACLE12_I-2053465567_TS-UNDOTBS1_FN
O-10_56skk8ks_961159836_166
recovering datafile copy file number=00011 name=/oracle/oracle12/RMAN_BACKUP/ORACLE12_data_D-ORACLE12_I-2053465567_TS-UNDOTBS1_FN
O-11_57skk813_961159843_167
recovering datafile copy file number=00012 name=/oracle/oracle12/RMAN_BACKUP/ORACLE12_data_D-ORACLE12_I-2053465567_TS-ORACLE12_FN
O-12_5askk81b_961159851_170
recovering datafile copy file number=00013 name=/oracle/oracle12/RMAN_BACKUP/ORACLE12_data_D-ORACLE12_I-2053465567_TS-ASO_TEST_FN
O-13_51skk8if_961159759_161
recovering datafile copy file number=00014 name=/oracle/oracle12/RMAN_BACKUP/ORACLE12_data_D-ORACLE12_I-2053465567_TS-UNIONE_ENC_
ARIA_FNO-14_52skk8iv_961159775_162
recovering datafile copy file number=00015 name=/oracle/oracle12/RMAN_BACKUP/ORACLE12_data_D-ORACLE12_I-2053465567_TS-UNIONE_ENC_
SEED_FNO-15_53skk8je_961159790_163
recovering datafile copy file number=00016 name=/oracle/oracle12/RMAN_BACKUP/ORACLE12_data_D-ORACLE12_I-2053465567_TS-UNIONE_ENC_
AES_FNO-16_54skk8jt_961159805_164
recovering datafile copy file number=00017 name=/oracle/oracle12/RMAN_BACKUP/ORACLE12_data_D-ORACLE12_I-2053465567_TS-UNIONE_ENC_
3DES_FNO-17_55skk8kd_961159821_165
channel ORA_DISK_1: reading from backup piece /oracle/oracle12/RMAN_BACKUP/ORACLE12_5eskkaks_1_1_961161884_174
channel ORA_DISK_1: piece handle=/oracle/oracle12/RMAN_BACKUP/ORACLE12_5eskkaks_1_1_961161884_174 tag=INCR_UPDATE
channel ORA_DISK_1: restored backup piece 1
channel ORA_DISK_1: restore complete, elapsed time: 00:00:03
Finished recover at 27-NOV-17
```

```
Starting backup at 27-NOV-17
using channel ORA_DISK_1
channel ORA_DISK_1: starting incremental level 1 datafile backup set
channel ORA_DISK_1: specifying datafile(s) in backup set
input datafile file number=00003 name=/oracle/oracle12/oradata/oracle12/sysaux01.dbf
input datafile file number=00002 name=+DATA/ORACLE12/DATAFILE/unione02.dbf
input datafile file number=00005 name=+DATA/ORACLE12/DATAFILE/unione01.dbf
input datafile file number=00008 name=+DATA/ORACLE12/DATAFILE/unione03.dbf
input datafile file number=00009 name=+DATA/ORACLE12/DATAFILE/unione04.dbf
input datafile file number=00004 name=/oracle/oracle12/oradata/oracle12/undotbs01.dbf
channel ORA_DISK_1: starting piece 1 at 27-NOV-17
channel ORA_DISK_1: finished piece 1 at 27-NOV-17
piece handle=/oracle/oracle12/RMAN_BACKUP/ORACLE12_5gskkb32_1_1_961162338_176 tag=INCR_UPDATE comment=NONE
channel ORA_DISK_1: backup set complete, elapsed time: 00:00:01
channel ORA_DISK_1: starting incremental level 1 datafile backup set
channel ORA_DISK_1: specifying datafile(s) in backup set
input datafile file number=00001 name=/oracle/oracle12/oradata/oracle12/system01.dbf
channel ORA_DISK_1: starting piece 1 at 27-NOV-17
channel ORA_DISK_1: finished piece 1 at 27-NOV-17
piece handle=/oracle/oracle12/RMAN_BACKUP/ORACLE12_5hskkb33_1_1_961162339_177 tag=INCR_UPDATE comment=NONE
channel ORA_DISK_1: backup set complete, elapsed time: 00:00:01
channel ORA_DISK_1: starting incremental level 1 datafile backup set
channel ORA_DISK_1: specifying datafile(s) in backup set
input datafile file number=00013 name=/oracle/oracle12/oradata/oracle12/aso_test01.dbf
input datafile file number=00014 name=/oracle/oracle12/oradata/oracle12/UNIONE_ENC_ARIA.dbf
input datafile file number=00015 name=/oracle/oracle12/oradata/oracle12/UNIONE_ENC_SEED.dbf
input datafile file number=00016 name=/oracle/oracle12/oradata/oracle12/UNIONE_ENC_AES.dbf
input datafile file number=00017 name=/oracle/oracle12/oradata/oracle12/UNIONE_ENC_3DES.dbf
input datafile file number=00010 name=/oracle/oracle12/oradata/oracle12/undotbs02.dbf
input datafile file number=00011 name=/oracle/oracle12/oradata/oracle12/undotbs03.dbf
input datafile file number=00007 name=/oracle/oracle12/oradata/oracle12/users01.dbf
input datafile file number=00012 name=/oracle/oracle12/oradata/oracle12/oracle12_01.dbf
channel ORA_DISK_1: starting piece 1 at 27-NOV-17
channel ORA_DISK_1: finished piece 1 at 27-NOV-17
piece handle=/oracle/oracle12/RMAN_BACKUP/ORACLE12_5iskkb34_1_1_961162340_178 tag=INCR_UPDATE comment=NONE
channel ORA_DISK_1: backup set complete, elapsed time: 00:00:01
Finished backup at 27-NOV-17
```

수행 결과를 살펴보면 가장 먼저 백업 된 파일을 복원(Restore) 시킵니다. 그리고 복원된 파일을 현재 시점으로 증분 복구(Recover) 시킵니다. 복구가 완료되면 "starting incremental level 1 datafile backup set" 메시지와 함께 다시 백업을 수행합니다.

테스트 결과를 보면 세 번째 백업부터 실제 운영 중인 DATA 파일을 읽어서 백업하는 과정이 생략되어 있음을 확인할 수 있습니다.

Database 서버와 백업 서버가 분리되어 있다면 운영 서버에 큰 부하없이 백업이 가능하다는 것을 확인할 수 있습니다.

2 백업된 파일을 사용한 복제 DB 생성

이미 백업이 완료된 백업된 파일을 이용하여 타겟 데이터베이스에 연결하지 않고 DUPLICATE 명령어를 사용해 복제 DB를 생성할 수 있습니다.

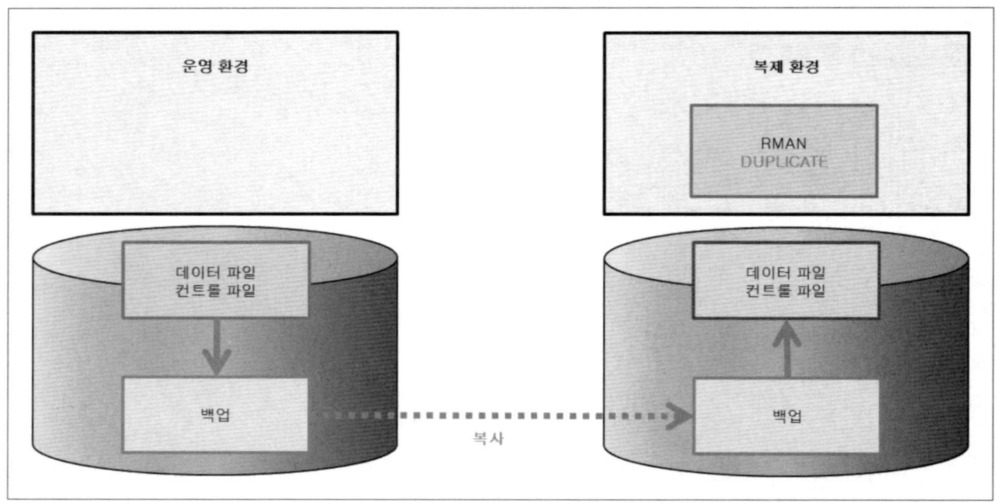

지금부터 백업된 파일을 사용하여 복제 DB를 생성하겠습니다.

먼저 현재 DB의 백업을 수행합니다.

```
RMAN> BACKUP DATABASE PLUS ARCHIVELOG ;
RMAN> BACKUP CURRENT CONTROLFILE ;
```

```
RMAN> BACKUP DATABASE PLUS ARCHIVELOG ;


Starting backup at 27-NOV-17
current log archived
using channel ORA_DISK_1
channel ORA_DISK_1: starting archived log backup set
channel ORA_DISK_1: specifying archived log(s) in backup set
input archived log thread=1 sequence=508 RECID=505 STAMP=961167581
input archived log thread=1 sequence=509 RECID=506 STAMP=961167582
input archived log thread=1 sequence=510 RECID=507 STAMP=961167584
input archived log thread=1 sequence=511 RECID=508 STAMP=961167585
input archived log thread=1 sequence=512 RECID=509 STAMP=961167587
input archived log thread=1 sequence=513 RECID=510 STAMP=961167662
channel ORA_DISK_1: starting piece 1 at 27-NOV-17
channel ORA_DISK_1: finished piece 1 at 27-NOV-17
piece handle=/oracle/oracle12/RMAN_BACKUP/ORACLE12_65skkg9i_1_1_961167666_197 tag=TAG20171127T150103 comment=NONE
channel ORA_DISK_1: backup set complete, elapsed time: 00:00:04
Finished backup at 27-NOV-17

Starting backup at 27-NOV-17
using channel ORA_DISK_1
channel ORA_DISK_1: starting full datafile backup set
channel ORA_DISK_1: specifying datafile(s) in backup set
input datafile file number=00003 name=/oracle/oracle12/oradata/oracle12/sysaux01.dbf
input datafile file number=00004 name=/oracle/oracle12/oradata/oracle12/undotbs01.dbf
input datafile file number=00001 name=/oracle/oracle12/oradata/oracle12/system01.dbf
input datafile file number=00002 name=/oracle/oracle12/oradata/oracle12/UNIONE/unione02.dbf
input datafile file number=00008 name=/oracle/oracle12/oradata/oracle12/UNIONE/unione03.dbf
input datafile file number=00009 name=/oracle/oracle12/oradata/oracle12/UNIONE/unione04.dbf
input datafile file number=00010 name=/oracle/oracle12/oradata/oracle12/undotbs02.dbf
input datafile file number=00011 name=/oracle/oracle12/oradata/oracle12/undotbs03.dbf
input datafile file number=00007 name=/oracle/oracle12/oradata/oracle12/users01.dbf
input datafile file number=00005 name=/oracle/oracle12/oradata/oracle12/UNIONE/unione01.dbf
input datafile file number=00012 name=/oracle/oracle12/oradata/oracle12/oracle12_01.dbf
channel ORA_DISK_1: starting piece 1 at 27-NOV-17
```

```
RMAN> BACKUP CURRENT CONTROLFILE ;

Starting backup at 27-NOV-17
using channel ORA_DISK_1
channel ORA_DISK_1: starting full datafile backup set
channel ORA_DISK_1: specifying datafile(s) in backup set
including current control file in backup set
channel ORA_DISK_1: starting piece 1 at 27-NOV-17
channel ORA_DISK_1: finished piece 1 at 27-NOV-17
piece handle=/oracle/oracle12/RMAN_BACKUP/ORACLE12_69skkgnc_1_1_961168108_201 tag=TAG20171127T150828 comment=NONE
channel ORA_DISK_1: backup set complete, elapsed time: 00:00:02
Finished backup at 27-NOV-17

Starting Control File and SPFILE Autobackup at 27-NOV-17
piece handle=/oracle/oracle12/FRA/ORACLE12/autobackup/2017_11_27/o1_mf_s_961168113_f1qbz30p_.bkp comment=NONE
Finished Control File and SPFILE Autobackup at 27-NOV-17

RMAN>
```

DB 복제할 기준 시간을 확인하고 Redo Log 파일을 스위칭합니다.

```
RMAN> SELECT SYSDATE CUR_TIME FROM DUAL ;
RMAN> ALTER SYSTEM SWITCH LOGFILE ;
RMAN> ALTER SYSTEM SWITCH LOGFILE ;
RMAN> ALTER SYSTEM SWITCH LOGFILE ;
RMAN> ALTER SYSTEM CHECKPOINT ;
```

```
RMAN> SELECT SYSDATE CUR_TIME FROM DUAL ;

CUR_TIME
-------------------
2017/11/27 15:09:16

RMAN> ALTER SYSTEM SWITCH LOGFILE ;

Statement processed

RMAN> ALTER SYSTEM SWITCH LOGFILE ;

Statement processed

RMAN> ALTER SYSTEM SWITCH LOGFILE ;

Statement processed

RMAN> ALTER SYSTEM CHECKPOINT ;

Statement processed

RMAN>
```

복제되어 구성할 DB 서버의 오라클 홈 영역에 있는 listener.ora 파일을 생성합니다.

```
vi $ORACLE_HOME/network/admin/listener.ora
UNIONE =
  (DESCRIPTION_LIST =
    (DESCRIPTION =
      (ADDRESS = (PROTOCOL = TCP)(HOST = yspark-linux)(PORT = 1577))
    )
  )
```

```
UNIONE =
  (DESCRIPTION_LIST =
    (DESCRIPTION =
      (ADDRESS = (PROTOCOL = TCP)(HOST = yspark-linux)(PORT = 1577))
    )
  )
[oracle12@yspark-linux admin]$ cat listener.ora
```

RMAN을 수행시킬 서버에 오라클 홈 영역에 있는 접속 파일 tnsnames.ora 파일에 추가합니다. 이때 UR=A라는 내용을 추가하여 nomount에서 접속이 가능하도록 설정합니다.

```
vi $ORACLE_HOME/network/admin/tnsnames.ora
UNIONE =
(DESCRIPTION =
(ADDRESS = (PROTOCOL = TCP)(HOST = yspark-linux)(PORT = 1577))
(CONNECT_DATA =
(SERVER = DEDICATED) (SERVICE_NAME = UNIONE)
(UR = A) ## Enable to connect into NOMOUNT database status
) )
```

```
UNIONE =
(DESCRIPTION =
(ADDRESS = (PROTOCOL = TCP)(HOST = yspark-linux)(PORT = 1577))
(CONNECT_DATA =
(SERVER = DEDICATED) (SERVICE_NAME = UNIONE)
(UR = A) ## Enable to connect into NOMOUNT database status
) )
[oracle12@yspark-linux admin]$ cat tnsnames.ora
```

준비가 되었다면 복제되어 구성할 DB 서버의 리스너를 기동시킵니다.

```
#lsnrctl start UNIONE
```

```
[oracle12@yspark-linux admin]$ lsnrctl start UNIONE

LSNRCTL for Linux: Version 12.2.0.1.0 - Production on 27-NOV-2017 15:12:37

Copyright (c) 1991, 2016, Oracle.  All rights reserved.

Starting /oracle/oracle12/app/oracle/product/12.2.0/dbhome_1/bin/tnslsnr: please wait...

TNSLSNR for Linux: Version 12.2.0.1.0 - Production
System parameter file is /oracle/oracle12/app/oracle/product/12.2.0/dbhome_1/network/admin/listener.ora
Log messages written to /oracle/oracle12/app/oracle/diag/tnslsnr/yspark-linux/unione/alert/log.xml
Listening on: (DESCRIPTION=(ADDRESS=(PROTOCOL=tcp)(HOST=yspark-linux)(PORT=1577)))

Connecting to (DESCRIPTION=(ADDRESS=(PROTOCOL=TCP)(HOST=yspark-linux)(PORT=1577)))
STATUS of the LISTENER
------------------------
Alias                     UNIONE
Version                   TNSLSNR for Linux: Version 12.2.0.1.0 - Production
Start Date                27-NOV-2017 15:12:37
Uptime                    0 days 0 hr. 0 min. 0 sec
Trace Level               off
Security                  ON: Local OS Authentication
SNMP                      OFF
Listener Parameter File   /oracle/oracle12/app/oracle/product/12.2.0/dbhome_1/network/admin/listener.ora
Listener Log File         /oracle/oracle12/app/oracle/diag/tnslsnr/yspark-linux/unione/alert/log.xml
Listening Endpoints Summary...
  (DESCRIPTION=(ADDRESS=(PROTOCOL=tcp)(HOST=yspark-linux)(PORT=1577)))
The listener supports no services
The command completed successfully
[oracle12@yspark-linux admin]$ 
```

복제해서 기동시킬 DB용 파리미터 파일을 만들기 위해 기존 DB 서버에서 pfile 파일을 생성합니다.

```
SQL> create pfile='initUNIONE.ora' from spfile ;
```

```
[oracle12@yspark-linux admin]$ sqlplus "/as sysdba"

SQL*Plus: Release 12.2.0.1.0 Production on Mon Nov 27 15:16:10 2017

Copyright (c) 1982, 2016, Oracle.  All rights reserved.


Connected to:
Oracle Database 12c Enterprise Edition Release 12.2.0.1.0 - 64bit Production

SQL> create pfile='initUNIONE.ora' from spfile ;

File created.

SQL> exit
Disconnected from Oracle Database 12c Enterprise Edition Release 12.2.0.1.0 - 64bit Production
[oracle12@yspark-linux admin]$ 
```

이제 만든 pfile을 db_file_name_convert 파라미터, log_file_name_convert 파라미터, 기타 메모리 파라미터 등 복제되는 서버의 구성에 맞게 수정하여 서버로 옮겨 놓습니다.

```
vi initUNIONE.ora
```

```
[oracle12@yspark-linux dbs]$ grep dest initUNIONE.ora
*._diag_adr_trace_dest='/oracle/oracle12/app/oracle/diag/rdbms/UNIONE/UNIONE/trace'
*.audit_file_dest='/oracle/oracle12/app/oracle/admin/UNIONE/adump'
*.core_dump_dest='/oracle/oracle12/app/oracle/diag/rdbms/UNIONE/UNIONE/cdump'
*.db_recovery_file_dest='/oracle/oracle12/FRA/UNIONE/'
*.db_recovery_file_dest_size=107374182400
*.diagnostic_dest='/oracle/oracle12/app/oracle'
*.log_archive_dest='/oracle/UNIONE/arch'
[oracle12@yspark-linux dbs]$ grep name initUNIONE.ora
*.db_name='UNIONE'
[oracle12@yspark-linux dbs]$ grep NAME initUNIONE.ora
*.DB_FILE_NAME_CONVERT='oracle12','UNIONE'
*.LOG_FILE_NAME_CONVERT='oracle12','UNIONE'
[oracle12@yspark-linux dbs]$ grep dump initUNIONE.ora
*.audit_file_dest='/oracle/oracle12/app/oracle/admin/UNIONE/adump'
*.core_dump_dest='/oracle/oracle12/app/oracle/diag/rdbms/UNIONE/UNIONE/cdump'
[oracle12@yspark-linux dbs]$ 
```

패스워드 파일과 Dump 디렉토리를 생성합니다.

```
# export ORACLE_SID=UNIONE
# cd $ORACLE_HOME/dbs
# orapwd file=orapwUNIONE password=P#ssw0rd entries=5 sys=y force=y
# mkdir -p /oracle/oracle12/app/oracle/diag/rdbms/UNIONE/UNIONE/trace
# mkdir -p /oracle/oracle12/app/oracle/admin/UNIONE/adump
# mkdir -p /oracle/oracle12/app/oracle/diag/rdbms/UNIONE/UNIONE/cdump
# mkdir -p /oracle/oracle12/FRA/UNIONE/
# mkdir -p /oracle/oracle12/UNIONE/arch
```

```
[UNIONE]yspark-linux:/oracle/oracle12/app/oracle/product/12.2.0/dbhome_1/dbs> export ORACLE_SID=UNIONE
[UNIONE]yspark-linux:/oracle/oracle12/app/oracle/product/12.2.0/dbhome_1/dbs> cd $ORACLE_HOME/dbs
[UNIONE]yspark-linux:/oracle/oracle12/app/oracle/product/12.2.0/dbhome_1/dbs> orapwd file=orapwUNIONE password=P@ssw0rd entries=5 sys=y force=y
[UNIONE]yspark-linux:/oracle/oracle12/app/oracle/product/12.2.0/dbhome_1/dbs>
[UNIONE]yspark-linux:/oracle/oracle12/app/oracle/product/12.2.0/dbhome_1/dbs>
```

```
[oracle12@yspark-linux dbs]$ mkdir -p /oracle/oracle12/app/oracle/diag/rdbms/UNIONE/UNIONE/trace
[oracle12@yspark-linux dbs]$ mkdir -p /oracle/oracle12/app/oracle/admin/UNIONE/adump
[oracle12@yspark-linux dbs]$ mkdir -p /oracle/oracle12/app/oracle/diag/rdbms/UNIONE/UNIONE/cdump
[oracle12@yspark-linux dbs]$ mkdir -p /oracle/oracle12/FRA/UNIONE/
[oracle12@yspark-linux dbs]$ mkdir -p /oracle/oracle12/UNIONE/arch
[oracle12@yspark-linux dbs]$
```

이제 NOMOUNT 상태로 복제 구성할 DB를 기동합니다.

```
# export ORACLE_SID=UNIONE
# sqlplus "/as sysdba"
SQL> startup nomount pfile=$ORACLE_HOME/dbs/initUNIONE.ora
```

```
[UNIONE]yspark-linux:/home/oracle12> echo $ORACLE_SID
UNIONE
[UNIONE]yspark-linux:/home/oracle12> sqlplus "/as sysdba"

SQL*Plus: Release 12.2.0.1.0 Production on Mon Nov 27 15:55:19 2017

Copyright (c) 1982, 2016, Oracle.  All rights reserved.

Connected to an idle instance.

SQL> startup nomount pfile=$ORACLE_HOME/dbs/initUNIONE.ora
ORACLE instance started.

Total System Global Area  746586112 bytes
Fixed Size                  8625176 bytes
Variable Size             587203560 bytes
Database Buffers           33554432 bytes
Redo Buffers                8151040 bytes
In-Memory Area            109051904 bytes
SQL>
```

복제할 사전 준비가 되었습니다. 복제할 서버에서 원래 DB 서버의 RMAN을 원격으로 연결하고 DB 복제를 하기 위해 접속합니다. 대상 DB 서버의 접속이 되면 auxiliary 옵션을 주어 복제 DB도 접속합니다.

```
# export ORACLE_SID=UNIONE
# rman target sys/oracle@oracle12 nocatalog
RMAN> backup archivelog all ;
RMAN> connect auxiliary sys/\”P#ssw0rd\”
```

```
[UNIONE]yspark-linux:/home/oracle12> export ORACLE_SID=UNIONE
[UNIONE]yspark-linux:/home/oracle12> rman target sys/oracle@oracle12 nocatalog

Recovery Manager: Release 12.2.0.1.0 - Production on Mon Nov 27 16:19:48 2017

Copyright (c) 1982, 2017, Oracle and/or its affiliates.  All rights reserved.

connected to target database: ORACLE12 (DBID=2053465567)
using target database control file instead of recovery catalog

RMAN> backup archivelog all ;

Starting backup at 27-NOV-17
current log archived
allocated channel: ORA_DISK_1
channel ORA_DISK_1: SID=171 device type=DISK
skipping archived logs of thread 1 from sequence 508 to 518; already backed up
channel ORA_DISK_1: starting archived log backup set
channel ORA_DISK_1: specifying archived log(s) in backup set
input archived log thread=1 sequence=519 RECID=516 STAMP=961172395
channel ORA_DISK_1: starting piece 1 at 27-NOV-17
channel ORA_DISK_1: finished piece 1 at 27-NOV-17
piece handle=/oracle/oracle12/RMAN_BACKUP/ORACLE12_6dskkktc_1_1_961172396_205 tag=TAG20171127T161956 comment=NONE
channel ORA_DISK_1: backup set complete, elapsed time: 00:00:01
Finished backup at 27-NOV-17

Starting Control File and SPFILE Autobackup at 27-NOV-17
piece handle=/oracle/oracle12/FRA/ORACLE12/autobackup/2017_11_27/o1_mf_s_961172397_f1qh4z3g_.bkp comment=NONE
Finished Control File and SPFILE Autobackup at 27-NOV-17

RMAN> connect auxiliary sys/\"P#ssw0rd\"

connected to auxiliary database: UNIONE (not mounted)

RMAN> █
```

이제 RUN 명령어를 조합하여 복제 명령을 실행합니다.

```
RUN
{
SET NEWNAME FOR DATABASE TO '/oracle/oracle12/oradata/UNIONE/%U' ;
sql 'alter session set nls_date_format="YYYY-MM-DD:HH24:MI:SS"';
DUPLICATE TARGET DATABASE TO UNIONE NOREDO
NOFILENAMECHECK
UNTIL TIME '<DB 복제할 기준 시간>'
LOGFILE
GROUP 1 ('/oracle/oracle12/oradata/UNIONE/redo01.log') SIZE 200M REUSE,
GROUP 2 ('/oracle/oracle12/oradata/UNIONE/redo02.log') SIZE 200M REUSE,
GROUP 3 ('/oracle/oracle12/oradata/UNIONE/redo03.log') SIZE 200M REUSE
SPFILE PARAMETER_VALUE_CONVERT 'oracle12','UNIONE'
SET control_files='/oracle/oracle12/oradata/UNIONE/control01.ctl'
SET db_recovery_file_dest='/oracle/oracle12/FRA/UNIONE/'
SET LOG_ARCHIVE_DEST='/oracle/oracle12/UNIONE/arch'
SET audit_file_dest='/oracle/oracle12/app/oracle/admin/UNIONE/adump' ;
}
```

```
RMAN> RUN
2> {
3> SET NEWNAME FOR DATABASE TO '/oracle/oracle12/oradata/UNIONE/%U' ;
4> sql 'alter session set nls_date_format="YYYY-MM-DD:HH24:MI:SS"';
5> DUPLICATE TARGET DATABASE TO UNIONE NOREDO
6> NOFILENAMECHECK
7> UNTIL TIME '2017-11-27:15:00:00'
8> LOGFILE
9> GROUP 1 ('/oracle/oracle12/oradata/UNIONE/redo01.log') SIZE 200M REUSE,
10> GROUP 2 ('/oracle/oracle12/oradata/UNIONE/redo02.log') SIZE 200M REUSE,
11> GROUP 3 ('/oracle/oracle12/oradata/UNIONE/redo03.log') SIZE 200M REUSE
12> SPFILE PARAMETER_VALUE_CONVERT 'oracle12','UNIONE'
13> SET control_files='/oracle/oracle12/oradata/UNIONE/control01.ctl'
14> SET db_recovery_file_dest='/oracle/oracle12/FRA/UNIONE/'
15> SET LOG_ARCHIVE_DEST='/oracle/oracle12/UNIONE/arch'
16> SET audit_file_dest='/oracle/oracle12/app/oracle/admin/UNIONE/adump' ;
17> }

executing command: SET NEWNAME
```

```
executing command: SET until clause

sql statement: alter system set  db_name =  ''ORACLE12'' comment= ''Modified by RMAN duplicate'' scope=spfile

sql statement: alter system set  db_unique_name =  ''UNIONE'' comment= ''Modified by RMAN duplicate'' scope=spfile

Oracle instance shut down

Oracle instance started

Total System Global Area     746586112 bytes

Fixed Size                     8625176 bytes
Variable Size                587203560 bytes
Database Buffers              33554432 bytes
Redo Buffers                   8151040 bytes
In-Memory Area               109051904 bytes

Starting restore at 27-NOV-17
allocated channel: ORA_AUX_DISK_1
channel ORA_AUX_DISK_1: SID=89 device type=DISK

channel ORA_AUX_DISK_1: starting datafile backup set restore
channel ORA_AUX_DISK_1: restoring control file
channel ORA_AUX_DISK_1: reading from backup piece /oracle/oracle12/FRA/ORACLE12/autobackup/2017_11_27/o1_mf_s_96116811
3_f1qbz30p_.bkp
channel ORA_AUX_DISK_1: piece handle=/oracle/oracle12/FRA/ORACLE12/autobackup/2017_11_27/o1_mf_s_961168113_f1qbz30p_.b
kp tag=TAG20171127T150833
channel ORA_AUX_DISK_1: restored backup piece 1
channel ORA_AUX_DISK_1: restore complete, elapsed time: 00:00:01
output file name=/oracle/oracle12/oradata/UNIONE/control01.ctl
Finished restore at 27-NOV-17

database mounted

contents of Memory Script:
{
```

```
sql statement: alter system set  db_name =  ''UNIONE'' comment= ''Reset to original value by RMAN'' scope=spfile

sql statement: alter system reset  db_unique_name scope=spfile
Oracle instance started

Total System Global Area     746586112 bytes

Fixed Size                     8625176 bytes
Variable Size                595592168 bytes
Database Buffers              25165824 bytes
Redo Buffers                   8151040 bytes
In-Memory Area               109051904 bytes
sql statement: CREATE CONTROLFILE REUSE SET DATABASE "UNIONE" RESETLOGS ARCHIVELOG
  MAXLOGFILES      16
  MAXLOGMEMBERS      3
  MAXDATAFILES      100
  MAXINSTANCES     8
  MAXLOGHISTORY      292
 LOGFILE
  GROUP   1 ( '/oracle/oracle12/oradata/UNIONE/redo01.log' ) SIZE 200 M  REUSE,
  GROUP   2 ( '/oracle/oracle12/oradata/UNIONE/redo02.log' ) SIZE 200 M  REUSE,
  GROUP   3 ( '/oracle/oracle12/oradata/UNIONE/redo03.log' ) SIZE 200 M  REUSE
 DATAFILE
  '/oracle/oracle12/oradata/UNIONE/data_D-UNIONE_TS-SYSTEM_FNO-1'
 CHARACTER SET AL32UTF8
```

```
datafile 3 switched to datafile copy
input datafile copy RECID=1 STAMP=961236701 file name=/oracle/oracle12/oradata/UNIONE/data_D-UNIONE_TS-SYSAUX_FNO-3
datafile 4 switched to datafile copy
input datafile copy RECID=2 STAMP=961236701 file name=/oracle/oracle12/oradata/UNIONE/data_D-UNIONE_TS-UNDOTBS1_FNO-4
datafile 7 switched to datafile copy
input datafile copy RECID=3 STAMP=961236701 file name=/oracle/oracle12/oradata/UNIONE/data_D-UNIONE_TS-USERS_FNO-7
datafile 10 switched to datafile copy
input datafile copy RECID=4 STAMP=961236702 file name=/oracle/oracle12/oradata/UNIONE/data_D-UNIONE_TS-UNDOTBS1_FNO-10
datafile 11 switched to datafile copy
input datafile copy RECID=5 STAMP=961236702 file name=/oracle/oracle12/oradata/UNIONE/data_D-UNIONE_TS-UNDOTBS1_FNO-11
datafile 12 switched to datafile copy
input datafile copy RECID=6 STAMP=961236702 file name=/oracle/oracle12/oradata/UNIONE/data_D-UNIONE_TS-ORACLE12_FNO-12
Reenabling controlfile options for auxiliary database
Executing: alter database enable block change tracking using file '/oracle/oracle12/oradata/UNIONE/bct_D-UNIONE_lbskmif4'

contents of Memory Script:
{
   Alter clone database open resetlogs;
}
executing Memory Script

database opened
Finished Duplicate Db at 28-NOV-17
```

마지막에 DB가 OPEN 되었다는 메시지와 함께 수행이 완료됩니다.

이제 복제된 DB의 상태를 확인합니다.

```
# export ORACLE_SID=UNIONE
# sqlplus "/as sysdba"
SQL> SELECT INSTANCE_NAME,STATUS FROM V$INSTANCE ;
SQL> SELECT MEMBER FROM V$LOGFILE ;
SQL> SELECT FILE_NAME FROM DBA_DATA_FILES ;
```

```
[UNIONE]yspark-linux:/home/oracle12> export ORACLE_SID=UNIONE
[UNIONE]yspark-linux:/home/oracle12> sqlplus "/as sysdba"

SQL*Plus: Release 12.2.0.1.0 Production on Tue Nov 28 10:25:24 2017

Copyright (c) 1982, 2016, Oracle.  All rights reserved.


Connected to:
Oracle Database 12c Enterprise Edition Release 12.2.0.1.0 - 64bit Production

SQL> select INSTANCE_NAME,STATUS from v$instance ;

INSTANCE_NAME    STATUS
---------------- ------------
UNIONE           OPEN

SQL> select member from v$logfile ;

MEMBER
--------------------------------------------------------------------------------
/oracle/oracle12/oradata/UNIONE/redo03.log
/oracle/oracle12/oradata/UNIONE/redo02.log
/oracle/oracle12/oradata/UNIONE/redo01.log

SQL> SELECT FILE_NAME FROM DBA_DATA_FILES ;

FILE_NAME
--------------------------------------------------------------------------------
/oracle/oracle12/oradata/UNIONE/data_D-UNIONE_TS-SYSTEM_FNO-1
/oracle/oracle12/oradata/UNIONE/data_D-UNIONE_TS-SYSAUX_FNO-3
/oracle/oracle12/oradata/UNIONE/data_D-UNIONE_TS-USERS_FNO-7
/oracle/oracle12/oradata/UNIONE/data_D-UNIONE_TS-UNDOTBS1_FNO-4
/oracle/oracle12/oradata/UNIONE/data_D-UNIONE_TS-UNDOTBS1_FNO-10
/oracle/oracle12/oradata/UNIONE/data_D-UNIONE_TS-UNDOTBS1_FNO-11
/oracle/oracle12/oradata/UNIONE/data_D-UNIONE_TS-ORACLE12_FNO-12

7 rows selected.

SQL> 
```

로그를 분석해 보면 백업 받은 데이터를 다른 서버에 복원시키고 복구하는 순서와 동일합니다. 차이가 있다면 명령 단계가 간소하게 수행이 되는 것과 RMAN의 여러 개 멀티채널을 OPEN 해서 수행하면 속도를 빠르게 진행된다는 것입니다.

CPU CORE 수가 많은 대용량 서버에서 복제 RMAN 명령어 내용에 allocate channel 명령어를 이용하여 채널을 최대 16개 설정 후 수행하면 진행 과정의 데이터 파일의 복원, 복구 과정을 병렬로 수행하게 되어 복제 수행 시간을 단축할 수 있습니다.

3 실제 운영 DB의 데이터 파일을 이용한 복제 DB 생성

RMAN 백업 파일에서 읽는 것이 아니라 실제 데이터 파일을 복사해서 복제 DB를 만들 수 있습니다.

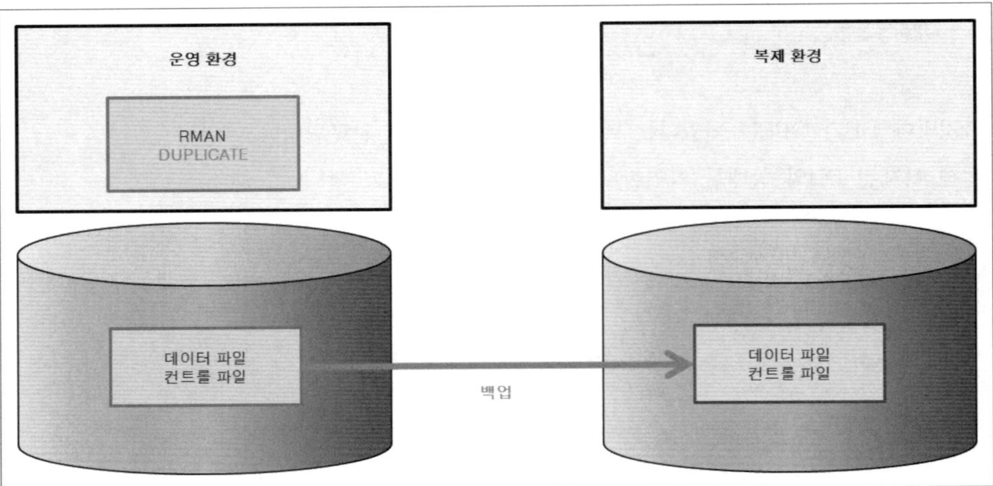

백업 데이터로 복제 할 경우 복제 환경에서 RMAN 명령이 수행되는데 실제 운영 DB를 이용한 복제 DB 생성은 운영 환경에서 RMAN 명령어로 수행합니다.

먼저 현재 DB의 백업이 존재하는지 확인합니다.

```
RMAN> LIST BACKUP ;
```

```
[oracle12]yspark-linux:/home/oracle12> rman target /
Recovery Manager: Release 12.2.0.1.0 - Production on Tue Nov 28 11:01:54 2017
Copyright (c) 1982, 2017, Oracle and/or its affiliates.  All rights reserved.
connected to target database: ORACLE12 (DBID=2053465567)
RMAN> LIST BACKUP ;
using target database control file instead of recovery catalog
specification does not match any backup in the repository
RMAN> █
```

복제되어 구성할 DB 서버의 오라클 홈 영역에 있는 listener.ora 파일을 생성합니다.

```
vi $ORACLE_HOME/network/admin/listener.ora
YONGSEOK =
  (DESCRIPTION_LIST =
    (DESCRIPTION =
      (ADDRESS = (PROTOCOL = TCP)(HOST = yspark-linux)(PORT = 1588))
    )
  )

SID_LIST_YONGSEOK =
  (SID_LIST =
    (SID_DESC =
      (GLOBAL_DBNAME = YONGSEOK)
      (ORACLE_HOME = /oracle/oracle12/app/oracle/product/12.2.0/dbhome_1)
      (SID_NAME = YONGSEOK)
    )
  )
```

```
YONGSEOK =
  (DESCRIPTION_LIST =
    (DESCRIPTION =
      (ADDRESS = (PROTOCOL = TCP)(HOST = yspark-linux)(PORT = 1588))
    )
  )

SID_LIST_YONGSEOK =
  (SID_LIST =
    (SID_DESC =
      (GLOBAL_DBNAME = YONGSEOK)
      (ORACLE_HOME = /oracle/oracle12/app/oracle/product/12.2.0/dbhome_1)
      (SID_NAME = YONGSEOK)
    )
  )
[oracle12]yspark-linux:/oracle/oracle12/app/oracle/product/12.2.0/dbhome_1/network/admin>
```

운영 중인 서버에서 RMAN을 수행하여 복제 서버로 접속해야 하므로 복제 DB 서버 정보를 접속 파일 tnsnames.ora 파일에 추가합니다. 이때 UR=A라는 내용을 추가하여 nomount에서 접속이 가능하도록 설정합니다.

```
vi $ORACLE_HOME/network/admin/tnsnames.ora
YONGSEOK =
  (DESCRIPTION =
        (ADDRESS = (PROTOCOL = TCP)(HOST = yspark-linux)(PORT = 1588))
        (CONNECT_DATA =
                (SERVER=DEDICATED)
                (SERVICE_NAME=YONGSEOK)
                (UR=A)
        )
)
```

```
ORACLE12 =
  (DESCRIPTION =
    (ADDRESS = (PROTOCOL = TCP)(HOST = yspark-linux)(PORT = 1512))
    (CONNECT_DATA =
      (SERVER = DEDICATED)
      (SERVICE_NAME = oracle12)
      (UR=A)
    )
  )

YONGSEOK =
  (DESCRIPTION =
        (ADDRESS = (PROTOCOL = TCP)(HOST = yspark-linux)(PORT = 1588))
        (CONNECT_DATA =
                (SERVER=DEDICATED)
                (SERVICE_NAME=YONGSEOK)
                (UR=A)
        )
)
[UNIONE]yspark-linux:/oracle/oracle12/app/oracle/product/12.2.0/dbhome_1/network/admin> cat tnsnames.ora
```

준비가 되었다면 복제되어 구성할 DB 서버의 리스너를 기동시킵니다.

```
#lsnrctl start YONGSEOK
```

```
[UNIONE]yspark-linux:/oracle/oracle12/app/oracle/product/12.2.0/dbhome_1/network/admin> lsnrctl start YONGSEOK

LSNRCTL for Linux: Version 12.2.0.1.0 - Production on 28-NOV-2017 11:21:55

Copyright (c) 1991, 2016, Oracle.  All rights reserved.

Starting /oracle/oracle12/app/oracle/product/12.2.0/dbhome_1/bin/tnslsnr: please wait...

TNSLSNR for Linux: Version 12.2.0.1.0 - Production
System parameter file is /oracle/oracle12/app/oracle/product/12.2.0/dbhome_1/network/admin/listener.ora
Log messages written to /oracle/oracle12/app/oracle/diag/tnslsnr/yspark-linux/yongseok/alert/log.xml
Listening on: (DESCRIPTION=(ADDRESS=(PROTOCOL=tcp)(HOST=yspark-linux)(PORT=1588)))

Connecting to (DESCRIPTION=(ADDRESS=(PROTOCOL=TCP)(HOST=yspark-linux)(PORT=1588)))
STATUS of the LISTENER
------------------------
Alias                     YONGSEOK
Version                   TNSLSNR for Linux: Version 12.2.0.1.0 - Production
Start Date                28-NOV-2017 11:21:56
Uptime                    0 days 0 hr. 0 min. 1 sec
Trace Level               off
Security                  ON: Local OS Authentication
SNMP                      OFF
Listener Parameter File   /oracle/oracle12/app/oracle/product/12.2.0/dbhome_1/network/admin/listener.ora
Listener Log File         /oracle/oracle12/app/oracle/diag/tnslsnr/yspark-linux/yongseok/alert/log.xml
Listening Endpoints Summary...
  (DESCRIPTION=(ADDRESS=(PROTOCOL=tcp)(HOST=yspark-linux)(PORT=1588)))
The listener supports no services
The command completed successfully
[UNIONE]yspark-linux:/oracle/oracle12/app/oracle/product/12.2.0/dbhome_1/network/admin>
```

복제해서 기동시킬 DB용 파라미터 파일을 만들기 위해 기존 DB 서버에서 pfile 파일을 생성합니다.

```
SQL> create pfile='initYONGSEOK.ora' from memory ;
```

```
[oracle12]yspark-linux:/home/oracle12> sqlplus "/as sysdba"

SQL*Plus: Release 12.2.0.1.0 Production on Tue Nov 28 11:29:16 2017

Copyright (c) 1982, 2016, Oracle.  All rights reserved.


Connected to:
Oracle Database 12c Enterprise Edition Release 12.2.0.1.0 - 64bit Production

SQL> create pfile='initYONGSEOK.ora' from memory ;

File created.

SQL> exit
Disconnected from Oracle Database 12c Enterprise Edition Release 12.2.0.1.0 - 64bit Production
[oracle12]yspark-linux:/home/oracle12>
```

이제 만든 pfile을 control_file, db_name, dest 파라미터, 메모리 파라미터 등 복제되는 서버의 구성에 맞게 수정하여 서버로 옮겨놓습니다.

```
vi initYONGSEOK.ora
```

```
[oracle12]yspark-linux:/oracle/oracle12/app/oracle/product/12.2.0/dbhome_1/dbs> grep name initYONGSEOK.ora
db_name='YONGSEOK'
[oracle12]yspark-linux:/oracle/oracle12/app/oracle/product/12.2.0/dbhome_1/dbs> grep dest initYONGSEOK.ora
_diag_adr_trace_dest='/oracle/oracle12/app/oracle/diag/rdbms/YONGSEOK/YONGSEOK/trace'
audit_file_dest='/oracle/oracle12/app/oracle/admin/YONGSEOK/adump'
core_dump_dest='/oracle/oracle12/app/oracle/diag/rdbms/YONGSEOK/YONGSEOK/cdump'
db_recovery_file_dest='/oracle/oracle12/FRA/YONGSEOK'
db_recovery_file_dest_size=100G
diagnostic_dest='/oracle/oracle12/app/oracle'
log_archive_dest='/oracle/oracle12/arch/YONGSEOK'
[oracle12]yspark-linux:/oracle/oracle12/app/oracle/product/12.2.0/dbhome_1/dbs>
```

```
[oracle12]yspark-linux:/oracle/oracle12/app/oracle/product/12.2.0/dbhome_1/dbs> grep control_files initYONGSEOK.ora
control_files='/oracle/oracle12/oradata/YONGSEOK/control01.ctl'
control_files='/oracle/oracle12/oradata/YONGSEOK/control02.ctl'
[oracle12]yspark-linux:/oracle/oracle12/app/oracle/product/12.2.0/dbhome_1/dbs>
[oracle12]yspark-linux:/oracle/oracle12/app/oracle/product/12.2.0/dbhome_1/dbs>
```

패스워드 파일과 Dump 디렉토리를 생성합니다.

```
# export ORACLE_SID=YONGSEOK
# cd $ORACLE_HOME/dbs
# orapwd file=orapwYONGSEOK password=P#ssw0rd entries=5 sys=y force=y
# mkdir -p /oracle/oracle12/app/oracle/diag/rdbms/YONGSEOK/YONGSEOK/trace
# mkdir -p /oracle/oracle12/app/oracle/admin/YONGSEOK/adump
# mkdir -p /oracle/oracle12/oradata/YONGSEOK/
# mkdir -p /oracle/oracle12/app/oracle/diag/rdbms/YONGSEOK/YONGSEOK/cdump
# mkdir -p /oracle/oracle12/FRA/YONGSEOK/
# mkdir -p /oracle/oracle12/arch/YONGSEOK
```

```
[oracle12]yspark-linux:/oracle/oracle12/app/oracle/product/12.2.0/dbhome_1/dbs> orapwd file=orapwYONGSEOK password=P#ssw0rd entries=5
 sys=y force=y
[oracle12]yspark-linux:/oracle/oracle12/app/oracle/product/12.2.0/dbhome_1/dbs> mkdir -p /oracle/oracle12/app/oracle/diag/rdbms/YONGS
EOK/YONGSEOK/trace
[oracle12]yspark-linux:/oracle/oracle12/app/oracle/product/12.2.0/dbhome_1/dbs> mkdir -p /oracle/oracle12/app/oracle/admin/YONGSEOK/a
dump
mkdir -p /oracle/oracle12/app/oracle/diag/rdbms/YONGSEOK/YONGSEOK/cdump
[oracle12]yspark-linux:/oracle/oracle12/app/oracle/product/12.2.0/dbhome_1/dbs> mkdir -p /oracle/oracle12/app/oracle/diag/rdbms/YONGS
EOK/YONGSEOK/cdump
[oracle12]yspark-linux:/oracle/oracle12/app/oracle/product/12.2.0/dbhome_1/dbs> mkdir -p /oracle/oracle12/FRA/YONGSEOK/
[oracle12]yspark-linux:/oracle/oracle12/app/oracle/product/12.2.0/dbhome_1/dbs> mkdir -p /oracle/oracle12/arch/YONGSEOK
[oracle12]yspark-linux:/oracle/oracle12/app/oracle/product/12.2.0/dbhome_1/dbs>
```

이제 NOMOUNT 상태로 복제 구성할 DB를 기동합니다.

```
# export ORACLE_SID=YONGSEOK
# sqlplus "/as sysdba"
SQL> startup nomount pfile=$ORACLE_HOME/dbs/initYONGSEOK.ora
```

```
[YONGSEOK]yspark-linux:/home/oracle12> export ORACLE_SID=YONGSEOK
[YONGSEOK]yspark-linux:/home/oracle12> sqlplus "/as sysdba"

SQL*Plus: Release 12.2.0.1.0 Production on Tue Nov 28 12:18:29 2017

Copyright (c) 1982, 2016, Oracle.  All rights reserved.

Connected to an idle instance.

SQL> startup nomount pfile=$ORACLE_HOME/dbs/initYONGSEOK.ora
ORACLE instance started.

Total System Global Area  746586112 bytes
Fixed Size                  8625176 bytes
Variable Size             587203560 bytes
Database Buffers           33554432 bytes
Redo Buffers                8151040 bytes
In-Memory Area            109051904 bytes
SQL> ▌
```

복제할 사전 준비가 되었습니다. 복제 할 서버에서 원래 DB 서버의 RMAN을 원격으로 연결하고 DB 복제를 하기 위해 접속합니다. 대상 DB 서버의 접속이 되면 auxiliary 옵션을 주어 복제 DB도 접속합니다.

```
# export ORACLE_SID=oracle12
# rman target sys/P#ssw0rd@ORACLE12 nocatalog auxiliary sys/P#ssw0rd@YONGSEOK
```

```
[oracle12]yspark-linux:/home/oracle12> export ORACLE_SID=oracle12
[oracle12]yspark-linux:/home/oracle12> rman target sys/P#ssw0rd@oracle12 nocatalog auxiliary sys/P#ssw0rd@YONGSEOK

Recovery Manager: Release 12.2.0.1.0 - Production on Tue Nov 28 12:55:12 2017

Copyright (c) 1982, 2017, Oracle and/or its affiliates.  All rights reserved.

connected to target database: ORACLE12 (DBID=2053465567)
using target database control file instead of recovery catalog
connected to auxiliary database: YONGSEOK (not mounted)

RMAN> ▌
```

주의할 점은 sys의 패스워드 설정 값이 원래 DB와 복제 DB가 같아야 복제가 됩니다. RMAN에서 DB 접속이 모두 완료되면 RUN 스크립트를 조합해 복제 명령을 수행합니다. 이제 RUN 명령어를 조합하여 복제 명령을 실행합니다.

```
RUN
{
SET NEWNAME FOR DATABASE TO '/oracle/oracle12/oradata/YONGSEOK/%U' ;
DUPLICATE TARGET DATABASE TO YONGSEOK FROM ACTIVE DATABASE
NOFILENAMECHECK
LOGFILE
GROUP 1 ('/oracle/oracle12/oradata/YONGSEOK/redo01.log') SIZE 200M REUSE,
GROUP 2 ('/oracle/oracle12/oradata/YONGSEOK/redo02.log') SIZE 200M REUSE,
GROUP 3 ('/oracle/oracle12/oradata/YONGSEOK/redo03.log') SIZE 200M REUSE
SPFILE PARAMETER_VALUE_CONVERT 'oracle12','YONGSEOK'
SET control_files='/oracle/oracle12/oradata/YONGSEOK/control01.ctl'
SET db_recovery_file_dest='/oracle/oracle12/FRA/YONGSEOK/'
SET LOCAL_LISTENER='YONGSEOK'
SET audit_file_dest='/oracle/oracle12/app/oracle/admin/YONGSEOK/adump';
}
```

```
RMAN> RUN
{
SET NEWNAME FOR DATABASE TO '/oracle/oracle12/oradata/YONGSEOK/%U' ;
DUPLICATE TARGET DATABASE TO YONGSEOK FROM ACTIVE DATABASE
NOFILENAMECHECK
2> 3> 4> 5> 6> LOGFILE
7> GROUP 1 ('/oracle/oracle12/oradata/YONGSEOK/redo01.log') SIZE 200M REUSE,
8> GROUP 2 ('/oracle/oracle12/oradata/YONGSEOK/redo02.log') SIZE 200M REUSE,
9> GROUP 3 ('/oracle/oracle12/oradata/YONGSEOK/redo03.log') SIZE 200M REUSE
10> SPFILE PARAMETER_VALUE_CONVERT 'oracle12','YONGSEOK'
11> SET control_files='/oracle/oracle12/oradata/YONGSEOK/control01.ctl'
12> SET db_recovery_file_dest='/oracle/oracle12/FRA/YONGSEOK/'
13> SET LOCAL_LISTENER='YONGSEOK'
14> SET audit_file_dest='/oracle/oracle12/app/oracle/admin/YONGSEOK/adump';
15> }

executing command: SET NEWNAME

Starting Duplicate Db at 28-NOV-17
allocated channel: ORA_AUX_DISK_1
channel ORA_AUX_DISK_1: SID=173 device type=DISK
current log archived

contents of Memory Script:
{
   restore clone from service  'ORACLE12' spfile to
 '/oracle/oracle12/app/oracle/product/12.2.0/dbhome_1/dbs/spfileYONGSEOK.ora';
   sql clone "alter system set spfile= ''/oracle/oracle12/app/oracle/product/12.2.0/dbhome_1/dbs/spfileYONGSEOK.ora''";
}
executing Memory Script

Starting restore at 28-NOV-17
using channel ORA_AUX_DISK_1

channel ORA_AUX_DISK_1: starting datafile backup set restore
channel ORA_AUX_DISK_1: using network backup set from service ORACLE12
channel ORA_AUX_DISK_1: restoring SPFILE
output file name=/oracle/oracle12/app/oracle/product/12.2.0/dbhome_1/dbs/spfileYONGSEOK.ora
channel ORA_AUX_DISK_1: restore complete, elapsed time: 00:00:18
Finished restore at 28-NOV-17
```

```
Oracle instance shut down

Oracle instance started

Total System Global Area     746586112 bytes

Fixed Size                     8625176 bytes
Variable Size                603980776 bytes
Database Buffers              16777216 bytes
Redo Buffers                   8151040 bytes
In-Memory Area               109051904 bytes

Starting restore at 28-NOV-17
allocated channel: ORA_AUX_DISK_1
channel ORA_AUX_DISK_1: SID=89 device type=DISK

channel ORA_AUX_DISK_1: starting datafile backup set restore
channel ORA_AUX_DISK_1: using network backup set from service ORACLE12
channel ORA_AUX_DISK_1: restoring control file
channel ORA_AUX_DISK_1: restore complete, elapsed time: 00:00:07
output file name=/oracle/oracle12/oradata/YONGSEOK/control01.ctl
Finished restore at 28-NOV-17

database mounted

contents of Memory Script:
{
   set newname for datafile  1 to
 "/oracle/oracle12/oradata/YONGSEOK/data_D-YONGSEOK_TS-SYSTEM_FNO-1";
   set newname for datafile  3 to
 "/oracle/oracle12/oradata/YONGSEOK/data_D-YONGSEOK_TS-SYSAUX_FNO-3";
   set newname for datafile  4 to
 "/oracle/oracle12/oradata/YONGSEOK/data_D-YONGSEOK_TS-UNDOTBS1_FNO-4";
   set newname for datafile  7 to
 "/oracle/oracle12/oradata/YONGSEOK/data_D-YONGSEOK_TS-USERS_FNO-7";
   set newname for datafile  10 to
 "/oracle/oracle12/oradata/YONGSEOK/data_D-YONGSEOK_TS-UNDOTBS1_FNO-10";
   set newname for datafile  11 to
 "/oracle/oracle12/oradata/YONGSEOK/data_D-YONGSEOK_TS-UNDOTBS1_FNO-11";
   set newname for datafile  12 to
 "/oracle/oracle12/oradata/YONGSEOK/data_D-YONGSEOK_TS-ORACLE12_FNO-12";
   restore
   from  nonsparse   from service
 'ORACLE12'   clone database
   ;
   sql 'alter system archive log current';
}
```

```
channel ORA_AUX_DISK_1: specifying datafile(s) to restore from backup set
channel ORA_AUX_DISK_1: restoring datafile 00001 to /oracle/oracle12/oradata/YONGSEOK/data_D-YONGSEOK_TS-SYSTEM_FNO-1
channel ORA_AUX_DISK_1: restore complete, elapsed time: 00:04:19
channel ORA_AUX_DISK_1: starting datafile backup set restore
channel ORA_AUX_DISK_1: using network backup set from service ORACLE12
channel ORA_AUX_DISK_1: specifying datafile(s) to restore from backup set
channel ORA_AUX_DISK_1: restoring datafile 00003 to /oracle/oracle12/oradata/YONGSEOK/data_D-YONGSEOK_TS-SYSAUX_FNO-3
channel ORA_AUX_DISK_1: restore complete, elapsed time: 00:05:40
channel ORA_AUX_DISK_1: starting datafile backup set restore
channel ORA_AUX_DISK_1: using network backup set from service ORACLE12
channel ORA_AUX_DISK_1: specifying datafile(s) to restore from backup set
channel ORA_AUX_DISK_1: restoring datafile 00004 to /oracle/oracle12/oradata/YONGSEOK/data_D-YONGSEOK_TS-UNDOTBS1_FNO-4
channel ORA_AUX_DISK_1: restore complete, elapsed time: 00:04:47
channel ORA_AUX_DISK_1: starting datafile backup set restore
channel ORA_AUX_DISK_1: using network backup set from service ORACLE12
channel ORA_AUX_DISK_1: specifying datafile(s) to restore from backup set
channel ORA_AUX_DISK_1: restoring datafile 00007 to /oracle/oracle12/oradata/YONGSEOK/data_D-YONGSEOK_TS-USERS_FNO-7
channel ORA_AUX_DISK_1: restore complete, elapsed time: 00:00:04
channel ORA_AUX_DISK_1: starting datafile backup set restore
channel ORA_AUX_DISK_1: using network backup set from service ORACLE12
channel ORA_AUX_DISK_1: specifying datafile(s) to restore from backup set
channel ORA_AUX_DISK_1: restoring datafile 00010 to /oracle/oracle12/oradata/YONGSEOK/data_D-YONGSEOK_TS-UNDOTBS1_FNO-10
channel ORA_AUX_DISK_1: restore complete, elapsed time: 00:00:04
channel ORA_AUX_DISK_1: starting datafile backup set restore
channel ORA_AUX_DISK_1: using network backup set from service ORACLE12
channel ORA_AUX_DISK_1: specifying datafile(s) to restore from backup set
channel ORA_AUX_DISK_1: restoring datafile 00011 to /oracle/oracle12/oradata/YONGSEOK/data_D-YONGSEOK_TS-UNDOTBS1_FNO-11
channel ORA_AUX_DISK_1: restore complete, elapsed time: 00:00:04
channel ORA_AUX_DISK_1: starting datafile backup set restore
channel ORA_AUX_DISK_1: using network backup set from service ORACLE12
channel ORA_AUX_DISK_1: specifying datafile(s) to restore from backup set
channel ORA_AUX_DISK_1: restoring datafile 00012 to /oracle/oracle12/oradata/YONGSEOK/data_D-YONGSEOK_TS-ORACLE12_FNO-12
channel ORA_AUX_DISK_1: restore complete, elapsed time: 00:00:02
Finished restore at 28-NOV-17
```

```
datafile 3 switched to datafile copy
input datafile copy RECID=1 STAMP=961252642 file name=/oracle/oracle12/oradata/YONGSEOK/data_D-YONGSEOK_TS-SYSAUX_FNO-3
datafile 4 switched to datafile copy
input datafile copy RECID=2 STAMP=961252643 file name=/oracle/oracle12/oradata/YONGSEOK/data_D-YONGSEOK_TS-UNDOTBS1_FNO-4
datafile 7 switched to datafile copy
input datafile copy RECID=3 STAMP=961252643 file name=/oracle/oracle12/oradata/YONGSEOK/data_D-YONGSEOK_TS-USERS_FNO-7
datafile 10 switched to datafile copy
input datafile copy RECID=4 STAMP=961252643 file name=/oracle/oracle12/oradata/YONGSEOK/data_D-YONGSEOK_TS-UNDOTBS1_FNO-10
datafile 11 switched to datafile copy
input datafile copy RECID=5 STAMP=961252643 file name=/oracle/oracle12/oradata/YONGSEOK/data_D-YONGSEOK_TS-UNDOTBS1_FNO-11
datafile 12 switched to datafile copy
input datafile copy RECID=6 STAMP=961252644 file name=/oracle/oracle12/oradata/YONGSEOK/data_D-YONGSEOK_TS-ORACLE12_FNO-12
Reenabling controlfile options for auxiliary database
Executing: alter database enable block change tracking using file '/oracle/oracle12/oradata/YONGSEOK/bct_D-YONGSEOK_ibskn29s'

contents of Memory Script:
{
   Alter clone database open resetlogs;
}
executing Memory Script

database opened
Finished Duplicate Db at 28-NOV-17

RMAN>
```

마지막에 DB가 OPEN 되었다는 메시지와 함께 수행이 완료됩니다.

이제 복제된 DB의 상태를 확인합니다.

```
# export ORACLE_SID=YONGSEOK
# sqlplus "/as sysdba"
SQL> SELECT INSTANCE_NAME,STATUS FROM V$INSTANCE ;
SQL> SELECT MEMBER FROM V$LOGFILE ;
SQL> SELECT FILE_NAME FROM DBA_DATA_FILES ;
```

```
[oracle12]yspark-linux:/home/oracle12> export ORACLE_SID=YONGSEOK
[YONGSEOK]yspark-linux:/home/oracle12> sqlplus "/as sysdba"

SQL*Plus: Release 12.2.0.1.0 Production on Tue Nov 28 15:14:00 2017

Copyright (c) 1982, 2016, Oracle.  All rights reserved.


Connected to:
Oracle Database 12c Enterprise Edition Release 12.2.0.1.0 - 64bit Production

SQL> SELECT INSTANCE_NAME,STATUS FROM V$INSTANCE ;

INSTANCE_NAME    STATUS
---------------- ------------
YONGSEOK         OPEN

SQL> SELECT MEMBER FROM V$LOGFILE ;

MEMBER
--------------------------------------------------------------------------------
/oracle/oracle12/oradata/YONGSEOK/redo03.log
/oracle/oracle12/oradata/YONGSEOK/redo02.log
/oracle/oracle12/oradata/YONGSEOK/redo01.log

SQL> SELECT FILE_NAME FROM DBA_DATA_FILES ;

FILE_NAME
--------------------------------------------------------------------------------
/oracle/oracle12/oradata/YONGSEOK/data_D-YONGSEOK_TS-SYSTEM_FNO-1
/oracle/oracle12/oradata/YONGSEOK/data_D-YONGSEOK_TS-SYSAUX_FNO-3
/oracle/oracle12/oradata/YONGSEOK/data_D-YONGSEOK_TS-USERS_FNO-7
/oracle/oracle12/oradata/YONGSEOK/data_D-YONGSEOK_TS-UNDOTBS1_FNO-4
/oracle/oracle12/oradata/YONGSEOK/data_D-YONGSEOK_TS-UNDOTBS1_FNO-10
/oracle/oracle12/oradata/YONGSEOK/data_D-YONGSEOK_TS-UNDOTBS1_FNO-11
/oracle/oracle12/oradata/YONGSEOK/data_D-YONGSEOK_TS-ORACLE12_FNO-12

7 rows selected.

SQL> ▮
```

로그를 분석해 보면 운영 중인 DATA 파일을 복제 서버로 COPY 후 RECOVER하는 순서와 동일합니다.

CPU CORE 수가 많은 대용량 서버에서 복제 RMAN 명령어 내용에 allocate channel 명령어를 이용하여 채널을 최대 16개 설정 후 수행 하면 진행 과정의 데이터 파일의 복원, 복구 과정을 병렬로 수행하게 되어 복제 수행 시간을 단축할 수 있습니다.

4 RECOVER TABLE 명령어를 이용한 백업 파일에서 특정 테이블 복구

여러 가지 데이터 손실에 대한 장애에 따른 FLASHBACK, LOGMINER, RECYCLEBIN 등 완전 복구 방법은 많습니다.

하지만 TRUNCATE TABLE에 대한 완전 복구하는 방법에 대해서는 앞에서 살펴본 백업본을 타 서버에 내려서 올려서 복구하는 방법 밖에 없었습니다.

Oracle 12C 버전에서는 특정 테이블만 백업 데이터에서 복구하는 RECOVER TABLE 기능이 제공됩니다.

지금부터 RECOVER TABLE 기능을 이용하여 복구하는 실습을 해보겠습니다.

```
SQL> 테스트 유저생성
SQL> 테스트 테이블 생성
SQL> 테스트 테이블에 테스트 데이터 생성
```

```
SQL> SELECT FILE_NAME , BYTES/1024/1024 MB , TABLESPACE_NAME
  2  FROM DBA_DATA_FILES
  3  WHERE TABLESPACE_NAME='ORACLE12' ;

FILE_NAME                                                                MB TABLESPACE_NAME
------------------------------------------------------------------- ---------- ------------------------------
/oracle/oracle12/oradata/oracle12/oracle12_01.dbf                          10 ORACLE12

SQL> 
```

```
SQL> create user YONGSEOK IDENTIFIED BY PARK
  2  DEFAULT TABLESPACE ORACLE12
  3  QUOTA UNLIMITED ON ORACLE12 ;

User created.

SQL> GRANT CONNECT,RESOURCE TO YONGSEOK ;

Grant succeeded.

SQL> CONN YONGSEOK/PARK
Connected.
SQL> 
```

```
SQL> CONN YONGSEOK/PARK
Connected.
SQL> SELECT * FROM EMP ;

     EMPNO ENAME      JOB              MGR HIREDATE                  SAL       COMM     DEPTNO
---------- ---------- --------- ---------- ------------------ ---------- ---------- ----------
      7369 SMITH      CLERK           7902 17-DEC-80                 800                    20
      7499 ALLEN      SALESMAN        7698 20-FEB-81                1600        300         30
      7521 WARD       SALESMAN        7698 22-FEB-81                1250        500         30
      7566 JONES      MANAGER         7839 02-APR-81                2975                    20
      7654 MARTIN     SALESMAN        7698 28-SEP-81                1250       1400         30
      7698 BLAKE      MANAGER         7839 01-MAY-81                2850                    30
      7782 CLARK      MANAGER         7839 09-JUN-81                2450                    10
      7788 SCOTT      ANALYST         7566 09-DEC-82                3000                    20
      7839 KING       PRESIDENT            17-NOV-81                5000                    10
      7844 TURNER     SALESMAN        7698 08-SEP-81                1500                    30
      7876 ADAMS      CLERK           7788 12-JAN-83                1100                    20

     EMPNO ENAME      JOB              MGR HIREDATE                  SAL       COMM     DEPTNO
---------- ---------- --------- ---------- ------------------ ---------- ---------- ----------
      7900 JAMES      CLERK           7698 03-DEC-81                 950                    30
      7902 FORD       ANALYST         7566 03-DEC-81                3000                    20
      7934 MILLER     CLERK           7782 23-JAN-82                1300                    10

14 rows selected.

SQL> 
```

이제 RMAN 백업을 수행합니다.

```
# rman target /
RMAN> BACKUP AS COMPRESSED BACKUPSET DATABASE ;
```

```
[oracle12]yspark-linux:/home/oracle12> rman target /

Recovery Manager: Release 12.2.0.1.0 - Production on Tue Nov 28 16:09:48 2017

Copyright (c) 1982, 2017, Oracle and/or its affiliates.  All rights reserved.

connected to target database: ORACLE12 (DBID=2053465567)

RMAN> backup as compressed backupset database ;

Starting backup at 28-NOV-17
using target database control file instead of recovery catalog
allocated channel: ORA_DISK_1
channel ORA_DISK_1: SID=8 device type=DISK
channel ORA_DISK_1: starting compressed full datafile backup set
channel ORA_DISK_1: specifying datafile(s) in backup set
input datafile file number=00003 name=/oracle/oracle12/oradata/oracle12/sysaux01.dbf
input datafile file number=00004 name=/oracle/oracle12/oradata/oracle12/undotbs01.dbf
input datafile file number=00001 name=/oracle/oracle12/oradata/oracle12/system01.dbf
input datafile file number=00010 name=/oracle/oracle12/oradata/oracle12/undotbs02.dbf
input datafile file number=00011 name=/oracle/oracle12/oradata/oracle12/undotbs03.dbf
input datafile file number=00007 name=/oracle/oracle12/oradata/oracle12/users01.dbf
input datafile file number=00012 name=/oracle/oracle12/oradata/oracle12/oracle12_01.dbf
channel ORA_DISK_1: starting piece 1 at 28-NOV-17
channel ORA_DISK_1: finished piece 1 at 28-NOV-17
piece handle=/oracle/oracle12/RMAN_BACKUP/ORACLE12_8bskn8ps_1_1_961258300_267 tag=TAG20171128T161140 comment=NONE
channel ORA_DISK_1: backup set complete, elapsed time: 00:01:45
Finished backup at 28-NOV-17

Starting Control File and SPFILE Autobackup at 28-NOV-17
piece handle=/oracle/oracle12/FRA/ORACLE12/autobackup/2017_11_28/o1_mf_s_961258406_f1t34r12_.bkp comment=NONE
Finished Control File and SPFILE Autobackup at 28-NOV-17

RMAN> 
```

이제 TRUNCATE TABLE 장애를 발생시킵니다.

```
SQL> ALTER SESSION SET NLS_DATE_FORMAT='YYYY/MM/DD HH24:MI:SS' ;
SQL> SELECT SYSDATE FROM DUAL ;
SQL> TRUNCATE TABLE EMP ;
```

```
16:18:06 SQL> CONN YONGSEOK/PARK
Connected.
16:18:12 SQL> ALTER SESSION SET NLS_DATE_FORMAT='YYYY/MM/DD HH24:MI:SS' ;

Session altered.

Elapsed: 00:00:00.00
16:18:15 SQL> SELECT SYSDATE FROM DUAL ;

SYSDATE
-------------------
2017/11/28 16:18:21

Elapsed: 00:00:00.00
16:18:21 SQL> TRUNCATE TABLE EMP ;

Table truncated.

Elapsed: 00:00:00.52
16:18:39 SQL> █
```

이제 RECOVER TABLE 명령으로 복구를 시작합니다. 운영 DB가 OPEN인 상태에서 실행합니다.

```
SQL> RENAME EMP TO EMP_BACK ;
RMAN> RECOVER TABLE YONGSEOK.EMP UNTIL TIME "TO_DATE('2017-11-28:16:18:21','yyyy-mm-
dd:hh24:mi:ss')" AUXILIARY DESTINATION '/oracle/oracle12/RECOVER_TAB_AREA' ;
```

```
16:24:11 SQL> conn YONGSEOK/PARK
Connected.
16:24:21 SQL> RENAME EMP TO EMP_BACK ;

Table renamed.

Elapsed: 00:00:00.92
16:24:36 SQL> █
```

```
RMAN> RECOVER TABLE YONGSEOK.EMP UNTIL TIME "TO_DATE('2017-11-28:16:18:21','yyyy-mm-dd:hh24:mi:ss')" AUXILIARY DESTINATION '/oracle/oracle12/REC
OVER_TAB_AREA';

Starting recover at 28-NOV-17
using channel ORA_DISK_1
RMAN-05026: warning: presuming following set of tablespaces applies to specified point-in-time

List of tablespaces expected to have UNDO segments
Tablespace SYSTEM
Tablespace UNDOTBS1

Creating automatic instance, with SID='Cfac'

initialization parameters used for automatic instance:
db_name=ORACLE12
db_unique_name=Cfac_pitr_ORACLE12
compatible=12.2.0
db_block_size=8192
db_files=200
diagnostic_dest=/oracle/oracle12/app/oracle
_system_trig_enabled=FALSE
sga_target=712M
processes=200
db_create_file_dest=/oracle/oracle12/RECOVER_TAB_AREA
log_archive_dest_1='location=/oracle/oracle12/RECOVER_TAB_AREA'
#No auxiliary parameter file used


starting up automatic instance ORACLE12

█
```

```
contents of Memory Script:
{
# set requested point in time
set until  time "TO_DATE('2017-11-28:16:18:21','yyyy-mm-dd:hh24:mi:ss')";
# set destinations for recovery set and auxiliary set datafiles
set newname for clone datafile  1 to new;
set newname for clone datafile  4 to new;
set newname for clone datafile  10 to new;
set newname for clone datafile  11 to new;
set newname for clone datafile  3 to new;
set newname for clone tempfile  1 to new;
set newname for clone tempfile  2 to new;
set newname for clone tempfile  3 to new;
set newname for clone tempfile  4 to new;
# switch all tempfiles
switch clone tempfile all;
# restore the tablespaces in the recovery set and the auxiliary set
restore clone datafile  1, 4, 10, 11, 3;

switch clone datafile all;
}
executing Memory Script

executing command: SET until clause

executing command: SET NEWNAME

executing command: SET NEWNAME

executing command: SET NEWNAME

executing command: SET NEWNAME
```

```
Starting restore at 28-NOV-17
using channel ORA_AUX_DISK_1

channel ORA_AUX_DISK_1: starting datafile backup set restore
channel ORA_AUX_DISK_1: specifying datafile(s) to restore from backup set
channel ORA_AUX_DISK_1: restoring datafile 00001 to /oracle/oracle12/RECOVER_TAB_AREA/ORACLE12/datafile/o1_mf_system_%u_.dbf
channel ORA_AUX_DISK_1: restoring datafile 00004 to /oracle/oracle12/RECOVER_TAB_AREA/ORACLE12/datafile/o1_mf_undotbs1_%u_.dbf
channel ORA_AUX_DISK_1: restoring datafile 00010 to /oracle/oracle12/RECOVER_TAB_AREA/ORACLE12/datafile/o1_mf_undotbs1_%u_.dbf
channel ORA_AUX_DISK_1: restoring datafile 00011 to /oracle/oracle12/RECOVER_TAB_AREA/ORACLE12/datafile/o1_mf_undotbs1_%u_.dbf
channel ORA_AUX_DISK_1: restoring datafile 00003 to /oracle/oracle12/RECOVER_TAB_AREA/ORACLE12/datafile/o1_mf_sysaux_%u_.dbf
channel ORA_AUX_DISK_1: reading from backup piece /oracle/oracle12/RMAN_BACKUP/ORACLE12_8bskn8ps_1_1_961258300_267
channel ORA_AUX_DISK_1: piece handle=/oracle/oracle12/RMAN_BACKUP/ORACLE12_8bskn8ps_1_1_961258300_267 tag=TAG20171128T161140
channel ORA_AUX_DISK_1: restored backup piece 1
channel ORA_AUX_DISK_1: restore complete, elapsed time: 00:16:35
Finished restore at 28-NOV-17

datafile 1 switched to datafile copy
input datafile copy RECID=228 STAMP=961260262 file name=/oracle/oracle12/RECOVER_TAB_AREA/ORACLE12/datafile/o1_mf_system_f1t3zlps_.dbf
datafile 4 switched to datafile copy
input datafile copy RECID=229 STAMP=961260262 file name=/oracle/oracle12/RECOVER_TAB_AREA/ORACLE12/datafile/o1_mf_undotbs1_f1t3zlhj_.dbf
datafile 10 switched to datafile copy
input datafile copy RECID=230 STAMP=961260263 file name=/oracle/oracle12/RECOVER_TAB_AREA/ORACLE12/datafile/o1_mf_undotbs1_f1t3zlvo_.dbf
datafile 11 switched to datafile copy
input datafile copy RECID=231 STAMP=961260263 file name=/oracle/oracle12/RECOVER_TAB_AREA/ORACLE12/datafile/o1_mf_undotbs1_f1t3zlwy_.dbf
datafile 3 switched to datafile copy
input datafile copy RECID=232 STAMP=961260263 file name=/oracle/oracle12/RECOVER_TAB_AREA/ORACLE12/datafile/o1_mf_sysaux_f1t3zlfy_.dbf
```

```
starting media recovery

archived log for thread 1 with sequence 559 is already on disk as file /oracle/oracle12/FRA/ORACLE12/archivelog/2017_11_28/o1_mf_1_559_f1t3p6hf_
.arc
archived log file name=/oracle/oracle12/FRA/ORACLE12/archivelog/2017_11_28/o1_mf_1_559_f1t3p6hf_.arc thread=1 sequence=559
media recovery complete, elapsed time: 00:00:01
Finished recover at 28-NOV-17

sql statement: alter database open read only

contents of Memory Script:
{
   sql clone "create spfile from memory";
   shutdown clone immediate;
   startup clone nomount;
   sql clone "alter system set  control_files =
  ''/oracle/oracle12/RECOVER_TAB_AREA/ORACLE12/controlfile/o1_mf_f1t3z5r3_.ctl'' comment=
 ''RMAN set'' scope=spfile";
   shutdown clone immediate;
   startup clone nomount;
# mount database
sql clone 'alter database mount clone database';
}
executing Memory Script
```

```
connected to auxiliary database (not started)
Oracle instance started

Total System Global Area     746586112 bytes

Fixed Size                     8625176 bytes
Variable Size                222299112 bytes
Database Buffers             507510784 bytes
Redo Buffers                   8151040 bytes

sql statement: alter database mount clone database

contents of Memory Script:
{
# set requested point in time
set until  time "TO_DATE('2017-11-28:16:18:21','yyyy-mm-dd:hh24:mi:ss')";
# set destinations for recovery set and auxiliary set datafiles
set newname for datafile  12 to new;
# restore the tablespaces in the recovery set and the auxiliary set
restore clone datafile  12;

switch clone datafile all;
}
executing Memory Script

executing command: SET until clause
```

```
database opened

contents of Memory Script:
{
# create directory for datapump import
sql "create or replace directory TSPITR_DIROBJ_DPDIR as ''
/oracle/oracle12/RECOVER_TAB_AREA''";
# create directory for datapump export
sql clone "create or replace directory TSPITR_DIROBJ_DPDIR as ''
/oracle/oracle12/RECOVER_TAB_AREA''";
}
executing Memory Script

sql statement: create or replace directory TSPITR_DIROBJ_DPDIR as ''/oracle/oracle12/RECOVER_TAB_AREA''

sql statement: create or replace directory TSPITR_DIROBJ_DPDIR as ''/oracle/oracle12/RECOVER_TAB_AREA''

Performing export of tables...
   EXPDP> Starting "SYS"."TSPITR_EXP_CfaC_adog":
   EXPDP> Processing object type TABLE_EXPORT/TABLE/TABLE_DATA
   EXPDP> Processing object type TABLE_EXPORT/TABLE/STATISTICS/TABLE_STATISTICS
   EXPDP> Processing object type TABLE_EXPORT/TABLE/STATISTICS/MARKER
   EXPDP> Processing object type TABLE_EXPORT/TABLE/TABLE
   EXPDP> . . exported "YONGSEOK"."EMP"                          8.781 KB      14 rows
   EXPDP> Master table "SYS"."TSPITR_EXP_CfaC_adog" successfully loaded/unloaded
   EXPDP> ******************************************************************************
   EXPDP> Dump file set for SYS.TSPITR_EXP_CfaC_adog is:
   EXPDP>   /oracle/oracle12/RECOVER_TAB_AREA/tspitr_CfaC_36635.dmp
   EXPDP> Job "SYS"."TSPITR_EXP_CfaC_adog" successfully completed at Tue Nov 28 16:54:22 2017 elapsed 0 00:06:19
Export completed


contents of Memory Script:
{
# shutdown clone before import
shutdown clone abort
}
executing Memory Script

Oracle instance shut down

Performing import of tables...
   IMPDP> Master table "SYS"."TSPITR_IMP_CfaC_aavi" successfully loaded/unloaded
   IMPDP> Starting "SYS"."TSPITR_IMP_CfaC_aavi":
   IMPDP> Processing object type TABLE_EXPORT/TABLE/TABLE
   IMPDP> Processing object type TABLE_EXPORT/TABLE/TABLE_DATA
   IMPDP> . . imported "YONGSEOK"."EMP"                          8.781 KB      14 rows
   IMPDP> Processing object type TABLE_EXPORT/TABLE/STATISTICS/TABLE_STATISTICS
   IMPDP> Processing object type TABLE_EXPORT/TABLE/STATISTICS/MARKER
```

RMAN의 RECOVER TABLE 명령어를 수행하면 해당 TABLE의 백업 시점에 필요한 테이블스페이스에 필요한 백업데이터 파일과 기본적으로 필요한 DB의 기본 테이블스페이스 SYSTEM, SYSAUX, UNDO 테이블스페이스와 함께 해당 영역에 복제 DB를 생성한다.

그리고나서 만들어진 복제 DB에서 해당 TABLE을 데이터펌프 EXPDP를 이용해 추출해서 원래 데이터베이스로 IMPDP 적재된다.

이전의 버전에서 DBA가 수작업으로 각 단계별로 복구해야 하는 일련의 과정들이 단 한 줄의 RMAN 명령어로 진행되었습니다.

이제 복구가 잘 되었는지 테이블을 조회합니다.

```
SQL> ALTER SESSION SET NLS_DATE_FORMAT='YYYY/MM/DD HH24:MI:SS' ;
SQL> SELECT SYSDATE FROM DUAL ;
SQL> SELECT * FROM EMP ;
```

```
16:58:27 SQL> conn YONGSEOK/PARK
Connected.
16:58:35 SQL> ALTER SESSION SET NLS_DATE_FORMAT='YYYY/MM/DD HH24:MI:SS' ;

Session altered.

Elapsed: 00:00:00.00
16:58:40 SQL> SELECT SYSDATE FROM DUAL ;

SYSDATE
-------------------
2017/11/28 16:58:47

Elapsed: 00:00:00.00
16:58:47 SQL> SET LINESIZE 500
16:58:59 SQL> SELECT * FROM EMP ;

     EMPNO ENAME      JOB              MGR HIREDATE                   SAL       COMM     DEPTNO
---------- ---------- --------- ---------- ------------------- ---------- ---------- ----------
      7369 SMITH      CLERK           7902 1980/12/17 00:00:00        800                    20
      7499 ALLEN      SALESMAN        7698 1981/02/20 00:00:00       1600        300         30
      7521 WARD       SALESMAN        7698 1981/02/22 00:00:00       1250        500         30
      7566 JONES      MANAGER         7839 1981/04/02 00:00:00       2975                    20
      7654 MARTIN     SALESMAN        7698 1981/09/28 00:00:00       1250       1400         30
      7698 BLAKE      MANAGER         7839 1981/05/01 00:00:00       2850                    30
      7782 CLARK      MANAGER         7839 1981/06/09 00:00:00       2450                    10
      7788 SCOTT      ANALYST         7566 1982/12/09 00:00:00       3000                    20
      7839 KING       PRESIDENT            1981/11/17 00:00:00       5000                    10
      7844 TURNER     SALESMAN        7698 1981/09/08 00:00:00       1500                    30
      7876 ADAMS      CLERK           7788 1983/01/12 00:00:00       1100                    20

     EMPNO ENAME      JOB              MGR HIREDATE                   SAL       COMM     DEPTNO
---------- ---------- --------- ---------- ------------------- ---------- ---------- ----------
      7900 JAMES      CLERK           7698 1981/12/03 00:00:00        950                    30
      7902 FORD       ANALYST         7566 1981/12/03 00:00:00       3000                    20
      7934 MILLER     CLERK           7782 1982/01/23 00:00:00       1300                    10

14 rows selected.

Elapsed: 00:00:00.00
16:59:07 SQL> █
```

간단한 RMAN 명령어로 테이블 복구가 완료되었습니다.

5 Flashback Database 기능을 이용한 Rewind 복구(타임 머신 복구)

Oracle Flashback Database를 사용하여 전체 데이터베이스를 과거 시간으로 되감을 수 있습니다. 미디어 복구와 달리 데이터베이스를 과거 상태로 되돌리려면 데이터 파일을 복원 할 필요가 없습니다.

지금부터 데이터베이스 시간을 돌려 장애를 복구하겠습니다.

먼저 FLASHBACK 기능을 활성화합니다.

```
SQL> SHUTDOWN IMMEDIATE ;
SQL> STARTUP MOUNT ;
SQL> ALTER DATABASE FLASHBACK ON ;
SQL> SHUTDOWN IMMEDIATE ;
SQL> STARTUP ;
SQL> SELECT NAME , FLASHBACK_ON FROM V$DATABASE ;
```

```
17:20:43 SYS@oracle12> SHUTDOWN IMMEDIATE ;
Database closed.
Database dismounted.
ORACLE instance shut down.
17:21:32 SYS@oracle12> STARTUP MOUNT ;
ORACLE instance started.

Total System Global Area  746586112 bytes
Fixed Size                  8625176 bytes
Variable Size             587203560 bytes
Database Buffers           33554432 bytes
Redo Buffers                8151040 bytes
In-Memory Area            109051904 bytes
Database mounted.
17:22:27 SYS@oracle12> ALTER DATABASE FLASHBACK ON ;

Database altered.

Elapsed: 00:00:02.59
17:22:48 SYS@oracle12> SHUTDOWN IMMEDIATE ;
ORA-01109: database not open


Database dismounted.
ORACLE instance shut down.
17:23:21 SYS@oracle12> STARTUP ;
ORACLE instance started.

Total System Global Area  746586112 bytes
Fixed Size                  8625176 bytes
Variable Size             587203560 bytes
Database Buffers           33554432 bytes
Redo Buffers                8151040 bytes
In-Memory Area            109051904 bytes
Database mounted.
Database opened.
17:24:05 SYS@oracle12>
```

```
17:26:26 SYS@oracle12> SELECT NAME ,FLASHBACK_ON FROM V$DATABASE ;

NAME      FLASHBACK_ON
--------- ------------------
ORACLE12  YES

1 row selected.

Elapsed: 00:00:00.03
17:26:40 SYS@oracle12>
```

이제 일반 유저 세션에서 장애 테스트 테이블과 현재 SCN 값을 확인합니다.

```
SQL> SELECT COUNT(*) FROM EMP ;
SQL> SELECT CURRENT_SCN FROM V$DATABASE;
```


```
17:20:43 SYS@oracle12> SHUTDOWN IMMEDIATE ;
Database closed.
Database dismounted.
ORACLE instance shut down.
17:21:32 SYS@oracle12> STARTUP MOUNT ;
ORACLE instance started.

Total System Global Area  746586112 bytes
Fixed Size                  8625176 bytes
Variable Size             587203560 bytes
Database Buffers           33554432 bytes
Redo Buffers                8151040 bytes
In-Memory Area            109051904 bytes
Database mounted.
17:22:27 SYS@oracle12> ALTER DATABASE FLASHBACK ON ;

Database altered.

Elapsed: 00:00:02.59
17:22:48 SYS@oracle12> SHUTDOWN IMMEDIATE ;
ORA-01109: database not open


Database dismounted.
ORACLE instance shut down.
17:23:21 SYS@oracle12> STARTUP ;
ORACLE instance started.

Total System Global Area  746586112 bytes
Fixed Size                  8625176 bytes
Variable Size             587203560 bytes
Database Buffers           33554432 bytes
Redo Buffers                8151040 bytes
In-Memory Area            109051904 bytes
Database mounted.
Database opened.
17:24:05 SYS@oracle12>
```


```
17:29:20 YONGSEOK@oracle12> SELECT COUNT(*) FROM EMP ;

  COUNT(*)
----------
      1792

1 row selected.

Elapsed: 00:00:00.00
17:29:33 YONGSEOK@oracle12> CONN SYSTEM/oracle
Connected.
17:29:53 SYSTEM@oracle12>
17:29:53 SYSTEM@oracle12> SELECT CURRENT_SCN FROM V$DATABASE;

CURRENT_SCN
-----------
 1437624389

1 row selected.

Elapsed: 00:00:00.09
```

이제 해당 테이블에 데이터 유실 장애를 발생합니다.

```
SQL> DELETE FROM EMP ;
SQL> COMMIT ;
```

```
17:34:42 YONGSEOK@oracle12> DELETE FROM EMP ;

1792 rows deleted.

Elapsed: 00:00:00.06
17:35:01 YONGSEOK@oracle12> COMMIT ;

Commit complete.
```

다시 돌아오기 위하여 현재의 SCN 값을 조회합니다.

```
SQL> SELECT CURRENT_SCN FROM V$DATABASE ;
```

```
17:39:53 SYS@oracle12> SELECT CURRENT_SCN FROM V$DATABASE;

CURRENT_SCN
-----------
 1437625126

1 row selected.

Elapsed: 00:00:00.23
```

이제 데이터베이스의 시간을 과거로 돌립니다.

```
SQL> SHUTDOWN IMMEDIATE ;
SQL> STARTUP MOUNT ;
RMAN> FLASHBACK DATABASE TO SCN <과거SCN 번호> ;
SQL> ALTER DATABASE OPEN READ ONLY ;
```

```
17:43:25 SYS@oracle12> SHUTDOWN IMMEDIATE ;
Database closed.
Database dismounted.
ORACLE instance shut down.
17:43:48 SYS@oracle12> STARTUP MOUNT ;
ORACLE instance started.

Total System Global Area  746586112 bytes
Fixed Size                  8625176 bytes
Variable Size             587203560 bytes
Database Buffers           33554432 bytes
Redo Buffers                8151040 bytes
In-Memory Area            109051904 bytes
Database mounted.
```

```
[oracle12]yspark-linux:/home/oracle12> rman target / nocatalog

Recovery Manager: Release 12.2.0.1.0 - Production on Tue Nov 28 17:45:37 2017

Copyright (c) 1982, 2017, Oracle and/or its affiliates.  All rights reserved.

connected to target database: ORACLE12 (DBID=2053465567, not open)
using target database control file instead of recovery catalog

RMAN> FLASHBACK DATABASE TO SCN 1437624389 ;

Starting flashback at 28-NOV-17
allocated channel: ORA_DISK_1
channel ORA_DISK_1: SID=91 device type=DISK


starting media recovery
media recovery complete, elapsed time: 00:00:07

Finished flashback at 28-NOV-17

RMAN> █
```

```
17:48:08 SYS@oracle12> ALTER DATABASE OPEN READ ONLY ;

Database altered.

Elapsed: 00:00:03.31
17:48:23 SYS@oracle12> █
```

이제 장애가 발생한 테이블을 조회합니다.

```
SQL> SELECT COUNT(*) FROM EMP ;
```

```
17:35:12 YONGSEOK@oracle12> CONNECT YONGSEOK/PARK
Connected.
17:50:19 YONGSEOK@oracle12>
17:50:19 YONGSEOK@oracle12> SELECT COUNT(*) FROM EMP ;

  COUNT(*)
----------
      1792

1 row selected.

Elapsed: 00:00:00.03
17:50:23 YONGSEOK@oracle12>
```

이제 테이블을 조회 한 테이블을 백업 받아 놓습니다.

```
# exp USERID=YONGSEOK/PARK TABLES=EMP FILE=EMP.DMP
```

```
[oracle12]yspark-linux:/home/oracle12> exp USERID=YONGSEOK/PARK TABLES=EMP FILE=EMP.DMP
Export: Release 12.2.0.1.0 - Production on Tue Nov 28 17:56:20 2017

Copyright (c) 1982, 2017, Oracle and/or its affiliates.  All rights reserved.


Connected to: Oracle Database 12c Enterprise Edition Release 12.2.0.1.0 - 64bit Production
Export done in AL32UTF8 character set and AL16UTF16 NCHAR character set

About to export specified tables via Conventional Path ...
. . exporting table                            EMP       1792 rows exported
Export terminated successfully without warnings.
[oracle12]yspark-linux:/home/oracle12>
```

이제 다시 원래의 DB 시간으로 돌아갑니다.

```
SQL> SHUTDOWN IMMEDIATE ;
SQL> STARTUP MOUNT ;
RMAN> FLASHBACK DATABASE TO SCN <현재SCN 번호> ;
SQL> ALTER DATABASE OPEN RESETLOGS ;
```

```
17:48:23 SYS@oracle12> SHUTDOWN IMMEDIATE ;
Database closed.
Database dismounted.
ORACLE instance shut down.
18:05:06 SYS@oracle12> STARTUP MOUNT ;
ORACLE instance started.

Total System Global Area  746586112 bytes
Fixed Size                  8625176 bytes
Variable Size             587203560 bytes
Database Buffers           33554432 bytes
Redo Buffers                8151040 bytes
In-Memory Area            109051904 bytes
Database mounted.
```

```
[oracle12]yspark-linux:/home/oracle12> rman target /

Recovery Manager: Release 12.2.0.1.0 - Production on Tue Nov 28 18:07:01 2017

Copyright (c) 1982, 2017, Oracle and/or its affiliates.  All rights reserved.

connected to target database: ORACLE12 (DBID=2053465567, not open)

RMAN> FLASHBACK DATABASE TO SCN 1437625126 ;

Starting flashback at 28-NOV-17
using target database control file instead of recovery catalog
allocated channel: ORA_DISK_1
channel ORA_DISK_1: SID=91 device type=DISK


starting media recovery
media recovery complete, elapsed time: 00:00:03

Finished flashback at 28-NOV-17

RMAN>
```

```
18:08:58 SYS@oracle12> ALTER DATABASE OPEN RESETLOGS ;

Database altered.

Elapsed: 00:00:49.35
18:10:07 SYS@oracle12>
```

RESETLOGS로 오픈하면 현재로 다시 돌아오게 됩니다.

이제 데이터 유실이 되어 장애 난 테이블을 다시 조회합니다.

```
SQL> SELECT COUNT(*) FROM EMP
```

```
17:53:57 YONGSEOK@oracle12> CONNECT YONGSEOK/PARK
Connected.
18:11:42 YONGSEOK@oracle12>
18:11:42 YONGSEOK@oracle12> SELECT COUNT(*) FROM EMP ;

  COUNT(*)
----------
         0

1 row selected.

Elapsed: 00:00:00.10
18:11:48 YONGSEOK@oracle12>
```

과거에 돌아가서 백업 받은 데이터를 복구합니다.

```
# imp USERID=YONGSEOK/PARK TABLES=EMP FILE=EMP.DMP IGNORE=Y
```

```
[oracle12]yspark-linux:/home/oracle12> imp USERID=YONGSEOK/PARK TABLES=EMP FILE=EMP.DMP IGNORE=Y

Import: Release 12.2.0.1.0 - Production on Tue Nov 28 18:14:28 2017

Copyright (c) 1982, 2017, Oracle and/or its affiliates.  All rights reserved.


Connected to: Oracle Database 12c Enterprise Edition Release 12.2.0.1.0 - 64bit Production

Export file created by EXPORT:V12.02.00 via conventional path
import done in AL32UTF8 character set and AL16UTF16 NCHAR character set
. importing YONGSEOK's objects into YONGSEOK
. importing YONGSEOK's objects into YONGSEOK
. . importing table                          "EMP"       1792 rows imported
Import terminated successfully without warnings.
[oracle12]yspark-linux:/home/oracle12>
```

마지막으로 장애 난 테이블을 조회하여 복구가 완료되었는지 확인합니다.

```
SQL> SELECT COUNT(*) FROM EMP ;
```

```
18:11:48 YONGSEOK@oracle12> SELECT COUNT(*) FROM EMP ;

  COUNT(*)
----------
      1792

1 row selected.

Elapsed: 00:00:00.01
18:15:48 YONGSEOK@oracle12>
```

CATALOG DB 환경의 RMAN 사용 방법

RMAN 백업으로 구성된 환경에서 카탈로그 정보를 컨트롤 파일에 두는 곳은 많지 않습니다. 대부분 백업 마스터 서버에 Oracle Database 설치 후 카탈로그 DB를 생성하여 백업 정보를 관리하게 됩니다.

Oracle Database 12C 기준 카탈로그 DB 서버의 라이선스는 별도의 추가 비용이 없이 사용 가능합니다.

Oracle Docs 사이트의 Database Licensing Information User Manual을 보면 다음과 같이 나와 있습니다.

Infrastructure Repository Databases

A separate single instance Oracle Database can be installed and used as an infrastructure repository for RMAN, Oracle Enterprise Manager Cloud Control, Automatic Workload Repository (AWR) Warehouse, Global Data Services Catalog, and Grid Infrastructure Management Repository without additional license requirements, provided that all the targets are correctly licensed. It may not be used or deployed for other uses.

출처 : https://docs.oracle.com/database/121/DBLIC/editions.htm#DBLIC109

이제부터 별도의 카탈로그 DB 환경에서의 백업/복구를 확인해 보겠습니다.

1 카탈로그 DB 기본 관리

RMAN 카탈로그 정보를 담을 DB를 생성합니다. Oracle Database S/W 설치 후 DBCA를 통해서 일반적으로 생성합니다. RMAN 카탈로그 정보를 담을 DB 생성 이후부터 진행하겠습니다.

```
# 만들어진 DB 상태확인
# export ORACLE_SID=rmandb
SQL> show parameter db_name
```

```
[oracle12]yspark-linux:/home/oracle12> ps -ef | grep rmandb
oracle12  3853     1  0 Nov28 ?        00:00:02 ora_pmon_rmandb
oracle12  3855     1  0 Nov28 ?        00:00:01 ora_clmn_rmandb
oracle12  3857     1  0 Nov28 ?        00:00:08 ora_psp0_rmandb
oracle12  3860     1  0 Nov28 ?        00:00:08 ora_vktm_rmandb
oracle12  3864     1  0 Nov28 ?        00:00:02 ora_gen0_rmandb
oracle12  3866     1  0 Nov28 ?        00:00:01 ora_mman_rmandb
oracle12  3870     1  0 Nov28 ?        00:00:07 ora_gen1_rmandb
oracle12  3874     1  0 Nov28 ?        00:00:02 ora_diag_rmandb
oracle12  3876     1  0 Nov28 ?        00:00:01 ora_ofsd_rmandb
oracle12  3880     1  0 Nov28 ?        00:00:08 ora_dbrm_rmandb
oracle12  3882     1  0 Nov28 ?        00:00:27 ora_vkrm_rmandb
oracle12  3884     1  0 Nov28 ?        00:00:02 ora_svcb_rmandb
oracle12  3886     1  0 Nov28 ?        00:00:03 ora_pman_rmandb
oracle12  3888     1  0 Nov28 ?        00:00:13 ora_dia0_rmandb
oracle12  3890     1  0 Nov28 ?        00:00:04 ora_dbw0_rmandb
oracle12  3892     1  0 Nov28 ?        00:00:02 ora_lgwr_rmandb
oracle12  3894     1  0 Nov28 ?        00:00:08 ora_ckpt_rmandb
oracle12  3896     1  0 Nov28 ?        00:00:03 ora_lg00_rmandb
oracle12  3898     1  0 Nov28 ?        00:00:01 ora_smon_rmandb
oracle12  3900     1  0 Nov28 ?        00:00:02 ora_lg01_rmandb
```

```
[oracle12]yspark-linux:/home/oracle12> export ORACLE_SID=rmandb
[rmandb]yspark-linux:/home/oracle12> sqlplus "/as sysdba"

SQL*Plus: Release 12.2.0.1.0 Production on Wed Nov 29 09:23:23 2017

Copyright (c) 1982, 2016, Oracle.  All rights reserved.


Connected to:
Oracle Database 12c Enterprise Edition Release 12.2.0.1.0 - 64bit Production

09:23:24 SYS@rmandb>
09:23:24 SYS@rmandb> show parameter db_name

NAME                                 TYPE        VALUE
------------------------------------ ----------- ------------------------------
db_name                              string      rmandb
09:23:30 SYS@rmandb>
```

RMAN CATALOG 테이블스페이스와 사용자를 생성합니다.

```
SQL> CREATE TABLESPACE RMAN_CATALOG DATAFILE SIZE 1G AUTOEXTEND ON ;
SQL> CREATE USER RMAN IDENTIFIED BY cat
     TEMPORARY TABLESPACE TEMP
     DEFAULT TABLESPACE RMAN_CATALOG
     QUOTA UNLIMITED ON RMAN_CATALOG;
SQL> GRANT RECOVERY_CATALOG_OWNER TO RMAN ;
SQL> GRANT CONNECT,RESOURCE TO RMAN ;
SQL> CONNECT RMAN
```

```
09:23:30 SYS@rmandb> CREATE TABLESPACE RMAN_CATALOG DATAFILE SIZE 1G AUTOEXTEND ON ;
09:43:50 SYS@rmandb> CREATE USER RMAN IDENTIFIED BY cat
09:44:40   2  TEMPORARY TABLESPACE TEMP
09:44:40   3  DEFAULT TABLESPACE RMAN_CATALOG
09:44:40   4  QUOTA UNLIMITED ON RMAN_CATALOG;
09:44:41 SYS@rmandb> GRANT RECOVERY_CATALOG_OWNER TO RMAN;
09:44:52 SYS@rmandb> GRANT CONNECT,RESOURCE TO RMAN ;
09:47:33 SYS@rmandb> CONNECT RMAN/cat
Connected.
09:47:52 RMAN@rmandb>
09:47:52 RMAN@rmandb>
```

RMAN을 수행하여 CATALOG DB 서버로 접속해야 하므로 접속 파일 tnsnames.ora 파일에 접속 정보를 추가합니다.

```
# vi $ORACLE_HOME/network/admin/tnsnames.ora
rmandb =
  (DESCRIPTION =
       (ADDRESS = (PROTOCOL = TCP)(HOST = yspark-linux)(PORT = 1588))
       (CONNECT_DATA =
              (SERVER=DEDICATED)
              (SERVICE_NAME=rmandb)
       )
)
# tnsping rmandb
# sqlplus rman@rmandb
```

```
rmandb =
  (DESCRIPTION =
        (ADDRESS = (PROTOCOL = TCP)(HOST = yspark-linux)(PORT = 1588))
        (CONNECT_DATA =
                (SERVER=DEDICATED)
                (SERVICE_NAME=rmandb)
        )
)
[oracle12]yspark-linux:/oracle/oracle12/app/oracle/product/12.2.0/dbhome_1/network/admin> tnsping rmandb

TNS Ping Utility for Linux: Version 12.2.0.1.0 - Production on 29-NOV-2017 09:55:32

Copyright (c) 1997, 2016, Oracle.  All rights reserved.

Used parameter files:
/oracle/oracle12/app/oracle/product/12.2.0/dbhome_1/network/admin/sqlnet.ora


Used TNSNAMES adapter to resolve the alias
Attempting to contact (DESCRIPTION = (ADDRESS = (PROTOCOL = TCP)(HOST = yspark-linux)(PORT = 1588)) (CONNECT_DATA = (SERVER=DEDICATED) (SERVICE_
NAME=rmandb)))
OK (80 msec)
[oracle12]yspark-linux:/oracle/oracle12/app/oracle/product/12.2.0/dbhome_1/network/admin> sqlplus rman/cat@rmandb

SQL*Plus: Release 12.2.0.1.0 Production on Wed Nov 29 09:55:38 2017

Copyright (c) 1982, 2016, Oracle.  All rights reserved.

Last Successful login time: Wed Nov 29 2017 09:47:51 +09:00

Connected to:
Oracle Database 12c Enterprise Edition Release 12.2.0.1.0 - 64bit Production

09:55:38 RMAN@rmandb>
09:55:38 RMAN@rmandb> █
```

Create catalog 단계입니다. RMAN 명령어를 이용하여 CATALOG를 생성합니다.

```
# export ORACLE_SID=<운영DB>
# rman CATALOG rman/cat@rmandb
RMAN> CREATE CATALOG ;
```

```
[oracle12]yspark-linux:/home/oracle12> export ORACLE_SID=oracle12
[oracle12]yspark-linux:/home/oracle12> rman CATALOG rman/cat@rmandb

Recovery Manager: Release 12.2.0.1.0 - Production on Wed Nov 29 09:58:42 2017

Copyright (c) 1982, 2017, Oracle and/or its affiliates.  All rights reserved.

connected to recovery catalog database

RMAN> CREATE CATALOG ;

recovery catalog created

RMAN> █
```

Register database 단계입니다. 백업이 필요한 운영 중인 데이터베이스를 Catalog Database에 등록합니다.

```
# rman TARGET sys/P#ssw0rd@oracle12 CATALOG rman/cat@rmandb
RMAN> REGISTER DATABASE ;
```

```
[oracle12]yspark-linux:/home/oracle12> rman TARGET sys/P#ssw0rd@oracle12 CATALOG rman/cat@rmandb

Recovery Manager: Release 12.2.0.1.0 - Production on Wed Nov 29 10:03:40 2017

Copyright (c) 1982, 2017, Oracle and/or its affiliates.  All rights reserved.

connected to target database: ORACLE12 (DBID=2053465567)
connected to recovery catalog database

RMAN> REGISTER DATABASE ;

database registered in recovery catalog
starting full resync of recovery catalog
full resync complete

RMAN>
```

Verify registration 단계입니다. 잘 등록되었는지 등록된 데이터베이스의 정보를 확인해 봅니다.

```
# rman TARGET sys/P#ssw0rd@oracle12 CATALOG rman/cat@rmandb
RMAN> REPORT SCHEMA ;
```

```
[oracle12]yspark-linux:/home/oracle12> rman TARGET sys/P#ssw0rd@oracle12 CATALOG rman/cat@rmandb

Recovery Manager: Release 12.2.0.1.0 - Production on Wed Nov 29 10:08:10 2017

Copyright (c) 1982, 2017, Oracle and/or its affiliates.  All rights reserved.

connected to target database: ORACLE12 (DBID=2053465567)
connected to recovery catalog database

RMAN> REPORT SCHEMA ;

Report of database schema for database with db_unique_name ORACLE12

List of Permanent Datafiles
===========================
File Size(MB) Tablespace           RB segs Datafile Name
---- -------- -------------------- ------- ------------------------
1    10240    SYSTEM               YES     /oracle/oracle12/oradata/oracle12/system01.dbf
3    30720    SYSAUX               NO      /oracle/oracle12/oradata/oracle12/sysaux01.dbf
4    30720    UNDOTBS1             YES     /oracle/oracle12/oradata/oracle12/undotbs01.dbf
7    70       USERS                NO      /oracle/oracle12/oradata/oracle12/users01.dbf
10   100      UNDOTBS1             YES     /oracle/oracle12/oradata/oracle12/undotbs02.dbf
11   100      UNDOTBS1             YES     /oracle/oracle12/oradata/oracle12/undotbs03.dbf
12   10       ORACLE12             NO      /oracle/oracle12/oradata/oracle12/oracle12_01.dbf

List of Temporary Files
=======================
File Size(MB) Tablespace           Maxsize(MB) Tempfile Name
---- -------- -------------------- ----------- --------------------
1    124      TEMP                 32767       /oracle/oracle12/oradata/oracle12/temp01.dbf
2    30720    TEMP                 30720       /oracle/oracle12/oradata/oracle12/temp02.dbf
3    30720    TEMP                 30720       /oracle/oracle12/oradata/oracle12/temp03.dbf
4    30720    TEMP                 30720       /oracle/oracle12/oradata/oracle12/temp04.dbf

RMAN>
```

이전 NOCATALOG로 백업 받은 데이터를 복구에 이용하기 위해서 Manual Backup Registration이 필요합니다.

NOCALTALOG mode로 Control File을 백업 후 Catalog에 수동으로 등록시켜 봅니다.

```
# rman TARGET sys/P#ssw0rd@oracle12 NOCATALOG
RMAN> backup current controlfile ;
RMAN> list backup ; #Piece Name : 백업파일명 확인
# rman TARGET sys/P#ssw0rd@oracle12 CATALOG rman/cat@rmandb
RMAN> CATALOG backuppiece '백업파일명' ;
```

```
[oracle12]yspark-linux:/home/oracle12> rman TARGET sys/P#ssw0rd@oracle12 NOCATALOG

Recovery Manager: Release 12.2.0.1.0 - Production on Wed Nov 29 10:12:42 2017

Copyright (c) 1982, 2017, Oracle and/or its affiliates.  All rights reserved.

connected to target database: ORACLE12 (DBID=2053465567)
using target database control file instead of recovery catalog

RMAN> backup current controlfile;

Starting backup at 29-NOV-17
allocated channel: ORA_DISK_1
channel ORA_DISK_1: SID=185 device type=DISK
channel ORA_DISK_1: starting full datafile backup set
channel ORA_DISK_1: specifying datafile(s) in backup set
including current control file in backup set
channel ORA_DISK_1: starting piece 1 at 29-NOV-17
channel ORA_DISK_1: finished piece 1 at 29-NOV-17
piece handle=/oracle/oracle12/RMAN_BACKUP/ORACLE12_8kskp879_1_1_961323241_276 tag=TAG20171129T101401 comment=NONE
channel ORA_DISK_1: backup set complete, elapsed time: 00:00:04
Finished backup at 29-NOV-17

Starting Control File and SPFILE Autobackup at 29-NOV-17
piece handle=/oracle/oracle12/FRA/ORACLE12/autobackup/2017_11_29/o1_mf_s_961323248_f1w2h2gh_.bkp comment=NONE
Finished Control File and SPFILE Autobackup at 29-NOV-17

RMAN>
```

```
RMAN> LIST BACKUP ;


List of Backup Sets
===================


BS Key  Type LV Size       Device Type Elapsed Time Completion Time
------- ---- -- ---------- ----------- ------------ ---------------
163     Full    10.84M     DISK        00:00:02     28-NOV-17
        BP Key: 163   Status: AVAILABLE  Compressed: NO  Tag: TAG20171128T173352
        Piece Name: /oracle/oracle12/FRA/ORACLE12/autobackup/2017_11_28/o1_mf_s_961263232_f1t7vlfq_.bkp
  SPFILE Included: Modification time: 28-NOV-17
  SPFILE db_unique_name: ORACLE12
  Control File Included: Ckp SCN: 1437624470   Ckp time: 28-NOV-17

BS Key  Type LV Size       Device Type Elapsed Time Completion Time
------- ---- -- ---------- ----------- ------------ ---------------
164     Full    10.84M     DISK        00:00:03     28-NOV-17
        BP Key: 164   Status: AVAILABLE  Compressed: NO  Tag: TAG20171128T181002
        Piece Name: /oracle/oracle12/FRA/ORACLE12/autobackup/2017_11_28/o1_mf_s_961265403_f1t9zfd9_.bkp
  SPFILE Included: Modification time: 28-NOV-17
  SPFILE db_unique_name: ORACLE12
  Control File Included: Ckp SCN: 1437626319   Ckp time: 28-NOV-17

BS Key  Type LV Size       Device Type Elapsed Time Completion Time
------- ---- -- ---------- ----------- ------------ ---------------
165     Full    666.27M    DISK        00:02:11     29-NOV-17
        BP Key: 165   Status: AVAILABLE  Compressed: YES  Tag: TAG20171129T011115
        Piece Name: /oracle/oracle12/RMAN_BACKUP/ORACLE12_8fsko8dk_1_1_961290676_271
  List of Datafiles in backup set 165
  File LV Type Ckp SCN    Ckp Time  Abs Fuz SCN Sparse Name
  ---- -- ---- ---------- --------- ----------- ------ ----
  1       Full 1437653245 29-NOV-17              NO     /oracle/oracle12/oradata/oracle12/system01.dbf
  3       Full 1437653245 29-NOV-17              NO     /oracle/oracle12/oradata/oracle12/sysaux01.dbf
  4       Full 1437653245 29-NOV-17              NO     /oracle/oracle12/oradata/oracle12/undotbs01.dbf
  7       Full 1437653245 29-NOV-17              NO     /oracle/oracle12/oradata/oracle12/users01.dbf
  10      Full 1437653245 29-NOV-17              NO     /oracle/oracle12/oradata/oracle12/undotbs02.dbf
  11      Full 1437653245 29-NOV-17              NO     /oracle/oracle12/oradata/oracle12/undotbs03.dbf
  12      Full 1437653245 29-NOV-17              NO     /oracle/oracle12/oradata/oracle12/oracle12_01.dbf

BS Key  Size       Device Type Elapsed Time Completion Time
------- ---------- ----------- ------------ ---------------
166     14.23M     DISK        00:00:03     29-NOV-17
        BP Key: 166   Status: AVAILABLE  Compressed: YES  Tag: TAG20171129T011344
        Piece Name: /oracle/oracle12/RMAN_BACKUP/ORACLE12_8gsko8i8_1_1_961290824_272
```

```
  Control File Included: Ckp SCN: 1437682508   Ckp time: 29-NOV-17

BS Key  Type LV Size       Device Type Elapsed Time Completion Time
------- ---- -- ---------- ----------- ------------ ---------------
171     Full    10.84M     DISK        00:00:02     29-NOV-17
        BP Key: 171   Status: AVAILABLE  Compressed: NO  Tag: TAG20171129T101408
        Piece Name: /oracle/oracle12/FRA/ORACLE12/autobackup/2017_11_29/o1_mf_s_961323248_f1w2h2gh_.bkp
  SPFILE Included: Modification time: 29-NOV-17
  SPFILE db_unique_name: ORACLE12
```

```
[oracle12]yspark-linux:/home/oracle12> rman TARGET sys/P#ssw0rd@oracle12 CATALOG rman/cat@rmandb

Recovery Manager: Release 12.2.0.1.0 - Production on Wed Nov 29 10:16:36 2017

Copyright (c) 1982, 2017, Oracle and/or its affiliates.  All rights reserved.

connected to target database: ORACLE12 (DBID=2053465567)
connected to recovery catalog database

RMAN> CATALOG backupPiece '/oracle/oracle12/FRA/ORACLE12/autobackup/2017_11_29/o1_mf_s_961323248_f1w2h2gh_.bkp' ;

cataloged backup piece
backup piece handle=/oracle/oracle12/FRA/ORACLE12/autobackup/2017_11_29/o1_mf_s_961323248_f1w2h2gh_.bkp RECID=172 STAMP=961323452

RMAN>
```

RMAN catalog에 RMAN Script를 저장할 수 있으며 이를 Global Script라고 합니다. RMAN Script를 저장하고 수행할 수 있습니다.

```
# rman TARGET sys/P#ssw0rd@oracle12 CATALOG rman/cat@rmandb
RMAN> CREATE GLOBAL SCRIPT global_full_backup COMMENT 'use only with ARCHIVELOG mode databases'
2> {
3>   BACKUP DATABASE PLUS ARCHIVELOG ;
4>   DELETE NOPROMPT OBSOLETE ;
5> }
RMAN> LIST GLOBAL SCRIPT NAMES ;
RMAN> PRINT GLOBAL SCRIPT global_full_backup ;
RMAN> RUN {
2> EXECUTE GLOBAL SCRIPT global_full_backup ;
3> }
```

```
[oracle12]yspark-linux:/home/oracle12> rman TARGET sys/P#ssw0rd@oracle12 CATALOG rman/cat@rmandb

Recovery Manager: Release 12.2.0.1.0 - Production on Wed Nov 29 10:25:00 2017

Copyright (c) 1982, 2017, Oracle and/or its affiliates.  All rights reserved.

connected to target database: ORACLE12 (DBID=2053465567)
connected to recovery catalog database

RMAN> CREATE GLOBAL SCRIPT global_full_backup COMMENT 'use only with ARCHIVELOG mode databases'
2> {
3>   BACKUP DATABASE PLUS ARCHIVELOG ;
4>   DELETE NOPROMPT OBSOLETE ;
5> }

created global script global_full_backup

RMAN> LIST GLOBAL SCRIPT NAMES ;

List of Stored Scripts in Recovery Catalog


    Global Scripts


       Script Name
       Description
       -----------------------------------------------------------------------
       global_full_backup
       use only with ARCHIVELOG mode databases

RMAN>
```

```
RMAN> PRINT GLOBAL SCRIPT global_full_backup ;

printing stored global script: global_full_backup
{
  BACKUP DATABASE PLUS ARCHIVELOG ;
  DELETE NOPROMPT OBSOLETE ;
}

RMAN>
```

```
RMAN> RUN {
2> EXECUTE GLOBAL SCRIPT global_full_backup ;
3> }

executing global script: global_full_backup


Starting backup at 29-NOV-17
current log archived
allocated channel: ORA_DISK_1
channel ORA_DISK_1: SID=100 device type=DISK
skipping archived logs of thread 1 from sequence 559 to 560; already backed up
channel ORA_DISK_1: starting archived log backup set
channel ORA_DISK_1: specifying archived log(s) in backup set
input archived log thread=1 sequence=2 RECID=562 STAMP=961324268
channel ORA_DISK_1: starting piece 1 at 29-NOV-17
channel ORA_DISK_1: finished piece 1 at 29-NOV-17
piece handle=/oracle/oracle12/RMAN_BACKUP/ORACLE12_8mskp97f_1_1_961324271_278 tag=TAG20171129T103111 comment=NONE
channel ORA_DISK_1: backup set complete, elapsed time: 00:00:03
Finished backup at 29-NOV-17
```

RMAN catalog 정보를 유실되면 백업 정보가 없으므로 복구가 불가능합니다. 일반적으로 exp 유틸을 사용하여 매일 백업을 받습니다.

```
# exp rman/cat@rmandb file=rman-catalog-export.dmp owner=rman feedback=100
```

```
[rmandb]yspark-linux:/oracle/oracle12> exp rman/cat@rmandb file=rman-catalog-export.dmp owner=rman feedback=100

Export: Release 12.2.0.1.0 - Production on Wed Nov 29 10:41:48 2017

Copyright (c) 1982, 2017, Oracle and/or its affiliates.  All rights reserved.


Connected to: Oracle Database 12c Enterprise Edition Release 12.2.0.1.0 - 64bit Production
Export done in AL32UTF8 character set and AL16UTF16 NCHAR character set
. exporting pre-schema procedural objects and actions
. exporting foreign function library names for user RMAN
. exporting PUBLIC type synonyms
. exporting private type synonyms
. exporting object type definitions for user RMAN
About to export RMAN's objects ...
. exporting database links
. exporting sequence numbers
. exporting cluster definitions
. about to export RMAN's tables via Conventional Path ...
. . exporting table                             AL
                                                          4 rows exported
. . exporting table                            BCB
                                                          0 rows exported
. . exporting table                            BCF
                                                          5 rows exported
. . exporting table                            BCR
                                                          0 rows exported
. . exporting table                            BDF
                                                          7 rows exported
. . exporting table                             BP
                                                         10 rows exported
. . exporting table                            BRL
                                                         19 rows exported
. . exporting table                             BS
                                                         10 rows exported
. . exporting table                            BSF
                                                          5 rows exported
. . exporting table                            CCB
                                                          0 rows exported
```

```
. . exporting table                             TF
                                                          4 rows exported
. . exporting table                             TS
                                                          6 rows exported
. . exporting table                          TSATT
                                                          6 rows exported
. . exporting table                  VPC_DATABASES
                                                          0 rows exported
. . exporting table                      VPC_USERS
                                                          0 rows exported
. . exporting table                     WATERMARKS
                                                          0 rows exported
. . exporting table                            XAL
                                                          0 rows exported
. . exporting table                            XCF
                                                          0 rows exported
. . exporting table                            XDF
                                                          0 rows exported
. . exporting table                       XMLSTORE
                                                          0 rows exported
. exporting synonyms
. exporting views
. exporting stored procedures
. exporting operators
. exporting referential integrity constraints
. exporting triggers
. exporting indextypes
. exporting bitmap, functional and extensible indexes
. exporting posttables actions
. exporting materialized views
. exporting snapshot logs
. exporting job queues
. exporting refresh groups and children
. exporting dimensions
. exporting post-schema procedural objects and actions
. exporting statistics
Export terminated successfully without warnings.
[rmandb]yspark-linux:/oracle/oracle12>
```

RMAN catalog에 직접 접속해 원하는 데이터베이스의 Database ID와 DB Key를 조회하여 Catalog Database에서 타겟 데이터베이스의 백업 상황을 확인할 수 있습니다.

```
운 영 DB SQL> CONNECT SYS
운 영 DB SQL> SELECT DBID FROM V$DATABASE ;
RMANDB SQL> CONNECT RMAN
RMANDB SQL> SELECT DB_KEY FROM RC_DATABASE WHERE DBID = <운영DB ID> ;
RMANDB SQL> SELECT DBINC_KEY,BS_KEY, BACKUP_TYPE, COMPLETION_TIME
FROM RC_DATABASE_INCARNATION i, RC_BACKUP_SET b
WHERE i.DB_KEY = <DB_KEY>
AND i.DB_KEY = b.DB_KEY ;
RMANDB SQL> EXECUTE DBMS_RCVMAN.SETDATABASE(null,null,null,<운영 DB ID>,null);
RMANDB SQL> SELECT BACKUP_TYPE,STATUS,TAG,BYTES,COMPLETION_TIME FROM RC_BACKUP_FILES ;
```

```
10:53:48 SYS@oracle12> select dbid from v$database ;

      DBID
----------
2053465567
10:53:55 SYS@oracle12>
```

```
10:55:16 RMAN@rmandb> SELECT DB_KEY FROM RC_DATABASE WHERE DBID = 2053465567 ;

    DB_KEY
----------
         1
10:56:10 RMAN@rmandb>
```

```
10:56:41 RMAN@rmandb> SELECT DBINC_KEY,BS_KEY, BACKUP_TYPE, COMPLETION_TIME
10:56:48   2  FROM RC_DATABASE_INCARNATION i, RC_BACKUP_SET b
10:56:48   3  WHERE i.DB_KEY = 1
10:56:48   4  AND i.DB_KEY = b.DB_KEY ;

 DBINC_KEY     BS_KEY B COMPLETION_TIME
---------- ---------- - -----------------
         2        880 D 28/11/17 17:33:54
       206        880 D 28/11/17 17:33:54
       205        880 D 28/11/17 17:33:54
         2        881 D 28/11/17 18:10:05
       206        881 D 28/11/17 18:10:05
       205        881 D 28/11/17 18:10:05
         2        883 L 29/11/17 01:13:47
       206        883 L 29/11/17 01:13:47
       205        883 L 29/11/17 01:13:47
         2        884 L 29/11/17 01:13:56
       206        884 L 29/11/17 01:13:56
       205        884 L 29/11/17 01:13:56
         2        885 D 29/11/17 01:14:06
       206        885 D 29/11/17 01:14:06
       205        885 D 29/11/17 01:14:06
         2       1111 D 29/11/17 10:14:10
       206       1111 D 29/11/17 10:14:10
       205       1111 D 29/11/17 10:14:10
         2       1141 L 29/11/17 10:31:12
       206       1141 L 29/11/17 10:31:12
       205       1141 L 29/11/17 10:31:12
         2       1153 D 29/11/17 10:32:46
       206       1153 D 29/11/17 10:32:46
       205       1153 D 29/11/17 10:32:46
         2       1169 L 29/11/17 10:32:55
       206       1169 L 29/11/17 10:32:55
       205       1169 L 29/11/17 10:32:55
         2       1185 D 29/11/17 10:32:59
       206       1185 D 29/11/17 10:32:59
       205       1185 D 29/11/17 10:32:59
```

```
10:56:48 RMAN@rmandb> EXECUTE DBMS_RCVMAN.SETDATABASE(null,null,null,2053465567,null);
10:57:36 RMAN@rmandb>
10:58:02 RMAN@rmandb>
10:58:04 RMAN@rmandb> SELECT BACKUP_TYPE,STATUS,TAG,BYTES,COMPLETION_TIME FROM RC_BACKUP_FILES ;

BACKUP_TYPE                      STATUS           TAG                                   BYTES COMPLETION_TIME
-------------------------------- ---------------- -------------------------------- ---------- -----------------
COPY                             AVAILABLE                                            9778688 28/11/17 16:22:46
COPY                             AVAILABLE                                              26624 28/11/17 16:27:44
BACKUP SET                                                                           11272192
BACKUP SET                                                                              32768
BACKUP SET                       AVAILABLE        TAG20171128T173352                 11370496 28/11/17 17:33:54
BACKUP SET                                                                              32768
BACKUP SET                                                                           11272192
BACKUP SET                       AVAILABLE        TAG20171128T181002                 11370496 28/11/17 18:10:06
BACKUP SET                                                                               8704
BACKUP SET                                                                             100864
BACKUP SET                                                                            4753408
BACKUP SET                                                                             256000
```

Catalog Database의 Catalog 버전을 조회합니다.

```
RMANDB SQL> SELECT * FROM RCVER ;
```

```
10:58:06 RMAN@rmandb> SELECT * FROM RCVER ;

VERSION
------------
12.02.00.01
11:08:34 RMAN@rmandb>
```

Catalog 버전을 마지막 버전으로 Upgrade합니다.

```
# rman TARGET sys/P#ssw0rd@oracle12 CATALOG rman/cat@rmandb
RMAN> UPGRADE CATALOG ;
RMAN> UPGRADE CATALOG ;
```

```
[oracle12]yspark-linux:/home/oracle12> rman TARGET sys/P#ssw0rd@oracle12 CATALOG rman/cat@rmandb

Recovery Manager: Release 12.2.0.1.0 - Production on Wed Nov 29 11:12:25 2017

Copyright (c) 1982, 2017, Oracle and/or its affiliates.  All rights reserved.

connected to target database: ORACLE12 (DBID=2053465567)
connected to recovery catalog database

RMAN> UPGRADE CATALOG ;

recovery catalog owner is RMAN
enter UPGRADE CATALOG command again to confirm catalog upgrade

RMAN> UPGRADE CATALOG ;

recovery catalog upgraded to version 12.02.00.01
DBMS_RCVMAN package upgraded to version 12.02.00.01
DBMS_RCVCAT package upgraded to version 12.02.00.01.

RMAN>
```

2 CATALOG 명령어

CATALOG 명령어는 과거에 수행 완료된 백업 대상 파일을 RMAN Repository에 등록합니다. Control File 전체 손상에 대해, 취득된 백업을 RMAN Repository에 수동으로 개별 등록하고 싶을 때 사용합니다.

아카이브 로그를 RMAN Repository에 등록합니다.

```
# rman TARGET sys/P#ssw0rd@oracle12 CATALOG rman/cat@rmandb
RMAN> CATALOG ARCHIVELOG '<아카이브경로/아카이브로그파일명>' ;
```

```
[oracle12]yspark-linux:/home/oracle12> rman TARGET sys/P#ssw0rd@oracle12 CATALOG rman/cat@rmandb

Recovery Manager: Release 12.2.0.1.0 - Production on Wed Nov 29 12:42:28 2017

Copyright (c) 1982, 2017, Oracle and/or its affiliates.  All rights reserved.

connected to target database: ORACLE12 (DBID=2053465567)
connected to recovery catalog database

RMAN> CATALOG ARCHIVELOG '/oracle/oracle12/FRA/ORACLE12/archivelog/2017_11_29/o1_mf_1_9_f1w93bfz_.arc' ;

cataloged archived log
archived log file name=/oracle/oracle12/FRA/ORACLE12/archivelog/2017_11_29/o1_mf_1_9_f1w93bfz_.arc RECID=570 STAMP=961332174

RMAN>
```

NOCATALOG로 받은 backup piece를 RMAN Repository에 등록합니다.

```
# rman TARGET / NOCATALOG
RMAN> backup as compressed backupset database format '/oracle/oracle12/TEMP_BACKUP/%U_%T';
# rman TARGET sys/P#ssw0rd@oracle12 CATALOG rman/cat@rmandb
RMAN> CATALOG BACKUPPIECE '<과거 backup piece 명>' ;
```

```
[oracle12]yspark-linux:/oracle/oracle12/RMAN_BACKUP> rman TARGET / NOCATALOG

Recovery Manager: Release 12.2.0.1.0 - Production on Wed Nov 29 12:31:32 2017

Copyright (c) 1982, 2017, Oracle and/or its affiliates.  All rights reserved.

connected to target database: ORACLE12 (DBID=2053465567)
using target database control file instead of recovery catalog

RMAN> backup as compressed backupset database format '/oracle/oracle12/TEMP_BACKUP/%U_%T';

Starting backup at 29-NOV-17
allocated channel: ORA_DISK_1
channel ORA_DISK_1: SID=178 device type=DISK
channel ORA_DISK_1: starting compressed full datafile backup set
channel ORA_DISK_1: specifying datafile(s) in backup set
input datafile file number=00003 name=/oracle/oracle12/oradata/oracle12/sysaux01.dbf
input datafile file number=00004 name=/oracle/oracle12/oradata/oracle12/undotbs01.dbf
input datafile file number=00001 name=/oracle/oracle12/oradata/oracle12/system01.dbf
input datafile file number=00002 name=/oracle/oracle12/oradata/oracle12/yongseok01.dbf
input datafile file number=00005 name=/oracle/oracle12/oradata/oracle12/unione01.dbf
input datafile file number=00010 name=/oracle/oracle12/oradata/oracle12/undotbs02.dbf
input datafile file number=00011 name=/oracle/oracle12/oradata/oracle12/undotbs03.dbf
input datafile file number=00007 name=/oracle/oracle12/oradata/oracle12/users01.dbf
input datafile file number=00012 name=/oracle/oracle12/oradata/oracle12/oracle12_01.dbf
channel ORA_DISK_1: starting piece 1 at 29-NOV-17
channel ORA_DISK_1: finished piece 1 at 29-NOV-17
piece handle=/oracle/oracle12/TEMP_BACKUP/8tskpg9b_1_1_20171129 tag=TAG20171129T123138 comment=NONE
channel ORA_DISK_1: backup set complete, elapsed time: 00:02:06
Finished backup at 29-NOV-17

Starting Control File and SPFILE Autobackup at 29-NOV-17
piece handle=/oracle/oracle12/FRA/ORACLE12/autobackup/2017_11_29/o1_mf_s_961331625_f1wbnvtx_.bkp comment=NONE
Finished Control File and SPFILE Autobackup at 29-NOV-17
```

```
[oracle12]yspark-linux:/home/oracle12> rman TARGET sys/P#ssw0rd@oracle12 CATALOG rman/cat@rmandb

Recovery Manager: Release 12.2.0.1.0 - Production on Wed Nov 29 12:45:28 2017

Copyright (c) 1982, 2017, Oracle and/or its affiliates.  All rights reserved.

connected to target database: ORACLE12 (DBID=2053465567)
connected to recovery catalog database

RMAN> CATALOG BACKUPPIECE '/oracle/oracle12/TEMP_BACKUP/8tskpg9b_1_1_20171129' ;

cataloged backup piece
backup piece handle=/oracle/oracle12/TEMP_BACKUP/8tskpg9b_1_1_20171129 RECID=183 STAMP=961332361
```

데이터 파일의 사본을 CATALOG 명령어로 레벨 0의 증분 백업으로 RMAN 리포지터리에 기록할 수 있습니다.

```
# rman TARGET sys/P#ssw0rd@oracle12 CATALOG rman/cat@rmandb
RMAN> CATALOG DATAFILECOPY  '<경로/파일명>' LEVEL 0 TAG ' ' ;
```

```
[oracle12]yspark-linux:/oracle/oracle12/TEMP_BACKUP> ls -al
total 10485772
drwxr-xr-x   2 oracle12 dba                26 Nov 30 01:13 .
drwxr-xr-x. 11 oracle12 dba              4096 Nov 29 12:19 ..
-rw-r-----   1 oracle12 oinstall 10737426432 Nov 29 13:03 system01.dbf
[oracle12]yspark-linux:/oracle/oracle12/TEMP_BACKUP> rman TARGET sys/P#ssw0rd@oracle12 CATALOG rman/cat@rmandb

Recovery Manager: Release 12.2.0.1.0 - Production on Tue Dec 19 10:55:37 2017

Copyright (c) 1982, 2017, Oracle and/or its affiliates.  All rights reserved.

connected to target database: ORACLE12 (DBID=2053465567)
connected to recovery catalog database

RMAN> CATALOG DATAFILECOPY
2> '/oracle/oracle12/TEMP_BACKUP/system01.dbf' LEVEL 0 TAG 'incr0_system' ;

cataloged datafile copy
datafile copy file name=/oracle/oracle12/TEMP_BACKUP/system01.dbf RECID=223 STAMP=963140197

RMAN>
```

3 CHANGE 명령어

CATALOG 명령어가 RMAN 리포지터리에 등록하는 명령어라면 CHANGE 명령어는 RMAN 백업 데이터를 복구 시 사용할 수 있게 하나거나 사용할 수 없도록 상태를 변경하는 명령어입니다.

CATALOG 명령어로 등록한 카피 본을 레파지토리 정보에서 삭제합니다.

```
# rman TARGET sys/P#ssw0rd@oracle12 CATALOG rman/cat@rmandb
RMAN> CHANGE DATAFILECOPY  '<경로/파일명>' UNCATALOG ;
```

```
[oracle12]yspark-linux:/home/oracle12> rman TARGET sys/P#ssw0rd@oracle12 CATALOG rman/cat@rmandb
Recovery Manager: Release 12.2.0.1.0 - Production on Tue Dec 19 11:19:03 2017

Copyright (c) 1982, 2017, Oracle and/or its affiliates.  All rights reserved.

connected to target database: ORACLE12 (DBID=2053465567)
connected to recovery catalog database

RMAN> CHANGE DATAFILECOPY
2> '/oracle/oracle12/TEMP_BACKUP/system01.dbf' UNCATALOG ;

uncataloged datafile copy
datafile copy file name=/oracle/oracle12/TEMP_BACKUP/system01.dbf RECID=223 STAMP=963140197
Uncataloged 1 objects

RMAN> █
```

CHANGE 명령어는 RMAN 리포지터리에서 정보를 변경하는 목적의 명령어입니다.
잘못 수행되거나 백업 시 사용자 실수로 데이터 유실에 대한 백업 데이터를 무효화시킬 때 사용합니다.

```
# rman TARGET sys/P#ssw0rd@oracle12 CATALOG rman/cat@rmandb
RMAN> LIST BACKUPSET <백업번호> ;
RMAN> CHANGE BACKUPSET <백업 번호> UNAVAILABLE ;
```

```
RMAN> list backupset 1971 ;


List of Backup Sets
===================


BS Key  Type LV Size       Device Type Elapsed Time Completion Time
------- ---- -- ---------- ----------- ------------ ---------------
1971    Full    673.72M    DISK        00:01:58     19-DEC-17
        BP Key: 1993   Status: AVAILABLE  Compressed: YES  Tag: TAG20171219T011119
        Piece Name: /oracle/oracle12/RMAN_BACKUP/ORACLE12_bbsmfk9o_1_1_963105080_363
  List of Datafiles in backup set 1971
  File LV Type Ckp SCN    Ckp Time  Abs Fuz SCN Sparse Name
  ---- -- ---- ---------- --------- ----------- ------ ----
  1       Full 1439287159 19-DEC-17             NO     /oracle/oracle12/oradata/oracle12/system01.dbf
  2       Full 1439287159 19-DEC-17             NO     /oracle/oracle12/oradata/oracle12/yongseok01.dbf
  3       Full 1439287159 19-DEC-17             NO     /oracle/oracle12/oradata/oracle12/sysaux01.dbf
  4       Full 1439287159 19-DEC-17             NO     /oracle/oracle12/oradata/oracle12/undotbs01.dbf
  5       Full 1439287159 19-DEC-17             NO     /oracle/oracle12/oradata/oracle12/unione01.dbf
  7       Full 1439287159 19-DEC-17             NO     /oracle/oracle12/oradata/oracle12/users01.dbf
  10      Full 1439287159 19-DEC-17             NO     /oracle/oracle12/oradata/oracle12/undotbs02.dbf
  11      Full 1439287159 19-DEC-17             NO     /oracle/oracle12/oradata/oracle12/undotbs03.dbf
  12      Full 1439287159 19-DEC-17             NO     /oracle/oracle12/oradata/oracle12/oracle12_01.dbf

RMAN> CHANGE BACKUPSET 1971 UNAVAILABLE ;

changed backup piece unavailable
backup piece handle=/oracle/oracle12/RMAN_BACKUP/ORACLE12_bbsmfk9o_1_1_963105080_363 RECID=260 STAMP=963105082
Changed 1 objects to UNAVAILABLE status

RMAN> █
```

장기간의 백업 상태로 특정 일자 백업 데이터를 보관하도록 변경할 수 있습니다.

```
# rman TARGET sys/P#ssw0rd@oracle12 CATALOG rman/cat@rmandb
RMAN> LIST BACKUPSET <백업번호> ;
RMAN> CHANGE BACKUP TAG '<태그 이름>' KEEP FOREVER NOLOGS;
```

```
RMAN> LIST BACKUPSET 1971 ;


List of Backup Sets
===================


BS Key  Type LV Size       Device Type Elapsed Time Completion Time
------- ---- -- ---------- ----------- ------------ ---------------
1971    Full    673.72M    DISK        00:01:58     19-DEC-17
        BP Key: 1993   Status: AVAILABLE  Compressed: YES  Tag: TAG20171219T011119
        Piece Name: /oracle/oracle12/RMAN_BACKUP/ORACLE12_bbsmfk9o_1_1_963105080_363
  List of Datafiles in backup set 1971
  File LV Type Ckp SCN    Ckp Time  Abs Fuz SCN Sparse Name
  ---- -- ---- ---------- --------- ----------- ------ ----
  1       Full 1439287159 19-DEC-17             NO     /oracle/oracle12/oradata/oracle12/system01.dbf
  2       Full 1439287159 19-DEC-17             NO     /oracle/oracle12/oradata/oracle12/yongseok01.dbf
  3       Full 1439287159 19-DEC-17             NO     /oracle/oracle12/oradata/oracle12/sysaux01.dbf
  4       Full 1439287159 19-DEC-17             NO     /oracle/oracle12/oradata/oracle12/undotbs01.dbf
  5       Full 1439287159 19-DEC-17             NO     /oracle/oracle12/oradata/oracle12/unione01.dbf
  7       Full 1439287159 19-DEC-17             NO     /oracle/oracle12/oradata/oracle12/users01.dbf
  10      Full 1439287159 19-DEC-17             NO     /oracle/oracle12/oradata/oracle12/undotbs02.dbf
  11      Full 1439287159 19-DEC-17             NO     /oracle/oracle12/oradata/oracle12/undotbs03.dbf
  12      Full 1439287159 19-DEC-17             NO     /oracle/oracle12/oradata/oracle12/oracle12_01.dbf

RMAN> CHANGE BACKUP TAG 'TAG20171219T011119' KEEP FOREVER NOLOGS;

using channel ORA_DISK_1
keep attributes for the backup are changed
backup will never be obsolete
archived logs will not be kept or backed up
backup set key=1971 RECID=260 STAMP=963105198

RMAN>
```

CHANGE 명령어는 백업 데이터 및 복사 데이터의 가용성 상태의 변경 가능합니다.

자동 진단 저장소(ADR)에 기록된 장애의 우선순위를 변경하거나 장애를 종료할 수 있습니다.

데이터 파일 유실 장애를 발생시킵니다.

```
[oracle12]yspark-linux:/oracle/oracle12/oradata/oracle12> ls
control01.ctl     redo01.log  sysaux01.dbf  temp02.dbf  undotbs01.dbf  UNIONE         yongseok01.dbf
control02.ctl     redo02.log  system01.dbf  temp03.dbf  undotbs02.dbf  unione01.dbf
oracle12_01.dbf   redo03.log  temp01.dbf    temp04.dbf  undotbs03.dbf  users01.dbf
[oracle12]yspark-linux:/oracle/oracle12/oradata/oracle12> mv users01.dbf users01.dbf.bak
```

```
13:01:31 SYS@oracle12> conn system/oracle
Connected.
13:01:40 SYSTEM@oracle12>
13:01:40 SYSTEM@oracle12> CREATE TABLE test_tab (id NUMBER) TABLESPACE USERS;
CREATE TABLE test_tab (id NUMBER) TABLESPACE USERS
*
ERROR at line 1:
ORA-01116: error in opening database file 7
ORA-01110: data file 7: '/oracle/oracle12/oradata/oracle12/users01.dbf'
ORA-27041: unable to open file
Linux-x86_64 Error: 2: No such file or directory
Additional information: 3

13:04:29 SYSTEM@oracle12>
```

이제 LIST 명령으로 장애 상황을 조회한 후 CHANGE 명령어로 우선순위를 변경 후에 조회합니다.

```
# rman TARGET sys/P#ssw0rd@oracle12 CATALOG rman/cat@rmandb
RMAN> LIST FAILURE ;
RMAN> CHANGE FAILURE 1662 PRIORITY LOW ;
```

```
RMAN> LIST FAILURE;

Database Role: PRIMARY

List of Database Failures
=========================

Failure ID Priority Status    Time Detected Summary
---------- -------- --------- ------------- -------
1662       HIGH     OPEN      19-DEC-17     One or more non-system datafiles are missing

RMAN> CHANGE FAILURE 1662 PRIORITY LOW;

Database Role: PRIMARY

List of Database Failures
=========================

Failure ID Priority Status    Time Detected Summary
---------- -------- --------- ------------- -------
1662       HIGH     OPEN      19-DEC-17     One or more non-system datafiles are missing

Do you really want to change the above failures (enter YES or NO)? YES
changed 1 failures to LOW priority

RMAN>  LIST FAILURE;

Database Role: PRIMARY

no failures found that match specification

RMAN>
```

다양한 DATA 유실 장애의 RMAN을 사용하는 대처 방법

많이 구성되어 운영되는 RMAN Catalog DB 백업 환경에서 오라클 DB 내의 DATA 유실 상황에서 어떻게 복구가 가능한지 각 상황 별 대처 방법을 알아보겠습니다.

1 SYSTEM TABLESPACE 유실 상황

SYSTEM TABLESPACE의 데이터 파일 유실 장애를 발생시킵니다.

```
[oracle12]yspark-linux:/oracle/oracle12/oradata/oracle12> mv system01.dbf system01.dbf.bak
[oracle12]yspark-linux:/oracle/oracle12/oradata/oracle12> sqlplus "/as sysdba"

SQL*Plus: Release 12.2.0.1.0 Production on Tue Dec 19 13:17:36 2017

Copyright (c) 1982, 2016, Oracle.  All rights reserved.

Connected.






13:17:38 SYS@oracle12>
13:17:38 SYS@oracle12> shutdown abort ;
ORACLE instance shut down.
13:18:03 SYS@oracle12> startup
ORACLE instance started.

Total System Global Area  746586112 bytes
Fixed Size                  8625176 bytes
Variable Size             587203560 bytes
Database Buffers           33554432 bytes
Redo Buffers                8151040 bytes
In-Memory Area            109051904 bytes
Database mounted.
ORA-01157: cannot identify/lock data file 1 - see DBWR trace file
ORA-01110: data file 1: '/oracle/oracle12/oradata/oracle12/system01.dbf'

13:18:34 SYS@oracle12>
```

이제 RMAN으로 유실된 SYSTEM TABLESPACE의 데이터 파일을 복구합니다.

```
# rman TARGET sys/P#ssw0rd@oracle12 CATALOG rman/cat@rmandb
RMAN> RESTORE DATAFILE 1 ;
RMAN> RECOVER DATAFILE 1 ;
RMAN> ALTER DATABASE OPEN ;
```

```
[oracle12]yspark-linux:/home/oracle12> rman TARGET sys/P#ssw0rd@oracle12 CATALOG rman/cat@rmandb
Recovery Manager: Release 12.2.0.1.0 - Production on Tue Dec 19 13:21:30 2017
Copyright (c) 1982, 2017, Oracle and/or its affiliates.  All rights reserved.
connected to target database: ORACLE12 (DBID=2053465567, not open)
connected to recovery catalog database
RMAN> RESTORE DATAFILE 1 ;
Starting restore at 19-DEC-17
allocated channel: ORA_DISK_1
channel ORA_DISK_1: SID=91 device type=DISK
channel ORA_DISK_1: starting datafile backup set restore
channel ORA_DISK_1: specifying datafile(s) to restore from backup set
channel ORA_DISK_1: restoring datafile 00001 to /oracle/oracle12/oradata/oracle12/system01.dbf
channel ORA_DISK_1: reading from backup piece /oracle/oracle12/RMAN_BACKUP/ORACLE12_bfsmgpah_1_1_963142993_367
channel ORA_DISK_1: piece handle=/oracle/oracle12/RMAN_BACKUP/ORACLE12_bfsmgpah_1_1_963142993_367 tag=TAG20171219T114313
channel ORA_DISK_1: restored backup piece 1
channel ORA_DISK_1: restore complete, elapsed time: 00:03:24
Finished restore at 19-DEC-17
RMAN>
RMAN> RECOVER DATAFILE 1 ;
Starting recover at 19-DEC-17
using channel ORA_DISK_1
starting media recovery
media recovery complete, elapsed time: 00:00:04
Finished recover at 19-DEC-17
RMAN> ALTER DATABASE OPEN ;
Statement processed
```

유실된 SYSTEM TABLESPACE의 데이터 파일이 복구가 정상 수행되었는지 조회합니다.

```
RMAN> SELECT FILE_NAME FROM DBA_DATA_FILES ;

FILE_NAME
--------------------------------------------------------------------------------
/oracle/oracle12/oradata/oracle12/system01.dbf

/oracle/oracle12/oradata/oracle12/sysaux01.dbf

/oracle/oracle12/oradata/oracle12/unione01.dbf

/oracle/oracle12/oradata/oracle12/users01.dbf

/oracle/oracle12/oradata/oracle12/yongseok01.dbf

/oracle/oracle12/oradata/oracle12/undotbs01.dbf

/oracle/oracle12/oradata/oracle12/undotbs02.dbf

/oracle/oracle12/oradata/oracle12/undotbs03.dbf

/oracle/oracle12/oradata/oracle12/oracle12_01.dbf

9 rows selected
RMAN> █
```

2 USER DATA FILE 유실 상황

일반적인 어플리케이션이 사용하는 TABLESPACE의 데이터 파일 유실 장애를 발생시킵니다.

```
[oracle12]yspark-linux:/oracle/oracle12/oradata/oracle12> mv unione01.dbf unione01.dbf.bak
[oracle12]yspark-linux:/oracle/oracle12/oradata/oracle12> sqlplus "/as sysdba"

SQL*Plus: Release 12.2.0.1.0 Production on Tue Dec 19 13:58:06 2017

Copyright (c) 1982, 2016, Oracle.  All rights reserved.


Connected to:
Oracle Database 12c Enterprise Edition Release 12.2.0.1.0 - 64bit Production

13:58:07 SYS@oracle12>
13:58:07 SYS@oracle12> CREATE TABLE test_tab (id NUMBER) TABLESPACE UNIONE ;
CREATE TABLE test_tab (id NUMBER) TABLESPACE UNIONE
*
ERROR at line 1:
ORA-01116: error in opening database file 5
ORA-01110: data file 5: '/oracle/oracle12/oradata/oracle12/unione01.dbf'
ORA-27041: unable to open file
Linux-x86_64 Error: 2: No such file or directory
Additional information: 3


13:58:29 SYS@oracle12>
```

이제 RMAN으로 유실된 일반 TABLESPACE의 데이터 파일을 ADR 정보를 이용하여 복구합니다.

```
# rman TARGET sys/P#ssw0rd@oracle12 CATALOG rman/cat@rmandb
RMAN> LIST FAILURE
RMAN> ADVISE FAILURE ;
RMAN> REPAIR FAILURE NOPROMPT ;
```

```
[oracle12]yspark-linux:/home/oracle12> rman TARGET sys/P#ssw0rd@oracle12 CATALOG rman/cat@rmandb

Recovery Manager: Release 12.2.0.1.0 - Production on Tue Dec 19 14:31:06 2017

Copyright (c) 1982, 2017, Oracle and/or its affiliates.  All rights reserved.

connected to target database: ORACLE12 (DBID=2053465567)
connected to recovery catalog database

RMAN> LIST FAILURE ;

Database Role: PRIMARY

List of Database Failures
=========================

Failure ID Priority Status    Time Detected Summary
---------- -------- --------- ------------- -------
1742       HIGH     OPEN      19-DEC-17     One or more non-system datafiles need media recovery
```

```
RMAN> ADVISE FAILURE ;

Database Role: PRIMARY

List of Database Failures
=========================

Failure ID Priority Status    Time Detected Summary
---------- -------- --------- ------------- -------
1742       HIGH     OPEN      19-DEC-17     One or more non-system datafiles need media recovery

analyzing automatic repair options; this may take some time
allocated channel: ORA_DISK_1
channel ORA_DISK_1: SID=101 device type=DISK
analyzing automatic repair options complete

Mandatory Manual Actions
========================
no manual actions available

Optional Manual Actions
=======================
1. If you restored the wrong version of data file /oracle/oracle12/oradata/oracle12/unione01.dbf, then replace it with the correct
 one

Automated Repair Options
========================
Option Repair Description
------ ------------------
1      Restore and recover datafile 5
  Strategy: The repair includes complete media recovery with no data loss
  Repair script: /oracle/oracle12/app/oracle/diag/rdbms/oracle12/oracle12/hm/reco_3345154672.hm
```

```
RMAN> REPAIR FAILURE NOPROMPT ;

Strategy: The repair includes complete media recovery with no data loss
Repair script: /oracle/oracle12/app/oracle/diag/rdbms/oracle12/oracle12/hm/reco_3345154672.hm

contents of repair script:
   # restore and recover datafile
   sql 'alter database datafile 5 offline';
   restore ( datafile 5 );
   recover datafile 5;
   sql 'alter database datafile 5 online';
executing repair script

sql statement: alter database datafile 5 offline

Starting restore at 19-DEC-17
using channel ORA_DISK_1

channel ORA_DISK_1: starting datafile backup set restore
channel ORA_DISK_1: specifying datafile(s) to restore from backup set
channel ORA_DISK_1: restoring datafile 00005 to /oracle/oracle12/oradata/oracle12/unione01.dbf
channel ORA_DISK_1: reading from backup piece /oracle/oracle12/RMAN_BACKUP/ORACLE12_bksmh2lp_1_1_963152569_372
channel ORA_DISK_1: piece handle=/oracle/oracle12/RMAN_BACKUP/ORACLE12_bksmh2lp_1_1_963152569_372 tag=TAG20171219T142243
channel ORA_DISK_1: restored backup piece 1
channel ORA_DISK_1: restore complete, elapsed time: 00:00:03
Finished restore at 19-DEC-17

Starting recover at 19-DEC-17
using channel ORA_DISK_1

starting media recovery
media recovery complete, elapsed time: 00:00:05

Finished recover at 19-DEC-17

sql statement: alter database datafile 5 online
repair failure complete

RMAN>
```

```
RMAN> CREATE TABLE test_tab (id NUMBER) TABLESPACE UNIONE ;

Statement processed

RMAN> SELECT * FROM test_tab ;

no rows selected

RMAN>
```

3 ONLINE REDO LOG FILE 유실 상황

온라인 리두 로그 파일이 모두 유실되었을 상황에서의 대처를 알아보겠습니다.

온라인 리두 로그 파일이 모두 유실되는 상황입니다.

```
[oracle12]yspark-linux:/oracle/oracle12/oradata/oracle12> mv redo01.log redo01.log.bak
[oracle12]yspark-linux:/oracle/oracle12/oradata/oracle12> mv redo02.log redo02.log.bak
[oracle12]yspark-linux:/oracle/oracle12/oradata/oracle12> mv redo03.log redo03.log.bak
[oracle12]yspark-linux:/oracle/oracle12/oradata/oracle12> sqlplus "/as sysdba"

SQL*Plus: Release 12.2.0.1.0 Production on Tue Dec 19 14:50:58 2017

Copyright (c) 1982, 2016, Oracle.  All rights reserved.

Connected to an idle instance.

14:50:59 SYS@oracle12> startup
ORACLE instance started.

Total System Global Area  746586112 bytes
Fixed Size                  8625176 bytes
Variable Size             587203560 bytes
Database Buffers           33554432 bytes
Redo Buffers                8151040 bytes
In-Memory Area            109051904 bytes
Database mounted.
ORA-03113: end-of-file on communication channel
Process ID: 11141
Session ID: 89 Serial number: 36308

14:53:09 SYS@oracle12> conn /as sysdba
Connected to an idle instance.

14:53:13 SYS@oracle12>
14:53:13 SYS@oracle12> shutdown abort ;
ORACLE instance shut down.
14:53:22 SYS@oracle12>
```

이제 백업 본을 이용하여 온라인 리두 로그가 유실되어 장애 중인 데이터베이스를 복구합니다.

```
# sqlplus "/as sysdba"
SQL> STARTUP MOUNT ;
# rman TARGET sys/P#ssw0rd@oracle12 CATALOG rman/cat@rmandb
RMAN> RESTORE DATABASE ;
RMAN> SELECT * FROM V$LOG ;  -- CURRENT SEQUENCE 번호조회
RMAN> RECOVER DATABASE UNTIL SEQUENCE <CURRENT SEQUENCE 번호> THREAD 1 ;
RMAN> ALTER DATABASE OPEN RESETLOGS ;
```

```
[oracle12]yspark-linux:/oracle/oracle12/oradata/oracle12> sqlplus "/as sysdba"

SQL*Plus: Release 12.2.0.1.0 Production on Tue Dec 19 14:58:20 2017

Copyright (c) 1982, 2016, Oracle.  All rights reserved.

Connected to an idle instance.

14:58:21 SYS@oracle12>
14:58:21 SYS@oracle12> startup mount ;
ORACLE instance started.

Total System Global Area  746586112 bytes
Fixed Size                  8625176 bytes
Variable Size             587203560 bytes
Database Buffers           33554432 bytes
Redo Buffers                8151040 bytes
In-Memory Area            109051904 bytes
Database mounted.
14:58:39 SYS@oracle12>
```

```
[oracle12]yspark-linux:/home/oracle12> rman TARGET sys/P#ssw0rd@oracle12 CATALOG rman/cat@rmandb

Recovery Manager: Release 12.2.0.1.0 - Production on Tue Dec 19 15:00:32 2017

Copyright (c) 1982, 2017, Oracle and/or its affiliates.  All rights reserved.

connected to target database: ORACLE12 (DBID=2053465567, not open)
connected to recovery catalog database

RMAN> RESTORE DATABASE ;

Starting restore at 19-DEC-17
allocated channel: ORA_DISK_1
channel ORA_DISK_1: SID=91 device type=DISK

channel ORA_DISK_1: starting datafile backup set restore
channel ORA_DISK_1: specifying datafile(s) to restore from backup set
channel ORA_DISK_1: restoring datafile 00001 to /oracle/oracle12/oradata/oracle12/system01.dbf
channel ORA_DISK_1: restoring datafile 00003 to /oracle/oracle12/oradata/oracle12/sysaux01.dbf
channel ORA_DISK_1: restoring datafile 00004 to /oracle/oracle12/oradata/oracle12/undotbs01.dbf
channel ORA_DISK_1: restoring datafile 00005 to /oracle/oracle12/oradata/oracle12/unione01.dbf
channel ORA_DISK_1: restoring datafile 00007 to /oracle/oracle12/oradata/oracle12/users01.dbf
channel ORA_DISK_1: restoring datafile 00010 to /oracle/oracle12/oradata/oracle12/undotbs02.dbf
channel ORA_DISK_1: restoring datafile 00011 to /oracle/oracle12/oradata/oracle12/undotbs03.dbf
channel ORA_DISK_1: restoring datafile 00012 to /oracle/oracle12/oradata/oracle12/oracle12_01.dbf
channel ORA_DISK_1: reading from backup piece /oracle/oracle12/RMAN_BACKUP/ORACLE12_bksmh2lp_1_1_963152569_372
channel ORA_DISK_1: piece handle=/oracle/oracle12/RMAN_BACKUP/ORACLE12_bksmh2lp_1_1_963152569_372 tag=TAG20171219T142243
channel ORA_DISK_1: restored backup piece 1
channel ORA_DISK_1: restore complete, elapsed time: 00:18:32
Finished restore at 19-DEC-17
```

```
15:27:09 SYS@oracle12> SELECT GROUP#,THREAD#,SEQUENCE#,STATUS FROM V$LOG ;

    GROUP#    THREAD#  SEQUENCE# STATUS
---------- ---------- ---------- ----------------
         1          1         49 INACTIVE
         3          1         48 INACTIVE
         2          1         50 CURRENT
15:28:56 SYS@oracle12>
```

```
RMAN> RECOVER DATABASE UNTIL SEQUENCE 50 THREAD 1 ;

Starting recover at 19-DEC-17
using channel ORA_DISK_1

starting media recovery
media recovery complete, elapsed time: 00:00:01

Finished recover at 19-DEC-17

RMAN>
```

4 CONTROL FILE 유실 상황

데이터베이스의 컨트롤 파일이 유실되었습니다. RMAN을 이용하여 장애를 복구하겠습니다. 컨트롤 유실 상황을 만듭니다.

```
16:05:16 SYS@oracle12> shutdown immediate ;
Database closed.
Database dismounted.
ORACLE instance shut down.
16:05:45 SYS@oracle12> exit
Disconnected from Oracle Database 12c Enterprise Edition Release 12.2.0.1.0 - 64bit Production
[oracle12]yspark-linux:/oracle/oracle12/oradata/oracle12> ls -al *.ctl
-rw-r-----. 1 oracle12 dba 11386880 Dec 19 16:05 control01.ctl
-rw-r-----. 1 oracle12 dba 11386880 Dec 19 16:05 control02.ctl
[oracle12]yspark-linux:/oracle/oracle12/oradata/oracle12> mv control01.ctl control01.ctl.bak

[oracle12]yspark-linux:/oracle/oracle12/oradata/oracle12> mv control02.ctl control02.ctl.bak
[oracle12]yspark-linux:/oracle/oracle12/oradata/oracle12> sqlplus "/as sysdba"

SQL*Plus: Release 12.2.0.1.0 Production on Tue Dec 19 16:31:09 2017

Copyright (c) 1982, 2016, Oracle.  All rights reserved.

Connected to an idle instance.

16:31:10 SYS@oracle12>
16:31:10 SYS@oracle12> startup
ORACLE instance started.

Total System Global Area  746586112 bytes
Fixed Size                  8625176 bytes
Variable Size             587203560 bytes
Database Buffers           33554432 bytes
Redo Buffers                8151040 bytes
In-Memory Area            109051904 bytes
ORA-00205: error in identifying control file, check alert log for more info

16:31:18 SYS@oracle12>
```

이제 백업 본을 이용하여 컨트롤 파일이 유실되어 장애 중인 데이터베이스를 복구합니다.

```
# rman TARGET sys/P#ssw0rd@oracle12 CATALOG rman/cat@rmandb
RMAN> RESTORE CONTROLFILE FROM AUTOBACKUP;
RMAN> ALTER DATABASE MOUNT ;
RMAN> RECOVER DATABASE;
RMAN> ALTER DATABASE OPEN RESETLOGS ;
```

```
[oracle12]yspark-linux:/home/oracle12> rman TARGET sys/P#ssw0rd@oracle12 CATALOG rman/cat@rmandb

Recovery Manager: Release 12.2.0.1.0 - Production on Tue Dec 19 16:39:49 2017

Copyright (c) 1982, 2017, Oracle and/or its affiliates.  All rights reserved.

connected to target database: ORACLE12 (not mounted)
connected to recovery catalog database

RMAN> RESTORE CONTROLFILE FROM AUTOBACKUP;

Starting restore at 19-DEC-17
allocated channel: ORA_DISK_1
channel ORA_DISK_1: SID=172 device type=DISK

recovery area destination: /oracle/oracle12/FRA/
database name (or database unique name) used for search: ORACLE12
channel ORA_DISK_1: AUTOBACKUP /oracle/oracle12/FRA/ORACLE12/autobackup/2017_12_19/o1_mf_s_963158238_f3kg2kb7_.bkp found in the re
covery area
channel ORA_DISK_1: looking for AUTOBACKUP on day: 20171219
channel ORA_DISK_1: restoring control file from AUTOBACKUP /oracle/oracle12/FRA/ORACLE12/autobackup/2017_12_19/o1_mf_s_963158238_f
3kg2kb7_.bkp
channel ORA_DISK_1: control file restore from AUTOBACKUP complete
output file name=/oracle/oracle12/oradata/oracle12/control01.ctl
output file name=/oracle/oracle12/oradata/oracle12/control02.ctl
Finished restore at 19-DEC-17

RMAN>
```

```
RMAN> ALTER DATABASE MOUNT ;

Statement processed
released channel: ORA_DISK_1

RMAN> RECOVER DATABASE;

Starting recover at 19-DEC-17
Starting implicit crosscheck backup at 19-DEC-17
allocated channel: ORA_DISK_1
channel ORA_DISK_1: SID=91 device type=DISK
Crosschecked 44 objects
Finished implicit crosscheck backup at 19-DEC-17

Starting implicit crosscheck copy at 19-DEC-17
using channel ORA_DISK_1
Finished implicit crosscheck copy at 19-DEC-17

searching for all files in the recovery area
cataloging files...
cataloging done

List of Cataloged Files
=======================
File Name: /oracle/oracle12/FRA/ORACLE12/autobackup/2017_12_19/o1_mf_s_963158238_f3kg2kb7_.bkp

using channel ORA_DISK_1

starting media recovery

archived log for thread 1 with sequence 3 is already on disk as file /oracle/oracle12/oradata/oracle12/redo03.log
archived log file name=/oracle/oracle12/oradata/oracle12/redo03.log thread=1 sequence=3
media recovery complete, elapsed time: 00:00:00
Finished recover at 19-DEC-17

RMAN> 
```

```
RMAN> ALTER DATABASE OPEN RESETLOGS ;

Statement processed
new incarnation of database registered in recovery catalog
starting full resync of recovery catalog
full resync complete

RMAN> 
```

5 DATABASE 전체 유실 상황

전체 데이터베이스의 관련된 파일을 모두 유실하였을 때 장애 상황에서 복구하는 방법을 알아보겠습니다.

모든 파일을 지우고 장애 상황을 만듭니다. 파라미터 파일, 컨트롤 파일, 데이터 파일, 온라인 리두 로그 파일 모두 유실된 상황입니다.

```
[oracle12]yspark-linux:/oracle/oracle12/app/oracle/product/12.2.0/dbhome_1/dbs> rm spfileoracle12.ora initoracle12.ora
[oracle12]yspark-linux:/oracle/oracle12/app/oracle/product/12.2.0/dbhome_1/dbs> ls *oracle12.ora
ls: cannot access *oracle12.ora: No such file or directory
[oracle12]yspark-linux:/oracle/oracle12/app/oracle/product/12.2.0/dbhome_1/dbs>
[oracle12]yspark-linux:/oracle/oracle12/app/oracle/product/12.2.0/dbhome_1/dbs> 
```

```
[oracle12]yspark-linux:/oracle/oracle12/oradata/oracle12> ls
control01.ctl      oracle12_01.dbf  redo02.log.bak  system01.dbf  temp04.dbf      UNIONE           users01.dbf.bak
control01.ctl.bak  redo01.log       redo03.log      temp01.dbf    undotbs01.dbf   unione01.dbf
control02.ctl      redo01.log.bak   redo03.log.bak  temp02.dbf    undotbs02.dbf   unione01.dbf.bak
control02.ctl.bak  redo02.log       sysaux01.dbf    temp03.dbf    undotbs03.dbf   users01.dbf
[oracle12]yspark-linux:/oracle/oracle12/oradata/oracle12> rm -rf *
[oracle12]yspark-linux:/oracle/oracle12/oradata/oracle12> ls
[oracle12]yspark-linux:/oracle/oracle12/oradata/oracle12> sqlplus "/as sysdba"

SQL*Plus: Release 12.2.0.1.0 Production on Tue Dec 19 17:28:48 2017

Copyright (c) 1982, 2016, Oracle.  All rights reserved.

Connected to an idle instance.

17:47:26 SYS@oracle12>
17:47:26 SYS@oracle12> startup
ORA-01078: failure in processing system parameters
LRM-00109: could not open parameter file '/oracle/oracle12/app/oracle/product/12.2.0/dbhome_1/dbs/initoracle12.ora'
17:47:29 SYS@oracle12> 
Ready                                   ssh2: AES-256-CTR   21, 24  21 Rows, 130 Cols  VT100   CAP NUM
```

이제 RMAN 백업 본을 이용하여 데이터베이스 전체를 복구하겠습니다.

```
# rman TARGET / CATALOG rman/cat@rmandb
RMAN> STARTUP NOMOUNT ;
RMAN> RESTORE SPFILE ;
RMAN> STARTUP FORCE NOMOUNT ;
RMAN> RESTORE CONTROLFILE ;
RMAN> ALTER DATABASE MOUNT ;
RMAN> SELECT * FROM V$LOG ;  -- CURRENT SEQUENCE 번호조회
RMAN> run {
2> SET UNTIL SEQUENCE 14 THREAD 1;
3> RESTORE DATABASE;
4> RECOVER DATABASE;
5> }
RMAN> ALTER DATABASE OPEN RESETLOGS ;
```

```
[oracle12]yspark-linux:/home/oracle12>  rman TARGET / CATALOG rman/cat@rmandb

Recovery Manager: Release 12.2.0.1.0 - Production on Tue Dec 19 17:49:42 2017

Copyright (c) 1982, 2017, Oracle and/or its affiliates.  All rights reserved.

connected to target database (not started)
connected to recovery catalog database

RMAN> STARTUP NOMOUNT;

startup failed: ORA-01078: failure in processing system parameters
LRM-00109: could not open parameter file '/oracle/oracle12/app/oracle/product/12.2.0/dbhome_1/dbs/initoracle12.ora'

starting Oracle instance without parameter file for retrieval of spfile
Oracle instance started

Total System Global Area    1073741824 bytes

Fixed Size                     8628936 bytes
Variable Size                293602616 bytes
Database Buffers             763363328 bytes
Redo Buffers                   8146944 bytes
```

```
RMAN> RESTORE SPFILE ;

Starting restore at 19-DEC-17
using channel ORA_DISK_1

channel ORA_DISK_1: starting datafile backup set restore
channel ORA_DISK_1: restoring SPFILE
output file name=/oracle/oracle12/app/oracle/product/12.2.0/dbhome_1/dbs/spfileoracle12.ora
channel ORA_DISK_1: reading from backup piece /oracle/oracle12/FRA/ORACLE12/autobackup/2017_12_19/o1_mf_s_963161564_f3kkbh7s_.bkp
channel ORA_DISK_1: piece handle=/oracle/oracle12/FRA/ORACLE12/autobackup/2017_12_19/o1_mf_s_963161564_f3kkbh7s_.bkp tag=TAG201712
19T165243
channel ORA_DISK_1: restored backup piece 1
channel ORA_DISK_1: restore complete, elapsed time: 00:00:03
Finished restore at 19-DEC-17

RMAN> █
```

```
RMAN> STARTUP FORCE NOMOUNT ;

Oracle instance started

Total System Global Area     746586112 bytes

Fixed Size                     8625176 bytes
Variable Size                587203560 bytes
Database Buffers              33554432 bytes
Redo Buffers                   8151040 bytes
In-Memory Area               109051904 bytes

RMAN> RESTORE CONTROLFILE ;

Starting restore at 19-DEC-17
allocated channel: ORA_DISK_1
channel ORA_DISK_1: SID=89 device type=DISK

channel ORA_DISK_1: starting datafile backup set restore
channel ORA_DISK_1: restoring control file
channel ORA_DISK_1: reading from backup piece /oracle/oracle12/FRA/ORACLE12/autobackup/2017_12_19/o1_mf_s_963161564_f3kkbh7s_.bkp
channel ORA_DISK_1: piece handle=/oracle/oracle12/FRA/ORACLE12/autobackup/2017_12_19/o1_mf_s_963161564_f3kkbh7s_.bkp tag=TAG201712
19T165243
channel ORA_DISK_1: restored backup piece 1
channel ORA_DISK_1: restore complete, elapsed time: 00:00:01
output file name=/oracle/oracle12/oradata/oracle12/control01.ctl
output file name=/oracle/oracle12/oradata/oracle12/control02.ctl
Finished restore at 19-DEC-17

RMAN> ALTER DATABASE MOUNT ;

Statement processed
released channel: ORA_DISK_1

RMAN> █
```

```
RMAN> SELECT * FROM V$LOG ;

    GROUP#    THREAD#  SEQUENCE#      BYTES  BLOCKSIZE    MEMBERS ARC
---------- ---------- ---------- ---------- ---------- ---------- ---
STATUS           FIRST_CHANGE# FIRST_TIM NEXT_CHANGE# NEXT_TIME     CON_ID
---------------- ------------- --------- ------------ --------- ----------
         1          1         13  209715200        512          1 YES
INACTIVE            1439641137 19-DEC-17   1439641238 19-DEC-17          0

         3          1         12  209715200        512          1 YES
INACTIVE            1439641015 19-DEC-17   1439641137 19-DEC-17          0

         2          1         14  209715200        512          1 NO
CURRENT             1439641238 19-DEC-17 184467440737                    0

RMAN>
```

```
RMAN> run {
2> SET UNTIL SEQUENCE 14 THREAD 1;
3> RESTORE DATABASE;
4> RECOVER DATABASE;
5> }

executing command: SET until clause

Starting restore at 19-DEC-17
Starting implicit crosscheck backup at 19-DEC-17
allocated channel: ORA_DISK_1
channel ORA_DISK_1: SID=11 device type=DISK
Crosschecked 50 objects
Finished implicit crosscheck backup at 19-DEC-17

Starting implicit crosscheck copy at 19-DEC-17
using channel ORA_DISK_1
Finished implicit crosscheck copy at 19-DEC-17

searching for all files in the recovery area
cataloging files...
cataloging done

List of Cataloged Files
=======================
File Name: /oracle/oracle12/FRA/ORACLE12/autobackup/2017_12_19/o1_mf_s_963161564_f3kkbh7s_.bkp

using channel ORA_DISK_1

channel ORA_DISK_1: starting datafile backup set restore
channel ORA_DISK_1: specifying datafile(s) to restore from backup set
channel ORA_DISK_1: restoring datafile 00001 to /oracle/oracle12/oradata/oracle12/system01.dbf
channel ORA_DISK_1: restoring datafile 00003 to /oracle/oracle12/oradata/oracle12/sysaux01.dbf
channel ORA_DISK_1: restoring datafile 00004 to /oracle/oracle12/oradata/oracle12/undotbs01.dbf
channel ORA_DISK_1: restoring datafile 00005 to /oracle/oracle12/oradata/oracle12/unione01.dbf
channel ORA_DISK_1: restoring datafile 00007 to /oracle/oracle12/oradata/oracle12/users01.dbf
channel ORA_DISK_1: restoring datafile 00010 to /oracle/oracle12/oradata/oracle12/undotbs02.dbf
channel ORA_DISK_1: restoring datafile 00011 to /oracle/oracle12/oradata/oracle12/undotbs03.dbf
channel ORA_DISK_1: restoring datafile 00012 to /oracle/oracle12/oradata/oracle12/oracle12_01.dbf
channel ORA_DISK_1: reading from backup piece /oracle/oracle12/RMAN_BACKUP/ORACLE12_c3smhb8l_1_1_963161365_387
channel ORA_DISK_1: piece handle=/oracle/oracle12/RMAN_BACKUP/ORACLE12_c3smhb8l_1_1_963161365_387 tag=TAG20171219T164923
channel ORA_DISK_1: restored backup piece 1
channel ORA_DISK_1: restore complete, elapsed time: 00:17:42
Finished restore at 19-DEC-17

Starting recover at 19-DEC-17
using channel ORA_DISK_1

starting media recovery

archived log for thread 1 with sequence 13 is already on disk as file /oracle/oracle12/FRA/ORACLE12/archivelog/2017_12_19/o1_mf_1_
13_f3kk9o7s_.arc
archived log file name=/oracle/oracle12/FRA/ORACLE12/archivelog/2017_12_19/o1_mf_1_13_f3kk9o7s_.arc thread=1 sequence=13
media recovery complete, elapsed time: 00:00:01
Finished recover at 19-DEC-17

RMAN>
```

```
RMAN> ALTER DATABASE OPEN RESETLOGS ;

Statement processed
new incarnation of database registered in recovery catalog
starting full resync of recovery catalog
full resync complete

RMAN>
```

복구가 완료되었습니다. 정상 복구되었는지 확인합니다.

```
[oracle12]yspark-linux:/oracle/oracle12/oradata/oracle12> ls
control01.ctl  oracle12_01.dbf  redo02.log  sysaux01.dbf  temp01.dbf  temp03.dbf  undotbs01.dbf  undotbs03.dbf  users01.dbf
control02.ctl  redo01.log       redo03.log  system01.dbf  temp02.dbf  temp04.dbf  undotbs02.dbf  unione01.dbf
[oracle12]yspark-linux:/oracle/oracle12/oradata/oracle12> sqlplus "/as sysdba"

SQL*Plus: Release 12.2.0.1.0 Production on Tue Dec 19 18:32:19 2017

Copyright (c) 1982, 2016, Oracle.  All rights reserved.


Connected to:
Oracle Database 12c Enterprise Edition Release 12.2.0.1.0 - 64bit Production

18:32:24 SYS@oracle12>
18:32:24 SYS@oracle12> SELECT STATUS FROM V$INSTANCE ;

STATUS
------------
OPEN
18:32:45 SYS@oracle12>
```

03
Chapter

ASM의 정석 편

많은 기업 들이 클러스터 구조의 파일 관리 솔루션(HACMP, MC Service Guard, GPFS, …)을 비싼 값을 들여 구매하고 이 솔루션을 이용하여 Raw Device 구조 형태로 오라클 데이터베이스를 구성/관리하고 있습니다.

오라클은 오라클 데이터베이스를 사용할 경우 최적의 스토리지 성능을 내기 위해 Oracle 10g 버전부터 출시한 ASM(Automatic Storage Management)을 출시하였고, 이 파일 관리 솔루션은 Oracle DB 구축 시 무료로 제공됩니다.

Oracle Database 12c Release 2Licensing Information User Manual 발췌

Oracle Automatic Storage Management (Oracle ASM)	Oracle ASM is free to use with all Oracle databases and Oracle ACFS file systems.

Oracle 12c 매뉴얼 상의 De-support로 명시된 것과는 별개로 Oracle 12c Database에서 기술적인 RAW device 지원여부는 "사용 불가"입니다.

Announcement of De-Support of using RAW devices in Oracle Database Version 12.1(MOS. 문서 ID 578455.1)

Oracle 12c부터 ASM 또는 FILE(RAC인 경우 클러스터 파일시스템)만 지원하게 되었습니다. 데이터사이즈 테라 급 이상 초대형 Oracle 데이터베이스에서는 컴퓨터 사이언스에서 I/O의 동기 방식인 FILE 구조는 CPU 사용이 관여하므로 CPU 사용을 최소화하는 I/O 비동기 방식인 ASM 저장 구조의 데이터베이스로 구성해야 합니다.

이제부터 ASM(Automatic Storage Management)의 장점에 대해서 자세히 알아보고 ASM 관리 방법에 대해 확인해 보겠습니다.

ASM 개요

"ASM(Automatic Storage Management, 이하 ASM)은 스토리지를 관리를 자동화해 주는 서비스입니다. 디스크 추가/삭제 작업 시 자동적으로 데이터를 재분배해 주며, striping 효과를 데이터파일 단위로 지정할 수 있는 고성능 클러스터 파일시스템입니다."

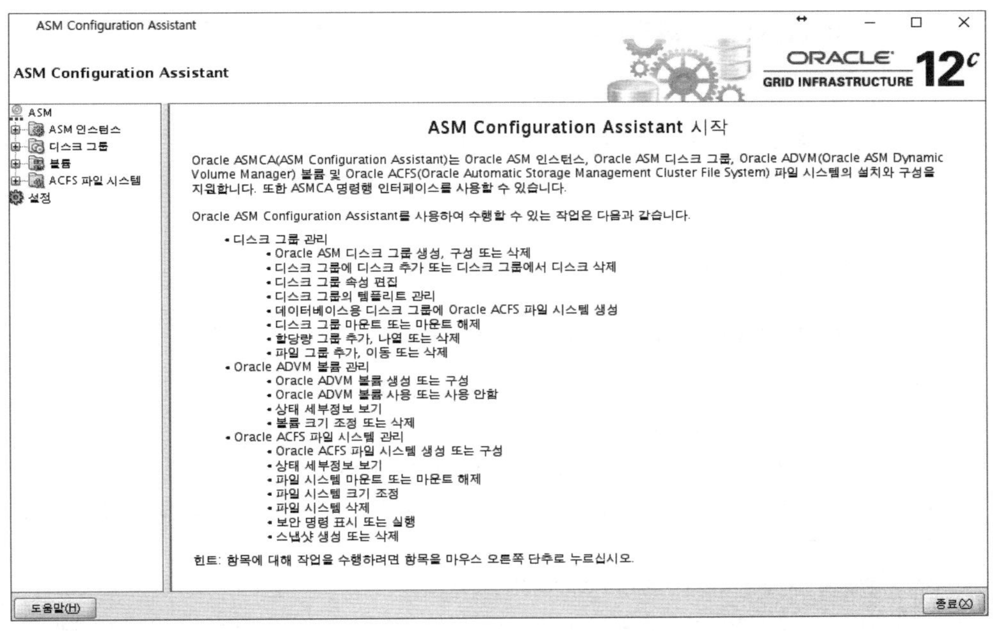

데이터베이스 구성 시 기본이 되는 디스크를 효율적으로 관리하기 위해 Oracle 10g에서 처음 선보인 데이터베이스를 위한 클러스터링 솔루션입니다. ASM은 하나의 SMP(Symmetric Multi-Processor) 장비뿐 아니라, RAC을 구성하는 모든 노드들에 대해서도 지원이 가능합니다.

1 ASM 소개

Oracle 데이터베이스 파일의 관리를 위해 특별히 구현된 storage 관리서비스입니다.

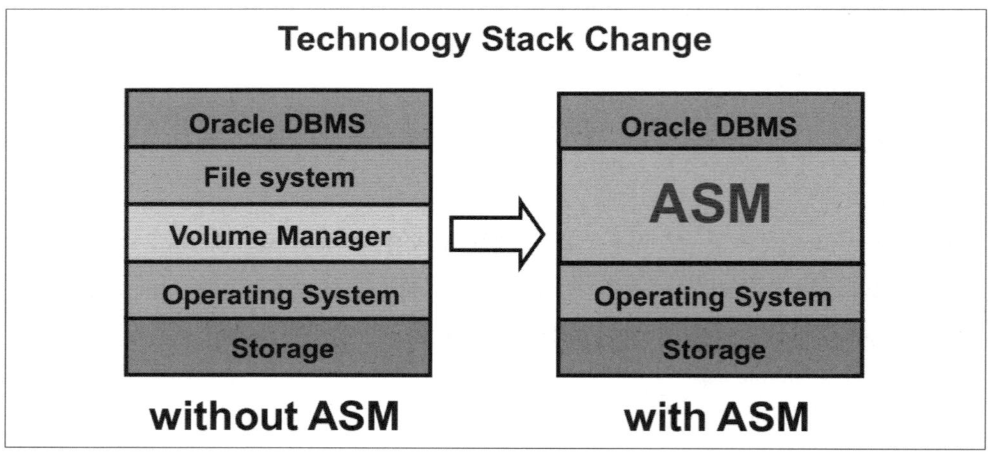

Oracle의 커널 내에 Volume 매니저 및 파일 시스템을 통합하였습니다.

2 ASM 주요 특징

1. 관리 복잡성이 제거됩니다(스토리지 관리가 단순해집니다).

- 매일 처리해야만 하는 스토리지 관리항목이 줄어들거나 제거됩니다.
- 모든 Application load에 대해 자동적인 I/O tuning이 수행됩니다.
- 생성되는 데이터파일에 대해 의미 있는 이름이 자동적으로 부여됩니다.
- 관리대상이 혁신적으로 줄어듭니다(파일시스템과 LVM 관리범위가 ASM Disk group으로 통합 관리됨).
- 디스크 구성 변경이 쉽습니다.
- 구성이 변경될 때, 자동적으로 데이터 재분배가 일어납니다.
- 파일시스템 상에 데이터파일이 있는 것이 아니기 때문에 실수로 파일을 삭제할 가능성이 배제됩니다.

2. 스토리지 제품 구입비용 절약

- Cluster Volume manager와 파일시스템 기능이 데이터베이스에 포함되어 있습니다.
- 저렴한 JBOD 형태의 디스크부터 고가의 SAN 디스크 array까지 지원합니다.

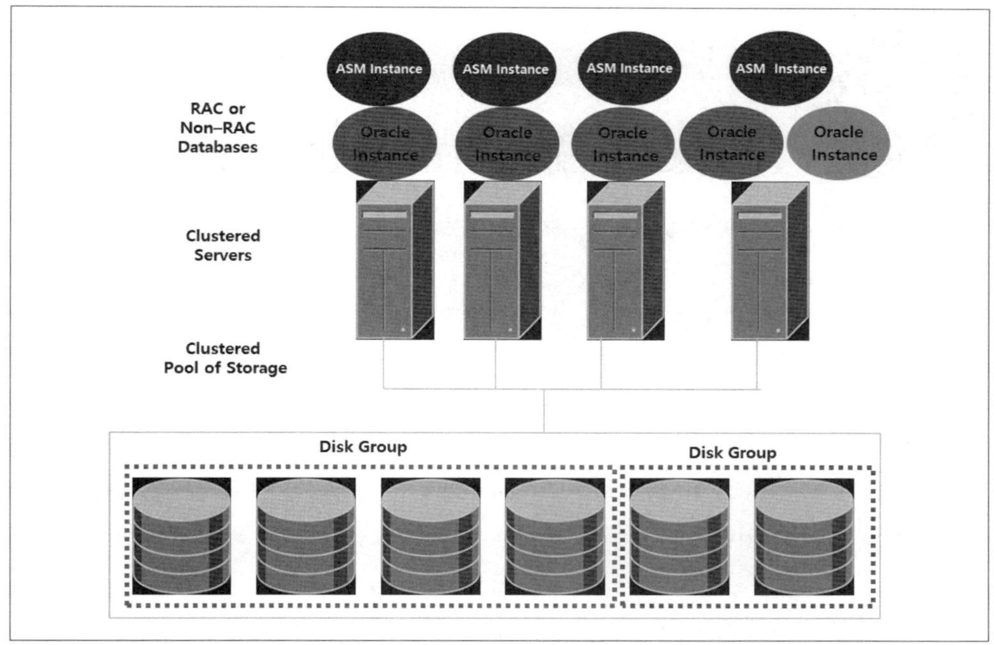

1. 성능/확장성/안정성 증대

- 모든 파일에 대해서 RAW disk 수준의 I/O 성능을 보장합니다.
- 다른 디스크 Array에 걸쳐 저장되어 있는 데이터 파일들에 대해 striping을 적용할 수 있습니다.
- Software mirroring이 지원됩니다.

2. RAC(Real Application Clusters) 지원

- 여타 Cluster Volume manager와 Cluster 파일시스템이 필요없습니다.

Oracle Grid Infrastructure

RAC을 구축하기 위해서 3rd party 클러스터 소프트웨어가 필요했었습니다. 하지만 복잡도는 커지고 비용이 많이 소요되었습니다. 이를 해결하기 위해 오라클이 클러스터웨어를 직접 만들어 제공합니다. (Integrated Clusterware Management)이 클러스터 웨어 제품 이름이 Oracle Grid Infrastructure입니다.

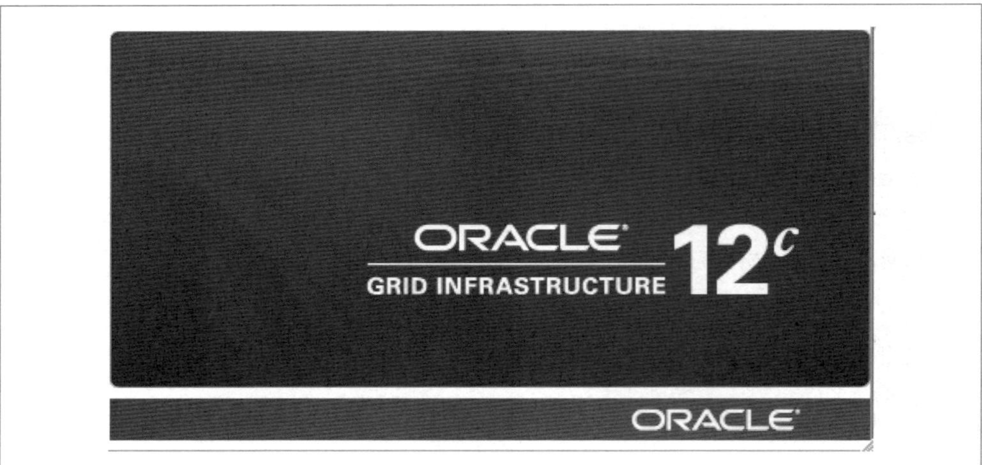

1 범용 클러스터 웨어

Oracle Database뿐만 아니라 Application을 위한 클러스터웨어(Clusterware)입니다. 오라클은 오라클 데이터베이스를 지원하는 모든 플랫폼에 대해 통합된 클러스터웨어(Cluster Ready Service, CRS)를 제공합니다.

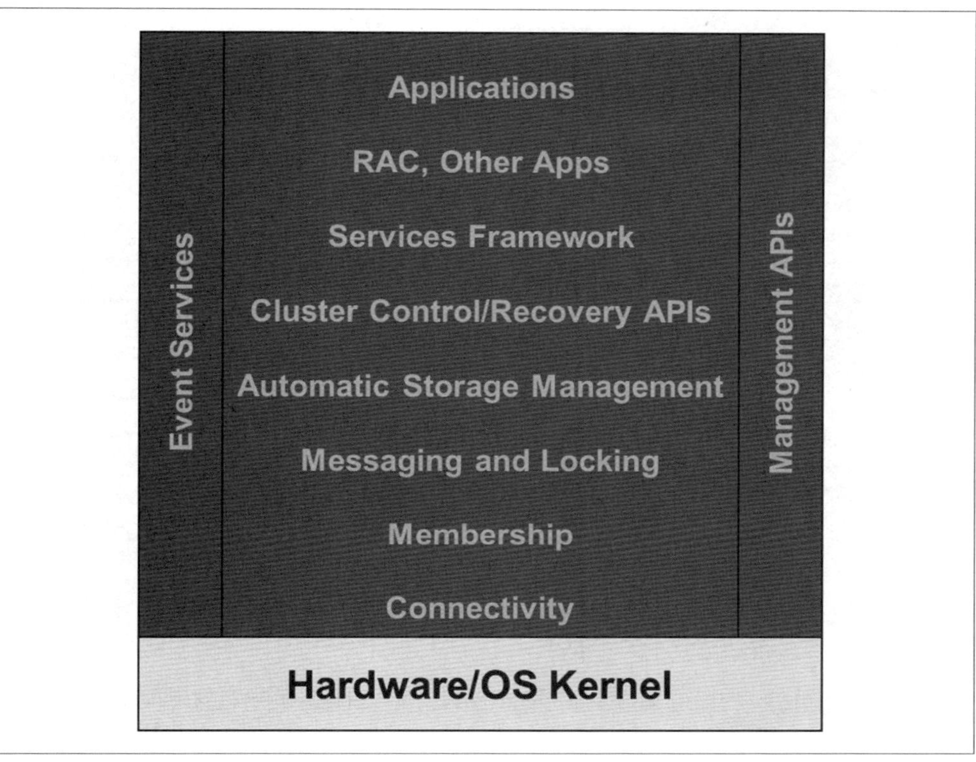

이 오라클 클러스터웨어의 기본 기능은 그림과 같이 클러스터웨어가 지녀야 할 기능들을 포함하고 있습니다.

오라클 Clusterware는 디스크를 공유하는 Active-Active 구조입니다.
오라클 RAC을 사용하면 한 노드에 장애가 발생하더라도 서비스는 지속됩니다. 클러스터 상의 다른 노드는 살아있고, 모든 사용자가 이 노드들을 통해 프로세싱을 계속할 수 있기 때문입니다. 클러스터가 아닌 하나의 SMP 서버로 운영한다면, OS 장애 등과 같은 장애 상황이 발생할 때, 전체 시스템은 다운되고 결국 모든 사용자들이 서비스를 받을 수 없게 됩니다.

다른 벤더의 데이터베이스를 사용하면서 프로세서의 장애와 같은 상황에 의한 서비스다운 현상을 막기 위해서는, 별도의 SMP 서버를 구매해서 대기 상태로 두어야 할 것입니다. 이러한 구성을 cold standby 혹은 active/passive 구성이라고 합니다. 이 구성은 단점은 장애 복구의 시간이 오래 걸린다는 것과 비용이 많이 든다는 것입니다.

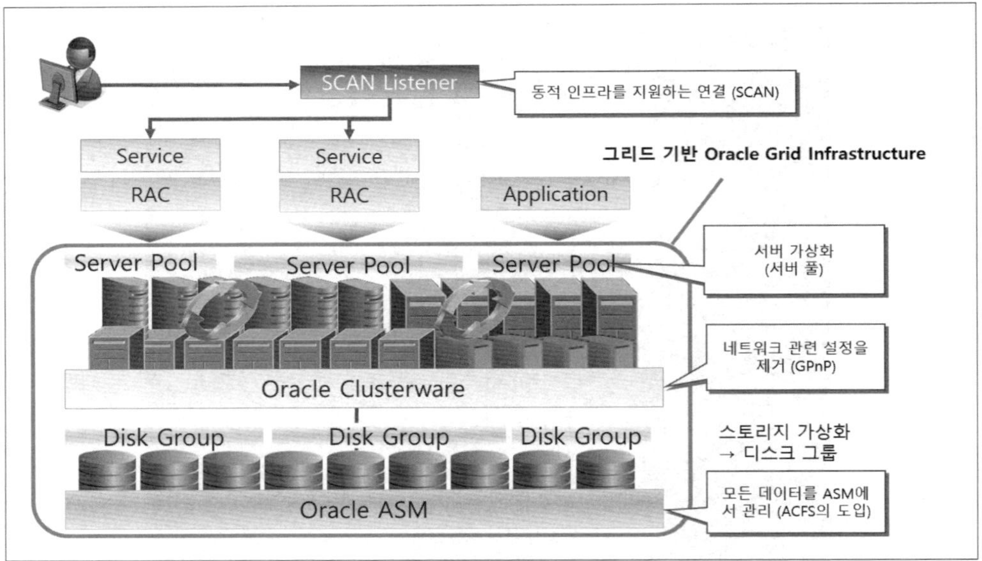

| 오라클이 제공하는 클러스터웨어

오라클이 제공하는 클러스터웨어를 사용함으로써 얻는 이점은 다음과 같습니다.

❶ **저비용**: 이 클러스터 웨어에 대해 별도의 비용이 소요되지 않습니다.

❷ **단일 벤더 지원**: 오라클이 클러스터웨어도 지원하므로, 3rd party 클러스터 소프트웨어 벤더의 지원이 필요없습니다.

❸ **단순한 설치, 구성, 유지보수**: 오라클 클러스터웨어는 오라클 데이터베이스의 표준 관리 툴을 사용해서 설치, 구성, 유지보수를 할 수 있습니다. 별도의 통합 절차가 필요없습니다.

❹ **모든 플랫폼에 일관된 고품질**: 오라클 자체적으로 클러스터웨어에 대한 집중적인 테스트를 수행할 수 있습니다.

❺ **모든 플랫폼에 일관된 기능**: 기존에는 3rd party 클러스터웨어의 제한에 의해 RAC를 구성할 수 있는 최대 노드수가 플랫폼마다 달랐습니다. Oracle 클러스터는 모든 플랫폼에 대해 최대 64 노드까지 지원됩니다. 그리고 사용자들은 노드의 장애, 인터커넥트(interconnect)의 장애, I/O fencing 등에 대해 모든 플랫폼에 걸쳐 일관된 응답속도를 기대할 수 있습니다.

❻ **향상된 기능**: 통합된 모니터링과 통지(notification) 기능이 포함되어 있어서, 장애 시 데이터베이스와 애플리케이션 단의 빠른 복구가 가능합니다.

2 구성 요소

Oracle 11g Release 2부터 Oracle Clusterware와 Oracle ASM(Automatic Storage Management)이 통합되어 Oracle Grid Infrastructure 불리는 별도의 Product 형태로 제공됩니다.

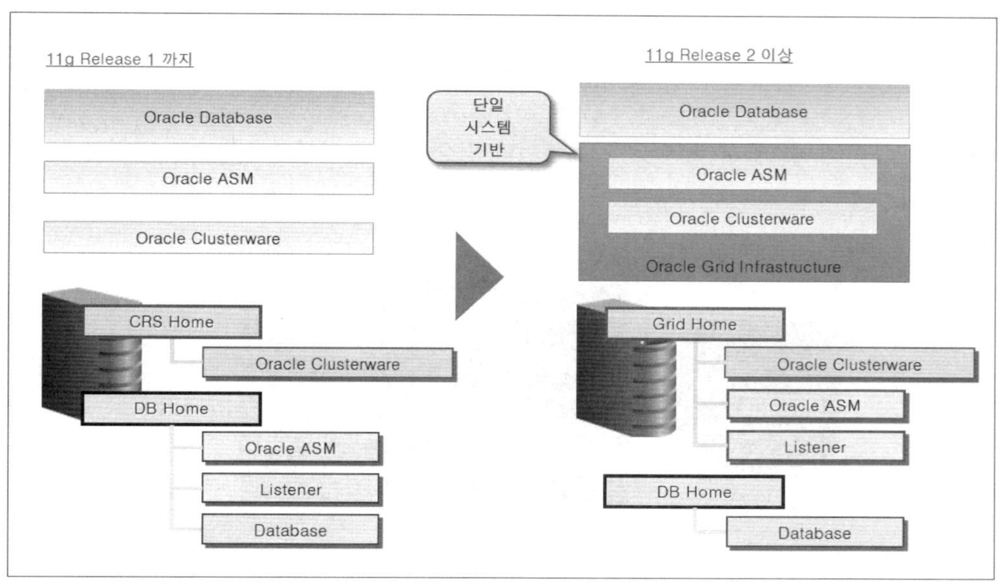

ASM 환경의 데이터베이스를 구성하기 위한 구성 순서는 Oracle 11g R2 Version 이상부터 Oracle ASM으로 데이터베이스를 구성하기 위해서는 오라클 그리드 인프라스트럭처 소프트웨어를 먼저 설치하여 ASM 환경을 구성하고 난 후 오라클 Database 소프트웨어를 설치하여 Database를 생성해야 합니다.

Oracle 스토리지 가상화

Oracle 데이터베이스를 위해 Oracle의 데이터 저장 전략을 어떻게 구성하고 구현하였는지 오라클의 스토리지 가상화 기준을 알아보겠습니다.

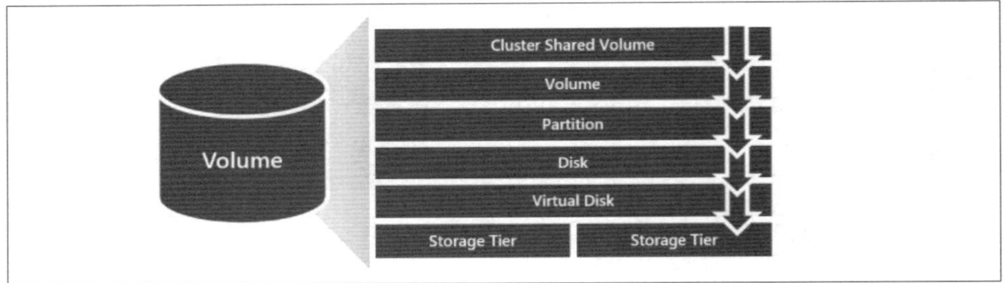

1 스토리지 가상화

Oracle 데이터베이스에 대해서 Volume 매니저 겸 파일 시스템기능을 제공하며 디스크 구성을 가상화해 DBA가 손쉽게 스토리지를 관리를 관리합니다.

Enterprise Edition /Standard Edtition 2에 관계없이 싱글 환경 및 클러스터 환경 모두 사용가능합니다.
Single ASM 환경으로 구성 후 클러스터 환경으로 변경 가능합니다.

Oracle Database에 스토리지 풀을 제공하여서 디스크 관리 시간, 비용을 대폭 절감하였습니다.

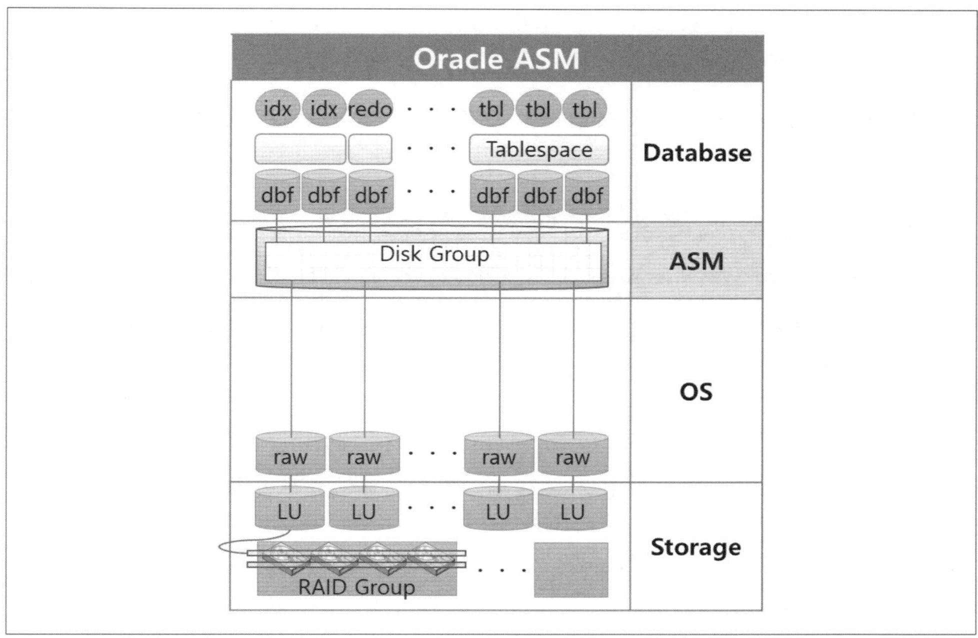

여러 디스크 Array에 디스크를 가상화하여 디스크 추가/제거해도 데이터를 투명하게 재분배가 됩니다.

2 데이터베이스 저장의 기본 사상

Oracle ASM의 설계 기본 사상은 Stripe And Mirror Everthing(S.A.M.E.)입니다.
전통적인 오라클 데이터베이스의 디스크 설계는 용도별로 디스크를 구별하여 설계하였습니다.

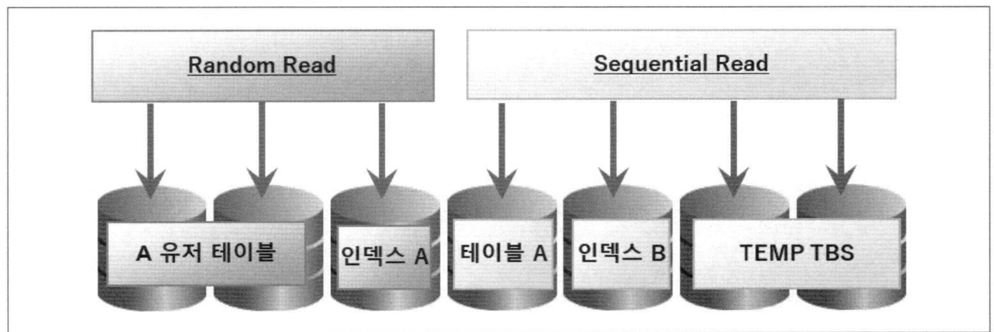

인덱스와 테이블을 분리하였고 스키마 단위, 서비스 단위로 구별하여 저장하였습니다. 이렇게 분리하여 구성하다 보니 디스크 별로 나누어진 성능 이슈가 큰 차이를 보였습니다. 오라클 ASM은 데이터를 그룹 내의 모든 디스크에 스트라이프 되도록 만들어졌습니다.

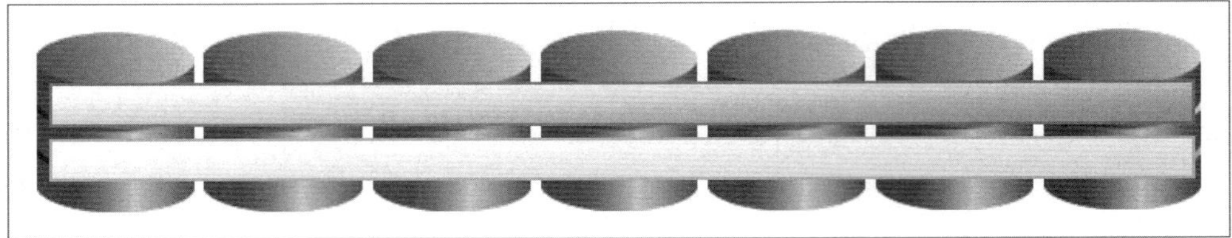

"모든 디스크가 균등하게 사용될 수 있도록 모든 디스크에 데이터를 스트라이프해 분산 배치하고, 미러링도 구현"하도록 스토리지 Volume 설계 기술을 만들었습니다.

이로 인하여 얻는 장점은 다음과 같습니다.

❶ **I/O 성능의 확보** : 모든 Disk의 I/O 대역폭을 최대한으로 활용이 가능합니다.

❷ **가용성을 보장** : 미러링 채용으로 디스크 장애 Risk에 대한 가용성을 확보합니다.

❸ **설계의 간소화** : 물리적 Disk 구성을 은폐해 특별한 설계가 불필요합니다.

ASM 디스크 관리 아키텍처

Oracle ASM은 추가 비용없이 데이터베이스 파일에 대한클러스터 파일 시스템 및 Volume 매니저 기능을 제공하는 Oracle 스토리지 플랫폼 관리 Product입니다. ASM의 스토리지 데이터 저장 측면의 핵심 기술을 알아보겠습니다.

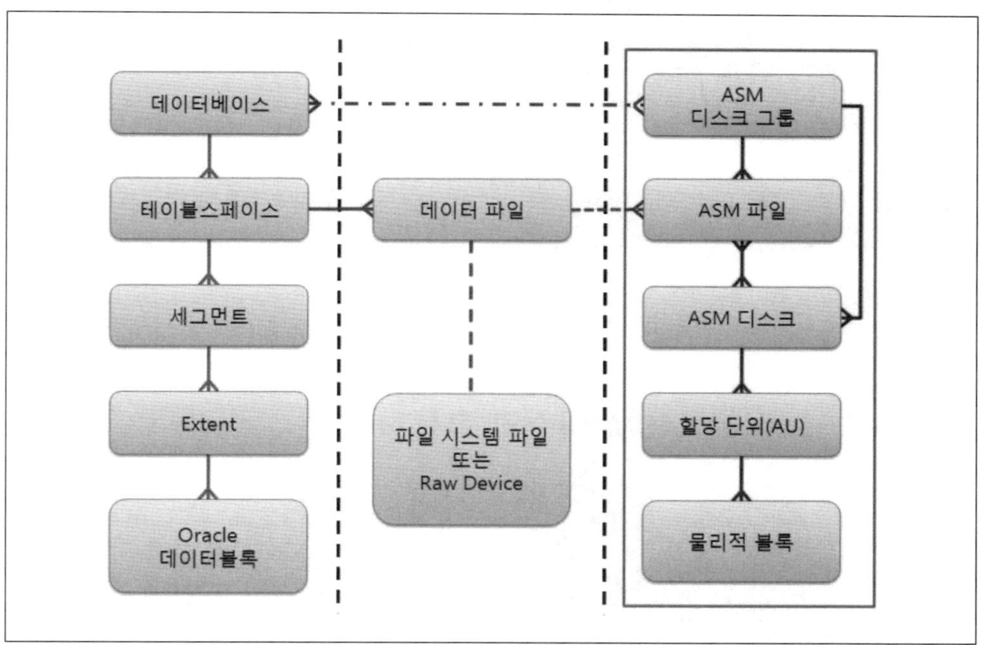

1 디스크 트라이핑

ASM의 주요 장점은 유연한 데이터 분산 Stripping이 된다는 점입니다.

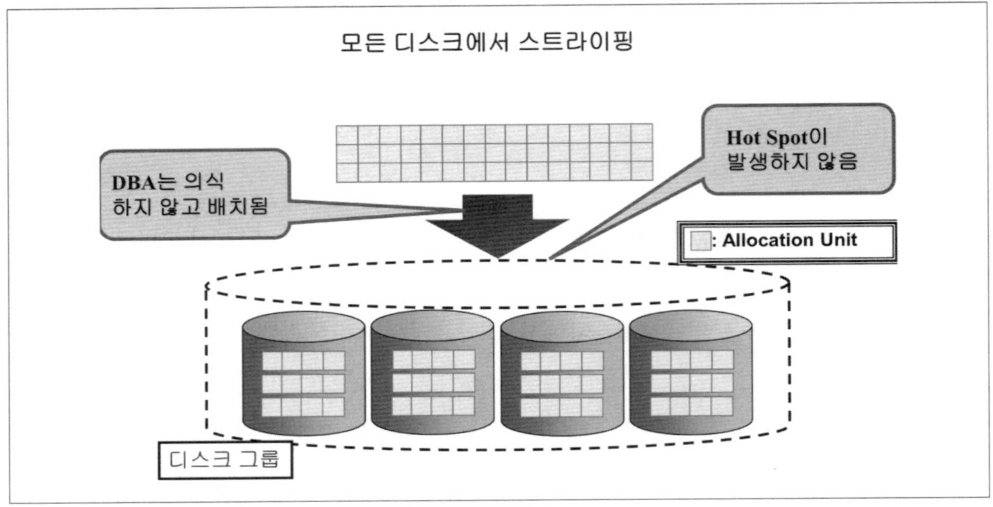

ASM이 관리하는 모든 디스크에 대해 load balancing 작업을 자동적으로 처리해 줌으로써, 특정 디스크에 load가 집중되는 hot spot 현상을 최소화할 수 있으며, 이로 인해 성능을 극대화할 수 있습니다.

또한, 데이터가 디스크에 균등한 크기로 저장/관리되어 fragmentation 현상이 발생하지 않습니다.

❶ Disk Group의 모든 디스크에서 스트라이핑(핫스팟이 발생하지 않음)

❷ 스토리지 서버의 크로스 스트라이핑도 가능

2 디스크 미러링

ASM은 특정 데이터에 대한 복사본을 자기 자신의 디스크에 유지할 수 있기 때문에 Software 미러링 효과를 볼 수 있습니다.

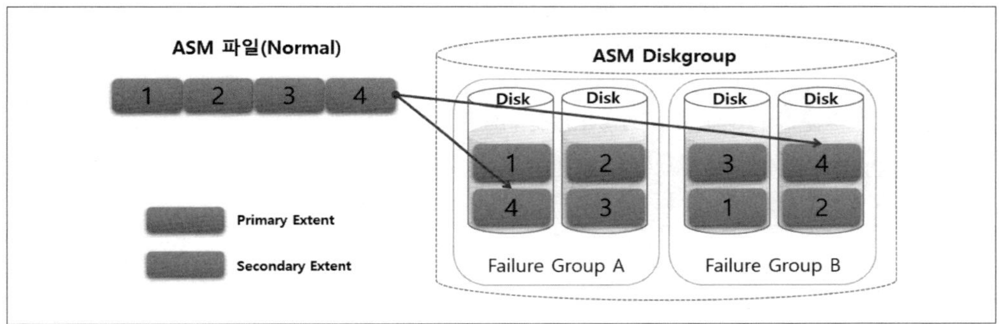

이처럼 ASM은 데이터에 대한 안정성, 그리고 성능을 어떻게 유지할 것인가에 대해 상당히 유연하게 달리 지정할 수 있습니다.

❶ 데이터베이스 수준의 software Mirroring을 제공합니다.

❷ 아래와 같은 3가지 방법을 제공합니다.

- External : Hardware mirroring을 사용하고자 할 때 사용합니다.
- Normal(2-way) : 특정 ASM Disk group이 적어도 2개 이상의 Failure Group을 갖게 되는 구성
- High(3-way) : 특정 ASM Disk group이 적어도 3개 이상의 Failure Group을 갖게 되는 구성

ASM Disk의 EXTENT에 대한 복사본이 다른 Failure Group에 저장/유지됩니다.

파일마다 다른 미러링(External/Normal/High)의 설정이 가능합니다.

❶ 다른 장애 그룹(Failure Group)에 속하는 ASM Disk 간에 보관 유지
❷ 일반적으로 자원(전원 등)을 공유하는 단위(케이스 / 컨트롤러)로 설정

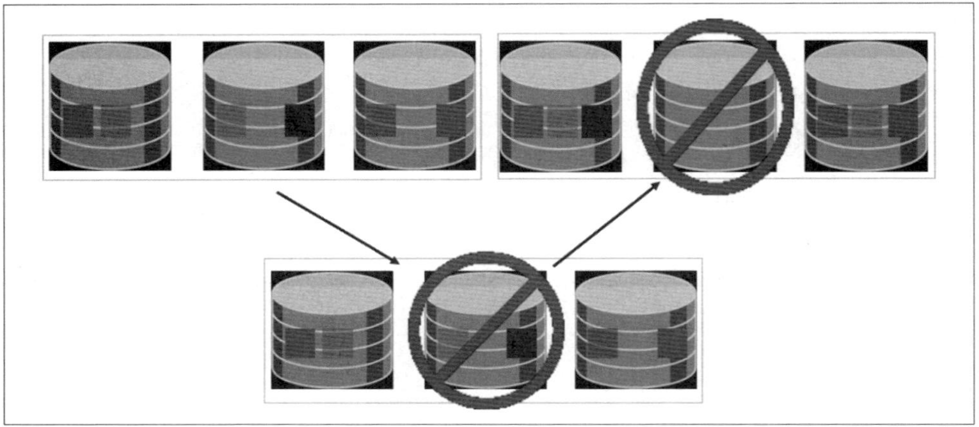

이러한 이유로 기존 Hardware Mirroring에서 사용되었던 Hot Spare 디스크는 필요치 않으며, 복사본 EXTENT를 유지할 수 있는 디스크 추가용량이 있으면 되는 것입니다.

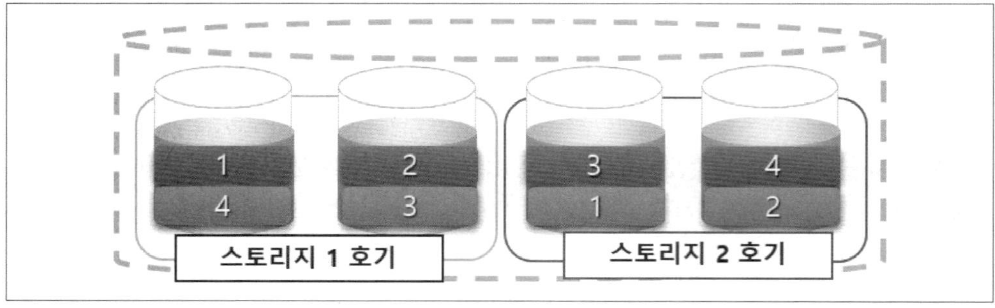

미러링의 대상을 다른 외부에 만드는 것으로 스토리지 서버의 장애 대책이 가능하게 구성할 수 있습니다.

| ASM의 Mirroring

❶ 파일의 중요도에 맞춘 다중화 구성이 가능합니다.
❷ 디스크 갱신/디스크 삽입 시 Redundancy에 따라 디스크 액세스가 증가됩니다.

3 동적 리밸런싱

ASM이 관리하는 영역에서 새로운 디스크가 추가되거나 삭제될 때마다, 기존 데이터들에 대해 재구성 작업이 자동적으로 일어납니다. 디스크의 추가/삭제 시 자동 및 동적으로 파일을 재배치가 온라인 중에 일어납니다.

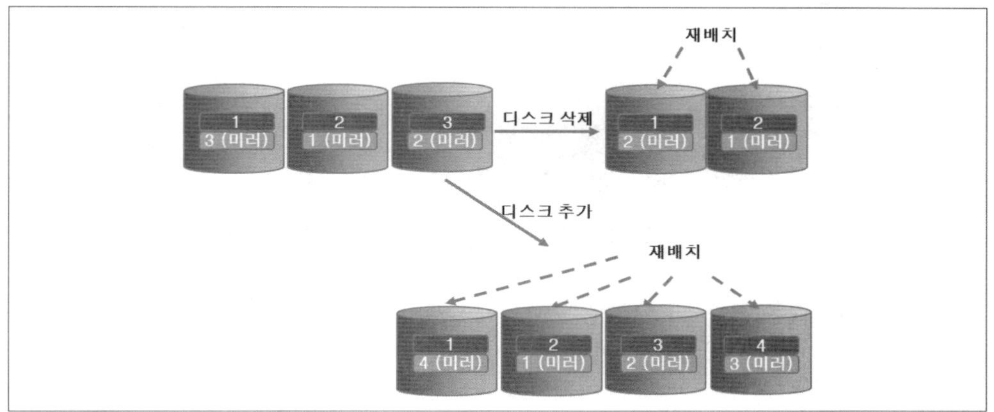

ASM은 기존데이터베이스 구성과 독립적으로 관리될 수 있습니다. 즉 기존 데이터베이스가 데이터 저장소로 파일시스템을 사용하고 있어도, 이와는 별도로 새로운 데이터파일을 ASM에 저장/관리할 수 있는 것입니다. 기존데이터 파일들은 ASM 관리영역으로 이관될 수도 있습니다.

부하의 정도에 따라 디스크를 순차적으로 추가하는 Small Start가 가능하며, 반대로 디스크 수를 줄이는 것도 데이터베이스 온라인 중에 가능합니다.

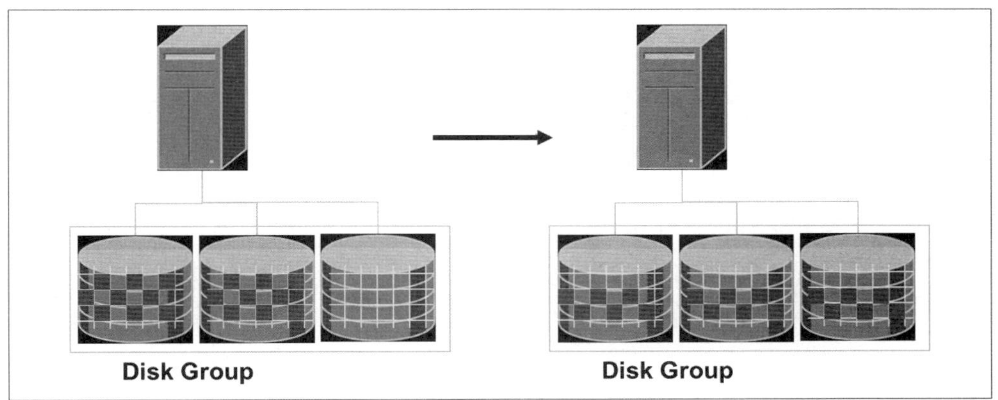

| ASM Rebalancing 정리

❶ Disk가 추가/삭제 또는 크기조정이 일어날 때, Disk group은 모든 Storage에 대한 load를 균등히 하기 위해 rebalancing 작업을 수행합니다.

❷ Disk group에 포함되는 Disk의 크기를 기준으로 해당 작업을 수행하게 됩니다.

❸ Storage의 구성정보가 변경될 때 자동적으로 수행되며, DBA에 의해 수동으로 발생될 수 있습니다.

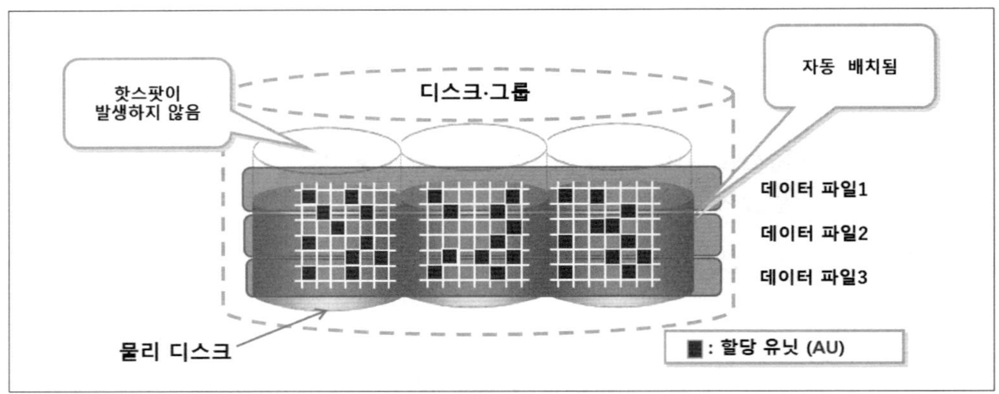

ASM 구성요소

Logical Volume/파일시스템 그리고 오라클 데이터파일에 대한 개념이 ASM에 의해 제거되었습니다. 이러한 관리 영역 제거는 장애요소가 그 만큼 줄어든 것이며, 관리비용을 획기적으로 줄일 수 있다는 것을 뜻합니다.

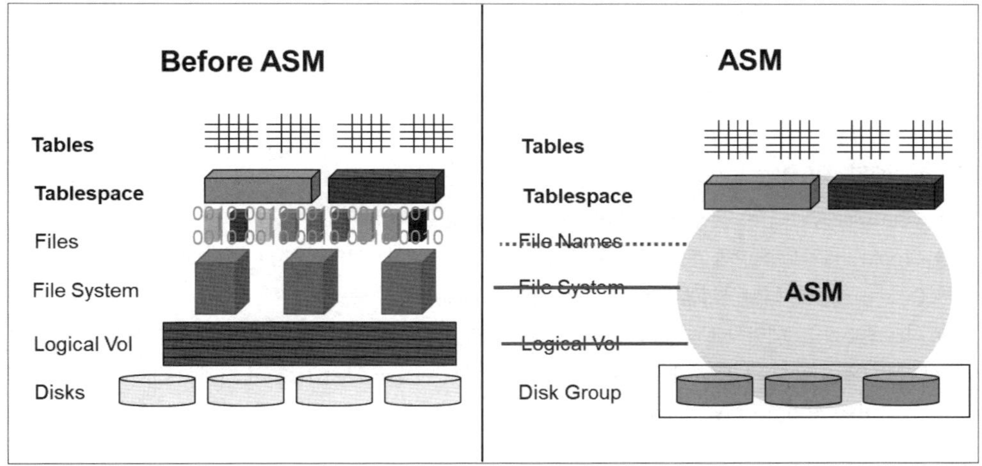

지금부터 ASM의 구성요소에 대해 알아보겠습니다.

1 ASM Architecture

Oracle ASM은 ASM Instance, CSS service, ASM Disk Group, ASM 디스크로 구성되어 있습니다.

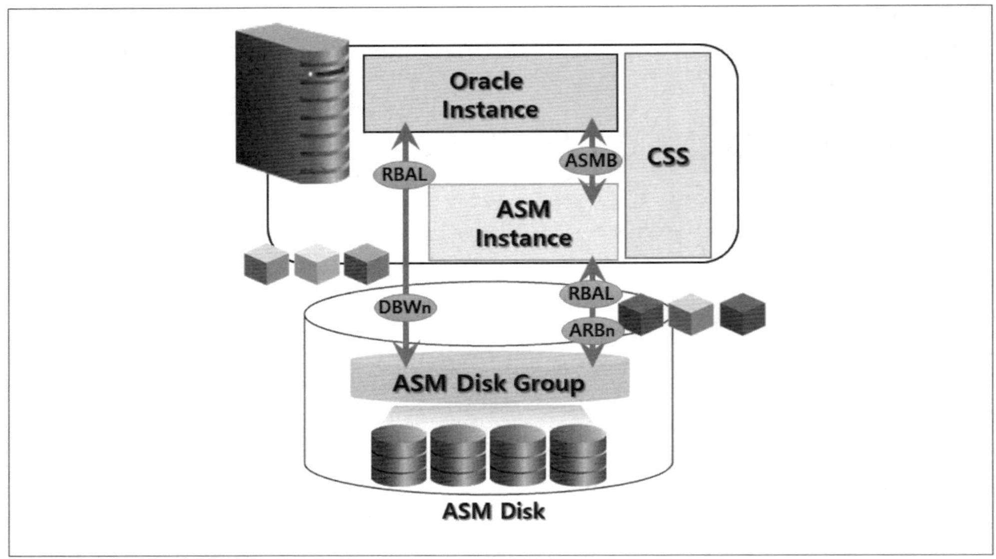

다음은 ASM 구성요소 별의 주요 특징입니다.

| ASM Instance

❶ ASM Disk Group을 관리하는 메모리와 프로세스 군으로 이루어져 있습니다.

❷ Oracle Instance의 형태로 스토리지 관리 목적으로 보완/개선하여 만든 것입니다.

❸ Disk Group에 대한 정보를 수집해 Database Instance에 제공합니다.

❹ 디스크에 있는 데이터에 대한 데이터(metadata)를 가지고 있는 디스크 관리를 위한 instance입니다.

❺ DB Buffer Cache와 같은 개념으로 디스크 안에 있는 내용을 Caching하여 최대한 디스크에 접근하지 않고 바로 작업할 수 있게 합니다.

| Cluster Synchronization Services

❶ Oracle Clusterware의 멤버십 관리를 서비스합니다.

❷ Oracle Instance와 ASM Instance의 존재를 통지하는 역할을 합니다.

| ASM Disk Group

❶ Oracle Instance에서 사용가능한 가상화 스토리지 풀입니다.

❷ 물리적으로 할당 받은 디스크를 묶어서 생성합니다.

❸ 기본적으로 할당된 디스크를 관리해주는 역할을 합니다.

| ASM Disk

❶ ASM Disk Group을 구성하는 개별 디스크(Logical Unit)입니다.

❷ 일반적으로 Disk Array의 LU를 그대로 사용합니다.

| ASM 관련 주요 Process

❶ **ASMB Process** : ASM Instance와 Database Instance 사이에서 정보를 교환해 주는 역할을 합니다.

❷ **RBAL Process** : 디스크가 추가, 삭제되었을 경우 Disk Group에 대한 Rebalance를 담당하는 역할로 ASM Instance의 요청이 있을 경우 디스크를 열고 닫는 프로세스입니다.

❸ **ARBn(ARB1~ARB9)** : RBAL Process의 요청을 받아 실질적으로 작업을 수행하는 Process입니다.

전반적인 ASM 프로세스는 다음과 같습니다.

```
>ps -ef |grep +ASM
grid 2047 1 08:48:38  0:02 asm_mmnl_+ASM # 활성 세션 이력정보 수집 및 변화율 계산.
grid 2022 1 08:48:38 0:00 asm_gen0_+ASM# 일반적인 TASK 실행 프로세스로 ASM 프로세스가 GEN0프로세스에게
                                         특정파일 블로킹 요청. Slave 프로세스와 본질적으로 유사
grid 2014 1 08:48:37 ? 0:02 asm_pmon_+ASM # 프로세스 모니터 프로세스
grid 2016 1 08:48:37 ? 0:03 asm_psp0_+ASM # Process 생성기
grid 2018 1 08:48:37 ? 4:48 asm_vktm_+ASM # 가상시간 유지기 프로세스
grid 2024 1 08:48:38 ? 0:01 asm_diag_+ASM # 진단기능 프로세스
grid 2026 1 08:48:38 ? 0:03 asm_dia0_+ASM # 진단기능 프로세스
grid 2028 1 08:48:38 ? 0:00 asm_mman_+ASM # 메모리 관리자 프로세스
grid 2030 1 08:48:38 ? 0:00 asm_dbw0_+ASM # DB Block writercheck point 프로세스Dirty 버퍼를 Data파일에 적용
grid 2032 1 08:48:38 ? 0:01 asm_lgwr_+ASM # 로그기록자 프로세스
grid 2034 1 08:48:38 ? 0:01 asm_ckpt_+ASM # 체크포인트 프로세스
grid 2036 1 08:48:38 ? 0:00 asm_smon_+ASM # 시스템모니터 프로세스
grid 2038 1 08:48:38 ? 0:01 asm_rbal_+ASM # ASM Disk Group에 디스크 추가하거나 제거할 때Rebalance 작업 처리
grid 2040 1 08:48:38 ? 0:01 asm_gmon_+ASM # 삭제 또는 오프라인과 같은 디스크 레벨 작업을 관리하고
                                          ASM Disk Group 호환성 개선
grid 2042 1 08:48:38 ? 0:02 asm_mmon_+ASM # SGA 통계수집 관리 및ADDM 분석 실행 작업 조정자.
root 2049 1 08:48:38 ? 0:00 ora_dism_+ASM # Solaris dynamic intimate shared memory
                                            메모리를 resize 함으로 가용성을 증대시켜주는 프로세스
```

2 ASM FILE

ASM File은 ASM Disk group에 저장되는 Oracle 데이터 파일입니다. 파일이 생성될 때, Mirroring을 어떻게 할 것인지, Striping은 어떻게 할 것인가에 대한 정보가 함께 적용됩니다.

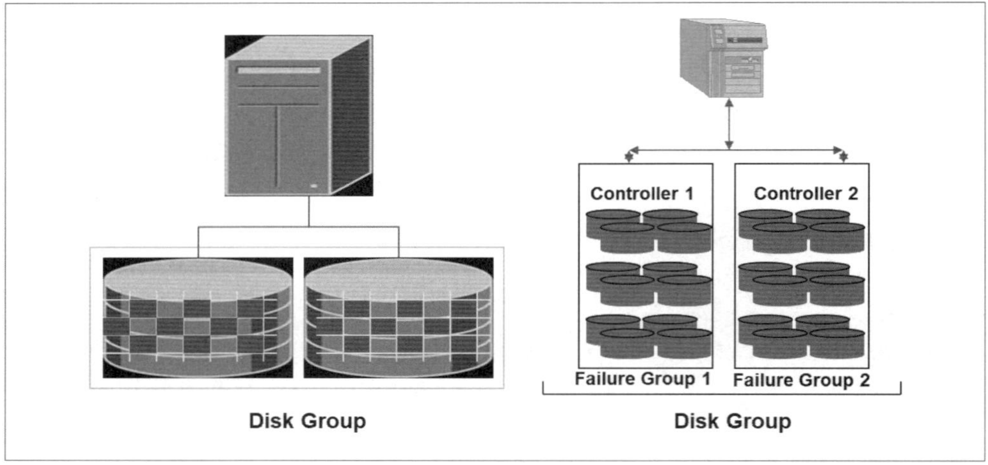

ASM File은 OS에 의해 확인될 수 없으며, RMAN이나 다른 Oracle 지원 툴에 의해 확인 가능합니다.

생성/삭제/읽기/쓰기/크기 변경이 가능하고, 하나의 ASM File은 하나의 Disk group에 분산 저장됩니다.

Disk group을 이루는 개별 파일들이 모든 disk에 분산 저장되기 때문에 하나의 disk에 대한 백업은 유용하지 않습니다. ASM File에 대한 백업은 RMAN을 이용하면 됩니다.

ASM File의 RAID 그룹과 이중화 패턴은 다음과 같습니다.

- 기본 구성 1 : "RAID1 +0"× External Redundancy
- 기본구성 2 : "RAID 없음 or RAID0"× Normal Redundancy
- 이중 장애 대응 구성 : "RAID 없음 or RAID0"× High Redundancy

Oracle 11g ASM부터 VLDB(Very Large Data Base)를 지원하여 최대 140페타 바이트까지 지원합니다.

❶ 1개의 ASM 인스턴스에 최대 만들 수 있는 Disk Group은 511개입니다(12c R1).
❷ 스토리지 시스템 안에 10,000 ASM disks를 만들 수 있습니다.
❸ 1개의Disk Group 내에 100만 개의 ASM File을 만들 수 있습니다.
❹ Disk Group의 호환성이 12.1 이상 AU의 단위에 따라 최대 만들 수 사이즈가 다릅니다.

- AU size 1Mb : 4Peta Byte
- AU size 2Mb : 8 Peta Byte
- AU size 4Mb : 16 Peta Byte
- AU size 8Mb : 32 Peta Byte

3 ASM 인스턴스와 Database 인스턴스의 동작

ASM Instance는 디스크 관리를 위한 instance로 Disk Group에 대한 정보를 수집해 Database Instance에 제공합니다.

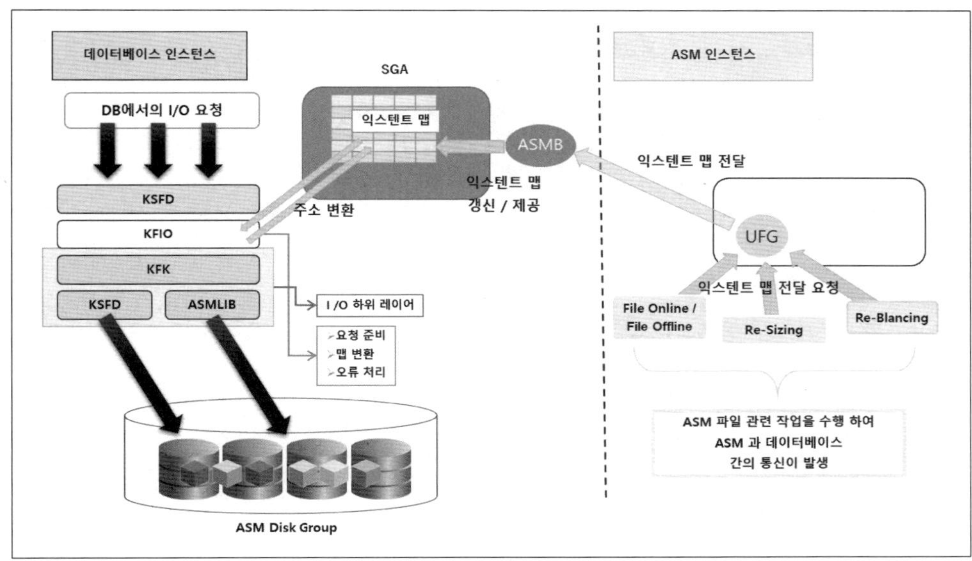

❶ UFG (Umbilicus Fore Ground) 프로세스는 데이터베이스마다 하나의 프로세스가 구동합니다.
❷ UFG 장애 시 데이터베이스 인스턴스가 영향을 받습니다.
❸ KFIO과 KFK가 RAWVolume을 사용하는 경우에는 없는 레이어입니다.
❹ KFK와 그 아래의 레이어는 I/O 하위 레이어는 I/O를 받아 전달합니다.
❺ KSFD는 ASMLIB를 사용하지 않는 경우에I/O는 여기를 통과합니다.
❻ ASMLIB는 Linux에서 ASMLiB를 사용하는 경우에 통과하며, KSFD보다 여분의 레이어가 생략되어 있기 때문에, 약간 고속의 처리가 됩니다.

Raw Device와 Oracle ASM

전통적인 방식의 디스크 저장 구조인 Raw Device 구조를 기준으로 ASM 구조가 어떻게 구성되어있는지 확인해보고 전통적인 Raw Device 구조의 한계점을 알아보겠습니다.

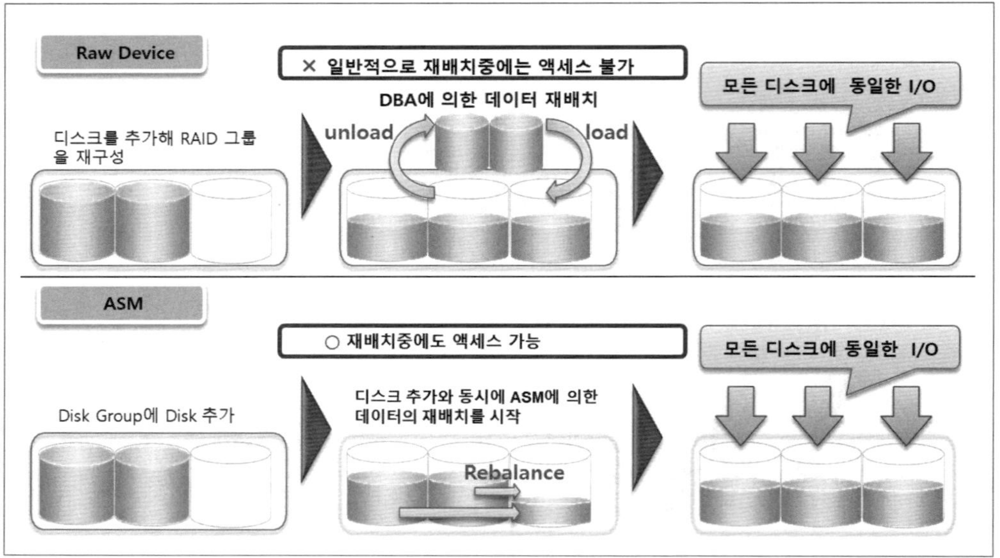

1 STACK 구성 비교

Raw Device는 스토리지 레이어에서 제공한 raw를 Volume 매니저(VM)를 통해 VG로 만들어서 Logical Volume을 만들어서 Oracle Database의 File로 사용하게 구성되어 있습니다.

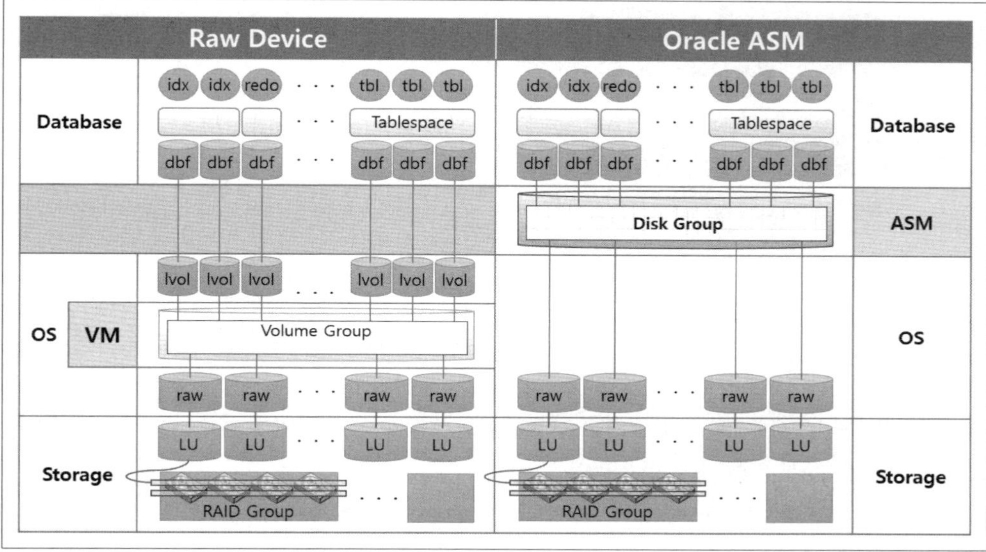

Oracle ASM은 Raw 형태의 디스크 디바이스를 직접 스토리지 가상화 Pool 영역인 ASM Disk Group으로 구성합니다. 가상의 스토리지 Pool인 Disk Group 안에서 Oracle Database의 File로 사용하게 되어 있습니다.

2 I/O Write 시의 처리 구조 비교

전통적인 Raw Device 시스템이 물리적인 블록에 논리적인 블록의 주소를 맵핑하는 hasing function을 이용한 Mapping을 사용하기 때문에 function을 위한 CPU 소비를 수반하고, disk 추가 시 bit 단위의 재배치 작업을 요구하게 됩니다.

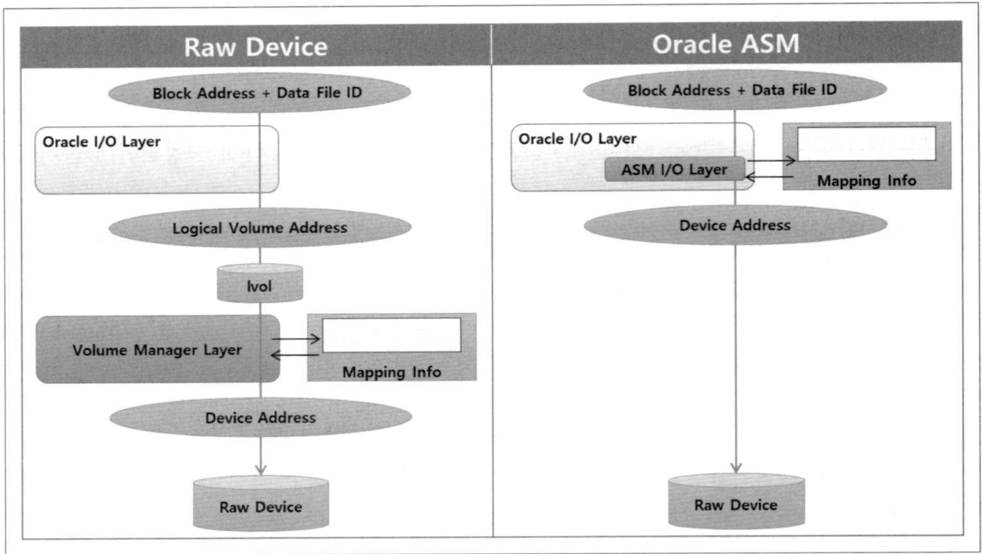

Raw Device 시스템은 블록 또는 버퍼 된 I/O를 사용하는 인터페이스입니다. OS Layer의 I/O caching에 광범위하게 사용됩니다.

Oracle ASM은 Buffer되지 않은 I/O를 사용합니다. OS 수준에서 Raw Device에 직접 사용하므로 I/O caching이 발생하지 않습니다.

ASM 시스템은 전체 디스크를 일정한 크기의 extents로 분할하여 물리적인 블록에 file extents를 Mapping합니다.

이 물리적인 디스크는 DISK GROUP 단위로 묶어서, 관리되므로 동일 DISK GROUP에 속하는 여러 디스크에 각각의 DATA FILE을 균등하게 분산시켜 I/O 성능에 향상을 가할 수 있습니다.

| ASM 구조 정리

❶ File extents가 자동 분배되므로 Online 중에 Disk 추가 가능
❷ OS 상에서 디스크 추가 후 ASM Disk group에 Disk를 add하면 완료
❸ I/O가 Disk group에 자동 분산됨으로, Hot spot을 피할 수 있음.
❹ 파일에 대한 striping의 크기를 적절히 설정할 수 있음(128kb(fine-grained) or 1MB(coarse)).
❺ Buffer를 거치지 않는 Direct Access로 I/O 수행(ASYNC I/O)
❻ ASM을 통해 Software mirroring 지원(extents mirror)
❼ Platform에 상관없이 ASM만 설치되면 구현이 가능

3 Raw Device 환경 구성

스토리지 시스템의 가장 큰 성능 저하 요소는 특정 디스크에 I/O Load가 몰려 성능 Bottleneck이 일어나는 Hot Spot 현상입니다.

결과적으로 Raw Device는 특정 디스크에 Load가 몰리는 Hot Spot 현상을 최소화하기 위한 스트라이핑 구조를 만들기 위해 다음의 스토리지 분할 작업을 합니다.

다수의 물리적 디스크(Physical Disk)를 묶어서 최대한의 여러 개수로 나누어 PV(Physical Volume)을 만듭니다. 그리고 다수의 PV를 묶어서 VG(Volume Group)으로 만든 후 VG를 나눠서 LV = Raw Volume을 만듭니다.

최대한 I/O를 분배하기 위하여 전통적인 Raw Device 구조는 같은 작업을 반복하여 신규 영역을 만듭니다.

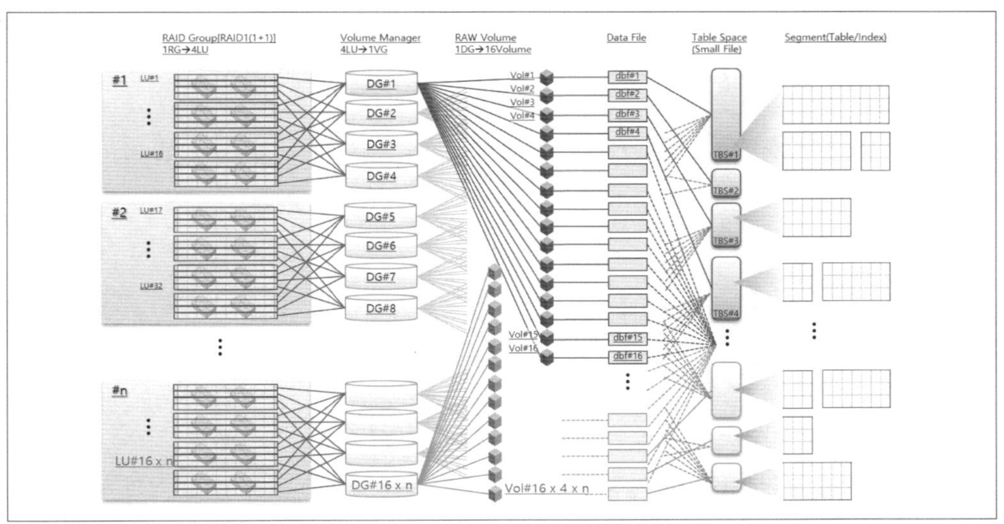

이러한 구조에서는 오라클 DBA가 다음과 같은 Rule 적용하여 관리해야 합니다.

❶ 테이블스페이스가 매우 세분화되어 있어야 합니다.

- 빈공간이 테이블스페이스마다 독립하고 있기 때문에, 낭비되는 공간이 증대됩니다.
- 감시대상(테이블스페이스)이 많아 자주 공간 부족이 발생해 운영 공수가 많아집니다.
- 데이터 파일 수가 많아, SQL의 성능저하나 파일처리 조작오류를 유발할 수 있습니다.
- 관리계층이 많기 때문에 운영 작업이 복잡합니다.

❷ 데이터 파일 추가 시에 기존 데이터를 리밸런스하지 않습니다.

- 빈 영역이 신규Volume에만 존재하기 때문에 새롭게 INSERT되는 레코드가 그 Volume에 집중함으로써 병목현상이 발생하기 쉽습니다.
- 기존 레코드는 기존 Volume에 저장되어 있기 때문에, 성능 개선 효과가 없습니다.

4 ASM 구성

ASM 구조는 물리적인 디스크 Physical Disk를 직접 가상화하여 Disk group을 만듭니다. 각각의 Physical Disk는 물리적인 개별 ASM Disk로 구성됩니다.

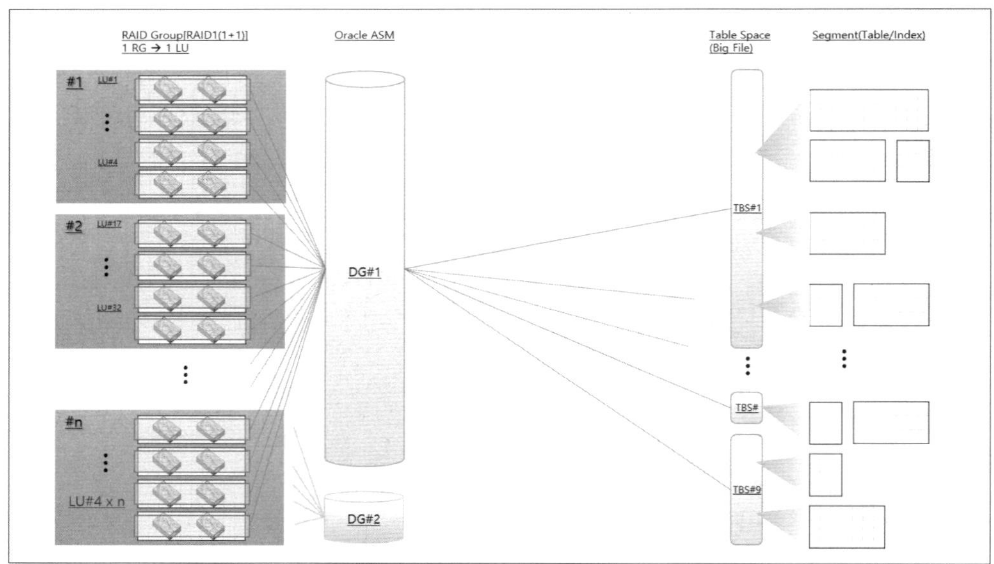

ASM 구성은 다음과 같은 장점이 있습니다.

- **효율적인 디스크 관리** : 관리자가 디스크 그룹에 새로운 디스크를 추가하거나 삭제 시 ASM은 DB의 중단 없이 자동으로 Rebalancing합니다.

- **디스크 I/O의 효과적 분산** : Raw Device 방식은 디스크 교체 또는 추가 시 데이터가 균등하게 분산되지 못하고 쏠림 현상이 발생하였으나, ASM은 AU(Allocation Unit)란 단위로 나누어서 서로 다른 디스크로 균등하게 분산시켜 저장합니다.
- **비용절감** : 소프트에어적으로 RAID 기능이 구현되기 때문에 별도의 RAID 장비를 구매해서 사용할 필요가 없어 비용 절감 효과가 있습니다.

가상화 된 ASM Disk Group에 테이블스페이스를 한 개 또는 하나 이상을 만들 수 있습니다.

❶ 하나의 RAID Group은 하나의 Logical Unit만 자릅니다.
❷ 가능한 한 많은 LU를 하나의 ASM Disk group으로 묶습니다.
❸ 각 ASM Disk group에 포함하는 ASM Disk(LU)는 동일한 성능 및 크기로 구성합니다.

기존 Raw Device 환경의 디스크와 신규 디스크 사이에 데이터가 균등하게 분산되지 못하고 기존디스크로 데이터가 몰리는 경우가 많았지만 ASM 구성은 위와 같이 Oracle이 직접 물리적인 디스크를 관리하는 구성이기 때문에 디스크가 교체되거나 디스크 제거/디스크 추가되면 저장 영역크기에 비례하는 데이터를 이동하여 파일을 균등하게 재분산(Re-Balancing)하고 디스크에서 로드가 균형을 이루도록 유지합니다.
Data File 단위로 구성된 각 ASM DISK에 대해 균등하게 File Extent(AU)를 할당합니다.

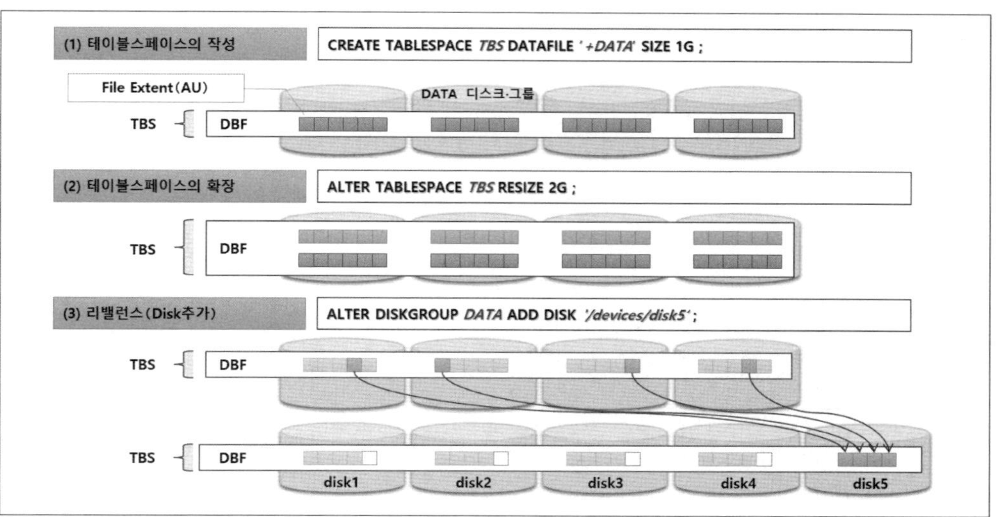

ASM Disk Group에 테이블스페이스를 생성하면 스트라이프 구조를 유지하기 위하여 모든 디스크의 사용 율이 동일하도록 할당합니다.

ASM Disk Group 관리

Oracle Database의 최적화된 운영을 위하여 ASM의 주요 구성 요소인 ASM Disk Group을 어떻게 생성하고 관리해야 하는지 알아보고 ASM Disk Group을 이루고 있는 ASM Disk의 주요 관리 방법에 대해 알아보겠습니다.

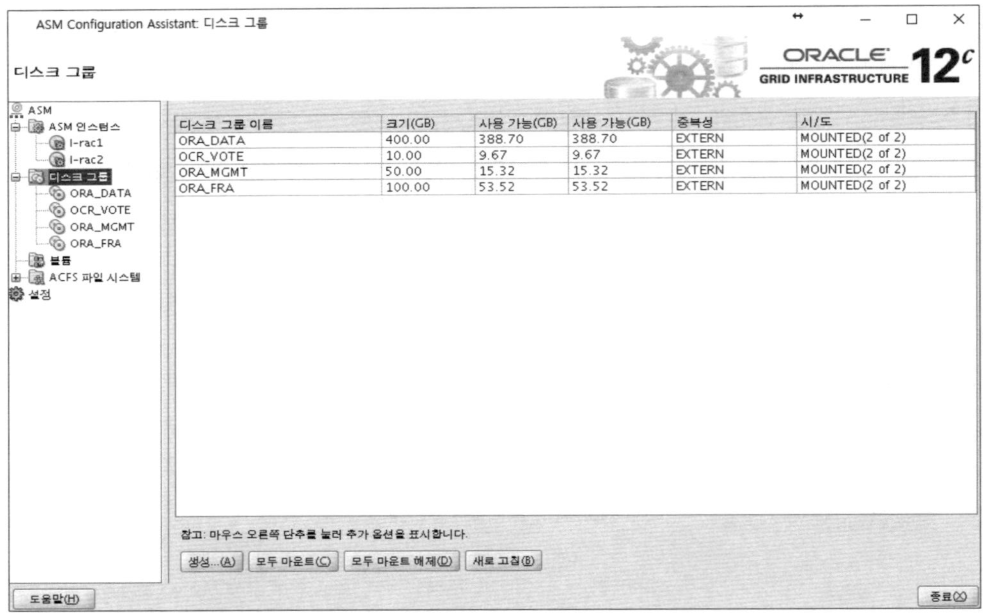

1 ASM Disk Group 생성

Oracle Grid Infrastructure 제품을 설치하고 나면 asmca라는 유틸을 통해 ASM Disk Group을 생성해야 합니다.

아래의 그림은 asmca라는 유틸을 실행 시 나오는 X Window System(X11) 화면입니다.

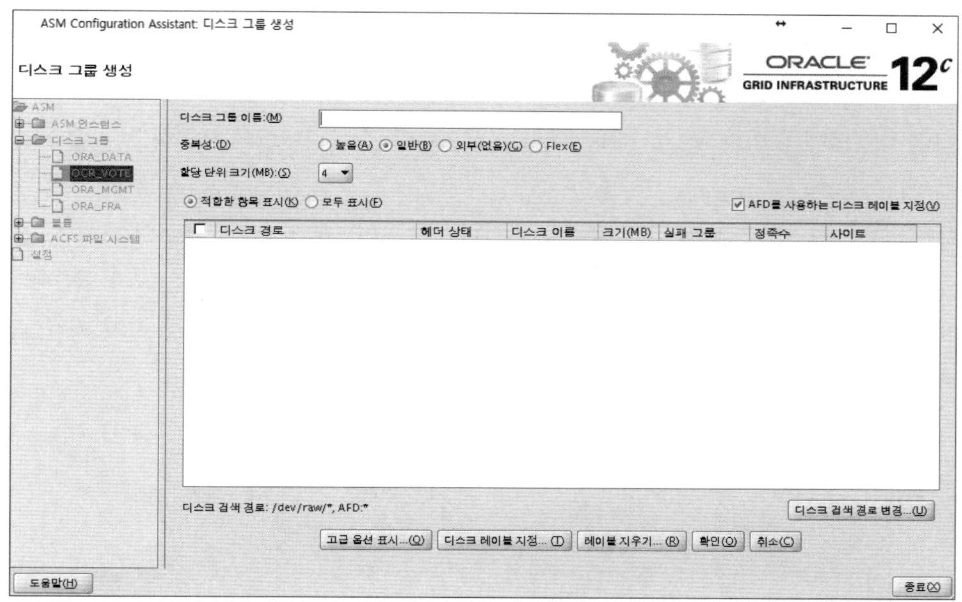

09. Section에서 asmca의 설명을 자세히 하겠습니다. 지금부터 Disk Group 생성의 기준에 대해서 알아보겠습니다.

ASM Disk Group 생성을 위한 일반가이드입니다.

❶ ASM의 스트라이핑은 용량 기준 때문에 하나의 Disk Group에는 같은 양의 ASM 디스크를 사용하는 것이 좋습니다.

❷ 요구 사항이 없는 경우 Disk Group은 2개의 운영하여 하나는 운영 데이터(데이터 파일 등) 용이고 다른 하나는 백업 데이터용으로 구성합니다.

❸ 데이터베이스의 백업 스토리지 기능을 이용하는 경우 등은 최소 3 개의 Disk Group으로 운영이 필요합니다.

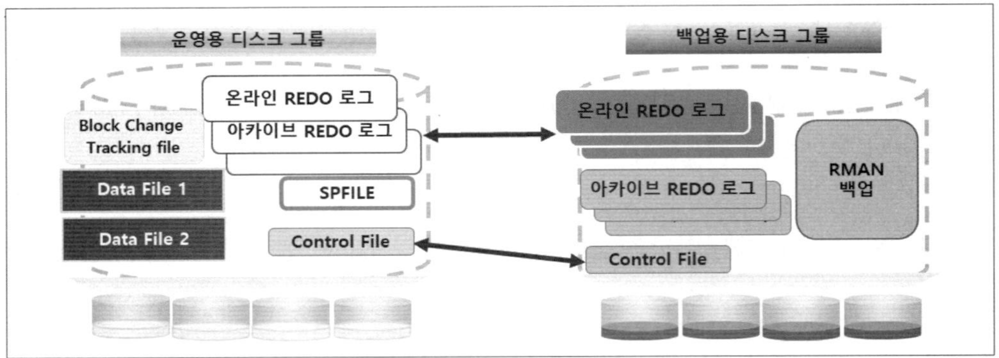

오라클 매뉴얼에는 일반적으로 하나 이상의 Disk Group을 나누도록 권고하고 있습니다.

ASM Disk Group은 스토리지를 기준으로 가상화된 Pool이므로 스토리지 종류와 스펙에 따라 구성 방법의 차이가 있을 수 있으므로 스토리지 제조사의 가이드를 살펴 볼 필요가 있습니다. 스토리지 제조사는 스토리지 종류별로 Oracle ASM Disk Group으로 구성 시의 최적화된 가이드 문서를 제공 배포하고 있습니다.

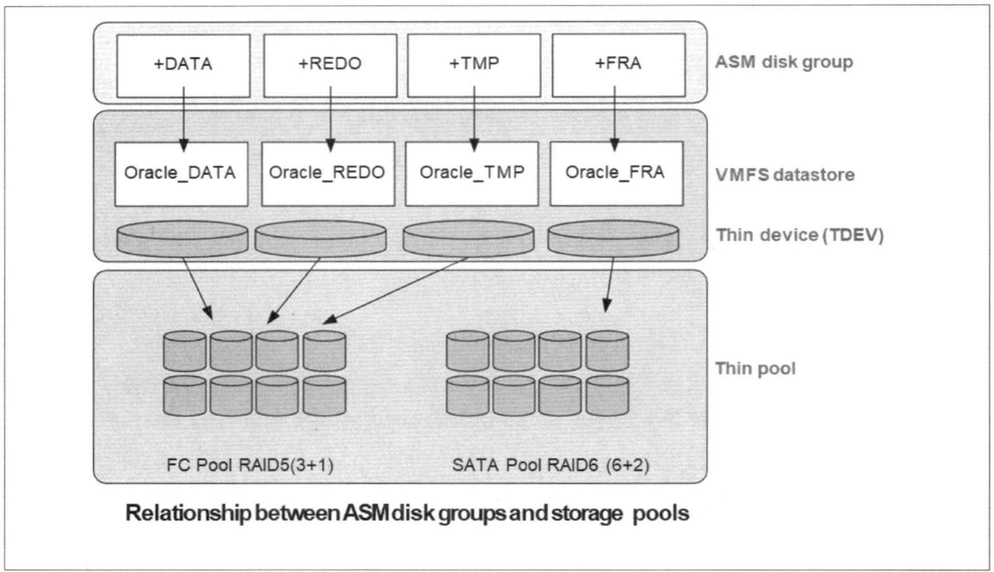

Relationship between ASM disk groups and storage pools

▲ Dell EMC SC Series Arrays and Oracle–White Papers

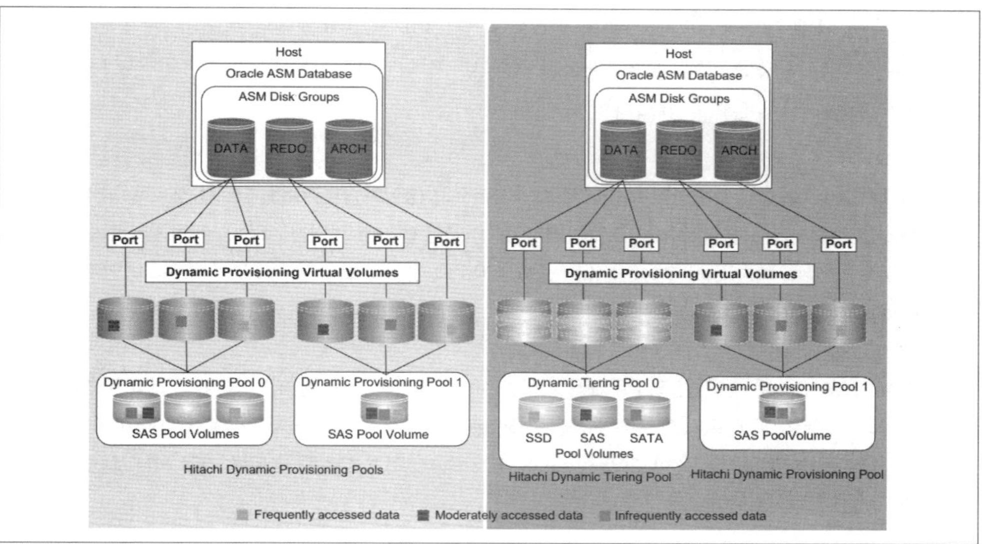

▲ Optimizing Oracle Database 11gR2 with Automatic Storage Management on Hitachi Virtual Storage Platform–Best Practices Guide

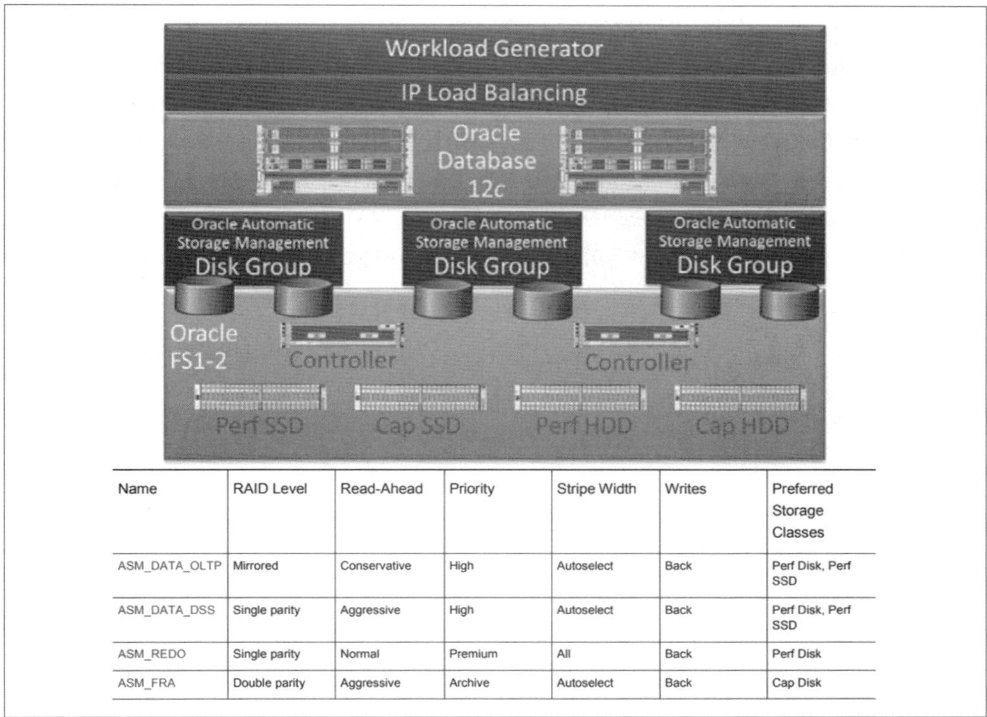

Name	RAID Level	Read-Ahead	Priority	Stripe Width	Writes	Preferred Storage Classes
ASM_DATA_OLTP	Mirrored	Conservative	High	Autoselect	Back	Perf Disk, Perf SSD
ASM_DATA_DSS	Single parity	Aggressive	High	Autoselect	Back	Perf Disk, Perf SSD
ASM_REDO	Single parity	Normal	Premium	All	Back	Perf Disk
ASM_FRA	Double parity	Aggressive	Archive	Autoselect	Back	Cap Disk

▲ Best Practices for Optimizing Storage for Oracle Automatic Storage Management with Oracle FS1 Series Storage – Oracle White Paper

특정 스토리지 제조사의 가이드 문서의 공통점과 저자가 직접 ASM 환경의 오라클 DB 구축 프로젝트, ASM 환경의 DB 유지 관리를 수행한 결과 ASM Disk Group을 구성하는 것이 일반적인 가이드는 다음과 합니다.

❶ **DATA Disk Group** : 순수하게 데이터베이스의 복구의 중심이 되는 Data File과 SP File과 1번 컨트롤 파일을 위치하게 구성합니다. 디스크의 RAID를 이용한 미러링 보다는 ASM이 직접 관리하도록 일반적으로 2중화(Normal Redundancy) 또는 중요 데이터이면서 스토리지 디스크가 충분하다면 3중화(High Redundancy)로 구성합니다.

❷ **REDO Disk Group** : 온라인 리두로그를 저장하는 REDODisk Group을 구성합니다. 리두 로그와 데이터 파일의 I/O 특성이 다르기 때문에 성능을 위해 분리해야 하고, 스토리지의 SSD or Flash Disk 영역이 있다면 오라클의 로깅을 위한 지연 현상(Log File Sync)이 발생하지 않도록 가장 빠른 디스크에 Disk Group을 위치시킵니다.

❸ **TEMP Disk Group** : Tempfile은 TEMP 테이블스페이스의 사이즈가 클수록 디스크 장애 시 복구하지 않고 그냥 다시 생성하는 편이 훨씬 빠르기 때문에 대용량 데이터베이스에서 별도의 Disk Group으로 빼내고 정렬 작업이 많을 경우 성능을 위해 +TEMP를 분리해야 합니다. ASM 미러링 형태는 External로 구성합니다.

❹ **FRA Disk Group** : 고속 복구 영역으로 2번 컨트롤 파일, 아카이브 로그, Flash Back 로그파일, RMAN 백업 세트 등을 저장합니다. 이 영역은 순차 쓰기만 일어나고 복구를 위한 용도로만 사용되기 때문에 SATA 디스크처럼 저렴한 디스크에 구성해도 됩니다. 고속 복구 영역을 별도의 ASM Disk Group으로 분리하는 것은 오라클의 권장 사항이기도 합니다. ASM 미러링 형태는 External로 구성합니다.

Oracle RAC로 구성 시 필요한 OCR, Voting Disk, Mgmt DB 등은 GRID Disk Group으로 분리하여 3중화(High Redundancy)로 구성합니다.

2 ASM Disk Group 할당 단위(Allocation Units)

모든 Oracle ASM Disk는 Allocation Units (AU)로 나누어집니다. AU size는 ASM Disk Group 내의 기본 할당 단위입니다. 파일 Extents는 하나 이상의 할당단위로 구성되었습니다. Oracle ASM 파일은 하나 이상의 파일 Extents로 구성됩니다.

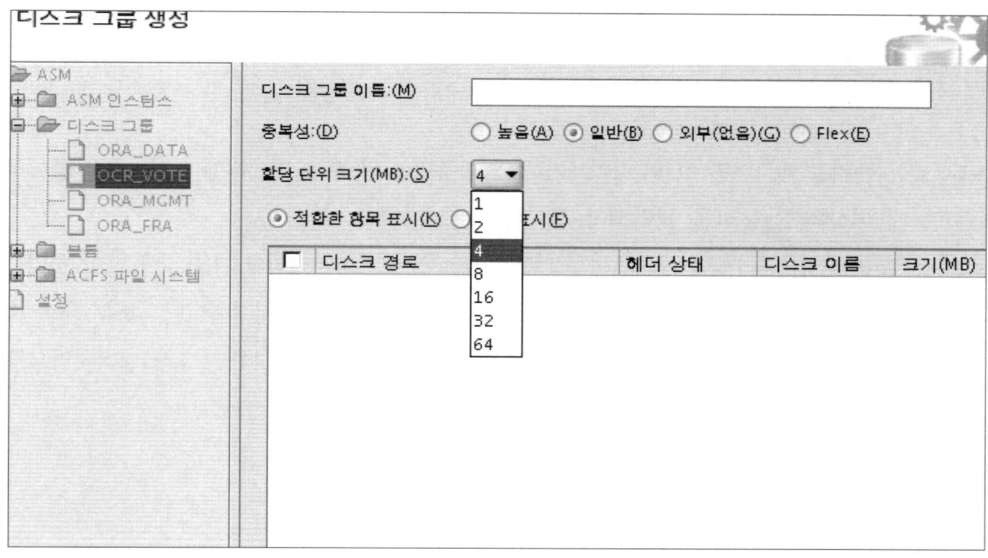

Disk Group을 생성할 때 Oracle ASM 할당 단위 크기인 AU SIZE를 Disk Group 속성 특정 Disk Group 호환성 수준에 따라 값을 1, 2, 4, 8, 16, 32, 64MB로 설정이 가능합니다. AU 크기가 클수록 일반적으로 큰 순차 읽기를 사용하는 DW 시스템에서 성능 이점이 있습니다.

Oracle 10g와 호환하는 Disk Group은 모든 Extent에 대해 공유 풀의 메모리를 요구합니다. 따라서 데이터베이스의 용량이 큰 경우라면 매우 많은 양의 메모리가 필요하게 됩니다.

```
new MEMORY_TARGET = current MEMORY_TARGET + 20 percent + growth of "shared pool"

column "current value" form a15

select MT "current value", (1.2*MT) + difference "new value"
from (select value as MT from v$parameter where name='memory_target'),
    (select (max_size - current_size) as difference
     from v$memory_dynamic_components where component='shared pool');
```

▲ ORA-04031 on ASM Instance-default memory parameters for 11.2 ASM instances are too low (MOS 문서 ID 1536039.1)

11.2.0.4 이하 Version의 ASM 인스턴스는 최소 2기가의 Memory Target로 확보해 주어야 합니다.

이와 같은 논리로 계산하면 AU의 사이즈가 1MB(디폴트)라면, 1TB 데이터베이스는 공유 풀에서 100만 개 이상의 Extent를 관리해야 합니다.
그래서 Oracle Grid Infrastructure 11g부터 Extent의 크기와 AU의 크기를 갖게 해야 한다는 요구조건이 없어졌습니다. 파일 생성 시 Extent의 크기는 1MB부터 시작합니다. ASM 내의 파일의 크기가 일정한 임계치에 도달하면 Extent 사이즈는 4MB, 16MB, 그리고 마지막으로 64MB로 증가합니다.

가변형 크기의 ASM 파일 임계치는 다음과 같습니다.

❶ 첫 20000 extent는(0-19999) disk group **동일 AU 사이즈와 항상 같게 설정됩니다.**
❷ 다음 20000 extent까지(20000-39999) **4 * AU 사이즈와 같습니다.**
❸ 다음 20000 extent부터(40000+) 그 이상은 **16 * AU 사이즈와 같게 설정됩니다.**

이와 같이 ASM 인스턴스가 자동으로 적절한 Extent 크기를 결정하기 때문에 AU 크기의 고민은 없어졌습니다. 보다 적은 수의 Extent로 많은 양의 데이터를 저장할 수 있게 되면서, 공유 풀에서 관리되는 Extent의 수가 줄어들고 따라서 성능을 몇 배로 개선하는 것이 가능해졌습니다.

하지만 가변 Extent 크기 설정으로 인해 파일의 용량이 급격하게 증가/감소하는 상황에서 조각(fragmentation) 현상이 발생할 수 있습니다. ASM은 필요한 경우 조각 모음을 자동으로 수행합니다. ASM의 조각 모임은 Online-Rebalancing입니다.

다음은 Disk Group 강제 REBALANCE를 수행방법입니다.

```
SQL> ALTER DISKGROUP <Disk Group명> REBALANCE POWER 5 WAIT;
```

```
SQL> ALTER DISKGROUP ORA_DATA REBALANCE POWER 5 WAIT ;
Diskgroup altered.
SQL> █
```

ASM POWER LIMIT은 Dynamic Rebalancing을 수행하는 ARBn 프로세스의 개수로 디폴트가 1개이며, 최대 11개까지 가능합니다.
앞의 명령어는 5개의 ARBn 프로세스를 사용하여 REBALANCE 작업을 수행하고, REBALANCE이 완료될 때까지 기다린 후에 메시지합니다.
Disk Group REBALANCE는 시간이 오래 걸리므로 디폴트(WAIT를 명시 안함)로 REBALANCE 작업이 완료되지 않더라도 명령어 실행 메세지를 표시합니다. 이때, V$ASM_OPERATION 뷰를 통해 REBALANCE 진행사항을 파악할 수 있습니다

3 ASM Disk Group 호환성(COMPATIBILITY)

ASM은 10g Version 이후부터 오라클 데이터베이스에 사용되는 스토리지 플랫폼입니다. 11g 기반 ASM 인스턴스는 10g Release 1, 10g Release 2, 11g Release 1 및 이후 Version의 데이터베이스를 지원합니다. 다시 말해, ASM Version이 데이터베이스 Version과 같거나 더 크다면, 해당 ASM Version에서 데이터베이스를 생성하는 것이 가능합니다.
반대로 작다면 데이터베이스 생성은 불가능합니다. 따라서 ASM Disk Group의 호환성 관리는 중요한 요소입니다.
ASM은 11g 이상 총 3가지 호환성이 있습니다.

❶ DATABASE COMPATIBILITY : Disk Group을 ASM 인스턴스에서 마운트하기 위해 인스턴스가 허락하는 RDBMS 인스턴스의 호환 가능한 최소 Version입니다. 이 호환성은 ASM과 데이터베이스 인스턴스 사이에 교환되는 메세지의 포맷을 결정합니다. ASM 인스턴스는 다른 호환성 설정으로 다른RDBMS 클라이언트 실행 지원이 가능합니다. 데이터베이스 호환 Version은 각 인스턴스 설정보다 크거나 해당 데이터베이스에 사용되는 모든 Disk Group의 RDBMS 호환성과 같아야 합니다. 데이터베이스 인스턴스는 전형적으로 ASM 인스턴스와 다른 오라클 홈에서 실행됩니다. 이 의미는 데이터베이스 인스턴스는 ASM 인스턴스가 아닌 다른 Version의 소프트웨어 Version에서 실행될 수 있습니다. 데이터베이스 인스턴스가 ASM 인스턴스에 먼저 연결되고 양쪽 다 지원 가능한 가장 높은 Version을 협상합니다. 호환성 매개변수를 데이터베이스에 설정하고, 데이터베이스 Version과 RDBMS 호환성이 Disk Group의 설정이 데이터베이스 인스턴스가 주어진 Disk Group을 마운트할 수 있는지 여부를 결정합니다.

❷ ASM COMPATIBILITY : 디스크에 ASM 메타데이터에 대한 데이터 구조의 형식의 제어로 지속적인 호환성 설정을 의미합니다. Disk Group의 ASM 호환성 레벨은 같은 Disk Group의 RDBMS 호환성 레벨과

같거나 그 이상이어야 합니다. ASM 호환성은 ASM 메타데이터의 형식에 관계가 있습니다. 파일 콘텐츠의 형식은 데이터베이스 인스턴스에 의해 결정된다. 예를 들면 RDBMS 호환성이 10.1로 설정될 수 있는 반면 Disk Group의 ASM 호환성은 11.0로 설정할 수 있습니다. 이것은 Disk Group에 사용되는 소프트웨어 Version이 10.1과 같거나 그 이상이라면, 소프트웨어 Version이 11.0 혹은 그 이상의 ASM 소프트웨어에 의해 Disk Group이 관리되는 것을 의미합니다.

❸ ADVM COMPATIBILITY : Oracle ASM Volume에 포함된 Disk Group을 통해 결정됩니다. 값은 11.2 이상이어야 합니다. 이 속성을 설정하기 전의 COMPATIBLE.ASM 값은 반드시 11.2 이상이어야 합니다. 또한 Oracle ADVM Volume 드라이버는 반드시 로드 되야 합니다. 기본으로 COMPATIBLE.ASM의 속성은 설정하기 전에 비어있습니다. Disk Group의 호환성은 프로토콜 메시지나 연속적인 디스크 구조의 변경에는 고급이 필요합니다. 그러나 향상된 Disk Group 호환성은 돌이킬 수 없습니다. 만약 향상된 Disk Group 호환성을 설정하였다면 이전 설정값으로 변경할 수 없습니다. 이전값으로 되돌리려면 예전 호환성 속성 설정으로 새로운 Disk Group을 생성하고 새로운 Disk Group에 이전 Disk Group의 데이터 파일을 복원합니다.

호환성 확인 방법은 다음과 같습니다.

```
SQL>SELECT NAME,COMPATIBILITY,DATABASE_COMPATIBILITY FROM V$ASM_DISKGROUP ;
```

```
SQL> set line 500
SQL> col COMPATIBILITY for a40
SQL> col NAME for a20
SQL> col DATABASE_COMPATIBILITY for a40
SQL> SELECT NAME,COMPATIBILITY,DATABASE_COMPATIBILITY FROM V$ASM_DISKGROUP ;

NAME                 COMPATIBILITY                            DATABASE_COMPATIBILITY
-------------------- ---------------------------------------- ----------------------------------------
OCR_VOTE             12.2.0.1.0                               10.1.0.0.0
ORA_DATA             12.2.0.1.0                               10.1.0.0.0
ORA_FRA              12.2.0.1.0                               10.1.0.0.0
ORA_MGMT             12.2.0.1.0                               10.1.0.0.0

SQL> ▌
```

호환성 변경 방법은 ALTER DISKGROUP 명령어로 가능합니다.

```
SQL>ALTER DISKGROUP ORA_DATA SET ATTRIBUTE 'compatible.rdbms'='11.1' ;
```

```
SQL> SELECT NAME,COMPATIBILITY,DATABASE_COMPATIBILITY FROM V$ASM_DISKGROUP ;

NAME                 COMPATIBILITY                            DATABASE_COMPATIBILITY
-------------------- ---------------------------------------- ----------------------------------------
OCR_VOTE             12.2.0.1.0                               10.1.0.0.0
ORA_DATA             12.2.0.1.0                               10.1.0.0.0
ORA_FRA              12.2.0.1.0                               10.1.0.0.0
ORA_MGMT             12.2.0.1.0                               10.1.0.0.0

SQL> ALTER DISKGROUP ORA_DATA SET ATTRIBUTE 'compatible.rdbms'='11.1' ;

Diskgroup altered.

SQL> SELECT NAME,COMPATIBILITY,DATABASE_COMPATIBILITY FROM V$ASM_DISKGROUP ;

NAME                 COMPATIBILITY                            DATABASE_COMPATIBILITY
-------------------- ---------------------------------------- ----------------------------------------
OCR_VOTE             12.2.0.1.0                               10.1.0.0.0
ORA_DATA             12.2.0.1.0                               11.1.0.0.0
ORA_FRA              12.2.0.1.0                               10.1.0.0.0
ORA_MGMT             12.2.0.1.0                               10.1.0.0.0

SQL> ▌
```

SQL*Plus 유틸리티를 이용한 ASM 관리 방법

지금까지는 Oracle ASM의 주요 기능과 구성 방법에 대해서 살펴보았습니다. 이제부터 실제 수행하는 가장 많이 사용하고 있고, 터미널 환경에서 사용이 가능한 SQL*Plus 유틸리티를 이용한 ASM 관리 명령과 수행 명령을 단계별 실습을 통해 습득해 보고 상황별 대응 방법에 대해 알아보겠습니다.

1 SYSASM

SYSASM 권한은 ASM 관리자 작업을 실행할 수 있는 목적으로 만들어진 특별한 권한입니다. SYSASM 권한은 데이터베이스 관리자로부터 ASM 관리를 분리 시켰습니다. SYSDBA 권한으로 ASM 인스턴스 관리 명령어의 수행에 제한이 있습니다. ASM 관리는 SYSASM 권한을 받은 유저로 해야 합니다. 권한이 분리되어 있는지 히든 파라미터를 조회해 봅니다.

```
SQL>SELECT RPAD(I.KSPPINM, 35) || ' = ' || V.KSPPSTVL AS PARAM
, I.KSPPDESC DESCRIPTION
FROM X$KSPPI I
, X$KSPPCV V
, V$PARAMETER P
WHERE V.INDX = I.INDX
AND V.INST_ID = I.INST_ID
AND I.KSPPINM = P.NAME(+)
AND I.KSPPINM ='_asm_admin_with_sysdba'
ORDER BY I.KSPPINM
```

```
SQL> SELECT RPAD(I.KSPPINM, 35) || ' = ' || V.KSPPSTVL AS PARAM
  2  , I.KSPPDESC DESCRIPTION
  3  FROM X$KSPPI I
  4  , X$KSPPCV V
  5  , V$PARAMETER P
  6  WHERE V.INDX = I.INDX
  7  AND V.INST_ID = I.INST_ID
  8  AND I.KSPPINM = P.NAME(+)
  9  AND I.KSPPINM ='_asm_admin_with_sysdba'
 10  ORDER BY I.KSPPINM ;

Parameter                                     Parameter
Name                                          Description
--------------------------------------------- ------------------------------------------------------------
_asm_admin_with_sysdba              = FALSE   Does the sysdba role have administrative privileges on ASM?

SQL>
```

새로운 OS-privileged Group인 OS ASM group은 ASM을 위해 사용됩니다. 이 그룹의 멤버는 OS 인증을 사용하여 SYSASM으로 접속할 수 있으며, ASM에 모든 접근/관리가 가능합니다.

V$PWFILE_USERS 뷰에 SYSASM 컬럼이 추가되었습니다.

```
$ ps -ef | grep pmon              -- ASM 인스턴스명 확인
$ . oraenv
ORACLE_SID = [인스턴스명] ? +ASM -- ASM 인스턴스명 입력으로 환경변수 세팅
$ sqlplus / as sysasm             -- ASM 관리자 권한으로 접속
SQL> desc v$pwfile_users
```

```
[root@yspark-linux ~]# su - oracle12
Last login: Tue Jan  2 08:12:44 KST 2018 on pts/0
[oracle12]yspark-linux:/home/oracle12> ps -ef | grep pmon
oracle12 16383     1  0  2017 ?        00:00:15 asm_pmon_+ASM
oracle12 22846 22788  0 09:54 pts/0    00:00:00 grep --color=auto pmon
[oracle12]yspark-linux:/home/oracle12> . oraenv
ORACLE_SID = [oracle12] ? +ASM
The Oracle base has been changed from /oracle/oracle12/app/oracle to /oracle/grid12/app/oracle
[+ASM]yspark-linux:/home/oracle12> sqlplus / as sysasm

SQL*Plus: Release 12.2.0.1.0 Production on Tue Jan 2 09:55:16 2018

Copyright (c) 1982, 2016, Oracle.  All rights reserved.


Connected to:
Oracle Database 12c Enterprise Edition Release 12.2.0.1.0 - 64bit Production

SQL> desc v$pwfile_users
 Name                                      Null?    Type
 ----------------------------------------- -------- ----------------------------
 USERNAME                                           VARCHAR2(128)
 SYSDBA                                             VARCHAR2(5)
 SYSOPER                                            VARCHAR2(5)
 SYSASM                                             VARCHAR2(5)
 SYSBACKUP                                          VARCHAR2(5)
 SYSDG                                              VARCHAR2(5)
 SYSKM                                              VARCHAR2(5)
 ACCOUNT_STATUS                                     VARCHAR2(30)
 PASSWORD_PROFILE                                   VARCHAR2(128)
 LAST_LOGIN                                         TIMESTAMP(9) WITH TIME ZONE
 LOCK_DATE                                          DATE
 EXPIRY_DATE                                        DATE
 EXTERNAL_NAME                                      VARCHAR2(1024)
 AUTHENTICATION_TYPE                                VARCHAR2(8)
 COMMON                                             VARCHAR2(3)
 CON_ID                                             NUMBER
```

이제부터 SYSASM 유저로 접속하여 ASM 관리 명령어 실습을 하겠습니다.
SYSASM 권한의 유저를 만들고 조회합니다.

```
$ orapwd file=$ORACLE_HOME/dbs/orapw+ASM entries=5 force=y   -- SYS암호세팅 (최초 1회)
$ sqlplus / as sysasm
SQL>CREATE USER new_user IDENTIFIED by new_user_passwd ;
SQL>GRANT SYSASM TO new_user ;
SQL>CONNECT new_user AS SYSASM ;
SQL> conn /as sysasm
SQL> select USERNAME,SYSDBA,SYSOPER,SYSASM FROM v$pwfile_users ;
```

```
[+ASM]yspark-linux:/oracle/grid12/bin_grid/dbs> orapwd file=orapw+ASM entries=5 force=y
Enter password for SYS:
[+ASM]yspark-linux:/oracle/grid12/bin_grid/dbs> sqlplus "/as sysasm"

SQL*Plus: Release 12.2.0.1.0 Production on Tue Jan 2 10:14:16 2018

Copyright (c) 1982, 2016, Oracle.  All rights reserved.


Connected to:
Oracle Database 12c Enterprise Edition Release 12.2.0.1.0 - 64bit Production

SQL> CREATE USER new_user IDENTIFIED by new_user_passwd ;

User created.

SQL> GRANT SYSASM TO new_user ;

Grant succeeded.

SQL> CONNECT new_user AS SYSASM ;
Enter password:
Connected.
SQL> conn /as sysasm
Connected.
```

```
SQL> conn /as sysasm
Connected.
SQL> select USERNAME,SYSDBA,SYSOPER,SYSASM FROM v$pwfile_users ;

USERNAME   SYSDBA          SYSOPER         SYSASM
---------- --------------- --------------- ---------------
SYS        TRUE            TRUE            FALSE
NEW_USER   FALSE           FALSE           TRUE

SQL>
```

2 신규 ASM Disk Group 생성

이제 신규 Disk Group을 생성해야 합니다. 본 실습은 Grid Infrastructure를 설치 후 클러스터 환경이 구성된 상태에서 실습합니다. Grid Infrastructure 설치 및 CRS 구성 방법은 본 장에서는 생략합니다.

먼저 현재 만들어진 Disk Group을 조회합니다.

```
$ sqlplus / as sysasm
SQL>SELECT NAME,TOTAL_MB,FREE_MB,USABLE_FILE_MB FROM V$ASM_DISKGROUP ;
```

```
[+ASM]yspark-linux:/oracle/grid12/bin_grid/dbs> sqlplus / as sysasm

SQL*Plus: Release 12.2.0.1.0 Production on Tue Jan 2 10:25:54 2018

Copyright (c) 1982, 2016, Oracle.  All rights reserved.


Connected to:
Oracle Database 12c Enterprise Edition Release 12.2.0.1.0 - 64bit Production

SQL> COLUMN NAME FOR A15
SQL> SELECT NAME,TOTAL_MB,FREE_MB,USABLE_FILE_MB FROM V$ASM_DISKGROUP ;

NAME              TOTAL_MB    FREE_MB USABLE_FILE_MB
--------------- ---------- ---------- --------------
CRS_DATA             48600      48512          48512

SQL> 
```

신규 Disk Group에 사용할 ASM DISK를 조회합니다.

```
SQL> CONNECT / AS SYSASM
SQL> SELECT PATH, NAME, MOUNT_STATUS, HEADER_STATUS, MODE_STATUS, STATE, TOTAL_MB FROM
V$ASM_DISK ORDER BY 1 ;
```

```
SQL> CONNECT / AS SYSASM
Connected.
SQL> SELECT PATH, NAME, MOUNT_STATUS, HEADER_STATUS, MODE_STATUS, STATE, TOTAL_MB FROM V$ASM_DISK ORDER BY 1 ;

PATH                 NAME             MOUNT_STATUS          HEADER_STATUS MODE_STATUS          STATE      TOTAL_MB
-------------------- ---------------- --------------------- ------------- -------------------- ---------- ----------
/dev/sdb1            CRS_DATA_0000    CACHED                MEMBER        ONLINE               NORMAL          48600
/dev/sdb2                             CLOSED                PROVISIONED   ONLINE               NORMAL              0
/dev/sdb3                             CLOSED                PROVISIONED   ONLINE               NORMAL              0
/dev/sdb5                             CLOSED                PROVISIONED   ONLINE               NORMAL              0
/dev/sdb6                             CLOSED                PROVISIONED   ONLINE               NORMAL              0

SQL> 
```

V$ASM_DISK 뷰에는 MOUNT_STATUS, HEADER_STATUS, MODE_STATUS, STATE의 총 4가지 상태 확인 컬럼이 있습니다.

ASM DISK 상태 컬럼 의미입니다.

❶ **MOUNT_STATUS** : GROUP MOUNT에 관련된 인스턴스 별 디스크의 상태정보입니다.

- MISSING : ASM 메타데이터에는 디스크가 ASM Disk Group의 일부로 표기되어 있으나, 실제로는 스토리지 시스템 내에 표기된 이름의 디스크가 존재하지 않는 상태
- CLOSED : 스토리지상에 디스크는 존재하나 ASM에서 디스크로의 ACCESS가 불가한 상태
- OPENED : 스토리지상에 디스크가 존재하고 ASM에서 디스크로의 ACCESS 되고 있는 상태로 현재 데이터베이스 인스턴스가 사용 중인 DISKGROUP에 속한 디스크
- CACHED : 스토리지상에 디스크가 존재하고 ASM에서 ACCESS되고 있는 상태로, 마운트된 DISKGROUP에 속한 ASM 인스턴스
- IGNORED : 시스템 상에 디스크가 존재하나, ASM으로부터 무시되고 있는 상태
- CLOSING : 종료 중인 디스크 상태

❷ **HEADER_STATUS** : DISCOVERY에 의해 보여지는 인스턴스 별 디스크의 상태정보입니다.

- UNKNOWN : ASM 인스턴스에 의해 디스크헤더가 아직 읽혀진 적이 없는 상태
- CANDIDATE : 디스크가 아직 DISKGROUP의 멤버가 아니며, ALTER DISKGRUOP 문으로 DISKGROUP에 추가될 수 있는 상태

- INCOMPATIBLE : 디스크 헤더의 Version이 ASM 소프트웨어 Version과 호환되지 않은 상태
- PROVISIONED : 디스크가 아직 DISKGROUP의 멤버가 아니며, ALTER DISKGRUOP 문으로 DISKGROUP에 추가될 수 있으며. CANDIDATE 상태와는 다르며, 관리자가 ASM에 적합한 디스크로 만들기 위해 플랫폼에 기반한 특정 액션이 가해진 상태
- MEMBER : 현재 존재하는 DISKGROUP의 포함된 상태
- FORMER : 디스크가 한 때 DISKGROUP의 멤버였다가, 해당 DISKGROUP에서 완전히 DROP된 상태로 재사용 가능
- CONFLICT : 충돌이 발생해 ASM 디스크에 마운트 되지 못한 상태
- FOREIGN : ASM이 아닌 다른 오라클 제품에 의해 생성된 데이터를 포함하고 있는 디스크(datafile, logfile, ocr 등)

❸ **MODE_STATUS : 디스크에 어떤 종류의 I/O 요청되고 있는지 전반적인 상태를 확인합니다.**
- ONLINE : 디스크가 ONLINE이며 정상적으로 동작하는 상태
- OFFLINE : 디스크가 OFFLINE이며 정상적으로 ACCESS되지 않는 상태

❹ **STATE : DISK GROUP에 대한 DISK의 전반적인 상태를 체크합니다.**
- UNKNOWN : 아직 mount되지 않은 경우의 디스크
- NORMAL : 디스크가 온라인이고 정상적으로 동작 가능
- ADDING : 디스크가 Disk Group에 추가되고 있는 중이며, 스트라이핑 Rebalancing 중인 상태
- DROPPING : 디스크가 명령으로 OFFLINE이 되는 중이며, 데이터를 DISKGRUOP 내의 다른 디스크로 옮기는 Rebalancing 중인 상태
- HUNG : DROP될 디스크로부터 데이터를 Relocate할 공간이 불충분하여 Drop 오퍼레이션을 수행할 수 없는 상태
- FORCING : 디스크가 데이터를 offload 하지 않고 DISK GROUP으로부터 제거되고 있는 상태. 데이터는 Redundant 카피로부터 recover되는 상태
- DROPPED : 디스크가 DISK GROUP에서 완전히 제거된 상태

이제 상태를 확인 후 현재 다른 Disk Group에서 사용 중이지 않고 사용가능한 디스크로 신규 디스크 그룹을 생성합니다.

먼저 추가 할 디스크의 OS 권한이 Grid Infrastructure 설치 유저에게 부여되어 있는지 확인합니다.

```
$ cd /dev/
$ ls -al <디스크 디바이스 이름>
```

```
[root@yspark-linux dev]# ls -al sdb*
brw-rw---- 1 root      disk 8, 16 Dec 28 17:20 sdb
brw-rw---- 1 oracle12 dba  8, 17 Jan  2 12:35 sdb1
brw-rw---- 1 oracle12 dba  8, 18 Jan  2 10:44 sdb2
brw-rw---- 1 oracle12 dba  8, 19 Jan  2 10:44 sdb3
brw-rw---- 1 oracle12 dba  8, 20 Jan  2 10:44 sdb4
brw-rw---- 1 oracle12 dba  8, 21 Jan  2 10:44 sdb5
brw-rw---- 1 oracle12 dba  8, 22 Jan  2 10:44 sdb6
[root@yspark-linux dev]#
```

FRA 디스크 그룹을 할당된 디스크 2개를 가지고 Normal Redundancy로 생성해 봅니다.

```
SQL> CONNECT / AS SYSASM
SQL> CREATE DISKGROUP FRA NORMAL REDUNDANCY
  2  FAILGROUP FRA1 DISK '/<디스크 경로/1번 디스크 이름>'
  3  FAILGROUP FAR2 DISK '/<디스크 경로/2번 디스크 이름>' ;
```

```
SQL> CONNECT / AS SYSASM
Connected.
SQL> CREATE DISKGROUP FRA NORMAL REDUNDANCY
  2  FAILGROUP FRA1 DISK '/dev/sdb2'
  3  FAILGROUP FAR2 DISK '/dev/sdb3' ;

Diskgroup created.

SQL>
```

Disk Group을 생성하고 정상적으로 생성되었는지 Disk Group과 Disk 상태를 확인합니다.

```
SQL> SELECT NAME, TYPE, TOTAL_MB, FREE_MB, USABLE_FILE_MB FROM V$ASM_DISKGROUP ;
SQL> SELECT PATH, NAME, MOUNT_STATUS, HEADER_STATUS, MODE_STATUS, STATE, TOTAL_MB  FROM
V$ASM_DISK ORDER BY 1 ;
```

```
SQL> SELECT NAME, TYPE, TOTAL_MB, FREE_MB, USABLE_FILE_MB FROM V$ASM_DISKGROUP ;

NAME                 TYPE                 TOTAL_MB    FREE_MB USABLE_FILE_MB
-------------------- -------------------- ---------- ---------- --------------
CRS_DATA             EXTERN                  48600      48512          48512
FRA                  NORMAL                  97204      97098          48549

SQL> SELECT PATH, NAME, MOUNT_STATUS, HEADER_STATUS, MODE_STATUS, STATE, TOTAL_MB  FROM V$ASM_DISK ORDER BY 1 ;

PATH       NAME                 MOUNT_STAT HEADER_STATUS        MODE_STA STATE        TOTAL_MB
---------- -------------------- ---------- -------------------- -------- ---------- ----------
/dev/sdb1  CRS_DATA_0000        CACHED     MEMBER               ONLINE   NORMAL          48600
/dev/sdb2  FRA_0000             CACHED     MEMBER               ONLINE   NORMAL          48602
/dev/sdb3  FRA_0001             CACHED     MEMBER               ONLINE   NORMAL          48602
/dev/sdb5                       CLOSED     PROVISIONED          ONLINE   NORMAL              0
/dev/sdb6                       CLOSED     PROVISIONED          ONLINE   NORMAL              0

SQL>
```

V$ASM_DISKGROUP 뷰에 새로 만든 Disk Group인 FRA이 존재하며 TYPE은 NORMAL로 되어있습니다.
V$ASM_DISK 뷰에 해당 디스크 디바이스의 HEADER_STATUS는 MEMBER 상태이고 MOUNT_STATUS는 CACHED로 바뀌었습니다.

3 기존 ASM Disk Group 삭제

FRA 영역은 Normal Redundancy 형태가 아닌 External Redundancy 형태로 만들어도 되는 것을 확인하고, 기존 Disk Group을 삭제하고 External Redundancy 형태의 Disk Group으로 생성합니다.

현재 만들어진 FRA Disk Group을 삭제합니다.

```
SQL> CONNECT / AS SYSASM
SQL> DROP DISKGROUP FRA ;
```

```
SQL> CONNECT / AS SYSASM
Connected.
SQL> DROP DISKGROUP FRA ;

Diskgroup dropped.

SQL>
```

삭제가 잘 되었는지 확인합니다.

```
SQL> SELECT NAME, TYPE, TOTAL_MB, FREE_MB, USABLE_FILE_MB FROM V$ASM_DISKGROUP ;
SQL> SELECT PATH, NAME, MOUNT_STATUS, HEADER_STATUS, MODE_STATUS, STATE, TOTAL_MB  FROM
V$ASM_DISK ORDER BY 1 ;
```

```
SQL> SELECT NAME, TYPE, TOTAL_MB, FREE_MB, USABLE_FILE_MB FROM V$ASM_DISKGROUP ;

NAME                 TYPE                 TOTAL_MB    FREE_MB USABLE_FILE_MB
-------------------- ------------------ ---------- ---------- --------------
CRS_DATA             EXTERN                  48600      48512          48512

SQL> SELECT PATH, NAME, MOUNT_STATUS, HEADER_STATUS, MODE_STATUS, STATE, TOTAL_MB  FROM V$ASM_DISK ORDER BY 1 ;

PATH       NAME                 MOUNT_STAT HEADER_STATUS        MODE_STA STATE        TOTAL_MB
---------- -------------------- ---------- -------------------- -------- ---------- ----------
/dev/sdb1  CRS_DATA_0000        CACHED     MEMBER               ONLINE   NORMAL          48600
/dev/sdb2                       CLOSED     FORMER               ONLINE   NORMAL              0
/dev/sdb3                       CLOSED     FORMER               ONLINE   NORMAL              0
/dev/sdb5                       CLOSED     PROVISIONED          ONLINE   NORMAL              0
/dev/sdb6                       CLOSED     PROVISIONED          ONLINE   NORMAL              0

SQL>
```

이전 신규 Disk Group 생성 전의 PROVISIONED 상태에서 FORMER 상태로 확인 가능합니다. 앞에서 설명하였지만 FORMER 상태는 ASM DISK로 한번 추가 되었다가 삭제된 상태로 다시 사용가능한 상태입니다.

External Redundancy 형태의 Disk Group의 FRA Disk Group을 생성합니다.

```
SQL> CONNECT / AS SYSASM
SQL> CREATE DISKGROUP FRA EXTERNAL REDUNDANCY DISK '/<디스크 경로/디스크 이름>' ;
```

```
SQL> CONNECT / AS SYSASM
Connected.
SQL> CREATE DISKGROUP FRA EXTERNAL REDUNDANCY DISK '/dev/sdb5' ;

Diskgroup created.

SQL>
```

Disk Group 생성 후 Disk Group과 Disk 상태를 확인합니다.

```
SQL> SELECT NAME, TYPE, TOTAL_MB, FREE_MB, USABLE_FILE_MB FROM V$ASM_DISKGROUP ;
SQL> SELECT PATH, NAME, MOUNT_STATUS, HEADER_STATUS, MODE_STATUS, STATE, TOTAL_MB  FROM
V$ASM_DISK ORDER BY 1 ;
```

```
SQL> SELECT NAME, TYPE, TOTAL_MB, FREE_MB, USABLE_FILE_MB FROM V$ASM_DISKGROUP ;

NAME                 TYPE                 TOTAL_MB    FREE_MB USABLE_FILE_MB
-------------------- ------------------ ---------- ---------- --------------
CRS_DATA             EXTERN                  48600      48512          48512
FRA                  EXTERN                  97652      97600          97600

SQL> SELECT PATH, NAME, MOUNT_STATUS, HEADER_STATUS, MODE_STATUS, STATE, TOTAL_MB  FROM V$ASM_DISK ORDER BY 1 ;

PATH       NAME                 MOUNT_STAT HEADER_STATUS        MODE_STA STATE        TOTAL_MB
---------- -------------------- ---------- -------------------- -------- ---------- ----------
/dev/sdb1  CRS_DATA_0000        CACHED     MEMBER               ONLINE   NORMAL          48600
/dev/sdb2                       CLOSED     FORMER               ONLINE   NORMAL              0
/dev/sdb3                       CLOSED     FORMER               ONLINE   NORMAL              0
/dev/sdb5  FRA_0000             CACHED     MEMBER               ONLINE   NORMAL          97652
/dev/sdb6                       CLOSED     PROVISIONED          ONLINE   NORMAL              0

SQL>
```

4 ASM Disk Group에 Disk 추가 / 삭제

이제 Disk Group에 Disk를 추가합니다.

신규 Disk Group인 REDO Disk Group을 EXTERNAL REDUNDANCY 타입으로 생성합니다.

```
SQL> CONNECT / AS SYSASM
SQL> CREATE DISKGROUP REDO EXTERNAL REDUNDANCY DISK '</디스크경로/디스크이름>';
```

```
SQL> CONNECT / AS SYSASM
Connected.
SQL> CREATE DISKGROUP REDO EXTERNAL REDUNDANCY DISK '/dev/sdb2' ;

Diskgroup created.

SQL>
```

Disk Group 생성 후 Disk Group과 Disk 상태를 확인합니다.

```
SQL> SELECT NAME, TYPE, TOTAL_MB, FREE_MB, USABLE_FILE_MB FROM V$ASM_DISKGROUP ;
SQL> SELECT PATH, NAME, MOUNT_STATUS, HEADER_STATUS, MODE_STATUS, STATE, TOTAL_MB  FROM
V$ASM_DISK ORDER BY 1 ;
```

```
SQL> CONNECT / AS SYSASM
Connected.
SQL> SELECT NAME, TYPE, TOTAL_MB, FREE_MB, USABLE_FILE_MB FROM V$ASM_DISKGROUP ;

NAME                 TYPE                 TOTAL_MB    FREE_MB USABLE_FILE_MB
-------------------- ------------------ ---------- ---------- --------------
CRS_DATA             EXTERN                  48600      48512          48512
FRA                  EXTERN                  97652      97600          97600
REDO                 EXTERN                  48602      48550          48550

SQL> SELECT PATH, NAME, MOUNT_STATUS, HEADER_STATUS, MODE_STATUS, STATE, TOTAL_MB  FROM V$ASM_DISK ORDER BY 1 ;

PATH       NAME                 MOUNT_STAT HEADER_STATUS        MODE_STA STATE        TOTAL_MB
---------- -------------------- ---------- -------------------- -------- ---------- ----------
/dev/sdb1  CRS_DATA_0000        CACHED     MEMBER               ONLINE   NORMAL          48600
/dev/sdb2  VOL2                 CACHED     MEMBER               ONLINE   NORMAL          48602
/dev/sdb3                       CLOSED     FORMER               ONLINE   NORMAL              0
/dev/sdb5  FRA_0000             CACHED     MEMBER               ONLINE   NORMAL          97652
/dev/sdb6                       CLOSED     PROVISIONED          ONLINE   NORMAL              0

SQL>
```

신규 DISK를 새로 만든 REDO Disk Group에 추가합니다.

```
SQL> CONNECT / AS SYSASM
SQL>ALTER DISKGROUP REDO ADD DISK '</디스크경로/디스크이름>' NAME VOL3 ;
```

```
SQL> CONNECT / AS SYSASM
Connected.
SQL> ALTER DISKGROUP REDO ADD DISK '/dev/sdb3' NAME VOL3 ;

Diskgroup altered.

SQL>
```

Disk Group에 Disk가 잘 추가되었는지 확인합니다.

```
SQL> SELECT NAME, TYPE, TOTAL_MB, FREE_MB, USABLE_FILE_MB FROM V$ASM_DISKGROUP ;
SQL> SELECT PATH, NAME, MOUNT_STATUS, HEADER_STATUS, MODE_STATUS, STATE, TOTAL_MB  FROM
V$ASM_DISK ORDER BY 1 ;
```

```
SQL> SELECT NAME, TYPE, TOTAL_MB, FREE_MB, USABLE_FILE_MB FROM V$ASM_DISKGROUP ;

NAME                 TYPE                 TOTAL_MB    FREE_MB USABLE_FILE_MB
-------------------- ------------------ ---------- ---------- --------------
CRS_DATA             EXTERN                  48600      48512          48512
FRA                  EXTERN                  97652      97600          97600
REDO                 EXTERN                  97204      97150          97150

SQL> SELECT PATH, NAME, MOUNT_STATUS, HEADER_STATUS, MODE_STATUS, STATE, TOTAL_MB  FROM V$ASM_DISK ORDER BY 1 ;

PATH       NAME                 MOUNT_STAT HEADER_STATUS        MODE_STA STATE        TOTAL_MB
---------- -------------------- ---------- -------------------- -------- ---------- ----------
/dev/sdb1  CRS_DATA_0000        CACHED     MEMBER               ONLINE   NORMAL          48600
/dev/sdb2  VOL2                 CACHED     MEMBER               ONLINE   NORMAL          48602
/dev/sdb3  VOL3                 CACHED     MEMBER               ONLINE   NORMAL          48602
/dev/sdb5  FRA_0000             CACHED     MEMBER               ONLINE   NORMAL          97652
/dev/sdb6                       CLOSED     PROVISIONED          ONLINE   NORMAL              0

SQL>
```

Disk Group의 사이즈는 늘었고 디스크는 잘 추가되었습니다.

이번에는 추가한 Disk가 아닌 기존에 있던 VOL2 Disk를 삭제합니다.

```
SQL> CONNECT / AS SYSASM
SQL>ALTER DISKGROUP REDO DROP DISK VOL2 ;
```

```
SQL> CONNECT / AS SYSASM
Connected.
SQL> ALTER DISKGROUP REDO DROP DISK VOL2 ;

Diskgroup altered.

SQL>
```

Disk Group에 Disk가 잘 삭제되었는지 확인합니다.

```
SQL> SELECT NAME, TYPE, TOTAL_MB, FREE_MB, USABLE_FILE_MB FROM V$ASM_DISKGROUP ;
SQL> SELECT PATH, NAME, MOUNT_STATUS, HEADER_STATUS, MODE_STATUS, STATE, TOTAL_MB  FROM
V$ASM_DISK ORDER BY 1 ;
```

```
SQL> SELECT NAME, TYPE, TOTAL_MB, FREE_MB, USABLE_FILE_MB FROM V$ASM_DISKGROUP ;

NAME                 TYPE                 TOTAL_MB    FREE_MB USABLE_FILE_MB
-------------------- ------------------ ---------- ---------- --------------
CRS_DATA             EXTERN                  48600      48512          48512
FRA                  EXTERN                  97652      97600          97600
REDO                 EXTERN                  48602      48550          48550

SQL> SELECT PATH, NAME, MOUNT_STATUS, HEADER_STATUS, MODE_STATUS, STATE, TOTAL_MB  FROM V$ASM_DISK ORDER BY 1 ;

PATH       NAME                 MOUNT_STAT HEADER_STATUS        MODE_STA STATE      TOTAL_MB
---------- -------------------- ---------- -------------------- -------- -------- ----------
/dev/sdb1  CRS_DATA_0000        CACHED     MEMBER               ONLINE   NORMAL        48600
/dev/sdb2                       CLOSED     FORMER               ONLINE   NORMAL            0
/dev/sdb3  VOL3                 CACHED     MEMBER               ONLINE   NORMAL        48602
/dev/sdb5  FRA_0000             CACHED     MEMBER               ONLINE   NORMAL        97652
/dev/sdb6                       CLOSED     PROVISIONED          ONLINE   NORMAL            0

SQL>
```

5 ASM Disk Group Rebalancing

Chapter 7 Disk Group 편에서 설명한 Rebalancing을 모니터링 방법을 알아보겠습니다. 주요 기능의 하나인 ASM Disk Group에 디스크를 추가하면 재배치가 일어납니다.

용량 큰 디스크를 추가하면서 Dynamic Rebalancing을 수행하는 ARBn 프로세스의 개수를 1개로 바꿔서 Rebalancing 지연이 일어나도록 수행 후 Rebalancing 모니터링을 합니다.

```
SQL>ALTER DISKGROUP REDO ADD DISK '/dev/sdb6' NAME VOL6 REBALANCE POWER 1 ;
SQL>SELECT GROUP_NUMBER,OPERATION,PASS,STATE,POWER,EST_MINUTES FROM V$ASM_OPERATION ;
```

```
SQL> ALTER DISKGROUP REDO ADD DISK '/dev/sdb6' NAME VOL6 REBALANCE POWER 1 ;

Diskgroup altered.

SQL> SELECT GROUP_NUMBER,OPERATION,PASS,STATE,POWER,EST_MINUTES FROM V$ASM_OPERATION ;

GROUP_NUMBER OPERATION       PASS                      STATE           POWER EST_MINUTES
------------ --------------- ------------------------- ---------- ---------- -----------
           3 REBAL           COMPACT                   WAIT                1           0
           3 REBAL           REBALANCE                 RUN                 1           0
           3 REBAL           REBUILD                   DONE                1           0
```

V$ASM_OPERATION 뷰는 재배치를 모니터링하는 뷰입니다. 실제 Disk Group에 명령을 수행 후 프롬프트가 떨어졌지만 내부적으로 디스크 재배치 수행 중인 상태를 확인합니다. 연속적으로 V$ASM_OPERATION 뷰를 조회합니다.

```
SQL>SELECT GROUP_NUMBER,OPERATION,PASS,STATE,POWER,EST_MINUTES FROM V$ASM_OPERATION ;
```

```
SQL> SELECT GROUP_NUMBER,OPERATION,PASS,STATE,POWER,EST_MINUTES FROM V$ASM_OPERATION ;

GROUP_NUMBER OPERATION       PASS                         STATE          POWER EST_MINUTES
------------ --------------- ---------------------------- ---------- ---------- -----------
           3 REBAL           COMPACT                      WAIT               1           0
           3 REBAL           REBALANCE                    RUN                1           0
           3 REBAL           REBUILD                      DONE               1           0

SQL> /

GROUP_NUMBER OPERATION       PASS                         STATE          POWER EST_MINUTES
------------ --------------- ---------------------------- ---------- ---------- -----------
           3 REBAL           COMPACT                      WAIT               1           0
           3 REBAL           REBALANCE                    RUN                1           0
           3 REBAL           REBUILD                      DONE               1           0

SQL> /

GROUP_NUMBER OPERATION       PASS                         STATE          POWER EST_MINUTES
------------ --------------- ---------------------------- ---------- ---------- -----------
           3 REBAL           COMPACT                      WAIT               1           0
           3 REBAL           REBALANCE                    RUN                1           0
           3 REBAL           REBUILD                      DONE               1           0

SQL> /

GROUP_NUMBER OPERATION       PASS                         STATE          POWER EST_MINUTES
------------ --------------- ---------------------------- ---------- ---------- -----------
           3 REBAL           COMPACT                      WAIT               1           0
           3 REBAL           REBALANCE                    RUN                1           0
           3 REBAL           REBUILD                      DONE               1           0

SQL> /

GROUP_NUMBER OPERATION       PASS                         STATE          POWER EST_MINUTES
------------ --------------- ---------------------------- ---------- ---------- -----------
           3 REBAL           COMPACT                      REAP               1           0
           3 REBAL           REBALANCE                    DONE               1           0
           3 REBAL           REBUILD                      DONE               1           0

SQL> /

GROUP_NUMBER OPERATION       PASS                         STATE          POWER EST_MINUTES
------------ --------------- ---------------------------- ---------- ---------- -----------
           3 REBAL           COMPACT                      REAP               1           0
           3 REBAL           REBALANCE                    DONE               1           0
           3 REBAL           REBUILD                      DONE               1           0

SQL> /

GROUP_NUMBER OPERATION       PASS                         STATE          POWER EST_MINUTES
------------ --------------- ---------------------------- ---------- ---------- -----------
           3 REBAL           COMPACT                      REAP               1           0
           3 REBAL           REBALANCE                    DONE               1           0
           3 REBAL           REBUILD                      DONE               1           0

SQL> /

no rows selected

SQL> ▮
```

시간이 지날수록 Rebalancing STATE 상태가 변경 되는 것을 확인할 수 있고 Rebalancing 완료 이후에는 조회가 안 되는 것을 볼 수 있습니다.

추가한 디스크를 삭제하면서 ARBn 프로세스의 개수를 11개로 바꿔서 빠른 Rebalancing이 일어나도록 수행하고 Rebalancing 모니터링을 합니다.

```
SQL> ALTER DISKGROUP REDO DROP DISK VOL6 REBALANCE POWER 11 ;
SQL> SELECT GROUP_NUMBER,OPERATION,PASS,STATE,POWER,EST_MINUTES FROM V$ASM_OPERATION ;
```

```
SQL> ALTER DISKGROUP REDO DROP DISK VOL6 REBALANCE POWER 11 ;

Diskgroup altered.

SQL> SELECT GROUP_NUMBER,OPERATION,PASS,STATE,POWER,EST_MINUTES FROM V$ASM_OPERATION ;

GROUP_NUMBER OPERATION       PASS                      STATE          POWER EST_MINUTES
------------ --------------- ------------------------- ---------- ---------- -----------
           3 REBAL           COMPACT                   WAIT              11           0
           3 REBAL           REBALANCE                 RUN               11           0
           3 REBAL           REBUILD                   DONE              11           0

SQL> SELECT GROUP_NUMBER,OPERATION,PASS,STATE,POWER,EST_MINUTES FROM V$ASM_OPERATION ;

GROUP_NUMBER OPERATION       PASS                      STATE          POWER EST_MINUTES
------------ --------------- ------------------------- ---------- ---------- -----------
           3 REBAL           COMPACT                   WAIT              11           0
           3 REBAL           REBALANCE                 RUN               11           0
           3 REBAL           REBUILD                   DONE              11           0

SQL> SELECT GROUP_NUMBER,OPERATION,PASS,STATE,POWER,EST_MINUTES FROM V$ASM_OPERATION ;

GROUP_NUMBER OPERATION       PASS                      STATE          POWER EST_MINUTES
------------ --------------- ------------------------- ---------- ---------- -----------
           3 REBAL           COMPACT                   WAIT              11           0
           3 REBAL           REBALANCE                 RUN               11           0
           3 REBAL           REBUILD                   DONE              11           0

SQL> SELECT GROUP_NUMBER,OPERATION,PASS,STATE,POWER,EST_MINUTES FROM V$ASM_OPERATION ;

GROUP_NUMBER OPERATION       PASS                      STATE          POWER EST_MINUTES
------------ --------------- ------------------------- ---------- ---------- -----------
           3 REBAL           COMPACT                   WAIT              11           0
           3 REBAL           REBALANCE                 RUN               11           0
           3 REBAL           REBUILD                   DONE              11           0

SQL> SELECT GROUP_NUMBER,OPERATION,PASS,STATE,POWER,EST_MINUTES FROM V$ASM_OPERATION ;

no rows selected

SQL> ▮
```

더 빠른 Rebalancing이 되었습니다. 하지만 서버의 리소스를 더 많이 할당하게 됩니다. 실제 운영환경에서 수행 시 적절한 POWER 값으로 작업해야 합니다.

ASM Disk 장애 상황 시 : Fast Mirror Resync(DISK_REPAIR_TIME)

Fast Mirror Resync가 지원되지 않는 Version에서는 ASM redundancy를 사용 시 Disk가 순간 failure(케이블, 전원, host bus adaptor, disk controller의 failure)로 Offline이 되면 ASM은 Disk Group으로부터 해당 디스크를 Drop 시키고 할당된 extents를 Member로 구성 된 다른 ASM Disk에 Re-Creating합니다. Oracle 11G 부터 출시된 ASM Fast Mirror Resync로 일시적인 disk의 failure 시 Resynchronize에 필요한 시간을 많이 줄였습니다. Disk가 순간 failure로 인하여 Offline되면 ASM은 해당 Extent를 추적하여 Disk가 복구된 후 변경된 extent만 Resync합니다.

Oracle Grid Infrastructure 11g부터 전체 디스크를 복사하는 대신 디스크의 손상된 부분만을 복구하는 작업이 수행됩니다. 디스크그룹 속성인 disk_repair_time을 사용하여 ASM 인스턴스가 디스크 그룹에서 디스크를 drop 처리하기 전에 얼마만큼의 에러를 허용하는지 결정하게 됩니다.

ASM Disk Group의 disk_repair_time을 조회합니다.

```
SQL> CONNECT / AS SYSASM
SQL>SELECT A.NAME , A.DATABASE_COMPATIBILITY , B.NAME , B.VALUE
    FROM V$ASM_DISKGROUP A , V$ASM_ATTRIBUTE B
  WHERE A.GROUP_NUMBER=B.GROUP_NUMBER
    AND B.NAME = 'disk_repair_time'
  ORDER BY A.NAME ;
```

```
SQL> SELECT A.NAME , A.DATABASE_COMPATIBILITY , B.NAME , B.VALUE
  2  FROM V$ASM_DISKGROUP A , V$ASM_ATTRIBUTE B
  3  WHERE A.GROUP_NUMBER=B.GROUP_NUMBER
  4  AND B.NAME = 'disk_repair_time'
  5  ORDER BY A.NAME ;

NAME                 DATABASE_COMPATIBILITY         NAME                 VALUE
-------------------- ------------------------------ -------------------- --------------------
CRS_DATA             10.1.0.0.0                     disk_repair_time     3.6h
DB_DATA              11.2.0.2.0                     disk_repair_time     3.6h
FRA                  10.1.0.0.0                     disk_repair_time     3.6h

SQL>
```

ASM disk path fail 시, ASM disk는 offline되지만 DISK_REPAIR_TIME에 설정한 값에 해당하는 시간이 지나기 전에는 Dropped되지는 않습니다. 이 값이 설정되면 수리를 완료한 후 resynchronize할 수 있을 때까지 ASM은 기다립니다.

Resync 시 많은 리소스가 추가 되어서 이 현상을 막기 위해서는 빠른 Disk 교체를 해주어야 하는데 신규 Disk의 교체 시간이 늦을 경우 기본인 3.6시간의 값을 변경해서 시간을 버는 방법이 있습니다.

```
SQL> CONNECT / AS SYSASM
SQL> ALTER DISKGROUP <장애 Disk Group> SET ATTRIBUTE 'disk_repair_time'='10h' ;
```

```
SQL> CONNECT / AS SYSASM
Connected.
SQL> ALTER DISKGROUP DB_DATA SET ATTRIBUTE 'disk_repair_time'='10h' ;

Diskgroup altered.

SQL> SELECT A.NAME , A.DATABASE_COMPATIBILITY , B.NAME , B.VALUE
  2  FROM V$ASM_DISKGROUP A , V$ASM_ATTRIBUTE B
  3  WHERE A.GROUP_NUMBER=B.GROUP_NUMBER
  4  AND B.NAME = 'disk_repair_time'
  5  ORDER BY A.NAME ;

NAME                 DATABASE_COMPATIBILITY         NAME                 VALUE
-------------------- ------------------------------ -------------------- --------------------
CRS_DATA             10.1.0.0.0                     disk_repair_time     3.6h
DB_DATA              11.2.0.2.0                     disk_repair_time     10h
FRA                  10.1.0.0.0                     disk_repair_time     3.6h

SQL>
```

Disk Group의 Repair Time 변경 기능은 11.1.0.0.0부터 나온 기능이므로 이하 버전 호환성의 Disk Group에서는 사용할 수 없습니다. ORA-15283 에러가 발생합니다. Disk Group의 버전 호환성을 변경해야 합니다.

```
SQL> CONNECT / AS SYSASM
Connected.
SQL> ALTER DISKGROUP FRA SET ATTRIBUTE 'disk_repair_time'='10h' ;
ALTER DISKGROUP FRA SET ATTRIBUTE 'disk_repair_time'='10h'
*
ERROR at line 1:
ORA-15032: not all alterations performed
ORA-15242: could not set attribute disk_repair_time
ORA-15283: ASM operation requires compatible.rdbms of 11.1.0.0.0 or higher

SQL>
```

6 ASM Disk Group 버전 호환성 변경

ASM Disk Group의 호환성 변경을 확인해 보겠습니다.

ASK Disk Group의 호환 여부를 조회합니다.

```
SQL>SELECT NAME, TYPE, TOTAL_MB,
FREE_MB, USABLE_FILE_MB,COMPATIBILITY,DATABASE_COMPATIBILITY FROM V$ASM_DISKGROUP ;
```

```
SQL> SELECT NAME, TYPE, TOTAL_MB, FREE_MB, USABLE_FILE_MB,COMPATIBILITY,DATABASE_COMPATIBILITY FROM V$ASM_DISKGROUP ;

NAME                 TYPE               TOTAL_MB    FREE_MB USABLE_FILE_MB COMPATIBILITY     DATABASE_COMPATIBILITY
-------------------- ------------------ ---------- ---------- -------------- ----------------- ------------------------------
CRS_DATA             EXTERN                 48600      48512          48512 12.2.0.1.0        10.1.0.0.0
FRA                  EXTERN                 97652      97600          97600 11.2.0.2.0        10.1.0.0.0
REDO                 EXTERN                 48602      48550          48550 11.2.0.2.0        10.1.0.0.0

SQL>
```

REDO Disk Group의 ASM COMPATIBILITY를 12.2.0.1로 변경합니다.

```
SQL> ALTER DISKGROUP REDO SET ATTRIBUTE 'compatible.asm'='12.2.0.1' ;
SQL> SELECT NAME, TYPE, TOTAL_MB, FREE_MB,
USABLE_FILE_MB,COMPATIBILITY,DATABASE_COMPATIBILITY FROM V$ASM_DISKGROUP ;
```

```
SQL> ALTER DISKGROUP REDO SET ATTRIBUTE 'compatible.asm'='12.2.0.1' ;

Diskgroup altered.

SQL> SELECT NAME, TYPE, TOTAL_MB, FREE_MB, USABLE_FILE_MB,COMPATIBILITY,DATABASE_COMPATIBILITY FROM V$ASM_DISKGROUP ;

NAME                 TYPE               TOTAL_MB    FREE_MB USABLE_FILE_MB COMPATIBILITY     DATABASE_COMPATIBILITY
-------------------- ------------------ ---------- ---------- -------------- ----------------- ------------------------------
CRS_DATA             EXTERN                 48600      48512          48512 12.2.0.1.0        10.1.0.0.0
FRA                  EXTERN                 97652      97600          97600 11.2.0.2.0        10.1.0.0.0
REDO                 EXTERN                 48602      48548          48548 12.2.0.1.0        10.1.0.0.0

SQL>
```

FRA Disk Group의 DBMS COMPATIBILITY를 12.2.0.1로 변경합니다.

```
SQL> ALTER DISKGROUP FRA SET ATTRIBUTE 'compatible.rdbms'='12.2.0.1' ;
```

```
SQL> ALTER DISKGROUP FRA SET ATTRIBUTE 'compatible.rdbms'='12.2.0.1' ;
ALTER DISKGROUP FRA SET ATTRIBUTE 'compatible.rdbms'='12.2.0.1'
*
ERROR at line 1:
ORA-15032: not all alterations performed
ORA-15242: could not set attribute compatible.rdbms
ORA-15234: target RDBMS compatibility (12.2.0.1.0) exceeds ASM compatibility (11.2.0.2.0)

SQL>
```

ASM compatibility의 호환 버전 초과 에러 ORA-15234가 발생합니다.

ASM Compatibility>= DBMS Compatibility의 규칙이 존재합니다.

이전의 REDO Disk Group의 ASM COMPATIBILITY를 11.2.0.2로 다시 낮춰 보겠습니다.

```
SQL>ALTER DISKGROUP REDO SET ATTRIBUTE 'compatible.asm'='11.2.0.2' ;
```

```
SQL> ALTER DISKGROUP REDO SET ATTRIBUTE 'compatible.asm'='11.2.0.2' ;
ALTER DISKGROUP REDO SET ATTRIBUTE 'compatible.asm'='11.2.0.2'
*
ERROR at line 1:
ORA-15032: not all alterations performed
ORA-15242: could not set attribute compatible.asm
ORA-15244: new compatibility setting less than current [12.2.0.1.0]

SQL>
```

현재 Compatibility보다 낮출 수 없다는 에러 ORA-15244가 발생합니다.

Compatibility는 값을 올릴 수는 있지만 낮출 수는 없습니다.

ASM instance 관리 Dictionary View

Oracle은 ASM 환경을 관리하기 위한 V$뷰를 통해 제공하고 있습니다.

```
SQL> SELECT * FROM V$ASM_ALIAS ;        # ASM DISK GROUP의 ALIAS 정보
SQL> SELECT * FROM V$ASM_DISK ;         # DISK 정보
SQL> SELECT * FROM V$ASM_DISKGROUP ;  # DISK 그룹 정보
SQL> SELECT * FROM V$ASM_OPERATION ;  # ASM 인스턴스 상에서 실행되는 작업 현황
SQL> SELECT * FROM V$ASM_CLIENT ;       # ASM을 사용하는 DB INSTANCE 정보
SQL> SELECT * FROM V$ASM_FILE ;         # ASM FILE 정보
SQL> SELECT * FROM V$ASM_TEMPLATE ;   # ASM의 모든 Disk Group에 설정된 템플릿 정보.
SQL> SELECT * FROM V$ASM_ATTRIBUTE ;   # ASM의 속성 정보.
SQL> SELECT * FROM V$ASM_DISK_IOSTAT ; # ASM DISK의 IO 상태정보
SQL> SELECT * FROM V$ASM_DISK_STAT ;   # ASM DISK의 상태 정보
SQL> SELECT * FROM V$PWFILE_USERS ;    # SYSASM 권한의 유저 확인
```

ASM Configuration Assistant를 이용한 ASM 관리 방법

X11 protocol을 이용한 X Window System 환경의 Graphical User Interface(GUI)인 화면을 이용하여 마우스를 사용하며 사용자가 쉽게 ASM 관리할 수 있도록 오라클은 인터페이스 프로그램인 Oracle ASM Configuration Assistant(ASMCA)를 제공하고 있습니다. 본 장에서는 ASM Configuration Assistant의 화면을 이용하여 ASM Disk Group과 ASM Disk을 관리하는 방법을 확인해 보겠습니다.

1 ASMCA 실행

ASMCA를 실행시키기 위해서는 DB 서버에 접속해야 할 PC/노트북에 X Window System의 클라이언트 프로그램이 설치/수행되어야 합니다. Mobaxterm은 Cygwin에 기반을 둔 Putty와 Cygwin 및 Xwindows 환경을 통합한 프로그램입니다. 본 장에서는 Mobaxterm은 GNU License Tool입니다. Mobaxterm을 이용하여 ASMCA를 실행 및 제어하겠습니다.

먼저 Mobaxterm 프로그램 Home Edition을 사이트에서 다운로드 한 후 프로그램을 설치합니다.

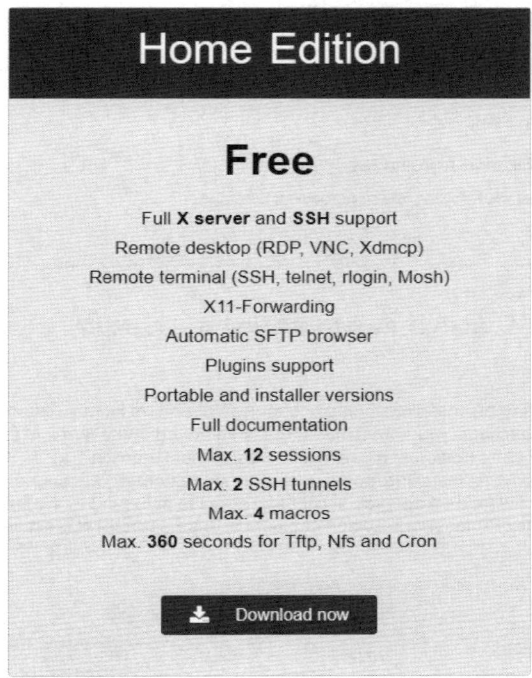
Home Edition
Free
Full X server and SSH support
Remote desktop (RDP, VNC, Xdmcp)
Remote terminal (SSH, telnet, rlogin, Mosh)
X11-Forwarding
Automatic SFTP browser
Plugins support
Portable and installer versions
Full documentation
Max. 12 sessions
Max. 2 SSH tunnels
Max. 4 macros
Max. 360 seconds for Tftp, Nfs and Cron
Download now

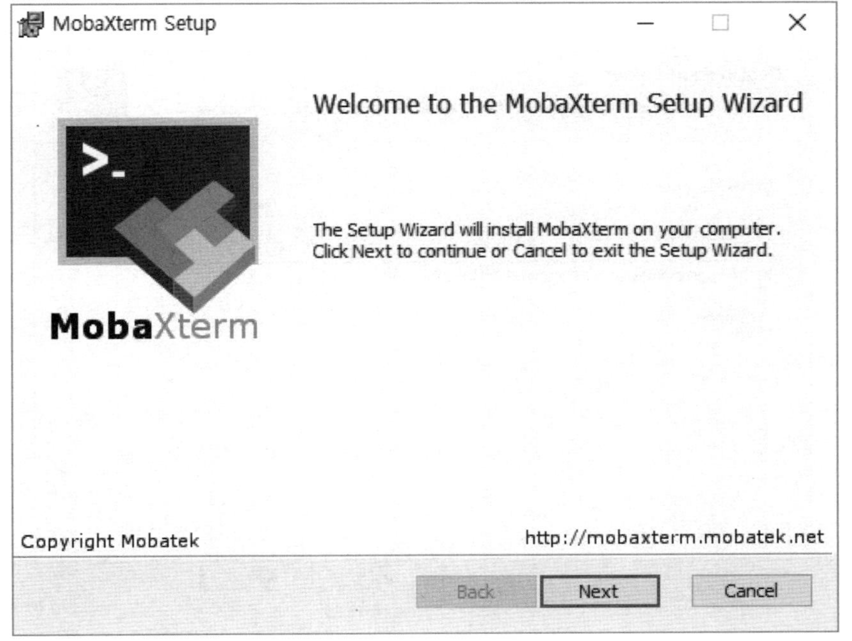
MobaXterm Setup
Welcome to the MobaXterm Setup Wizard
The Setup Wizard will install MobaXterm on your computer.
Click Next to continue or Cancel to exit the Setup Wizard.
MobaXterm
Copyright Mobatek
http://mobaxterm.mobatek.net
Back
Next
Cancel

Mobaxterm 프로그램 설치 주요 화면입니다.

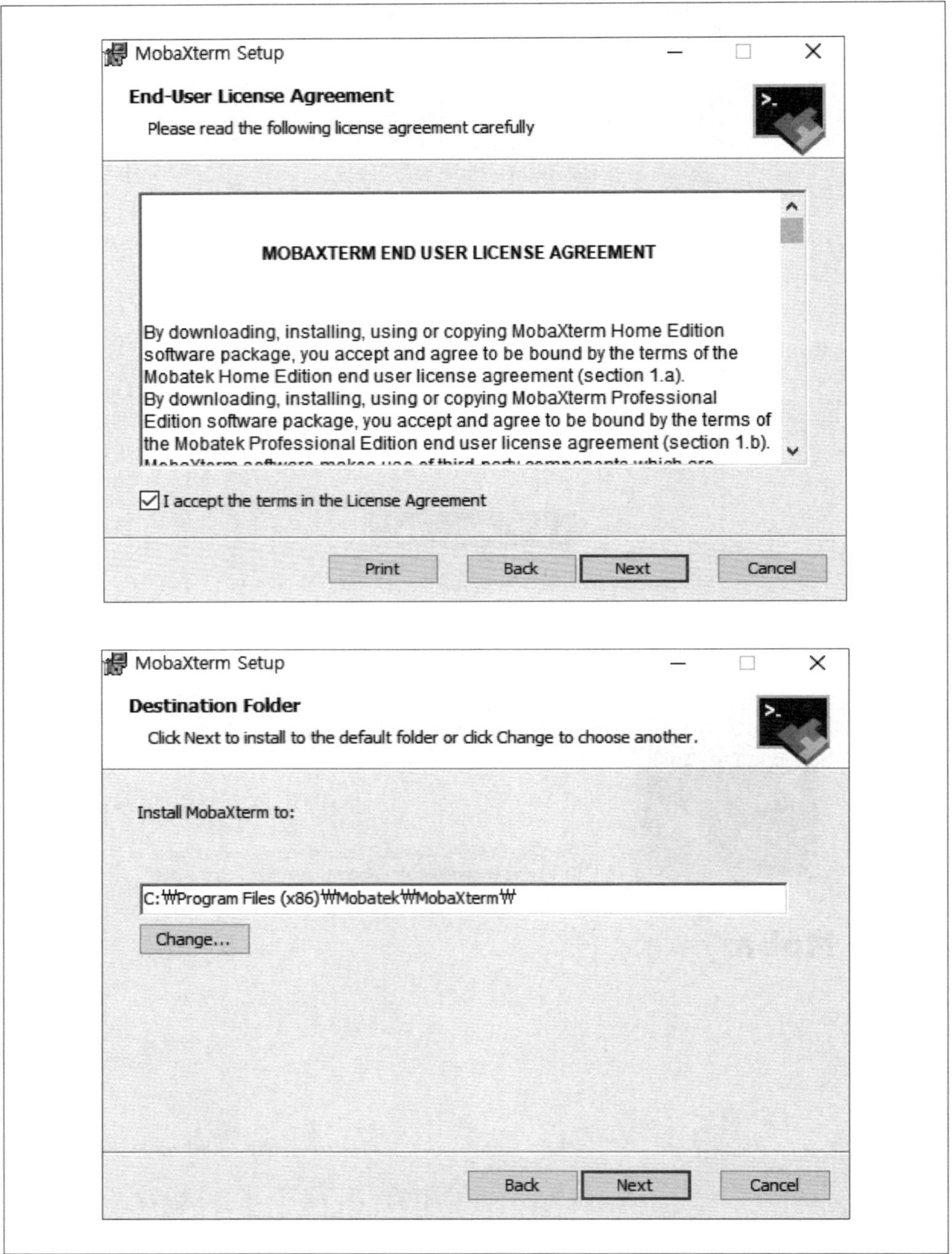

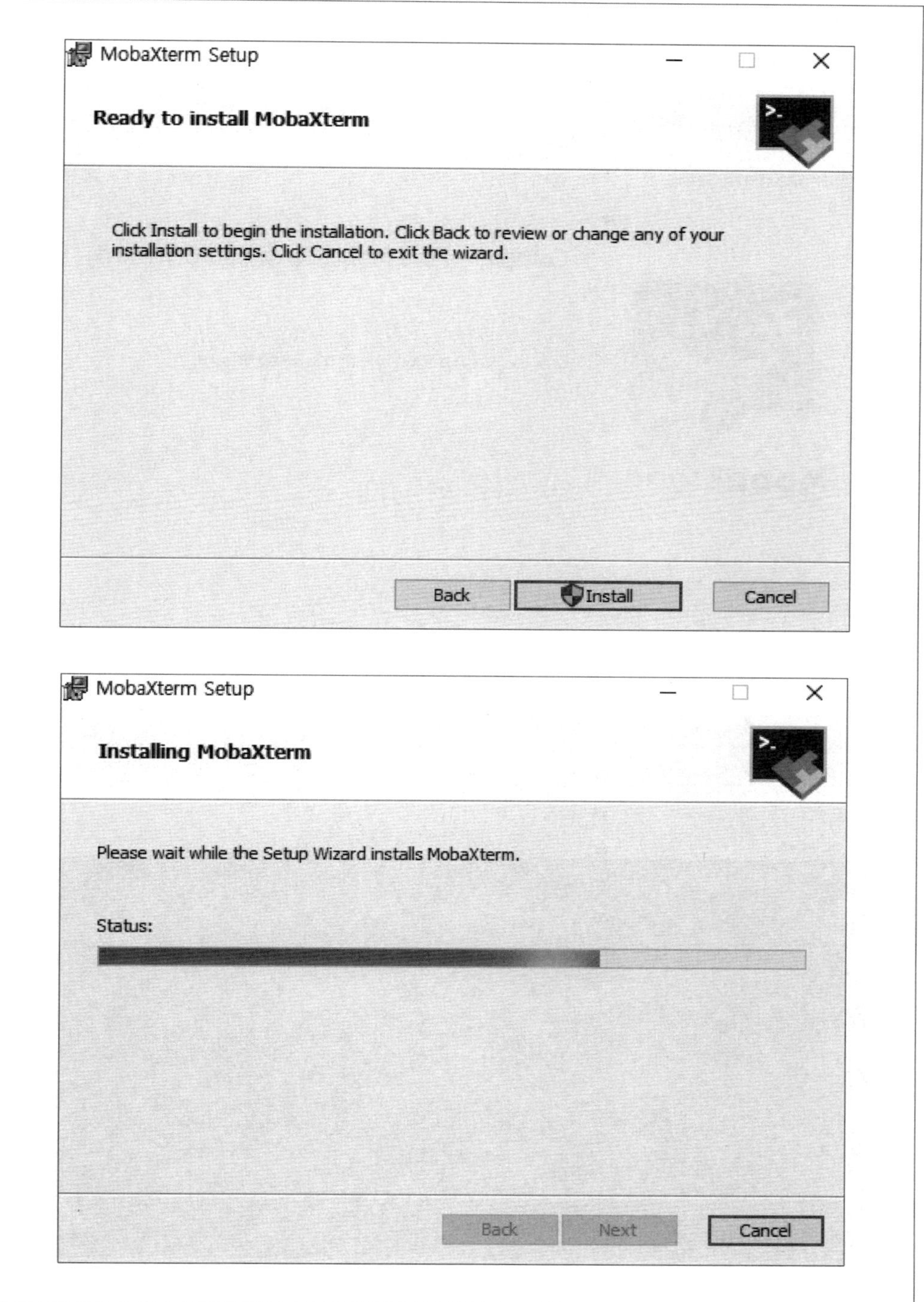
MobaXterm Setup
Ready to install MobaXterm
Click Install to begin the installation. Click Back to review or change any of your installation settings. Click Cancel to exit the wizard.
Back
Install
Cancel
MobaXterm Setup
Installing MobaXterm
Please wait while the Setup Wizard installs MobaXterm.
Status:
Back
Next
Cancel

MobaXterm 프로그램 설치가 완료 되었습니다. 이제 서버에 접속하려는 클라이언트 PC의 IP를 확인합니다.

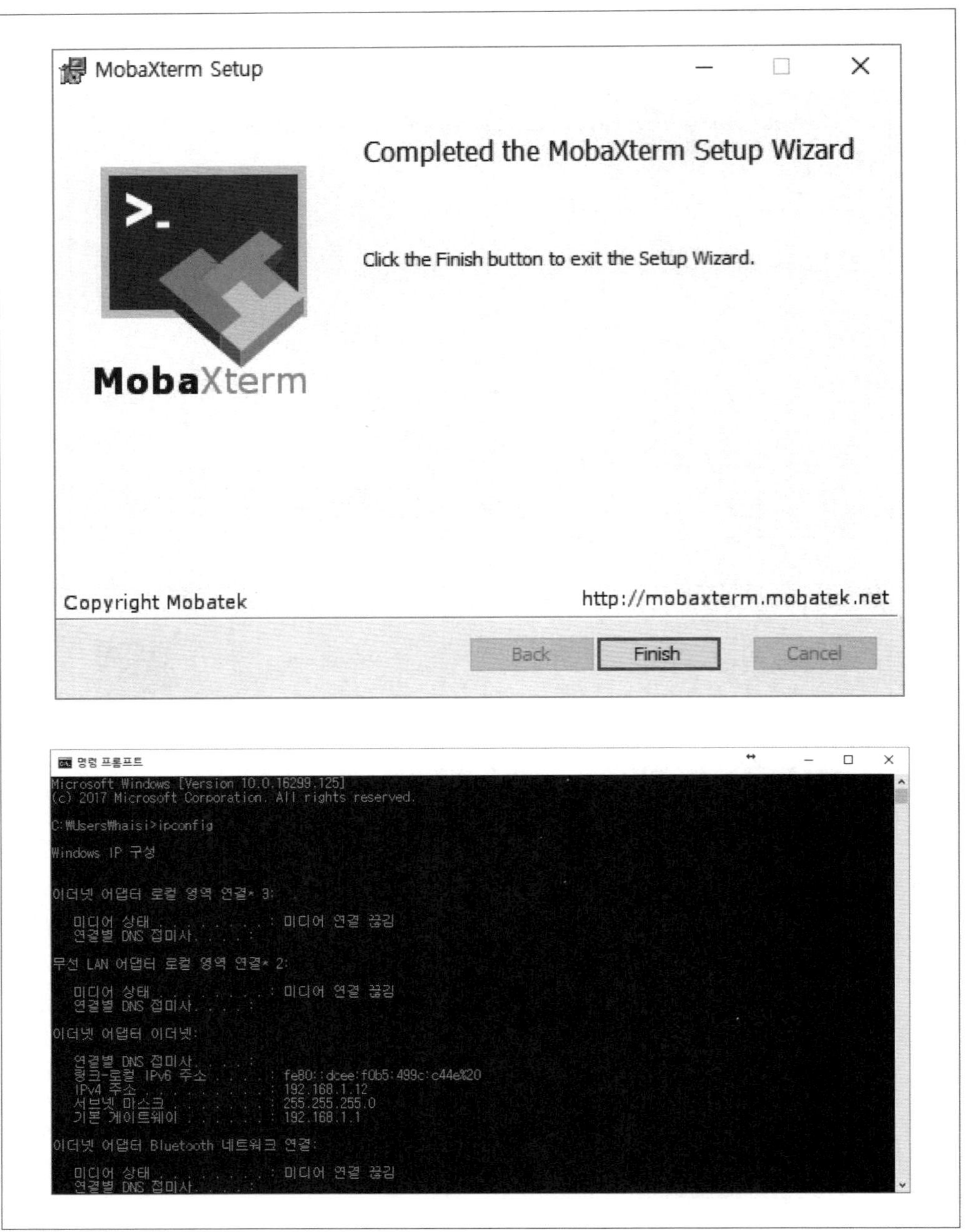

IP 확인 후에는 X window System에 접속하여 통신하기 위한 X client Display 값을 확인해야 합니다.

hostname : D.S로 확인합니다. 앞의 D 절에 오는 값은 디스플레이의 X 서버는 TCP 포트 6000 + D 포트 번호입니다. 뒤의 S는 호스트 디스플레이의 화면 값 S를 의미합니다.

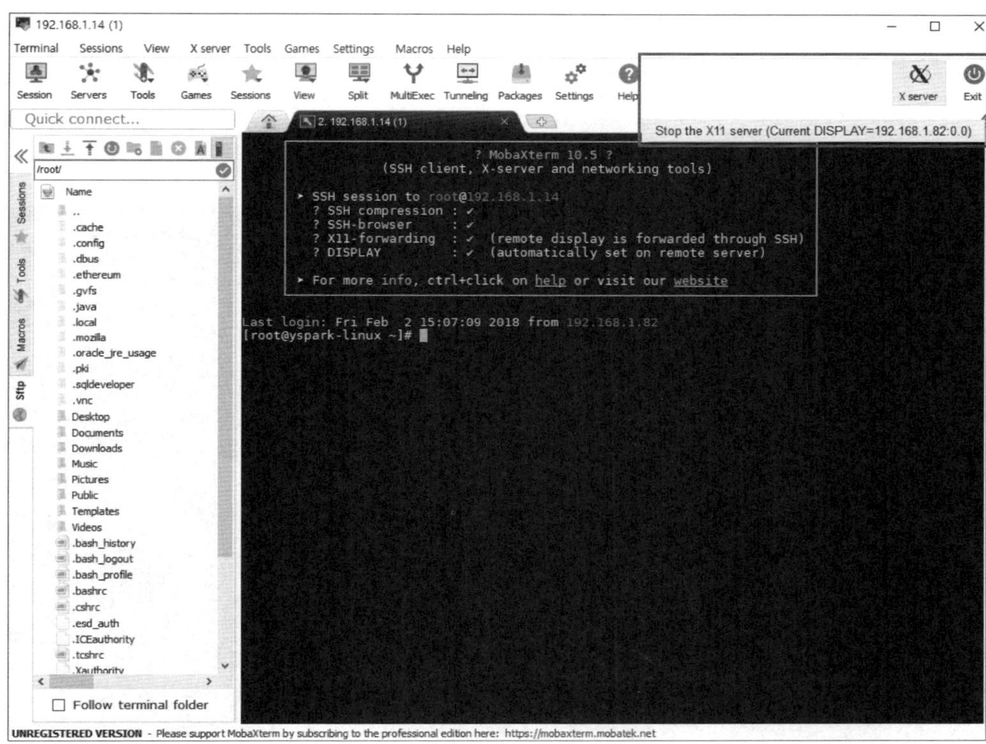

Mobaxterm 프로그램 우측 상단에 X server 마우스를 클릭하면 X windows Display 설정값을 확인할 수 있습니다.

이제 클라이언트 PC의 접속 준비는 완료 되었습니다.

터미널에 접속해 아래와 같이 수행하면 PC 화면에 Mobaxterm 프로그램을 통해 X windows 화면이 생성됩니다.

```
# su - oracle12                          -- Grid Infrastructure 설치 유저 접속
# . oraenv  -- 환경변수 세팅
ORACLE_SID = [oracle12] ? +ASM           -- ASM 인스턴스명 입력
# export DISPLAY=192.168.1.12:0.0        -- 클라이언트 IP와 Mobaxterm 프로그램 log 확인 Value 입력
# asmca                                  -- ASMCA 프로그램 실행
```

```
[root@yspark-linux ~]# su - oracle12
Last login: Tue Jan  2 12:46:22 KST 2018 on pts/2
[oracle12]yspark-linux:/home/oracle12> . oraenv
ORACLE_SID = [oracle12] ? +ASM
The Oracle base has been changed from /oracle/oracle12/app/oracle to /oracle/grid12/app/oracle
[+ASM]yspark-linux:/home/oracle12> echo $ORACLE_SID
+ASM
[+ASM]yspark-linux:/home/oracle12> echo $ORACLE_HOME
/oracle/grid12/bin_grid
[+ASM]yspark-linux:/home/oracle12> export DISPLAY=192.168.1.12:0.0
[+ASM]yspark-linux:/home/oracle12>
[+ASM]yspark-linux:/home/oracle12> asmca
```

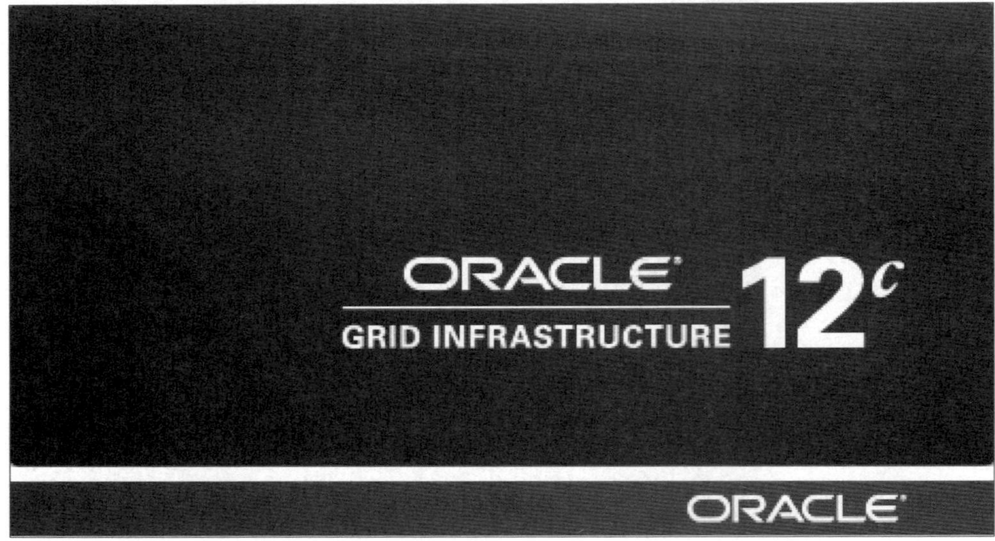

2 ASM Disk Group 조회

ASMCA의 화면에서 좌측 메뉴의 Disk Groups를 마우스로 클릭하면 우측 Main 화면에 ASM Disk Group을 한눈에 확인할 수 있습니다.

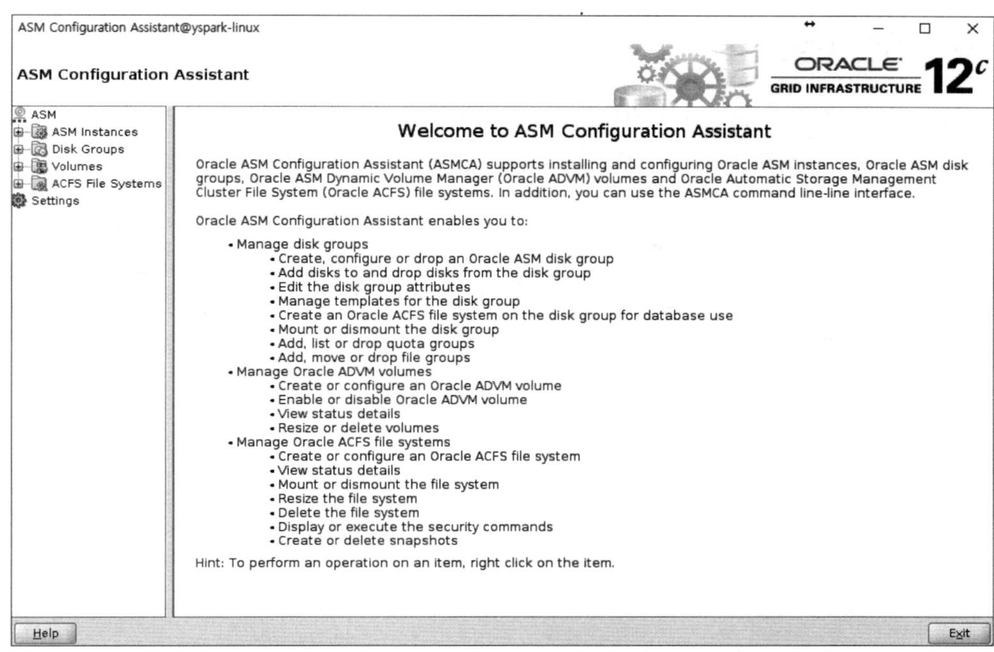
ASM Configuration Assistant@yspark-linux
ASM Configuration Assistant
ORACLE
GRID INFRASTRUCTURE
12c
ASM
ASM Instances
Disk Groups
Volumes
ACFS File Systems
Settings
Welcome to ASM Configuration Assistant
Oracle ASM Configuration Assistant (ASMCA) supports installing and configuring Oracle ASM instances, Oracle ASM disk groups, Oracle ASM Dynamic Volume Manager (Oracle ADVM) volumes and Oracle Automatic Storage Management Cluster File System (Oracle ACFS) file systems. In addition, you can use the ASMCA command line-line interface.
Oracle ASM Configuration Assistant enables you to:
• Manage disk groups
• Create, configure or drop an Oracle ASM disk group
• Add disks to and drop disks from the disk group
• Edit the disk group attributes
• Manage templates for the disk group
• Create an Oracle ACFS file system on the disk group for database use
• Mount or dismount the disk group
• Add, list or drop quota groups
• Add, move or drop file groups
• Manage Oracle ADVM volumes
• Create or configure an Oracle ADVM volume
• Enable or disable Oracle ADVM volume
• View status details
• Resize or delete volumes
• Manage Oracle ACFS file systems
• Create or configure an Oracle ACFS file system
• View status details
• Mount or dismount the file system
• Resize the file system
• Delete the file system
• Display or execute the security commands
• Create or delete snapshots
Hint: To perform an operation on an item, right click on the item.
Help
Exit

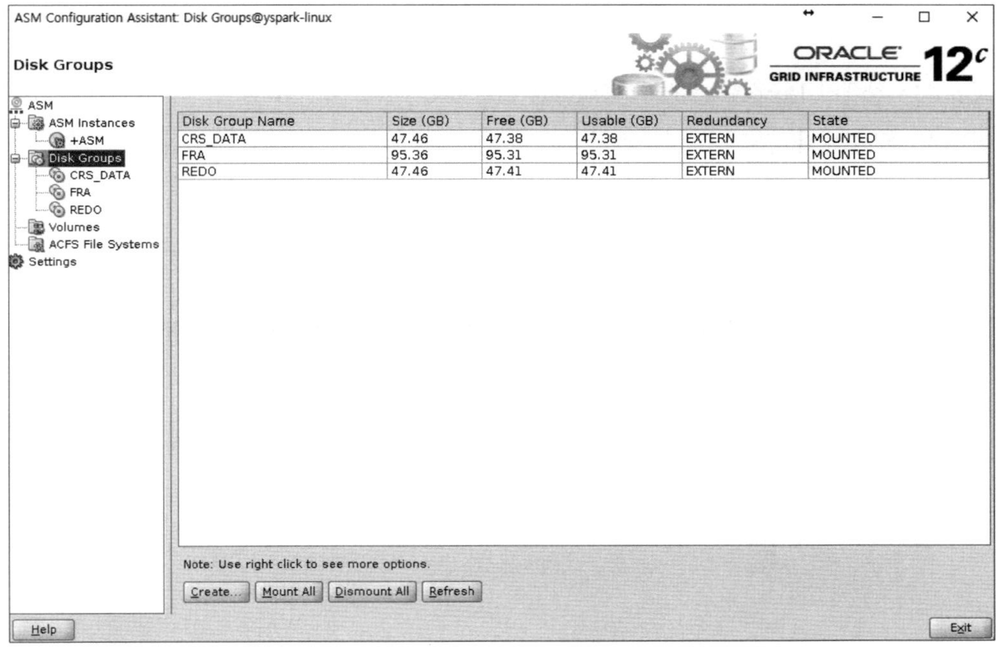
ASM Configuration Assistant: Disk Groups@yspark-linux
Disk Groups
ORACLE
GRID INFRASTRUCTURE
12c
ASM
ASM Instances
+ASM
Disk Groups
CRS_DATA
FRA
REDO
Volumes
ACFS File Systems
Settings
Disk Group Name | Size (GB) | Free (GB) | Usable (GB) | Redundancy | State
CRS_DATA | 47.46 | 47.38 | 47.38 | EXTERN | MOUNTED
FRA | 95.36 | 95.31 | 95.31 | EXTERN | MOUNTED
REDO | 47.46 | 47.41 | 47.41 | EXTERN | MOUNTED
Note: Use right click to see more options.
Create...
Mount All
Dismount All
Refresh
Help
Exit

3 ASM Disk Group 삭제

ASMCA을 통해 이미 만들어진 기존 Disk Group을 삭제하겠습니다. 먼저 삭제할 REDO Disk Group을 선택하고 우측 마우스 버튼을 누르면 Pop-Up 창이 생성됩니다.

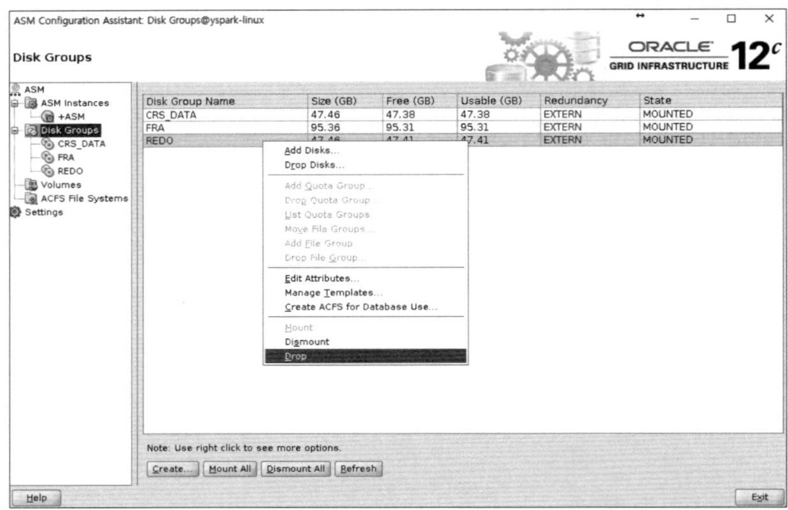

Pop-Up 창에서 Drop을 선택 후 클릭하면 Confirm Drop 팝업이 한 번 더 생성되고 Yes 버튼을 클릭합니다.

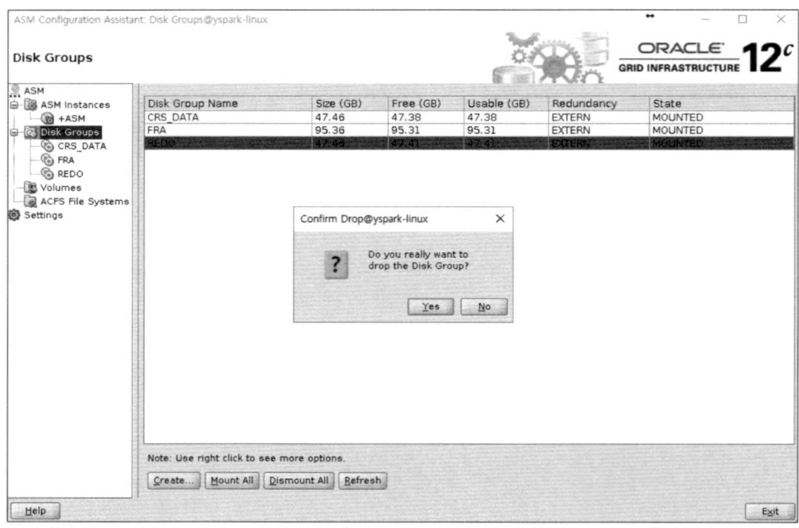

Performing operation이라는 진행 중인 창이 생성된 후 다시 Disk Group 조회 화면으로 돌아옵니다.

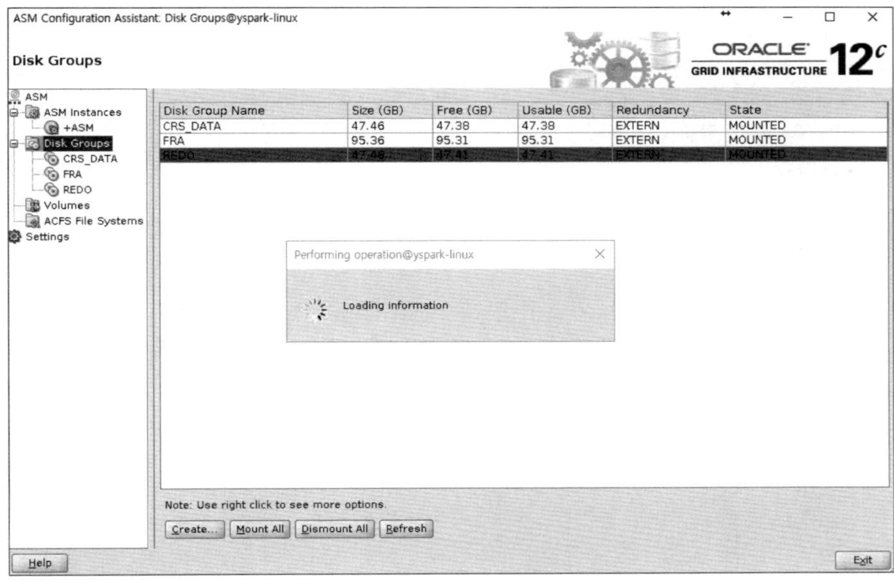

선택한 REDO Disk Group은 삭제가 되었고, 나머지 Disk Group만 조회가 됩니다.

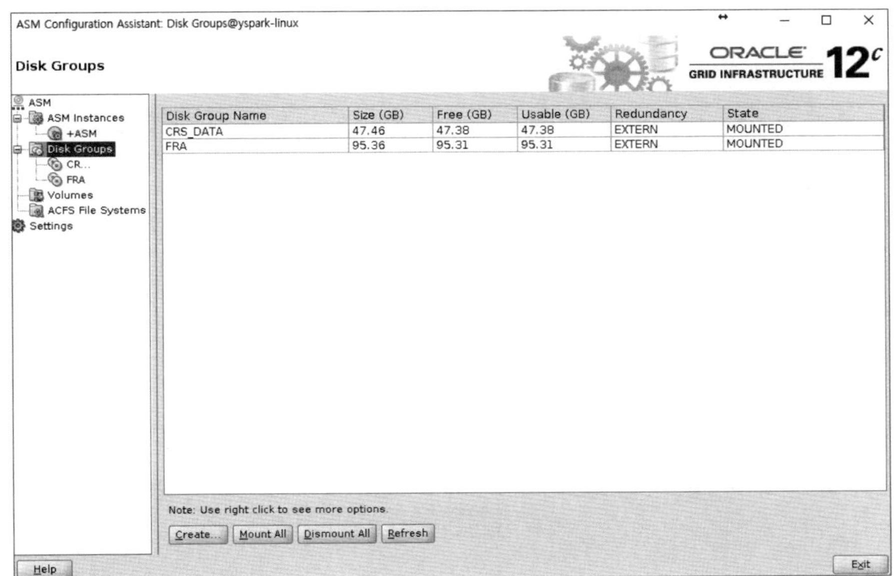

4 ASM Disk Group 생성

ASMCA을 통해 신규 Disk Group을 생성하겠습니다. DB_DATA라는 신규 Disk Group을 만들어 보겠습니다.

하단에 Create 버튼을 클릭합니다.

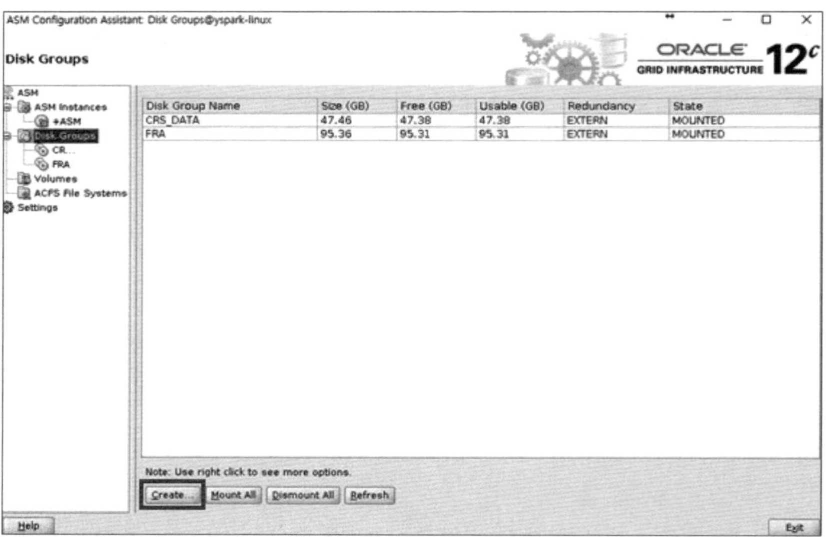

Create Disk Group 화면으로 이동됩니다.

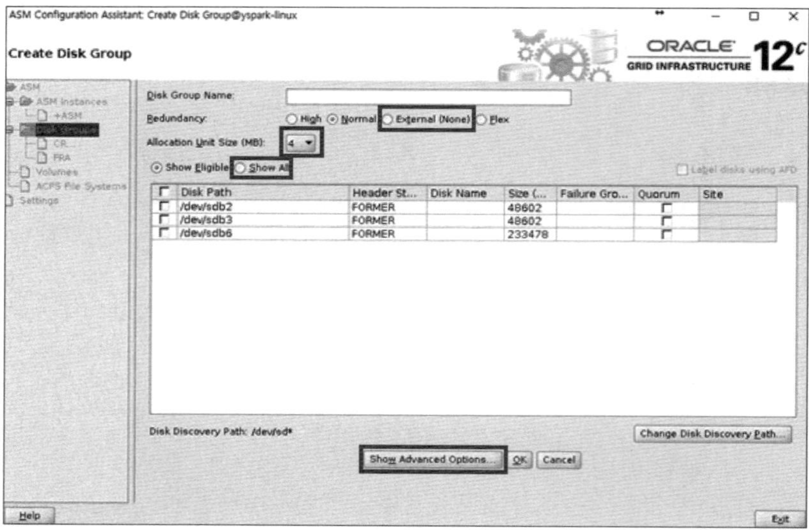

Redundancy는 External로 선택하고 AU size는 4 MB로 선택합니다.

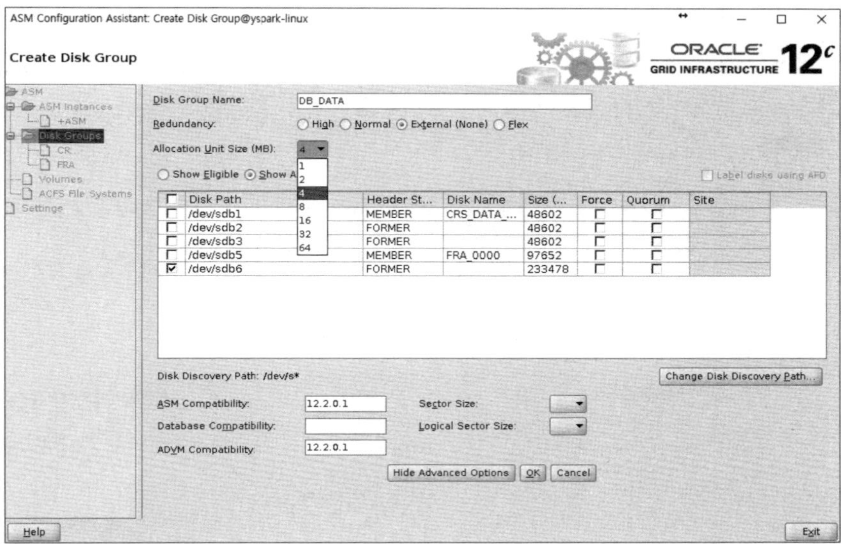

하단의 Show Advanced Options 버튼을 클릭하면 Compatibility와 Sector Size를 선택할 수 있는 창으로 확장됩니다. 원하는 값으로 설정 후에 OK 버튼을 클릭합니다.

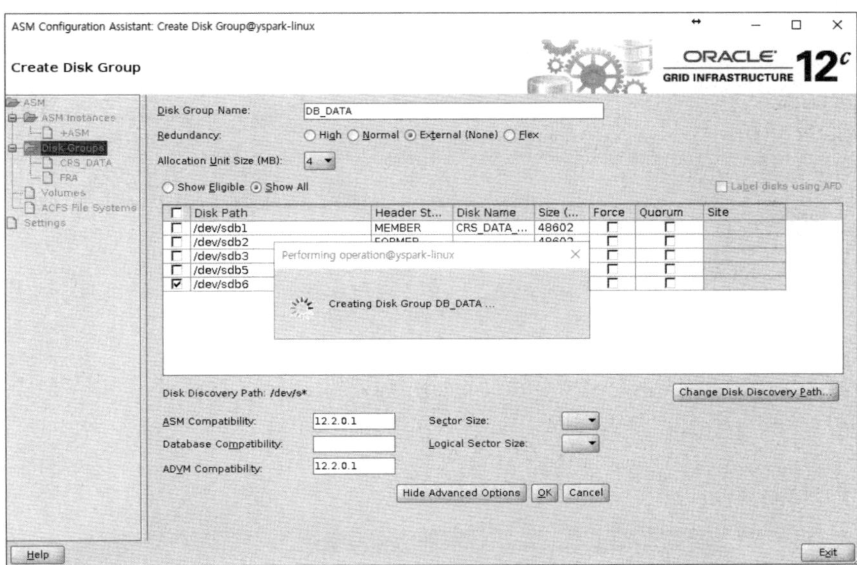

Creating Disk Group이라는 내용으로 Performing operation Pop-Up 창이 생성됩니다.

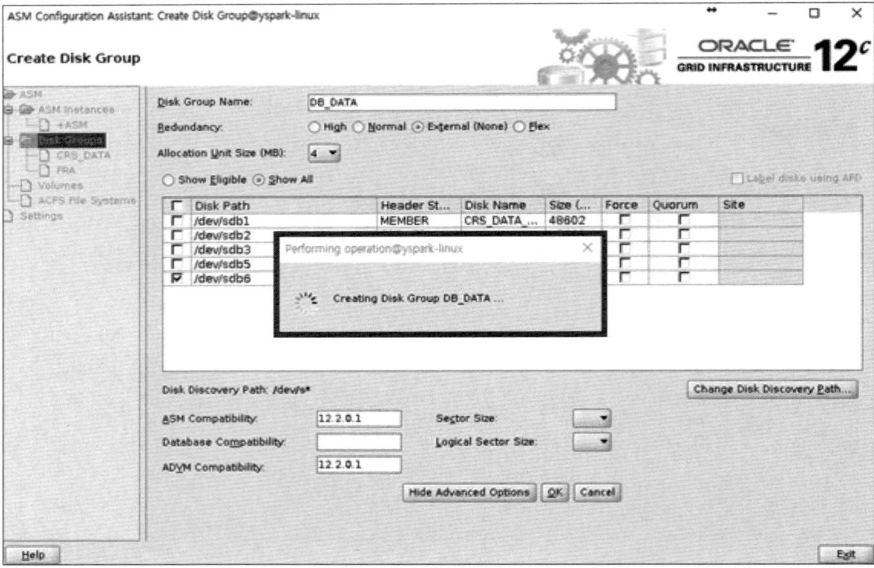

Disk Groups 조회 창으로 이동되면서 DB_DATA 라는 신규 Disk Group이 생성된 것을 확인할 수 있습니다.

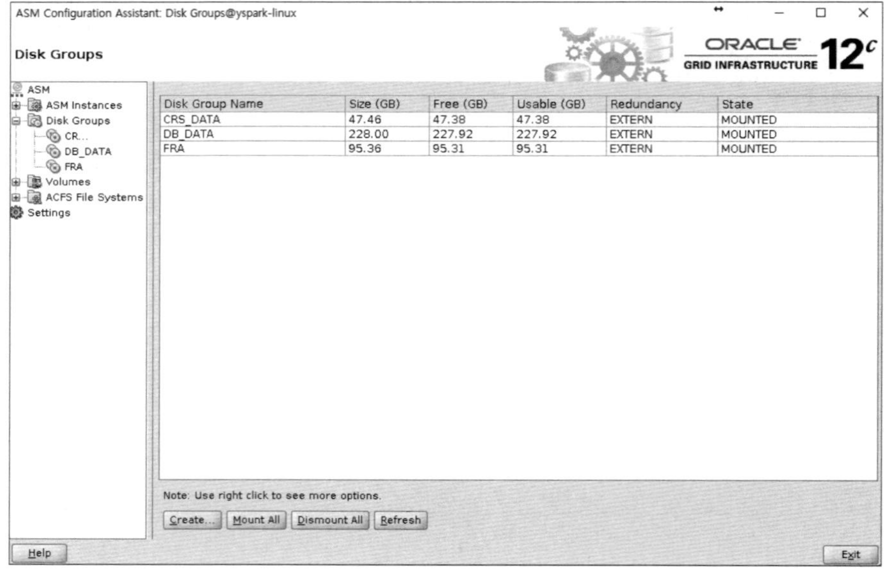

5 ASM Disk 추가

만들어진 기존 Disk Group에 ASM Disk를 추가하겠습니다.

먼저 디스크를 추가할 DB_DATA Disk Group을 선택하고 우측 마우스 버튼을 누르면 Pop-Up 창이 생성됩니다.

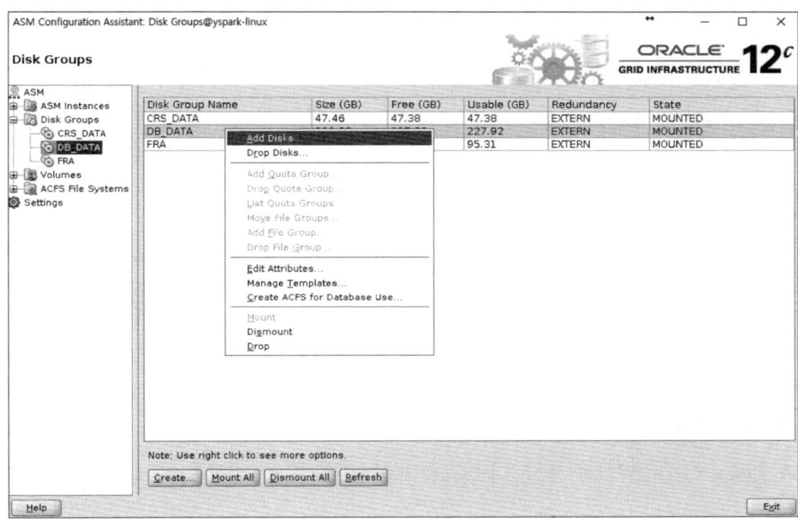

Pop-Up 창에서 Add Disks를 선택하면 Add Disks 창으로 이동됩니다.

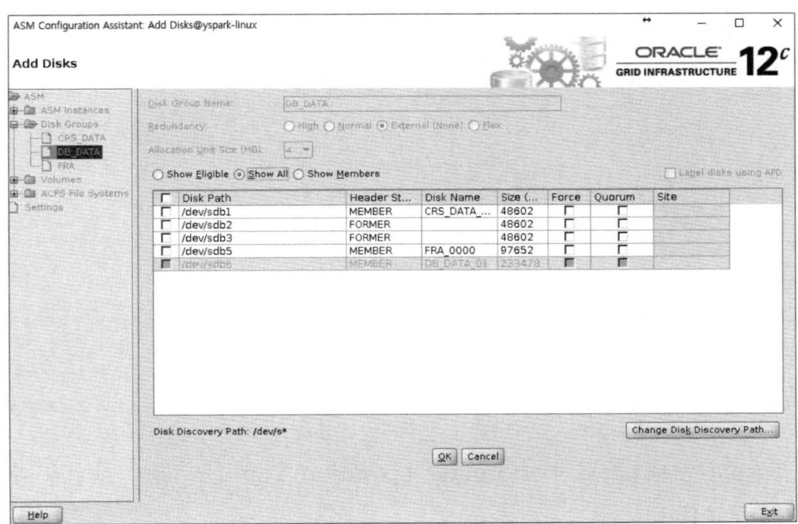

Pop-Up 창에서 Add Disks를 선택하면 Add Disks 창으로 이동됩니다.

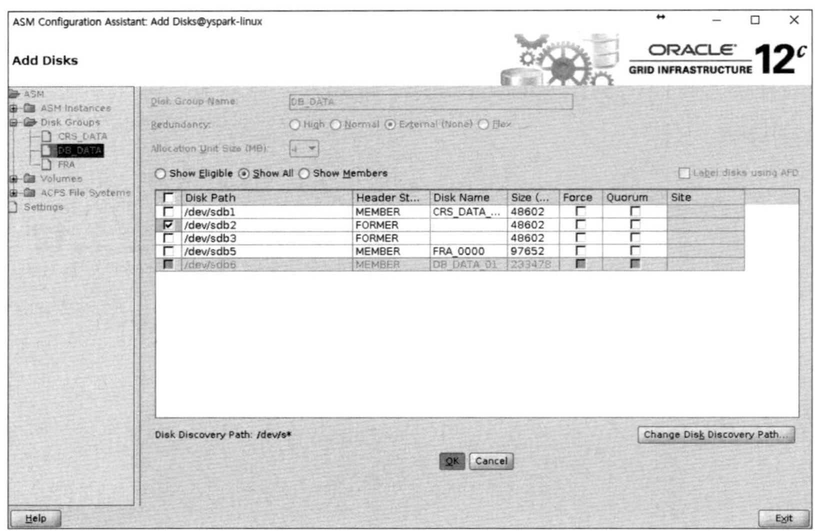

Show All을 클릭하면 모든 할당 된 ASM Disk와 미 할당된 디스크를 확인할 수 있습니다. DB_DATA Disk Group에 추가할 디스크를 선택하고 OK 버튼을 클릭합니다.

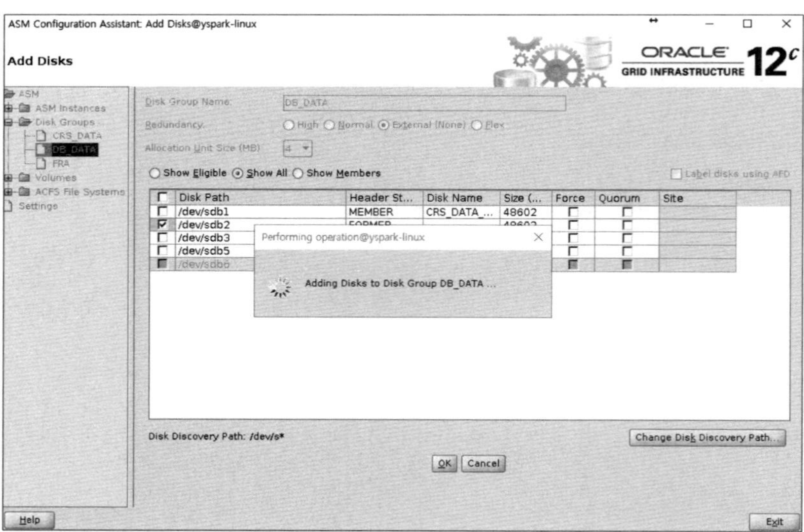

Adding Disks라는 내용으로 Performing operation Pop-Up 창이 생성된 후에 Disk Groups 창으로 이동됩니다.

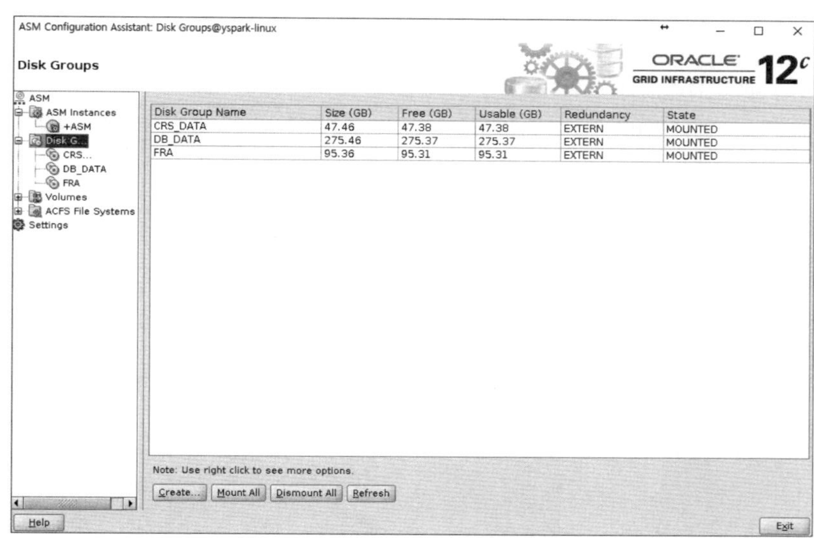

DB_DATA Disk Group의 디스크가 추가가 완료되어 Disk Group의 Size가 커졌습니다.

6 ASM Disk 삭제

만들어진 기존 Disk Group에 ASM Disk를 삭제하겠습니다.
먼저 디스크를 추가할 DB_DATA Disk Group을 선택하고 우측 마우스 버튼을 누르면 Pop-Up 창이 생성됩니다.

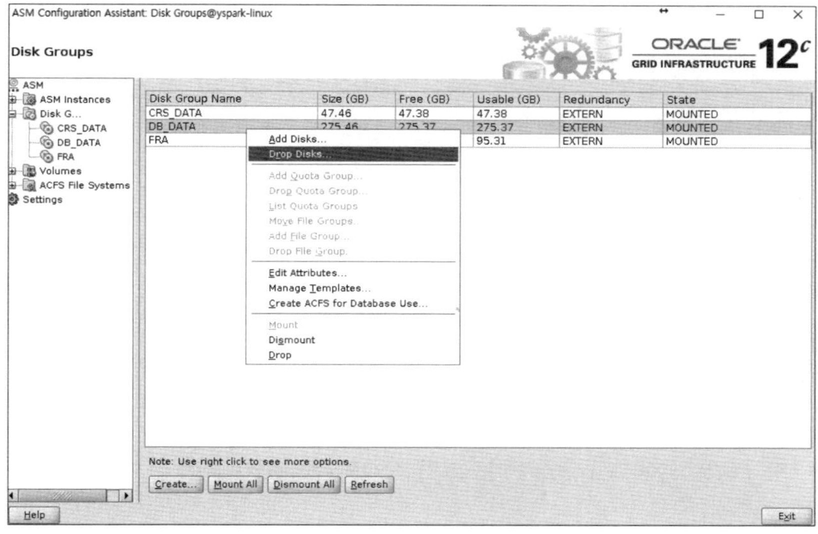

Pop-Up 창에서 Drop Disks를 선택하고 클릭하면 Drop Disks 창으로 이동됩니다.

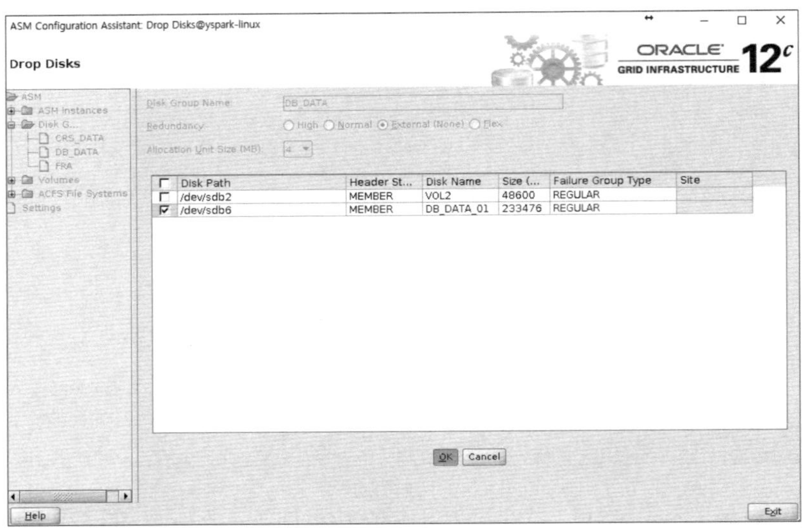

삭제할 ASM Disk를 선택하고 OK 버튼을 클릭하면 Dropping Disks라는 내용으로 Performing operation Pop-Up 창이 생성된 후에 Disk Groups 창으로 이동됩니다.

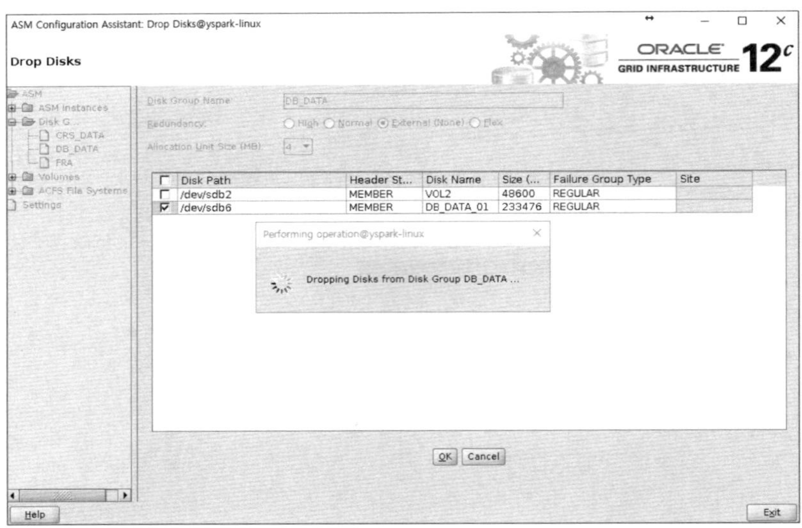

완료되면 DB_DATA Disk Group의 디스크가 삭제되어 Size가 줄어 든 것을 확인할 수 있습니다.

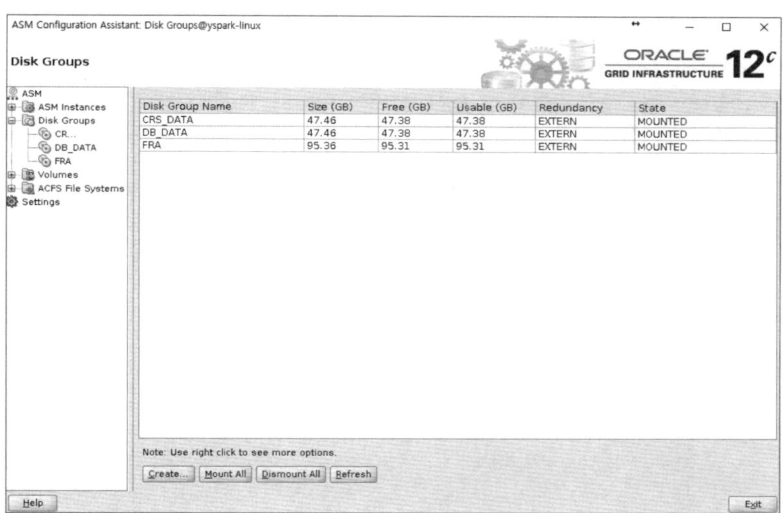

7 ASM Disk Group 속성 값 변경

ASMCA를 통해 ASM Disk Group의 속성 값 변경을 하겠습니다.

Disk Groups 창에서 DB_DATA의 속성 값을 변경하기 위해 선택 후 우측 마우스 클릭합니다.

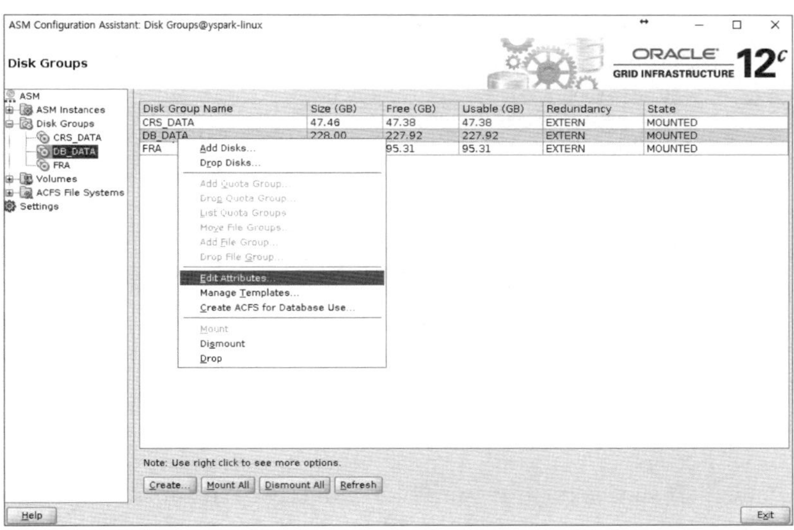

Pop-Up 창에서 Edit Attributes 항목을 선택하여 클릭하면 Edit Attributes for Disk Group 창으로 이동합니다.

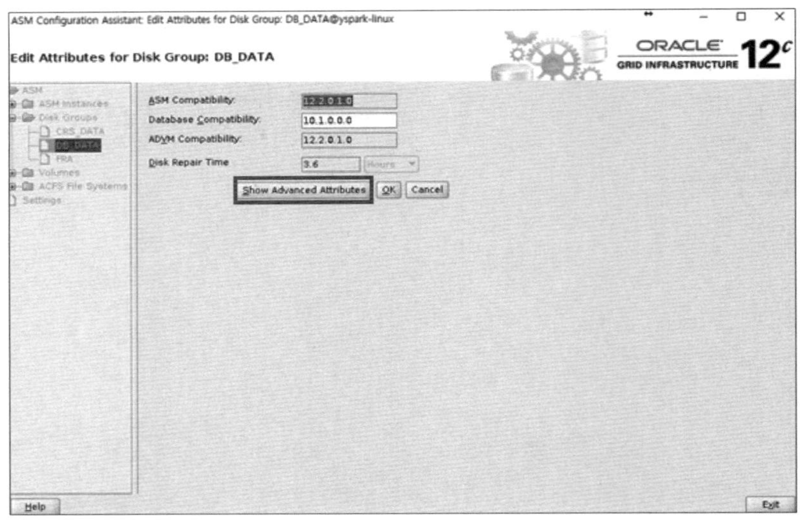

Show Advanced Attributes 버튼을 클릭하면 ASM Disk Group의 상세한 속성값을 설정할 수 있는 숨어 있는 창이 표시됩니다.

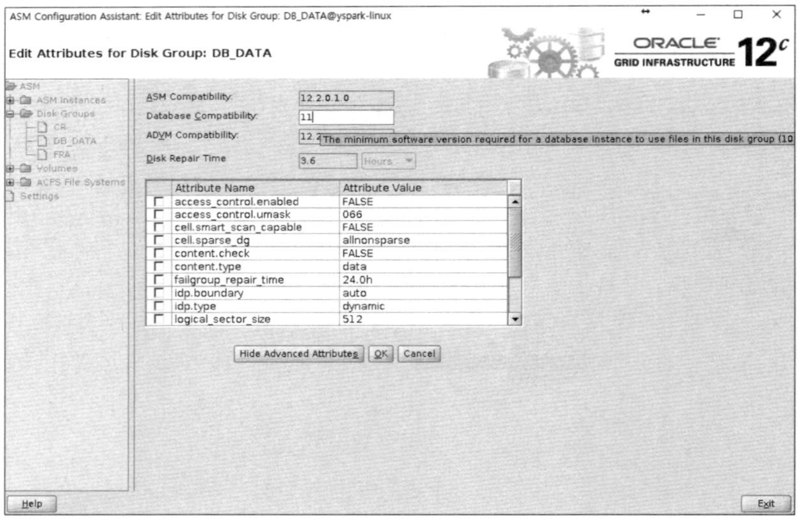

"The minimum software version required for a database instance to use files in this disk group (10.1 and above)" Database Compatibility 값을 입력하려고 하면 해당 Disk Group에 구성할 Database 인스턴스 버전으로 최소한 동일하게 맞추어야 한다는 경고 문구 내용이 Pop-Up 창 메시지가 나옵니다.

Database Compatibility 값에 11.2.0.2 을 입력하면 Disk Repair Time 속성 값이 Disable 되어 있다가 Enable되어 변경이 가능하게 되었습니다.

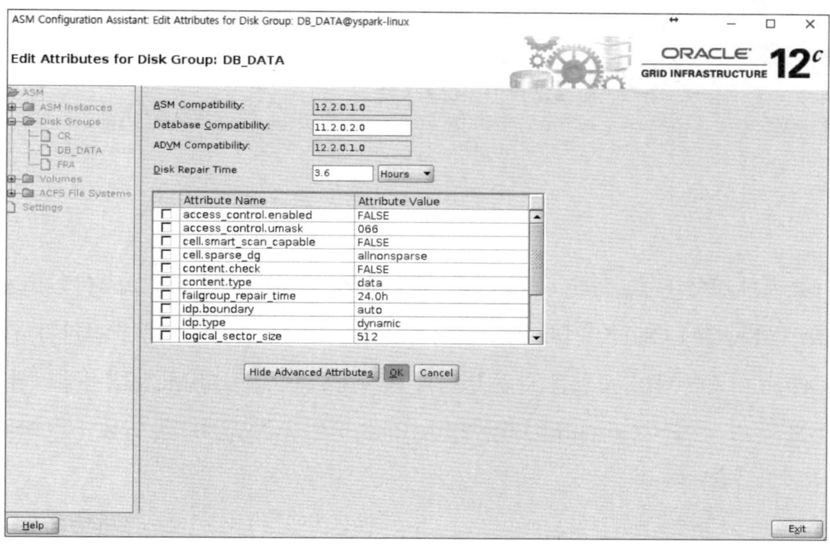

Disk Repair Time 값을 10 Hours로 변경합니다. 나머지 속성 변경 값을 입력하고 OK를 버튼을 클릭하면 Warning Pop-up 창이 나옵니다. Yes 버튼을 눌러서 ASM Disk Group의 속성 변경을 완료합니다.

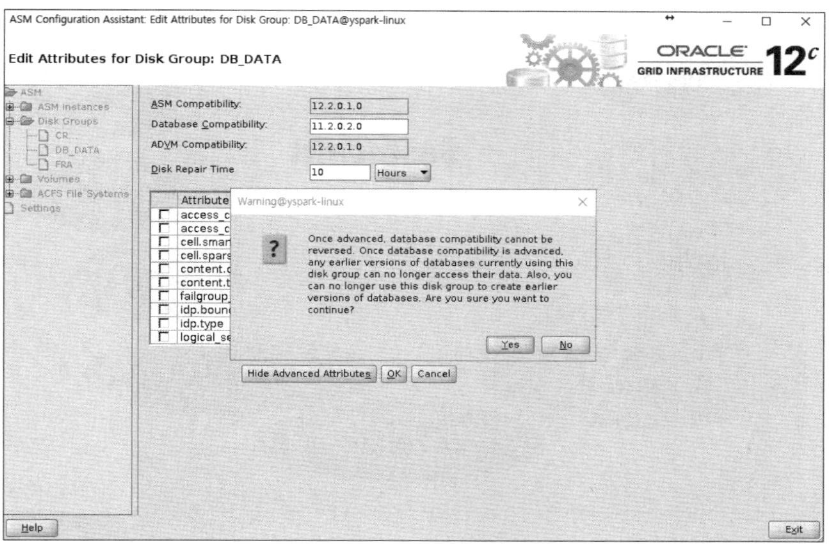

ASMCMD를 이용한 ASM 관리 방법

오라클 DBA에게 친숙한 SQL*Plus 유틸리티, 일반 사용자가 관리하기 쉬운 ASM Configuration Assistant (ASMCA) GUI 인터페이스 이외에 전통적인 UNIX 시스템 관리자가 관리하기 쉽도록 Oracle이 OS 파일 시스템 관리 명령과 유사하도록 만든 ASMCMD 유틸리티가 있습니다. ASM 관리 전용 Command Line Interface 툴인 ASMCMD를 이용하여 ASM 관리 방법을 알아보겠습니다.

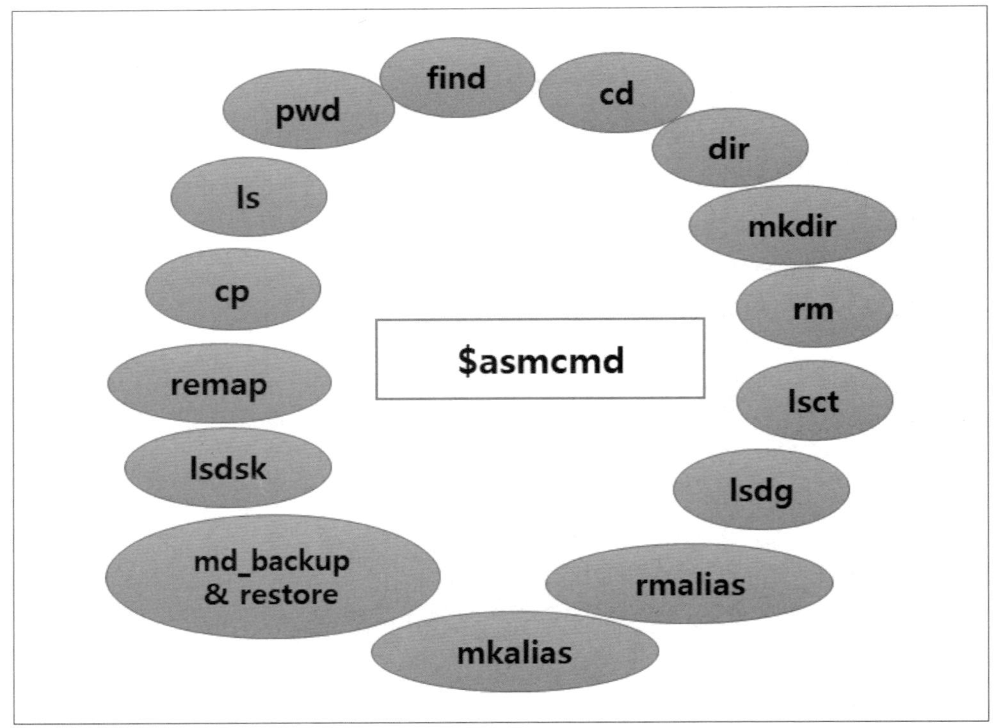

1 ASMCMD 실행

ASMCMD는 Oracle ASM 볼륨내의 디스크 관리, 데이터 관리, 백업 등의 작업을 ASM Instance에서의 SQL 명령어가 아닌 OS 파일 시스템 명령과 유사하도록 구현된 유틸리티입니다. 대화식 모드로 UNIX 쉘 명령어와 유사한 작업이 가능합니다. ASMCMD를 실행하겠습니다.

```
# su - oracle12                    -- Grid Infrastructure 설치 유저 접속
# . oraenv  -- 환경변수 세팅
ORACLE_SID = [oracle12] ? +ASM     -- ASM 인스턴스명 입력
#asmcmd -p                         -- ASMCMD 유틸리티 실행
```

```
[root@yspark-linux ~]# su - oracle12
Last login: Wed Jan  3 12:51:48 KST 2018 on pts/2
[oracle12]yspark-linux:/home/oracle12> . oraenv
ORACLE_SID = [oracle12] ? +ASM
The Oracle base has been changed from /oracle/oracle12/app/oracle to /oracle/grid12/app/oracle
[+ASM]yspark-linux:/home/oracle12> asmcmd -p
ASMCMD [+] >
```

2 ASM Disk Group 조회

ASMCMD의 ls 명령어를 이용하여 ASM Disk Group을 조회합니다.

```
#asmcmd -p
ASMCMD > ls -l
```

```
[+ASM]yspark-linux:/home/oracle12> asmcmd -p
ASMCMD [+] > ls -l
State    Type    Rebal  Name
MOUNTED  EXTERN  N      CRS_DATA/
MOUNTED  EXTERN  N      DB_DATA/
MOUNTED  EXTERN  N      FRA/
MOUNTED  EXTERN  N      REDO/
MOUNTED  EXTERN  N      TEMP/
ASMCMD [+] >
```

ASMCMD의 lsdg 명령어를 이용하여 전반적인 ASM Disk Group 사용 현황을 조회합니다.

```
#asmcmd -p
ASMCMD > lsdg
```

```
[+ASM]yspark-linux:/home/oracle12> asmcmd -p
ASMCMD [+] > lsdg
State    Type    Rebal  Sector  Logical_Sector  Block       AU  Total_MB  Free_MB  Req_mir_free_MB  Usable_file_MB  Offline_disks  Voting_files  Name
MOUNTED  EXTERN  N         512             512   4096  4194304     48600    48512                0           48512              0             N  CRS_DATA/
MOUNTED  EXTERN  N         512             512   4096  4194304    233476   230968                0          230968              0             N  DB_DATA/
MOUNTED  EXTERN  N         512             512   4096  1048576     97652    94491                0           94491              0             N  FRA/
MOUNTED  EXTERN  N         512             512   4096  4194304     48600    45412                0           45412              0             N  REDO/
MOUNTED  EXTERN  N         512             512   4096  4194304     48600    48444                0           48444              0             N  TEMP/
ASMCMD [+] >
```

ASMCMD는 기존 shell prompt와 비슷한 인터페이스로 만들어져서 정보가 제공됩니다.

❶ Total_MB : 디스크 그룹 전체의 용량입니다.

❷ Free_MB : 중복을 고려하지 않은 순수 공간의 용량입니다.

❸ Req_mir_free_MB : 중복 (Redundancy) 구성 시 만일 디스크 장애가 발생해도 데이터를 성공적으로 재배치할 수 있는 영역을 고려했을 경우의 공간의 용량입니다.

❹ Usable_file_MB : 물리적으로 파일 작성이 가능한 공간의 용량입니다.

3 ASM File ↔ OS 파일 시스템 복사

ASMCMD의 cp 명령어를 이용하여 ASM Disk Group 안의 ASM File을 OS 파일 시스템으로 복사합니다.

```
# asmcmd -p
ASMCMD > cp <source 파일 이름> <OS 절대경로/Target 파일 이름>
```

```
[+ASM]yspark-linux:/home/oracle12> asmcmd -p
ASMCMD [+] > cd DB_DATA
ASMCMD [+DB_DATA] > cp spfileORACLE12.ora /tmp/spfileORACLE12.ora
copying +DB_DATA/spfileORACLE12.ora -> /tmp/spfileORACLE12.ora
ASMCMD [+DB_DATA] > exit
[+ASM]yspark-linux:/home/oracle12> ls -al /tmp/spfileORACLE12.ora
-rw-r----- 1 oracle12 oinstall 3584 Jan  3 16:14 /tmp/spfileORACLE12.ora
[+ASM]yspark-linux:/home/oracle12>
```

이번에는 반대로 OS 파일 시스템의 File을 ASM DISK Group의 File로 복사합니다.

```
# asmcmd -p
ASMCMD > cp <OS 절대경로/Target 파일 이름><Source 파일 이름>
```

```
[+ASM]yspark-linux:/tmp> asmcmd -p
ASMCMD [+] > cd /FRA
ASMCMD [+FRA] > cp /tmp/spfileORACLE12.ora +FRA/spfileORACLE12.ora
copying /tmp/spfileORACLE12.ora -> +FRA/spfileORACLE12.ora
ASMCMD [+FRA] > ls -l +FRA/spfileORACLE12.ora
Type           Redund  Striped  Time             Sys  Name
PARAMETERFILE  UNPROT  COARSE   JAN 03 16:00:00  N    spfileORACLE12.ora => +FRA/ASM/PARAMETERFILE/spfileORACLE
12.ora.260.964456163
ASMCMD [+FRA] > █
```

4 ASM Disk 관리

ASMCMD의 lsdsk 명령어를 이용하여 ASM Disk의 상태를 모니터링합니다.

```
# asmcmd -p
ASMCMD >lsdsk --statistics
```

```
[+ASM]yspark-linux:/tmp> asmcmd -p
ASMCMD [+] > lsdsk --statistics
Reads   Write  Read_Errs  Write_Errs    Read_time      Write_Time  Bytes_Read  Bytes_Written  Voting_File  Path
 5588  169085          0           0    33.568475  414880.622866    30826496      692572160            N  /dev/sdb1
 2595   11851          0           0    15.824378   15994.917027    12341760     3345672192            N  /dev/sdb2
 2841    6437          0           0    40.826838   13855.015684    28352512       99229696            N  /dev/sdb3
 1902   44710          0           0    21.879625    55642.18973    15356416     3581714944            N  /dev/sdb5
51307   17569          0           0   680.287137    6738.391013   715125760     2917980672            N  /dev/sdb6
ASMCMD [+] >
```

ASMCMD의 iostat 명령어를 이용하여 ASM Disk Group의 ASM Disk I/O의 통계를 모니터링합니다.

```
# asmcmd -p
ASMCMD >iostat
```

```
[+ASM]yspark-linux:/tmp> asmcmd -p
ASMCMD [+] > iostat
Group_Name  Dsk_Name        Reads      Writes
CRS_DATA    CRS_DATA_0000   30908416   693198848
DB_DATA     VOL6            715207680  2918611456
FRA         FRA_0000        15380992   3582341632
REDO        VOL2            12423680   3346290688
TEMP        VOL3            28430336   99856384
ASMCMD [+] >
```

iostat 명령어를 이용하여 ASM Disk가 포함된 DB_DATA Disk Group의 I/O 통계정보(바이트)를 1초 간격으로 표시하면서 모니터링합니다.

```
# asmcmd -p
ASMCMD >iostat -G <디스크 그룹명><간격(초)>
```

```
[+ASM]yspark-linux:/tmp> asmcmd -p
ASMCMD [+] > iostat -G DB_DATA 1
Group_Name  Dsk_Name  Reads      Writes
DB_DATA     VOL6      715209728  2918824448

Group_Name  Dsk_Name  Reads  Writes
DB_DATA     VOL6      0.00   8192.00

Group_Name  Dsk_Name  Reads  Writes
DB_DATA     VOL6      0.00   0.00

Group_Name  Dsk_Name  Reads  Writes
DB_DATA     VOL6      0.00   0.00

Group_Name  Dsk_Name  Reads    Writes
DB_DATA     VOL6      4096.00  4096.00

Group_Name  Dsk_Name  Reads  Writes
DB_DATA     VOL6      0.00   0.00

Group_Name  Dsk_Name  Reads  Writes
DB_DATA     VOL6      0.00   0.00

Group_Name  Dsk_Name  Reads  Writes
DB_DATA     VOL6      0.00   8192.00

Group_Name  Dsk_Name  Reads  Writes
DB_DATA     VOL6      0.00   4096.00

Group_Name  Dsk_Name  Reads  Writes
DB_DATA     VOL6      0.00   0.00
```

비 대화식 모드로 ASMCMD 명령어를 실행하면 명령어를 간소화하여 모니터링 할 수 있습니다.

```
# asmcmd iostat -G <디스크 그룹명><간격(초)> -et
```

```
[+ASM]yspark-linux:/tmp> asmcmd iostat -G DB_DATA 1 -et
Group_Name  Dsk_Name  Reads       Writes      Read_Err  Write_Err  Read_Time   Write_Time
DB_DATA     VOL6      826826752   2928096768  0         0          779.833849  7017.970602

Group_Name  Dsk_Name  Reads       Writes      Read_Err  Write_Err  Read_Time  Write_Time
DB_DATA     VOL6      1400832.00  524288.00   0.00      0.00       0.35       0.31

Group_Name  Dsk_Name  Reads      Writes  Read_Err  Write_Err  Read_Time  Write_Time
DB_DATA     VOL6      540672.00  0.00    0.00      0.00       0.21       0.00

Group_Name  Dsk_Name  Reads     Writes    Read_Err  Write_Err  Read_Time  Write_Time
DB_DATA     VOL6      31744.00  15360.00  0.00      0.00       0.06       0.29

Group_Name  Dsk_Name  Reads       Writes    Read_Err  Write_Err  Read_Time  Write_Time
DB_DATA     VOL6      2908160.00  16384.00  0.00      0.00       0.71       0.05

Group_Name  Dsk_Name  Reads       Writes  Read_Err  Write_Err  Read_Time  Write_Time
DB_DATA     VOL6      1654784.00  0.00    0.00      0.00       4.61       0.00

Group_Name  Dsk_Name  Reads       Writes    Read_Err  Write_Err  Read_Time  Write_Time
DB_DATA     VOL6      6072320.00  16384.00  0.00      0.00       2.56       0.05

Group_Name  Dsk_Name  Reads       Writes    Read_Err  Write_Err  Read_Time  Write_Time
DB_DATA     VOL6      7361536.00  11264.00  0.00      0.00       6.10       0.72

Group_Name  Dsk_Name  Reads       Writes  Read_Err  Write_Err  Read_Time  Write_Time
DB_DATA     VOL6      5214208.00  0.00    0.00      0.00       6.66       0.00
```

5 ASM Disk Group 백업과 복원

ASMCMD에서 md_backup 명령어를 통하여 만들어진 ASM Disk Group의 구성 정보를 백업 파일에 저장할 수 있습니다.

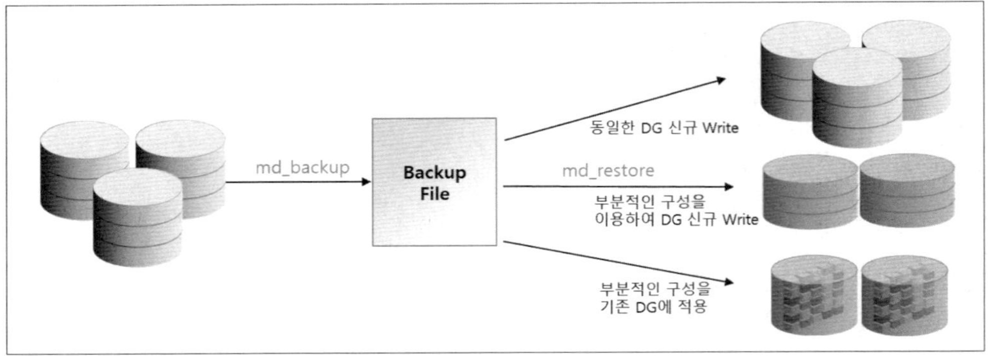

ASMCMD에서 md_restore 명령어를 통하여 만들어진 Backup File을 사용하여 ASM Disk Group을 다시 작성하고 기존의 ASM Disk Group에 같은 구성을 적용하여 복원 시킬 수 있습니다.

이를 실습을 통해 확인해 보겠습니다.

ASMCMD를 실행하여 TEMP Disk Group의 구성 정보를 특정 영역에 백업합니다.

```
# asmcmd -p
ASMCMD >md_backup <백업 받을 절대 경로>/<Disk Group 구성 정보 백업 파일명> -G <Disk Group 명>
```

```
[+ASM]yspark-linux:/oracle/asmcmd_backup> asmcmd
ASMCMD> md_backup /oracle/asmcmd_backup/backup_tempdg -G TEMP
Disk group metadata to be backed up: TEMP
Current alias directory path: orclcle12/TEMPFILE
Current alias directory path: orclcle12
ASMCMD> exit
[+ASM]yspark-linux:/oracle/asmcmd_backup> ls -l
total 16
-rw-r--r-- 1 oracle12 dba 12827 Jan  3 17:52 backup_tempdg
[+ASM]yspark-linux:/oracle/asmcmd_backup>
```

백업 받은 파일의 내용을 확인해 봅니다.

```
# cat <백업 받을 절대 경로>/<Disk Group 구성 정보 백업 파일명>
```

```
[+ASM]yspark-linux:/oracle/asmcmd_backup> cat backup_tempdg
@diskgroup_set = (
                   {
                     'ALIASINFO' => {
                                      '0' => {
                                               'ALIASNAME' => 'orclcle12',
                                               'REFERENCE_INDEX' => '83886133',
                                               'LEVEL' => 0,
                                               'DGNAME' => 'TEMP'
                                             }
                                    },
                     'DGINFO' => {
                                   'DGAUSZ' => '4194304',
                                   'DGTYPE' => 'EXTERN',
                                   'DGTORESTORE' => 0,
                                   'DGDBCOMPAT' => '10.1.0.0.0',
                                   'DGNAME' => 'TEMP',
                                   'DGCOMPAT' => '12.2.0.1.0'
                                 },
                     'TEMPLATEINFO' => {
                                         '2' => {
                                                  'SYSTEM' => 'Y',
                                                  'TEMPNAME' => 'AUDIT_SPILLFILES',
                                                  'REDUNDANCY' => 'UNPROT',
                                                  'DGNAME' => 'TEMP',
                                                  'STRIPE' => 'COARSE'
                                                },
                                         '10' => {
                                                   'TEMPNAME' => 'XTRANSPORT BACKUPSET',
                                                   'SYSTEM' => 'Y',
                                                   'REDUNDANCY' => 'UNPROT',
                                                   'DGNAME' => 'TEMP',
                                                   'STRIPE' => 'COARSE'
                                                 },
                                         '9' => {
                                                  'REDUNDANCY' => 'UNPROT',
                                                  'TEMPNAME' => 'INCR XTRANSPORT BACKUPSET',
                                                  'SYSTEM' => 'Y',
                                                  'STRIPE' => 'COARSE',
                                                  'DGNAME' => 'TEMP'
                                                },
                                         '1' => {
                                                  'REDUNDANCY' => 'UNPROT',
                                                  'TEMPNAME' => 'OCRFILE',
                                                  'SYSTEM' => 'Y',
                                                  'STRIPE' => 'COARSE',
```

```
                'DISKSINFO' => {
                                'VOL3' => {
                                           'VOL3' => {
                                                      'FAILGROUP' => 'VOL3',
                                                      'TOTAL_MB' => '48600',
                                                      'NAME' => 'VOL3',
                                                      'QUORUM' => 'REGULAR',
                                                      'PATH' => '/dev/sdb3',
                                                      'DGNAME' => 'TEMP'
                                                    }
                                         }
                              },
                'ATTRINFO' => {
                               'AU_SIZE' => '4194304',
                               'CELL.SPARSE_DG' => 'allnonsparse',
                               'COMPATIBLE.ASM' => '12.2.0.1.0',
                               '_._DIRVERSION' => '12.2.0.1.0',
                               'COMPATIBLE.ADVM' => '12.2.0.1.0',
                               'APPLIANCE._PARTNERING_TYPE' => 'GENERIC',
                               '_USD.LIST_SIZE' => '4',
                               'PHYS_META_REPLICATED' => 'true',
                               'COMPATIBLE.RDBMS' => '10.1.0.0.0'
                             }
              }
            );
[+ASM]yspark-linux:/oracle/asmcmd_backup>
```

이제 md_restore 명령어를 이용한 ASM Disk Group 복구 테스트를 위해 TEMP DISK GROUP을 삭제하겠습니다. SQL*Plus 유틸리티를 이용하여 TEMP Disk Group을 삭제합니다.

```
# sqlplus "/as sysasm"
SQL> DROP DISKGROUP TEMP  INCLUDING CONTENTS ;
```

```
[+ASM]yspark-linux:/home/oracle12> sqlplus "/as sysasm"
SQL*Plus: Release 12.2.0.1.0 Production on Wed Jan 3 18:02:54 2018
Copyright (c) 1982, 2016, Oracle.  All rights reserved.

Connected to:
Oracle Database 12c Enterprise Edition Release 12.2.0.1.0 - 64bit Production
SQL> DROP DISKGROUP TEMP  INCLUDING CONTENTS ;
Diskgroup dropped.
SQL>
```

ASM Disk Group의 삭제를 확인합니다.

```
[+ASM]yspark-linux:/oracle/asmcmd_backup> asmcmd ls
CRS_DATA/
DB_DATA/
FRA/
REDO/
[+ASM]yspark-linux:/oracle/asmcmd_backup>
```

TEMP Disk Group이 삭제된 것을 확인 하였습니다. md_restore 명령어로 삭제된 Disk Group을 복구합니다.

```
# asmcmd -p
ASMCMD >md_restore <백업 받을 절대 경로>/<Disk Group 구성 정보 백업 파일명> --full
```

```
[+ASM]yspark-linux:/oracle/asmcmd_backup> asmcmd -p
ASMCMD [+] > md_restore /oracle/asmcmd_backup/backup_tempdg --full
Current Diskgroup metadata being restored: TEMP
Diskgroup TEMP created!
```

```
[+ASM]yspark-linux:/oracle/asmcmd_backup> asmcmd ls
CRS_DATA/
DB_DATA/
FRA/
REDO/
TEMP/
[+ASM]yspark-linux:/oracle/asmcmd_backup> █
```

삭제한 TEMP Disk Group의 복구가 완료된 것을 확인하였습니다.

ASMCMD 여러 종류의 명령어가 있습니다.

관리 대상	명령어
ASM 인스턴스	dsget / dsset / lsct / lsop / lspwusr / orapwusr / shutdown / spbackup / spcopy / spget / spmove / spset / startup
ASM 디스크 그룹	chdg / chkdg / dropdg / iostat / lsattr / lsdg / lsdsk / lsod / md_backup / md_restore / mkdg / mount / offline / online / rebal / remap / setattr / umount
DG 템플릿	chtmpl / lstmpl / mktmpl / rmtmpl
ASM파일	cd / cp / du / find / ls / lsof / mkalias / pwd / rm /rmalias
ASM 파일 액세스 제어	chgrp / chmod / chown / groups / grpmod / lsgrp / lsusr / mkgrp / mkusr / passwd / rmgrp / rmusr
ADVM 볼륨	volcreate / voldelete / voldisable / volenable / volinfo / volresize / volset / volstat
명령 목록 표시	help

ASM Cluster File System(ACFS)

Oracle Automatic Storage Management Cluster File System(Oracle ACFS)는 멀티-플랫폼, 확장 가능한 File System, 그리고 오라클 데이터베이스 밖에서 유지되고 있는 고객 File들을 지원하기 위해 Oracle Automatic Storage Management(Oracle ASM)을 확장한 스토리지 관리 기술입니다.

Oracle ACFS는 많은 데이터베이스와 실행 File, 데이터베이스 TraceFile, 데이터베이스 alert Log File, 애플리케이션 보고서, BFILES 그리고 설정 File 등을 포함하는 애플리케이션 File들을 지원합니다.

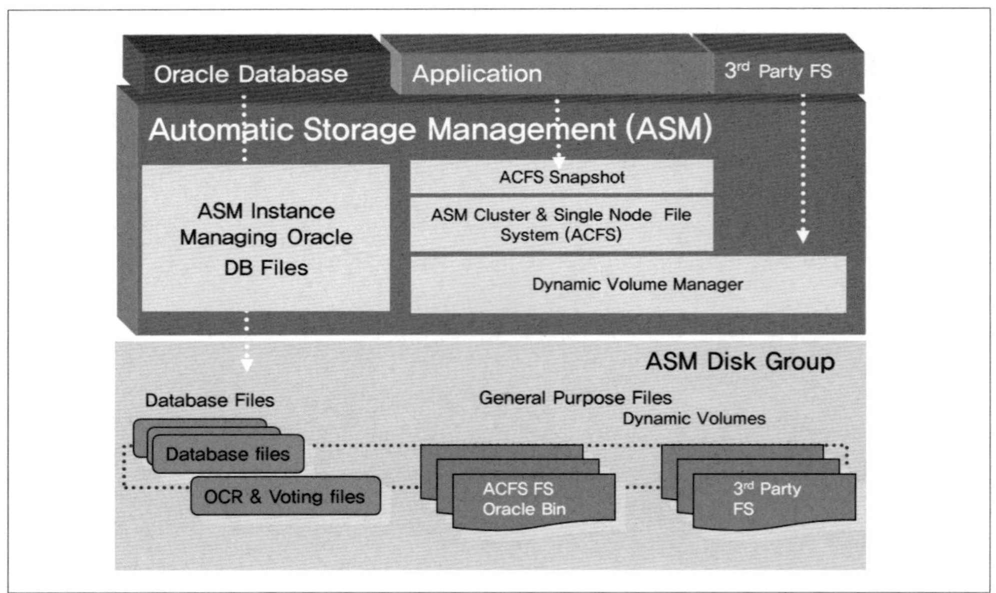

1 ASM 볼륨생성

SQL*Plus 유틸리티를 이용하여 ASM에 접속해서 ACFS에서 사용할 볼륨을 생성하겠습니다. ACFS_TEST Disk Group을 생성합니다.

```
# sqlplus "/as sysasm"
SQL>CREATE DISKGROUP ACFS_TEST EXTERNAL REDUNDANCY DISK '/dev/sdb3' ;
```

```
[+ASM]yspark-linux:/home/oracle12> sqlplus "/as sysasm"
SQL*Plus: Release 12.2.0.1.0 Production on Wed Jan 3 20:17:31 2018
Copyright (c) 1982, 2016, Oracle.  All rights reserved.

Connected to:
Oracle Database 12c Enterprise Edition Release 12.2.0.1.0 - 64bit Production
SQL> CREATE DISKGROUP ACFS_TEST EXTERNAL REDUNDANCY DISK '/dev/sdb3' ;
Diskgroup created.
SQL> ■
```

10000Mb 사이즈의 DBA_WORK라는 볼륨을 ACFS_TEST Disk Group에 생성합니다.

```
# sqlplus "/as sysasm"
SQL>ALTER DISKGROUP ACFS_TEST ADD VOLUME DBA_WORK SIZE 10000M ;
```

```
[+ASM]yspark-linux:/home/oracle12> sqlplus "/as sysasm"
SQL*Plus: Release 12.2.0.1.0 Production on Wed Jan 3 20:21:13 2018
Copyright (c) 1982, 2016, Oracle.  All rights reserved.

Connected to:
Oracle Database 12c Enterprise Edition Release 12.2.0.1.0 - 64bit Production
SQL> ALTER DISKGROUP ACFS_TEST ADD VOLUME DBA_WORK SIZE 10000M ;
Diskgroup altered.
```

생성이 완료 된 후 OS File System에서 /dev/asm을 조회하면 OS 디바이스가 생성된 것을 확인할 수 있습니다.

```
#cd /dev/asm
# ls -l
```

```
[+ASM]yspark-linux:/home/oracle12> cd /dev/asm
[+ASM]yspark-linux:/dev/asm> ls -l
total 0
brwxrwx--- 1 root dba 248, 107009 Jan  3 20:21 dba_work-209
[+ASM]yspark-linux:/dev/asm> ■
```

dba_work-209로 디바이스가 생성되었으며 209는 디스크 그룹에 대한 고유 번호입니다. 이 번호는 Oracle에 의해 자동으로 할당됩니다.

이제 ASM 볼륨상태를 조회합니다.

```
SQL>SELECT VOLUME_NAME, SIZE_MB, VOLUME_NUMBER, STATE, USAGE, VOLUME_DEVICE, MOUNTPATH
FROM V$ASM_VOLUME ;
```

```
SQL> SELECT VOLUME_NAME, SIZE_MB, VOLUME_NUMBER, STATE, USAGE, VOLUME_DEVICE, MOUNTPATH
  2  FROM V$ASM_VOLUME ;

VOLUME_NAM    SIZE_MB VOLUME_NUMBER STATE      USAGE      VOLUME_DEVICE                  MOUNTPATH
---------- ---------- ------------- ---------- ---------- ------------------------------ ------------------------------
DBA_WORK        10048             1 ENABLED               /dev/asm/dba_work-209

SQL>
```

2 ASM 볼륨을 이용한 OS 일반 File system 생성

ASM 볼륨이 준비되었으니 이제 File System으로 사용하도록 mount합니다.

root 유저로 mount 할 위치를 생성하고 mkfs 수행한 후 mount를 실행합니다.

```
# cd /
# mkdir /dba_work
# mkfs -t ext3 /dev/asm/dba_work-209
# mount /dev/asm/dba_work-209 /dba_work
```

```
[root@yspark-linux ~]# cd /
[root@yspark-linux /]# mkdir /dba_work
[root@yspark-linux /]# mkfs -t ext3 /dev/asm/dba_work-209
mke2fs 1.42.9 (28-Dec-2013)
Filesystem label=
OS type: Linux
Block size=4096 (log=2)
Fragment size=4096 (log=2)
Stride=0 blocks, Stripe width=0 blocks
643376 inodes, 2572288 blocks
128614 blocks (5.00%) reserved for the super user
First data block=0
Maximum filesystem blocks=2634022912
79 block groups
32768 blocks per group, 32768 fragments per group
8144 inodes per group
Superblock backups stored on blocks:
        32768, 98304, 163840, 229376, 294912, 819200, 884736, 1605632

Allocating group tables: done
Writing inode tables: done
Creating journal (32768 blocks): done
Writing superblocks and filesystem accounting information: done

[root@yspark-linux /]# mount /dev/asm/dba_work-209 /dba_work
[root@yspark-linux /]#
```

df -h 명령어를 통하여 정상적으로 /dba_work File System이 mount 되었는지 확인합니다.

```
# df -h
```

```
[root@yspark-linux /]# df -h
Filesystem                               Size  Used Avail Use% Mounted on
devtmpfs                                 768M     0  768M   0% /dev
tmpfs                                    4.0G  644M  3.4G  16% /dev/shm
tmpfs                                    793M   20M  774M   3% /run
tmpfs                                    793M     0  793M   0% /sys/fs/cgroup
/dev/mapper/ol_yspark--linux-root         50G   11G   40G  22% /
/dev/mapper/ol_yspark--linux-home         50G   47M   50G   1% /home
/dev/mapper/ol_yspark--linux-oracle      417G   69G  349G  17% /oracle
/dev/sda1                               1014M  276M  739M  28% /boot
tmpfs                                    159M  8.0K  159M   1% /run/user/42
tmpfs                                    159M   36K  159M   1% /run/user/0
/dev/sde1                                932G  854G   79G  92% /usb_hdd
/dev/asm/dba_work-209                    9.6G   23M  9.1G   1% /dba_work
[root@yspark-linux /]#
```

3 ASM 볼륨을 이용한 ASM Cluster File Systems(ACFS) 생성

이번에는 ACFS 파일 시스템을 만들겠습니다. 10000Mb 사이즈의 MONITORING라는 볼륨을 ACFS_TEST Disk Group에 생성합니다.

```
#sqlplus "/as sysasm"
SQL>ALTER DISKGROUP ACFS_TEST ADD VOLUME MONITORING SIZE 10000M ;
```

```
[+ASM]yspark-linux:/home/oracle12sqlplus "/as sysasm"

SQL*Plus: Release 12.2.0.1.0 Production on Wed Jan 3 20:54:09 2018

Copyright (c) 1982, 2016, Oracle.  All rights reserved.

Connected to:
Oracle Database 12c Enterprise Edition Release 12.2.0.1.0 - 64bit Production

SQL> ALTER DISKGROUP ACFS_TEST ADD VOLUME MONITORING SIZE 10000M ;

Diskgroup altered.

SQL>
```

ASM 볼륨이 생성되었는지 조회합니다.

```
SQL>SELECT VOLUME_NAME, SIZE_MB, VOLUME_NUMBER, STATE, USAGE, VOLUME_DEVICE, MOUNTPATH
FROM V$ASM_VOLUME ;
```

```
SQL> SELECT VOLUME_NAME, SIZE_MB, VOLUME_NUMBER, STATE, USAGE, VOLUME_DEVICE, MOUNTPATH
  2  FROM V$ASM_VOLUME ;

VOLUME_NAM    SIZE_MB VOLUME_NUMBER STATE      USAGE      VOLUME_DEVICE                  MOUNTPATH
---------- ---------- ------------- ---------- ---------- ------------------------------ ------------------------------
DBA_WORK        10048             1 ENABLED               /dev/asm/dba_work-209
MONITORING      10048             2 ENABLED               /dev/asm/monitoring-209

SQL>
```

root 유저로 mount 할 위치를 생성하고 mkfs 수행한 후 mount를 실행합니다.

```
# cd /
# mkdir /oracle/monitoring
# mkfs -t acfs /dev/asm/monitoring-209
# mount -t acfs /dev/asm/monitoring-209 /oracle/monitoring
```

```
[root@yspark-linux /]# mkdir /oracle/monitoring
[root@yspark-linux /]# mkfs -t acfs /dev/asm/monitoring-209
mkfs.acfs: version                   = 12.2.0.1.0
mkfs.acfs: on-disk version           = 39.0
mkfs.acfs: volume                    = /dev/asm/monitoring-209
mkfs.acfs: volume size               = 10536091648  (   9.81 GB )
mkfs.acfs: Format complete.
[root@yspark-linux /]# mount -t acfs /dev/asm/monitoring-209 /oracle/monitoring
[root@yspark-linux /]#
```

df -h 명령어를 통하여 정상적으로 ACFS File System이 mount 되었는지 확인합니다.

```
# df -h
```

```
[root@yspark-linux /]# df -h
Filesystem                            Size  Used Avail Use% Mounted on
devtmpfs                              768M     0  768M   0% /dev
tmpfs                                 4.0G  644M  3.4G  16% /dev/shm
tmpfs                                 793M   20M  774M   3% /run
tmpfs                                 793M     0  793M   0% /sys/fs/cgroup
/dev/mapper/ol_yspark--linux-root      50G   11G   40G  22% /
/dev/mapper/ol_yspark--linux-home      50G   47M   50G   1% /home
/dev/mapper/ol_yspark--linux-oracle  417G   69G  349G  17% /oracle
/dev/sda1                            1014M  276M  739M  28% /boot
tmpfs                                 159M  8.0K  159M   1% /run/user/42
tmpfs                                 159M   36K  159M   1% /run/user/0
/dev/sde1                             932G  854G   79G  92% /usb_hdd
/dev/asm/dba_work-209                 9.6G   23M  9.1G   1% /dba_work
/dev/asm/monitoring-209               9.9G   59M  9.8G   1% /oracle/monitoring
[root@yspark-linux /]#
```

ASM 볼륨을 정보를 다시 조회합니다.

```
SQL>SELECT VOLUME_NAME, SIZE_MB, VOLUME_NUMBER, STATE, USAGE, VOLUME_DEVICE, MOUNTPATH
FROM V$ASM_VOLUME ;
```

```
SQL> SELECT VOLUME_NAME, SIZE_MB, VOLUME_NUMBER, STATE, USAGE, VOLUME_DEVICE, MOUNTPATH
  2  FROM V$ASM_VOLUME ;

VOLUME_NAM    SIZE_MB VOLUME_NUMBER STATE      USAGE      VOLUME_DEVICE                  MOUNTPATH
---------- ---------- ------------- ---------- ---------- ------------------------------ ------------------------------
DBA_WORK        10048             1 ENABLED               /dev/asm/dba_work-209
MONITORING      10048             2 ENABLED    ACFS       /dev/asm/monitoring-209        /oracle/monitoring

SQL>
```

ASM 인스턴스에서 조회하면 일반 OS File System을 만든 볼륨과는 다르게 USAGE 컬럼에는 ACFS로 MOUNTPATH 컬럼에는 /oracle/monitoring 볼륨 정보에 대한 정보 조회가 가능합니다.

```
acfsutil 유틸리티의 info fs 옵션으로 확인할 수 있습니다.
#acfsutil info fs
```

```
[+ASM]yspark-linux:/home/oracle12> acfsutil info fs
/oracle/monitoring
    ACFS Version: 12.2.0.1.0
    on-disk version:       39.0
    compatible.advm:       11.2.0.2.0
    ACFS compatibility:    11.2.0.2.0
    flags:        MountPoint,Available
    mount time:   Wed Jan  3 21:02:27 2018
    mount sequence number: 0
    allocation unit:       4096
    metadata block size:   512
    volumes:      1
    total size:   10536091648  (   9.81 GB )
    total free:   10474958848  (   9.76 GB )
    file entry table allocation: 32768
    primary volume: /dev/asm/monitoring-209
        label:
        state:                 Available
        major, minor:          248, 107010
        logical sector size:   512
        size:                  10536091648  (   9.81 GB )
        free:                  10474958848  (   9.76 GB )
        metadata read I/O count:         360
        metadata write I/O count:        32
        total metadata bytes read:       209408   ( 204.50 KB )
        total metadata bytes written:    120832   ( 118.00 KB )
        ADVM diskgroup:        ACFS_TEST
        ADVM resize increment: 67108864
        ADVM redundancy:       unprotected
        ADVM stripe columns:   8
        ADVM stripe width:     1048576
    number of snapshots:  0
    snapshot space usage: 0  ( 0.00 )
    replication status: DISABLED
    compression status: DISABLED
[+ASM]yspark-linux:/home/oracle12>
```

4 ASM Cluster File Systems(ACFS)의 Online Resize

비싼 3rd party 볼륨 매니저 제품에서 제공하던 File System의 Online Resize 기능이 ACFS에서 제공되는지 확인하여 보겠습니다.

10000m로 만들었던 monitoring 볼륨으로 mount한 /oracle/monitoring 디렉토리의 사이즈를 15000m으로 증가시킵니다.

```
#acfsutil size 15000m /oracle/monitoring
```

```
[+ASM]yspark-linux:/home/oracle12> df -h /oracle/monitoring
Filesystem               Size  Used Avail Use% Mounted on
/dev/asm/monitoring-209  9.9G   59M  9.8G   1% /oracle/monitoring
[+ASM]yspark-linux:/home/oracle12> acfsutil size 15000m /oracle/monitoring
acfsutil size: new file system size: 15770583040 (15040MB)
[+ASM]yspark-linux:/home/oracle12> df -h /oracle/monitoring
Filesystem               Size  Used Avail Use% Mounted on
/dev/asm/monitoring-209   15G   69M   15G   1% /oracle/monitoring
[+ASM]yspark-linux:/home/oracle12>
```

umount 없이 1초 미만의 처리 속도로 파일 mount되어 있는 디렉토리의 사이즈가 증가되었습니다.

ASM 인스턴스 내에서 ASM Volume을 조회하면 다음과 같이 MONITORING 볼륨 사이즈도 같이 늘어난 것을 확인할 수 있습니다.

```
SQL>SELECT VOLUME_NAME, SIZE_MB, VOLUME_NUMBER, STATE, USAGE, VOLUME_DEVICE, MOUNTPATH
FROM V$ASM_VOLUME
```

```
SQL> SELECT VOLUME_NAME, SIZE_MB, VOLUME_NUMBER, STATE, USAGE, VOLUME_DEVICE, MOUNTPATH
  2  FROM V$ASM_VOLUME ;

VOLUME_NAM    SIZE_MB VOLUME_NUMBER STATE      USAGE      VOLUME_DEVICE                   MOUNTPATH
---------- ---------- ------------- ---------- ---------- ------------------------------- ------------------------------
DBA_WORK        10048             1 ENABLED               /dev/asm/dba_work-209
MONITORING      15040             2 ENABLED    ACFS       /dev/asm/monitoring-209         /oracle/monitoring

SQL>
```

acfstuil 명령어

Linux/Unix의 ACFS 명령어입니다.

```
acfsutil info fs  - Display ACFS file and file system features and information
acfsutil snapshot  - create and display ACFS snapshots
acfsutil registry  - Registry an ACFS file system with the ACFS mount registry
acfsutil rmfs  - Remove unmounted ACFS file system
acfsutil size - resize an ACFS file system
```

Windows의 ACFS 명령어입니다.

```
acfsformat [/vf] [/b blksz] [/n name] device [blocks]- ACFS 파일 시스템 Create
acfsmountvol [/all] [/v]- ACFS 파일 시스템 Mount
acfsdismount [/v] [/p] [/P] path- ACFS 파일 시스템 Unmount
acfschkdsk [/a] [/v] [/n] [/f] [info] device- ACFS 파일 시스템체크 및 수정
```

5 ASM Cluster File Systems 정리

ASM Cluster File System(CFS)는 클러스터의 모든 노드들이 공유할 수 있는 클러스터 파일 시스템을 ASM 위에 둘 수 있습니다. 따라서 고가의 타벤더 CFS 솔루션을 사용할 필요가 없습니다.

클러스터의 모든 노드들이 공유할 수 있는 클러스터 파일 시스템을 ASM 위에 둘 수 있습니다. ACFS 파일시스템은 NFS 및 CIFS와 같은 산업 표준 프로토콜을 이용하여 원격 클라이언트에게 제공될 수도 있습니다.

Oracle Grid Infrastructure 환경의 서버라면 추가로 고가의 타 벤더 CFS 솔루션을 구매할 필요가 없습니다.

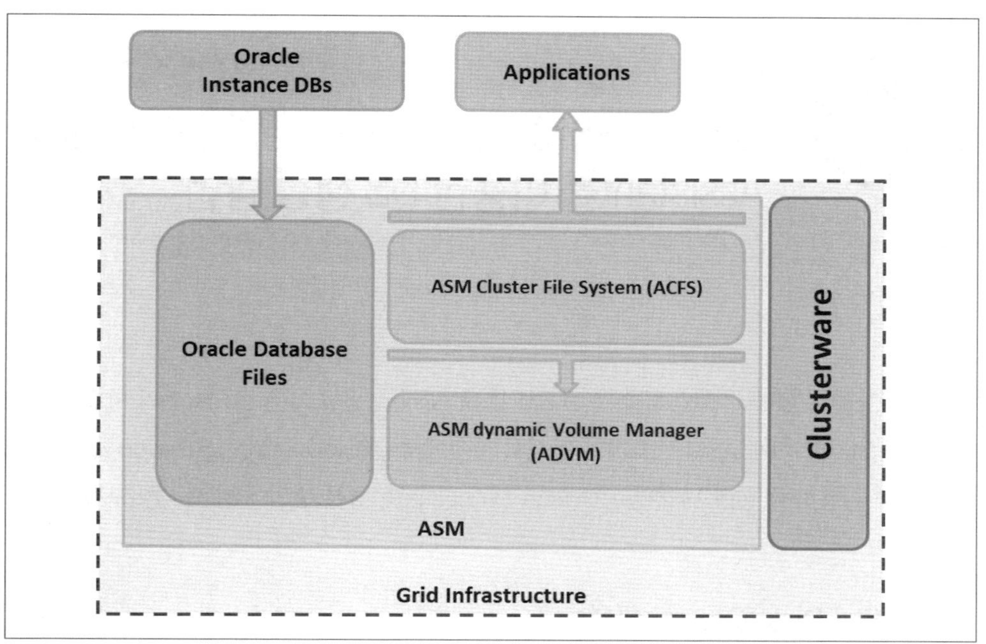
Oracle
Instance DBs
Applications
ASM Cluster File System (ACFS)
Oracle Database
Files
ASM dynamic Volume Manager
(ADVM)
Clusterware
ASM
Grid Infrastructure

Oracle ASM 환경의 Database Configuration Assistant를 이용한 DB 생성 방법

지금까지 Oracle ASM 스토리지 구조, ASM Disk Group 생성 기준, ASM 관리 방법에 대해서 알아봤습니다. 이제 ASM 스토리지 방식의 환경에서 Database Configuration Assistant (DBCA)을 사용하여 진행 단계별로 Oracle Database를 생성 방법에 대해 알아보겠습니다.

1 ASM Disk Group 생성

클러스터웨어 정보 File (OCR, VOTING)을 저장하는 CRS_DATA, Database File을 저장하는 DB_DATA, 고속 복구 영역을 저장하는 FRA, 온라인 리두 로그 파일을 저장하는 REDO, Temp File을 저장하는 TEMP 디스크 그룹을 생성합니다.

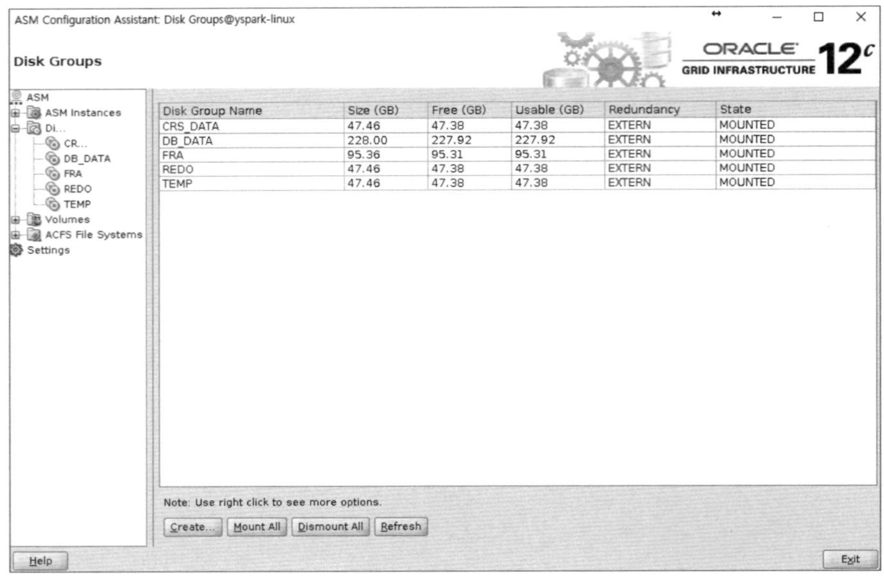

2 Database Configuration Assistant(DBCA) 실행

터미널에 접속해 아래와 같이 수행하면 PC 화면에 Mobaxterm 프로그램을 통해 X windows 화면이 생성됩니다. Mobaxterm 프로그램 설치 방법은 Chapter 9. ASMCA를 이용한 ASM 관리 방법 편에서 설명하였습니다.

```
# su - oracle12                          -- Grid Infrastructure 설치 유저 접속
# . oraenv  -- 환경변수 세팅
ORACLE_SID = [oracle12] ? oracle12       -- DB인스턴스명 입력
# export DISPLAY=192.168.1.12:0.0        -- 클라이언트 IP와 Mobaxterm 프로그램 log 확인 Value 입력
# dbca                                   -- ASMCA 프로그램 실행
```

```
[+ASM]yspark-linux:/home/oracle12> . oraenv
ORACLE_SID = [+ASM] ? oracle12
The Oracle base has been changed from /oracle/grid12/app/oracle to /oracle/oracle12/app/oracle
[oracle12]yspark-linux:/home/oracle12> export DISPLAY=192.168.1.12:0.0
[oracle12]yspark-linux:/home/oracle12> dbca
```

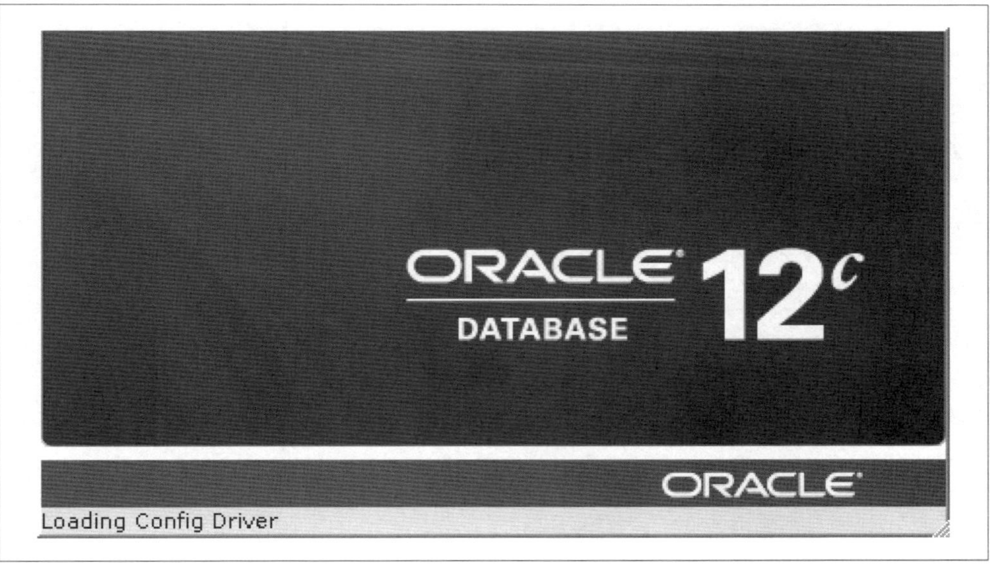

3 Select Database Operation

DB를 신규로 생성해야 하기 때문에 Create a database를 선택합니다.

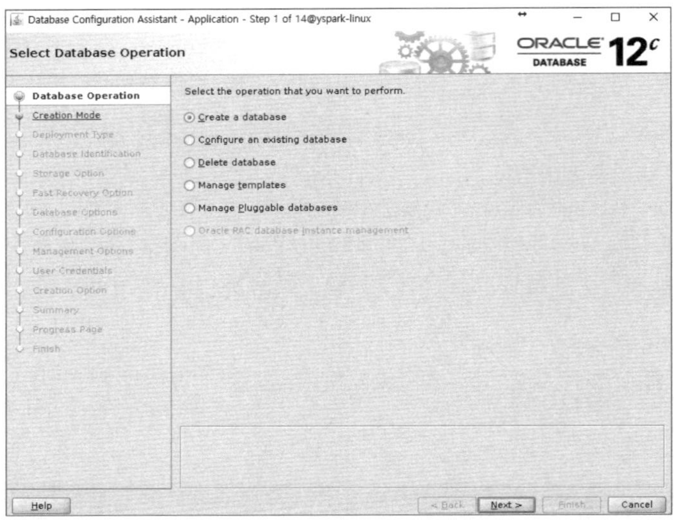

4 Select Database Creation Mode

Database 관련 파일을 적절한 ASM Disk Group에 배치시켜야 하므로 Advanced configuration을 선택합니다.

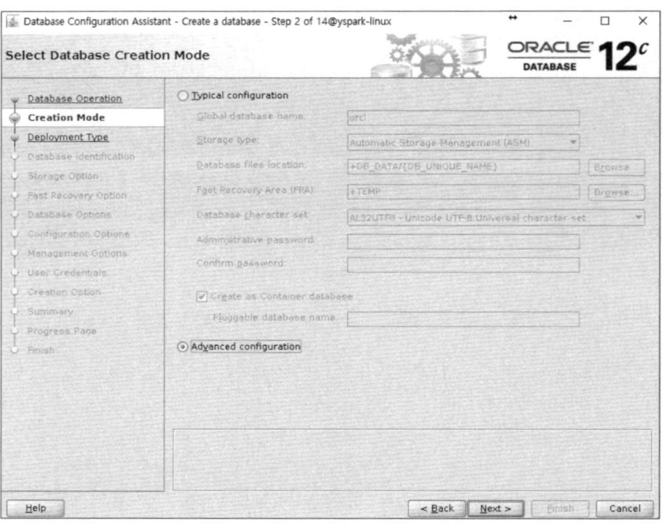

5 Select Database Deployment Type

Database type을 정합니다. Single ASM 환경의 DB이므로 Database Type은 Single Instance database를 선택합니다. RAC ASM 환경인 경우 여기서 RAC database를 선택합니다.

보통 일반적인 DB를 생성 시 Template는 General Purpose or Transaction Processing을 선택합니다.

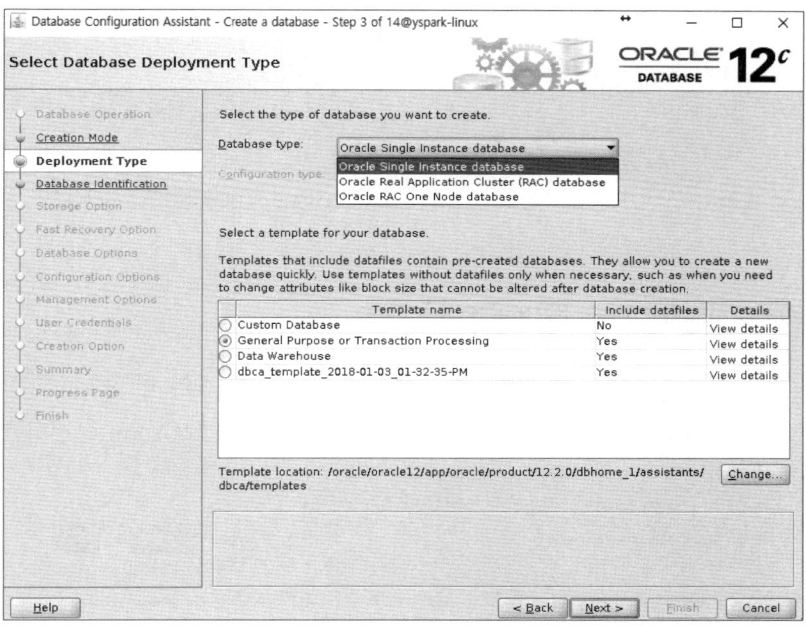

6 Select Database Deployment Type

Database 이름을 정합니다. 12c부터 멀티태넌트 Option 기능이 제공되어 CDB를 만드는 옵션이 있습니다.

선택하지 않고 Disable로 만듭니다.

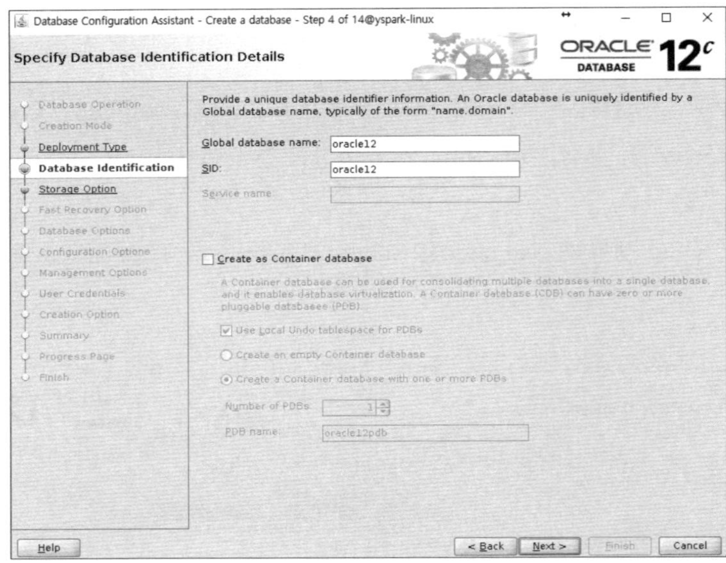

7 Select Database Storage Option

스토리지 구성 방법을 정하는 화면입니다. ASM 환경으로 구성해야 하므로 ASM으로 선택 후 Database file location은 Browse 클릭 후 DB_DATA Disk Group을 선택합니다.

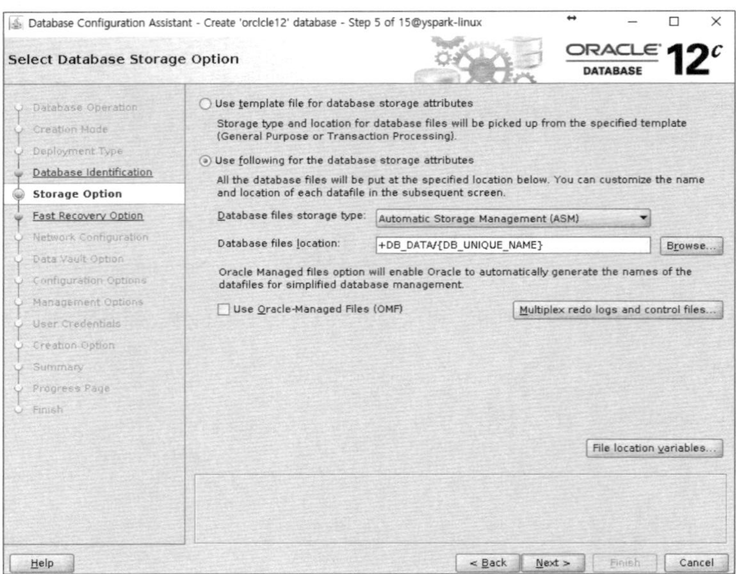

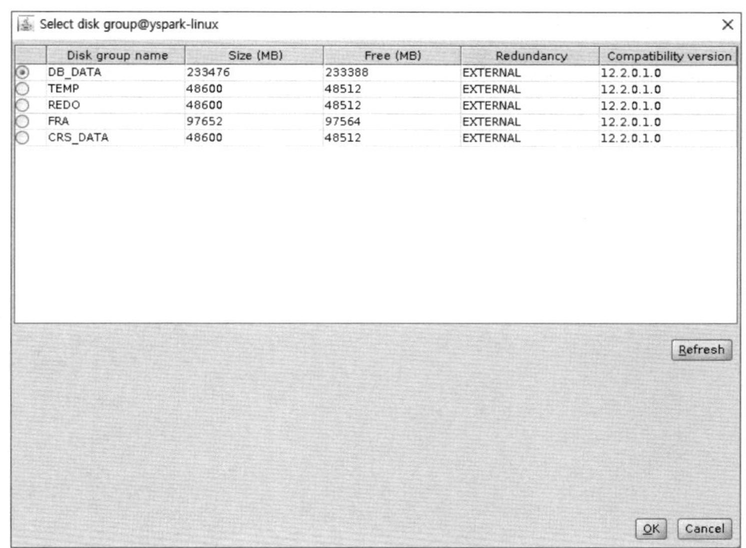

8 Select Fast Recovery Option

고속 복구 영역을 설정하는 화면입니다. ASM 환경의 백업은 RMAN 백업을 DB 백업을 구성해야 합니다. 고속 복구 영역의 설명은 RMAN의 정석 편에서 설명하였습니다. Browse 클릭 후 FRA Disk Group을 선택합니다. Enable archiving을 선택합니다. 고속 복구 영역의 사이즈는 FRA Disk Group 사이즈만큼 설정합니다.

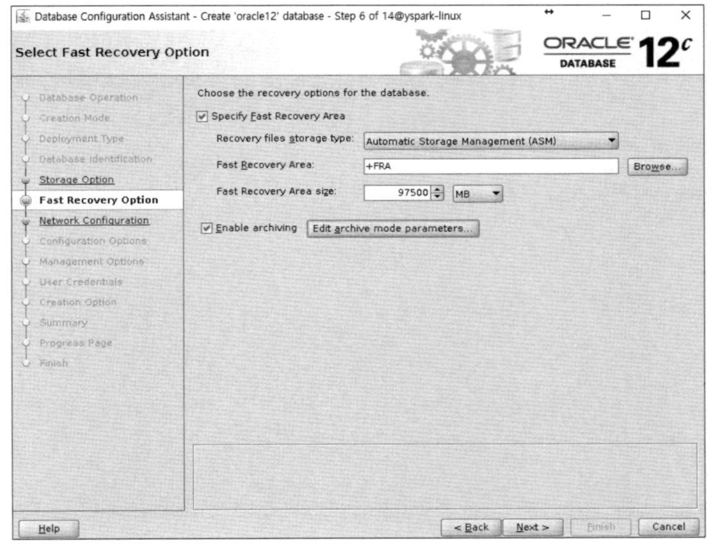

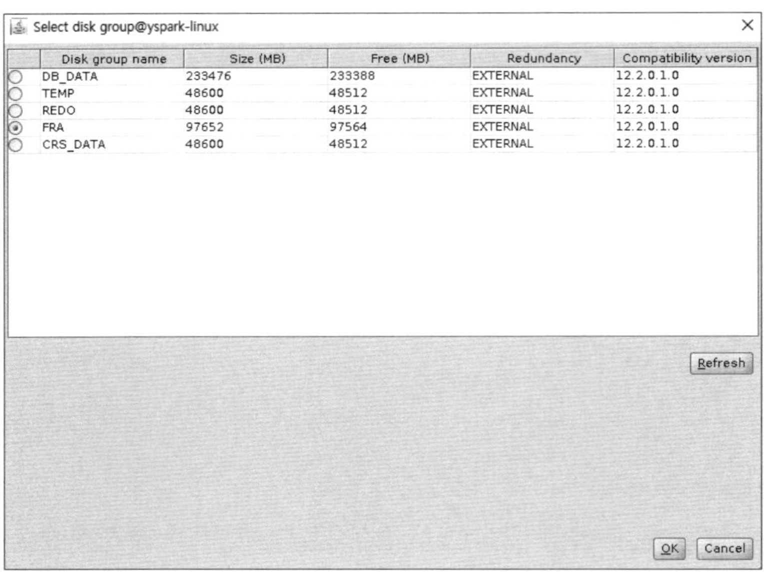

9 Specify Network Configuration Details

신규로 생성하는 Database의 접속을 담당할 리스너를 설정하는 화면입니다. Grid Infrastructure를 구성 후 만들어진 리스너를 선택합니다.

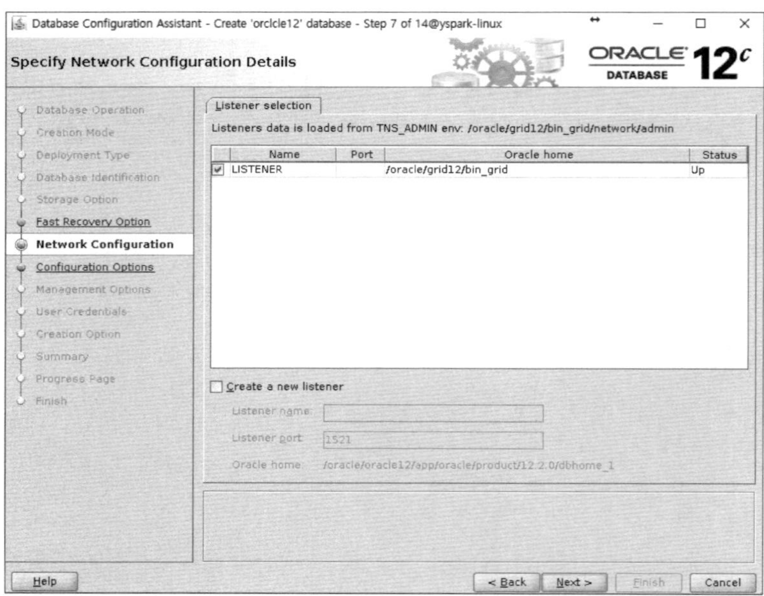

10 Select Oracle Data Vault Config Option

신규로 생성하는 Database의 보안 Advanced Security Option 기능인 DB Vault와 Label Security 설정하는 화면입니다. 구매하지 않았다면 Disable하고 Next를 클릭합니다.

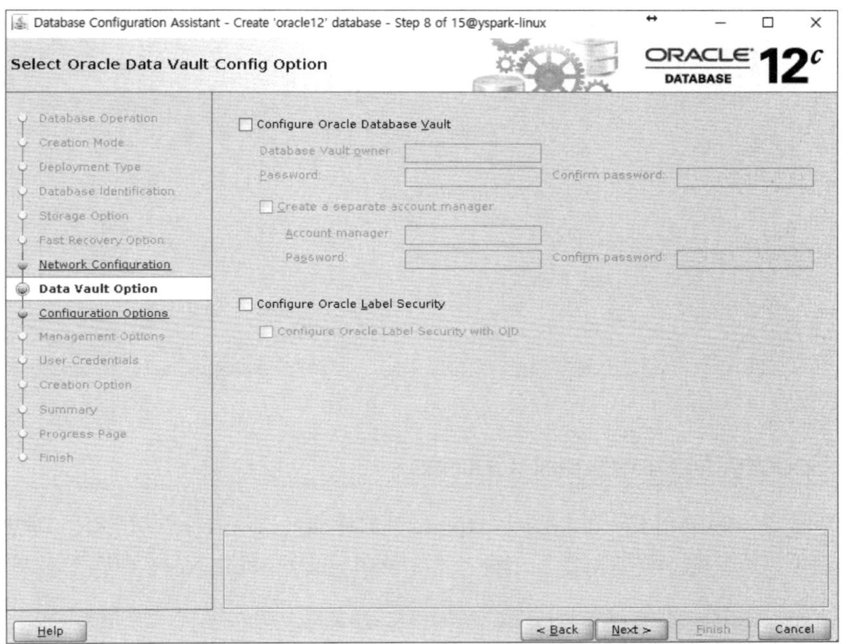

11 Specify Configuration Options

신규로 생성하는 Database의 메모리 크기, Process, 캐릭터셋을 설정하는 화면입니다. ASM 스토리지 구성과 관련이 없어 Next를 눌러 넘어가지만 서버 환경에 맞게 가장 많은 설정을 해주어야 합니다.

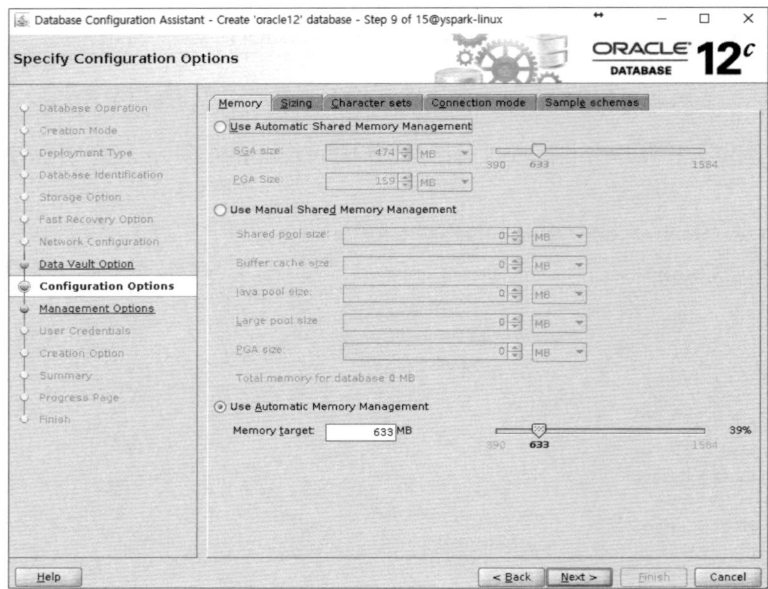

12 Specify Management Options

신규로 만들 Database의 EM database express와 EM cloud control을 설정하는 화면입니다. 옵션을 구매하지 않았거나 EM을 도입하지 않았으면 disable하고 Next 버튼을 클릭합니다.

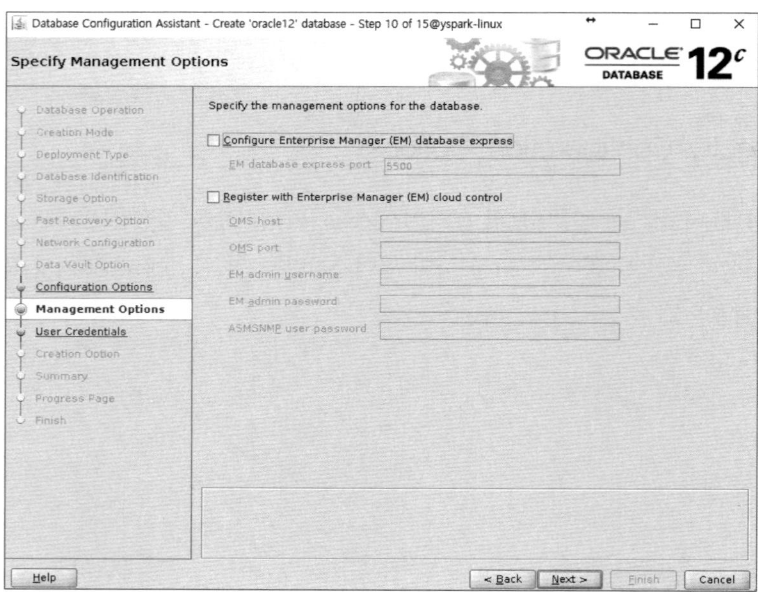

13 Specify Database User Credentials

신규로 만들 Database의 패스워드를 입력하는 화면입니다. 패스워드는 보통의 경우 DB를 생성하고 어플리케이션 설정 후 최종 변경하기 때문에 쉬운 패스워드로 입력하고 Next 버튼을 클릭합니다.

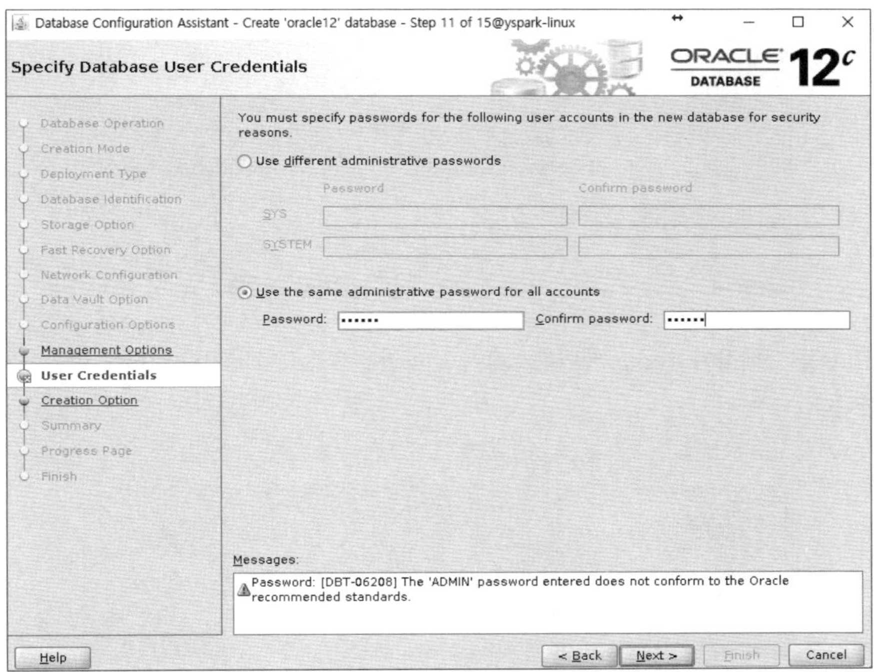

14 Select Database Creation Option

신규로 만들 Database의 Database File 위치를 설정하는 화면입니다.
이전 버전과는 다르게 Customize Storage Locations를 클릭해서 Pop-Up 창에서 선택해야 합니다.

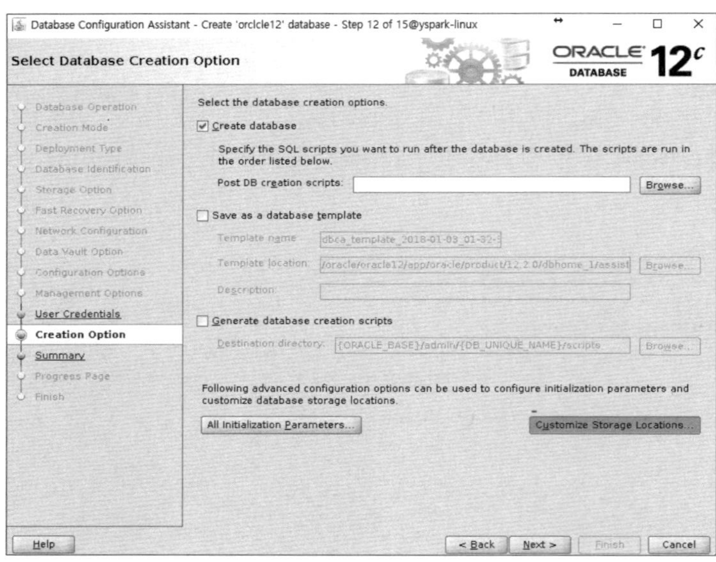

Datafiles를 선택하여 Temp 테이블스페이스 파일은 TEMP Disk Group에 만들어지도록 선택합니다.

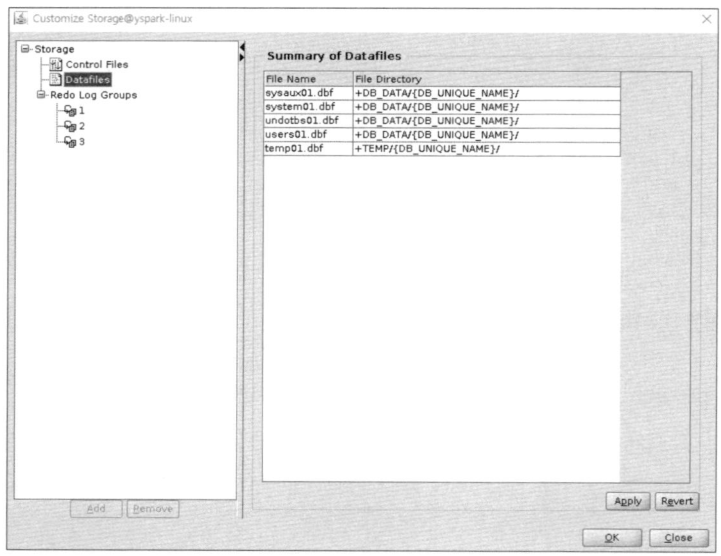

Datafiles를 선택하여 Temp 테이블스페이스 파일은 TEMP Disk Group에 만들어지도록 선택합니다.

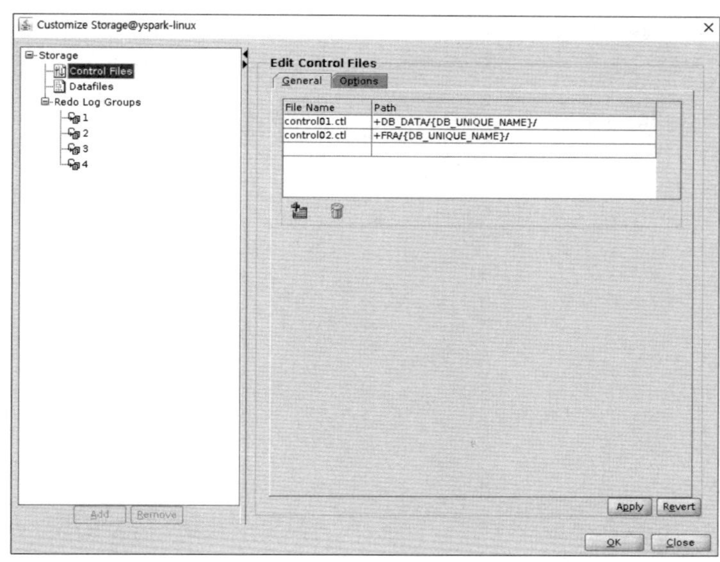

Redo Log Groups를 선택하여 Size를 1024M으로 설정합니다. 저자는 온라인 리두 로그는 사이즈가 작을 때 발생하는 이슈를 많이 경험하여 기본적으로 1G 이상으로 만듭니다.

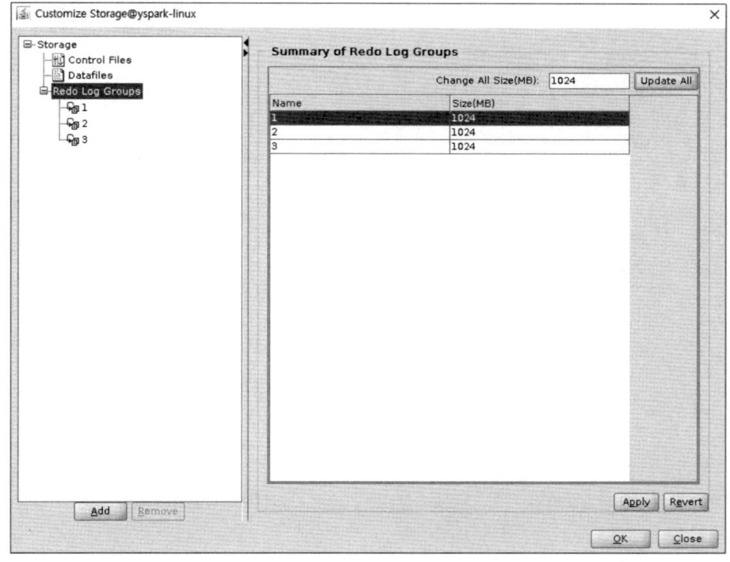

Redo Log Groups를 선택하여 Size를 설정하고 Group을 4번까지 추가하고 Member를 2개로 만들어 첫 번째 Member는 REDO Disk Group에 만들고 두 번째 Member는 FRA Disk Group에 만들도록 세팅하고 Apply 버튼을 클릭합니다.

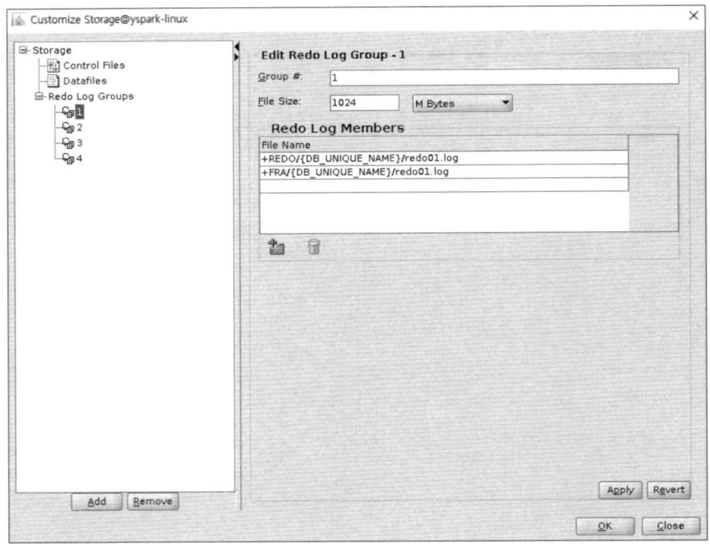

Database Storage File 위치 설정이 완료되면 원래의 화면으로 돌아와 Next 버튼을 클릭합니다.

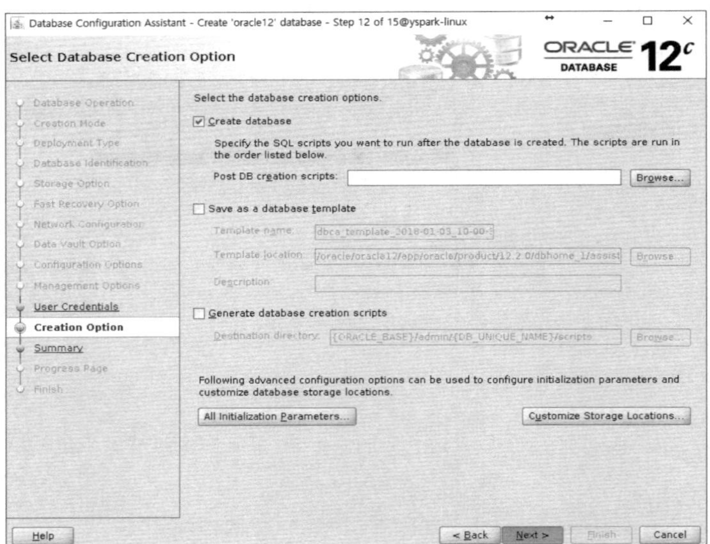

15 Select Database Creation Option

Database 생성 마지막 화면입니다. 파일 위치가 잘 놓여졌는지 다른 설정 값은 이상이 없는지 확인합니다. 설정에 이상이 없다면 Finish 버튼을 클릭합니다.

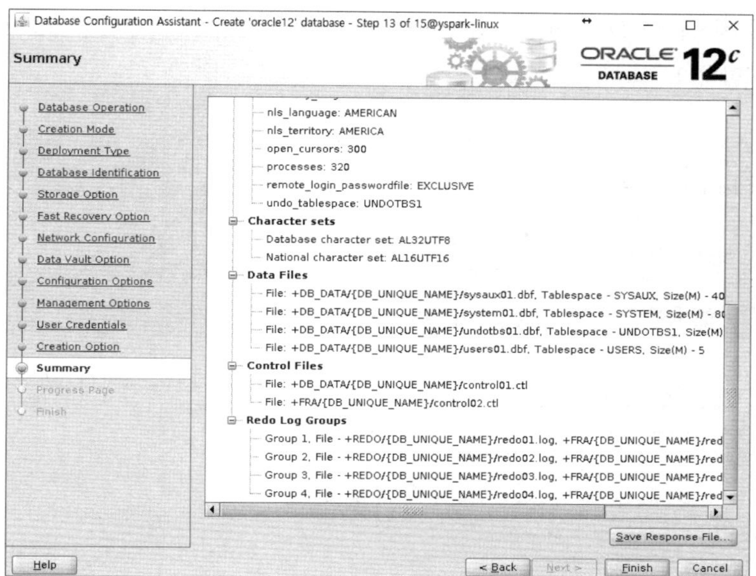

16 최종 마무리

OK 버튼을 클릭해서 설정을 마무리하고 Progress Page로 넘어갑니다. 이제 Database가 생성될 때까지 기다립니다.

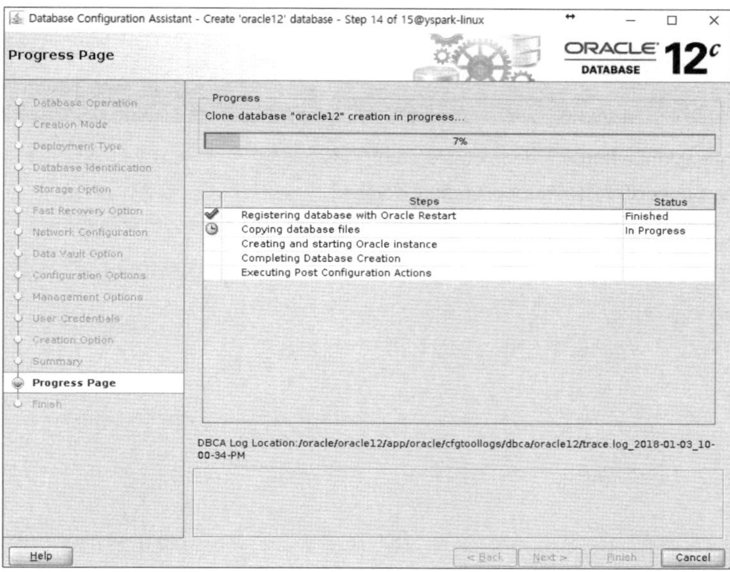

Database가 생성된 후 Database에 접속하여 쿼리를 통해 Database 관련 File들이 잘 만들어졌는지 확인합니다.

```
# sqlplus "/as sysdba"
SQL>SELECT NAME FROM V$DATAFILE
     UNION
     SELECT MEMBER FROM V$LOGFILE
     UNION
     SELECT NAME FROM V$TEMPFILE ;
```

```
[oracle12]yspark-linux:/home/oracle12> dbca
[oracle12]yspark-linux:/home/oracle12> sqlplus "/as sysdba"

SQL*Plus: Release 12.2.0.1.0 Production on Thu Jan 4 00:16:59 2018

Copyright (c) 1982, 2016, Oracle.  All rights reserved.


Connected to:
Oracle Database 12c Enterprise Edition Release 12.2.0.1.0 - 64bit Production

00:16:59 SYS@oracle12>
00:16:59 SYS@oracle12> SELECT NAME FROM V$DATAFILE
00:17:41   2  UNION
00:17:42   3  SELECT MEMBER FROM V$LOGFILE
00:17:42   4  UNION
00:17:42   5  SELECT NAME FROM V$TEMPFILE ;

NAME
--------------------------------------------------------------------------------
+DB_DATA/oracle12/sysaux01.dbf
+DB_DATA/oracle12/system01.dbf
+DB_DATA/oracle12/undotbs01.dbf
+DB_DATA/oracle12/users01.dbf
+FRA/oracle12/redo01.log
+FRA/oracle12/redo02.log
+FRA/oracle12/redo03.log
+FRA/oracle12/redo04.log
+REDO/oracle12/redo01.log
+REDO/oracle12/redo02.log
+REDO/oracle12/redo03.log
+REDO/oracle12/redo04.log
+TEMP/oracle12/temp01.dbf
00:17:42 SYS@oracle12>
```

▶ 참고자료

참고	참고문헌
[1] Oracle OnlineManual(https://docs.oracle.com) [2] My Oracle Support(https://support.oracle.com)	

찾아보기

INDEX

【C】

【D】

【E】

【F】

【G】

【H】

【I】

【L】

【M】

【O】

【P】

【R】

【S】

【T】

【U】

【V】

【기 타】